CONTEMPORARY GREECE AND EUROPE

This book would not have been possible without the support of the late Yannos Kranidiotis

Contemporary Greece and Europe

Edited by
ACHILLEAS MITSOS and ELIAS MOSSIALOS
The London School of Economics and Political Science

Routledge
Taylor & Francis Group
LONDON AND NEW YORK

First published 2000 by Ashgate Publishing

Reissued 2019 by Routledge
2 Park Square, Milton Park, Abingdon, Oxon, OX14 4RN
52 Vanderbilt Avenue, New York, NY 10017

Routledge is an imprint of the Taylor & Francis Group, an informa business

A Library of Congress record exists under LC control number:

ISBN 13: 978-1-138-73406-7 (hbk)
ISBN 13: 978-1-138-73402-9 (pbk)
ISBN 13: 978-1-315-18739-6 (ebk)

Contents

PART V: FOREIGN POLICIES AND EXTERNAL RELATIONS

About the Authors

George Alogoskoufis is Professor of Economics at the Athens School of Economics, and a Member of the Greek Parliament. Since 1997 he has been economics spokesman for New Democracy, the opposition party in Greece.

Michael G. Arghyrou is Lecturer in Economics at Brunel University, London. His research interests and publications are in international macroeconomics, monetary economics and Greek marcroeconomic performance.

Nicos Christodoulakis is Professor of Economics at the Athens School of Economics, Member of the Greek Parliament and Deputy Minister of Finance in Greece.

Dimitris N. Chryssochoou is Reader in European Integration at the University of Exeter. For 1999–2000 he is Visiting Fellow at the Centre of International Studies at Cambridge University and Visiting Scholar at the Institute on Western Europe at Columbia University.

Theodore A. Couloumbis is Professor of International Relations at the University of Athens and Director General of the Hellenic Foundation for European and Foreign Policy (ELIAMEP).

Efterpe Fokas is a PhD candidate in the European Institute at the London School of Economics and Political Science and co-editor of the ASEN Bulletin (Association for the Study of Ethnicity and Nationalism).

Nikolas C. Garganas is the Deputy Governor of the Bank of Greece and an Honorary Fellow of the London School of Economics and Political Science. His research interests and publications include monetary union and the Greek monetary system.

Harris C. Georgiades is a PhD candidate at the Centre for Euro-Mediterranean Studies at the University of Reading working on EU-Turkish relations.

Panagiotis C. Ioakimidis is Professor of European Policy and Institutions at the University of Athens and has been a senior policy advisor on European Union affairs for the Greek Ministry of Foreign Affairs.

The late **Yannos Kranidiotis** was the Alternate Foreign Affairs Minister and Minister for European Affairs in Greece. His life was cut short in a tragic airplane accident on 16th September 1999.

Lois Labrianidis is Professor of Economics at the University of Macedonia in Thessaloniki. His research and publications focus on industrial location, regional incentives and the spatial aspects of subcontracting.

Panagiotis Liargovas is Visiting Assistant Professor at the the Athens School of Economics. He had previously worked at the European Commission, the Greek Ministry of Finance and the Hellenic Centre for European Studies.

Emmanouel C. Mamatzakis is Lecturer in Economics at Queen Mary and Westfield College. His current research focuses on the link between public infrastructure and productivity growth of the EU in general and of the Greek economy in particular.

Achilleas Mitsos is a Director-General at the European Commission and Robert Schuman Visiting Fellow at the European Institute at the London School of Economics and Political Science.

Andreas Moschonas is Associate Professor of Political Sociology and holds the Jean Monnet Chair in European Studies at the University of Crete, Greece. His research focuses on political parties, European elections and trade unions and European integration.

Elias Mossialos is Reader in European health policy at the Department of Social Policy, London School of Economics and Political Science and Director of LSE Health.

George Pagoulatos is a Post-doctoral Fellow at Princeton University after obtaining his doctorate from St. Anthony's College, Oxford.

Christos J. Paraskevopoulos has a PhD from the London School of Economics and Political Science. His academic interests and publications focus on institutions, EU regional policy and integration theory.

Maria Petmesidou is Professor of Social Policy at Democritus University in Thrace. Her research and publications focus on social policy, industrial change, labour markets and social exclusion.

Stelios Stavridis holds the Jean Monnet Chair in the International Dimension of European Integration, and is Director of the Euro-Mediterranean Centre at The University of Reading.

Panos Tsakloglou is Associate Professor in the Department of International and European Economic Studies at the the Athens School of Economics.

Loukas Tsoukalis holds the Eleftherios Venizelos Chair of Contemporary Greek Studies and is also Director of the Hellenic Observatory of the European Institute at the London School of Economics and Political Science.

Aristotle Tziampiris has a PhD from the London School of Economics and currently is working for the Institute of Defence Analysis in Athens.

Thanos Veremis is Professor of Modern History at the University of Athens and President of the Board at the Hellenic Foundation of European and Foreign Policy (ELIAMEP).

Axel Sotiris Wallden has served as General Secretary of the Greek Ministry of National Economy and as visiting professor at the Panteion University, Athens. He is currently working in the European Commission.

PART I
CONTEMPORARY GREECE AND EUROPE

1 Contemporary Greece and Europe: Introduction and Synopsis

ELIAS MOSSIALOS AND ACHILLEAS MITSOS

Contemporary Greek society is characterised by an all embracing trend for reform. As in all European economies, it should modernise in order to survive the inevitable structural changes taking place in the international system as a result of globalisation. However, for Greece this task is additionally constrained by the need to overcome continual problems which characterise the Greek polity, and are rooted in the historical and political culture of the country: institutional centralisation combined with ineffective policy-making and implementation, intense politicisation of economic and social relations, an absence of stratagem, an overwhelming public sector, a weak but paternalistic state and a ubiquitous network of clientelistic relations, are all features of the contemporary Greek polity. (Mouzelis, 1990; Tsoukalas, 1983; Charalambis, 1989; Diamandouros, 1994). In addition, as highlighted by Mouzelis (1995) the Greek political system is also distinguished by 'the uneasy co-existence of clientelism and populism; both entail a vertical, authoritarian integration of the people into the national political arena and indicate an extremely weak civic society.' This in turn is characterised by an atmosphere of disbelief and scepticism concerning the longevity, fairness and trustworthiness of the political system. In this context, the project and process of transforming Greek society and generating a public and political consensus toward modernisation becomes a very difficult, though not impossible, task.

A significant outcome of these features is the tangible weakness of civil society primarily manifested through the command of party interests in almost all spheres of public life. Moreover, the resolution of economic and social issues in Greek politics has traditionally taken place within a multiple framework of political relations characterised by the competition for state favours between coalitions of political parties, professions, unions, business interests and public sector officials. Such institutional patterns and political customs have created a diverse set of political and economic stakes expressed by powerful groups (both within and outside the public sector) which favour the *status quo* and have proved able to hinder the formation and implementation of effective state policies. It is evident that in this context the policies of reform are perceived as a danger to the vested interests of certain parts of Greek society which would forcefully oppose any reform. (Pappas, 1999; Sotiropoulos, 1996; Spourdalakis, 1988).

Until quite recently Greece was considered the European Union's odd man out. The country had failed to respond adequately to the EMU project and reform its economic public administration and social policies. Its external relations with almost all neighbouring countries were at an all-time low since the Second World War, and nationalism was on the rise.

The effective integration of Greece into the European Union has not only been an extremely long and non-linear process, but remains incomplete. The initial major disparities – in terms of the level of economic development, social and economic structure, macroeconomic performance – and, even more importantly, the perception of national interest in international relations, have impeded this process. In addition, the functioning of some of the most evident mechanisms of integration, in particular the trade and capital movement sectors, made convergence even more difficult. It was this need for a full and effective integration that made the modernisation of both the Greek economy and Greek society an urgent and imperative objective, and the process of integration synonymous with the process of modernisation.

The process of European Union integration has led to increasing internal disparities which challenge certain existing mechanisms of integration. Conversely it has contributed to raising issues that have provided more maturity to the European Union; issues such as solidarity, the redistribution of resources and factors of production and minority foreign policy positions are of vital importance for particular member states. All are elements of an advanced union. Hence, paradoxically, the existence of a permanent, important and increasing gap between Greece and the European Union led to both the mobilisation and consolidation of domestic forces in favour of modernisation, and to the inclusion of elements of economic and political solidarity in the main structure of the EU.

Against this background, in the 1990s significant economic reforms were introduced. These were combined with attempts to rationalise public administration, external relations and forms of political contact. Could Greece have performed better? The present government has been criticised, not without substance, for not being sufficiently daring in its reforms. This is particularly the case with public administration and social policy. Yet the impact of the reforms and policy changes related to economic policies and external relations was significant, and is depicted in the analysis presented in several essays included in this volume. Nonetheless, differing opinions prevail among the contributors of this volume concerning the potential efficacy of these reforms and policy changes.

This book aims to explore some of the most important facets of divergence between Greece and the EU. It examines the process through which they affect the relative performance of the country in the economic, social, political and international relations fronts, together with the recent significant attempts to modernise and rationalise internal and external policies and structures.

The book has been divided into five parts. In the introductory section, Greece's Alternate Minister of Foreign Affairs, the late Yannos Kranidiotis, analyses the fundamental objectives of Greek foreign policy. Tsoukalis examines the challenges and implications associated with EU membership for Greek domestic and foreign politics, and Mitsos explores Greece's participation in the process of European integration. Part II deals with Greece and the EMU, Part III analyses the issues related to state modernisation and adjustment, Part IV examines the welfare state and related policies and finally Part V analyses Greece's foreign policy and external relations with particular emphasis on the Balkans and Greek-Turkish relations.

The late Yannos Kranidiotis (*The Fundamental Objectives of Greek Foreign Policy*) emphasises the importance of EU membership for the development of Greece's regional and international role. Greek foreign policy is defined by the political and economic considerations emanating from the country's position within three broader and interrelated systems: the European Union, the regional subsystem of Southeastern Europe and the international system. In this context, Kranidiotis argues that Greece has the potential to play an important regional and international role by promoting peace, stability and cooperation in the Southeastern region and Europe as a whole.

To this end, a determining variable is the further development of Greece's EU membership. The importance of European cooperation for

Greece's economy and politics renders the EU the defining framework for the formulation of the country's foreign policy. In this respect, Greece's foreign policy objectives cannot be perceived in isolation to the development of an overall and consistent policy toward deepening and widening the country's EU membership. EMU participation is one major step in this direction. For Kranidiotis, EMU participation is not only an economic, but also a political cause, as it will allow Greece to participate in the future decision making and policy formulating structures of the EU.

Kranidiotis suggests that for the Union's evolution, Greece's policy should consolidate the EU's political dimension toward the eventual crystallisation of a political system of governance, the deepening of integration of Common Foreign and Security Policy issues, and the development of institutional structures that will not only allow flexibility, but also equality in terms of 'integration involvement'. With respect to enlargement, Kranidiotis considers the accession of Central and Eastern European countries, in addition to the Balkan countries, to the EU as an opportunity to cement democracy, stability and prosperity, not only in these countries, but in Europe as a whole. The accession of Cyprus is an important consideration for Greece as it will contribute to achieving both economic prosperity and security in the island and the wider region.

Finally, for Kraniditiotis the development of inter-regional cooperation toward stability and democracy in Southeastern Europe is a primary foreign policy objective for Greece. Greece's status as one of the most developed countries in this area will allow it to play a defining role within such a framework of cooperation. An important aspect of inter-regional cooperation in Southeastern Europe is the development of a peaceful and cooperative relationship with Turkey. To this end, strengthening Turkey's European orientation will contribute both to the improvement of Greek-Turkish relations, and to the stabilisation and economic development of the wider Southeastern region.

Tsoukalis (*Greece in the EU: Domestic Reform Coalitions, External Constraints and High Politics*) argues that Greece's membership entails not only the challenge of economic adjustment, but that of transforming the functioning of its political institutions towards a system which would provide transparency, flexibility, stability and the development of new forms of social solidarity. He also argues that fundamentally, membership of the EU would require a radical change between the state and the market in Greece.

It is also argued that EU membership has acted as a powerful catalyst for the development of policy reform. The late 1990s witnessed an acceleration of the process of modernisation in both economic and political terms. The political scene is characterised by decreased polarisation, and the issue of modernisation/reform cuts right across the two main political parties, while a broader change in the forms of political contact is manifested in the 'mushrooming of citizen's movements'. Regarding economic developments, achieving the EMU target could be seen as a firm indicator of Greece's economic advancement. However, much is still required to implement structural reforms. Greece's effective performance within this new EMU environment is dependent upon the success of important structural reforms. In this respect, it is argued that using EMU requirements and the external constraints associated with EU membership to introduce reforming policies, could prove dangerous. In terms of foreign policy, EU membership has strengthened Greece's economic and political weight. However, the author agrees with Ioakimidis (see *The Europeanisation of Greece's Foreign Policy: Progress and Problems* in this volume) that there is a gap between the EU's expectations of Greece, and the actual ability of the European cooperation framework to pursue coherent foreign and security policies. A small country like Greece should pursue high politics less and view the EU as providing a coherent institutional framework for careful diplomacy, identifying common interests with other countries, building coalitions and creating economic and political alliances.

Overall, Tsoukalis argues that EU membership has had a positive impact on Greek society and economy, and that despite its delay, Greece has entered the process of reform and modernisation. However, there is still much to be done in terms of economic advancement. In the field of foreign policy, Greece faces distinct challenges in comparison to other EU members. Given the nature of the EU, Greece's successful membership will require a combination of more domestic reforms, careful diplomacy and less high politics abroad. It is the author's strong impression that 'Greece has been slowly but steadily moving in this direction'.

Finally, Mitsos (*Maximising Contribution to the European Integration Process as a Prerequisite for the Maximisation of Gains*) explores Greece's participation in the process of European integration and argues that it is in the country's national interest to pursue a pro-integrationist, federalist approach in the European Union. According to Mitsos, the maximisation of gains from EU membership is only possible if Greece's long-term goals coincide with the other member states and Greek governments adopt a federalist outlook and practices.

Greece's approach to the European integration process has been characterised by a certain intergovernmentalism. Nonetheless, in recent years, the realisation of the economic gains to be expected from EU membership has resulted in a more European approach. This is reflected in a political and social consensus in favour of European integration.

Despite this fact however, Greece continues to adopt a strong intergovernmentalist stance regarding major decisions on the direction of the integration process, diverging significantly from other member states. As a result, Greece remains a marginal country with respect to the decision-making process within the European framework. The driving force behind Greece's intergovernmental approach to the integration process is to be found in its foreign policy considerations, and in particular in its relation to Turkey which affects the entire spectrum of Greek policies. Greece's success in economic issues lies in the development of a gradual convergence between national and Community long term goals. In the field of foreign policy issues such a condition is difficult to achieve: this difficulty is exacerbated by Greece's reluctance to promote a long term approach emphasising closer ties between the EU and Turkey.

It is also argued that it is in Greece's interest to adopt a consistent pro-integrationist stance in its overall political action within Community processes. Isolating a particular policy area and adopting contradictory strategies, tactics and approaches regarding the EU's various policy areas, is not only impossible, but will eventually prove detrimental to Greek interests. Greece's stance on the extent, depth and form of the Community's sectoral policies, or their financial consequences needs to be compatible with its internal economic policy, as well as its foreign policy. Moreover, Greece must recognise the need to promote the identification of long-term goals with a strong European dimension. This will lead to the acceptance of the federalist logic in everyday Community practices which, in turn, will permit the maximisation of gains from participation in the process of European integration. A federalist approach is not just an ideological choice but an imperative of the national interest.

The second part of the book deals with issues related to Greece's membership of the European Monetary Union (EMU). All contributors suggest that Greece has made significant economic progress during the late 1990s and it is highly likely that it will achieve EMU participation by the year 2001. In order to ensure survival within, and benefit from EMU participation and the ability to deal with possible economic shocks within the single currency area, contributors also suggest that Greece facilitate structural reforms and privatisation, and focus on improving labour market flexibility. More specifically, Christodoulakis suggests that Greece has made substantial progress towards both real and nominal convergence but stresses the need for structural reforms and in particular, labour market policies. Garganas is satisfied with the initiatives taken for the introduction of structural reforms and believes that Greece's prospects within EMU are very good. Alogoskoufis, in contrast, argues that the Government's performance with regard to structural reforms is very poor, and unless more radical policies towards real convergence are introduced, it is likely that Greece will face major problems within EMU.

Christodoulakis (*The Greek Economy Converging Towards EMU*) is generally optimistic about Greece's economic performance. He examines the development of the Greek economy towards convergence with the EU and argues that recent economic developments (1995–1999) suggest that Greece has entered a period of increasing growth, a balanced fiscal position and is certain to join EMU. All economic estimates and indicators show that Greece will be able to achieve the Maastricht Treaty convergence criteria for participating in EMU by the year 2001.

The author argues that apart from the progress in nominal convergence, the economic indicators of the last five years also suggest a development towards macro-economic stability and real convergence. The recent economic stabilisation was accompanied by measures aimed at the country's competitiveness as well as the market's ability to respond to country-specific shocks within EMU; coupled with the Simitis government's successful implementation of its privatisation programme and a broad class of structural measures to improve labour market flexibility.

The author emphasises that economic stability and convergence is not only a necessary condition for entering EMU, but also that within EMU a country which no longer suffers from macroeconomic impediments is more capable of absorbing shocks and achieving growth and employment. After EMU, Greek governments will not be able to use an autonomous monetary policy as a policy instrument to handle a possible adverse shock to its national economy. Therefore, not only Greece, but other member states, will have to rely on the increased flexibility of wages and prices to facilitate adjustment to country-specific disturbances. In this context, for the next few years Greek governments should focus on the deregulation of the labour market and the welfare state. Greek policy makers should try to increase the degree of flexibility in labour markets and invest heavily in education and training in order to create a competent labour force. Finally, Greek policy makers should also try to reinforce social cohesion mechanisms and support systems. Reconciling efficiency with social equity emerges as the major political challenge of the future. In this way, the material gains of greater efficiency could be used to create a mechanism for reconciling the economy with society.

Garganas (*Greece and EMU: Prospects and Challenges*) is even more optimistic regarding the development of the Greek economy. He also emphasises the fact that Greece should speed up its privatisation programmes and structural reforms in order to ensure that EMU participation will be beneficial. However, he believes that Greece not only has made remarkable progress in terms of nominal convergence criteria but also that the structural reforms that are already in place will ensure Greece's successful performance within EMU.

Garganas argues that with the introduction of the Euro, attention will shift from issues of transition to the challenges posed by EMU for Euro-area economies and what they need to do over the next 10–15 years. As the option of using monetary policies disappears, EMU members will find themselves constrained in their ability to respond to macroeconomic shocks or to changes in local economic conditions. As EU countries do not possess homogeneous economic structures, asymmetric shocks may occur and the risks of such shocks are of particular importance for small open economies, such as Greece.

The author argues that Greece should ensure that the adjustments made are sustainable after EMU and that the country will be able to cope effectively with macro-economic shocks. The Greek economy will face two main challenges after EMU. The first is the continuing need for fiscal consolidation post 1999. The second is the demand for more labour market flexibility. Although to achieve this public expenditure would need to be substantially limited, it would still be realistic for the government to speed up and expand its privatisation plans and press ahead in earnest with its programmes for reforming the social security system and the wider public sector, rationalising public expenditure, and reducing tax evasion. It is also argued that policy measures aimed at enhancing competition in product markets and improving labour market flexibility need to be pursued as a matter of urgency. Garganas maintains that there are some positive developments such as: the social dialogue programme on economic growth, competitiveness and employment, the structural measures in public enterprises to improve quality and reduce the costs of services, and the new (1998) legislation on labour flexibility. The author's view is that Greece is moving forward to be able to meet the challenges of the future. Due to the requirements of prospective participation in EMU, important progress has been made during the last few years in terms of macro-economic adjustment. Moreover, he suggests 'that structural changes are already being implemented to help ensure that Greece will not only survive in EMU, but it will be able to thrive in the EMU'.

Alogoskoufis (*The Greek Economy and the Euro*) is more moderate in his hypotheses for the future successful performance of Greece within EMU. Like Christodoulakis, he also emphasises the importance of EMU membership for a small country with macroeconomic imbalances such as Greece. Apart from tackling the root causes of Greece's inflation problem, EMU participation would also be politically advantageous, as it would allow Greece to become fully integrated within the EU. It is currently widely expected that Greece will achieve EMU participation before the year 2002. Alogoskoufis suggests that despite the delays and weaknesses of the convergence programmes introduced during the 1990s, it is highly likely that Greece will make it into the Euro zone. However, although Alogoskoufis recognises the significant progress made by the Greek economy, he stresses that in terms of nominal convergence there are still significant problems to be tackled, whilst in terms of structural adjustment, Greece's performance has been particularly poor. Unless Greece speeds up its structural reforms we cannot be optimistic about the country's prospects within EMU. Thus, in the next few years Greece must focus on achieving the required nominal convergence for EMU participation, whilst elaborating on the nature of domestic structural reforms to achieve real convergence with the EU and ensure sustainable economic and social advancement.

It is argued that the structural reforms of the 1990s have not been sufficiently bold to help reverse expectations and lead to a new wave of investment and growth that would help close the gap in living standards between Greece and the EU. The government's record with regard to measures for making room for private investment and for better utilisation of EU funds has been rather unsatisfactory.

In this context, the author claims that not only will entry into EMU cost the country more than necessary due to delays and policy failures, but also that Greece will be relatively unprepared for the challenges of life in EMU. He recommends the following seven priorities as a means of accelerating reforms: a) consolidation of public finances; b) simplification of tax system; c) reform of public administration; d) serious reform in education; e) reform of the health and social security systems; f) dramatic reforms of the state enterprise sector, and g) new regional policy.

Finally, Arghyrou (*EMU and Greek Macro-economic Policy in the 1990s*) examines why the macro-economic strategy in the 1990s failed to achieve EMU participation in 1999, and seeks to identify the macro-economic strategy that would maximise the chances of Greece joining the single currency in 2001.

Arghyrou argues that Greece's inability to qualify for EMU in 1999 stemmed from its policy of limited potential. This policy could not compensate for the lack of determination to undertake the political cost necessary to modernise the public sector, and promote long-overdue structural adjustments in the supply section of the Greek economy.

Arghyrou suggests that in order to secure EMU participation in 2001, the Greek government should follow a macro-economic strategy which is based upon: a) reduction of public consumption to achieve stabilisation; b) the implementation of measures to ensure real convergence (privatisation, labour and product market flexibility, welfare reforms, infrastructure projects); and c) a fiscal and income policy with a 2 per cent inflation objective.

In relation to the latter, it is argued that the prospect of Greece joining EMU in 2001 will increase if authorities consolidate their decision to reduce public consumption and promote structural adjustment, with a decision to abandon the highly risky exchange rate pegging monetary framework and replace it with one involving formal inflation targets.

Finally, it is suggested that as the prospect of joining EMU is well received by Greek society the Greek government has the opportunity to take the necessary measures to correct the serious macroeconomic imbalances and structural weaknesses of the economy with minimum social reaction.

Part III deals with issues related to state modernisation and adjustment. Chryssochoou, Stravridis and Moschonas (*Greece and the European Union after Amsterdam*) examine the Amsterdam Treaty (AMT) reforms and their implications for both the European integration process and Greek politics. It is argued that the AMT represents the outcome of a largely managerial type of reform with no important developments on the issues that it was initially expected to address, mainly enlargement and institutional reform. The reason for this lies in the fundamental intergovernmentalist nature of the EU system of governance. In the authors' view, although the creation of a Single Market has resulted in new forms of interest group organisation and patterns of large-scale civil society-formation, the member governments are still capable of exercising managerial control over integration. In this sense, the EU remains a 'contractual union' sustained by an informal culture of consensus created by the elite. Thus, 'as long as EU constitutional change is controlled by a management coalition of states the prospects for substantive institutional reforms will remain particularly moderate'.

Since the signing of the Treaty of European Union in 1992 (the Maastricht Treaty), the political climate surrounding Greece's European perspective is characterised by a wide consensus among the majority of the political forces in Greece that support the process of European integration. In this context, Greece adopted a strong pro-integrationist approach in the 1996/97 IGC promoting the federalisation of EU structures and its democratic legitimisation. With respect to Greek objectives, it is argued that as the 1996/97 Intergovernmental Conference provided for an intergovernmental mechanism of multilateral bargaining and negotiation, it is difficult to assess the extent to which Greece's original aspirations have been incorporated in the AMT. However, the reforms introduced in relation to issues of social policy, employment, the flexibility clause and the incorporation of the Schengen Agreement into the community framework generally indicate that 'what was actually achieved brings Greece closer to EU governance structures whilst increasing the pressure for substantive domestic reforms toward modernisation'.

The AMT includes many of the proposals supported by Greece with the exception of the key issue of territorial integrity – which failed to materialise. Greece's key objectives for external reform were the protection of borders and the inclusion of a mutual assistance clause. Although these objectives would fit into the EU's rhetoric as an extension of economic and monetary union, such issues would also represent a clear move toward a more federal Europe: thus they were accepted as difficult to achieve in a context where the majority of member states are reluctant to move in this direction.

Liargovas (*The Changing Role of the Greek State in View of EMU*) examines the changing role of the Greek state in view of EMU and argues that EU membership had a significant impact on Greece's economic and social development. This impact is particularly evident in the more flexible, yet decreased role of the state in the Greek economy and society. The author examines the reasons for the delay in adopting economic and structural reforms in Greece, and how during the 1990s, Greek public authorities finally started to implement wide-scale reforms aimed at improving the state's effectiveness and efficiency. He argues that the shift in Greece's economic policy towards the adoption of structural reforms can be attributed to the impact of 'the EMU factor' in Greek economy and society.

The author suggests that according to 'new political economy' theory there are three main reasons why, during the 1980s, successive Greek governments displayed such irrational and myopic behaviour regarding macroeconomic policies. Firstly, the significant ideological differences regarding redistributive priorities among the main political parties meant that governments were using their control over a macro-economic variable to influence the choices available to future governments, or for attracting votes in pre-election periods. Secondly, great uncertainty over the potential gains and losses limited public support for structural reforms and privatisation programmes. And finally, the weak civil society and the clientelistic mode of political organisation in Greece meant that particular groups had a relatively stronger organisational and interventionist capacity and thus were able to resist policies that were perceived as detrimental to their interests.

The EMU factor played a significant role in the development of policies for structural reforms and privatisation. The EMU target put pressure on Greek governments to implement institutional reforms. It therefore helped to increase policy makers' credibility and the degree of commitment, thereafter reducing the level of public uncertainty. In addition, the process of economic convergence had a positive effect on the ideological convergence of the different political parties regarding alternative economic policies. Moreover, the institutional reforms and the measures taken for rationalising policy making created obstacles for the influence exercised by interest groups. The author argues that overall 'EMU has acted as an external shock increasing public authorities' commitment to implement changes, and paving the way to institutional reforms, thus destroying the influence of interest groups in Greece'. In this sense, it can be argued that the development of specific policies that will drive Greece into the euro zone have not only an economic dimension, but also represent important changes in Greek society and politics.

Pagoulatos (*The Six Syndromes of Structural Adjustments. Or What*

Greek Privatisation Can Teach Us) argues that the 'new political economy' theories that pessimistically view policy reform programmes as 'plagued by self-interested politicians, opportunists, bureaucrats and rent-seeking coalitions', are not very helpful in studying the case of privatisation in Greece. The most important question is not how policies will be imposed within an unfavourable setting, but how they will be sustained. In this context, his main concern is to explain why the Simitis government, in comparison to previous governments, has enjoyed a political advantage in the implementation of its economic adjustment and privatisation policies. He argues that three factors explain this fact: a) a policy learning process where the government of 1996 was able to draw upon the experience of previous privatisation enterprises, b) the presumption of left-wing sensibility and undisputed social-democratic credentials that the Simitis government enjoyed among the public and interest groups, allowed the implementation of privatisation against limited sociopolitical reaction, and c) the external constraints factor associated with EMU participation allowed the Simitis government to implement structural reforms and privatisation by almost defying political costs.

The author argues that we must consider that privatisation policies are only one part of a process toward the transition from an interventionist to a new regulatory state and should not be regarded as the ticket to a 'free for all' capitalism. The most compelling justifications put forward for these policies in Greece 'concern not their intrinsic desirability, but their pragmatic necessity'. However, after the question of desirability has been resolved, the implementation of privatisation alone does not necessarily imply that they will have a positive effect. The author emphasises that 'privatisation should be followed by a strengthening and expansion rather that a weakening of public regulatory authority'. If new regulatory authorities fail to emerge the concentration of power within a small number of private interests is highly likely to prove as detrimental to the economy and society as the traditional clientelism of the public sector.

Mamatzakis (*Public Infrastructure as a Determinant Factor of the Economic Performance of Greek Industrial Output*) offers an empirical estimation of the effects of public capital stock on private sector productivity in Greek industry. His study reveals that the effect of infrastructure on private sector productivity is positive and far reaching. Thus it is reasonable to expect that building up infrastructure enhances the productivity of the industrial sector, and benefits the Greek economy as a whole. The author emphasises that the importance of the empirical findings of this study rests on the underlying policy suggestions that Greece is still a developing country with anachronistic infrastructure in the periphery of the EU.

Low productivity growth in Greece during the 1970s and 1980s was a major problem, and resulted in a widening productivity gap between Greece and the EU. The stagnation of government investment in the 1980s meant that there was no substantial progress in the implementation of major infrastructure projects. This occurred despite the widespread recognition of the importance of several major infrastructure projects for the country's economic restructuring. Mamatzakis argues that infrastructure might be the missing link in macroeconomic policy. It could enhance the attractiveness and competitiveness of the Greek economy by restoring many economically inactive regions created over the last twenty years through a process of de-industrialisation. Moreover, the poor services derived from infrastructure largely affect the Greek economy in its development towards convergence with the rest of the EU partners. The European Commission seems to realise this as the priority of the EU support framework for Greece is the creation of the appropriate infrastructure as a necessary condition for the development of the country and its convergence to European standards. Moreover, infrastructure is a determining factor in Greece's role in the South-eastern region of Europe since the development of proper infrastructure is almost a precondition for the realisation of Greece's ambition to become a business and transport hub linking South-east Europe with the EU.

Paraskevopoulos (*Institutional Networks, Learning and Greece's Adaptation within European Regional Policy*) examines the process of the Europeanisation of regional policy, and argues that Greece's centralised state structure and weak civil society are major impediments to the adaptation processes that are required for taking full advantage of the benefits associated with EU's structural policy.

The empowerment of subnational governments through European regional policies has significant effects for local government and community structures. Regional and local systems of government are increasingly affected by supranational linkages, and by their capacity to exploit the challenges that those linkages present. In this context, the effectiveness and efficiency of policy making at regional level depends on adaptation ability; that is, the learning institutional infrastructure at the local level, rather than on the protective role of the state.

It is argued that despite the major reforms in local administration imposed in Greece by the Europeanisation process of the 1980s and 1990s, policy making is still characterised by centralised administration and hierarchical intergovernmental relations. This structure affects the distribution of resources and power among local actors and subsequently constitutes a major impediment to the building of horizontal cooperative networks, thus inhibiting Greece's adjustment to the European environment. Moreover, the weak civil society in Greece associated with administrative weaknesses and the clientelistic political system, is a main characteristic of Greek sociopolitical structure which substantially limits the capability for collective action.

The author argues that due to state centralisation and weak civil society in Greece, the Europeanisation process at the local level relies decisively upon the above initiatives to create a more rapid structural adjustment to the European environment. The Europeanisation process is interpreted as an external shock for the 'inward looking political class', society and the economy. The challenge of Europeanisation and the involvement of EU programmes and initiatives constitutes a positive external shock for the local systems of governance resulting in the amelioration of local institutional infrastructure, even where the pre-existing local capacity in terms of learning and institution-building is poor. However, in the long-term, these developments cannot sustain the process of Europeanisation. Local partnerships and networking enabling regional actors to participate in cooperative relations and the provision of public goods, constitute the crucial factors for facilitating adaptation in the less favoured regions of Europe.

Finally, Fokas (*Orthodoxy and the EU*) challenges those approaches, developed both in Greece and abroad, that recognise Orthodoxy as a national tradition forming a barrier between Greece and the EU. She argues that the appropriation of religion by politics is a dangerous trend that may lead to the regionalisation of Europe according to religion, and to the peripheralisation of Greece.

The author points to a political and academic discourse which, in its search for the quintessential elements of a 'European identity', accepts the dichotomy between Catholic and Orthodox Christianity as the fundamental dividing line in the cultural demarcation of Europe, and designates Orthodoxy as un-European and incompatible with the integration process. In the absence of an official European Union cultural-religious agenda, the centrality of religion in shaping the boundaries of European civilisation is of significant importance for those nations, such as Greece, which lie outside particular narrow definitions of such an identity.

However, such ideas are reflected in, or even spurred by, facts and opinions within Greece. The special relationship between church, the state and ethnicity in Greece has rendered Orthodox faith a strong element of political conscience. The development of a certain anti-Western populism is based on a set of ideological distortions of the centrality that Orthodoxy has for Greek national identity. There is a widespread perception of Greek identity which has also been analysed and argued over by academics, politicians and other public figures who regard faith as a barrier between Greece and the rest of Europe and considers European Modernity as a threat to Greek culture and society.

This popular dichotomy and incompatibility between Orthodoxy and the West that is deliberated in both domestic and international discussions, not only facilitates the trend towards the religious regionalisation of Europe, but also serves to provide the intellectual basis for those restricting membership in the New European political, economic and security architectures and resisting the changes in Greek society associated with such membership.

Fokas argues that this manipulation of religion both in Greece and abroad is a very dangerous trend. Regardless of the direction in which the prejudice is flowing (to, or from the West) the potential results are the same: a regionalisation of Europe according to religious, cultural and civilisation differences and the peripheralisation of Greece by these factors.

Part IV addresses the area of social policies in Greece. Whilst welfare systems vary across different countries, their differences are also related to central nation state-building processes such as the development of social and economic patterns, political and social culture and a concept of national citizenship. In this respect, welfare crisis in Greece is explained largely in terms of the internal qualities of the Greek statist/clientelistic model of social organisation, and reflects the serious institutional and social deadlocks it created during the 1980s. Petmesidou (*Social Protection in Greece in the Nineties: Reforming the 'Weak' Welfare State*) argues that the qualitative characteristics of the welfare state crisis in Greece make the success of reform, aimed at solving economic and social problems, conditional upon the development of a wide social consensus regarding a new mode for the economy, and a new social contract for the redefinition of the relationship between civil society, and the state. The inherent relationship between welfare crisis, and the peculiarities of the political and social culture that permeate the state and society in Greece, suggests that reforming the social protection system towards a universalistic approach requires a broader transformation of the socioeconomic regime. The most important prerequisite for such a transformation is a consensus-building process that will both assign importance to and support the reform of public policies, and promote agreement between social partners.

The legal reforms introduced during the 1990s with respect to the pension system, the labour market, health care and social welfare represent a decisive attempt to meet the challenges facing the Greek model of social protection. The social dialogue programme is an important development towards social consensus building. However, disagreement between social partners still prevails and the process of change with respect to social concentration, in favour of large scale and effective reform, is slow. In addition, the domination of the fiscal imperative surrounding EMU over the social effects of the reforming measures further exacerbates the incapacity of social partners to become significant forces of transformation. The author suggests that 'it is highly likely that a persistent policy along these lines will cause serious confrontations and a stalemate within social dialogue in Greece'. In this respect, the development of supranational policies for improving social quality at EU level, and promoting reciprocity between European economic and social policies might prove to be of crucial importance towards social concentration for a thorough regime transformation in Greece.

The link between the Greek model of social protection, and the peculiarities of the Greek model of social organisation, may lead us to conclusions about the 'uniqueness' of the Greek situation. However, the evidence presented in Tsakloglou's chapter (*Poverty and Anti-poverty Policies in Greece and a Comparison with Other Mediterranean and EU Member States*) suggest that such a claim cannot be sustained. In his paper, he examines the patterns of poverty and anti-poverty policies in Greece and argues that the issues of inequality and poverty cannot be analysed with reference to the 'uniqueness' of the Greek situation. The author uses comparative analysis to challenge the assertions about the 'Greek uniqueness'. He demonstrates that considerable similarities can be found between Greece and the rest of the Southern Mediterranean EU member states both in the structure and patterns of poverty, and in the development of anti-poverty policies. The evidence presented in this study is indicative of the existence of a distinct Southern European model of welfare based upon a number of socioeconomic factors that are common to these countries. Such factors are dualist economic structures, strong family links, the operation of political clientelism and vested interests, and low efficiency and corruption of the public sector. These factors create a situation where the provision of social welfare is only sufficient for segments of the population with strong links with the labour market. However, family links prevent the emergence of extreme forms of material deprivation. In this context the author concludes that, at least in the fields of social policy in general and poverty and anti-poverty policies in particular, the Greek case rather than being 'unique', presents many similarities with other Southern EU member states that have developed a distinct model of the welfare state.

As Petmesidou points out in her own chapter, during the 1990s, the remaining Southern European states introduced successful reform policies. This indicates that an effective process of consensus building on changing the mode of governance has already taken place. However, in Greece such a development is still very slow and disagreement among social patterns seems to prevail.

Part V deals with Greece's external relations. Most of the contributors agree that the Greek political system, its economy and society is undergoing a process of change as a result of the requirements of adjusting to the European integration process. Ioakimidis (*The Europeanisation of Greece's Foreign Policy: Progress and Problems*) demonstrates how this process of Europeanisation can also be identified in the field of foreign policy as Greece adjusts to the objectives, policy styles, procedural and institutional requirements of the Common Foreign and Security Policy (CFSP). Since 1995, as its foreign policy objectives and goals seem to have acquired a strong European dimension, Greece has almost ceased to be perceived as a 'heretical' awkward partner in the EU framework. The Europeanisation process can be identified in that the thematic and geographic scope of Greece's foreign policy agenda has been expanded beyond 'high politics issues' to include, more generally, elements of 'low politics' such as trade environment, technology, agriculture and culture, and to account for problems of remote countries and regions. The prevailing style of foreign policy has also transformed as Greece gradually abandons its rhetorical, populist and strong nationalistic mode for a more pragmatic, problem-solving and issue-oriented approach. This integrates the concepts of negotiations and compromise as principle diplomatic techniques for solving problems and promoting interests. There is also an attempt to rationalise foreign policy making structures with the establishment of new bodies to institutionalise policy making processes and promote a less personalised approach. Overall, the requirements of EU membership instigated substantive change to the objectives and orientation of foreign policy, and public perceptions and attitudes about Greece's global position and its external relations.

However, Ioakimidis also argues that the Europeanisation of Greece's foreign policy by no means implies that Greece is satisfied with the performance and policy outputs of Common Foreign and Security Policy (CFSP), especially with respect to the management of regional or international crises, and with the ability of its partners to address its fundamental security concerns. It is argued that there is still a 'capability expectations gap' associated with Greece's tendency to over-estimate the potential security benefits to be gained by membership of the EU. Greece appears to sustain far greater expectations of the CFSP, than the policy it is capable of delivering. Despite the fact that considerable progress has been made towards the rationalisation of Greece's foreign policy, a traditional perception of European countries as the 'protector powers' still characterises Greece's participation in the CFSP. The author argues that it is in Greece's interest to adjust its expectations in line with the CFSP's existing capabilities, while adopting a strong pro-integrationist stance for the strengthening of the policy's institutional, political and military qualities.

The two major and interrelated foreign policy objectives for Greece concern the questions of its potential role in the Balkan region and its policy vis-à-vis Turkey. Couloumbis (*Greece in a Post-Cold War Environment*) examines the challenges facing Greece in this respect, and the possibilities for developing policies aimed at the stabilisation and democratisation of the Balkans, and the establishment of a climate of reconciliation and cooperation towards Turkey.

He argues that successive Greek governments since 1974 have adopted a cautious and pragmatic set of external policies expressing a consensual approach to Greek foreign policy challenges. Whilst trying to maintain a military balance of power towards Turkey, Greece has managed to promote its integration within a zone of global stability (EU, Western European Union – WEU and the North Atlantic Treaty Organisation – NATO) and to act as a stabilising party in the Balkans, promoting multilateral and multilevelled cooperation in the region.

The author argues that post Cold War conditions present Greece with many challenges, but also with significant opportunities to enhance its strategic political and economic place in the international environment. As Greece emerged as the only consolidated democracy with an advanced market economy in the Balkan region, its interest lies in becoming an active contributor to peace, promoting the processes of democratisation and economic liberalisation. Greece should actively promote, both in the context of EU, NATO and the Organisation for Security and cooperation in Europe – OSCE, and through bilateral and regional initiatives, policies aimed at peace and cooperation in the southeast. Such programmes will link economic aid, technical assistance, free trade and investment with respect for the inviolability of international boundaries, the consolidation of democratic institutions, protection of human rights and a free market economy. A successful strategy of peace and mutually advantageous cooperation in the Balkans is likely to ameliorate the troubled Greek-Turkish relationship. As the strategic importance of Turkey has declined, the post Cold War era offers Greece and Cyprus a) the opportunity to pursue a consensual foreign policy that will combine a defence strategy designed to avoid war and safeguard the territorial status quo in the Aegean, Thrace and Cyprus; and b) a diplomatic strategy that combines the use of politico-economic instruments of leverage on Turkey with a comprehensive and long term set of proposals for mutually acceptable settlements in Cyprus and the Aegean.

Overall, it is argued that as the post Cold War environment creates many opportunities for Greece to advance its international economic and strategic position, the country should avoid the single issue and reactive policies of the past and follow a consistent foreign policy aimed at the stabilisation of the Balkan region, with Greece becoming an important economic and political power, and the establishment of a climate of reconciliation and cooperation with Turkey.

Veremis (*Kosovo: A Greek Appraisal*) is also preoccupied with the issue of stabilisation and peace in the Balkan area. Yugoslavia can be regarded as an example of what Couloumbis describes in his paper as the 'democratic paradox', a phenomenon that characterises the processes of social and economic liberalisation in many post-communist countries where democratisation is correlated with violent ethnic and social conflicts. Veremis examines the historical and political developments that led to both the outbreak of the Kosovo conflict in Yugoslavia, and NATO military operations against Yugoslavia. He argues that this case represents an example of how a small and middle-ranking state, undergoing a period of significant socioeconomic transformation and facing important domestic problems, fails to come to terms with the reality of great power politics. However, the great powers also failed to convince Serbia to comply with Western demands, and military action emerged as the only solution to terminate the continuing violation of the rights of Albanians, despite the fact that similar violations taking place in other parts of the world are only decried.

The cleavage on the preferred solutions amongst all negotiating sides, the refusal to proceed to more intensive negotiations, and the failure of international institutional frameworks to accommodate the conflict, were the primary reasons that led Western powers to resort to NATO military intervention. There was an important difference between the autonomy offered by the international community to the Kosovo Albanians, and the full independence they demanded. While the Serbs would have agreed to a partitioning of the region, this was not seen as a viable solution to the West.

Eventually, the use of force became the only solution that Western powers proved capable of delivering. This highlighted the failure of the international community to understand the complicated dynamics of Balkan conflicts, and underlined the weakness of the European framework of cooperation in playing a decisive role in the resolution of conflicts taking place in the region. Regarding the future of a post-Milosevic Yugoslavia, Western governments may witness either the disintegration of Yugoslavia into a number of non-viable micro-states, or a decimated Serbia with its present leadership still lodged in power. However, the most important question is whether the rest of South-eastern Europe can pursue its development and linkage with the European Union without Yugoslavia. The author suggests that the stabilisation and consolidation of boundaries amongst Serbia and its Southern neighbours ought to become a major western priority as the disintegration of Yugoslavia could release a chain-reaction of similar phenomena in the region.

In the recent history of Greece's external relations, the issue of the Former Yugoslav Republic of Macedonia (FYROM) has been widely regarded as an instance where Greece failed to realise the requirements of its participation in a broader European system of cooperation, and preferred to compromise its long-term interests in the Balkan area by adopting a narrow definition of national interest. Greek policies with respect to FYROM have seriously damaged its reputation as a European partner and have reinforced a perception of Greece as a country with a strong non cooperative approach.

Against these claims, Tziampiris (*Greece's Contribution to European Political Cooperation Policies Towards Former Yugoslavia, June 1991 – January 1992: An Institutional Analysis*) argues that within the context of the European Political Cooperation (EPC) arrangements for the resolution of the Yugoslav conflict, the Greek government of the period, from June 1991 to January 1992, pursued politics of cooperation rather than displaying counter-productive behaviour as has often been purported. The author argues that, viewed through the theoretical lenses of institutionalism, during this short period Greece contributed in a conducive way to the efforts that took place to contain and end the war in Yugoslavia in the context of the EPC international regime, while its behaviour towards FYROM was primarily marked by moderation and willingness to cooperate.

According to institutionalist theories, contentions about reputational concerns, side payments, reciprocity and anticipated regime decisions, the Greek cooperative attitude was mostly driven by the common belief among Greek decision makers that it was essential that their state be viewed by its EPC partners as contributing to the solution of the Yugoslav conflict. They also desired to portray Greece as a country with legitimate concerns in the region, and to create a reputation of trustworthiness and responsibility. Greece's foreign policy goals concerning monetary compensation for losses suffered by the war in Yugoslavia, the expectations of the upcoming Maastricht Summit, the establishment of the Cohesion Fund and accession to the WEU, superseded what amounted to a kind of traditional Greco-Serbian special relationship, and explain Greece's politics of cooperation towards the former Yugoslavia and FYROM. Tziampiris argues that the EPC operated as an international regime, which by linking the present with the future, created reputational concerns and ultimately increased pressures for cooperation between the different parts.

However, Tziampiris's chapter does not deal with the eventual transformation of the politics of cooperation, to the politics of confrontation regarding the 'name issue'. He briefly mentions that after January 1992, where domestic developments in Greece such as the rise of intense popular passions, increased partisanship and the split between the then Prime Minister Mitsotakis and then Foreign Affairs Minister Samaras, brought about the adoption of a restrictive position on the New Republic's name that eventually became non-negotiable and paramount to any other foreign policy goals. According to Tziampiris this change is better explained on the basis of a 'domestic politics approach', rather than through institutionalism.

Georgiades (*Greece and the EU-Turkish Relationship*) concurs that Greece's foreign policy has become more rationalised and flexible, acquiring a strong European dimension. He assesses the role of Greece in the EU-Turkish relationship, and argues that since 1995, Greece has adopted a more flexible approach and can no longer be accused of blocking Turkey's EU perspective. The author examines the role of Greece in the context of a controversial debate on whether Turkey was unwisely and unjustly shunned by the EU on the grounds of cultural differences and subjective notions of democracy, or whether the EU has simply set some self-evident prerequisites for membership that Turkey should try and meet.

During the 1980s, Greece reacted negatively and inflexibly towards any attempt to strengthen EC-Turkish relations, adopting an absolute stance and over-utilising its veto power, thus failing to secure the support of its European partners. Although one would have expected that the coming to power in 1990 of the more pro-European New democracy party would improve the Greek position within the EC, foreign policy continued to be driven by a myopic and narrow definition of the country's national interest, and engagement in the dispute over the name of FYROM served to further deteriorate Greece's negotiating leverage within the EC framework. Since the succession to government of Constantine Simitis, Greece has shown signs of a new and more constructive approach towards Turkey. This reached its pinnacle at the Luxembourg Summit in 1997 when Greece expressed its support for Turkey's eventual participation in the EU, and convinced its partners to codify a set of rules mainly regarding democratic institutions that, once met by Ankara, would facilitate the progress of EU-Turkish relations.

It is suggested that Greece should realise that it will benefit from having a democratic, prosperous and Europeanised Eastern neighbour and should adopt a proactive stance, with capable diplomacy aimed in this direction. Greece also needs to be a reliable EU partner as has been recently demonstrated through its more constructive foreign policy and honest efforts for economic convergence. Greece should move beyond the adoption of a 'conditionality' policy and be ready to show flexibility on issues such as the release of financial assistance to Turkey. It must also continue to try to convince its EU partners that a prosperous and democratic Turkey would only serve European interests. What remains to be seen is whether Turkey will share this vision.

Both Walldén (*Greece and the Balkans: Economic Relations*) and

Labrianidis (*Are Greek Companies that Invest in the Balkans in the 1990s Transnational Companies?*) emphasise the increasing importance of economic initiatives not only in terms of economic gains, but also for achieving its foreign policy objectives. In addition, Christodoulakis (*The Greek Economy Converging Towards EMU*) suggests that the recent economic activity developed in the area by Greek economic agents has significantly aided the overall improvement of the Greek economy. The opening of the Balkan markets is an obvious political and economic benefit for all the European nations and markets, and Greece already has a pivotal role in this process with a great number of investment projects in the Balkan area. Moreover, Christodoulakis suggests that this development is no substitute for the need for Greek firms to remain competitive in the European single market but it will help to achieve better size and capacity. Additionally, it will help with economic, political and institutional upgrading in the Balkan countries which is the best means towards their eventual accession to the European Union.

As Greece's economic relations with the Balkans have begun to receive considerable publicity, Walldén examines the country's economic performance in the region and considers the extent to which this economic activity can prove essentially beneficial for both Greece, and its Balkan neighbours.

It is argued that Greece's post-1989 performance in the Southern Balkans has been remarkable, and that political developments regarding both Greece's poor political record in the area, and the unfavourable political and economic climate in these countries, have not been able to arrest the development of economic relations. Although in some cases, such as transport, over-ambitious plans do not always seem based upon a long term assessment of the region's comparative advantages. Overall, Greek economic agents appear to have effectively exploited the opportunities offered by the process of economic and social restructuring in the Balkan area.

However, the economic opening in the Balkans may have a negative impact on Greece's economy and politics. Greece's economic orientation away from the demanding EU market to easier outlets in the Balkans may imply a qualitative downgrading of Greek production with both serious economic, and political consequences. Moreover, there is also great uncertainty regarding the Balkans' European perspective. The fact that Greece has developed stronger economic interests in countries that are either wholly excluded, or seem less promising as participants in the enlargement process may have negative consequences for Greece. The author argues that Greece should recognise that its economic future lies in Europe, EMU and global competitiveness. Nevertheless, an enhanced Greek role in the Balkans, which would be moving closer to the EU itself, could be a precious asset whilst proving beneficial to both the Union, and its Balkan partners. Greece has to resist a certain arrogance regarding its economic role in the Balkans and promote initiatives which are well prepared and less subordinated to power politics. Essentially, such a programme could prove profitable for both Greece and the other Balkan countries provided that there is a minimum of political and economic stability in the region, and that Greece resists the 'downgrading effect' of the Balkan and Eastern opening by improving the overall efficiency of its economy.

The last word belongs to Labrianidis who suggests that as a significant number of investment projects have been initiated in the region within a very short period of time, Greece seems to have effectively taken advantage of the economic opportunities offered in the Balkans. Similarly, he also points to the possible negative effects that these low market standards can have on Greece's effort to restructure its industry towards the production of high quality, internationally competitive products. In this chapter, he examines the operation of Greek companies in Central and Easter European Countries (CEECs) in order to identify whether the investment plans developed by Greek companies in the CEECs resemble conventional types of Transnational Companies – TNCs – ('true transnationals') or Transnational Companies from Underdeveloped Countries (UDCs). The author claims that this discussion is not simply concerned with 'the theoretical classification of Greek investment projects, but with the understanding of the mechanisms causing this internationalisation'. From this starting point Labrianidis 'attempts to reveal the comparative advantages of Greek investments in the CEECs that render their realisation feasible and whether they can be sustained in the long run'. The author argues that the characteristics of the companies concerned, and the type of Greek foreign investment in CEECs suggest that these investment projects cannot be classified either as 'true' (TNCs), or 'new' (TNCs from UDCs) transnationals. The majority are labour intensive, small scale operations predominantly attracted by the opportunities given by CEEC markets to reduce production costs, and in these markets, competition is based on price rather that quality. As both Walden and Labrianidis argue, the success of Greek economic ventures lies largely in the flexibility of Greek economic actors in volatile political and economic environments, and in intermediate prices and quality within conditions of limited income and domestic production recovering from collapse. As these factors are likely to erode, Greek investment projects will have to compete with domestic and Western economic actors. However, the evidence of this study suggests only a very limited number of the Greek companies investing in the CEECs have the opportunity to become new TNCs and less so 'true TNCs'.

Most of the papers being published in this collection are the revised presentations of the papers initially presented in a conference organised by the editors in 1998. The papers went through a rigorous review process (only 50 per cent of the papers submitted for review were finally selected for publication) and were updated to reflect changes since the conference took place.

We would like to acknowledge the work of the following referees whose help to the editors and authors was invaluable: Christopher Brewin, Dina Davaki, Spiros Economides, Geoffrey Edwards, Chryssafis Iordanoglou, Charlie Jeffrey, Kristis Konnaris, Lois Labrianidis, George Mavrotas, Nicos Mouzelis, Christos Papatheodorou, Chris Pissarides, Axel-Sotiris Walden, Stelios Stavridis, Elias Tzavalis, Panos Tsakloglou and Loukas Tsoukalis. We would also like to thank Anna Maresso for editorial coordination of the volume papers and Kennedy Stewart and Maria Komninou for their editorial assistance.

Finally, we would like to thank the authors of the chapters in this volume for a stimulating and productive collaboration. The political twists of the past three years gave the project many more twists and turns than we could have predicted at the outset. Their willingness to accommodate our many requests for yet another round of revisions has been greatly appreciated, as was their enthusiasm throughout the project.

London and Brussels, September 1999

References

Charalambis, D. (1989), *Clientelistic Relations and Populism: The Extra-Institutional Consensus Formation in the Greek Political System.* Athens: Exantas [in Greek].

Diamandouros, P.N. (1994), *Cultural Dualism and Political Change in Postauthoritarian Greece.* Madrid: Instituto Juan March de Estudios e Investigaciones, Working Paper.

Mouzelis, N.P. (1995), 'Greece in the Twenty-first Century: Institutions and Political Culture' in Constas, D. and Stavrou, T. (eds), *Greece Prepares for the Twenty-first Century*. Washington: The Woodrow Wilson Center Press.
Mouzelis, N.P. (1990), *Post Marxist Alternatives: The Construction of Social Orders*. London: Macmillan.
Pappas, T. (1999), *Making Party Democracy in Greece*. New York: St Martin's Press.
Sotiropoulos, D. (1996), *Populism and Bureaucracy: The Case of Greece under PASOK, 1981–1989*. Notre Dame: University of Notre Dame Press.
Spourdalakis, M. (1988), *The Rise of the Greek Socialist Party*. London: Routledge.
Tsoukalas, C. (1983), *Social Development and the State*. Athens: Themelio [in Greek].

2 The Fundamental Objectives of Greek Foreign Policy

YANNOS KRANIDIOTIS[1]

Modern Greek foreign policy unfolds in three co-centric circles that define Greece's position in the international system. The inner circle is formed by the European Union, to which Greece belongs organically and institutionally as a full member. The second circle is the regional sub-system of Southeastern Europe, where Greece finds itself geographically and culturally located. The third, outermost circle consists of the wider international system in which Greece participates by virtue of its membership in various international fora – including the United Nations and the open, globalised economic system. Placed within this context, there are essentially two fundamental objectives underpinning Greece's foreign policy today: (1) the objective of turning foreign policy into an operational instrument for promoting the interests of Greece as a member of the EU and of the area of Southeastern Europe; and (2) the desire to actively contribute to promoting the principles of peace, stability and cooperative patterns of behaviour, especially in the Balkans and the wider area of the Eastern Mediterranean.

It goes without saying that the European Union constitutes the bedrock and provides the defining framework of Greece's foreign policy. It is the springboard from which Greece seeks to develop its regional and international role. Membership of the European Union has solved a perennial problem for Greece: namely where Greece belongs, to the East or to the West. European Union membership means that Greece belongs to Europe and from this privileged position it can develop its links with the rest of the world. However one must remember that although a European country, Greece is simultaneously a Balkan and a Mediterranean country with historical, cultural and social features specific to this part of the world.

One notable development of recent years is that Greece has come to finally accept that its stability, prosperity and welfare are inextricably linked to its membership of the European Union. The future of Greece lies in the EU. As a result, Greece is determined to be part of the inner core of countries that would form the decision-making centre of the European Union in the 21st century, especially after the establishment of the Economic and Monetary Union (EMU) and the single currency – Euros. To that end, Greece has set as an overriding priority its participation in the single currency. For Greece, participation in the well-known single currency is not merely an economic issue, it is primarily a political one. It relates to Greece's role in the wider European architecture and its institutional place in the policy-formulating and decision-making process of the European Union.

Greece was not amongst the first group of countries which launched the Euro, since at this stage it did not meet the well-known 'convergence criteria' laid down in the Maasticht Treaty for joining the single currency. However the Greek economy has made considerable progress over the last four years in reducing the inflation rate and public deficits through the vigorous implementation of the 'convergence programme' as well as a programme of structural reforms. It is expected therefore that Greece will meet the criteria and become qualified to join the single currency by the year 2001. For the Greek government, this is a political objective of paramount importance which has to be obtained by all necessary political action and sacrifices. Otherwise, Greece feels that it runs the risk of being marginalised in the European Union context.

In political and economic terms, Greece has already substantially benefited from EU membership. Economically, Greece draws considerable resources from the EU budget – amounting to around 4 billion Euros per year. These funds have contributed to the economic modernisation of the country and the achievement of economic and social cohesion which constitutes a pivotal objective of the European Union. It also counterbalances the cost of the single European market and economic antagonism from some of the strongest countries of the Union. Therefore it is important that this effort on the part of the Union should continue in the future, particularly after the next enlargement. Politically, because of Greece's membership in the EU, the country has strengthened its bargaining power in the regional and the wider international system. Moreover, EU membership has assisted Greece in the process of building stable democratic institutions.

Greece has also significantly contributed to the growth and well-being of the EU. For example, in terms of European integration, suffice it to say that Greece has championed new ideas and principles – such as the need for economic and social cohesion embodied in the provisions of the Single

European Act. In addition, during its presidency in 1994 Greece worked successfully to enlarge the EU – adding Scandinavian countries and Austria. During this period it also initiated the Euromediterranean ('Barcelona') process in the European Council of Corfu and actively supported the deepening of integration in the IGC that drew up the Amsterdam Treaty.

With respect to future evolution of the EU, Greece's policy can be summed in the following main points:

EU Integration

Greece favours the process of deepening European integration and further developing the European Union. The new Treaty of Amsterdam is an important step in the right direction. Yet, much more is needed in order to eliminate the 'institutional deficit' which faces the European Union. For example, the institutional structures and decision-making mechanisms should be strengthened to accommodate the enlargement of the Union – such as when Cyprus and Central and Eastern Europe countries join the endeavour. The European Union must eventually acquire a genuine 'political government' capable of running the EMU and the enlarged economic and political responsibilities. Greece, therefore, advocates the revision of the treaties with the aim of strengthening the institutional system of the Union. Similarly, Greece actively supports the idea of developing further the Union's external capabilities for effective action. The Amsterdam Treaty makes a good contribution to enhancing the Union's common foreign and security policy (CFSP), but, again, much more is needed in order to enable the Union to confront new challenges, effectively manage crises and play a more decisive role in the international system, commensurate with its economic and commercial weight. The Kosovo crisis highlighted the need for enhancing the CFSP and endowing the EU with military capabilities. Finally, although a certain measure of flexibility might be necessary in an expanded Union, it would nevertheless be dangerous for the EU to pursue a 'policy of flexible integration' that would split the Union into groups of countries with different levels of 'integration involvement'. The institutionalisation of a multi-tiered Europe is not part of Greece's European strategy.

EU Enlargement

With regard to enlargement, Greece thinks that the accession of Central and Eastern European Countries to the EU represents an indispensable opportunity to cement democracy, stability and prosperity in a politically united Europe. The same applies to all Balkan countries including the countries that have emerged from the dissolution of Yugoslavia. Their accession to the European Union, would be the best strategy for eliminating the sources of instability in the region. Similarly, Greece believes that the European orientation of Turkey is both necessary and possible. It should be emphasised that Greece does not see the issue of the European orientation of Turkey in a dogmatic way – Greek concerns are purely political. Greece is prepared to welcome its eastern neighbour to the European family of nations, provided that it complies with the principles and norms upon which the EU is built.

The accession of Cyprus to the EU will contribute to the economic prosperity of the island and will reinforce the sense of security of its population. This would be particularly so in the case of the Turkish Cypriot community. It must also be made clear that the political question should not be related to the accession of Cyprus to the EU. It would be, of course, desirable to find a solution to the problem well before the end of the accession process. Every effort needs to be made in this respect and all parties concerned should be encouraged to show moderation and work within the UN framework for a just, viable and lasting solution of the Cyprus problem. The solution of the political problem, however, should not be a precondition. Cyprus' accession to the EU coupled with a comprehensive plan for the demilitarisation of the island will go a long way to the resolution of the Cyprus problem, guaranteeing peace and prosperity to all the citizens of the Republic, while transforming Cyprus into an island of stability in the region.

Inter-regional Cooperation

The establishment of a system of inter-regional cooperation embracing all countries of Southeastern Europe remains one of the principal objectives of Greece's foreign policy. Inter-regional cooperation conceived as an intermediate step towards eventual full accession to the European Union could enhance the conditions for cementing stability, democracy and economic development and welfare in the region. Especially after the Kosovo crisis, the stabilisation of Southeastern Europe through the promotion of advanced schemes of cooperation constitute a fundamental objective of Greece's foreign policy.

With respect to bilateral relations with Turkey, Greece is committed to developing a friendly, cooperative relationship. While this will be in the interest of both countries, it will be of special benefit to Turkey, immensely facilitating the Turkish drive to join the European Union. Of course, a pattern of cooperative relations must be based on the respect of the fundamental principles of international law and treaties and the legitimate rights of each country concerning its sovereignty and independence. Any dispute or claim can be resolved within the legal framework defined by international law, treaties and instruments including the International Court of Justice.

In spite of their differences, in August, 1999, Greece and Turkey started a dialogue on a set of low intensity issues – such as the environment, tourism, and culture – in the hope that this would contribute to shaping the appropriate climate for tackling more complex issues relating to aspects of sovereignty. Moreover, following the devastating earthquake in Turkey in August 1999, Greece was quick to offer humanitarian assistance, something which also contributed to the improvement of relations between the two countries. No doubt, the solution of the Cyprus problem could be a central determinant for a radical breakthrough in Greek-Turkish relations. And as the regions of Southeastern Europe, Mediterranean and Middle East are steadily moving towards the settlement of long-drawn disputes and the old walls of hatred and confrontation fall one after the other, the green, dividing line in Cyprus appears more and more to be a political anachronism and begs to be replaced by a system of cooperation, reconciliation and human exchanges.

In short, Greece's status as one of the more developed countries in the Southeastern European region, and a member of the EU and all major institutions of the international system has handed Greece a special responsibility. Recognising the important role that can be played, Greece has geared its foreign policy – after adjusting to EU requirements – to promote stability, democracy and integration in the sub-region and Europe as whole. It is an ethical foreign policy driven by the fundamental principles of international law, respect of human rights, cooperation and peace.

Note

1. This short piece was the last written by the late alternate Minister for Foreign Affairs and Minister for European Affairs before his life was cut short in a tragic airplane accident on 16th September, 1999.

3 Greece in the EU: Domestic Reform Coalitions, External Constraints and High Politics

LOUKAS TSOUKALIS

European Challenge

The title of this paper reminds us of a Woody Allen film: everything one wanted to know about Greece and the EU and never dared to ask. Short and simple messages, however, sometimes hide behind long and obscure titles. Let judgement be pronounced after the whole story has been told.

I shall start with some preliminary remarks about membership of the EU and what it concretely entails for a country like Greece. It is well known that the Union is now much more than the incomplete common market it had been for many years. Integration has both widened and deepened; and high politics has been added, albeit half-heartedly, to what had been wrongly described in the past as low politics. Yet, the fundamental characteristic of the European construction has not changed much: it is still mainly about economics in the wider sense of the term. European economic integration encompasses three processes: the opening (and regulation) of the internal market for goods, services, persons and capital; the redistribution of resources, mainly through structural policies; and now, economic and monetary union (EMU) which covers the whole macroeconomic dimension. Thus, integration is not only about economic liberalisation; it should also be seen as an attempt to establish a new form of governance between the nation-state and increasingly global markets (Tsoukalis, 1997a).

The success or failure of a country's EU membership depends largely on the ability of its economic agents to survive in a highly competitive environment, and hence to cope with continuous change. It also depends on its collective ability to play an active part in a never ending process of negotiations that take place at different levels and that involve representatives of both governments and private interests. The everyday functioning of the EU is still more about diplomacy than it is about democracy (Laffan, 1996). Each country needs to actively defend its interests, however defined, in negotiations where arguments interact with power politics and shifting alliances against the background of jointly established rules.

Membership of the EU constitutes a formidable challenge for Greece. The country has had a long history of high external protection and extensive state intervention in the economy, usually arbitrary and non-transparent, which had survived the Association Agreement signed with the EEC of Six back in 1961. Tariffs had come down as a result, but various forms of non-tariff protection proved their long endurance: they survived even some years after Greece's accession to what was still then the European Community (EC) in 1981.

As a member of the EC and now the EU, Greece has had to adjust to open and highly competitive markets. It also has had to adjust to the requirements of joint rule-setting in Brussels, which now covers not only different barriers to entry into the domestic market but also inflation, budget deficits and interest rates. Economic sovereignty in the Union has become indeed a relative concept. Greece has experienced considerable difficulties in adjusting to the new economic reality, much more so than the two Iberian countries that joined five years later.[1] Greece's economic maladjustment, which lasted for several years, at least partly explains the tensions that developed between it and both European institutions and partner countries.[2]

Greece often asked for exceptions in order to protect its domestic producers. Either deliberately or because of administrative inefficiency, Greece was slow in implementing European directives and regulations and was sometimes accused of wasting the money allocated to it through the Structural Funds. In the meantime, trade deficits kept on growing, financed in part through EU transfers, while the figures for inflation, budget deficits and interest rates remained way above those of any other EU country.

It was certainly not just a question of economic adjustment. The problems experienced by Greece as a member of the EU had also much to do with the functioning of the state and its institutions. The modern Greek state is both omnipresent and fundamentally weak. Its pervasive influence is intimately linked to a clientele system, which it has been precisely intended to serve. It is extremely vulnerable to political parties and organised groups, while its institutions remain weak, inflexible and inefficient in performing the traditional Weberian functions. The Greek state has been aptly described as a colossus with feet of clay (Sotiropoulos, 1993).

Instead of catering for particularistic interests and the perpetuation of the clientele system, Greece needs state institutions which provide stable and transparent rules of the game, flexible regulation of markets, monetary stability, the promotion and management of economic change, and, last but not least, the development of new forms of social solidarity for the losers. The above would imply a radical change in the relationship between the state and the market in Greece, which is mainly what membership of the EU is all about.

Building Reform Coalitions

This brings me to the first part of the sub-title: what kind of political coalitions could carry out the reforms necessary for Greece's successful adjustment to EU membership and the rapidly changing international environment? The term reform is, of course, rather neutral. Others may prefer politically loaded terms such as modernisation. What matters, of course, is not the name but the contents.

The reform process has been long and difficult, characterised by strong domestic resistance to change. It is only natural that resistance to change should come from those who expect to lose it from it. Thus, any political economy analysis of reform needs to identify potential losers, which is also what politicians carrying the banner of reform need to do. Once identified, potential losers can be dealt with in different ways. Divide and rule is an old and frequently practised method. There is also the possibility of compensation, usually in a limited number of cases, or even incorporation in a wider, positive-sum game. The experience of Greece during the 1980s and 1990s suggests that potential losers from the kind of reform associated with EU membership were numerous – and that some of them were politically powerful. Although potential winners were perhaps the majority in absolute numbers, they were generally dispersed and badly organised.

A non-exhaustive list of potential losers from adjustment to EU membership would include a significant part of Greek business, accustomed to external protection and heavily dependent on state favouritism, especially through public procurement contracts. Who said that all businesspeople believe in free competition? It would also include most of organised labour, which can be found in the large state-controlled sector, characterised by over-employment, relatively high pay and low productivity. It would certainly include a large part of the political class, which has developed and exploited its comparative advantage in the operation of the clientele system, a system that flourishes in protected markets and under non-transparent rules. The list of losers would also include other, less well-organised groups of society, such as many small businesses and the lesser skilled. Unable to adjust to a very competitive environment, but also unable to offer effective political resistance, they are, unavoidably, being sacrificed on the altar of economic restructuring.

Faced with such a situation, Greek governments tried for more than ten years following accession to avoid or simply postpone adjustment, which would have been politically costly. At the same time, they showed great readiness to throw money at any group of society able to make enough noise around it. In the process, they have created another category of losers, one that conveniently happened to be disenfranchised because of age. By that, I mean the younger generations and those not born as yet, who will have to bear the full burden of delayed adjustment, not to mention the burden of servicing the large public debt accumulated mostly during the 1980s. The welfare state in Greece has been largely built on the basis of inter-generational redistribution, and this is certainly not something the post-1974 political system should be proud of.

In more recent years, the process of reform/modernisation has acquired a new momentum. The turning point came around 1993, when Greece entered a phase of economic stabilisation and convergence with the rest of the EU, coupled with a more determined effort at privatisation and restructuring. Previous attempts in this direction had proved short-lived; but the margin of manoeuvre has become increasingly narrower with time. The prospect of economic marginalisation in the context of the EU, the rapidly rising cost of the servicing of the debt, and the increasing difficulties in the financing of deficits left Greek governments with very limited options.

This new phase has been characterised by a substantial improvement in terms of economic growth. Inflation and budget deficits have registered a sharp decline, thus rapidly converging towards the EU average. This convergence finally led to Greece's admission to the European exchange rate mechanism in March 1998. Although Greece failed to be admitted to the final stage of economic and monetary union (EMU) on the basis of the 1997 figures, the chances are very good indeed that it will be able to satisfy the criteria for admission soon and thus be allowed to enter the euro-zone in

January 2001.

The transformation of the economic scene has been truly remarkable; and the accompanying transformation of the political scene, although less spectacular, should not be underestimated. Domestic politics have become less polarised and personalised – and perhaps verging on the boring for the taste of some Greeks, used to charismatic leaders and interminable fights between good and evil. Although gradually shifting, the dividing line between reform/modernisation on the one hand and conservatism/populism on the other continues to cut right across the two main political parties in Greece (Tsoukalis, 1997b). The Socialists, under the leadership of Mr Simitis, have taken the lead in this process; and this has led to the progressive marginalisation of the populist section which used to dominate the party in the years of Andreas Papandreou. The main opposition party, New Democracy, has tended to adopt a more populist stance, and internal divisions have often been strongly pronounced. Power has a welding effect on those who share it, and the lack of it breeds dissension.

Should we expect a realignment of political forces in the future? Until now, the two biggest parties have shown remarkable resilience. Defectors have almost invariably been punished by the electorate, while attempts to create new parties have not survived the test of time. Among the small parties, only the Communists have so far succeeded in remaining comfortably and consistently above the 3 per cent barrier below which admission to the national parliament is denied.[3]

In a country where politics has been about anything and everything, and where political parties, either directly or through state institutions, try to exercise control over everything from admission to hospitals to the running of universities and sports, civil society has remained underdeveloped. The quality of democracy in Greece largely depends on the strengthening of independent groups and associations of citizens, which can act as effective controls on the all-expansive tendencies of the state. The relatively recent mushrooming of citizens' movements, mainly on environmental and human rights issues, is therefore a most encouraging sign.

External Constraints and Scapegoats

This brings me to the second part of the sub-title: the role of external constraints. EU membership brings with it numerous such constraints, be they the product of open markets, of common rules for bank assets and the protection of the environment, or the need to conform with the convergence criteria as an entry ticket for the final stage of EMU. On the other hand, EU policies and rules can sometimes serve as a convenient scapegoat for unpopular policies at home. Greek governments have frequently made use of the European scapegoat, whenever domestic support was in short supply. They have tried to capitalise on the generally high levels of public support for the EU at home, thus sometimes risking a boomerang effect.

EU membership does indeed enjoy high levels of support in Greece. This support has been repeatedly confirmed in opinion polls conducted in the country, and it has also been manifested in the attitude of most political parties and in the votes taken in the Greek Parliament. In fact, there seems to be a contradiction between the apparent love for the EU manifested by the large majority of Greeks and the strong resistance offered by many of the same people to the things that membership of the Union actually implies. This apparent contradiction, or paradox which is, of course, a Greek word, may suggest that the Greeks have tended to adopt a rather selective approach to EU membership. If so, it has not always worked.

For the cynical observer, Greek popular support for the EU could be explained in terms of the transfers of funds which now represent approximately 4–5 per cent (net transfers) of GDP per annum. There is, of course, something real in this argument, which equally well applies to a country like Ireland where membership of the Union is also very popular. Nevertheless, in the case of Greece transfers through the Structural Funds and the CAP have also had a negative aspect. Coupled with Greece's improved access to external borrowing, linked to membership of this club of advanced European economies, transfers from the EU have enabled Greek politicians to delay adjustment, while also providing an extra breathing space for the old clientele system.

For Greece, there is much more to EU membership than access to funds. The Union is generally seen as providing a stable political environment for a country with a turbulent history; a catalyst for political, economic and social modernisation, which is, of course, resisted by potential losers; and a valuable alliance, even without military means, for a country which finds itself in a very unstable neighbourhood and which perceives a serious threat to its external security. In other words, many Greeks consider the EU as a protection mechanism against their own bad, collective self and also a kind of insurance, inadequate though admittedly it may be, against external risks. For some Greeks, membership of the EU has always been considered as a means of changing the internal balance of forces and thus strengthening the political coalition for reform/modernisation. The number of reformers/ modernisers has been steadily on the increase over the years. Thus, Greece combines some of the characteristics of Ireland and Portugal (the pursuit of economic development and modernisation) with the feeling of external vulnerability found in a country like Finland. There is undoubtedly much more at stake in Greece with EU membership than in most other countries of the Union.

Attitudes towards EMU provide a good illustration of the above. With the exception of the Communist party, all other parties represented in the Greek parliament are in favour of Greece's participation in EMU. Disagreements among them have been about specific measures and the speed of the necessary economic adjustment. The popularity of Greece's membership of EMU has been repeatedly confirmed by large majorities in opinion polls, although here again we come up against the old problem of consistency, namely that every Greek in favour of EMU is not necessarily prepared to pay the price associated with membership. Support for EMU is easy to explain. The search for a collective shield against the enormous instability of exchange markets is coupled with the fear of the political marginalisation that would follow should Greece be left out for long from the most important part of the European construction. And experience seems to suggest that monetary stability would be more effectively guaranteed if responsibility for decisions in the area of monetary policy were to be transferred to the European Central Bank in Frankfurt. In this respect, Greece is not very different from most other members of the EU. On the other hand, stabilisation policies have a price, and it is therefore dangerous to try to pass on to Brussels the blame for austerity measures linked to the preparation stage for EMU.

When the target of EMU membership is accomplished – financial markets have been betting heavily on it – it will serve as a psychological boost as well as a sure sign that, having erred for several years in the economic wilderness, Greece is coming back to the fold. But it will be one thing to secure membership of EMU, and another to ensure that the Greek economy performs well in this new environment. Greece has entered a long and difficult phase of structural reform, including cutting the state-controlled sector of the economy down to size, overhauling the social security system, and adjusting Greek public administration to the rapidly shifting reality of

European integration and globalisation.[4] There is still a long distance to travel in this direction.

Frustration with High Politics

If in economic and political terms Greece is gradually becoming like any other European country, this is certainly not true of foreign policy. The reason is simple: the Greeks live in the rough neighbourhood of the Balkans, where nation-states have a relatively short history, national frontiers are not generally considered as sacrosanct, and ethnic minorities are frequently manipulated in order to destabilise neighbours and thus lay claims on a possible future redrawing of political maps.

The collapse of the old communist order on Greece's northern frontier may have opened the way for the establishment of democratic regimes. But its first affect has been to unleash the old nationalist (and irredentist) forces which had been kept in deep freeze during the Cold War. Thus, several communist leaders (Mr. Milosevic certainly not being alone in this respect) have decided to don the nationalist cloak in order to survive politically. This new environment has presented Greece with many problems and risks, but also with new opportunities (Veremis, 1995). In the early years, it tended to exaggerate the former and ignore the latter.

There have been, of course, real problems. The disintegration of Yugoslavia and the civil war which broke up in several parts of its territory, the breakdown of law and order in Albania, the rapid deterioration of economic conditions in all the former communist countries of the region – all these have had important negative consequences for Greece. Transport links with its trading partners in the EU have suffered badly; immigrants in Greece (many of them still illegal) now represent more than 5 per cent of the total population of a country which had been for long a net exporter of people; and the Greek armed forces have had to remain on pretty well constant alert.

At the same time, the Greek political class – a few notable exceptions apart – became obsessed with the name of what is still officially called the Former Yugoslav Republic of Macedonia, thus confusing irredentism (a real issue for many members of the political class in Skopje) with the name of the new republic. Opportunities for an honourable compromise on the name were lost in the early years, largely because of Greek obduracy. Greece's sensationalist press, aided by a group of professional patriots, succeeded in convincing public opinion that there was a real risk to Greece's territorial integrity. Pursuing a maximalist policy and employing a rhetoric which sounded very Greek to most foreigners, Greece became completely isolated on the issue.

On the other hand, Greece was not always helped by the attitude adopted by its allies and partners. The intervention of Western powers in the region, and more concretely in former Yugoslavia, has been strongly influenced by short-term considerations, while also reflecting a remarkable lack of understanding of the history and the political realities in this troubled part of the world (Woodward, 1995; Glenny, 1999). Adding insult to injury, Western allies seemed often to be chastising the Greeks for not behaving like Scandinavians – and in the Balkans at that!

Growing awareness of the deadlock created has led to a considerable shift in Greek official attitudes. Greece has thus begun to act as a stabilising factor in the region, through its participation in the peace-keeping force in Albania, its constructive role in the collective efforts to prevent the escalation of conflict in former Yugoslavia, its decision to improve relations and engage in regular dialogue with the still 'unnamed republic', and perhaps, most importantly, through trade and investment.

Although relatively poor by EU standards, Greece is an economic giant in the region. In money terms, its GDP is now bigger than the GDP of Albania, Bulgaria, Romania, the FYR of Macedonia, and new Yugoslavia put together, with a population approximately five times that of Greece. At current exchange rates, Greek GDP per capita is also approximately four times the GDP per capita of Turkey. Trade with its northern neighbours has grown, despite the economic difficulties experienced by the countries in the region; and Greek investment has also increased rapidly – arguably the most important contribution that Greece can make to stabilisation in the region (see also Kazakos and Liargovas, 1996). Greece's economic and political weight is further strengthened by its membership of both the EU and NATO, as long as the policies pursued by Athens do not diverge widely from those of its partners and allies. This has become increasingly true in recent times. Greece is now playing an active part inside the EU and international fora in collective efforts leading to Balkan reconstruction and the progressive integration of all countries into the European system (Gligorov, Kaldor and Tsoukalis, 1999).

Greece is fundamentally a status quo country in a part of the world where the status quo is being challenged from many directions. Worried about the instability on its northern frontier, it also perceives a direct threat to its territorial integrity emanating from Turkey. While this threat may be sometimes exaggerated by the Greeks, it is nonetheless real. The long list of unresolved bilateral issues between Greece and what is formally its NATO ally on the other side of the Aegean sea, the continuing problem of Cyprus affecting directly both Greece and Turkey, the military build-up on both sides, and the repeated threats of war from Turkish generals and politicians are not a figment of the otherwise fertile imagination of the Greeks. Indeed, living with Turkey as a neighbour is by no means a guarantee of an easy and comfortable life for most of the countries sharing a frontier with Turkey. The relatively recent memory of an empire, the large size and strategic position of the country, the serious instability of its political system, coupled with huge internal disparities and the threat of Islamic fundamentalism, the dominant position of the army in domestic politics, and the institutionalisation of state violence, all combine to make Turkey a very difficult country to deal with.

Nobody could, of course, seriously argue that Greece has no share of responsibility for the poor state of relations with its eastern neighbour. For Greece has a vested interest in the economic development and political stability of Turkey. The last thing that Greeks should want is a poor and internally divided Turkey, one more vulnerable to the temptation offered by political Islam and military adventures abroad. In this respect, Greece has a common interest with its European and American allies.

Support for Turkey's close association with the EU, leading eventually to full membership of the Union, should be entirely consistent with the above objectives. This should receive the full support of Greece; and the latter has done so on occasions, although not consistently. Still, Turkey's rapprochement with European institutions is and should be dependent on the fulfilment of certain criteria, including most notably the proper functioning of democratic institutions, the rule of law, the protection of human rights and the respect of minorities. The EU is not a simple common market, nor is it a military alliance like NATO in which the emphasis – at least, until recently – had been on the defence of frontiers and not on the defence of democratic institutions and the rights of citizens in its member countries (see the example of Greece and Portugal in the past, or Turkey until the present time).

Turkey's democratic record leaves an enormous amount to be desired, which has presented European countries with great difficulties regarding the policy to be pursued towards Turkey. On this issue, European and American attitudes have often diverged. For Washington, Turkey is basically a strategic ally, while for the Europeans it is also an associate and potential partner in what is considered by many Europeans as an emerging federation. This fundamentally different perspective is bound to lead sometimes to diverging policies.

Greece, from its side, has tended to overplay and misplay the EU card in relations with Turkey. As long as it does not fulfil the economic and political criteria set by the Union, Turkey will not be considered for membership of the EU, irrespective of whether Greece wants it or not. Thus, Greece's loud objections, usually intended for domestic consumption, have sometimes only served the purpose of providing a fig-leaf for some of its European partners who did not want to incur any political or economic cost in their relations with Ankara.

But Greece has gone further, by establishing a link between Greek-Turkish bilateral issues and the resolution of the Cyprus problem on the one hand, and the strengthening of EU relations with Turkey on the other. The latter includes the granting of EU financial aid to Turkey. Not always succeeding in persuading its partners about the desirability of such a link, Greek governments have therefore had to resort to the use of veto in order to block a particular measure or policy statement concerning relations with Turkey. More often than not, Greek vetoes have had a symbolic rather than practical significance.

Greek politicians have thus tended to forget an important principle, namely that vetoes inside the EU can only be used in exceptional circumstances and for short periods; and this is a general rule which should apply even more to small- and medium-sized countries. Playing to the gallery at home has sometimes proved a more powerful incentive for Greek politicians than the cost associated with the country's isolation in European councils; and this may be a high cost for a country which, largely because of geography, needs to rely more on diplomacy than military strength for the defence of its territory. Even worse, this policy has hardly produced any tangible benefits in relations with Turkey.[5]

With a strong perception of an external threat, Greece has looked to EU membership as a means of strengthening its own security; and in this respect, it has been deeply frustrated. The Union's common foreign and security policy is not common, and it still has little to do with security (Bildt et al., 1997; Zielonka, 1998). This has been confirmed time and time again. Rightly or wrongly, most European countries have until now preferred to leave the responsibility for collective actions in this area to the Atlantic alliance. Furthermore, the majority of EU members have tried to avoid becoming involved in bilateral disputes between Greece and Turkey. Greek appeals to Community solidarity and the arguments based on law and right have not always proved to be sufficiently persuasive. This has undoubtedly added to Greek frustration; and it helps much to explain the periodic outbursts of anti-European feelings in Greece, which spring from the darker parts of the collective Greek psyche, stirred by populist politicians and the country's sensationalist mass media. On such occasions, one is painfully reminded of the vulnerability of many Greeks to conspiracy theories and the persistence of what Diamantouros calls an 'underdog culture' (1994). This may in turn suggest that public support for the EU may not be as deep as those not very careful readers of opinion polls may think.

Much though they may have liked, EU countries cannot simply afford to stay away from the problems generated by the complex reality of Southeastern Europe, be they Kosovo, Bosnia or Cyprus. The Union has started negotiating with the officially recognised government in Cyprus on the latter's accession. Cyprus is one of the six countries in the so-called fast track leading to membership of the EU, and it can arguably fulfil the basic criteria for membership more easily than any of the other candidates.

Yet, it remains a divided country, and the crucial question is whether early accession to the EU can act as a catalyst for an internal political settlement between the two communities on the island or whether the internal settlement should be considered as a pre-condition for accession. Not surprisingly, the governments in Athens and Nicosia have opted for the former, fearing that if accession were to be made conditional on an internal settlement, which in turns means conditional on the willingness of Turkish Cypriots and Turkey to play the game, the accession of Cyprus would risk being written off *ad calendas Graecas*. This is another important reason why the Union will have to become more directly involved in the search for a viable solution to the problem of this divided island, which would also contribute much to the improvement of bilateral Greek-Turkish relations.

Adjustment: Better Late Than Never

Greece has travelled a long distance since the fall of the colonels' dictatorship in 1974. Democracy has been consolidated, and this has been achieved in an extremely peaceful manner. Greek democracy has had its share of demagogues, and public opinion sometimes has fallen prey to populist rhetoric. This is, of course, not totally unknown in other democracies. It could be argued that, for several years, economic stabilisation and much needed structural reforms were sacrificed on the altar of democratic consolidation.

Membership of the European Union has acted as a powerful catalyst for domestic reform/modernisation. Adjustment to the requirements of membership of this very unusual club, in which the most advanced democracies and mixed economies of Europe experiment in new forms of pooling of sovereignty, has been difficult and rather painful for Greece. Resistance to change from organised groups proved powerful enough to delay the process of adjustment for many years. The forces of reform/modernisation have now taken the upper hand, although there is still much that needs to be done.

Greece does not have the luxury enjoyed by many Western European countries for whom external threat has become a rather abstract notion since the disintegration of the Soviet empire. Developments in the Balkans, coupled with the continuing tension in relations with Turkey, reaching sometimes dangerous peaks, have tended to create a siege mentality in Greek society. In the early 1990s, and to a much lesser extent now, this was cultivated by a group of politicians across the political spectrum, who apparently decided to invest in nationalist shares. They were strongly encouraged by a large section of the media. Again, this is, undoubtedly, no Greek monopoly.

In general, Greek diplomacy has experienced difficulties in finding the right combination of the language of might, right and common interests. It has often placed almost exclusive emphasis on what it perceives as right on issues of foreign policy, while not paying enough attention to the need for building coalitions and identifying common interests with other countries. It has failed to appreciate that moralising in international relations is mostly the privilege of the strong, as so many US politicians never fail to remind us.

For Greece, membership of the EU certainly constitutes the most important element of its domestic and foreign policy. But the country happens to exist in an unstable neighbourhood; and no kind of foreign policy can transport it away from that location. Moreover, it will, unfortunately, remain on the frontier of the Union for many years to come, because none of its neighbours is likely to be able to fulfil the criteria for membership for some time. Guarding frontier posts requires continuous vigilance and *sang-froid*. It also requires skilful diplomacy. Greece needs to act as a stabilising force in the region.

Greece will need to combine domestic reforms with careful diplomacy abroad. Structural reforms can only succeed if social cohesion is preserved. This will be a difficult task for reformers/modernisers. On the other hand, national interests can only be defended successfully through alliances, formal or ad hoc. Given the nature of the European Union, the recipe for a successful membership of Greece should contain more domestic reform and less high politics – the external constraints being more or less given, although they should not be exaggerated. It is my strong impression that Greece has been slowly but steadily moving in this direction.

Notes

1. For a comparative study, see Maravall (1997).
2. Several works exist on the difficulties of Greece's adjustment to EU membership. See, for example, Featherstone and Ifantis (1996) and Kazakos and Ioakimidis (1994).
3. In the parliamentary elections which took place in April 2000, Mr Simitis succeeded in renewing his popular mandate, although with only a very small difference in terms of votes from the main opposition party. These elections also saw a further move in the direction of a two party system, with the two main parties representing almost 90 per cent of the vote.
4. The most comprehensive policy proposals in this direction were made by a committee of experts chaired by Professor John Spraos. The complete set of reports was published by the National Bank of Greece in 1998.
5. There was a significant shift in Greek policy, following the big earthquakes which hit the two countries in the summer of 1999. Greek gestures of friendship and solidarity were reciprocated by the other side, and this quickly led to a spectacular (and sustainable?) improvement in bilateral relations. The shift in Greek policy also opened the way for the formal adoption of Turkey as a candidate country by the European Council at Helsinki in December 1999. Thus, Greece's policy has been moving in the direction suggested.

References

Bildt, C., Cheysson, C., Jordan, B., Lindsey, L.B., Tsoukalis, L. and Vranitzky, F. (1997), *What Global Role for the EU?*, Philip Morris Institute Discussion Paper No. 13, (September).

Diamantouros, N.P., (1994), *Cultural Dualism and Political Change in Post-Authoritarian Greece*, Madrid: Centro Juan March de Estudios Avanzados en Ciencias Sociales.

Featherstone, K. and Ifantis, K. (1996), *Greece in a Changing Europe: Between European Integration and Balkan Disintegration?*, Manchester: Manchester University Press.

Glenny, M. (1999) *The Balkans 1804–1999*, London: Granta.

Gligorov, V., Kaldor, M. and Tsoukalis, L. (1999) *Balkan Reconstruction and European Integration.* The Hellenic Observatory Discussion Paper. London School of Economics and Political Science.

Kazakos, P. and Ioakimidis, P.C. (1994), *Greece and EC Membership Evaluated*, London: Pinter.

Kazakos, P. and Liargovas, P. (1996), *Transition and Economic Cooperation in Southeast Europe*, Athens: Gnossi [in Greek].

Laffan, B. (1996), 'The Politics of Identity and Political Order in Europe', *Journal of Common Market Studies*, (March).

Maravall, J.M (1997), *Regimes, Politics and Markets: Democratization and Economic Change in Southern and Eastern Europe*, Oxford: Oxford University Press.

Sotiropoulos, D. (1993), 'A Colossus with Feet of Clay: The State in Post-Authoritarian Greece', in Psomiades, H.G and Thomadakis, S. (eds), *Greece, the New Europe and the Changing International Order*, New York: Pella Publishing.

Tsoukalis, L (1997a), *The New European Economy Revisited*, Oxford: Oxford University Press.

Tsoukalis, L. (1997b), 'Beyond the Greek Paradox', in Allison, G.T and Nicolaïdis, K. (eds), *The Greek Paradox: Promise vs. Performance*, Cambridge: The MIT Press.

Veremis, T. (1995), *Greece's Balkan Entanglement*, Athens: Hellenic Foundation for European and Foreign Policy.

Woodward, S. (1995), *Balkan Tragedy: Chaos and Dissolution After the Cold War*, Washington D.C.: The Brookings Institution.

Zielonka, J. (1998), *Explaining Euro-Paralysis: Why Europe is Unable to Act in International Politics*, London: Macmillan St Antony's Series.

4 Maximising Contribution to the European Integration Process as a Prerequisite for the Maximisation of Gains

ACHILLEAS MITSOS[1]

Greece's participation in the European Union presents a paradox. The Greek people, in its entirety according to a number of opinion polls, are among European integration's warmest supporters yet the Greek governments' positions on major European integration issues significantly diverge from those of the other member states, and often, Greece is considered marginal to the process of European integration.[2]

The distinctiveness of the Greek case vis-à-vis other states which either formed or joined the European Union should not be sought in a different relationship between the elites and the people as the decision for Greek accession, like almost all major steps of European construction, was an *elite driven* one. If there is one distinguishing characteristic from other elite driven decisions it lies in the absence of even the basic elements of a 'permissive consensus'[3] as a few months after accession, the people gave power to a party that did not just disagree with accession but had made its anti-communitarian rhetoric a central element of its political platform. Let it be reminded that in the 1981 elections, the losers were not confined to Nea *Dimokratia*, a party which had identified itself with accession to the EC, but also included the smaller parties which had supported that prospect. Indicatively, the vote ratio between the two parties of the Left, KKE (strongly anti-western and anti-EC) and *KKE Esoterikou* (of a 'euro-communist' orientation and with a clear Europeanist ideology) was transformed from three to one in 1977 to eight to one in 1981.

Eighteen years after accession, the parties' Europeanist orientation is a given (excluding KKE whose power base however has been stabilised at around 5 per cent) and is in line with the Greek people's wider acceptance of a European perspective. *Europe* nevertheless remains someone else's creation. Its decisions are considered as imposed from the outside and Greek participation in Economic and Monetary Union, although a 'national goal', is considered more as a trophy in recognition and less as a prospect that will permit a substantial participation at the decision-making core.

In order to explain the co-existence of the wholehearted acceptance of European integration with the Greek governments' conscious choice of marginalising the country with respect to certain major decisions, one has to look at the special character of the main gains Greece expected from EC membership. All countries that participate in an integration procedure face an 'integration dilemma',[4] where the main benefits from integration are compared with the main drawbacks that should be avoided. In the case of Greece, the main drawbacks were found *within* the main benefits from membership. The nature of the Greek aims was such that their pursuit and the maximisation of benefits passed though a 'federalist logic', i.e. the transposition of power to the supranational level. On the flip side of this 'federalist logic' however, the loss of national sovereignty is considered as the main drawback, which the Greek governments should have fought to avoid.

The interdependence between maximising gains and minimising costs and the mutual negation of these goals is inherent in both crucial sectors where Greece expected major gains from membership in the (then) EEC namely, the support and modernisation of the Greek economy and, especially, the upgrading of the country's international position vis-à-vis Turkey.[5] In the financial sector, maximising the influx of Community funds requires that the development of the Union's less developed regions becomes a goal of the Union proper. This development however, is contradictory to the need to maintain an autonomous economic policy.[6] With respect to relations with Turkey, if gain maximisation passes through the 'communitisation' of the problem (i.e. transforming Greco-Turkish problems into EU-Turkish ones), a 'federalist' approach is clearly at odds with maintaining the archetypal intergovernmental instrument of the national veto, an instrument that Greece has not yet had the courage to abandon.

Thus, the demonisation of the loss of national sovereignty in economic policy matters and the diffidence to abandon the intergovernmental arsenal in Greco-Turkish relations only leave the intergovernmental approach open to the Greek governments. And if in the economic sector the gradual coincidence of national and community goals has led to an ever increasing use of a federalist rhetoric and argumentation, in relations with Turkey the course from the 'intergovernmental' to the 'federalist' logic has been fragmented and regressive with one logic's ammunition disabling the other's. Thus the solution of the chronic problems has been pushed back, impeding Greece's full, unequivocal participation at the Community's decision-making core.

This article's position is that the actual goal of maximising national gains from European integration leads to the necessity to maximise one's contribution to it. Analysing the dynamics of the relationship between Greece and the European Union shows that gain maximisation is only possible if Greece's long-term goals coincide with the other member states' and Greek governments adopt a federalist outlook and practices.

In the following section, the methodological distinction between the federalist and intergovernmental logic is examined with an attempt to classify the possible stances available to member states. The classification is made according to the type of stance adopted. This may be defensive, offensive, active or passive, and is seen in conjunction with the policy production phase at which a specific intervention is attempted. These methodological distinctions are used in the next section in order to understand Greece's European course from its inception to its current 'coming of age'. In the last section, an attempt is made to analyse the relationship between the various types of convergence and put forward the notion that real convergence, one that is based on results, is directly related to the convergence of policies and presupposes the convergence of long-term goals.

Active and Passive Participation: Intergovernmental and 'Federal' Approaches

The analysis of the creation and development of the European polity and the 'ontological' identification of its core characteristics, have preoccupied and divided researchers in the fields of political science, economic analysis and international relations for decades. Moreover, the number of potential appellations for this unique and constantly re-moulded form of governance is constantly on the increase.[7] What is certain is that, in this continuously evolving situation, two elements – Intergovernmental coordination and Supranational 'Constitutionality' – always co-exist and are, more or less, in competition with each other. Overall EU policy, as well as within the various sectors, reflects the current balance of social, economic and political forces of the widest possible spectrum regardless of whether their expression at the European level is direct or effectuated through state, supranational or sub-national institutions. This interplay may be either static or dynamic in character. A *static* interplay expresses the lowest common denominator, while a *dynamic synthesis* exceeds the algebraic sum of the various positions and allows, and sometimes imposes a forward orientation with an increased role for supranational institutions, the arch proponents of European integration's forward stride.

This *sui generis* co-responsibility between state and supranational modes of governance is expressed at all stages of policy production and member states choose the form, intensity and stage or level of intervention depending on the ever-changing balance of power. The final stage of EU policy making, and the lowest level of intervention, is found at the *policy implementation* level. The State is responsible for the implementation of legislative decisions taken at the European level. The margins for genuine 'national' policies are quite narrow, although they vary from sector to sector. In sectors with a strong EU presence, like the Common Agricultural Policy, the margins for action after the decisions have been taken at the European level are virtually non-existent, while in other sectors where the EU role is not consolidated (for example, and despite the recent pronouncements, in combating unemployment), a Community 'decision' differs little from a stated wish, allowing, in effect, any national policy.

The next level up for policy intervention is during the *formulation of policy*. Although recognising the point where policy 'formulation' ends and policy 'implementation' begins is often artificial,[8] the distinction exists, if only semantically. However, due to the remarkably complex decision-making mechanisms at the European level, recognising in advance the time and place at which member states intervene is by itself very complicated. Although a 'typical' Community decision is formally initiated by the European Commission and taken by the Council of Ministers (and the European Parliament, in the cases where 'co-decision' is foreseen), neither the actual starting point nor the end result and the intermediate stages are as clear-cut. The Treaties do not unequivocally define the European Commission's scope for policy initiation and the relative role of persons, circumstance, financial and social pressures, member state interjections, as well as 'mandates' from other EU institutions, varies from sector to sector as well as through time.[9] Moreover, from the initial proposal to the final decision there may be interventions by the European Parliament (with the Plenary session's final position, but also earlier in committees, political groups, etc.), the other less influential institutions (such as the Economic and Social Committee and the Committee of Regions) as well as discussions at the Council's various organs (the Committee of Permanent Representatives and the various Working Groups) were the distinctions between the roles of the member states, the European Commission, the Presidency and the Council's Secretariat are not always clearly defined.[10]

When a member state's intentions are more ambitious, then the aim is not to formulate policy, or even make *political proposals*, but instead, to define the objective of political decision, i.e. set the decision-making organs' *agenda*. By reiterating their claim to 'have our money back', Mrs Thatcher's government did not just achieve Britain's partial budget rebate but also placed the more general issue of the net results of member states' budgetary contributions/receipts on the top of the European agenda. Similarly, when the countries of the periphery, in alliance with the political forces advocating the re-balancing of the relationship between public intervention and market forces at the European level, achieved the introduction of economic and social cohesion as a key pillar of the European construction, they didn't just make some budgetary gains but radically transformed the European Union's agenda.[11]

In the long run however, the only way to effectively influence the agenda is by influencing the *institutional balance*, which, in turn, sets the agenda. For example, the choice of the Commission President is also based on the relative role member states want to grant the Commission at a given time. A strengthened role for the Commission entails initiatives and agenda items which will be different to those put forward by a Commission acting as 'caretaker/manager'.[12]

Finally, the institutional balance depends less on circumstantial balances of power and tactical manoeuvres, and more on the promotion of one or the other, *model of European integration*. A federal perspective obviously leads to a different balance between supranational and intergovernmental institutions than, say, the need for intergovernmental cooperation aiming at the unhindered operation of market forces. Intervention at this stage, the stage of collision between alternative philosophies, is the most demanding both in terms of the need for a long-term strategy, and with respect to that strategy's role and consistency which itself determines the various positions, coalitions and tactics.

The existence or not of a long-term strategy regarding the future of European integration and the extent to which it takes precedence over short-term considerations of relative gains determine the stage of intervention, the

Table 1 Forms of State Intervention

	INTERGOVERNMENTAL STANCE		SUPRANATIONAL STANCE	
	PASSIVE	ACTIVE	PASSIVE	ACTIVE
Long-Term Goal	Europe as intergovernmental entity		European integration	
European Strategy	Limited range of issues. Defensive intervention. Emphasis on veto use.	National distinctiveness. Intergovernmental alliances.	Passive acceptance of decisions.	Long-term gains considerations overcome short-term problems.
Institutions/Organs	Council of Ministers (and its organs). European Parliament only as forum for promotion of national interests. European Commission seen as purely executive institutions.		Emphasis on supranational institutions.	
Decision-Making Procedure	Unanimity		Majority	
Stages Policy-Making	Special importance on implementation margins.	Intervention on final decision-making stages.	Trust initiatives. European Commission.	Emphasis on priority setting agenda.

degree of an *active* or *passive* presence, as well as the scope of intervention. The latter may be *horizontal*, that is, cover the entirety of issues under discussion, or *vertical*, that is, limited to certain issues with which the national interest has been identified. A vertical presence, especially on issues of marginal importance to the main issue of European integration, is by definition confined in scope because, even if performed diligently and with effective coalition building, it places the particular member state outside the decision-making core. As is often said, relatively small countries like Belgium or the Netherlands are more influential in European affairs than certain larger ones (the United Kingdom being a prime example) precisely due to their *a priori* positioning at the core through their *horizontal* approach and involvement.

Based on the above thoughts regarding the horizontal or vertical type of intervention, the active or passive character of intervention and the supranational or intergovernmental long-term aspirations, a typology of the possible stances available to member states can be attempted:

On one end we have a *passive intergovernmental* intervention: The state chooses an isolated, defensive approach from the 'outside'; emphasises its national distinctiveness and can only intervene at the policy formulation stage. In essence, it does not participate in the overall negotiations. Instead, it's on the look-out, bides its time, blocks decisions when able to, and wages a 'Holy War' by placing asterisks and footnotes to decisions taken *in absentia* and which are often considered the result of 'conspiracies at the top'. All issues not directly of its concern are ignored, coalitions are depreciated, and the supranational organs and institutions are only used as added fora to highlight and reconfirm its national 'distinctiveness'. Any gains are circumstantial and short-term (but with the advantage of their potential domestic exploitation) while the state's effect on the overall balance of power is either negligible or, when its relative weight and power permit, negative.

At the other end, we find the *passive supranational stance*: When circumstances lead to a coincidence of main goals, a totally passive stance is chosen. Such a state's effect is similarly negligible on coalition building, agenda setting, the institutional balance, etc. Issues of national importance are delegated to the 'automatic pilot' with the obvious risk of a sudden realisation that the direction has changed and the ability to intervene has been lost.

In between the two extremes, we find *active stances* of an either *intergovernmental* or *supranational* character. Here, the scope of intervention covers a wide spectrum of issues, influence is sought at multiple levels and as early as possible, and the coalition-building game is played effectively and from the 'inside'. Maximising gains however is only possible if long-term supranational aspirations permit the exercise of influence through the supranational institutions and especially, the European Commission and the European Parliament. The greater the adherence to the 'federal', supranational dimension, the easier it becomes to accept an increased role for supranational institutions in setting the agenda and in 'supranationally' addressing a variety of issues.[13] In the case of an *active intergovernmental stance*, whatever divergences exist on either economic or international issues, they are promoted by the diverger and their solution becomes part of wider negotiations. Conversely, in cases of an *active supranational stance*, divergences are seen as a common problem and convergence becomes a goal of the European Union *per se*.

Greece's Course Through the European Integration Process

The first period of Greek participation in the – then – European Communities, from 1981 and for the next three or four years, is undoubtedly characterised by its highlighting of a 'Greek distinctiveness'. The Greek government, a few months after coming into office following the October 1981 elections, submitted to the Commission and the Council, the celebrated 'Greek Memorandum'.[14] In reality the memorandum represented nothing more than a synopsis of the problems the Greek economy was, and would be, facing in the EC and a simple juxtaposition of possible solutions that 'constitute the minimum possible for creating conditions for Greek membership of the European Communities which will not be in conflict with basic Greek national interests'.[15]

The demand for an increased, and qualitatively different, intervention by the Community's funds was at the centre of the Greek Memorandum. Emphasis was placed on two considerations: First, on the need for special adjustments which would allow the Greek economy's development, as well as Greece's relations with the EC in general, without contradictions and confrontations,[16] and second, on the 'real' divergence and not on the 'nominal', monetary, divergence. Besides, the Greek economy's distance from the subsequent 'convergence criteria' of the Maastricht Treaty was, at that time, considerably smaller than it would eventually become. As shown in the Appendix Table (and the figures), inflation was almost double the Community average only to later become four and five-times that; the budget deficit was lower than the Community average prior to accession but rose sharply and consistently in later years (and exploded during the election years); while public debt was significantly *lower* than the community average and, despite its steep increase, remained until 1988, at levels compatible even with the currently unreachable target, of 60 per cent of GDP.

The Community's structural policy was, at the time of Greek accession, at an almost symbolic phase.[17] Its allocation among states was largely predetermined; decisions regarding the financing of projects were taken on the basis of a very basic eligibility control; the main aims were confined to simply supporting and complementing the national regional policies; and its macroeconomic relevance was limited, representing only 0.6 per cent of Ireland's GDP or 0.2 per cent of Italy's.[18]

In all, it was a period of stagnation for European integration in general. The need for a great leap forward was becoming increasingly apparent but did not suffice for the solution of the fundamental budgetary, and hence redistributive, issues (such as the size and type of Community budgetary resources, CAP reform, and the United Kingdom's budget rebate). The Commission may have been in the process of compiling its proposals in response to the 'Mandate of 30th May 1980',[19] solutions had indeed appeared in the horizon but the balance of power did not yet permit their application.

As regards the Greek stance, the crucial element was undoubtedly found in the domestic political scene. *PASOK* had just won the elections, having beaten *Nea Dimokratia* in an electoral contest dominated by the issue of accession to the EEC. And although few believed that A. Papandreou actually envisaged leaving the EEC,[20] the new government's – and its Prime Minister's – political rhetoric remained anti-communitarian and the need for a face-saving pretext remained obvious.

During the first period of Greek membership its ministers and officials focused, almost exclusively, on issues of a narrowly defined Greek interest and the promotion of Greek 'distinctiveness'.[21] All discussions within the European Community were approached from a strictly helleno-centric point of view and in a defensive manner. Ministers at the Council, and especially officials in the various committees, acted like observers to decisions taken by others. According to the officially presented view of the time regarding a *Directoire*, decisions were taken by others through unknown and opaque procedures. The Greek representative was simply a privileged member of the club, and hence privy to the decisions before non-members. The smallest the reference to issues of an, even indirect, Greek interest the better because sustaining Greek autonomy on even minor issues was, despite EC accession, the major objective. Success was judged by the degree of resistance to the others' decisions and as a result, the greater the number of Greek vetoes or asterisks underlining Greece's distinctiveness, and the more marginalised the country found itself, the greater the success was deemed.

This wholly intergovernmental and defensive stance did not leave the possibility for any kind of influence at the supranational organs. And even though the European Parliament was occasionally used as a forum for the promotion of the celebrated 'distinctiveness', the European Commission was completely ignored. The non-recognition of the Commission as a player in its own right stemmed from Greece's intergovernmental approach, but, at the same time, also resulted from an ignorance of the rules of the game; an ignorance which was fed, worsened and perpetuated by the Greeks' conceited self-belief in their approach. This attitude led, and was influenced by, the complete lack of, an even personal communication with the then Greek Commissioner.[22] Even issues undoubtedly positive for Greek long-term interests were dealt with defensively, according to short-term considerations, and in resistance to their 'enforcement' that was seen as imposed from above and outside. The most classic example comes from the Greek approach to the negotiations regarding the Iberian enlargement. Instead of promoting a shift in the inter-communitarian balance of power towards the South and the periphery, Greece stressed the dangers for its agriculture and industry resulting, once again, in a Greek stance that was defensive, negative and obstructive.

If one had to choose the *nadir* in Greece's relationship as an EC-member state with the Community organs, procedures, laws, and practices, and therefore in the effectiveness of Greece's European policy, then this would be its January 1983 decision to devalue the Drachma and take a series of accompanying measures regarding quantitative restrictions on imports, exports promotion, etc.[23] It wasn't so much the devaluation *per se*, but the nature, extent and remarkable slipshodness of the accompanying measures, and the way decisions were taken and communicated to Community organs, were considered as defiantly outside the Community's norms.[24] This resulted in a strong negative climate for Greece in the European capitals and institutions, worsened its already low negotiating position and significantly hindered the satisfaction of its demands, even when they were fully compatible with Community laws and practices.

Treating the EC as the champion of adversarial interests, against which the only possible stances were aversion, resistance and a 'guerrilla warfare' clearly characterised the first years of membership, although not without exceptions: Two individuals – Gr. Varfis, Deputy Foreign Minister responsible for European affairs, and K. Simitis, Minister of Agriculture – were considered Europeanists and found themselves on the receiving end of attacks by both the pro-government press and, often quite openly, other fellow ministers.[25] These ministers were Europeanists by 'nature and position' in that both their Europeanist views were known (to K. Simitis they had cost him his seat in PASOK's Executive Office) and the ministries they headed were 'community ministries' *par excellence*. This coincidence of ideologically Europeanist philosophies in the ministries that required them was obviously purposeful and shows Prime Minister Papandreou's intention to gradually move towards more communitarian positions despite, and in complete contrast to, his political rhetoric of the time.

The prospect of the first Greek presidency in the second half of 1983 was presented as a great opportunity to advance the 'Greek distinctiveness'. Thus, Greek efforts at the 'historic' European Council in Stuttgart in June 1983 centred exclusively on the phrasing of a couple of favourable, for the Greek Memorandum, remarks in the official *communiqué*, when the same Council's 'Solemn Declaration' set the foundations for the intergovernmental conference which would result a year later, at the Fontainbleau Summit and the EC's disengagement from the major problems, which for over a decade, obstructed its take-off.[26]

The Greek presidency represents an interesting, and in many respects, unique case. Its uniqueness is not due to the Greek government's efforts to promote Greek interests, nor is it due to the exploitation of the various international and domestic promotion opportunities it can offer. It wasn't even due to the Greek authorities' relative inexperience in the handling of major international issues. Many small countries, many diplomatically 'inexperienced' countries, many countries with particular, divergent from the median, interests, have handled the Council's Presidency with great success, exactly because of their size (which allowed them increased effectiveness in the role of mediator), their distinctiveness (which allowed them on one hand, the choice of the right moment to put forward their particular demands, and on the other, the minimisation of domestic political cost following the acceptance of a compromise), or even their inexperience (which allowed them to delegate a significant part of the Presidency's tasks to the effective and experienced Council Secretariat services without the complexes of a great power).[27] Instead, the uniqueness of the Greek presidency of 1983 is due to the fact that it combined all these characteristics to the extreme. In 1983, Greece was *at once* a small country, completely inexperienced in European affairs (an inexperience which, despite the important exceptions mentioned above, was intensified by the prevailing attitude which equated accepting the rules of the game with 'capitulating' to their 'use as a front for the power of the *Directoire*'), and with distinctive characteristics which were objective but also unduly promoted for domestic political reasons; and all this, immediately following the German Presidency which had managed to establish the links between the various issues, thus allowing, following pre-determined and ambitious procedures, the striking of 'package deals'; and immediately preceding the French presidency, President Mitterrand's first, which aimed, and achieved, to be a truly 'historic presidency' which solved the long-standing 'Gordian knots' and allowed the EC to move to a higher level.

Rightly or wrongly, a presidency's success is judged by the success or failure of the European Summit that closes its six-month tenure. The Athens European Council, in December 1983, was negatively 'historic' and is often referred to as 'catastrophic', 'an example to avoid', 'the nadir of European integration', etc.[28] The reason was that it was the first official European Council that reached no decisions and made no declaration on even the most pressing and least controversial issues. It must however be noted that, from the moment the Athens Summit failed to address the strand of major issues, the non-publication of a declaration aimed at covering the deep crisis of European integration was a deliberate decision by the Greek presidency. Although the consequences regarding the Greek presidency's legacy and the country's credibility were obviously under-calculated, this decision was, in some respects, a brave one, which helped everyone realise the depth of the crisis.[29] Furthermore, due to the responsibility undertaken by Greece for European affairs, it paved the way for a responsible, active and 'from the inside' approach to European integration. Let it finally be noted that the differences between the 'historic' decisions at Fontainbleau and the Athens Summit's draft conclusions were marginal and unimportant.[30]

As regards Greece's relations with the European Community, the Greek presidency's contribution is, in essence, that it forced the Greek government to come to terms with the reality of the Community's decision-making process and the *sui generis* balance of rights and obligations inherent in this process. Despite the Summit's failure, the Greek government tentatively started to shift the focus away from the need to re-balance Greece's position in the EC and towards the promotion of changes within the Community. For the first time a new perspective made its appearance, albeit tentatively and inconsistently; namely that the 'battle from the outside' may be succeeded by one from 'the inside'.

The turning point in EC-Greek relations came following the 1985 general election. A. Papandreou's government was triumphantly returned to office but two important changes had taken place. First, the issue of relations with the EC was no longer the subject of a polarising domestic dispute and second, K. Karamanlis was no longer politically active. Moreover, the Commission had already replied, albeit ambiguously, to the Greek Memorandum[31] and the feeling that all can be achieved from 'the inside' dominated. This view was reinforced by the Greek politicians' and officials' learning process and by the prevailing atmosphere of a general dynamism around Europe. The new European Commission, in office since January 1985, headed by Jacques Delors, whose abilities and ambitions are already visible, and with Gr. Varfis (former deputy-minister for European affairs and knowledgeable of Greek sensitivities) replacing G. Kontogiorgis as the Greek commissioner, highlights this new atmosphere and the Greek government is, for the first time, in open communication with the Commission.[32]

An added, and especially important, element explaining and signalling this historical turn in the Greek government's stance, is found in the internal economic situation which necessitated the adoption of medium-term stabilising measures, with the Community accepting to grant a long-term loan in the context of a *quasi* agreement/contract with the Greek government. The successful negotiation for the granting of a long-term EC loan, part and parcel of National Economy Minister K. Simitis' stabilisation programme,[33] is also significantly due to the European Commission and its President, who did not hesitate to exert his personal influence towards any member states still not trusting the Papandreou government. His success thus 'locked' the Greek government even more on the chariot of the European Community and the Commission.

If however one had to choose the one, single most important aspect of this historic turn, then that would be the Integrated Mediterranean Programmes (IMPs). Discussions concerning the IMPs had started prior to Greek accession, not just in Greece's absence, but in order to address the competitiveness problems some regions of Italy and southern France would face as a result of the EC's southern enlargement. The IMPs later became a central element in the Commission's reply to the Greek memorandum in 1983, and finally developed into Greece's main negotiating demand, practically equated by the Greek government with the sought-after EC reform.[34] The IMP issue culminated at the December 1984 Dublin Summit with the Greek veto over the Iberian enlargement, and later became the precursor and guiding force behind the shift in the Community's philosophy in the field of structural interventions.[35]

From the moment of the IMPs' adoption, the Greek government abandoned its anti-EC stance and – especially – rhetoric and adopted a more 'communitarian' approach. Thus, it increasingly expressed its trust towards the supranational institutions, and eventually rested almost all its hopes for the settlement of the crucial Greek issues on the European Commission, whose president is considered by 'nature and position' a Greek ally, and whose Greek commissioner is responsible for Greece's top economic priority – the Structural Funds.

The Single European Act of 1987 and European integration's great leap forward heralded by the euphoria from the imminent completion of the internal market, lead to the search for new balances. The new term of 'economic and social cohesion' replaced older, often ambiguous terms, and the need to achieve real economic results from the structural funds defined their logic and philosophy and replaced the previous goal of simply complementing national regional policies. Importantly, the aim of cohesion and, in particular, 'the reduction of disparities between the levels of development of the various regions' was upgraded and became a fundamental goal of the new Treaty.[36] This search for real *economic results* stemming from the actions of the Structural Funds was reflected in the massive increase of their resources and the radical reform of their operational framework with the establishment of certain basic principles, including the concentration of resources on specific community goals, their medium-term planning, the celebrated 'partnership' between the periphery, the state and supranational institutions, etc.[37]

The Greek government naturally realised the gains to be made following the Structural Funds' significant increase. It especially realised the opportunity of an immediate, 'consumption' dimension: i.e. the relatively low-cost financing of balance of payments' deficits and the state budget, as well as the opportunities for political exploitation offered by the announcement, foundation, progress, completion, etc. of the public works financed by the Funds. Furthermore, because of these gains it ungrudgingly accepted, effectively without negotiation, and in contrast to other countries also benefiting from the new cohesion policy, the establishment of various procedures regarding programming, monitoring, evaluation, control etc.,[38] simply considering such measures as a necessary evil and nothing else.

Hence Greece becomes a 'communitarian' country *par excellence*. Not only does it accept the increased role for the supranational institutions but even pushes towards that direction itself. In reality however, this supranational approach characterises the Greek presence in the Community's organs but not the domestic policies and practices. The Greek government promoted the need for real convergence and insisted the EC actually apply the principles for the reduction in inequalities that it preaches, but did nothing internally towards that aim. The reduction in the development chasm between Greece and the other member states is convincingly put forward as the principle that should guide community policy and as a community 'right' of the poorest country. At the same time though, the right does not seem to entail any obligations for the country. Economic policy remained – or rather, was re-established following the 1985–87 interlude – short-term and 'myopic', while real convergence moved increasingly further away.

If the first Greek presidency of 1983 contributed to the beginning of the shift in the Greek stance, then the second presidency in 1988 symbolises the beginning of the period of a passive presence within the Community. While the first European Council under a Greek Presidency was considered historic in a negative way, as it failed to reach any decision, the Rhodes European Council was a 'smooth', managerial style, Summit, without high expectations.[39] The Prime Minister's illness at the time was undoubtedly a catalytic factor for that 'passive' involvement.

The political instability of the 1988–91 period, with its exclusive emphasis on the major political issue of the financial and moral scandals and the constant election battles, seriously undermined Greece's search for a place in the Community's balance of power. Although Greece had secured the Community resources it aimed for, the effective implementation of the decisions regarding their use remained subject to the concerted action of the two paralysing characteristics of Greek society: the clientelistic logic of the political system, still the main factor in determining priorities; and the inadequacy of the public administration. These two factors, in conjunction with the almost ubiquitous corruption phenomena, managed to neutralise, in effect, the Structural Funds' modernising/developmental logic.

At the same time, the constant 'electoral cycles' lead to a greater than usual 'myopic' approach to economic policy and consequently, the even greater divergence of all macroeconomic indicators from the community averages. Greece, once again, found itself absent from European developments, but no longer as an outside observer. Instead, it is a major recipient of important budgetary resources but unable to incorporate them in the appropriate macroeconomic framework, or stimulate the endogenous development potential, both necessary conditions for the maximisation of the multiplier consequences and the reversal, of divergence. This 'passivity from within' becomes a permanent characteristic of Greece's Community stance with respect to inter-community negotiations, even including those leading to the establishment of the rules governing the Structural Funds. Greece, unique among the 'cohesion countries', not only accepted that the main (or even only) role regarding developmental strategies belongs to the European Commission, but often strove to increase that role, no doubt calculating that the solution of its chronic structural problems is easier, and with lesser domestic consequences, if imposed from above. The Community was thus used both as a shield and as an offensive weapon in solving internal difficulties.[40]

The elections of April 1990 and the government of *Nea Dimokratia* did not bring about a significant shift in the passive (albeit from within) stance, although for altogether different reasons. *Nea Dimokratia's* ideologically Europeanist outlook and the party's historic role in Greek accession to the EC were expected to lead to a clear, unreserved, presence within the Community. Instead, Greece's marginalisation was exacerbated. The explanation however, is to be found in an entirely different domain: Yugoslav disintegration, the armed conflicts that ensued, initially following Croatian independence and then the independence of Bosnia-Herzegovina and the reapparition, in a new form, of the 'Macedonian' problem which had tormented the region in the first half of the century, and which most international observers considered, not just dormant, but solved by history once and for all.

Greece's position vis-à-vis the 'Macedonian' problem did not just diverge from its partners' but remained completely inexplicable in their eyes. This attitude was in direct contrast to the Greco-Turkish problems, which the other member states' governments at least understood, even when they adopted positions contrary to the Greek ones. However the real explosive in Greece's relations with its partners came from the Greek attitude towards Serbia. These lines do not envisage to critically appraise the Greek stance as regards the recognition of the 'Former Yugoslav Republic of Macedonia'; neither do they aim to explain the 'friendship' and 'camaraderie' with Slobodan Milosevic's Serbia be it the result of a 'common religious and cultural tradition' (a much neglected facet as regards the 'F.Y.R. of Macedonia', despite the fact that a majority of its population is also Christian Orthodox); or the consequence of Serbia's stance towards the 'F.Y.R. of Macedonia'; or even, the extreme but not entirely dismissable hypothesis, that the friendship towards S. Milosevic, or rather S. Milosevic's friendship towards Greece, and certain promises regarding a 'common Greco-Serbian border'[41] were the *real cause* behind the Greek stance towards the 'F.Y.R. of Macedonia'.

What is important for these lines is that, regardless of the causes and intentions, Greece did not just fail to capitalise on its privileged position as the only EC-member country in the region, but managed to become part of the rekindled Balkan problem.[42] Once again, the result was its complete isolation and marginalisation in the European arena and the condemnation to failure of any attempts to improve the balance of power in its favour.[43]

The passive approach to European affairs became even more pronounced following the 1993 elections and A. Papandreou's return to power. Greece's marginalisation intensified and reached heights verging on resentment following its unilateral trade embargo against the 'F.Y.R. of Macedonia's products in February 1994[44] and the subsequent (original to say the least, but nevertheless eventually unsuccessful) recourse by the Commission to the European Court of Justice.

This especially negative climate was gradually, but fundamentally, altered following the swearing into office of the Simitis' government in January 1996. The combination of an unambiguously Europeanist rhetoric with the clear devaluation of the Macedonian issue, and especially an economic policy characterised by a complete convergence of goals and a gradual nominal convergence with the other EU member states, led to Greece's reinstatement in the European game. The *Interim Agreement* with the 'F.Y.R. of Macedonia' in September 1995, and the Imia islets' crisis in January 1996 re-established Greece's international policy within the well-charted waters of the complete dominance of Greco-Turkish issues, with their perennial detrimental effect on the development of the EU-Greek relationship.

Already since Greek accession (and even before), Greco-Turkish relations, including the Cyprus issue, were strongly 'evident' and deeply affected Greece's overall position in European affairs. Their influence however remained 'structural' in nature in that, due to these relations, the complete convergence of goals between Greece and the EU was an impossible undertaking. In contrast however to, for example, the 'Macedonian issue', Greco-Turkish relations, despite their fluctuations and the successive periods of crisis and relative détente, rarely influenced Greece's overall stance in a circumstantial way. In other words, they set the level of goal convergence and imposed certain limits to Greece's convergence capability, but did not significantly influence the dynamic of this convergence.[45]

If the Greek government's economic policy convergence followed, despite some ephemeral fluctuations, a *linear progression*, from an outsider's reactionary stance towards an incorporation of EU goals and policies, the 'europeanisation' of Greco-Turkish relations did not follow a similar course. Sometimes Greece would emphasise its EC-partners' inability to comprehend the Greek positions and focus on the use of the veto and an autonomous Greek stance, while other times, Greece would choose to completely shift Greco-Turkish differences to the European level and transform them into differences between Europe and Turkey. These oscillations reflected tactical considerations (when not simply reacting to domestic political ones) and not the expression of a long-term strategy, and resulted in the mutual neutralisation of both positions. The example of the Luxembourg European Council in December 1997 is a case in point. Greece's applied efforts contributed (along with other factors) to the prospect of Turkish accession being treated by the European Union as subject to the solution of some of the Greco-Turkish differences. But the effort was neutralised by Greece's insistence, even after the European Council, to veto Turkey's financing according to the Customs Union regime between the EU and Turkey. Hence, the attempt to 'europeanise' Greco-Turkish differences had only an ephemeral impact due to its neutralisation by a contradictory approach of hindering community policy.

This inconsistency in the europeanisation of Greco-Turkish differences may have affected the Greek government's efficiency in dealing with them, but is not sufficient to alter the realisation of an all-round, long-term, centripetal Greek approach to European Union issues including European Political Cooperation and the Common Foreign and Security Policy. Here the Greek government's about-turn from an intergovernmental 'outsider' stance to a supranational one from 'within' was indeed spectacular.[46] This centripetal direction is noticeable in the designation of goals, the means utilised even, and perhaps especially, in the rhetoric and style adopted in the pursuit of improvements in the country's relative overall position. Moreover, this 'centripetality' is evident regardless of whether an aggressive or passive stance was adopted for any given issue.

In the last two major inter-Community negotiations (that which led to the Treaty of Amsterdam in June 1997, and that regarding the Union's finances, codified as 'Agenda 2000'[47]) the Greek government seems to have opted for an active, low key participation, of a strongly 'federalist' orientation. On the financial front this stance bore fruit since by reinforcing the image of the credible, moderate, interlocutor, Greece was in a position to exploit its advantageous position – stemming from combining the lowest level of development in the EU with the need to concentrate community funds in the regions with the sharpest problems – on the issues under negotiation.[48]

Nominal Convergence, Real Convergence, Convergence of Goals and Convergence of Policies

The historical review of Greece's 'European adventure' has shown that, in its two main areas of interest – the upgrading of its international position vis-à-vis Turkey, and the financial receipts from the Community budget – Greece has been largely successful. As regards the former, there is no doubt that such considerations were central in Greece's calculations from the outset despite never being officially emphasised. Empirically proving this upgrading of Greece's international position is impossible, as it would require a comparison between the two countries' international position with what it would have been had Greece not joined the European Union. Greece's international upgrading however, is a widely recognised fact and constitutes a central element of Turkey's appreciation of Greco-Turkish relations.

The financial gains, on the other hand, were clearly underrated, as a goal – reflecting the Community budget's structure in the late 1970s. Since then, the budget's size and structure have been transformed through a number of reforms, which have almost always been in a direction favourable to Greek interests. The most important reform is found in the Structural Funds' massive increase. Their rise both in real terms, and as a percentage of total budgetary expenditure (see Figure 1), in conjunction with their concentration in the states and regions most in need have disproportionally benefited Greece. However, one must not underestimate other reforms with important financial repercussions, such as the re-balancing of CAP in favour of the products of the southern periphery or the increasing importance of GDP based national contributions to the Community budget.

Figure 1 Agricultural and Structural Spending of the Community (% of EC Budget, 1980–1997)

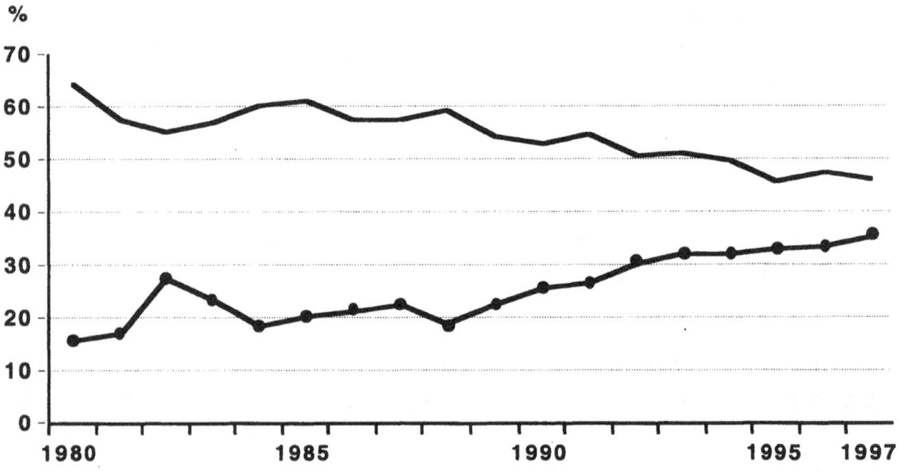

These modifications have resulted in Greece's *per capita* financial gains being particularly high (although significantly lower than Ireland's[49]) and constantly rising (Figures 2 and 3). However, it must be stressed that Greece played an important role in transforming these EU budget mechanisms. As shown earlier, the Greek governments, either through 'reactionary', 'outsider', interventions, or in coalition with others, contributed significantly towards a more re-distributive function of the Community

Figure 2 Greece's Net Per Capita Receipts From The Community Budget

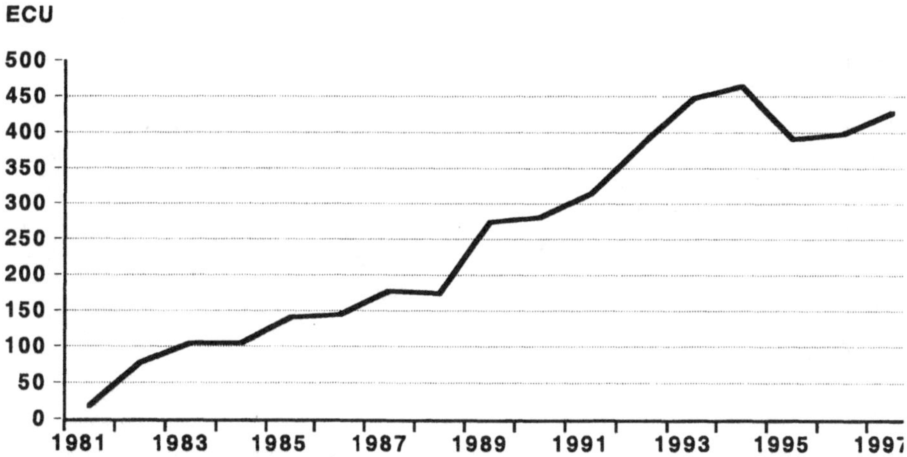

Figure 3 Greek Receipts/Contributions From/To The Community Budget

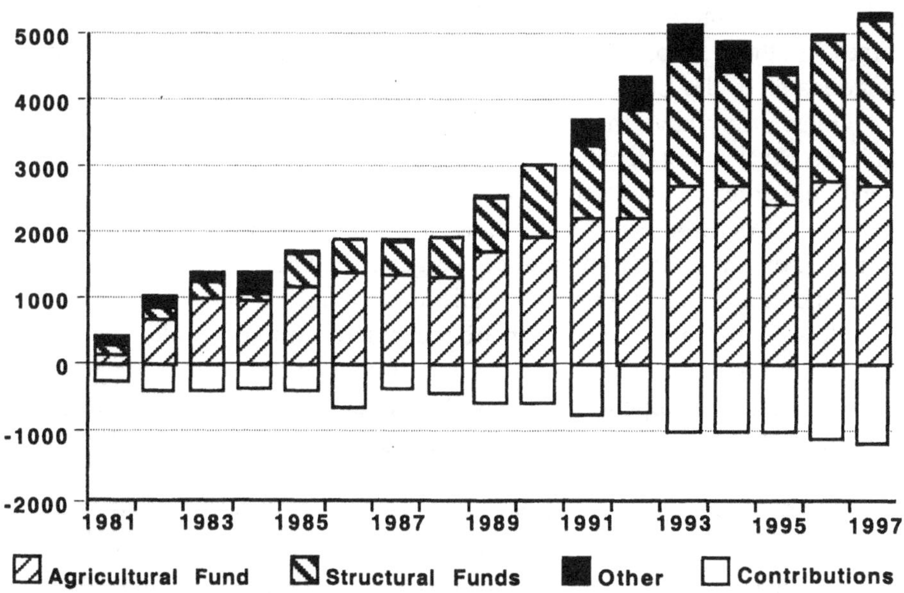

Figure 4 Greece-EU Convergence of GDP Per Capita

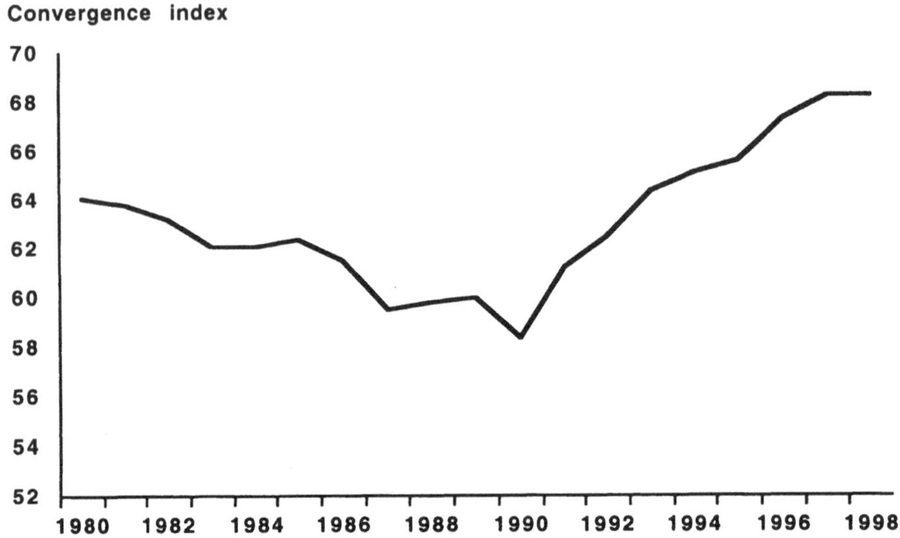

budget, and the transformation in the Structural Funds' philosophy. Greece was successful on this issue because its long term strategy, aimed at maximising its financial gains, coincided with the ideologically Europeanist forces and those who, for various reasons, sought to shift the supply of public goods on to the EC level.

Greece may have made considerable financial gains but convergence with the EU was not achieved: Per capita income was diverging until 1990 ('real convergence', see Figure 4) and only since then, clearly as a consequence of the Structural Funds, does it manifest an almost linear reduction.[50] The relation between real convergence and convergence of inflation rates and other macroeconomic indicators (nominal convergence[51]) has been low,[52] and an examination of the macroeconomic indicators since accession shows that they have, in fact, diverged rather than converged. Figure 5 – and the Appendix – shows the Greek macroeconomic indicators' relative development to the EC average as regards the 'Maastricht Convergence Criteria'.

Without wanting to dwell too much on this development,[53] two observations can nevertheless be made: The first, based on simple reading of the relevant data, shows the clearly detrimental effect of the 1985 and 1989–91

Figure 5 Greece-EU Comparison According to the Main Monetary Indicators (inflation rate, budget deficit, public debt, exchange rate in relation to the community average, 1980–1998)

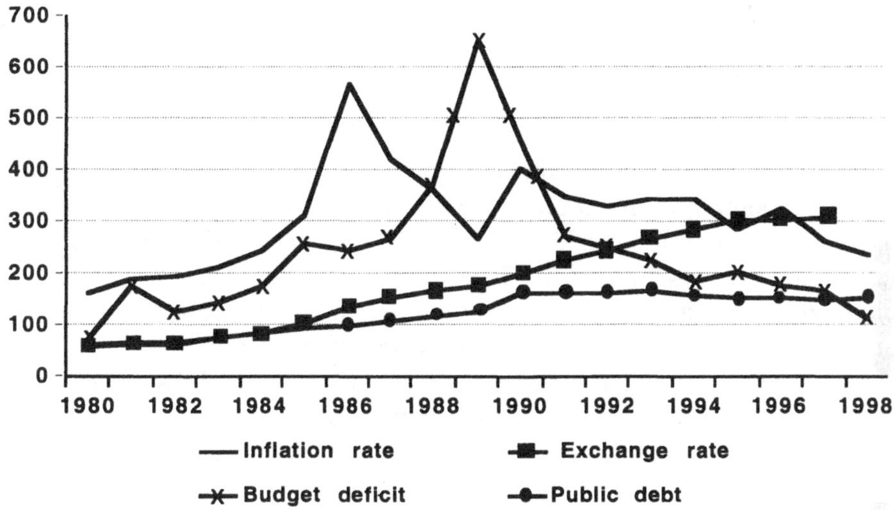

election periods on the inflation rate and Public Debt.[54] The second observation concerns the relationship between nominal convergence and the convergence of policies. In the first fifteen years of Greek EU membership, no effort was made to harmonise economic policy with that of its partners. Only in the last two or three years, due to the necessity of meeting the criteria for Greek participation in Economic and Monetary Union before its final phase in 2002, have there been efforts to adopt an economic policy that is compatible with that goal and similar with the policies followed by other countries. In reality however, as already mentioned, divergence in per capita income is used – effectively – to argue for the maximisation of receipts from the community budget, but not to guide domestic policy.

It is however certain that striving to maintain an unaltered domestic/national policy (or simply changing it just enough to avoid an incompatibility with EU law) while at the same time aiming to maximise the community's support, assistance, and solidarity is no longer a viable proposition. Convergence is a two-way street and requires mutual commitments in confronting short-term divergences, as well as common long-term goals.

The coincidence of long-term goals may no longer pose serious problems in economic policy[55] but is much harder to achieve in the field of foreign policy. Relations with Turkey are clearly the sources of the greatest concern. Although the other EU states' positions vis-à-vis Turkey may not always coincide with each other, either due to a different geopolitical starting point, or due to different economic or trade interests, they do converge in recognising the need for tightened economic, diplomatic, security, etc. relations with Turkey. For some EU countries such tightening should aim at Turkey's eventual accession to the EU, while for others this final goal poses serious concerns. Greece, although the country that has the most to gain from a smooth, dynamic improvement of relations with Turkey, hesitates to use its position within the EU to that end, and prefers using the veto card, hampering the tightening of EU-Turkish relations and sustaining the vicious circle where the issues dividing the two neighbouring countries, when not at crisis point, are left to stagnate and poison them both.

Greece's hard-line policies vis-à-vis Turkey often allow some of its partners to 'hide' behind the Greek positions and thus avoid antagonising Turkey; while at other times they push towards the invention of extra-EU methods to strengthen and support Turkey. Whatever the outcome though, the end result is Greece's marginalisation. Such a vicious circle prohibits both the improvement of EU-Turkish relations and Greece's complete 'integration' within the EU, precludes the possibility of a full coincidence of long-term goals and dooms any efforts to achieve policy convergence to ineffectiveness.

On this issue, like on all other issues where European integration divides the member states and marginalises at least one of them, the existence (and unequivocal formulation) of common long-term goals is a pre-requisite for the joint search of the most fruitful approach to whatever transient and partial divergences may occur. Confronting these divergences is achieved within the dynamic power balances of the day, reflects them, and may lead to a differentiation of the speed of progress[56] or even, when the diverger has significant impeding capabilities, to certain forms of compensation.[57] Otherwise, when divergences are either ignored and 'exorcised', or their solution is passively left to an invisible hand, they poison the overall process and lead, at best, to negative compromises.

Conclusions

This article aimed at the exploration of Greece's participation in the process of European integration. The course, from the decision to accede, which polarised the Greek political parties, to today's virtual consensus in favour of European integration, has been neither linear nor smooth. The significant, and increasing, financial gains undoubtedly contributed to this change of heart and the effort to maximise them led to the increased use of a communitarian rhetoric within a communitarian logic. In fact, this effort led Greece to play a crucial role in developing the philosophy and scope of the redistributive and structural character of community interventions. Despite all that though, Greece remains a marginal country as regards the decision-making procedures partly by choice, as it has not been disposed to abandon its intergovernmental and from the 'outside' approach to the process of European integration.

The main factor imposing this approach and prohibiting the Greek governments from acting as an integral ingredient of European integration's central core has to be searched in Greece's foreign policy and especially its relations with Turkey which poison the entire spectrum of Greek politics and condemn Greece to a marginal role in European developments. These problems are, by their nature, inherently difficult to solve but their solution has been made even more difficult by the hesitation to approach them within a long-term framework emphasising the need for increasingly closer ties between the EU and Turkey through which to solve the existing problems instead of the, by definition, short-term and tactical exploitation of Greece's current advantageous position in order to hamper any efforts strengthening these ties.

These thoughts lead to the first of this article's main conclusions. To isolate one sector which will focus the national interest and determine the overall political action within the community processes is simply impossible. A member state's stance with respect to the extent, depth and form of the community's sectoral policies, or their financial consequences, needs to be compatible with its internal economic policy as well as its foreign policy. It is increasingly utopian for a country to consider that it can focus its efforts on the parts of the overall EU policy that are of interest, or to consider that it can adopt contradictory strategies, tactics and approaches regarding the EU's various policies.

The second main conclusion regards the fundamental choice of the intergovernmental approach in contradistinction to the federalist one. An intergovernmental approach, that is, one which limits a member state's scope of action to intergovernmental contacts, cooperations and negotiations while ignoring the supranational organs and institutions, is limited in range because it denies the member state the opportunity to intervene in agenda-setting and the institutional balance which defines it. These limitations occur even when the intergovernmental approach is active, consistent and long-term in nature and execution and horizontally covers the entire spectrum of community policies.

The third conclusion concerns the federal approach proper and its pre-requisites. The convergence of levels of development, the reduction of the chasm of monetary indicators, the consistency of national policies all undoubtedly contribute to the promotion of the federalist logic. The real pre-requisite however has to be searched in the convergence of long-term goals. Common action in confronting and solving the transient and partial divergences, and a sharing of the costs (be they political, social or economic) is only possible if there is convergence of long-term objectives. Greek society's recognition of the need to promote this twin approach – that is, identification of long-term goals, and confronting divergences in common – will lead to the acceptance of the federalist logic in everyday community practices which, in turn, will permit the maximisation of gains from participation in the process of European integration. A federalist approach is not just an ideological choice but an imperative of the national interest.

Notes

1. The thoughts and analyses contained in this paper are, of course, entirely personal and, although clearly influenced by my experiences as Commission official, they do not reflect in any way the views of the Commission. The initial version of the article was written in Greek and I owe to Yannos Mitsos not just the translation and the overall improvement of style but also a number of valuable comments on the content. Very useful comments have also been provided by Artemis Kourtessis.
2. Beyers-Dierickx (1997), for example, in their attempt to analyse the communication behaviour of the member states' representatives in the working groups of the Council, found that the Greeks attract less communication than all other representatives.
3. On 'elite driven' decisions and the permissive or conscious popular consensus on European integration, see *inter alia* Eichenberg-Dalton (1993), Anderson (1995), Wessels (1995).
4. Petersen (1998).
5. Strengthening democracy was also among the main goals of Greek accession to the

European Communities, but the democratic regime was considered at the time much more vulnerable than later.

6. The great and increasing flow of funds is, without a doubt, an important explanatory factor of the ever-increasing popular acceptance of participation in Europe. See also Vaubel (1994).
7. See for example, Wessels (1997, p. 268) as well as the collection of representative articles in Nugent (1997).
8. 'Policy-makers are at the mercy of the implementers' [Meny-Muller-Quermonne (1996b, p. 7)]. 'Street-level bureaucrats can reshape policy' [Rhodes-Bache-George (1996, p. 375)].
9. For example, in the field of structural policy, the scope of initiative and the European Commission's ability to enforce its position have been transformed in recent years. In addition, in certain fields, a 'casual glance' at the Treaty's relevant articles may give the impression of a total Commission hegemony, but in practice, this hegemony is increasingly in doubt. For example, with regard to state aids, it appears that the Commission's jurisdiction is unchallenged. In practice however, the Commission is ineffective because its jurisdiction is confined to setting maximum limits and does not extend to checking the actual national resources that have been committed [Mitsos (forthcoming)].
10. On the role of the Council's 'working groups' see, Beyers (1998), Beyers-Dierickx (1998). On 'Committology', i.e. the role of committees with member state participation which are called to monitor, advise, or even, co-decide with the Commission on matters concerning the implementation of the Council's Decisions, Peterson (1995), Heinels (1996), Dogan (1997). For a general discussion on the Council's decision-making methods, see Hayes-Renshaw – Wallace (1995).
11. Even more, according to Liesbet Hooghe and Gary Marks (1997) the 'Cohesion Policy', encompassing three key aspects of 'controlled capitalism' (positive, i.e. market-friendly adjustment intervention by the European Union, multi-level partnership, and substantial redistribution) was an important victory against the 'neo-liberal plan'.
12. Around the time of the Single European Act (1986–1988) 'the Commission had moved from being the prisoner of governments determined to limit its autonomy to the position of an entrepreneur able to pyramid its role as broker of a 12-level chess game'. (In the words of John Major, as reproduced in Ross (1995, p. 33).) Recently, under the banner of 'doing less but better', the Commission has itself curbed its role to that of a conscientious manager. On the role of the Commission as a 'policy entrepreneur' and a 'purposeful opportunist' see *inter alia* Cram (1993), Cram (1994), Peterson (1995a), Marks-Hooghe-Blank (1996), Marks (1996).
13. Increasing the number of decisions requiring majority voting and not unanimity clearly strengthens the European Union's supranational character. [See, however, Marks (1996, p. 397).]
14. The memorandum, entitled 'Position of the Greek Government on Greece's Relations with the European Communities' was submitted by the Greek government to both the Commission and the Council of Ministers on 19-3-1982. See also Mitsos (1989, p. 394). For a very comprehensive bibliography of the development of Greece's position in the European Union, see Ioakimidis (1997).
15. 'Greek Memorandum's' closing lines, *op. cit.*
16. *op. cit.*
17. In 1980 the Regional Fund represented just 6.5 per cent of the Community budget. Court of Auditors' 'Annual Report', *Official Journal of the EC*, issue C 344, 31-12-1981.
18. Court of Auditors' (*op. cit.*) data regarding the size of the Regional Fund; EUROSTAT for the two countries' GDP.
19. The Council's 'mandate' represents the first identification of the need to conceptualise

all the important issues dividing the Community at the time. This 'mandate' initiated, in effect, what was to later become the so called 'Grand Negotiation'. A detailed and enlightening account of all facets of this negotiation is found in Ioakimidis (1988).

20. Besides, the *evolution* of A. Papandreou's political rhetoric (from calling for immediate withdrawal, to stressing the need for a special agreement prior to full membership, to a referendum so that the Greek people could decide once and for all, to the need for special arrangements within the EC) showed a great deal more about the new Prime Minister's real intentions than his proclamations of the moment. In addition, one must not forget that K. Karamanlis, the architect of Greek accession to the EC, was President of the Republic at the time and would surely not have stood passively by, while the country's radical repositioning on such a major issue was taking place. For a general discussion of Papandreou's government foreign policy at the time, see *inter alia* Loulis (1984), Melakopides (1987).
21. The author, advisor at the time to the Deputy Minister of Foreign Affairs and head of the 'inter-ministerial committee for EC affairs', recalls the surprise, bemusement and suspicions of 'serving community interests' with which positions, later considered evident, were then received. Such issues included the increasing of the EC budget, or supporting the southern enlargement as a prerequisite for a shift in the inter-communitarian balance of power (not to mention an initial attempt to *horizontally* represent the Greek government, supporting the Danish position on Greenland's rights following its departure from the EEC).
22. In defence of the Greek stance at the time however, it has to be noted that the European Commission's standing was at a particularly low ebb. Furthermore, among the factors explaining the Greek stance towards the Commission, one could add the Commission's negative 'Opinion' about Greek accession, the overcoming of which had required a major diplomatic effort, led personally by the then Prime Minister K. Karamanlis [Syrianos (1979), Mitsos (1981)]. This factor however, could not be put forward by the PASOK government as the 'Opinion's' publication had been enthusiastically greeted by PASOK, then in opposition, as a triumphant confirmation of its own positions.
23. The legal basis for the accompanying measures came from the 'safeguard clause' in Art. 130 of the Treaty on Greece's accession. See Mitsos (1989, p. 413).
24. The Commission's vice-president, Christofer Tugendhat's, official visit to Athens which coincided with the government decisions, personified the negative views that both the Commission and member states had of the Greek government as he was kept completely uninformed (!) both in his meetings with various ministers and with the Administration of the Bank of Greece.
25. The dispute between Europeanists and anti-Europeanists often became strenuous and took public dimensions as happened with Gr. Varfis' rumoured resignation following his confrontation with National Economy Minister, G. Arsenis in early 1983.
26. For its partners, and others, the prospect of a Greek Presidency raised important questions to say the least. The revelations in Attali (1993) about the highest-level discussions (including correspondence between Presidents Reagan and Mitterrand) concerning the timing of the G7 Summit at Williamsburg, USA are of a great historical interest and a case in point: President Mitterrand insisted that the Summit take place in the second half of 1983 so that A. Papandreou could attend as President of the EC and 'I will not be the only Socialist there' (*op. cit. p. 317)*. President Reagan, on the other hand, insisted that the Summit does not coincide with the Greek presidency exactly because of the undesirability of A. Papandreou's presence. Needless to say, the Summit took place before the opening of the Greek presidency, on 29 May 1983.
27. On the role of the Council's Presidency, see Kirchner (1992). For a general discussion with reference to the Greek presidencies, see Ioakimidis (1995b), Mitsos (1995),

Stavridis (1995).

28. See, for example, Ross (1995, p. 28). On the first Greek presidency, see Mitsos (1984), Tsakaloyannis (1985), Ioakimidis (1988), Kranidiotis and Perrakis (1987), TEPSA (1988).
29. In the words of J. Attali, advisor to President Mitterrand: 'Athènes a formidablement déblayé le terrain, poussant si bien la crise a son apogée que tout redevient possible' [Attali (1993, p. 561)].
30. Indulging in a personal account as I was privileged to attend the greatest part of that Council's meetings, I recall the bitterness of all those who, after through-the-night efforts to compose a final draft, witnessed the rejection of the compromise, not by Mrs Thatcher like most expected, but by President Mitterrand. Six months later, he would go down in the history of European integration on the back of a compromise not dissimilar to the one he had rejected in Athens.
31. *COM(82)348*, 18.6.1982 and *COM(83)134*, 29.3.1983.
32. A noteworthy exception to the complete lack of governmental communication with the previous Commissioner was the Ministry of Agriculture which, both for practical reasons and due to a conscious policy decision by the Agriculture Minister, K. Simitis, had always kept channels of communication open.
33. Interestingly, and in contrast to the 1983 measures, the Greek government's procedure of choice focused on the escape clause of the EC Treaty (Article 108), and not the Treaty of Accession. Although the totality of Greek demands was fulfilled there was a crucial qualification in that the loan would be granted in two instalments [*Official Journal of the EC, L373*, 31.12.1985 and *L357*, 18.12.1986], thus requiring the observation of both the Greek economic policy and the degree to which the specific immediate goals (now *jointly* set by the Commission and the Greek government) have been fulfilled. [Mitsos (1989), p. 413.]
34. On 23.3.1983 the Commission adopted the 'Report on the Integrated Mediterranean Programmes' [COM(83) 24]. The first Proposal for appropriate legislation was adopted on 16.8.1983 [COM(83) 495], *Official Journal of the EC, C251*, 19.9.1983, p. 1.
35. See Hooghe (1996b) which mentions that the origins of the modern cohesion policy should be traced back to Greece's threat to block the Iberian Enlargement. See also the very interesting analyses by Smyrl (1998) and Heinelt (1996). The Greek veto was withdrawn following the adoption in principle of the IMPs at the Brussels European Council in March 1985, and consequently, the Commission submitted its new formal proposals a month later [COM(85)180, Official Journal of the EC, L197], and the Council decided accordingly [Reg. 2099/85, *Official Journal of the EC, L197*, 27.7.1985, p. 1]. For a history of the IMPs, their linkage with the restructuring of the funds, and the history of the community's Regional Policy, see also Ioakimidis (1988), Mitsos (1989), Cheshire et al. (1991), Andrikopoulou (1995).
36. Article 130a of the Single European Act.
37. For an analysis of the qualitative shifts in the structural funds' actions, see *inter alia* Mendes (1990), Cheshire et al. (1991), Hannequart (1992), Marks (1992), Marks (1993), Andrikopoulou (1995), Bougas (1996), Hooghe (1996), Mitsos (forthcoming).
38. Greece would later be called to 'pay' for its casual acceptance of these rules and mechanisms when the state apparatus proved unable to implement them. Greece (and only Greece) was then driven to delegate to the Commission, not just the responsibility for solving the country's structural development problems, but also for solving the totality of the Greek economy's and society's structural 'Gordian knots'.
39. On the second Greek presidency, see Kranidiotis (1993).
40. See in Pagoulatos' contribution to this volume his 'Ulysses and the Sirens' syndrome. Just like Ulysses tied himself to the mast of his ship to avoid the temptation of the sirens,

the Greek government chose an imposed disciplinary mechanism which increased the cost of non-compliance.

41. For the relevant 'revelations' of the advisor to Foreign Minister A. Samaras, see Tarkas (1995). See also the next Foreign Minister's diary, Papakonstantinou (1994).
42. Characteristic of that situation is the immediate (as well as short-lived) shift in international attitudes towards Greece following the Greek government's only major peacemaking initiative with the *Vouliagmeni Conference* on 1 May 1993 [Owen (1995, p. 148)].
43. I submit my personal experience of the immense difficulties encountered in the arrangement of a meeting between Foreign Minister M. Papakostantinou and J. Delors to discuss the Greek positions regarding the upcoming crucial financial decisions. Under ordinary circumstances, setting up such a meeting would have been a formality but it became a major endeavour (!) at that moment in time due to the 'Macedonian issue'. Eventually the meeting did take place but covered, almost exclusively...the 'Macedonian issue'.
44. Prior to this official 'embargo', in August 1992 Greece had also cut off all supplies of oil to the countries of former Yugoslavia which resulted in 'Gligorov writhing' (as, according to his then advisor, Prime Minister Mitsotakis is reported to have said) [Skylakakis (1995, p. 182)]. In addition, an 'unofficial' embargo of Dutch products had also been implemented following the Dutch government's 'anti-hellenic' stance.
45. For Greco-Turkish relations, see Veremis (1998), Alexandris, et al. (1988), Papahadjopoulos (1998a). For their effects on the relations between the EU and Turkey, see Akagul (1998), Papahadjopoulos (1998b).
46. For a general discussion on the Greek stance at European Political Cooperation and especially Greece's linking the acceptance of the Maastricht Treaty with the decision to join the Western European Union, see Ioakimides (1993).
47. These negotiations concern the size and nature of the Union's budgetary resources, the future of the CAP (and the degree of participation of national and community budgets in supporting agricultural incomes), as well as the future of the structural funds, in light of the 'forthcoming' enlargement to include the former Eastern European countries and Cyprus. The Berlin European Council on 25 April 1999 reached decisions regarding the major financial issues, centring on the institutionalisation of objective principles, with, in effect, parallel measures for each member state.
48. For the Greek stance in the intergovernmental conference which led to the Treaty of Amsterdam, see Ioakimidis (1998) as well as Ioakimidis (1995), Yataganas (1996), Ioakimidis (1996) and Chrysochoou (1999). On the Amsterdam Treaty in general see (*inter alia*) Chrysochoou et al. (1999), as well as Moravcsik-Nicolaidis (1998) and the other articles in the *Journal of Common Market Studies*, vol. 36, Annual Report, 1999.
49. According to the author's calculations based on the 'Court of Auditors Annual Report for the 1998 Budget' [*Official Journal of the EC, C 349*, 17.11.1998], the net *per capita* receipts for the European Union's poorest countries were: ECU 430 for Greece, ECU 767 for Ireland, ECU 276 for Portugal and ECU 161 for Spain.
50. According to the the various econometric analyses commissioned by the European Commission for the appraisal of the Structural Funds actions, the second Community Support Framework, covering the 1994–1999 period will increase Greece's annual rate of GDP growth by between one and two percentage points. See also Cour des Comptes (1998).
51. For the various definitions and types of convergence, see Mitsos (forthcoming).
52. Indicatively, the correlation coefficient between Greece's 'real divergence' (GDP per capita divergence from the Community's average) and the divergence of inflation rates is 0.400, while the correlation coefficient between the same 'real divergence' and the divergence of budget deficits is 0.644.

53. See the articles by Christodoulakis, Alogoskoufis and Garganas in this volume. See also Alogoskoufis (1997).
54. On the connection between macroeconomic indicators, Greek economic policy and electoral cycles see Thomadakis-Seremetis (1993).
55. The real moment of truth for the community's goals will come when the policy of economic and social cohesion will have to be implemented in an easternly enlarged Union where Greece will no longer be the poorest country and hence, will have the greatest interest in the implementation of strict, objective criteria in the distribution of funds.
56. On the various forms of flexibility, variable geometry, etc., see the classification and exhaustive review in Stubb (1996).
57. On the functioning of the Structural Funds as a form of compensation or 'bribing' of member states of the European periphery, see Marks (1992), Marks (1993), Laursen (1995), Wishdale (1995), Mitsos (forthcoming).

References

Akagûl, P.D. (1998), 'Le cinquième élargissement de l'Union Européenne et la question de la canditature turque. La fin d'un cycle, mais quelles perspectives?'. *Revue du Marché Commun et de l'Union Européenne*, No. 419 (Juin), pp. 359–69.

Alexandris,A., et al. (1988), *I Ellinotourkikes Sheseis 1923–1987* (*Greek-Turkish Relations 1923–1987*), Athens: Ekdoseis Gnosi, ELIAMEP, [in Greek].

Alogoskoufis, G. (1997), 'To Provlima tis Oikonomikis kai Pragmatikis Syglisis' ('The Problem of Economic and Real Convergence'), in *Kintis*, Volume A, pp. 78–98 [in Greek].

Anderson, C. (1995), 'Economic Uncertainty and European Solidarity. Revisited Trends in Public Support for European Integration', in Rhodes-Mazey (1995), pp. 111–34.

Andrikopoulou, E. (1995), *I Perifereies stin Evropaiki Enosi. I Exelixi tis Perfiferiakis Politikis apo ti Synthiki tis Romis eos to Maastricht* (*The Regions in the European Union. The Evolution of Regional Policy from the Treaty of Rome to Maastricht*), Athens: Themelio, [in Greek].

Attali, J. (1993), *Verbatim, Tome 1: Chronique des annees 1981–1986*, Paris: Fayard.

Beyers, J. (1998), *'Where Does Supranationalism Come from? Ideas Floating through the Working Groups of the Council of the European Union'. European Integration online Papers*, Vol. 2, No. 9, http://eiop.or.at/eiop/texte/1998-009a.htm.

Beyers, J. and Dierickx, G. (1997), 'Nationality and European Negotiations: The Working Groups of the Council of Ministers', *European Journal of International Relations*, Vol. 3, No. 4, pp. 435–71.

Beyers, J. and Dierickx, G. (1998), 'The Working Groups of the Council of the European Union: Supranational or Intergovernmental Negotiations?' *Journal of Common Market Studies*, Vol. 36, No. 3 (Sept), pp. 289–317.

Bougas, A. (1996), 'Evropaikes Diarthrotikes Politikes' ('European Structural Policies'), *Synhrona Themata*, Vol. 60–61, (Dec.), pp. 169–78 [in Greek].

Cafruny, A.W. and Rosenthal, G.G. (eds) (1993), *The State of the European Community. The Maastricht Treaty and Beyond, Vol. 2*, London: Longman.

Cheshire. P., Camagni, R.P., Gaudemar, J.-P.de, and Cuadrado Roura, J.R. (1991), '1957 to 1992: Moving toward a Europe of Regions and Regional Policy', in Rodwin-Sazanami, pp. 268–300.

Chrysochoou, D.N., Tsinisizelis, M., Stavridis, S. and Ifantis, K. (1999), *Europe in Change.*

Theory and Reform in the European Union, Manchester: Manchester University Press.
Council of the European Union, General Secretariat (1998), *Intergovernmental Conference on the Revision of the Treaties. Dutch Presidency. Collected Texts*, Luxembourg: Office for Official Publications of the European Communities.
Cour des Comptes (1998), *Observations preliminaires presentées en vertu de l'article 188c, paragraphe 4, deuxième alinea, du Traité CE, relatives a l'évaluation des interventions des Fonds structurels concernant les periodes 1989–1993 et 1994–1999*, 28 Mai.
Cram, L. (1993), 'Calling the Tune without Paying the Pipe?, Social Policy Regulation: The Role of the Commission in EC Social Policy', *Policy & Politics*, Vol. 21, No. 2, pp. 135–46.
Cram, L. (1994), 'The European Commission as a Multi-Organisation, Social Policy and IT Policy in the EU', *Journal of European Public Policy*, Vol. 1, No. 2 (Autumn), pp. 195–217.
Dogan, R. (1997), 'Comitology: Little Procedures with Big Implications'. *West European Politics*, Vol. 20, No. 3 (July), pp. 31–60,.
Eichenberg, R.C. and Dalton, R.J. (1993), 'Europeans and the EC. The Dynamics of Public Support for European Integration', *International Organization*, Vol. 47, No. 4 (Summer), pp. 507–34.
Frangakis, N., Papayannides, A.D. and Apostolides, R. (eds) (1994), *The Third Greek Presidency of the Council of the European Union*, Athens: Hestia.
Gibson, H. (ed), (forthcoming), *Economic Change in Southern Europe*, Baltimore: Johns Hopkins University Press.
Golub, J. (1996), 'State Power and Institutional Influence in European Integration, Lessons from the Packaging Waste Directive', *Journal of Common Market Studies*, Vol. 34, No. 3 (Sept.), pp. 313–39.
Hannequart, A. (ed) (1992), *Economic and Social Cohesion in Europe, A New Objective for Integration*, London: Routledge.
Hayes-Renshaw, F. and Wallace, H. (1995), 'Executive Power in the European Union: The Functions and Limits of the Council of Ministers', *Journal of European Public Policy*, Vol. 2, No. 4 (Dec.), pp. 559–82.
Heinelt, H. (1996), 'Multilevel Governance in the European Union and the Structural Funds'. In Heinelt-Smith, pp. 9–25.
Heinelt, H. and Smith, R. (eds) (1996), *Policy Networks and European Structural Funds*, Brookfield: Avebury, Ashgate Publishing Company.
Hooghe, L. (ed) (1996a), *Cohesion Policy and European Integration: Building Multi-Level Governance*, New York: Oxford University Press.
Hooghe, L. (1996b), 'Building a Europe with the Regions: The Changing Role of the European Commission', in Hooghe, pp. 89–128.
Hooghe, L. and Marks, G. (1997), 'The Making of a Polity: The Struggle over European Integration', *European Integration online Papers*, Vol. 1, no.4, http://eiop.or.at/eiop/texte/1997-004a.htm.
Ioakimidis, P.C. (1988), *O Metashimatismos tis EOK. Apo tin 'Entoli' stin Eniaia Evropaiki Praxi. I Metexelixi tis Evropaikis Koinotitas kai o Rolos tis Elladas* (*The Transformation of the EEC. From the 'Mandate' to the European Single Act. The Evolution of the European Community and the Role of Greece*, Athens: Papazisis, [in Greek].
Ioakimidis, P.K. (1993), *Evropaiki Politiki Enosi. Theoria – Diapragmatefsi – Thesmi kai Politikes. I Synthiki tou Maastricht kai I Ellada* (*European Political Union. Theory – Negotiation – Institutions and Policies. The Maastricht Treaty and Greece*), Athens: Themelio, [in Greek].
Ioakimidis, P.K. (1995a), *I Anatheorisi tis Synthikis tou Maastricht* (*The Revision of the Treaty of Maastricht*, Athens: Themelio, [in Greek].

Ioakimidis, P.C. (1995b), *The Evolution of the Third Greek Presidency in the E.U.*, University of Bristol, Centre for Mediterranean Studies, Occasional Paper No. 12 (Sept.).
Ioakimidis, P.K. (1996), 'I Anatheorisi tis Synthikis gia tin Evropaiki Enosi' ('The Revision of the Treaty on the European Union'), *Synhrona Themata*, Vol. 60–61 (Dec.), pp. 74–87 [in Greek].
Ioakimidis, P.K. (1997), *I Ellada stin Evropaiki Enosi 1981–1996, Epilogi Vivliografias* (*Greece in the European Union 1981–1996, Selection of Bibliography*), Athens: Themelio, [in Greek].
Ioakimidis, P.K. (1998), *I Synthiki tou Amsterdam. Neo Protypo Oloklirosis I Symptoma Apo-Oloklirosis;* (*The Amsterdam Treaty. New Model of Integration or Symptom of Disintegration?*, Athens: Themelio, [in Greek].
Kintis, A. (ed) (1997), *To Paron kai to Mellon tis Ellinikis Ekonomias* (*The Present and Future of the Greek Economy*, in Greek), Athens: Gutenberg.
Kirchner, E.J. (1992), *Decision-Making in the European Community, The Council Presidency and European Integration*, Manchester: Manchester Univ. Press.
Kranidiotis, Y.N. (1993), *I Exelixi tis Ellinikis Politikis sti Defteri Elliniki Proedria tou Symvouliou tis Evropaikis Koinotitas* (*The Evolution of Greek Policy during the Second Greek Presidency of the Council of the European Community*), Athens: Komotini, Sakkoulas [in Greek].
Kranidiotis, Y.N. and Perrakis, S. (eds) (1987), *I Proti Elliniki Proedria stin E.K.* (*The First Greek Presidency of the EC*), Athens: Ministry of Foreign Affairs [in Greek].
Laursen, F. (ed) (1995a), *The Political Economy of European Integration*, The Hague: Kluwer Law International European Institute Public Administration.
Laursen, F. (1995b), 'On Studying European Integration. Integration Theory and Political Economy', in Laursen (1995a), pp. 3–29.
Loulis, J.C. (1984), 'Papandreou's Foreign Policy'. *Foreign Affairs*, Vol. 63, No. 2 (Winter), pp. 375–91.
Marks, G. (1992), 'Structural Policy in the European Community', in Sbraglia, pp. 191–224.
Marks, G. (1993), 'Structural Policy and Multilevel Government in the EC', in Cafruny-Rosenthal, pp. 391–410.
Marks, G. (1996), 'Exploring and Explaining Variation in EU Cohesion Policy', in Hooghe, pp. 388–422.
Marks, G., Hooghe, L. and Blank, K. (1996), 'European Integration from the 1980s, State-Centric v. Multi-level Governance', *Journal of Common Market Studies*, Vol. 34, No. 3 (Sept.), pp. 341–78.
Melakopides, C. (1987), 'The Logic of Papandreou's Foreign Policy', *International Journal*, Vol. XLII (Summer), pp. 559–84.
Mendes, A.J.M. (1990), 'Economic Cohesion in Europe, The Impact of the Delors Plan', *Journal of Common Market Studies*, Vol. XXIX, No. 1 (Sept.), pp. 18–36.
Meny, Y., Muller, P. and Quermonne, J.-L. (eds) (1996a), *Adjusting to Europe. The Impact of the European Union on National Institutions and Policies*, London: Routledge.
Meny, Y., Muller, P. and Quermonne, J.-L. (1996b), 'Introduction', In Meny-Muller-Quermonne,, pp. 1–22.
Mitsos, A. (1981), *I Proshorisi stis Evropaikes Koinotites* (*The Accession to the European Communities*, in Greek), Thessaloniki: Ekdoseis Synhrona Themata.
Mitsos, A. (1984), 'Se Anazitisi Evropaikis Stratigikis' ('In Search of a European Strategy', in Greek), *Synhrona Themata*, Vol. 21, pp. 11–14.
Mitsos, A. (1989), *I Elliniki Viomihania sti Diethni Agora. Kratiki Prostasia kai Antagonistiki Thesi tis Eghorias Paragogis prin kai meta tin Entaxi stin Evropaiki Koinotita* (*The Greek Industry in the International Market. State Protection and Competitive Position of the Domestic Production before and after Accession to the

European Community), Athens: Themelio, [in Greek].

Mitsos, A. (1995), *Aims and Policies of the Greek Presidency: The Brussels Perspective.* University of Bristol, Centre for Mediterranean Studies, Occasional Paper No. 12, Sept.

Mitsos, A. (ed) (1996), 'I Evropaiki Oloklirosi meta ti Diakyvernitiki Diaskepsi' ('European Integration after the Intergovernmental Conference, *Synhrona Themata*, Vol. 60–61 (Dec.), pp. 19–192 [in Greek].

Mitsos, A. (forthcoming), 'The Community's Redistributive and Development Role and the Southern European Countries', in Gibson, chapter 9.

Moravcsik, A. and Nicolaidis, K. 'Federal Ideals and Constitutional Realities in the Treaty of Amsterdam. Keynote Article', *Journal of Common Market Studies*, Vol. 36 (Sept.), Annual Review, pp. 13–38.

Niedermayer, O. and Sinnott, R. (eds) (1995), *Beliefs in Government, Volume Two. Public Opinion and Internationalized Governance*, Oxford University Press, Oxford.

Nugent, N. (ed) (1997), *The European Union. Volume I: Perspectives and Theoretical Interpretations*, Dartmouth Publishing Company, Brookfield.

O'Nuallain, C. (1985), *The Presidency of the European Council of Ministers, Impacts and implications for National Governments*, London: Croom Helm.

Owen, D. (1995), *Balkan Odyssey*, London: Victor Gollancz.

Papahadjopoulos, D. (1998a), *Greek Foreign Policy in the Post-Cold War Era.* CEPS Paper No. 72.

Papahadjopoulos, D. (rapporteur) (1998b), *EU-Turkish Relations: Meeting the Challenges ahead.* Proceedings of a CEPS-TUSIAD Conference, 6.11.1997, Brussels: CEPS.

Papakonstantinou, M. (1994), *To Imerologio Enos Politikou* (*The Diary of a Politician*), Athens: Estia [in Greek].

Petersen, N. (1998), 'National Strategies in the Integration Dilemma: An Adaptation Approach', *Journal of Common Market Studies*, Vol. 36, No. 1 (March), pp. 33–54.

Peterson, J. (1995), 'EU Research Policy: The Politics of Expertise', in Rhodes-Mazey, pp. 391–412.

Peterson, J. (1995a), 'Playing the Transparency Game, Consultation and Policy-Making in the European Commission', *Public Administration*, Vol. 73 (Autumn), pp. 473–92.

Rhodes, C. and Mazey, S. (eds) (1995), *The State of the European Union. Building a European Polity?* London: Longman.

Rhodes, R.A.W., Bache, I. and George, S. (1996), 'Policy Networks and Policy-Making in the European Union: A Critical Appraisal', in Hooghe, pp. 367–87.

Rodwin, L. and Sazanami. (eds) (1991), *Industrial Change and Regional Economic Transformation. The Experience of Western Europe*, London: Harper Collins Academic.

Ross, G. (1995), *Jacques Delors and European Integration*, Cambridge: Polity Press.

Sbragia, A.M. (ed) (1992), *Euro-Politics Institutions and Policy-Making in the 'New' European Community*, Washington, D.C.: Brookings Institute.

Schmitter, P.C. (1996), 'Some Alternative Futures for the European Polity and their Implications for European Public Policy', in *Meny-Muller-Quermonne*, pp. 25–40.

Skylakakis, Th. (1995), *Sto Onoma tis Makedonias* (*In the Name of Macedonia*), Athens: Evroekdotiki [in Greek].

Stavridis, S. (1995), *Foreign Policy Issues and the 1994 Greek Presidency*, University of Bristol, Centre for Mediterranean Studies, Occasional Paper No. 12, Sept.

Stubb, A.C.- G. (1996), 'A Categorization of Differentiated Integration', *Journal of Common Market Studies*, Vol. 34, No. 2, pp. 283–95.

Smyrl, M.E. (1998), 'When (and How), Do the Commission's Preferences Matter?', *Journal of Common Market Studies*, Vol. 36, No. 1 (March), pp. 79–99.

Syrianos, M. (1979), 'I Poreia pros tin Entaxi' ('The Road to Accession'), *Synhrona Themata*, Vol. 5 (May), pp. 4–16 [in Greek].

Tarkas, A.G. (1995), *Athina – Skopia piso apo tis Kleistes Portes* (*Athens – Skopje behind Closed Doors*), Athens: Lavyrinthos [in Greek].
TEPSA (1988), *La Grèce et la Communauté Européenne. Experiences et Perspectives*, Bruxelles: TEPSA.
Thomadakis, S.B. and Seremetis, D.B. (1993), 'I Apostatheropiitiki Dynamiki tou Ellinikou Eklogikou – Dimosionomikou Kyklou' ('The Destabilizing Dynamics of the Greek Electoral – Fiscal Cycle'), *Elliniki Epitheorisi Politikis Epistimis*, Vol. 2, pp. 48–82 [in Greek].
Tsakaloyannis, P. (1985), 'Greece's First Term in the Presidency of the EC: A Preliminary Assessment', in O'Nuallain, pp. 101–18.
Vaubel, R. (1994), 'The Public Choice Analysis of European Integration: A Survey', *European Journal Political Economy*, Vol. 10, pp. 227–49.
Veremis, Th. (1998), *Istoria ton Ellinotourkikon Sheseon 1453–1998*, (*History of Greek-Turkish Relations 1453–1998*), Athens: I. Sideris, ELIAMEP [in Greek].
Wessels, B. (1995), 'Evaluations of the EC: Elite or Mass-Driven'. In Niedermayer-Sinnott (1995), pp. 137–62.
Wessels, W. (1997), 'An Ever Closer Fusion?, A Dynamic Macropolitical View on Integration Processes'. *Journal of Common Market Studies*, Vol. 35, No. 2 (June), pp. 267–99.
Wishdale, F. (1996), 'EU Cohesion Policy: Facts, Figures, and Issues', in Hooghe, pp. 27–58.
Yataganas, X. (1996), 'To Thesmiko Provlima tis Evropaikis Enoseos kai I Diakyvernitiki Syndiaskepsi' ('The Institutional Problem of the European Union and the Intergovernmental Conference'), *Synhrona Themata*, Vol. 60–61 (Dec.), pp. 88–96 [in Greek].

Appendix 1: Greece's Convergence/Divergence from Community Average as Regards GDP per Capita and the Main Monetary Convergence Criteria (1980–98)

	1980	1981	1982	1983	1984	1985	1986	1987
Greece's GDP per capita with respect to EU-15 (PPS. EU-15 = 100)	64.1	63.8	63.2	62.1	62.1	62.4	61.5	59.5
Price deflator private consumption								
Greece	21.9	22.7	20.7	18.1	17.9	18.3	22.1	15.7
EU-15	13.2	11.9	10.6	8.5	7.3	5.8	3.9	3.7
Greece/EU	165.9	190.8	195.3	212.9	245.2	315.5	566.7	424.3
Net lending (+) or net borrowing (-) of general government (percentage of GDP at market prices)								
Greece	-2.4	-8.4	-6.3	-7.1	-8.3	-11.6	-10.3	-9.6
EU-15	-3.3	-4.7	-5.0	-4.9	-4.7	-4.5	-4.2	-3.6
Greece/EU	72.7	178.7	126.0	144.9	176.6	257.8	245.2	266.7
General government consolidated gross debt (percentage of GDP at market prices)								
Greece	23.8	28.3	31.9	36.6	43.9	51.6	53.7	59.7
EU-15	38.4	41.9	45.5	48.7	51.5	53.6	54.5	55.6
Greece/EU	62.0	67.5	70.1	75.2	85.2	96.3	98.5	107.4
Drachma Exchange Rate (drachmas per ecu, annual average)	59.4	61.6	65.3	78.1	88.4	105.7	137.4	156.3
Nominal Long-term Interest Rates (%)								
Greece	17.1	17.7	15.4	18.2	18.5	15.8	15.8	17.4
EU-15	12.8	14.9	14.1	12.5	11.8	10.9	9.2	9.4
Greece/EU	133.6	118.8	109.2	145.6	156.8	145.0	171.7	185.1

Primary Data Source: European Commission. European Economy, no. 65, 1998.

Data on the EC average until 1991 does not include the then, East Germany.

Data on interest rates are not fully comparable.

1988	1989	1990	1991	1992	1993	1994	1995	1996	1997	1998
59.8	60.0	58.4	61.2	62.5	64.4	65.1	65.6	67.3	68.3	68.3
14.2	13.5	19.9	19.7	15.6	14.2	11.0	8.6	8.5	5.5	4.5
3.9	5.0	4.9	5.6	4.7	4.1	3.2	3.0	2.6	2.1	1.9
364.1	270.0	406.1	351.8	331.9	346.3	343.8	286.7	326.9	261.9	236.8
-11.5	-14.4	-16.1	-11.5	-12.8	-13.8	-10.0	-10.3	-7.5	-4.0	-2.2
-3.1	-2.2	-3.5	-4.2	-5.1	-6.1	-5.4	-5.0	-4.2	-2.4	-1.9
371.0	654.5	460.0	273.8	251.0	226.2	185.2	206.0	178.6	166.7	115.8
65.8	69.2	90.1	92.3	98.8	111.6	109.3	110.1	111.6	108.7	107.7
54.9	54.1	55.2	56.0	60.4	65.9	68.0	71.0	73.0	72.1	70.5
119.9	127.9	163.2	164.8	163.6	169.3	160.7	155.1	152.9	150.8	152.8
167.6	178.8	201.4	225.2	247.0	268.6	288.0	303.0	305.6	309.4	...
16.6	...	...	...	...	23.3	20.8	17.4	14.4	9.9	...
9.3	9.8	11.1	10.3	9.8	7.8	8.2	8.6	7.3	6.2	...
178.5	...	...	...	...	298.7	253.7	202.3	197.3	159.7	...

PART II
GREECE AND EMU

5 The Greek Economy Converging Towards EMU

NICOS CHRISTODOULAKIS

After two decades of stagnation, during recent years Greece has entered a period of increasing growth, fiscal stability and low inflation. Structural reforms have assisted the reinvigoration of the real economy and, in addition to these, entry into the ERM in 1998 has contributed in making Greece the last convergence player in the EU. All economic estimates and indicators now show that Greece will be able to achieve the Maastricht Treaty criteria by the end of 1999, and therefore, will be ready to enter the euro-zone and participate together with the other member states in the third stage of the EMU in 2001.

This chapter delineates the main developments in the economy and shows the course that Greece has taken from the early post-war period of growth to the era of stagflation, and most recently back again on the track of development. The first section focuses on post-war growth, the second highlights the main characteristics of the economy, while the third section sheds some light on why previous stabilisation policies have failed. The fourth concentrates on recent developments followed by a discussion of Greece's new role in the Balkans. The final section offers concluding remarks.

Post-War Economic Growth

In the first two decades of the post-war period, Greece had the lowest per capita income among 16 OECD countries, but the country's income was growing at rates that was much higher than the European average. The average rate was 6.2 per cent per annum, and had this process been continued it would have led the Greek economy to converge in per capita terms with the European economies shortly after the end of the century. In the 1960s, per capita GDP in Greece was growing at 7 per cent per year against 4 per cent

Table 1 Greece: Main Macroeconomic Indicators

Variable	1951–74	1975–94	1995–99
Output (% change)	6.4	2.0	3.0
Public investment (% change)	6.0	1.0	11.0
Private investment (% change)	8.0	1.3	9.0
Unemployment (%)	4.0	6.0	10.0
Tradable sector output (% change)	9.0	1.4	n.a.
Non-tradable sector output (% change)	7.0	3.2	n.a.
Inflation (%)	6.0	17.0	6.0
Public deficit (GDP %)	n.a.	8.0	5.0
Public debt (GDP %), end of period	n.a.	110.0	105.0

Notes: Public deficit is not available before 1973 on a comparable basis. Unemployment rates for period 1960–74 and public debt for period 1961–74 are not available.

Source: Long-run macroeconomic time-series, Greek Ministry of Health and Author's calculations.

of the European average, and – with such a difference – convergence in per capita income would have taken 42 years. In the 1970s, Greece had a growth rate of 3.7 per cent, still out-performing the European average of 2 per cent but full convergence this time would have required a period of 81 years. In the 1980s the process was reversed and Greek per capita GDP was growing at only 1 per cent per annum, much lower than the European counterpart of 1.8 per cent. Still with the lowest per capita income among these countries, Greece was systematically diverging from the rest of the European economies. The decline of growth during the twenty years between 1975 and 1994 did not come alone. The halt of economic growth after 1974 was associated with major changes in institutional factors, such as wage-setting negotiations, accommodative exchange rate policy and a lack of fiscal discipline, which contributed significantly to the reversal of the growth trend that lasted until 1973 (Table 1). Due to the remarkable acceleration of the Greek GDP growth rate during the last five years (1995–99) per capita GDP in Greece is again converging towards the European average. From less than 60% in 1990, Greek per capita GDP is about to reach 70% of the European average by the end of 1999 (Figure 1).

Unemployment was very low in the 1970s, but then started to rise sharply, reaching over 10 per cent in 1980s. The stagnation of economic activity meant that new jobs were not enough for an expanding labour sup-

Figure 1 Greek GDP per capita as a percentage of GDP per capita in the European Union (ECUs PPP)

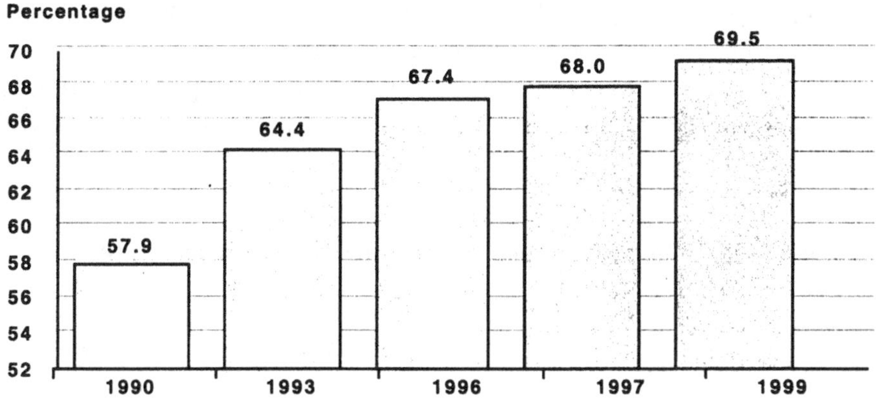

Source: Long-run macroeconomic time-series, Greek Ministry of Health and Author's calculations.

ply, while labour market rigidities prevented firms from restructuring employment. The opposite developments of growth rates and unemployment are demonstrated in Figure 2. The unemployment rate seems to have declined only in 1999 after the reappearance of fast growth.

Figure 2 Output Growth Rate and Urban Unemployment Rate

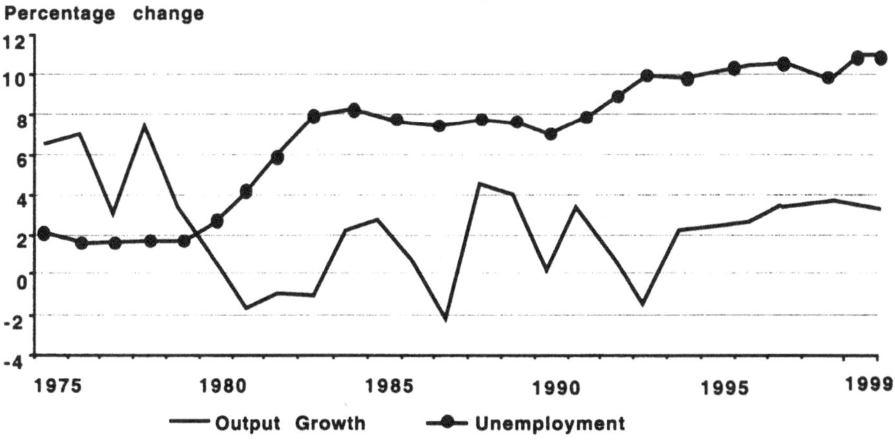

Source: Long-run macroeconomic time-series, Greek Ministry of Health and Author's calculations.

Until 1973 inflation in Greece was one of the lowest amongst OECD countries but it then jumped to unprecedented levels and up until 1998 remained one of the highest figures in the European Union. The initial cause for the rise in inflation was the oil shocks of 1973 and 1978 that coincided with real wage increases in the seventies and early eighties. However, despite the fact that wage inflation remained lower than price inflation for most of the recent period, a dramatic fall in inflation did not occur until 1994 (see Figure 3).

Figure 3 Wage Increases and Consumer Price Inflation Rate

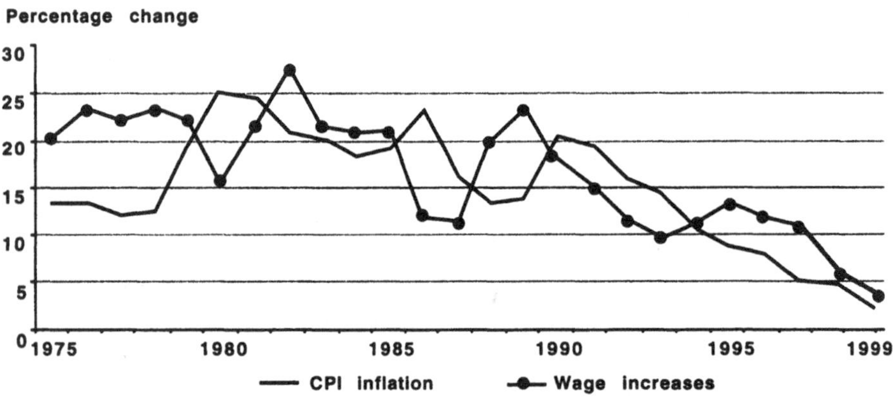

Source: Long-run macroeconomic time-series, Greek Ministry of Health and Author's calculations.

Other factors such as low productivity, lack of new investment and the imperfect functioning of markets seem to have contributed to the persistence of inflation. In the absence of growth, various governments during the last twenty years viewed public spending as a possible hedge against unemployment. The result was a rise in budget deficits that generated an explosive public debt (Figure 4) but produced only negligible gains in activity.

What have been the factors which led to a halt in high growth rates? To a large extent, the history of high growth rates in post-war Greece can be explained by low wages and low initial capital stock which helped to attract investment from countries with a highly paid labour force and low returns to capital. During the 1950s and 1960s, foreign investors found Greece to be a country with a workforce that was effectively disciplined through the

Figure 4 The Twin Deficits: Public and Trade Deficits

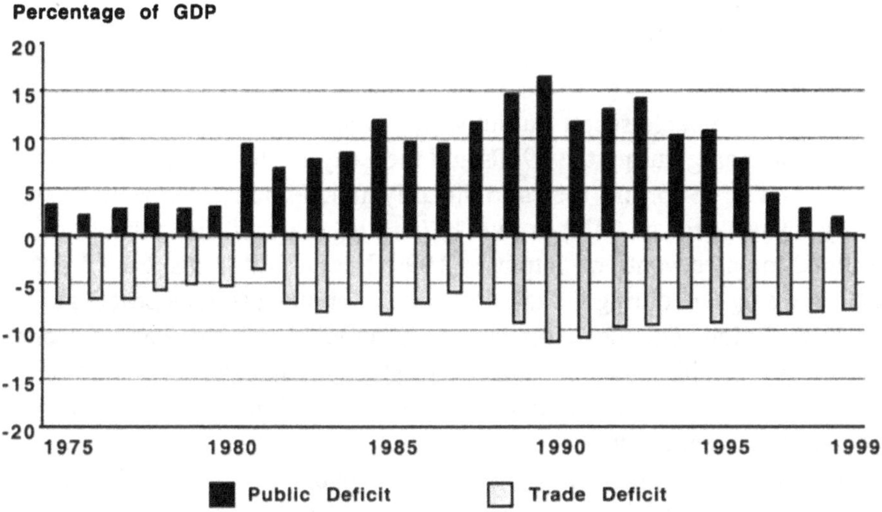

Source: Long-run macroeconomic time-series, Greek Ministry of Health and Author's calculations.

combination of enhancing labour supply from the agricultural sector and repressing trade union activity. Meanwhile, the state managed to keep an adequate level of aggregate demand, which in combination with import barriers and factor availability, helped to maintain high levels of employment.

A series of events in the mid-1970s put an end to the growth process. The oil price shocks of 1973 and 1979 meant a reorientation of world production towards more advanced technologies, the implementation of which required a different economic environment than previously. Fixed capital investment became scarce and started to concentrate in countries that could offer a highly skilled workforce, modern infrastructure to support the changing modes of production and a stable institutional framework to minimise the uncertainty of expected returns.

None of them was readily and adequately available in Greece at that time and the economy entered a period of prolonged stagnation. The situation was aggravated by domestic demandpush policies which were conceived to boost economic activity and increase employment. Predictably, without supplyside incentives the rise in demand simply led to more imports and higher inflation.

Basic Features of the Greek Economy

Performance by Sector

The share of tradable sector output which consists of mining and manufacturing, was rising during the 1960s and the early 1970s, but the process was reversed after 1975 and the ratio steadily fell. Figure 4 shows that from nearly 23 per cent of GDP in late 1970s, the share of the tradable sector declined to one seventh of output by 1999. In constant terms, traded output remained stagnant during the last 15 years, implying a serious process of de-industrialisation. On the contrary, the nontradable sector was constantly increasing, reaching nearly half of total economic activity (Figure 5). Output in agriculture declined as a share in total GDP from 17 per cent in 1975 to 8 per cent in 1999. At the same time employment in agriculture fell from 36 per cent to one fifth of the total. The public sector involving administration, health and education activities, as well as other services, kept more or less the same share of total output.

Figure 5 Tradable and Non-Tradable Sector Output

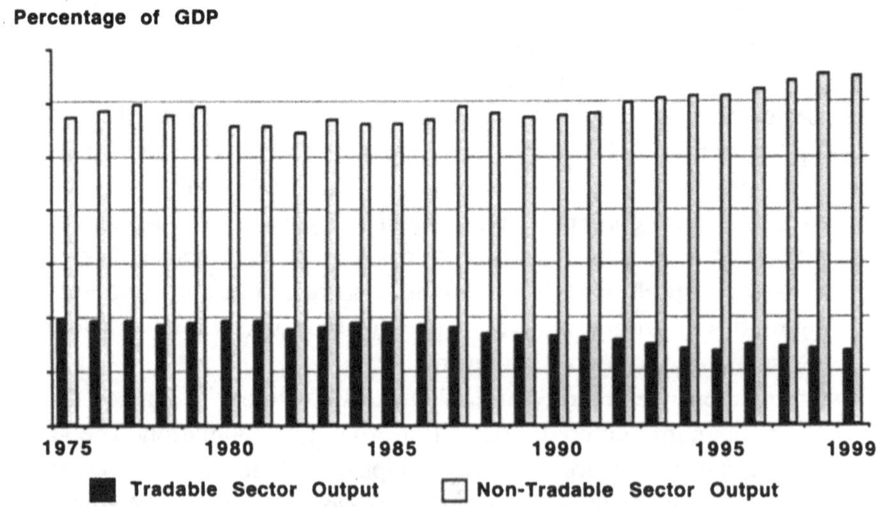

Source: Long-run macroeconomic time-series, Greek Ministry of Health and Author's calculations.

Employment in manufacturing remained virtually constant during the last decade. Combined with stagnant output, this implies that average labour productivity did not rise. In contrast, employment in the non-tradable sector increased less rapidly than output and, as a result, the average productivity in the non-tradable sector has risen sharply. Figure 6 contrasts productivity in the two sectors starting from the same normalised basis in 1975. The two indices moved in parallel until 1981, but then started to diverge sharply and in 1997, productivity in the non-tradable sector exceeded that of the tradable sector by 30 per cent. In the agricultural sector, productivity increased only mildly while a similar measure in the public sector fell substantially since public employment increased sharply.

Figure 6 Average Productivity in Tradable and Non-Tradable Sectors

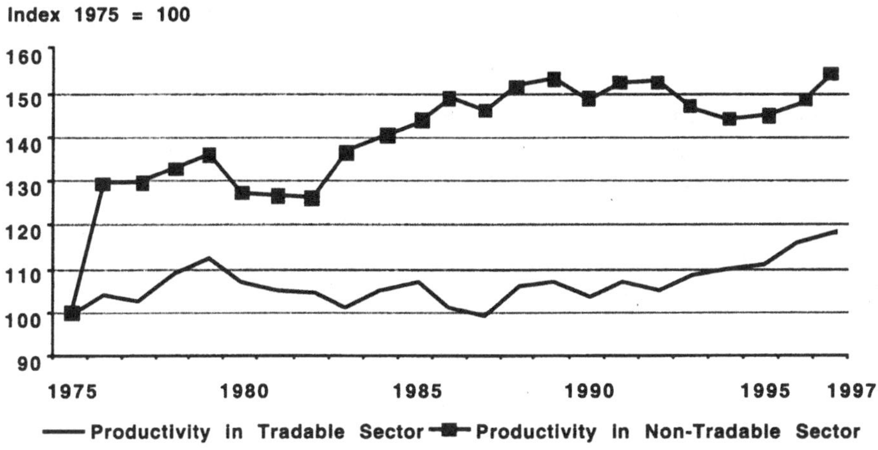

Source: Long-run macroeconomic time-series, Greek Ministry of Health and Author's calculations.

Of the above developments, the most worrying was the shrinking of the industrial sector which lasted until a few years ago. Greek manufacturing was characterised by a small productive capacity, and value-added was only one third of sector's output. Fixed capital investment was in real terms at the same level as in 1980, R&D activities were not substantially endorsed by Greek industry and the various forms of technology transfer and management innovation were limited. Despite the fact that unit labour cost has been

Figure 7 Real Unit Labour Cost

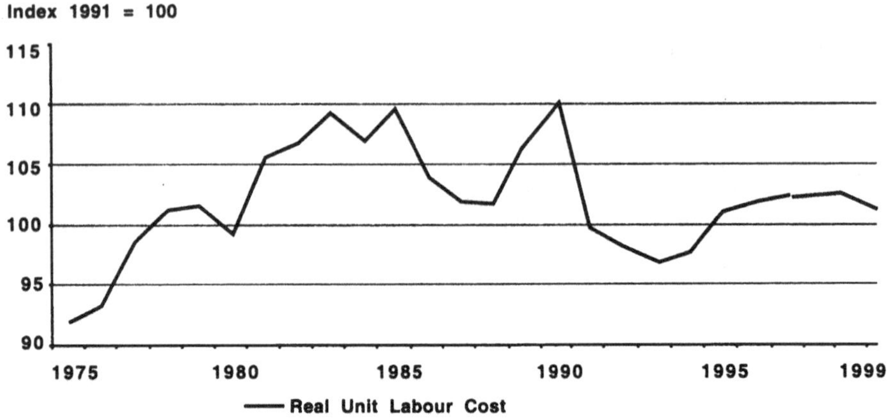

Source: Long-run macroeconomic time-series, Greek Ministry of Health and Author's calculations.

declining in real terms since 1985 (Figure 7), competitiveness did not rise sufficiently to compensate for the removal of protection brought about by the single European market.

However, a dynamic part of Greek manufacturing is moving in the opposite direction. During the last ten years, a considerable number of Greek firms have managed to adopt new technologies, modernise their management and succeed in highly competitive international markets. In 1998 industry rose by 6 per cent and by 8 per cent in 1999, signalling a new era of growth.

Employment

Employment in Greece has a number of idiosyncratic characteristics: Total unemployment has increased sharply since 1983 and remains at around 10 per cent. One of the key decisions that adversely affected labour market conditions was the decision of the government in 1982 to increase the minimum level of wages by 35 per cent as a means of compensating for past real wage losses. Implemented in a period of increasing openness to foreign competition after Greece's accession to the EU, the measure meant a serious fall in competitiveness. Unit labour costs rose by 26 per cent in 1982

Figure 8 Growth Rates of Employment in General Government and the Rest of the Economy

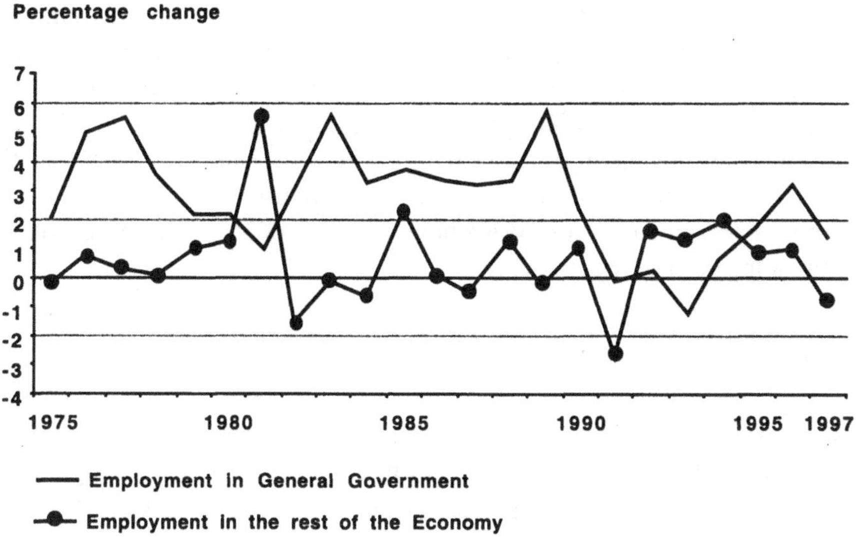

Source: Long-run macroeconomic time-series, Greek Ministry of Health and Author's calculations.

and after a while several firms – especially of medium size – were out of business. Unemployment started soaring to levels never experienced in Greece in the past and still remains at relatively high levels. The lack of adequate new investment by firms, restrictive labour market practices and the sizeable immigration flows during the 1990s have made a drastic reduction of unemployment unattainable.

Variability of employment over the business cycle is much lower than the variability of output, suggesting the presence of strong labour hoarding practices in Greece.[1] This finding suggests that increases in output will be translated to smaller shifts in employment.

Public employment is excessively high compared with depended employment in the private sector. In 1985, the number of employees in the general government rose by 18 per cent relative to 1981. During the last decade employment in general government has been stabilised to around 11 per cent of the total work force.

The agricultural population in Greece is falling and shows considerable variation between successive periods of low and high land fertility. Self-employment is widespread and rising. Finally, regarding skill composition, evidence suggests that there is a shortage of skilled and highly trained workforce, whilst there is an abundance of unskilled labour. The situation did not seriously improve over the last decade, despite the rise in demand and training opportunities available. According to a recent study on the expost effects of the Community Support Framework, during the period 1989–92 Greece had the lowest allocation of funds and the least efficiency for the training of its workforce in new skills. The situation started changing only recently after fundamental reforms have taken place in the training process and the allocation of incentives.

Investment and Infrastructure

Public capital accumulation in post war Greece can be divided into two main subperiods. From 1950 until 1973 the country experienced high accumulation rates – with an impressive average of 6 per cent per year. After the civil war ended in 1950, the economy started with a low level of capital which implied a potential for high factor returns. Increased public investment in conjunction with foreign investment flows from abroad during the 1950s (shielded by protective legislation) boosted economic growth. For the remaining years until 1973 infrastructure investment remained at high levels with emphasis given to transportation and communications. On the contrary, the most important characteristic of the Greek economy in the post-1974 period was the gradual reduction of national resources allocated to investment. From 1974 until the mid 1990s, the capital growth rate fell to an average rate of 1 per cent per year.

One important feature of this 'regime change' was the slowdown of private investment. Between 1950 and 1973 the private investment to output ratio averaged 16 per cent and then fell to an average of 14 per cent for the period 1974–94. In Figure 9 the development of infrastructure formation during the last three decades in Greece is compared with the share of private investment in output, where infrastructure is defined as the total stock of public capital. The picture reveals a very strong correlation between the two series. Periods of increases in public infrastructure are associated with rising private investment; when the former declines after 1975, the latter also falls.[2]

At the same time, public infrastructure was not sufficiently modernised

Figure 9 Infrastructure Formation (Rate of Change of Public Capital) and Private Investment

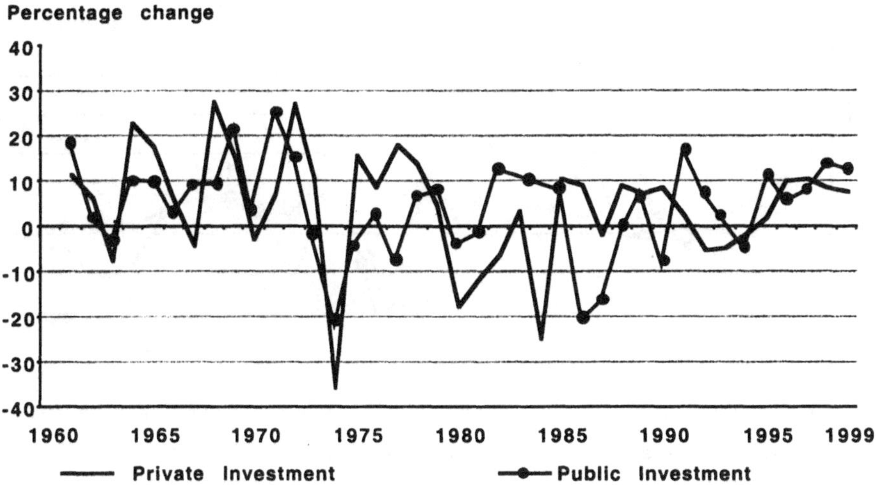

Source: Long-run macroeconomic time-series, Greek Ministry of Health and Author's calculations.

and, combined with the decline in private investment, it contributed to the erosion of competitiveness.[3] Since 1980 the structure of public expenditure in Greece has shifted away from investment finance to consumption spending. As a result, infrastructure in crucial sectors failed to come up with the need for improvement in order to facilitate economic activity and attract new investors.

Public Debt and Deficits

One of the most severe problems of the Greek economy since 1979 has been the rise of public debt as a result of unsustainable fiscal policies. Public consumption rose considerably in the 1980s reaching 29 per cent of output in 1994, after a peak of 32 per cent in 1985. Revenues were rising to a lesser extent, indicating the difficulty of extending the tax base and monitoring the timely collection of taxes. With regard to the structure of revenues, indirect taxes accounted for around 60 per cent of total tax revenues and amounted

Figure 10 Public Spending and Revenues

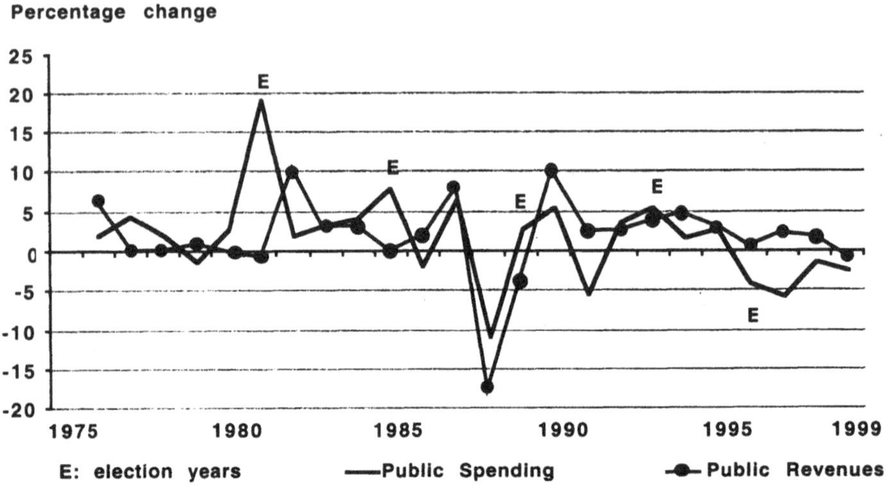

Source: Long-run macroeconomic time-series, Greek Ministry of Health and Author's calculations.

Figure 11 Direct and Indirect Taxes

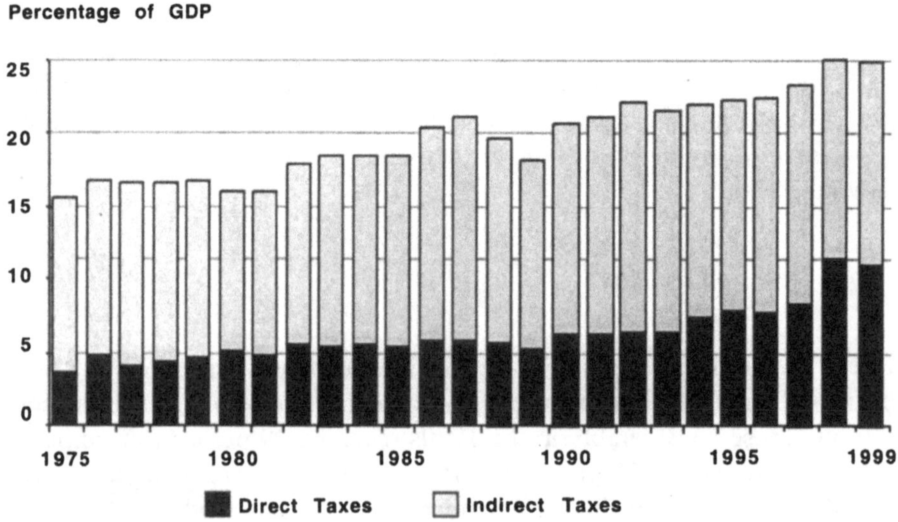

Source: Long-run macroeconomic time-series, Greek Ministry of Health and Author's calculations.

to 15 per cent of output in 1999, while direct taxes amounted to 10 per cent of output (Figure 11). More than 50 per cent of the indirect tax revenues were revenues from VAT and the remaining came from other indirect taxes and duties. Peaks in expenditure and troughs in revenues occurred mainly during the election years 1981, 1985, 1989 and 1990, pointing to the existence of strong political cycles (Figure 10).

To finance its widening deficits, the government had to borrow, thereby increasing public debt from 29 per cent of output in 1980 – one of the lowest in EU at that time – to the alarming level of 112 per cent in 1996. Interest payments as a ratio to GDP also rose rapidly due to an increase in real interest rates and the absence of any serious economic growth in that period. The explosive path of public debt made the options tougher as time went by and necessitated several stabilisation measures.

The External Sector

Figure 12 displays imports and exports of goods and services as a percentage of output. Being in a permanent state of trade account deficit, the external sector was mainly held in equilibrium by invisible receipts and capital

Figure 12 Exports and Imports of Goods and Services

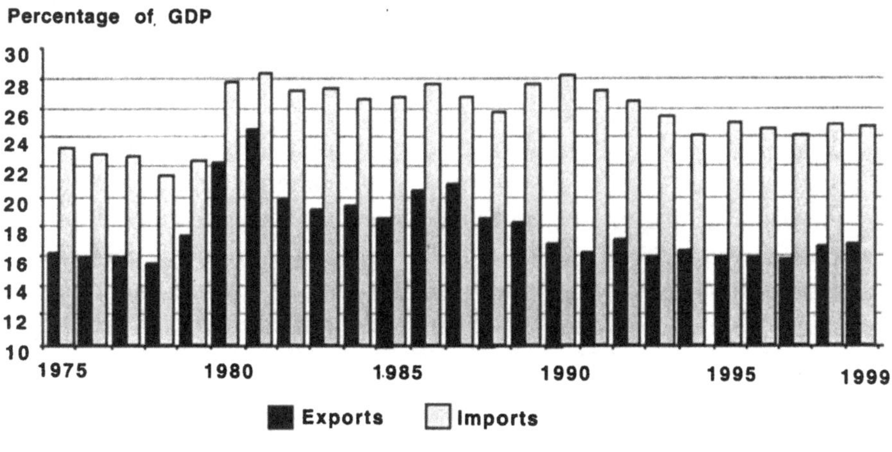

Source: Long-run macroeconomic time-series, Greek Ministry of Health and Author's calculations.

inflows. The boost in demand during the 1970s and 1980s led to an increase of imports that reached 24.6 per cent of output in 1999 that more than offset the rise in exports. As Figure 4 suggests, the trade deficit closely follows developments in the public deficit, lending support to the twin-deficits hypothesis. The deficit widened sharply in the early 1980s after Greece's accession to the EU, and was slimmed down between 1985–88 as a result of the stabilisation measures instigated during that period.

As far as exchange rate policy is concerned, Greece abandoned the fixed rate regime in 1974 and the monetary authorities adopted a crawling peg policy where the exchange was targeted to cover most of the inflation differential between Greece and its competitor countries. The exchange rate target was achieved via a system of exchange and capital restrictions which insulated the economy from occasional pressures in the foreign exchange market. The abolition of capital controls in June 1994 forced monetary authorities to rely more on short-term interest rates and the use of foreign exchange reserves in order to achieve the exchange rate target.

The Long History of Stabilisation Policies

Economic policy during the last twenty years in Greece was characterised mainly by a series of fiscal expansions and subsequent stabilisation measures that attempted to control the process of rising public debt and deficits. Below we examine the major episodes of fiscal expansion and the stabilisation programmes that attempted to control the imbalances.

The first major departure from prudent fiscal policy was initiated by the government in 1980–81, with an increase in public spending, lower taxation and a sharp expansion of credit. The new government started a fresh round of spending sprees in 1982 by raising wages, enlarging public employment and the public sector, and expanding both the benefits and the claimants of the welfare system. Total spending by the general government rose by more than 5 percentage units of GDP between 1981 and 1985 while total revenues did not follow the pace; as a result, the public deficit rose by 7 per cent of GDP (see Figures 4 and 10).

A mild stabilisation programme was first introduced in January 1983 in an attempt to control fiscal imbalances and the widening trade deficit by means of postponing wage increases and devaluing the currency by 10 per cent. The results of the programme were poor and private investment did not recover. Instead it fell further to 11 per cent of GDP in 1985, from 13 per cent in 1983. Inflation was 20 per cent in 1983 and economic activity remained stagnant with a growth rate of only 0.4 per cent per annum, while budget and trade deficits continued to widen.

To finance its persisting deficits, the government increasingly borrowed from abroad. In 1985 foreign debt had risen to USD 12 billion, compared with USD 7 billion in 1980. The process of foreign debt accumulation appeared to be unstable due to the fact that real world interest rates were becoming much higher than domestic growth rates and current account deficits were showing no sign of reversal. A new Stabilisation Programme was called for in October 1985 with the main purpose of correcting the external imbalance. The key ingredient of the programme was a currency devaluation by 15 per cent, accompanied by a tough incomes policy that ruled out pay rises in both the public and the private sector. The programme coincided with a number of favourable developments in the world economy such as the decline of interest rates, the fall in oil prices and a recovery of economic activity in the major OECD economies.

However, the programme achieved only part of the announced targets. Inflation fell below 13 per cent at the end of 1987, its lowest level since 1977, and the improvement of unit labour costs allowed exports to rise from 22 per cent of GDP in 1985 to 29 per cent in 1987. Total imports fell from 37 per cent of GDP in 1985 to 35 per cent in 1988 but this was mainly due to the dramatic reduction of oil prices. Non-oil imports actually increased from USD 7 billion in 1985 to 10 billion in 1987, confirming the hypothesis of the very low price elasticity of imported goods in Greece. Private investment in 1988 reached 12 per cent of GDP, compared with 11 per cent in 1985 and the economy grew by 4.5 per cent in 1988, the highest rate since 1978. However, public capital formation fell from 7 per cent of GDP in 1985 to around 5 per cent in 1987.

The stabilisation programme was abandoned in 1988 in a situation of increased political uncertainty. Three successive elections between 1989 and 1990 meant that no long-lasting measures could be enforced and as a result, the fiscal imbalance deteriorated further. In 1990, public debt was above 95 per cent of GDP while the budget deficit had reached 15 per cent. The government finally took some action: it imposed an emergency tax surcharge, raised the prices of public utilities and cancelled a number of early-retirement schemes. In the longer-run it set targets to reduce the size of the public sector by cutting a number of services, privatising public corporations and liquidating ailing firms under state control.

Primary deficits were indeed reduced in 1991, but not to the extent envisaged in the Budget and public debt continued to rise. A new stabilisation plan was then introduced in 1992 which included a heavy increase in petrol tax as a means of increasing revenues, reforms in the property tax system, a speed-up of privatisation and a typical pledge for a thorough curb of tax-evasion practices. The budget deficit was reduced, leading for the first time to a primary surplus of 1.5 per cent of GDP but the programme was, once again, halted by the early elections in 1993.

Public finances again deteriorated in 1993 and the new government pledged the need for fiscal redress. Deficit-curbing policies relied on extending the tax base and rationalising public expenditure rather than raising tax rates. The government introduced plans to curtail spending by imposing restrictions on new public employment, restraining wage increases to considerably below the rate of inflation and curbing abuses of the welfare system.

Stabilisation Ushers Growth

During the last four years (1995–99) the Greek economy has shown considerable and continuous progress paving the way to Greece's participation in EMU by 2001. This progress is reflected by the fact that in the last four years the budget deficit has been reduced by more than 12 percentage points of GDP, from 13.8 per cent in 1993 to 1.6 per cent in 1999. The improvement came from the increase in the primary surpluses to GDP ratio, as well as from the drastic reduction in interest payments as a percentage of GDP from 14 per cent in 1994 to 8.7 per cent in 1999. Compared with a nominal rise of GDP by 6.7 per cent, total revenues increased by almost 10 per cent, while total expenditures rose by less than 6 per cent, showing a mild trimming of state involvement in economic activity.

General Government debt as a ratio to GDP has declined by 7.4 per cent since 1996 and reached 104 per cent at the end of 1999. This is the largest decline that has ever taken place in Greece and equals the average reduction among the EU member states over the same period. The decline is due to the large primary surplus and significant privatisation revenues, which outweighed the debt-augmenting effects of the drachma devaluation in 1998. The sharp reduction of public guarantees for lending to public enterprises over the last few years means that traditional debt-increasing factors are now contained.

In addition, inflation has declined dramatically by around 12 percentage points, from 14.4 per cent in 1993 to an annual average of 2.4 per cent in 1999. The containment is due to higher competitiveness, a restricted incomes policy for both the public and private sector and the recent one-off decreases in indirect taxation on fuels, cars and electricity. Influenced by both the decline in inflation and the level of public borrowing, interest rates have taken a downward trend which is consistent with their convergence to the European average. The 10-year bond rate has been steadily converging to the European average and in 1999 was only 1.6% above the corresponding rates of the three best inflation-performing countries of the EU.

A hallmark in exchange rate policy was the decision in 1998 to join the European Exchange Rate Mechanism (ERM). By joining the ERM, Greece made a decisive step towards Economic and Monetary Union by the year 2001, since one of the prerequisites of full participation is a two-year exchange rate stability within ERM. By joining ERM, Greece effectively decided on the band within which the drachma will be converted into Euro. On the other hand, the adjustment implied a stronger long-term competitive position, thus ensuring that the rate of growth and therefore real convergence with the EU will be maintained.

Participation in the ERM was combined with fiscal and structural measures aimed at neutralising the side effects of the drachma adjustment and to give the economy all the impetus for competitive growth.

It is important to note that recent economic stabilisation was achieved without recession. Consistent economic policies and stable macroeconomic conditions promoted growth. GDP growth has gradually accelerated from negative in 1993 to 3.7 per cent in 1998 and 3.5 per cent in 1999, that is, more than one percentage unit above the European average. Thus, the Greek economy has finally started to converge towards the European average (Figure 13 overleaf).

The recent growth rates are mainly supported by endogenous factors, such as accumulated private investment, strong industrial activity, and a continuous flow of the Community Support Framework (CSF) funds. The growth rate of total investment was around 9 per cent in 1999, (12.4 per cent for public investment and 7.7 per cent for private investment) and has exhibited steady growth since 1995. In the European Union the average growth rate of investment was around 4.5 per cent in 1998. Thus, the mod-

Figure 13 From Divergence to Convergence (Average Growth Rates)

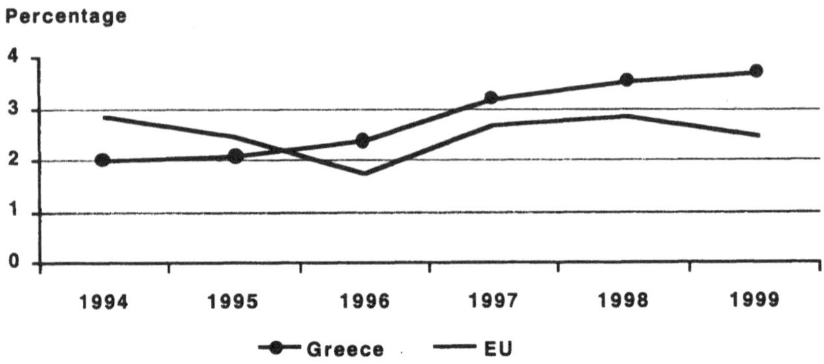

Source: Long-run macroeconomic time-series, Greek Ministry of Health and Author's calculations.

ernisation of the productive sector has been accelerated and industry grew by 6 per cent in 1998 and 8 per cent in 1999.

The acceleration in the absorption of structural funds from the European Union CSF targeted at financing large infrastructure projects have created a favourable environment for business activity. In general, the CSF is expected to have important supply-side effects that stem from the improvement of factor productivity through better infrastructure or by augmenting labour productivity through training. Employment is set to rise sharply and around 200 thousand jobs are expected to be created by the end of 2000.

Greece has a New Role in Southern Europe

Economic growth is also supported by the new geopolitical situation in the Balkans. In the past, Greece was confronted with an unfavourable situation not found anywhere else in Europe: the northern borders of the country were absolute barriers to communication, trade and investment with neighbouring countries. This generated two serious problems. First, it increased the economic distance between Greece and the EU and second, it did not allow economies of scale to develop. As a result, there was limited market accessibility for exporting industries and thin prospects for export-led growth.

The geopolitical isolation of Greece, combined with the small size of the domestic market perpetuated structural deficiencies in the economy and resulted in a situation that was singular in Europe:

- Greek industry was one of the most fragmented and small-sized in EU.
- Trade with other EU countries was taking place between sectors, on the traditional pattern of comparative advantage.
- Business alliances and partnerships with foreign counterparts were rare, especially in the industrial sector.
- In several sectors, where economies of scale were present, there was either no domestic activity or the state had to provide protection, thus leading to an economy with a high degree of state activism and ownership.

Political tensions apart, these disconnections had produced economic distortions for Greece and perhaps for the other countries of the area. The rehabilitation of these distortions is an obvious political and economic benefit for all European nations and markets, and Greece has a pivotal role to play in this process. From the moment the economic border of Eastern Europe and the Balkans opened to international competition, the Greeks again took up the traditional trade roads to the Balkans and to the rest of the countries in the area.

So far, the results are encouraging: in no more than ten years, Greek companies thrive in Albania, Bulgaria, Romania, Ukraine, Russia, the Black Sea region and other Balkan countries.

There are already positive developments in trade between Greece and Balkan countries. Not only have exports risen since 1990, leading to an amelioration of the current account, measured on a customs basis, but more importantly, two thirds of Greek-Balkan trade now have an intra-industry character – that is, trade within broadly similar sectors. This will create the conditions for economies of scale, enabling an increase in the average size of industry as compared to the currently small size of firms and the establishment of firms in sectors so far deemed improbable because of the insufficient size of markets.

It needs to be stressed that this should not be taken as a substitute for Greek firms needing to play a competitive role within the European single market. Simply, it will help to achieve better size and capacity. Additionally, a more efficient structure in the economies of neighbouring countries will have major benefits for the European Union, including:

- the creation of modern dynamic markets in the vicinity of the EU, thus enhancing trade potential, welfare prospects and stabilising workforce movements to the richest countries.
- economic, political and institutional upgrading in the Balkan countries, which is the best means towards their eventual accession to the European Union.
- it creates better conditions for an efficient utilisation of structural programmes for Balkan countries and Eastern Europe.

Structural Adjustment and Convergence

One of the most important goals of economic policy in recent years has been to increase the country's competitiveness as well as markets' ability to respond to country-specific shocks in unified Europe. Recently, the government has started to implement a broad class of structural measures in both the labour and the product market. As far as the labour market is concerned, the aim is to make employment rules more flexible by introducing legislation which allows wage bargaining at the local and company level so as to obtain competitive wage settings, part-time work in the public sector and public utilities so as to economise on labour and administration costs, and the gradual easing of restrictive labour practices in public corporations.

The privatisation programme of 1998 included stock market floatations or sale of 11 state enterprises, banks and public utilities. In 1998 privatisation proceeds reached nearly 3 per cent of GDP – one of the highest volumes ever achieved in a European country in a single year. The privatisation programme continued for the year 1999 with more public corporations and public utilities. The restructuring of loss-making public corporations (mainly in the transport, post office and defence sectors) is already paying-off and involves the elimination of restrictive labour practices in order to increase productivity and competitiveness, the removal of surplus personnel to other areas and the formation of strategic alliances with domestic or foreign firms.

After a long period of stagnation, Greece has finally started to exhibit significant growth rates. The process of convergence offers important opportunities for structural changes in the Greek economy with the development of markets, a new role for a state that is less in favour of public ownership and more in favour of regulating and modernising the financial system.

Convergence also implies a more coordinated and effective response to international crises. For example the 1998 turmoil, which started with the rescheduling of Russian debt, had only limited and short-term effects on the Greek bond and stock markets.

Economic stability and convergence is a necessary condition for entering EMU. Within EMU a country should be prepared to be able to absorb shocks and achieve growth and employment in a different macroeconomic environment. After EMU, Greek governments will not be able to have an autonomous monetary policy. The ability of a country to devalue its currency in order to improve competitiveness or act as a shock absorber to asymmetric shocks is an option that is no longer available under EMU. In the absence of an independent national monetary policy and a flexible nominal exchange rate, an adverse shock to a national economy could be handled through the use of national fiscal policy. However, contrary to what they would like to do, governments are not free to use this policy. They should maintain budgetary discipline in order to underpin the stability of the single currency and allow a more favourable policy mix. The Stability Pact establishes that member states shall avoid excessive deficits and provides two yardsticks for deficit and debt – namely 3 per cent and 60 per cent of GDP, respectively – on the basis of which the budgetary positions of the countries should be assessed. The Pact recognises that in order to respect the 3 per cent deficit ceiling even in unfavourable economic circumstances, government budgets should be close to balance or in surplus in the medium run.

Therefore, Greece (as well as other member states) will not be able to resort to local demand management for stabilisation purposes except for exceptional recessions. Policy may have to rely on increased price and market flexibility to facilitate adjustment to country-specific disturbances. Thus, Greek governments should try to ease labour markets further and cut non-wage labour costs. The arrival of the single currency makes broader structural reforms more urgent in Greece.

Greece should invest heavily in education and training in order to create a competent labour force. Flexibility, which is necessary in order to face the changing patterns of work organisation, should be combined with security based on the acquisition of the necessary skills for finding employment.

Focusing attention on education and training will promote employability and the acceptance of change within the labour force.

Finally, Greece will also try to reinforce social cohesion mechanisms and support systems. Reconciling efficiency with social cohesion emerges as the major political challenge of the times ahead.

Notes

1. According to Christodoulakis et al. (1995) the variability of employment is found to be more than three times lower than the respective figure for output.
2. Over the period 1964–90, the correlation coefficient between the two variables is found to be 0.70. For the 1960s, 1970s and 1980s it is found to be 0.93, 0.77 and 0.43, respectively.
3. For example, several international surveys recognise that the lack of modern telecommunications creates '...disincentives for new business to settle in Greece. See, among many others, OECD, 1992.

References

Christodoulakis, N. (1994), 'Fiscal Developments in Greece and the Scope for Budget Consolidation', *European Economy*, Vol. 3, pp. 97–134.

Christodoulakis, N. and Kalyvitis, S. (1998), 'Achieving Convergence within the European Union: the Role of Structural Funds in the Case of Greece' *European Planning Studies*, Vol. 6, pp. 695–707.

Christodoulakis, N., Dimelis, S.P. and Kollintzas, T. (1995), 'Comparisons of Business Cycles in the EC: Idiosyncrasies and Regularities', *Economica,* Vol. 62, pp. 1–27.

Christodoulakis, N. and Petrakos, G. (1999), 'Transition in the Balkans: Patterns of Change and Policies to Overcome Marginalisation and Disintegration', University of Thessaly Discussion Paper.

OECD (1992), 'Greece', *Economic Surveys*, Paris.

6 Greece and EMU: Prospects and Challenges

NIKOLAS C. GARGANAS[1]

Introduction

The creation of EMU is one of the most profound developments in the history of the international monetary system. On January 1, 1999 eleven 'first-wave' EU countries will hitch their economic destinies to the creation of a single currency and a common monetary policy. This action will represent a regime change for these first-wave countries, for other prospective members of EMU, and for the world as a whole.

This chapter addresses the prospects and challenges of joining EMU from the perspective of a prospective member – Greece. The chapter is divided into five sections. The second section deals with the criteria that need to be fulfilled to join EMU – the Maastricht Treaty criteria – and assesses Greece's progress in satisfying the criteria. The section also discusses the main challenges that lie ahead with respect to satisfying the Maastricht criteria. The third section deals with the crucial issue of asymmetric shocks. Optimum-currency-area theory has emphasised that countries forming a monetary union should have similar economic structures and institutions so as to lessen the likelihood and/or incidence of asymmetric shocks, which would warrant differentiated responses from monetary policy. This section argues that the issue of asymmetric shocks is likely to be particularly important in EMU, since such adjustment mechanisms as labour market flexibility and endogenous fiscal transfers do not yet operate to the degree necessary to take the place of exchange rate adjustments between EU countries. The section also argues, however, that the often-expressed concern that shocks will be frequent and asymmetric in EMU has been exaggerated. Nevertheless, EU countries do not possess strictly homogeneous economic structures, leaving some scope for asymmetric shocks to operate. The fourth section, therefore, discusses measures that need to be taken – in the light of optimum-currency-area theory – by Greece so that its economy is less vulnerable to asymmetric shocks and so that the challenges of joining, and prospering in, EMU can be met. The final section presents concluding comments.

Progress in Meeting the Maastricht Criteria

The process leading to EMU is well-known and does not warrant extensive repetition. To summarise briefly, the Maastricht Treaty was signed in February 1992 and, following ratification in the parliaments of all EU countries, came into effect on 1 November 1993. Article 109j(1) of the Treaty sets out a number of economic criteria related to the development of prices, government financial positions, exchange rates and long-term interest rates under which a country would be eligible to join the Third Stage of EMU. In order to examine the progress made by Greece in achieving a high degree of sustainable convergence, the following points are a synopsis of these criteria:

(1) Average consumer price inflation in the country should not be more than 1.5 percentage points above that of the three best-performing countries in terms of price stability.

(2) (a) A country should not have an excessive budget deficit with the reference rate being that it should not exceed 3 per cent of gross domestic product.

(b) The outstanding government debt of the country should not exceed 60 per cent of gross domestic product.

(3) A country should have observed the normal fluctuation margins of the exchange rate mechanism (ERM), for at least two years, without devaluing against the currency of any other member state.

(4) The average nominal long-term interest rate in the year of examination should not be more than 2 percentage points above that of the three best-performing countries in terms of price stability.

With regard to the fiscal and debt criteria, there is some scope for allowing performance that is in breach of these reference values, notably where the deficit is elevated owing to exceptional and temporary circumstances or the ratio of government debt is sufficiently diminishing and approaching the reference value of 60 per cent at a satisfactory pace (Maastricht Treaty, 1992, Articles 104c and associated Protocol No. 5).

Since the Maastricht Treaty came into force, Greece has made remarkable progress towards the achievement of a high degree of convergence.[2] Consumer price inflation decreased markedly, from above 10 per cent in 1994, to 4.3 per cent in February, 1998. The deceleration of inflation was temporarily interrupted in April-May, 1998, following the devaluation of the drachma, effective from 16 March (see below), but resumed thereafter (Figure 1).[3] This clear trend of disinflation reflects a number of important policy choices, most notably the tightening of monetary policy since the mid-1990s with a view to reducing inflation and ultimately achieving price

Figure 1 Consumer Price Inflation (percentage change over twelve months)

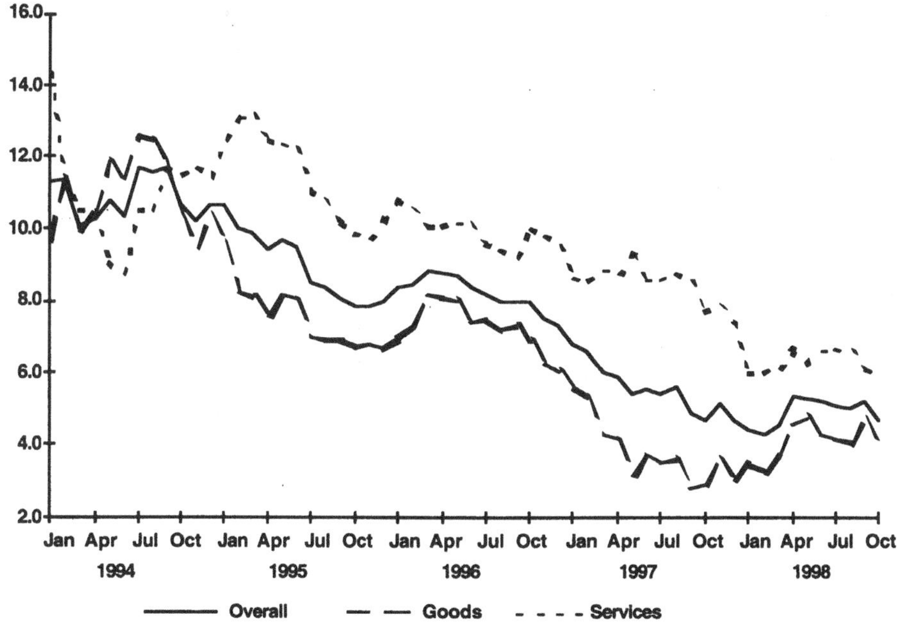

Source: National Statistical Service of Greece and Bank of Greece.

stability. Monetary policy has been guided by an exchange rate target as the main intermediate target and, prior to 1998, a target for broad money supply (M3). The exchange rate target initially provided for a depreciation of the nominal exchange rate which did not fully accommodate the difference between the targeted rate of domestic inflation and forecast inflation of Greece's main trading partners, and broad stability thereafter. These targets were broadly achieved; after a cumulative depreciation of some 11 per cent in 1994–95, against the ECU, the drachma was broadly stable in 1996 and 1997 (Figure 2).

Figure 2 Exchange Rate of the Drachma against the ECU

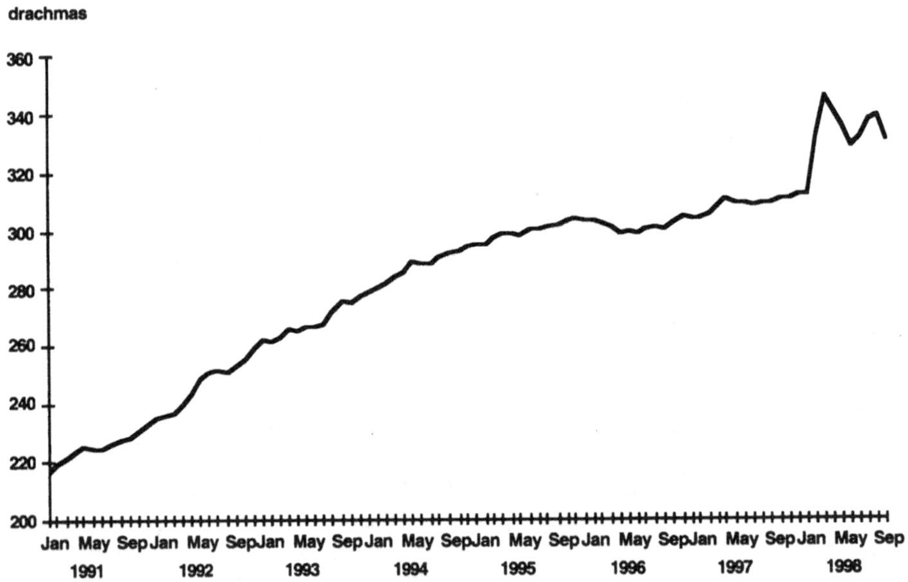

Source: Bank of Greece.

The objective of monetary policy to reduce inflation has been facilitated by adjustments in fiscal policy which aim, *inter alia*, at satisfying the Maastricht conditions. Since 1994, the first year of the Revised Convergence Programme, the government undertook a considerable budgetary effort which reduced the deficit from 13.8 per cent of GDP in 1993 to 4 per cent in 1997. The target for 1998 is 2.4 per cent, and on the evidence so far, it is expected that it will be attained.[4] The deficit-to-GDP ratio is projected to decline to 2.1 per cent in 1999.[5] The government debt ratio, which peaked at 111.6 per cent of GDP in 1993, broadly stabilised thereafter, decreasing to 108.6 per cent in 1997, and is projected to decline to 107.8 per cent in 1998.[6]

The stability task of monetary policy has been facilitated by the prohibition of monetary financing of government deficits and the prohibition of privileged access of the public sector to credit institutions, which entered into force with the start of the Second Stage of EMU, as required by the Maastricht Treaty. The reduction in inflation was also supported by the deceleration in unit labour cost growth. Both increases in compensation per employee and growth in unit labour costs were reduced, but still grew at 11.5 per cent and 10 per cent, respectively, in 1996, thus hindering a more rapid headway towards price stability. The rate of growth of unit labour costs was reduced to 6.5 per cent in 1997, but wage increases (of 10.7 per cent) again sharply outpaced inflation.[7]

The combination of nominal exchange rate stability with rapidly rising wage costs over a number of years raised doubts about the viability of the hard drachma policy. The perception by the markets that the drachma was overvalued and the expectation that an exchange rate correction and entry of the drachma into the ERM would be needed two years before the intended adoption of the euro in January 2001 fed speculative pressures on the drachma beginning in late October 1997 in the wake of the financial crisis in Asia.

Although the countermeasures taken by the Bank of Greece were successful in stabilising the currency in 1997, pressures, albeit less intense, continued in the period up to ERM entry in March 1998. For example, three-month Treasury bill rates rose by over 4 percentage points, from 8.4 per cent before the outbreak of the turmoil, to 12.8 per cent in March 1998. This sharp rise in interest rates, if maintained, risked undermining growth and fiscal targets, placing Greece's commitment to attain the Maastricht eligibility criteria by 1999 (the year of judgement for EMU entry as from January 2001) in jeopardy. A smooth exit from an unsustainable relatively fixed exchange rate regime had, therefore, become a necessity.

Effective March 16, 1998, the Greek drachma joined the ERM of the European Monetary System at a central rate that implied a 12.3 per cent devaluation against the ECU. At the same time, the government announced a supportive package of fiscal and structural measures. The drachma's entry into the ERM, at a central rate that was judged both by international organisations and by financial markets as appropriate and sustainable on the basis of a firm implementation of accompanying policy measures, represents a fundamental change in 'policy regime', signalling a strengthening of policies, which had clearly enhanced the prospects of success in the drive to EMU participation by January 1, 2001. Financial markets reacted favourably to ERM entry. The drachma appreciated quickly within the ERM band. Interest rates declined and the stock market surged.

In its monetary policy report for 1998, the Bank of Greece set price stability (defined as an increase in consumer prices of less than 2 per cent) as the main objective to be achieved by the end of 1999. The Bank set exchange rate stability within the ERM as the main intermediate objective, with the drachma expected to fluctuate within a narrow band from its central rate against the other currencies participating in the ERM. However, in the event of a conflict between the objectives of disinflation and exchange rate stability, the Bank stated that priority would be assigned to the inflation target. Consequently, the drachma could be allowed to appreciate, exceeding the envisaged narrow margins of fluctuation. In fact, following the drachma's entry into the ERM the currency appreciated by as much as 8 per cent above its central rate against the ECU.

Long-term interest rates have been on a broadly declining trend, converging towards the rates prevailing in the EU countries since the mid-1990s, with the exception of 1997 (Figure 3), although the differential remains significantly positive. The main factors underlying this trend were the significant decline in the inflation differential and the reduction in risk premia on drachma-denominated financial instruments.[8]

Beginning in 1999, the drachma will be part of ERM–2, with the euro at the centre of the system.[9] Consequently, stability of the exchange rate within the ERM will be gauged against the euro. To ensure that such stability is achieved, it is essential that the Bank's inflation objective for 1999 is reached. To that end, following the drachma's entry into the ERM, real short-term interest rates have been kept at very high levels (about 8 per cent).

To summarise briefly, all of the convergence criteria are within reach by 1999. The fiscal deficit will be well below the 3 per cent of GDP reference value and the public debt-to-GDP ratio is declining. The exchange rate criterion will be fulfilled as the drachma has been successfully participating

Figure 3 Greece: Long-term Interest Rate (monthly averages; in percentages)

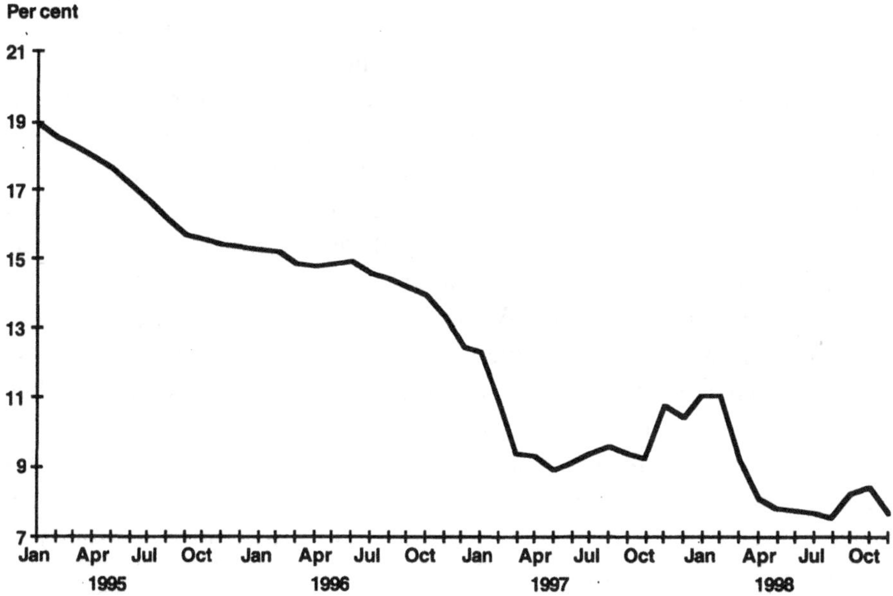

Source: Bank of Greece

Note: The harmonised series for Greece starts in mid-1997. Before this, data were based on best available proxies; for the period from March to June 1997, yield data for long-term bonds with shorter maturities than the harmonised series were used; before that, period yields at issue for long-term bonds with shorter maturities than the harmonised series were used.

in ERM. The main challenge with respect to the Maastricht criteria is inflation. The satisfaction of the Bank's inflation objective in 1999 would lower inflation expectations and, along with lower risk premia due to exchange rate stability, will help ensure the attainment of the interest-rate convergence criterion. To meet this challenge, the stance of monetary policy will have to remain tight and fiscal adjustment and wage moderation continue.

The Role of Asymmetric Shocks

With the introduction of the euro, attention will shift from issues of transition to monetary union and satisfaction of the Maastricht criteria to the challenges posed by EMU for the euro area economies. EMU will represent a change in the monetary policy regime since the scope for using national monetary policies – which countries have retained, albeit constrained by the central objective of exchange rate stability – will disappear after EMU.

The institutional architecture of EMU includes the decision to assign the instrument of monetary policy to the ECB in pursuit of the objective of price stability, the Stability and Growth Pact, and the requirement to comply with the convergence criteria to demonstrate that fiscal soundness has been achieved. This architecture is designed to ensure that an environment conducive to price stability has been established and that the adjustments that have been achieved are sustainable. It is one thing for a country to meet the Maastricht criteria and qualify for joining the single currency area, and quite another for it to survive there. So the frame of attention is moving away from what countries have achieved in the run-up to EMU to what they need to do over the next 10 to 15 years.

The celebrated theory of optimum currency areas sheds light on this issue. A central insight of this theory is that countries or regions that experience a high incidence of asymmetric shocks need a lot of flexibility in their labour markets and/or scope for adjusting fiscal policy if they want to form a monetary union (Garganas, 1993). Put differently, the more differentiated the structural characteristics of the economies, the greater the need for flexibility in the labour markets and endogeneity of fiscal transfers to make possible a smoothly functioning monetary union. In what follows, I discuss the likelihood for asymmetric shocks in EMU and the availability of labour market and fiscal adjustment mechanisms.

The risks of asymmetric shocks are particularly important to small, open economies such as Greece. Having renounced the option of varying the exchange rate and pursuing an independent monetary policy, members of EMU may find themselves constrained in responding to macroeconomic shocks. The absence of exchange risk, together with a high degree of financial market integration, implies that (in the absence of credit risk) approximately the same level of short-term rates must prevail in all participating countries. Consequently, it will no longer be possible to use monetary policy to vary those rates in response to changes in local economic conditions. The ability to use stabilisation policy will be constrained (Garganas, 1993).

There are, however several qualifications that need to be made to this argument. First, monetary-cum-interest rate policy may not be an *effective* response to cyclical disturbances, especially if real wages do not respond to price level changes (Eichengreen, 1994). Second, even if monetary policy is effective, a common monetary policy could suffice if the members of EMU experience similar shocks. Third, as noted above, forsaking monetary independence will be less costly when there are other adjustment mechanisms, such as labour mobility and fiscal transfers, to take up the slack (Eichengreen, 1994).

With regard to the issue of real wage rigidity, there is abundant academic research showing that real wages in European countries are less flexible than in the United States (Grubb et al., 1983; Bruno and Sachs, 1985). With real wages shown to be rigid, recent studies by Erkel-Rousse and Melitz (1995) and Canzoneri et al. (1996) have cast doubt on the ability of national monetary policies to affect real variables in most EU countries. Therefore, forsaking the exchange rate tool may be less costly for European economies than it would be for the United States economy (De Grauwe, 1997). Consider, next, the issue of asymmetric shocks and the roles of labour mobility and fiscal transfers as adjustment mechanisms in the event of such shocks.

It is certainly true that an asymmetric economic shock could indeed hit an EMU member, in which case adjustment through labour mobility and/or fiscal transfers, customary in a federal system such as that of the United States, will not be available to the extent that they are in the United States. National authorities will have to rely on alternative instruments for absorbing such shocks. How important are such asymmetric shocks likely to be in EMU?

There are several reasons why the often-expressed concern about the effects of asymmetric shocks in EMU may have been exaggerated. First, demand shocks in EMU will become more highly correlated because of the common monetary and fiscal policies pursued. In this connection, Artis and Zhang (1995) show that the business cycles of EU countries have become much more correlated since the early 1980s; there are now fewer asymmetric shocks among EU countries than fifteen years ago. Second, greater openness and the elimination of trade barriers may well increase the sectoral similarity of different countries and, hence, the likely correlation of the shocks faced by their national economies. That is, openness and trade integration are leading to a structure of trade in which countries increasingly buy and sell to each other the same categories of goods (De Grauwe, 1997). Third, a number of empirical studies have found that a large part of the asymmetric shocks in the EU countries occur at the sectoral level (as noted above, sectoral similarity between EU countries may be expected to increase), and not at the national level. Put differently, a large part of the changes in output and employment in a country are the result of different developments as between sectors (e.g., due to demand shifts or to differential technological changes). These shocks cannot be dealt with by exchange rate changes. (See Bini-Smaghi and Vori 1993; Bayoumi and Prassad, 1995; and Gros, 1996.) Finally, the greater openness and intra-European trade will increase cross-country spillovers and further stimulate policy coordination at all levels – including structural policies.

Nevertheless, asymmetric shocks will not disappear altogether. Indeed, theoretical considerations suggest that the effect of integration on the incidence of asymmetric shocks could go either way, because after integration there is likely to be more agglomeration (i.e., geographical specialisation of production). With more agglomeration, small shocks could have big asymmetries if they hit only some sectors of an economy. Furthermore, even if the role of asymmetric shocks were to be mitigated, another asymmetry is likely to arise in the face of shocks since there will be differences among countries in how changes in a common monetary policy are transmitted to the real economy. This transmission mechanism may vary because of institutional differences or differences in the process of financial intermediation – for instance, differences in the importance of bank lending relative to other forms of financing, and differences in the level and maturity structure of debt (Begg, 1997). Consequently, countries' abilities to adjust to shocks will continue to depend on their structural flexibility.

The Challenges Ahead

Countries such as Greece and Italy, with high public debt, face the unpalatable choice of engaging in further efforts of fiscal consolidation in order to reduce the level of overall debt so that it poses no further problem to public finances. Countries close to the 3 per cent limit for budget deficits will also be constrained by the Stability Pact. It will, therefore, take some time for these countries to establish fiscal positions sufficiently sound to allow some flexibility in the face of country-specific circumstances. Consequently, under EMU, countries like Greece and Italy will have to rely on alternative adjustment channels to respond to local disturbances.

The main challenge ahead in the case of Greece concerns the fiscal consolidation that needs to be continued after 1999 in order to comply with the medium-term objective of the Stability and Growth Pact of achieving a budgetary position close to balance or in surplus. There are several essential reasons why further fiscal consolidation will be beneficial. First, lower labour mobility in Europe compared with the United States and the inability of national governments to use monetary policy to mitigate the effects of country specific shocks mean that automatic fiscal stabilisers will have an important role to play in accommodating shocks. A key question is whether Greece will be able to keep its underlying fiscal balance in surplus or close to balance. If Greece accomplishes such a fiscal position, historical experience suggests that the reference value (i.e., a deficit-to-GDP ratio of 3 per cent of GDP) of the Stability and Growth Pact will allow adequate room for stabilisation. Second, it is necessary to bring the debt/GDP ratio down to 60 per cent of GDP, so that it poses no problem to the public finances. Third, the fact that interest rates will converge towards the lower German level implies some inherent loosening of monetary policy. An offsetting tightening of fiscal policy will ensure that the gains made in reducing inflation will be maintained. Fourth, fiscal expenditures tend to impact on nontraded goods, pushing up the prices of such goods (which are not subject to international competition to the same extent as traded goods). Consequently, to the extent that fiscal consolidation involves expenditure retrenchment, nontraded goods' prices will fall and real competitiveness will improve (i.e., the real exchange rate will decline in value).

The current size of public debt is the more immediate concern. As noted above, when Greece joins the euro-area interest rates will fall (towards German rates), which will cut interest payments. But the concern is that, unless the debt is reduced fairly quickly, Greece will later be exposed to sudden rises in short-term interest rates that increase the cost of debt servicing and make it hard to keep the annual budget within the terms of the Stability Pact on economic policy after the start of monetary union. Moreover, a speedy reduction in the public debt is essential because Greece, like other EU member states, will face increased pension liabilities in the second decade of the next century when, because of a marked ageing of the population, a large number of people start to retire. As a result, public pension spending is likely to increase sharply in relation to GDP, particularly if there is no reform of the social security system.

An exercise in the dynamics of the debt ratio carried out under certain assumptions and starting from 2000 onwards suggests that it would take ten to twelve years for the debt-to-GDP ratio to be brought down to 60 per cent. To achieve this result, it has been assumed that: Greece would need growth in nominal GDP of 3.5 per cent a year; a cost of public borrowing at 5 per cent; and a primary surplus of general government (excluding interest payments) of 6.7 per cent of GDP.

How likely is it that such assumptions can be met? In 1997, Greece's primary surplus was 5.7 per cent[10] and maintaining it at this level for ten to twelve years would virtually remove the scope for easing the high tax burden on Greek citizens over the next decade. It would also imply that there could be little room for public spending increases. It would be more realistic for the government to speed up and expand its privatisation plans, using the proceeds to reduce the debt stock. The government could also press ahead as fast as possible with the reform of the social security system. The government must also intensify its efforts to reduce tax evasion, to rationalise public expenditure and to reform the wider public sector.

As noted above, the labour market has also been stressed in the optimal currency areas literature. Two types of labour market mechanisms are relevant. These are real wage flexibility and labour mobility, respectively. The persistently high structural unemployment in the EU – estimated by the IMF at 8 to 9 per cent of the labour force – points to the limited progress made in many EU countries in addressing structural weaknesses in labour markets. There is a need for more comprehensive and sustained efforts to increase incentives for work, acquire skills, and create productive jobs. Nevertheless, the successful operation of EMU will, in large part, hinge on market flexibility more generally, especially that in the goods market. The smoothness of longer-run inter regional adjustment within the United States is often attributed to its open goods markets. This suggests that a successful currency area must have extensive trading of products – uninhibited by trade distortions – within the area. This means that Greece (and, indeed, many other countries in Europe) must continue to implement measures that improve competition in product markets.

It should also be stressed that labour market and goods market flexibility cannot be taken as exogenous with respect to the exchange regime any more than can monetary shocks. As Eichengreen (1994) has pointed out, when the government has resort to the exchange rate tool, and is prepared to adjust the nominal exchange rate in response to shocks, workers and firms will have less reason to write contracts allowing for changes in money wages. In other words, workers and firms will leave it to the government to restore a desired level of competitiveness through manipulation of the nominal exchange rate. If governments opt for monetary unification, however, workers and firms will realise that an inappropriate level of money wages can no longer be accommodated through nominal exchange rate adjustments; workers and firms are more likely to write contracts that deliver a greater degree of wage flexibility. Italy's abolition of its *scala mobile* in advance of EMU may be seen as an example of the tendency of labour market flexibility to be endogenous with respect to the exchange rate regime (Eichengreen, 1994).

Nevertheless, in the absence of specific measures, labour market and product mobility in Greece (and in other countries) will retain a degree of inflexibility regardless of the exchange rate regime. The main challenge for Greece is to recognise that policy measures aimed at enhancing competition in product markets and improving labour market flexibility need to be pursued as a matter of urgency.[11] Greater market flexibility will not only allow Greece to cope with idiosyncratic shocks more easily, but also, by strengthening competitiveness vis-à-vis EU partner countries will increase its attractiveness as a location for scale-intensive industries producing for an integrated market; Greece will thus benefit from joining EMU.

In this connection, an important development has been the social dialogue on economic growth, competitiveness and employment, which started in May 1997 and was concluded in November 1997 when the 'Pact of Mutual Trust towards the year 2000' was signed by the government and the social partners. This process has included discussions of policy guidelines to enhance competition in commodity markets, improve flexibility of labour markets, and strengthen the competitiveness of the Greek economy in general. For some of the guidelines, points of common approval were reached. For others, the government will assume the initiative for introducing legislation.

Structural measures are already being promoted in public enterprises to improve the quality and reduce the costs of services. These measures include the amendment of internal labour regulations in loss-making public enterprises, with a view to increasing adaptability of labour organisation (in terms of working hours, staff internal mobility, etc.). In compliance with European Union guidelines, this effort is linked with gradual market deregulation in the fields of telecommunications, energy and transportation.

More generally, new legislation was passed in August 1998, that covers areas such as the rearrangement of working time on an annual basis and the introduction of part-time employment in public enterprises and the public sector as a whole (e.g. local authorities, hospitals). By enhancing the flexibility of working time and linking working time to firms' needs, labour costs will be reduced and employment stimulated. Moreover, current hiring rules concerning the mandatory recruitment of handicapped persons have been revised, in order to make hiring procedures more transparent and thus prevent abuses. Finally, working arrangements between local authorities and social partners will be encouraged to take into account local conditions so as to help reduce unemployment.

Conclusions

In sum, Greece is moving forward so as to be able to meet the challenges of the future. Progress has been made in the past few years in terms of macroeconomic adjustment, a necessary prerequisite for Greece to qualify for EMU. Moreover, structural changes are being implemented to help ensure that Greece will not only *survive* in EMU, but that it will be able to *thrive* in EMU. The twin pillars of macroeconomic adjustment and structural change are necessary so that Greece will be able to compete effectively and reap the benefits of economic integration as the country moves forward into a more integrated Europe and the Twenty-first Century.

Notes

1. The author wishes to thank George Tavlas and two anonymous referees for helpful comments.
2. The data reported in the text represent data available as of March, 1998, when this address was delivered. Updates of these data are provided in footnotes, reflecting data that subsequently became available.
3. Inflation fell to 2.6 per cent in November 1999.
4. The government deficit-to-GDP ratio fell to 2.5 per cent in 1998.
5. According to the most recent (December 1999) projections, the deficit-to-GDP ratio will fall to 1.5 per cent in 1999.
6. The government debt-to-GDP ratio fell to 108.5 per cent in 1997 and 105.4 per cent in 1998, and is expected to be 104.2 per cent in 1999.
7. According to more recent figures, average wages grew by 10.5 per cent in 1997 and 6.3 per cent in 1998 and are expected to grow by 4.6 per cent in 1999; unit labour costs grew by 7.2 per cent and 3.9 per cent in 1997 and 1998 respectively and the figure for 1999 is

expected to be around 2.5 per cent.

8. In late 1999, yields on ten year government bonds have fallen to around 6.2 per cent, from 10.1 per cent just prior to the drachma's entry into the ERM in March 1998. The differential with Deutschemark instruments fell to about 120 basis points in late 1999 from over 500 basis points just prior to the drachma's entry into the ERM.
9. In late 1999, the drachma had appreciated by 7-8 per cent relative to its central rate against the euro.
10. According to more recent figures, Greece's primary surplus was 6.4 per cent in 1998 and is expected to be 7 per cent in 1999.
11. Legislation was passed in 1998 which sought to remove some of the key rigidities in the labour market (including inflexibility of working time, wages, ineffectiveness of job matching mechanisms). However, these changes have not yet had a material impact on the labour market. The 1999 *National Action Plan for Employment* includes a number of initiatives designed to improve flexibility, although more emphasis on improving the quality and job-relevance of vocational training is still needed.

References

Artis, M. and Zhang, W. (1995), *International Business Cycles and the ERM: Is There a European Business Cycle?*, CEPR Discussion Paper, No. 1191.

Bayoumi, T. and Prassad, E. (1995), *Currency Unions, Economic Fluctuations and Adjustment: Some Empirical Evidence*, CEPR Discussion Paper, No. 1172.

Begg, D. (1997), 'The Design of EMU', *Staff Studies for the World Economic Outlook*, Washington D.C.: International Monetary Fund.

Bini-Smaghi, L. and Vori, S. (1993), *Rating the EC as an Optimal Currency Area: Is it Worse than the US?*, Banca d'Italia Discussion Paper, No. 187.

Bruno, M. and Sachs, J. (1985), *Economics of Worldwide Stagflation*, Oxford: Basil Blackwell.

Canzoneri, M., Valles, J. and Vinals, J. (1996), *Do Exchange Rates Have to Address International Macroeconomic Imbalances?*, CEPR Discussion Paper, No. 1498.

De Grauwe, P. (1997), *The Economics of Monetary Integration* (3rd edition), Oxford: Oxford University Press.

Eichengreen, B. (1994), *International Monetary Arrangements for the 21st Century*, Washington D.C.: Brookings.

Erkel-Rousse, H. and Melitz, J. (1995), *New Empirical Evidence on the Costs of Monetary Union*, CEPR Discussion Paper, No. 1169.

Garganas, N. (1993), *The Implications of a Single European Currency and Monetary Policy: Prospects and Policy Issues*, Working Document, Centre for European Policy Studies (revised version published in Klein, 1998).

Gros, D. (1996), *A Reconsideration of the Optimum Currency Area Approach: The Role of External Shocks and Labour Mobility*, Brussels: Center for Economic Policy Studies.

Grubb, D., Jackman, R. and Laylard, R. (1983), 'Wage Rigidity and Unemployment in OECD Countries', *European Economic Review*.

Klein, L.R. (ed) (1998), *LINK Proceedings: Volume I*, 1991, 1992, Singapore: World Scientific Publishing Co., pp. 1–36.

7 The Greek Economy and the Euro

GEORGE ALOGOSKOUFIS

The importance of Greece's participation in Economic and Monetary Union cannot be underestimated. The Greek economy has had a dismal inflationary record in the last twenty years, it has accumulated public debt at an unprecedented rate, it has been characterised by very high nominal and real interest rates, and its growth record has been unimpressive. As an economy with such macroeconomic imbalances, Greece has a lot to gain from EMU participation.

First of all, Greece will tackle the roots of its inflation problem, by relying on the credibility and independence of the European Central Bank. As a result, it will import low nominal and real interest rates, something which will allow higher growth rates, lower servicing costs for public debt, and more resources for important social services which are currently underfunded. In addition, Greece, which is the poorer European economy, will be in a better position to reap the potential benefits of the single European market. Finally, EMU participation will have important political advantages for Greece, as it will be fully integrated again in the European Union.

Because it failed to achieve any of the nominal convergence criteria that were stipulated in the Maastricht treaty, Greece was not included in the group of eleven European countries that proceeded to adopt the new currency, the euro, in January 1999. Thus, Greece has two tasks in the next few years. The first is to ensure its inclusion in EMU as soon as possible. The Greek government aims for January 2001, one year before the euro fully replaces national currencies in the European Union. The second, and most important task, is for Greece to achieve real convergence with the European Union. Greece is the poorer European Union economy, and its per capita GDP is currently about 60 per cent of the European Union average. Growth rates need to be accelerated sharply, and to achieve this, Greece needs to introduce important domestic structural reforms. The successful introduction of these reforms must become the most important priority for Greece in the first few years of the next century.

How can Greece achieve this dual task of EMU entry and real convergence? Why did it fail to achieve these targets up to now? What is the nature of the reforms that need to be introduced? These are the questions that I try to answer in this chapter. However, before we proceed, we need to provide a brief survey and analysis of post-war economic developments in Greece. This is important in order to understand the nature of the policy recommendations that follow.

The Two Faces of Janus: The Greek Economy in the Post-War Period

For a number of years after World War II, the macroeconomic performance of Greece was one of the most impressive in Europe and the world as a whole. This lasted until the early 1970s but was subsequently reversed. While Greece recovered relatively quickly in the aftermath of the first oil shock, following the second oil shock and admission to the European Community, it entered a period of persistent stagflation from which it has yet to fully recover.

Like Janus, the Greek economy has thus displayed two faces in the post-war period (see Table 1 and Figure 1, which speak for themselves). In the twenty years between 1954 and 1973 the average rate of growth was around 7 per cent with an average rate of inflation of around 4 per cent. Growth exceeded the average for the OECD by about 2 percentage points per annum, while inflation was the same as the OECD average. In the next twenty years the situation changed dramatically. Growth started slowing down in the late 1970s and collapsed during the 1980s and early 1990s. At the same time inflation shot up and remained stubbornly high. The average growth rate for the period 1974–93 was only about 2 per cent per annum, slightly lower than the OECD average. Average inflation rose to 16 per cent, a level higher by about ten percentage points when compared with the average for the OECD. In the post-1973 period Greece also suffered from periodic balance of payments crises, such as the ones during 1973–74, 1980–81, 1984–85 and 1989–90. These developments are summarised in Table 1.[1]

What caused the transformation of one of the 'success stories' of the post-war world to one of the most problematic economies? What are the lessons implied by this sharp transformation? It is important to understand these issues, before one proceeds to make policy recommendations.

Table 1 From Non-Inflationary Growth to Persistent Stagflation Greece 1954–98

	1954–73	1974–98
Average Annual GDP Growth (%)	7.1	2.2
Average Annual Price Inflation (%)	3.8	16.0
Average Current Account (% of GDP)	-2.1	-4.2

Source: OECD, *Economic Outlook*, various issues.[2]

Two key aspects of Greece's experience need to be explained. The first is the slowdown of economic growth after 1974 and its virtual collapse after 1979, and the second is the failure to control inflation, when, in almost all the European countries of the OECD inflation rates fell sharply during the 1980s.

Greece displays much larger differences between the 'golden era' of the 1950s and 1960s and the subsequent period than the rest of the OECD. At the same time, it shares many features with two other southern European economies, Portugal and Spain, which displayed a much more impressive macroeconomic performance, especially since the mid-1980s. These three economies, which are among the poorest OECD countries, have experienced a relatively smooth transition from dictatorship to democracy in the mid-1970s and they all entered the European Community in the 1980s.

Clearly, the causes of the deterioration in Greece's macroeconomic performance cannot be solely external or global in origin, since the performance of Greece deteriorated not only absolutely, but also relative to that of its OECD partners (Figure 1). Also, the causes cannot be related simply to the transition from a largely authoritarian to a liberal democratic political regime, since Portugal and Spain experienced much more radical political transformations at a lower economic cost. Finally, the problem is not one of temporary shocks, like the oil shocks, or short-run macroeconomic management. The combination of low growth with high inflation persisted for about twenty-five years, which suggests that something deeper and more permanent has been at work.

My main thesis is that the deterioration in Greece's macroeconomic performance reflects a sharp domestic regime change in the early 1970s. The pre-1974 and the post-1974 regimes were characterised by radically

Figure 1 Growth and Inflation Differential between Greece and the OECD

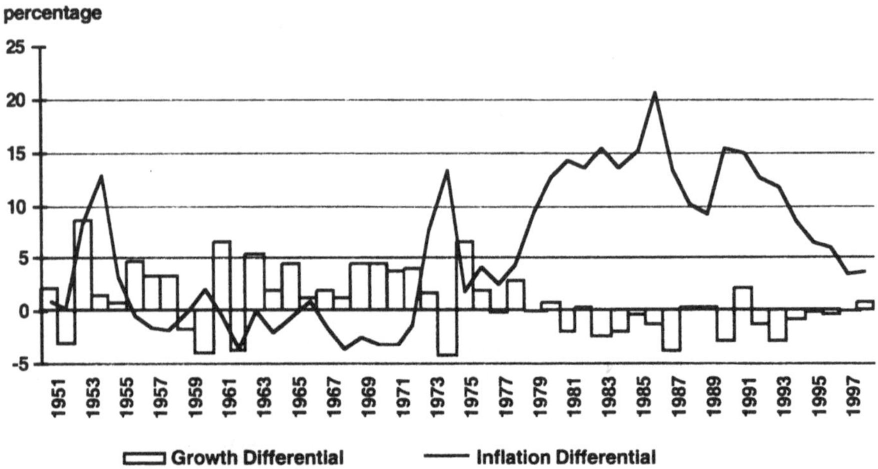

Source: OECD *Economic Outlook*, various issues.[2]

different economic and political institutions.

The first regime was characterised by commitment and coordination mechanisms that led to high investment and growth as well as low inflation. The commitment mechanisms for private investors included the guarantees of property rights in the constitution and the law, the tax laws and their implementation as well as the direct control of the state over labour unions. The above mechanisms guaranteed high returns to capital accumulation. Through the drachma's participation in the Bretton Woods system of fixed exchange rates, this regime also provided for a stable and predictable monetary standard, as well as a measure of fiscal discipline. In addition, through the market liberalisation that took place in the early 1950s and the powerful Currency Committee that allocated credit, the system provided two effective coordination mechanisms that allocated resources and savings relatively effectively.

On the other hand, the pre-1974 regime had been politically autocratic, having emerged in the aftermath of Greece's civil war. It degenerated into dictatorship in 1967. During the dictatorship, many of its elements were carried to unsustainable extremes. Thus, the regime broke down completely following the restoration of democracy in 1974.

The regime that took its place failed to develop the commitment and coordination mechanisms and institutions that would guarantee sufficiently high returns to the accumulation of capital. In addition, since the collapse of Bretton Woods, no domestic or international institution succeeded in guaranteeing a stable monetary standard. Labour unions acquired power that for a long time was not mitigated by institutional checks and balances. The public demanded redistribution and an expansion of the economic role of the state, but no mechanisms were put in place to ensure efficiency. Distortionary taxation and indebtedness rose to finance redistribution and the bigger state. The post-1974 regime resulted in a number of distortions that not only discouraged private investment but also caused a reduction in the social rate of return of the investment projects that were actually undertaken. The aspects of the second regime that appear to have generated most of the distortions include the financial system, monetary and fiscal policy, the labour market, the 'natural' monopolies and public enterprises, public administration, investment grants and EC transfers. In the next section, we shall analyse some of the most important factors.

Economic Policy: 1974–90

In analysing Greek economic policy since the fall of the dictatorship, we shall distinguish between the period before and after 1990. 1990 was the year when there was a clear change of policies. This change of policies was triggered by another crisis in the balance of payments. It was helped by the change in government and the EMU project.

We shall concentrate on fiscal policy and monetary and exchange rate policy, both microeconomic policies that led to an expansion of the role of the state. Policy in this period failed to provide the necessary credibility to investors, wage setters and savers, and resulted in a combination of low investment and growth as well as high inflation.

Fiscal Policy

Up until the mid-1970s, Greek governments followed the so-called 'golden rule' of fiscal policy, allowing deficits only in the government investment budget. Since 1978, they started breaking this rule, especially in election

Figure 2 Borrowing Requirement of the General Government

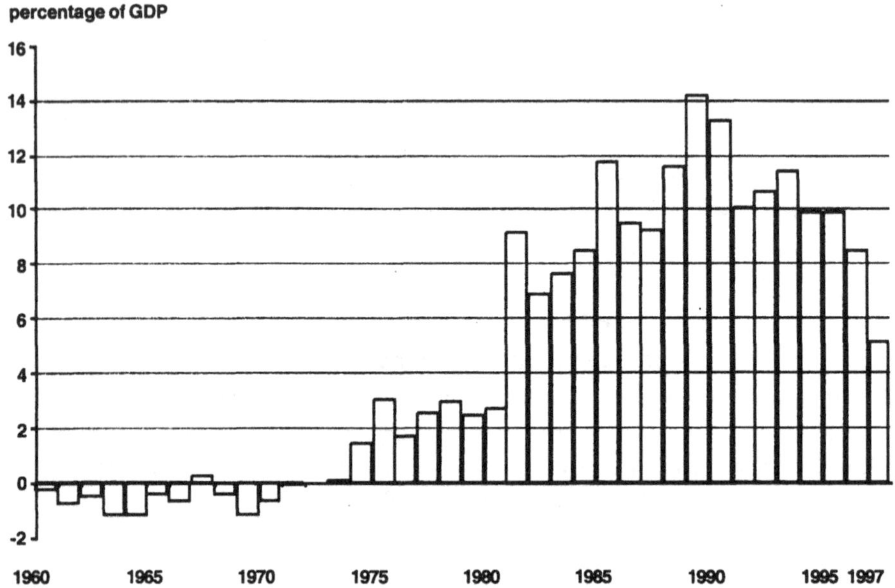

Source: Ministry of National Economy,[3] OECD.[2]

years. Fiscal deficits increased significantly in view of the attempts of governments to satisfy the general demand for income redistribution, social spending and a wider role for the state. Following a large pre-election deficit in 1981 by the outgoing liberal administration, the incoming socialists embarked on a programme of high public spending that caused that deficit to persist (see Figure 2).

In 1981, the General Government Borrowing Requirement (GGBR) rose to 9.1 per cent of GDP, from 2.6 per cent in 1980. It fell in 1982, but started rising again in 1983, to peak at 11.7 per cent in 1985, another election year. A short-lived attempt to control the deficits of the general government followed after the 1985 elections and the balance of payments crisis that ensued. However, in 1989, another election year, the borrowing requirement of the general government rose to 14 per cent of GDP.

Such large deficits caused a very rapid rise in government debt (see Figure 3). The rise in general government debt during the 1980s was mainly due to large primary deficits. The Papandreou governments engineered

Figure 3 The Rise in the Debt of the General Government

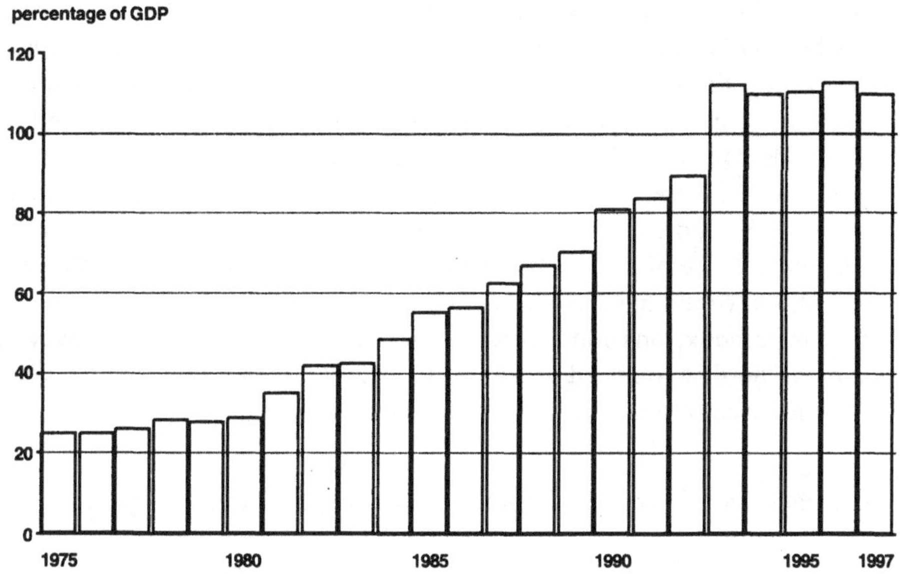

Source: Ministry of National Economy,[3] OECD.[2]

an expansion of the welfare state and grants and subsidies, which was mainly financed through domestic and external borrowing and EC transfers.

The second source of the rise in government deficits and debts, was the increase in nominal interest rates, after the gradual liberalisation of financial markets since the mid-1980s. Nominal and real interest rates rose significantly.

The third source of the rise in the debt to GDP ratio was the halt in economic growth. This caused a further widening of the gap between real interest rates and the GDP growth rate, and accelerated the process of debt accumulation.

Finally, and in addition to the three factors above, during the 1980s there was an explosion in government guarantees for loans by various private and public firms and agencies, as well as an explosion in the debts of agricultural cooperatives. In 1989 government guarantees amounted to 32 per cent of GDP and in the next three years, about half had lapsed and had been transformed into government debt.

Normally, these fiscal developments would have led to a very sharp rise in the current account deficit. In particular, with a continuously rising public debt to GDP ratio one would have expected a continuously rising external debt to GDP ratio and an external crisis that would have forced a much more drastic fiscal adjustment. One would also have expected a continuously falling private consumption to GDP ratio, which may have led to political demands for fiscal adjustment. In fact, in the case of Greece we saw neither of these, with the exception of two brief balance of payments crises in 1985 and 1989–90. However, despite these developments, neither the Greek balance of payments nor private consumption has shown the pattern that one would have expected under the circumstances. To explain this apparent paradox, one must consider the role of EC transfers. However, before we do that, we need to take a closer look at the interaction between wage and price setting and monetary and exchange rate policy.

The Wage-Price Spiral and Monetary and Exchange Rate Policy

Greece's inflation rate accelerated sharply in 1973. That rise in inflation can be attributed to the commodity and oil price shocks and the depreciation of the drachma which remained tied to the depreciating US dollar. Inflation peaked in 1974 and was brought under some control in the 1975–78 period. However, the second oil shock brought about another sharp acceleration of inflation. That acceleration proved more persistent, because it was accommodated by monetary and exchange rate policy, which in turn set off a vicious wage-price spiral. That wage price spiral remained uncontrolled until 1986, when a two-year wage freeze was imposed. After 1988, there was an attempt to catch-up with the real wage losses of 1986–87, which caused a resumption of the inflation spiral.

The persistent rise in inflation can be seen as an attempt by the governments of the late 1970s and early 1980s to use monetary and exchange rate policy to fine-tune the economy in the face of rising unemployment rates. The concern with unemployment was also enshrined in the 1975 constitution, which included a clause that defined the responsibility of the government for maintaining full employment. The previous constitution of 1952 contained no such clause.

It was facilitated by the fact that after 1975, Greece followed an independent monetary and exchange rate policy. In the period between 1954 and

1972, Greece participated fully in the Bretton Woods system of fixed exchange rates. Greece took full part in this regime after a devaluation of the drachma by 50 per cent in 1953. The drachma was made convertible for current transactions in May 1959, shortly after the introduction of convertibility in the rest of Western Europe. Between 1955 and the collapse of the Bretton Woods system in 1972, Greece enjoyed extremely low inflation. In fact, as Figure 1 shows, its inflation rate was lower than the OECD average.

After 1975, instead of participating in European attempts at monetary cooperation and exchange rate stabilisation, like the 'snake in the tunnel' or later the EMS, Greece followed an independent 'crawling peg' exchange rate policy of accommodating inflation differentials with its trading partners (see Figure 4). Its inflation rate has since soared, while unemployment rose significantly after the second oil shock. The monetary independence afforded to Greek governments since the collapse of Bretton Woods seems to have resulted in persistently high inflation, without any visible benefits on economic growth, the unemployment rate or the current account. This should not come as a surprise, and is in accordance with modern theories of inflation.

Figure 4 The Depreciation of the Drachma and Inflation Differentials

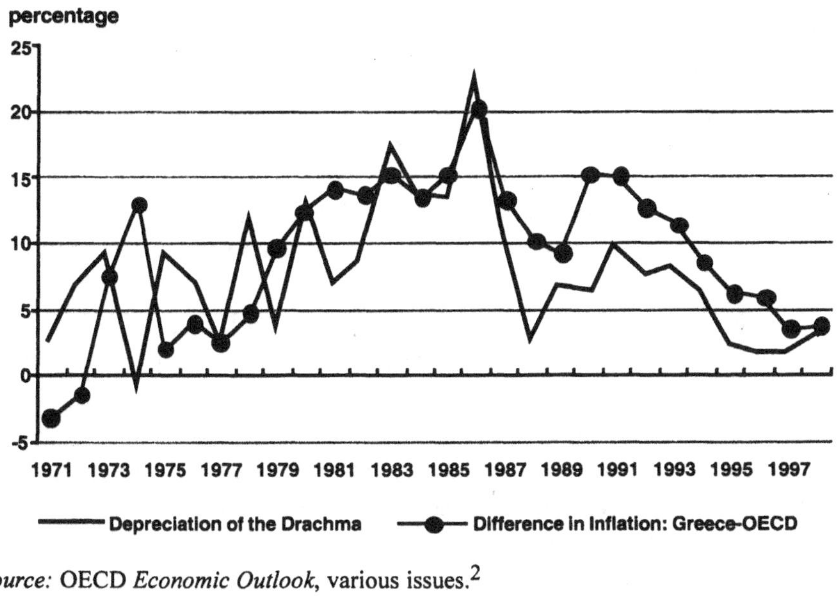

Source: OECD *Economic Outlook*, various issues.[2]

These theories suggest that whereas the mechanism through which inflation persists is excess monetary growth, its deeper determinants are distortions in the labour, product and capital markets. These distortions generate incentives for governments to try and correct them through unanticipated inflation. As these incentives are known to the private sector, they affect inflationary expectations. Through the determination of wages, prices and interest rates these expectations in turn affect the actual inflation rate. As a result, inflation becomes anticipated, and cannot therefore correct the distortions that the governments are concerned with.

In Greece's case, one example of such distortions was the high public deficits and debts that we have already examined. An acceleration in the rate of monetary creation provides a cheap method of avoiding some of the distortions associated with a rise in tax rates or in interest bearing government debt. If this monetisation and the subsequent inflation are initially unanticipated, they will not be reflected immediately in nominal interest rates. Thus, they will not affect the monetary base as a percentage of GDP and they will not cause an increase in interest payments on the public debt. Thus, the government has much to gain and little to lose. However, when this policy becomes anticipated, as it did indeed become, and nominal interest rates rise, the government gains little. A large part of the interest saved from the monetisation will be compensated by the higher interest payments on public debt. In addition, there will be a reduction in the monetary base as a percentage of GDP.

Similar problems arise from high unemployment or current account deficits. If wage increases are low, then the government has an incentive to devalue the currency in order to reduce relative unit labour costs, unemployment and the current account deficit. However, if the devaluation is anticipated it will be reflected in wage and price setting, and it will not affect the real exchange rate, the unemployment rate or the current account. Its main effect will be an increase in inflation.

Thus, in an economy with high public debt, high unemployment and high current account deficits, monetary sovereignty may cause an increase in average inflation as well. This will be the case when the private sector feels that the government would otherwise have incentives to use unanticipated money growth and a sudden depreciation of the exchange rate.

This seems to have been the case in Greece. As long as Greece participated in Bretton Woods, inflationary expectations were contained, even in the face of an overheating economy in 1971–72. When the institutional constraint of Bretton Woods was removed, inflation and, subsequently, inflationary expectations soared.

Microeconomic Distortions and the Role of the State

A number of microeconomic distortions operated during this period as well.

The first was related to the failure of labour market reform after 1974 to provide sufficient commitment mechanisms guaranteeing satisfactory returns for private investors. The switch from the suppression of labour unions to a regime of full accommodation of union demands resulted in a large increase in real unit labour costs between 1975 and 1985. This reduced international competitiveness and helped depress investment and growth rates. In conjunction with the collapse of the Bretton Woods system of fixed exchange rates, it also led to an accommodating regime for monetary and exchange rate policy which caused inflation to persist.

The second domestic institutional development was related to the loss of credibility of the tax authorities vis-à-vis investors and firms. This followed the significant increase of the tax burden in order to finance the expansion of the role of the state. It appears to have depressed domestic private investment, especially as some of the tax increases were retroactive levies on business profits.

A number of other microeconomic distortions appear as likely candidates for the fall in the growth rate, as a large part of this was due not just to the drop in investment rates but also a fall in the social productivity of capital. These include the oil price shocks, which operated in two distinct periods and have affected all OECD economies.

The nationalisations of the 1970s and 1980s, and the expansion of the role of the state were also very negative factors. Apart from their effects on property rights, nationalisations and the creation of a host of government agencies appear to have contributed to lower efficiency in production. In addition, distortions associated with monopoly, and inefficient production, even dumping, were introduced. For example, a number of ailing industrial firms were included in the Industrial Restructuring Organisation. These producers were subsidised by the state, operated inefficiently and reduced the rate of return and investment rates for other firms in the same sector. In addition, the pricing, production, investment and employment programmes of nationalised industries, old and new, were undertaken on the basis of political rather than purely economic considerations. Management was ineffective, as it changed quite often, their pricing policies were used for distributional and electoral objectives, their unions and suppliers achieved significant privileges, extracting large rents and the governing political party used them in order to find jobs for their supporters.

Further distortions were introduced through the financial system. Until the first oil shock, the Currency Committee provided a central coordinating mechanism that allocated savings to firms and sectors that promised high investment returns and growth rates. Although this system has been criticised as being inefficient, it seems to have helped the development of the Greek economy in the conditions that prevailed in the 1950s and the 1960s. After the first oil shock, the increase in unit labour costs and the growing importance of the nationalised industries, the drawbacks of the Currency Committee, which controlled the financial system, became apparent. Under pressure to avoid layoffs and closures of large firms that had been hit by the oil shock and the real wage increases, government ministers in the Currency Committee decided to extend loans to such firms not for investment purposes but to cover their operating deficits. There was also more emphasis on the financing of the nationalised industries, while compulsory investment of commercial banks in government paper increased. Thus, credit was extended to inefficient firms and the public sector, at low interest rates, and the rest of the economy faced a credit crunch. This contributed to the reduction in investment and growth rates. With time, these practices led to the creation of the so called 'problematic' or 'ailing' firms, many of which were included in the Industrial Restructuring Organisation that was created in the 1980s.

In addition, there is evidence that not only the quantity but the quality of public investment programmes deteriorated, especially in the 1980s. A number of large infrastructure programmes, especially in Athens, like the metro and the new airport were postponed in 1981, while the national road network, the telecommunications and the electricity networks suffered from lack of investment. There was a shift in the 1980s towards the improvement in the social infrastructure, with a large proportion of the investment budget spent on small-scale projects outside the large cities. Old age housing, local hospitals, squares and pavements formed a large part of public investment, a lot of it financed through EC grants and subsidies.

Further distortions were introduced through government grants and subsidies. Since the late 1970s a series of laws purporting to encourage regional development were applied, shifting the emphasis from tax breaks to grants and subsidies for firms that invested in less developed regions of the country. In addition, subsidies for public enterprises and entities kept growing, even for current expenditure. Finally, there were extensive transfers from the EEC since 1981. Transfers and subsidies of the general government rose from about 8.5 per cent of GDP in 1970 to 11 per cent in 1979 and 20 per cent of GDP in 1985. If not applied and monitored carefully, such transfers can result in investment projects, with low or even negative social productivity and minimal effects on the growth rate.

The Role of EU Transfers

The persistence of macroeconomic and structural imbalances as those that Greece experienced during the 1980s would have been impossible had Greece not become a member of the European Economic Community. EEC membership averted a generalised crisis in external confidence, which would have forced a change in policy. In addition, the EC provided Greece with funds that kept the balance of payments under control and increased private consumption, despite the flat growth rate.

Greece entered the European Economic Community in 1981, having applied in June 1975. The issue of membership was hotly debated for a number of years, with the socialist opposition firmly against membership. EC entry was quickly followed by the election victory of the socialist government of Andreas Papandreou, which proceeded to renegotiate some of the entry conditions and gained additional protection for Greek industry in the form of additional grace periods and extra financial assistance.

EC entry also coincided with the beginning of the explosion of public sector deficits and debts. This started in 1981, the election year, and continued throughout the 1980s.

Greece's balance of payments deteriorated during the 1980s due to domestic fiscal policy. However, EC transfers worked in the opposite direction, as they relieved the pressure on the balance of payments and helped sustain private consumption, despite the growth slowdown and the rising tax burden. These transfers that initially amounted to less than 1 per cent of Greece's GDP, gradually rose to more than 3 per cent during the 1980s.

Despite their benefits, in the case of Greece, EC transfers have had important negative side effects. By relaxing the external constraint and

Figure 5 European Union Transfers to Greece

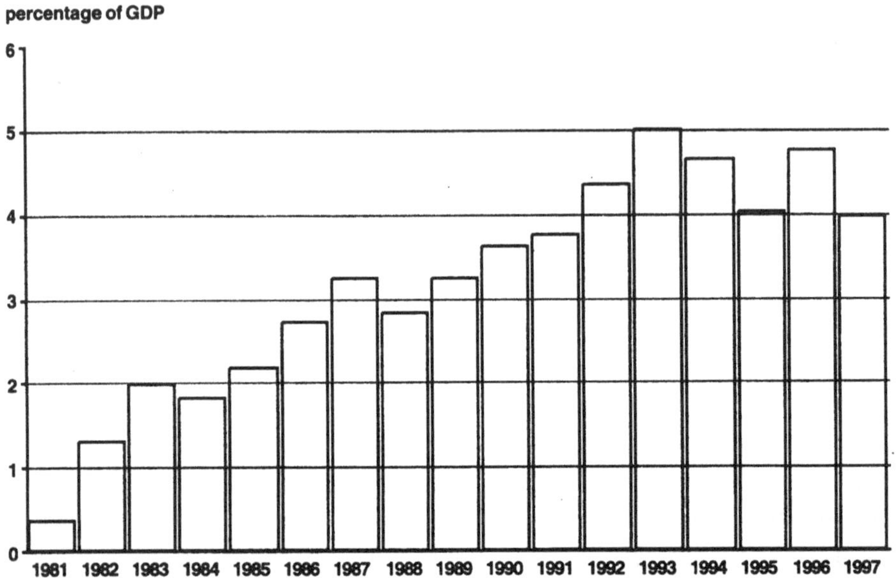

Source: Ministry of National Economy.[4]

allowing high private consumption they have helped delay the necessary fiscal and wage adjustment. Thus, they have crowded out the traded goods sector on account of both the looser fiscal policy that was followed and the higher real wages (lower competitiveness) that they helped sustain. On the basis of this interpretation, the decline in Greek manufacturing that has been documented by a number of authors and international organisations, as well as the growing trade imbalance is mainly due to the indirect effects of the sizeable transfers from abroad rather than trade liberalisation per se.

In addition, since the EC transfers were given almost unconditionally, they did not create incentives that would counteract the relaxation of the external constraint. The exceptions were the two instances in which Greece sought explicit balance of payments assistance from the EC, namely the 1985 and 1991 stabilisation programmes. The 1985 programme was abandoned prematurely at the end of 1987, while the 1991 programme was even more short lived.

EC transfers may also have caused additional microeconomic distortions. The programmes that were funded by these transfers, such as the

CAP, training, regional assistance, were not particularly well designed and it is not at all certain that they even had a positive contribution to a more efficient operation of the economy. These additional microeconomic distortions are additional to the other distortions that I have highlighted. Similarly, the fact that Greece had been gaining additional grace periods before conforming to the rest of the European Union in trade and financial market liberalisation has also helped delay the necessary structural adjustment.

The Challenge of Nominal and Real Convergence

Since 1990 there have been attempts to deal with many of the distortions that were introduced in the previous fifteen years. There was a gradual, though insufficient, reduction in government deficits. The nationalisations have given way to a few privatisations. Price controls have been relaxed and the labour market has been partially liberalised. Monetary financing of the state has been reduced and monetary policy in general became tighter. Inflation fell throughout the 1990s, as the policy of accommodating inflation differentials through the exchange rate was abandoned. Independence was granted to the Bank of Greece.

Yet, Greece failed to satisfy the nominal convergence criteria set out in the Maastricht treaty in 1998. It is currently widely expected to participate in EMU before the year 2002. However, important problems remain to be tackled in the years to come.

In addition, the structural reforms of the 1990s have not been sufficiently bold to help reverse expectations and lead to a new wave of investment and growth that would help close the gap in living standards between Greece and the European Union.

Nominal Convergence Efforts in the 1990s

The attempts to control fiscal deficits, inflation and the structural imbalances that grew in the 1970s and the 1980s started with the election of the New Democracy government in 1990.

The macroeconomic situation in 1990 was critical. Government deficits were getting out of control, 'hidden' debts had accumulated throughout the public sector, the social security system was on the brink of collapse, foreign exchange reserves had been depleted and inflation was accelerating.

The nominal convergence efforts that started in 1990 were reinforced through the two convergence programmes that were submitted to the European Union in 1993, and in 1994, after the socialists returned to power. Those programmes, which were similar in the priorities that they set, although not in the time frame for the completion of these priorities, have been guiding Greek macroeconomic policy throughout the 1990s. The priorities were as follows:

> To gradually reduce the General Government Borrowing Requirement to the 3 per cent of GDP required by the Maastricht treaty.
>
> To stabilise and reduce the General Government Debt to GDP ratio.
>
> To reduce inflation within 1.5 percentage points of the average of the three EU economies with the lowest inflation rate.
>
> To reduce the fluctuations of the drachma exchange rate vis-à-vis European Union currencies.
>
> To reduce long-term interest rates within 1.5 percentage points of the average of the three EU economies with the lowest long-term interest rates.

The international recession of 1993 and the early elections, which led to a change in government, derailed the first convergence programme. It lasted for less than 8 months. The new government, after a delay of about one year, submitted a revised convergence programme, which stipulated a much more gradual adjustment effort, and took account of the possibility of elections around 1996. The revised programme stated explicitly that the aim was for Greece to participate in EMU from the 1st of January 1999, but it failed to take into account that this required satisfaction of the five nominal convergence criteria by mid-1998. Thus, although the fiscal targets were officially realised, and the discrepancy in the inflation targets was not significant, Greece failed to satisfy the criteria for participation in EMU from the start.

It is worth going over the nominal convergence process of the 1990s, as it highlights some of the potential problems that will haunt Greece after it finally participates in the single currency.

We start with fiscal adjustment. Table 2 contains the main data. As is evident from the data presented, the General Government Borrowing

Table 2 Fiscal Adjustment in Greece 1989-1998

	1989	1990	1991	1992	1993	1994	1995	1996	1997	1998
Current Revenues	29.2	32.1	32.9	33.7	35.0	36.6	37.7	38.0	38.9	39.3
Direct Taxes	4.6	5.5	5.6	5.5	5.8	6.9	7.3	7.1	7.5	8.0
Indirect Taxes	11.5	13.2	13.8	14.6	14.0	13.6	13.5	13.7	14.2	14.3
Social Security Contribution	11.4	11.7	11.2	11.1	12.1	12.3	12.6	12.7	12.6	12.7
Current Expenditure	39.5	41.7	39.4	40.8	43.0	43.7	44.2	43.9	40.6	39.8
Public Consumption	15.2	15.3	14.4	13.9	14.4	13.9	14.8	15.5	14.8	14.4
Grants and Subsidies	16.7	16.2	15.6	15.2	15.8	15.7	16.4	16.4	16.2	16.3
Current Primary Expenditure	31.9	31.5	30.0	29.1	30.2	29.6	31.2	31.9	31.0	30.7
Interest Payments	7.6	10.2	9.4	11.7	12.8	14.1	12.9	12.0	9.6	9.1
Net Capital Transfers	0.8	0.8	0.4	0.0	0.3	-0.2	0.1	-0.9	0.0	-0.3
Fixed Investment	3.0	2.8	3.1	3.5	3.1	3.0	3.3	3.4	3.4	3.7
Borrowing Requirement	14.1	13.2	10.0	10.6	11.4	9.9	9.9	8.4	5.1	3.9
Primary Deficit	6.5	3	0.6	-1.1	-1.4	-4.2	-3.0	-3.6	-4.5	-5.2
'New' Accounting Items	0.3	2.9	1.5	2.2	2.4	0.1	0.7	-0.9	-1.1	-1.7
Government Guarantees	0.3	2.9	1.5	2.2	2.4	0.1	0.0	0.0	0.4	0.0
Past Budgets	0.0	0.0	0.0	0.0	0.0	0.0	0.7	-0.9	0.0	0.0
Equity Participations	0.0	0.0	0.0	0.0	0.0	0.0	0.0	0.0	-1.5	-.17
'Official' GGBR	*14.4*	*16.1*	*11.5*	*12.8*	*13.8*	*10.0*	*10.6*	*7.5*	*4.0*	*2.2*
'Official' Primary Deficit	*6.8*	*6.0*	*2.1*	*1.1*	*1.0*	*4.1*	*2.3*	*4.5*	*5.7*	*6.9*

Source: Author's estimates based on OECD data.[2]

Requirement (GGBR) has fallen from 14.1 per cent of GDP in 1989 to 3.9 per cent of GDP in 1998. This reduction was due to an impressive improvement in the primary balance. The primary deficit (which excludes interest payments) was 6.5 per cent of GDP in 1989. This primary deficit was reduced quickly in the 1990–93 period. In 1993 it had become a primary surplus of 1.4 per cent of GDP, an improvement of 8 percentage points. Three quarters of that improvement were on account of the increase in government revenues, from 29.2 per cent of GDP in 1989 to 35 per cent of GDP in 1993. One quarter was due to the reduction of current primary expenditure from 31.9 per cent of GDP in 1989 to 30.2 per cent of GDP in 1993.

There was a further, albeit smaller, improvement in the primary deficit between 1994 and 1998. The primary surplus was increased from 1.4 per cent of GDP in 1993 to 5.2 per cent in 1998. This was due solely to increases in government revenue, from 35 per cent of GDP in 1993 to 39.3 per cent of GDP in 1998. Current primary expenditure in fact increased slightly relative to GDP during this period.

Although most of the improvement in the primary deficit took place in the first part of the 1990s, this improvement was initially only partly reflected on the General Government Borrowing Requirement. The reason was interest payments, which originally rose as a share of GDP. This was due to the fact that after 1990 the government started servicing the debt properly, at market determined interest rates. This was not the case during the 1980s, and as a result the deficits of that period underestimate the true deficits. Interest payments peaked at 14.1 per cent of GDP in 1994, and have been declining ever since, mainly due to the fall in inflation and nominal interest rates.

In addition, the public debt to GDP ratio was stabilised around that time, as the bulk of the 'hidden' debts of the 1980s were incorporated in the official debt figures by 1993. Thus, about half of the true fiscal adjustment between 1994 and 1998 is attributed to the reduction in interest payments from 14.1 per cent of GDP in 1994 to 9.1 per cent of GDP in 1998.

The second element of the nominal convergence efforts of the 1990s was the reduction in inflation. After the Papandreou government abandoned the short-lived stabilisation programme of 1986–87, inflationary pressures returned. The New Democracy government, that came to power in April 1990 initiated a new anti-inflationary strategy, based on a gradual reduction of the rate of depreciation of the drachma below the difference between Greek and OECD inflation. Thus, it stopped accommodating inflation dif-

Figure 6 Inflation in Greece November 1990-December 1998

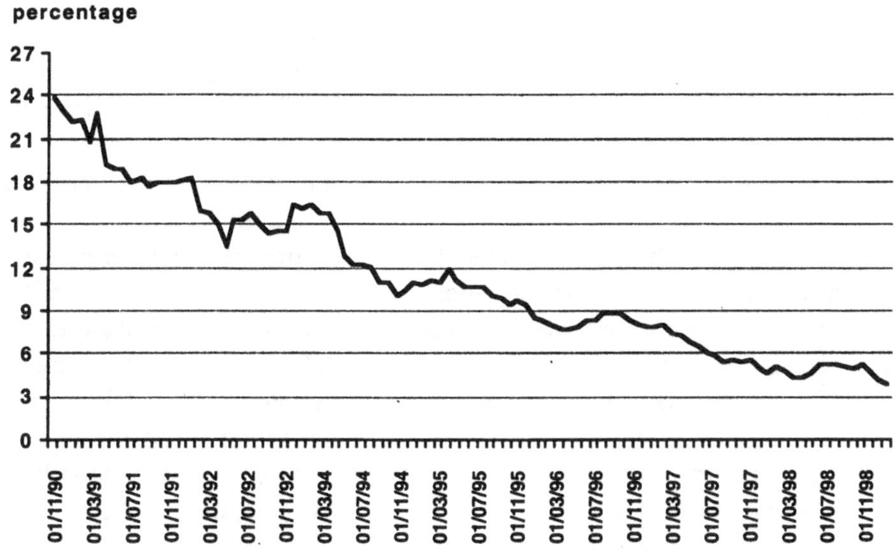

Source: Ministry of National Economy.[3]

ferentials. This was a policy that was gradually tightened and brought a reduction in inflation. Inflation peaked at around 20 per cent in November 1990 and has been falling ever since.

As already mentioned, the reduction in inflation was due to the fact that the rate of depreciation of the drachma stopped accommodating inflation differentials between Greece and its trading partners. This policy was facilitated by the fact that fiscal deficits were on a downward trend. It was also made possible by the gradual elimination of financing of government deficits by the Bank of Greece. Financing of the government by the Bank of Greece was eliminated between 1990 and 1993.

There were a few instances in which the downward path of inflation was interrupted. The first was the 1992–93 period, when measured inflation temporarily rose as a result of indirect tax increases aimed at boosting government revenue. This was planned for and was temporary. The second was the second half of 1994, due to a relaxation of monetary policy in the previous six months. That relaxation had brought about a drachma crisis, that caused a sustained rise in short-term interest rates throughout the summer of 1994. The monetary relaxation was accompanied by a very lax wage round. In the end, both monetary and exchange rate policy were tightened, and inflation resumed its downward path. Inflation rose temporarily in two other instances. In the 1996 pre-election period, due to high wage increases in the public sector that also affected the private sector, and in 1998, after the drachma devaluation of March 1998.

The devaluation of March 1998 came about after a sustained crisis of confidence, which forced the Bank of Greece to maintain short-term interest rates high for about six months. The devaluation relieved the pressure and also allowed the drachma to enter the exchange rate mechanism of the European Monetary System. The stock market rally that followed and the perception that Greece would eventually take part in EMU caused a virtuous circle sparked by expectations of falling interest rates, falling government deficits, a stronger drachma and falling inflation. At the time of writing (February 1999), it looks quite likely that Greece will eventually be in a position to take part in EMU before the year 2002, despite the fact that it did not make it from the start.

The Challenges of Real Convergence and Structural Reform

If nominal convergence was a slow process, structural reform and real convergence has been even slower. Even after the international recession of 1993, Greece's growth rate failed to rise sufficiently to ensure a fast rate of real convergence. Greece's per capita GDP stands at about 60 per cent of the average per capita GDP of the European Union. Even if the rate of growth of 1998 were to be maintained, it would take about half a century for Greece to achieve the average living standards of the European Union. Growth rates have to accelerate sharply if Greece wishes to have a faster rate of real convergence. However, for growth rates to accelerate, Greece needs a fast rate of structural reform that will make room for private investment in sectors that have hitherto been the exclusive domain of the state. It also needs a better utilisation of European Union funds that are being transferred to Greece, in order for the country to improve its economic and social infrastructure. Unfortunately, although both convergence programmes gave emphasis to structural reform, the record in the 1990s has been rather unsatisfactory.

It is worth looking at the priorities of the revised convergence programme, regarding economic growth and structural reform. The projections of the programme for economic growth were rather modest. The average projected growth rate for the 1994–99 period was 2.2 per cent, about the same as the projected growth rate of the European Union. Thus the programme did not consider real convergence as a priority. The hope of course was that growth would prove higher that projected, which started happening after 1996. In fact, on current OECD estimates, the average growth rate for the 1994–98 period is about 2.5 per cent, slightly higher than projected. For the same period, the average EU growth rate is estimated at 2.5 per cent as well. Thus, no progress was made on the issue of real convergence in the last five years. The slight acceleration in Greece's economic growth in recent years can be attributed more to the acceleration of growth in the European Union, relative to the first few years of the 1990s, rather than domestic factors.

This conclusion is strengthened if one examines the record of structural reform. The revised convergence programme highlighted five priorities for structural reform in order to help economic growth and real convergence.

The first priority was to exploit the transfers of funds from the European Union. In the last few years, these exceeded 4 per cent of GDP on average, and were meant to help Greece upgrade its economic and social infrastructure. These transfers do not appear to have had a major impact on Greece's growth rate up to now. Until 1998, Greece managed to absorb less than 50 per cent of the available funds and the projects that were funded were characterised by major inefficiencies.[4] In important priorities, like training and education absorption rates have been dismal. Major projects like the new Athens Airport, the Athens Metro, bridges and roadworks have been characterised by major delays. Therefore, the EU structural funds did not play the role that was envisaged.

The second stated priority of the programme was a new system of regional investment grants, aimed at fostering investment by large firms, in new products and the utilisation of state of the art technologies. Unfortunately, this also failed. Although the available funds have been spent, the results were more or less disappointing, and the government revised the system of investment incentives once more in 1998, shifting its priorities from grants to tax credits.

The third priority was the rise in the productivity and competitiveness of public enterprises. The means envisaged was the introduction of private sector management skills, floating in the stock exchange, restructuring programmes for loss making enterprises and new investment priorities. The national telecommunications organisation (OTE) was floated in the stock exchange in 1996, after a failed attempt in 1994, but the results in terms of growth and investment have been less than expected. 30 per cent of OTE is now privately held, but the government exercises tight control over its management. 23 per cent of Hellenic Petroleum has been sold in the stock market in 1998, but for all purposes it operates as a public enterprise. Public monopolies are maintained in important areas like electricity generation, natural gas, telecommunications, water and sewage, postal services, urban transport, rail transport. Important sectors such as banking, oil refining and air transport are dominated by public enterprises. Liberalisation has proceed slowly, the pricing policy of public enterprises is decided by the government, inflexible labour arrangements and high labour costs have not been affected much, even in loss making enterprises, obscure accounting practices remain, and, despite huge capital injections, their investment programmes are insufficient and badly planned. It is worth quoting the recent OECD survey of Greece on this:

> Despite substantial investment expenditure, which has averaged annually about 3.5% of GDP since the early 1980s, most public enterprises have not succeeded in updating to modern technologies or maintaining properly their infrastructure and/or equipment. Partly due to these modernisation delays, Greece has received a derogation from most EC directives related to the liberalisation of key sectors such as telecommunications, electricity, natural gas and air transportation. Since the beginning of the 1990s, a more significant effort has been made to narrow the existing large investment and technology gaps. … Despite some progress, critical investment lags remain. (OECD 1999, p. 107).[5]

In that same report, the OECD attempts to quantify the likely growth effects from liberalisation of the state enterprise sector and privatisation. It estimates the effects at around 9–11 per cent of GDP. Thus, if reforms are introduced in a period of three to four years, it would not be impossible to imagine that growth rates can be doubled solely on account of reform of the public enterprise sector. A lot remains to be done in this area, and this will be critical even after Greece's participation in the single currency.

A fourth element of the programme has been emphasis on education and training. However, this has remained more or less on paper. Utilisation of EU funds has been insufficient and few useful reforms have been introduced. University education remains a public monopoly. As a result universities are poorly funded and badly managed. Despite initiatives in some institutions and some firms, universities are not sensitive to the needs of the economy, and most training programmes are designed with the sole aim of absorbing EU funds. Thus, an important element of a coherent long-term growth strategy for Greece remains unexploited.

The same remarks can be made about the fifth priority of the programme, namely the initiatives to help small and medium sized enterprises (SMEs). Attempts to help SMEs, which are the backbone of the Greek economy have been badly planned. There is no coherent strategy to help SMEs, which face numerous obstacles in their attempts to obtain finance, in their tax treatment and in public procurement. As a result, a potentially dynamic growth source has not been tapped.

Conclusions and Policy Recommendations

Every Greek hopes that despite the delays and the weaknesses of the convergence efforts of the 1990s, Greece will finally make it into the euro zone as soon as possible. Two facts are for certain though. First, EMU entry will have cost the country much more than necessary, due to the delays and policy failures. Second, Greece will be relatively unprepared for the challenges of life in EMU. Thus, reform efforts must be accelerated, with a view of increasing the competitiveness of the economy and increasing the rate of economic growth.

There are seven important priorities for the years ahead.

- First, the consolidation of public finances. This will probably be the most immediate priority, given that the recorded reduction in the public deficit is to a large extent due to the heavy use of creative accounting, and there will be a need to normalise the fiscal accounts. Despite the reduction in interest rates that the euro will bring about, there will still be a need to control primary expenditure and the deficits of loss making public enterprises.
- Second, the simplification of the tax system. There is a pressing need for a tax reform that would simplify the tax system, deal with corrup-

tion and relieve the tax burden on low income families, especially young wage earners and pensioners, as well as private enterprises.

- Third, the reform of public administration. The Greek state has ceased to function even in its traditional tasks of security, justice and social protection. In addition, it puts too many obstacles in the operation of private enterprises, small and large, slowing down the growth process. Incentives have to be introduced in public administration, monitoring of performance ought to be introduced and the infrastructure of the state ought to be improved dramatically. In addition, privatisation and outsourcing ought to be introduced as soon as possible. The economy will never become competitive enough if the state is not made leaner and more efficient in its core tasks.
- Fourth, a serious reform is required in education. Education is one of the major engines of growth and the most efficient mechanism of intergenerational redistribution. It is still hindered by lack of funding and the presence of the state. The reform must proceed as a matter of national urgency, and must be decided on grounds of consensus so that it can be durable. The direction should be to create a more balanced system, with a large state presence in primary and secondary education, but more private involvement and funding as well.
- Fifth, the health and social security systems ought to be reformed as well. The state has neither the administrative skills nor the tax resources to be the sole provider of such services. A mixed system ought to be designed, with a view of encouraging new investment in health, more incentives for health workers, higher reliance on private insurance.
- Sixth, the state enterprise sector ought to forego dramatic reforms. Privatisation, liberalisation and competition are the key directions. This reform is likely to have the more immediate growth dividends. Sectors like banking, telecommunications, electricity and transport can become important engines of growth in the first years of the new century.
- Finally, a new regional policy is required. A policy aiming at creating scale economies in selected regions outside Athens and Thesaloniki has to be designed. The present policy of spreading regional aid thin redistributes income but does not generate growth. A rebalancing is thus needed.

Although the difficulties in introducing so many reforms at the same time have to be acknowledged, Greece has little time to spare. A substantial acceleration is needed in the pace of policy implementation in order to make up for the lost ground and ensure a satisfactory performance of Greece in the single currency area. The necessary social dialogue ought to take place on concrete government proposals and have a short duration. At the end of the day, the concurrent reform of several areas is likely to have the best results, through the reinforcement of the growth effects of several interlinked changes.

Notes

1. The analysis in this and the next section are based on Alogoskoufis G. (1995) 'The Two Faces of Janus: Institutions, Policy Regimes and Macroeconomic Performance in Greece', *Economic Policy,* April, p. 20.
2. OECD. *OECD Economic Outlook*. Paris: OECD, (various issues).
3. Ministry of National Economy. *Long-term Statistical Data for the Greek Economy.* Athens: Ministry of National Economy, (several years).
4. Ministry of National Economy. *Reports on the Community Support Framework.* Athens: Ministry of National Economy, (several years).
5. OECD. *Economic Surveys: Greece 1997–98*. Paris: OECD Publications, February 1999.

8 EMU and Greek Macroeconomic Policy in the 1990s

MICHAEL G. ARGHYROU

Introduction

There is little doubt that the Greek economy entered the 1990s with a number of serious macroecomomic imbalances. It is beyond our scope to provide here explanations for the rather disappointing macroeconomic performance of Greece during the period 1975–90. A great deal of research has been dedicated to this topic and the emerging consensus is that after 1975 (and especially in the 1980s) Greek authorities implemented a sub-optimal course of economic policy (involving substantial fiscal and monetary expansion) which affected the Greek economy in a number of negative ways, and according to Alogoskoufis and Christodoulakis (1991), brought Greece to the brink of insolvency in the late 1980s.[1]

Against this background, in 1990 the Greek authorities launched a stabilisation effort with the aim of correcting the mounting macroeconomic imbalances and achieving the participation of Greece in European Monetary Union (EMU) in 1999. However, despite the progress achieved in the 1990s, the second target was not achieved. As a result, the Greek government has now announced its intention to pursue EMU participation by 2001. The above define a clear agenda for Greek economic policy makers upon which the present chapter is focused. More specifically, I am concerned with the following two questions: (a) why the macroeconomic policy implemented in the 1990s failed to secure an EMU place for Greece in 1999; and (b) what macroeconomic strategy would maximise the chances of Greece joining the EMU in 2001?

The remainder of the chapter is structured as follows: the second section presents the main lines of Greek macroeconomic policy in the 1990s. The third section is dedicated to an assessment of this policy, while the fourth section presents my views on the issue of macroeconomic strategy towards EMU participation. The last section offers concluding remarks.

Greek Macroeconomic Policy in the 1990s: A Brief Overview

In the 1990s the Greek authorities implemented three stabilisation/convergence programmes: the three-year Medium Term Adjustment Programme (MTAP) 1991–93; the Convergence Programme (CP) 1993–98; and the Revised Convergence Programme (RCP) 1994–99. The MTAP and the CP 1993–98 were implemented by the conservative party New Democracy whereas the RCP 1994–99 was implemented by the socialist party PASOK. Despite the existence of differences on various points of lesser importance, both parties set the same set of objectives: (a) a reduction in inflation; (b) a reduction in budget deficits and public debt; and (c) the restructuring of the supply side of the Greek economy.

In reality, in the 1990s inflation reduction was mainly pursued by means of a two-step monetary strategy, the strong-drachma policy. Introduced in 1988, this policy involved a rate of depreciation of the drachma against the ECU smaller than the inflation differential existing between Greece and the EU average, effectively creating a fixed exchange rate regime during the period 1995–97. On the other hand, fiscal consolidation was mainly pursued by means of an increase in public revenue, that is through an increase in taxation revenue and an effort to reduce widespread tax evasion. The restructuring of the supply side of the Greek economy was mainly attempted through a higher level of public investment in the areas of transportation, telecommunications and energy, which are largely financed by the funds which Greece receives in the context of EU transfers. Finally, in the 1990s the Greek authorities proceeded to enact a number of institutional changes, including full financial liberalisation and granting independence to the Bank of Greece (BOG) in December 1997.

Without any doubt, the three convergence programmes of the 1990s have achieved some positive results which have been recognised by all international economic organisations.[2] The recent GDP growth rates are much higher compared to those of the early 1990s, inflation has declined significantly to historically low levels and the fiscal position of the country is improving steadily as a result of the considerable reduction in the public deficit. However, as Table 1 suggests, in 1997 Greece did not manage to satisfy any of the Maastricht criteria of nominal convergence and was left out of the first wave of EMU participants. This was largely the result of some substantial differences between the figures planned by the programmes and those actually realised. More specifically, most of the outcomes achieved by

Table 1 Nominal Convergence Among EU Member States

	Inflation	Fiscal position of General Government (% of GDP in 1997)		Long term interest rates	ERM participation	EMU founding member
	Jan 1998	Budget Deficit (+)	Public Debt	Jan 1998	May 1998	
Maastricht Reference Value	*2.7*	*3.0*	*60.0*	*7.8*		
Austria	1.1	2.5	66.1	5.6	Yes	Yes
Belgium	1.4	2.1	122.2	5.7	Yes	Yes
Denmark	1.9	-0.7	65.1	6.2	Yes	No
Finland	1.3	0.9	55.8	5.9	Yes	Yes
France	1.2	3.0	58.0	5.5	Yes	Yes
Germany	1.4	2.7	61.3	5.6	Yes	Yes
Greece	5.2	4.0	108.7	9.8	Yes	No
Ireland	1.2	-0.9	66.3	6.2	Yes	Yes
Italy	1.8	2.7	121.6	6.7	Yes	Yes
Luxembourg	1.4	-1.7	6.7	5.6	Yes	Yes
Netherlands	1.8	1.4	72.1	5.5	Yes	Yes
Portugal	1.8	2.5	62.0	6.2	Yes	Yes
Spain	1.8	2.6	68.8	6.3	Yes	Yes
Sweden	1.9	0.8	76.6	6.5	No	No
UK	1.8	1.9	53.4	7.0	No	No
EU	15	1.6	2.4	72.1	N/A	N/A

Source: European Commission.

Table 2 The Year 1993 Performance of the Convergence Programme 1993–98

	Planned	Outcome
Annual growth rates		
GDP real prices	2.0	0.2
Unemployment	9.8	8.6
Private consumption deflator	12.6	13.8
Compensation per employee	10.5	8.1
Per cent of GDP		
Current Account balance	-2.1	-1.7
General government net borrowing	8.6	14.2
Primary surplus	5.1	1.4
Public debt	107.5	111.8

Source for planned values: OECD Economic Survey of Greece, 1992–93, p. 49.

Source for outcomes: European Economy No. 64, Statistical Appendix.

the MTAP and the CP 1993–98 fell short of their projections, particularly in the field of fiscal consolidation but also in the field of inflation (see Table 2). The major overshooting of the fiscal targets in 1993 invalidated the CP and obliged the socialists, who took office in October 1993, to replace it with the RCP 1994–99. However, like the CP, the RCP fell short of its projections on many occasions, particularly in the field of prices and wages inflation but also in the areas of public consumption and budget deficit (see Table 3 overleaf).

Given that the progress achieved by the RCP was not enough to secure an EMU position for Greece in 1999, the authorities decided to intensify the convergence effort and pursue EMU participation by 2001. To that end, after the exchange rate crisis of November 1997, the Greek government decided to take the following steps:

(a) to join the ERM on 14 March, 1998. The price of ERM admission was the discontinuation of the strong drachma policy, that is, a 14 per cent discrete devaluation of the drachma vis-à-vis the ECU. At the same time, the BOG announced a 2 per cent inflation objective for 1999.[3] However, the BOG had already announced that the main target of monetary policy for the following two years (1999–2000) remained the maintenance of exchange rate stability against the post-devaluation central rate against the ECU and the euro after 1/1/1999.

(b) to introduce the Updated Revised Convergence Programme (URCP), aiming at a more active reduction in public expenditure, the speeding-up of the planned privatisations, promoting legislation aimed at a higher degree of labour market flexibility and a strict incomes policy in the public sector of the economy providing for salary increases which will not exceed a 2.5 per cent threshold over the next four years.

Greek Macroeconomic Policy in the 1990s: An Assessment

Fiscal Policy

Not surprisingly, one of the priorities of Greek policy makers in the 1990s was to achieve a reduction in public deficits and public debt whose high existing stock obliges the authorities to dedicate to its service a very significant amount of funds and maintain interest rates on public securities at high levels, making the meeting of the fiscal Maastricht criteria even more difficult.[4] As standard theory of public debt stabilisation suggests, in the presence of a non-zero growth rate for the economy, a reduction in the ratio of public debt to national income is conditional upon the realisation of primary surpluses or/and monetisation.[5] However, the latter option would certainly lead to inflationary outcomes, which would be incompatible with the requirements of the Maastricht Treaty. Furthermore, systematic monetisation of the debt would affect the economy's rate of growth and would hinder fiscal consolidation by means of (i) disturbing the operation of the price mechanism as a guide to the efficient allocation of sources; and (ii) putting pressure on interest rates which would suppress investment spending and increase the cost of servicing public debt.

Therefore, excluding monetary expansion as a means of financing public debt, the only available option is the creation of primary surpluses. These can be achieved by means of increasing public revenues or reducing public expenditure or a combination of both. In the early 1990s some economists (e.g. Katseli, 1990; Vaitsos, 1993) argued that the authorities should pursue primary surpluses through increased public revenue, that is, by means of

Table 3 The Revised Convergence Programme of Greece, 1994–99[a]

	1994	1995	1996	1997	1998	1999
GDP at constant prices	1.1	1.2	1.7	2.6	3.0	3.5
Outcome	*2.2*	*2.0*	*2.6*	*3.1*		
Private consumption	1.2	1.3	1.7	1.7	1.8	2.0
Outcome	*1.5*	*1.6*	*2.2*	*2.1*		
Public consumption	0.0	-0.5	-0.5	-0.5	-0.5	-0.5
Outcome[b]	*3.5*	*1.5*	*1.4*	*0.6*		
Private investment	2.5	0.9	3.5	6.8	8.4	10.1
Outcome[b]	*0.6*	*5.3*	*11.0*	*9.4*		
Public investment	6.0	8.0	9.5	11.0	12.0	14.0
Outcome[b]	*0.2*	*7.4*	*14.9*	*18.0*		
GDP deflator	10.7	8.0	6.3	4.0	3.6	3.3
Outcome	*10.1*	*9.3*	*8.9*	*6.7*		
Private consumption deflator	10.8	7.9	6.1	3.9	3.5	3.3
Outcome	*10.8*	*9.3*	*8.3*	*6.0*		
Real disposal private income	2.9	-1.1	-1.2	-0.7	1.4	2.5
Outcome[c]	*1.2*	*2.9*	*3.1*	*3.2*		
Real unit labour cost	0.5	-0.5	-0.5	-0.7	-0.8	-0.9
Outcome	*1.6*	*1.8*	*1.1*	*0.6*		
Change in the parity of drachma against the ECU	7.5	3.0	1.0	0.0	0.0	0.0
Outcome[d]	*7.2*	*4.0*	*0.5*	*0.0*		
Long-term interest rate	19.5	15.6	11.0	8.5	7.6	7.2
Outcome	*N/A*	*N/A*	*N/A*	*N/A*		
Outcome for average annual deposit rate[e]	*19.0*	*15.7*	*13.5*	*11.0*		
GDP deflator of EU members	3.0	2.9	2.7	2.6	2.6	2.6
Outcome	*2.6*	*2.9*	*2.6*	*1.9*		
GDP of EU member states at constant prices	1.2	2.0	3.0	3.4	3.6	3.6
Outcome	*2.9*	*2.4*	*1.6*	*2.4*		

	1994	1995	1996	1997	1998	1999
Long term interest rate of EU member states	6.9	6.8	6.7	6.4	6.4	6.4
Outcome	*8.2*	*8.6*	*7.3*	*6.5*		
Borrowing requirements of general government excluding interest payments (per cent of GDP)[f]	0.7	2.9	4.3	5.1	5.4	6.1
Outcome	*2.1*	*3.2*	*4.1*	*5.6*		
Interest payments on public debt (per cent of GDP)	13.9	13.6	11.9	9.3	7.8	7.0
Outcome	*14.2*	*12.4*	*11.5*	*10.5*		
General government debt (per cent of GDP)	112.1	115.2	115.3	113.4	109.3	103.4
Outcome	*110.4*	*111.8*	*111.8*	*108.3*		
Current account balance (per cent of GDP)	-2.9	-2.5	-2.2	-2.0	-1.8	-1.8
Outcome	*-1.0*	*-2.7*	*-3.5*	*-3.7*		
Unemployment (per cent of labour force)	10.1	10.4	10.2	9.7	8.9	7.9
Outcome	*8.9*	*9.1*	*9.0*	*8.9*		
Private sector's average propensity to save (per cent of disposal income)	22.1	20.2	17.9	15.9	15.6	16.0
Outcome (private gross saving, per cent of GDP at market prices)	*28.6*	*25.1*	*25.0*	*23.3*		

a *Source:* 'The Greek Economic Convergence Program', Bank of Greece, Economic Bulletin, November, 1994. *Source for outcomes:* European Economy No. 64, Statistical Appendix. Outcomes referring to 1997 represent provisional estimates.

b *Source:* Bank of Greece, Economic Bulletin No. 9 (March, 1997).

c Percentage change of real compensation per employee, total economy (CPI deflator).

d The Revised Convergence programme planned the accession of the Drachma to the ERM in 1996. This target was not met.

e *Source:* International Financial Statistics, Yearbook, 1997.

f Excluding revenue from privatisation.

curbing tax-evasion and imposing higher taxation on personal incomes and firms' profits. At first sight, it would appear that Greek governments in the first part of the 1990s adopted this strategy while a reduction in public consumption was not pursued very actively (in fact, Table 3 reveals that instead of the planned reduction in real public consumption, slight increases took place). However, it is not quite clear that such a strategy was a first-best choice.

Greece is not the only country which has faced the problem of public debt stabilisation. The existence of fiscal problems in a number of countries has encouraged the development of a growing empirical literature on this issue (among others see Manage and Marlow, 1986; Anderson et al., 1986; Ram, 1986, 1988; von Furstenberg et al., 1991; Hoover and Sheffrin, 1992). It is generally accepted that the selection of an appropriate fiscal strategy aiming to cope with fiscal problems crucially depends on the knowledge of the true causal relationship between public expenditure and public receipts.[6] Recent econometric evidence (see Katrakilidis, 1997; Arghyrou, 1998, 1999) suggests the existence of a long-run relationship between the two variables (that is, the existence of cointegration) and the existence of a causality pattern running from public receipts to public expenditure. In terms of evaluation of the fiscal policy followed in the first part of the 1990s, what is quite important is that the hypothesis of cointegration is not rejected. If that was the case, the implication would be that an increase in taxation would *definitely* lead to a reduction in deficit because public expenditure increases would not follow. *Only then* the policy of increasing tax revenues would be *unquestionably* effective. However, the existence of cointegration and the causality pattern mentioned above implies that increases in tax revenues are followed in time by increases in expenditure. Now, whether the deficit as *percentage of GDP* will decline as a result of an increase in taxation depends on three factors: (a) the elasticity of the response of public expenditure to changes in taxation revenue; (b) the initial level of the two variables; and (c) the rate of growth of GDP.

With regard to (a), if the estimated long-run elasticity of expenditure in changes of revenue were greater than one, the implication would be clear-cut: the deficit (both in terms of levels and percentage in GDP) would increase. For Greece, however, this does not seem to be the case: the existing econometric evidence (see Arghyrou, 1999) suggests a long-run elasticity coefficient ranging between 0.49 and 0.65. However, this is not enough to guarantee a reduction in deficit in the event of an increase in public receipts: if the initial level of expenditure is significantly higher than the one of receipts, a 10 per cent increase in receipts accompanied by a 7 per cent increase in expenditure may still give rise to an increase in the level of deficit. In that case, the deficit as a percentage of GDP could only decline if the rate of growth of GDP is sufficiently high. If it is not, the deficit could continue to increase *both in terms of levels and in terms of percentage in GDP* and, as a result, public debt will not be declining.[7] The case of Greece seems to be consistent with this scenario. The country entered the 1990s with a level of public receipts considerably lower than the one of public expenditure, while GDP growth in the early 1990s was very modest, in the range of 1.5–2.0 per cent. As a result, despite increasing revenues, public debt continued to increase. Therefore, it would appear that the convergence programmes implemented in the 1990s did not achieve enough fiscal progress because they placed too little emphasis on reducing public expenditure and, in particular, public consumption. The recent movements of pubic debt provides further evidence in favour of this view. In the early 1990s, the latter continued to increase. After 1995, when a more determined effort to control public expenditure was undertaken, public debt stopped increasing and has even displayed a modest decline (see Figure 1). To that

Figure 1 Public Debt (per cent of GDP)

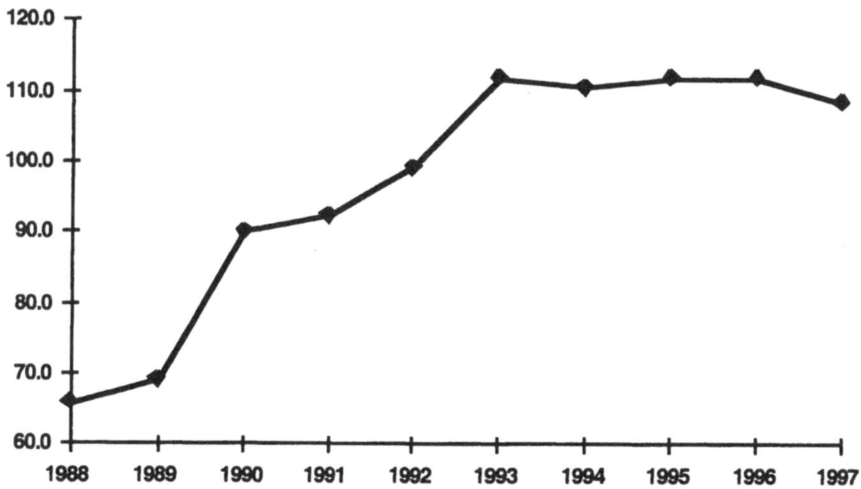

Source: European Economy No. 64, Statistical Appendix.

end, the reduction in interest rates which started in 1995 together with the increase in the rate of growth of GDP (see Table 3) certainly played a positive role.

Monetary/Exchange Rate Policy

As argued in the second section of this chapter, in the 1990s a reduction in Greek inflation was mainly pursued by means of the strong drachma policy.[8] A strong currency policy aims to reduce inflation by means of the following three channels: (a) by reducing the prices of imported and domestic final goods made of imported raw materials; (b) by reducing the prices of the products of the traded sector of the economy. Firms exposed to international competition cannot rely on competitiveness-inducing exchange rate policies, rather they are expected to restraint their own costs and increase their production efficiency; and (c) by operating as a *nominal anchor* for the economy and, as a result, reducing inflationary expectations (see Giavazzi and Pagano, 1988).

The choice to introduce a strong currency policy in the late 1980s was not surprising. 1988–90 was a period of particularly strong fiscal expansion and political uncertainty which aggravated the already mounting imbalances of the Greek economy and led to a substantial increase in inflation in 1990–91. Under such circumstances, the Greek authorities had to adopt a nominal anchor which would be easily understood by the general public and whose movements would be easily observed by agents so that the appropriate signals with regards to the shift in the authorities' preferences would be quickly recognised and inflation expectations would be rapidly stabilised. Without any doubt, the strong drachma has indeed contributed to a reduction in the rate of growth of prices: as Figure 2 suggests, CPI inflation in 1997 went down to 6 per cent compared with 14 per cent in 1988 and almost 20 per cent in 1991. This reduction allowed fiscal authorities to reduce the Treasury Bill rate and, as a result, reduce interest payments on public debt.

However, the improvement mentioned above has come at a cost and this is an issue which, until recently, had not been adequately addressed in Greece. The point is that as economic theory suggests, by its very nature, a strong currency policy has certain limits which in the case of Greece had become increasingly evident and were indicating that eventually, it would not be possible to avoid a devaluation of the drachma, despite the fact that

Figure 2 Annual CPI inflation, Inflation Differential against the EU and Nominal Depreciation against the ECU

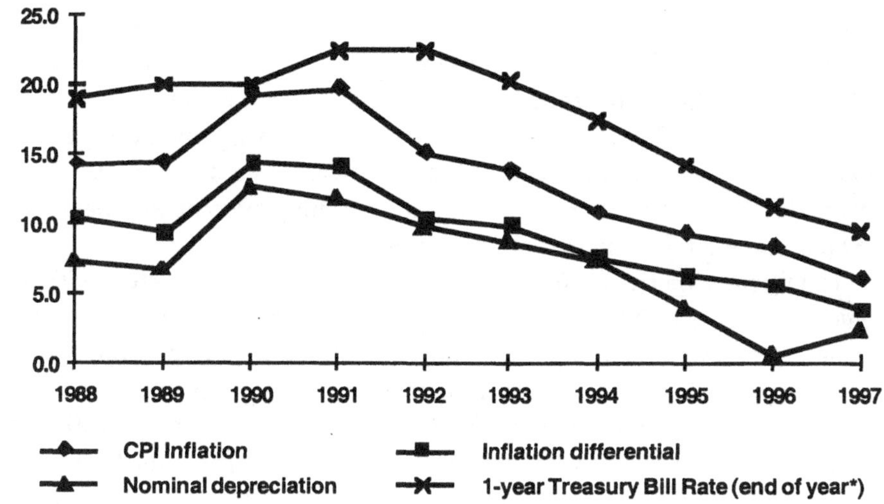

* *Note:* 1-year Treasury Bill Rate in September, 1997.

Source: European Economy No. 64, Statistical Appendix and Bank of Greece, Economic Bulletin, various editions.

before 1997 the BOG had managed to beat speculators on four occasions of exchange rate turbulence.[9] Space limitations do not allow a thorough discussion of this issue. However, it is important to mention that an exchange rate pegging regime lacks credibility in the face of substantial structural, inflation, and productivity differences among the countries participating in the system (see De Grauwe, 1996 and Persson and Tabellini, 1996). Under such circumstances, a high-inflation, low-productivity country can sustain an exchange rate peg to the currency of a low-inflation country only by means of maintaining a significant nominal and real interest rate differential. However, in the absence of structural adjustments aiming to reduce distortions in the goods and labour market and without a disciplined incomes policy and a bold attempt to address fiscal imbalances, a strong currency policy, if held for too long, leads to currency overvaluation which damages the international competitiveness of the economy, puts pressure on the current account and attracts short-term portfolio inflows. By increasing liquidity, such inflows tend to jeopardise the anti-inflationary character of monetary policy while, at the same time, making the country vulnerable to speculative attacks. Furthermore, the high levels of nominal and real interest rates which are necessary in order to sustain a strong currency policy put pressure on the cost of servicing the public debt, thus making fiscal consolidation even more difficult. In other words, the exchange rate makes sense as a nominal anchor in the medium-term, but as historic experience (e.g. the EMS crisis of 1992–93, the exchange rate crises in Spain, Portugal and Mexico in 1995 and, more recently, the south-east Asia crisis in 1997) has shown, if the peg is maintained for too long, it may become *self-defeating* and could create real dangers to the economy.

The Greek experience in 1997 and 1998 seems to be consistent with the scenario described above. It would appear that Greece did not take full advantage of the breathing space provided by the ten-year old strong drachma policy. The fight against inflation was not accompanied by a very disciplined incomes policy as, with the exception of the period 1991–93, nominal wage increases systematically exceeded CPI inflation (see Table 3). In addition, there was no substantial improvement in terms of promoting competition in the goods and labour market, something which is also evident by the downwards rigidity which inflation has exhibited during the period 1994–97, despite increasing exchange rate stability. One might say that in the face of the reaction of the too powerful trade unions of the public sector, both parties which ruled Greece in the 1990s seemed to be very reluctant in promoting the promised, and necessary, privatisations of a number of loss-making, debt-accumulating stated-owned firms. The strong drachma policy led to currency overvalution (see Arghyrou, 2000) which, consequently, put pressure on the current account and contributed to significant short-term capital inflows. These created extra difficulties to the BOG as the latter was pursuing two intermediate targets (exchange rate stability and limited money supply growth) using one policy instrument (interest rates).[10] The dangers involved in a policy mix where exchange rate policy had been given a role beyond its potential that would finally lead to a forced devaluation had been suggested in due course (see e.g. Mourmouras, 1997a and Mourmouras and Arghyrou, 1997). The crisis of October–November, 1997 and the drachma devaluation of March, 1998 confirmed those predictions. The November 1997 crisis clearly showed that in view of the limited progress in the field of fiscal and structural adjustment achieved by Greece in the 1990s, the markets had lost confidence in the pre-March 1998

Figure 3 Drachmas per ECU: Spot and 1-year Forward Exchange Rates

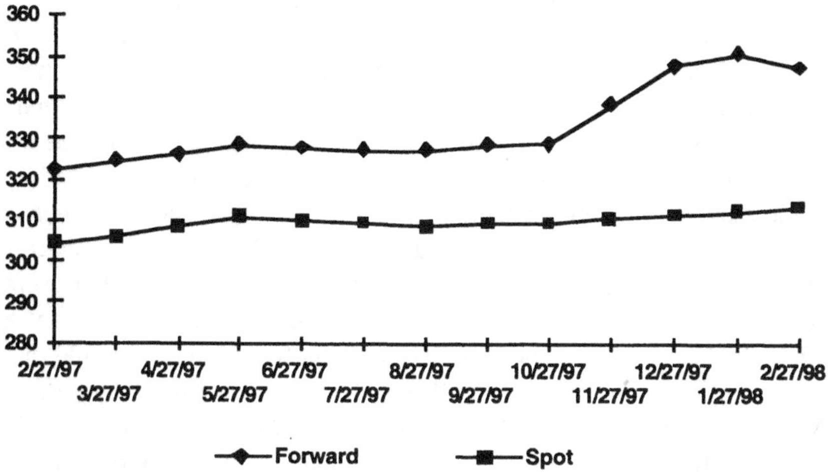

Source: Datastream.

exchange rate of the drachma vis-à-vis the ECU. Further evidence in favour of this view is provided by Figure 3 which presents the movements of the spot and 1-year forward drachma/ECU exchange rate. Even before the crisis, the 1-year forward rate was in the range of 320 drachmas per ECU, as opposed to an approximately 300 drachmas per ECU spot rate. This 6.5 per cent difference can be interpreted as a risk premium demanded by market participants to commit themselves to future drachma holdings, suggesting that even before October 1997 the future stability of the drachma against the ECU was not unquestionable. However, after the crisis of October 1997, the 1-year forward rate increased substantially, reaching the level of 347 drachmas per ECU in February 1997, that is 15 per cent higher than the corresponding spot rate. This suggests that after the crisis of October 1997 the markets completely lost confidence in the commitment of the Greek authorities to maintain an exchange rate against the ECU in the range of 300 drachmas per ECU. That would imply further increases in interest rates without guaranteeing that a forced devaluation would be avoided in the event of a new exchange rate crisis.[11]

It would appear that the realisation of these rather unfavourable markets' perceptions prompted (or rather obliged) the Greek authorities to proceed to a drachma devaluation and ERM accession in March 1998. Both choices do not seem to have been part of the authorities' immediate intentions. This view is based on a number of government official statements which took place before and after the November 1997 crisis but also on the argument that if the authorities had indeed decided to proceed to a devaluation of the drachma long ago, there was no reason to defend the national currency in such a determined way as they did in November 1997. If that was indeed the case, there is little doubt that the BOG would have let the drachma float during the crisis. The reason is that the cost of defending the national currency at that particular point in time, expressed by higher interest payments on public debt and a partial loss of the authorities' credibility (caused by the discontinuation of the strong drachma policy after so many official statements expressing the authorities' commitment to it) seems to be much higher compared to the benefits resulting from four additional months of exchange rate stability. All in all, the devaluation of the Greek drachma in March 1998 was the result of the limits of a policy mix which had succeeded in achieving stabilisation but had reached a point where its potential had been exhausted.

Greek Macroeconomic Policy on the Road to the Single Currency: The Way Forward

Fiscal Strategy

As argued earlier, the Greek government announced its intention to pursue a more active reduction in public consumption and the promotion of privatisation. Given the econometric findings mentioned earlier, I fully endorse this announcement. In addition, there is a number of further reasons making a case for a reduction in public consumption. These include the following:

(a) if Greece is to achieve real convergence with the rest of the EU countries by means of higher growth rates, the primary target of economic policy should be the stabilisation of the economy along with the creation of conditions for the attraction of foreign direct investment and for a higher amount of domestic sources to be directed to investment purposes. Increasing corporate taxes is not the best way to achieve this goal. In relation to this, Alesina and Perotti, (1995, 1996) suggest that successful fiscal consolidation programmes are characterised by public expenditure cuts and not by tax increases. The latter policy appears not only to be ineffective in reducing the deficit but also contractionary with regard to GDP growth.

(b) Alogoskoufis and Christodoulakis (1991) have formally shown that stabilisation through an increase in public revenues would result in the stabilisation of the external debt at a level higher than the one which would be achieved if primary surpluses were pursued through expenditure cuts.

(c) If Greece is to join EMU in the foreseeable future, it should observe the rather strict provisions of the recently signed Budget Stability Pact (EMU countries should run public deficits less than 3 per cent of GDP). Obviously, this will not be possible only by means of increasing existing taxes and imposing new ones, many of which (according to Greece's own government) are of a temporary nature (such as the system of objective taxation criteria).

(d) Finally, one should not underestimate the practical difficulties associated with an increase in public revenue: Greece is a country characterised by widespread tax evasion and in spite of all past efforts to reduce it, it seems that so far, the problem has not been tackled in an effective way.[12]

Monetary/Exchange Rate Strategy

As argued earlier, the BOG already announced a 2 per cent inflation objective for 1999. The monetary strategy through which this objective will be pursued involves exchange rate stability against the ECU (the euro after 1999) around the post-devaluation central parity (354 drachmas per euro). The drachma is to participate in the ERM (the ERM–II after 1999) until the accession of Greece to EMU in 2001 with a 15 per cent formal band of allowed fluctuation. However, according to the announcements of the BOG, the effective band of fluctuation will be restricted to 2 per cent.

Given the existing inflation differential between Greece and the EU average the above can be interpreted as a maintenance of the exchange rate nominal anchor (that is a continuation of the strong drachma policy), albeit around a new reference point (the post-devaluation level of the exchange rate). However, it is not clear to us that the participation of the drachma in the ERM with a 2 per cent effective band of fluctuation will be immune to exchange rate turbulence.[13] The crux of the argument is that given the prolonged character of the strong drachma policy and the uncertainty regarding the drachma overvaluation it had caused (i.e. the well known uncertainty regarding the definition of the exact level of the equilibrium exchange rate), it is very difficult to suggest with certainty that the recent realignment was enough to restore the drachma at its long-run equilibrium. In other words, given that the cumulative overvaluation of the drachma against the ECU during the period 1988–97 appears to be above 20 per cent (see Figure 2), how can one can guarantee that 357 drachmas per ECU is the drachma's equilibrium exchange rate?[14] If this is not the case, the problems discussed earlier will continue to exist and a second forced devaluation of the drachma may not be out of the question. Historic experience from the rest of the countries of *club-Med*, that is Italy, Portugal and Spain seem to confirm this view.[15]

Having such an experience, I cannot see why one should exclude completely the possibility that history will repeat itself in the case of Greece, a country where, after all, despite the progress achieved in the 1990s, fiscal imbalances are more pronounced and structural adjustments in the 1990s have been pursued in a more gradual way than in Portugal and Spain (see Table 1). Finally, one should also mention that the consequences of any possible overvaluation will be more pronounced in the future because (a) participation in the ERM has increased the degree of international exposure of the Greek national currency; and (b) the euro may well follow an appreciating pattern after 1999.[16] Given the productivity differences existing between Greece and the hard core of EMU, under such circumstances, the shadowing of the euro will result in extra pressure on the real exchange rate and the current account, similar to the one of 1983–84 which followed the drachma's attempt to shadow the then appreciating US dollar and resulted to the drachma's devaluation in 1985. In brief, it is not clear to us that the commitment of the Greek authorities to retain exchange rate stability until the accession of Greece to EMU is going in the right direction. By saying this, I do not imply that the drachma will definitely be subject to speculative attacks during the run-up to the euro. But I do imply that the economic theory suggests, and historic experience confirms, that this is a possibility which cannot be excluded. By formally committing itself to a 2 per cent band of fluctuation the BOG, for credibility reasons, is taking a considerable risk. In this context, the role of the other economic authority of the country, the government, is critical. The government should follow fiscal and incomes policy consistent with the 2 per cent inflation objective for 1999. It should also proceed without delay to the implementation of all the announced measures aiming to achieve the real convergence of the Greek economy to those of the hard-core of the EMU (privatisations, promotion of legislation aiming at more flexible goods and labour markets, bold, although unpopular, changes in the pension and social insurance system of the country, completion of the big infrastructure projects etc.). If the government fails to achieve the above, there exists the risk that the markets will form the impression that the fundamentals of the Greek economy are not improving fast enough to support the current exchange rate. Under such circumstances, the drachma may experience pressures like those of November 1997 and, in that case, a new forced devaluation of the Greek national currency may follow.

Of course, two powerful objections against this view, are the following: (a) as the Maastricht Treaty refers to exchange rate stability as one of the nominal convergence criteria, the BOG had no other option than to commit itself to exchange rate stability; and (b) a new realignment could generate expectations about a resumption of a crawling peg policy, similar to the one employed during the 1974–87 period (when monetary policy in Greece was a rather passive exercise meant to accommodate increasing public deficits); and the adoption of a wide band of fluctuation might intensify such expectations because it would deprive the economy of its exchange rate nominal anchor.

However, it is not clear to us that such criticism would be valid. As far as the first point above is concerned, one should not forget that there is still some confusion with regard to the interpretation of the exchange rate criterion, which may, after all, not be taken into consideration.[17] But even if the criterion is to be taken into consideration, it makes reference to exchange rate stability for a period of two years. Greece, however, will not join the EMU before 2001, which implies that the BOG retains maximum degrees of freedom in the field of exchange rate policy for more than one year and a half.

With regard to the second point, indeed, given the 'inflation culture' which has been developed in Greece during the last twenty years, one cannot ignore the dangers described by (b) above. However, there are two important differences between the policy mix which was employed between 1974 and 1987 and the policy mix which is proposed here. The first one is that during the 1974–87 period, fiscal policy was expansionary whereas in the policy framework suggested here it should not be so. The second refers to the new monetary framework which has been established in Greece after the announcement of a specific inflation objective for 1999 and the upgrading of the role of the Bank of Greece, that is the granting of independence to the monetary authority, in December 1997. The announcement of a 2 per cent specific quantitative inflation objective for 1999 sends a clear signal with regard to the policy intentions of the monetary authority. As a result, in the face of its introduction, the abolition of the formal commitment to a narrow band of fluctuation will not deprive the economy of a nominal anchor. However, for the recently introduced inflation objective to operate as such, it must represent a credible policy commitment. This is where Central Bank Independence (CBI) may operate as a useful, credibility-inducing, external policy constraint as suggested by the seminal paper by Rogoff (1985), and in the context of Greece, by Mourmouras (1994, 1997a) and Mourmouras and Arghyrou (2000).[18]

In Mourmouras and Arghyrou (2000) we present a full proposal for a new monetary policy framework in Greece and we argue that the problems associated with the presently implemented exchange-rate targeting monetary policy could be addressed by means of granting the BOG full political and economic independence and upgrading the recently announced inflation objective to a credible policy commitment through the introduction of formal *inflation targets*.[19] One of the main attractions of such a monetary framework, originally proposed by the seminal papers by Svensson (1997a and 1997b), is that inflation targets are a superior nominal anchor to intermediate monetary targets as they are unambiguous and better understood by the public. Furthermore, they provide an independent Central Bank 'constraint discretion' which might be useful in terms of coping with non-anticipated disturbances and a better incentive structure to achieve price stability because, by establishing a more open and transparent framework of monetary policy, they allow all agents to see what the Central Bank attempts to do and how it pursues its objectives (see Bernanke and Miskin, 1997). Finally, the introduction of inflation targets reduces the possibility of speculative attacks because under such a monetary framework, the level of the exchange rate does not constitute the intermediate target of monetary policy but assumes the status of a monetary instrument, along with other instruments which the Central Bank has at its disposal to meet the inflation target. From that point of view, the Central Bank is not bound to defend the national currency when the latter is under pressure and, as a result, speculation profits emerging from obliging the Central Bank to proceed to an unwanted devaluation (like the one of the sterling pound on 'Black Wednesday' in October, 1992) are not possible. In terms of inflation performance, the experience from the countries which have adopted inflation targets is rather impressive. Furthermore, some of them (i.e. Finland, Sweden and the United Kingdom) have managed to meet the inflation criterion set by the Maastricht Treaty, showing that an exchange rate arrangement like the ERM is not a one-way road for the meeting of the requirement.

The replacement of the exchange rate nominal anchor with an inflation target anchor may well suit the economic interests of Greece and the rest of the EMU Outs better than an exchange-rate pegging regime (see also Arghyrou and Mourmouras, 1998). Given that core inflation in Greece is mainly structural (in the sense that it is due to high budget deficits and inefficiencies in the labour and goods markets) a medium-term convergence programme that aims to remove such inefficiencies combined with a monetary programme involving higher than the EU average but gradually converging to it inflation targets could prove more effective than the nominal anchor of the ERM–II. Perhaps more importantly, it would allow the BOG to retain its valuable (in terms of stabilising inflationary expectations) formal commitment to future price stability without having to stick to the highly risky strategy of supporting the present level of the exchange rate. If exchange rate stability remains the point of attention for monetary policy in Greece, a second forced devaluation (whose probability cannot be ruled out) might be enough to destroy Greece's bid for EMU in 2001. We fail to see the reason why Greece has to choose this risky way to the single currency when another one is available. We also believe that a convergence plan involving inflation targets would be less painful in terms of output loss, firstly because of its gradual character and secondly because of the restoration of the competitiveness through the adjustment of the nominal exchange rate which would help the 'ailing' external sector of the economy.

Concluding Remarks

This chapter has examined the course of Greek macroeconomic policy in the 1990s and Greece's future prospects on the road to EMU participation. The two main messages emerging from our analysis are the following:

(a) despite the progress achieved by the three convergence programmes implemented after 1990, Greece did not manage to qualify for the EMU in 1999 because it followed a policy of limited potential which could not compensate for the lack of determination to undertake the political cost necessary to modernise the public sector and promote the long overdue structural adjustments in the supply side of the Greek economy.

(b) Greece's chances to join the EMU in 2001 may increase if the authorities accompany their correct decision to proceed to a reduction in public consumption and promote structural adjustment with a decision to abandon the highly risky exchange-rate pegging monetary framework and replace it with one involving formal inflation-targets.

Above all, and this is our final argument, it should be kept in mind that the Greek economy suffers from serious macroeconomic imbalances and structural weaknesses whose correction necessitate bold (and politically costly) decisions. The highly popular prospect of EMU in the foreseeable future provides the Greek authorities a first-class opportunity to proceed to the necessary steps with the minimum possible social reaction.

Notes

1. See Papademos (1990), Larre and Torres (1991), Halikias (1993, 1996), Tsoukalis (1993), Christodoulakis (1994) and Alogoskoufis (1995).
2. See e.g. European Economy, Annual Economic Report and the OECD Surveys of Greece for years 1996 and 1997.
3. See Bank of Greece, Monetary Programme, 1998.
4. A high stock of public debt contributes to the maintenance of high interest rates in a number of ways, including the following: (a) the government has to attract a large amount of domestic and foreign savings in order to cover the high level of interest payments (b) a highly indebted country has a motive to engineer a high level of inflation (i.e. impose the well-known inflation tax) in order to eliminate part of its debt. Inflation can be seen as a form of taxation in the following sense: interest payments on public bonds are usually denominated in non-indexed nominal terms. Therefore, as inflation erodes the purchasing power of money, it also reduces the real value of future nominal interest payments and results in a reduced real debt stock. The government also has the motivation to proceed to a devaluation of its national currency in order to reduce its external debt (provided that a substantial part of the latter is denominated in terms of national currency). Under such circumstances, interest rates on public securities should include a risk premium to compensate for the perceived inflation/devaluation risk (c) in the same spirit, interest rates should include a risk premium to compensate for the perceived small but existent risk of national default.
5. Monetary stabilisation of public debt works through two interrelated channels. Firstly seignorage, i.e. the increase in nominal money stock which allows the authorities to

finance part of the recorded deficits without adding to the existing stock of public bonds. Secondly the inflation tax, which follows the initial increase in nominal money (see above).

6. Evidence of one-way causality from tax receipts to spending would suggest that tax increases result in higher spending levels and possibly to larger deficits. Therefore, an increase in taxation would have an ambiguous impact on the deficit. Evidence of no significant causal relation would suggest that tax increases do not lead to higher spending or deficit growth, therefore the government can safely proceed to the imposition of new taxation. Evidence of two-way causality would suggest that one could not reject the hypothesis that higher spending levels result from higher revenue levels and would complicate the results for inference purposes. Finally, evidence of one-way causality from government consumption to tax receipts would imply that the dual aim to control the deficit and limit the role of the state in economic life should primarily be pursued by means of reducing public expenditure.
7. Perhaps a numerical example could make this point more clear. In 1995, total public expenditure in Greece was equal to 12.633 trillion drachmas. Total public revenue was equal to 6.753 tr. drachmas. The deficit was equal to 5.883 tr. drachmas (see Bank of Greece, Monthly Statistical Bulletin, December, 1997, p. 55). Without loss of generality, let us assume that 1995 is the base year of our analysis, therefore these figures represent both nominal and real values. Let us now assume a 10 per cent increase in revenue, followed by a 6.5 per cent increase in expenditure. That would result in expenditure equal to 13.475 tr., revenue equal to 7.428 tr. and deficit equal to 6.047. The level of the deficit would then increase by 2.8 per cent. If the rate of growth of GDP is less than 2.8 per cent, this implies that the deficit *as a percentage of GDP* will also increase. It might be of interest to mention that in 1995 the rate of growth of GDP in Greece was 2 per cent.
8. Of course, the fiscal tightening which took place in the 1990s, together with the improvement of long-term inflation expectations (as reflected by the reduction in long-term interest rates), must have made a positive contribution towards reducing actual Greek inflation. However, I cannot say the same with regard to fiscal policy: during the period 1994–97 increases in nominal wages in Greece were consistently higher than the level of the inflation rate.
9. The two EMS crises in 1992–93, the exchange rate crisis which followed the full liberilisation of capital movements in May, 1994 and the European monetary upheavals of March, 1995.
10. Just before the October 1997 exchange rate crisis the foreign exchange reserves of the BOG were equal to 17.9 billion US Dollars compared to 3 billion US Dollars in December, 1990. Brissimis and Gibson (1997) have estimated that over the period 1991–95 the BOG managed to sterilise 65 per cent of total capital inflows.
11. In order to beat the speculators during the crisis of October 1997 the BOG increased its intervention rate to 150 per cent compared to an 11 per cent intervention rate in September, 1997. This obliged the Treasury to increase the interest rates on public securities by almost two percentage points (from 9.5 per cent in September, 1997 to 11.3 per cent in October, 1997), something which implies that in 1998 interest payments on public debt will be significantly higher than previously anticipated. Finally, in an effort to support the parity of the drachma the BOG proceeded to intervention in the foreign exchange market. As a result, the Bank lost a third of its foreign exchange reserves. On 7/11/97, i.e. at the end of the crisis, the foreign exchange reserves of the Bank were down to approximately 10.5 billion.
12. The underground economy is currently estimated to represent a figure above 30 per cent of Greek GDP (see Pavlopoulos, 1987; Kanellopoulos, 1992).
13. A thorough discussion of the difficulties associated with a narrow band of fluctuation can

be found in Kenen (1995).

14. For every year, the drachma's overvaluation is defined as the difference between the nominal depreciation of the drachma against the ECU and the inflation differential existing between Greece and the EU average.
15. Like Greece in 1997–98, Italy, Portugal and Spain had achieved a certain degree of inflation convergence with Germany before 1992. However, all three countries experienced *forced* devaluations within the ERM in 1992–93. Furthermore, Spain and Portugal, despite three discrete devaluations in 1992–93 (of a cumulative order of 19 per cent and 12 per cent respectively), had to proceed to a further 7 per cent (forced) devaluation two years later, i.e. in 1995.
16. This prediction is based on a number of arguments including the view that the European Central Bank which will undertake the conduct of monetary policy in the EMU on 1 January, 1999 will follow a rather tight monetary policy in order to establish quickly its anti-inflation credentials.
17. The Maastricht Treaty mentions that EMU participation implies exchange rate stability defined as the fluctuation of the exchange parity within the 'normal' band of fluctuation without, however, defining quantitatively what is meant by the word 'normal'. This has given rise to voices which claim that a legal case can be made against the view that exchange rate stability implies a 2.25 per cent fluctuation against the central rate (see e.g. National Institute Economic Review, October, 1996, p. 68 and p. 76).
18. See also Lohmann (1992), Alesina and Gati (1995) and Walsh (1995). For an excellent review of the literature on Central Bank Independence see Mourmouras (1997b).
19. Political (or goal) independence is the ability of the Central Bank to define, without interventions from the government, the goals of monetary policy; economic (or instrument) independence, which is the ability of the Central Bank to choose the instruments of monetary policy to achieve the targets of monetary policy.

References

Alesina A. and Gatti R. (1995), 'Independent Central Banks: Low Inflation at No Cost?', *American Economic Review Papers and Proceedings*, Vol. 85, pp. 196–200.

Alesina A. and Perotti R. (1995), 'Fiscal Expansions and Adjustments in OECD Countries', *Economic Policy*, Vol. 20, pp. 207–48.

Alesina A. and Perotti R. (1996), *Fiscal Adjustments in OECD Countries: Composition and Macroeconomic Effects*, NBER Working Paper, No. 5730, Cambridge, Massachusetts: National Bureau of Economic Research.

Alogoskoufis G. (1995), 'The two faces of Janus: Institutions, Policy Regimes and Macroeconomic Performance in Greece', *Economic Policy*, Vol. 20, pp. 149–92.

Alogoskoufis G. and Christodoulakis N. (1991), 'Fiscal deficits, seigniorage and external debt: the case of Greece', in Alogoskoufis G., Papademos L. and Portes R. (eds), *External Constraints on Macroeconomic Policy: the European Experience*, Cambridge: Cambridge University Press.

Anderson W., Wallace M. and Warner J. (1986), 'Government Spending and Taxation: What Causes What?', *Southern Economic Journal*, Vol. 52, pp. 630–39.

Arghyrou M.G. (2000), 'Strong-currency policy and long-run PPP: the drachma devaluation of 1998', mimeo, Department of Economics and Finance, Brunel University.

Arghyrou M.G. (1999), *Fiscal Strategy and Public Debt Reduction: The Greek Experience in the 1990s*, Department of Economics and Finance, Brunel University, Discussion

Paper 99–12.
Arghyrou M.G. (1998), 'Causal relationships between public expenditure, public receipts and Gross Domestic Product: Greece 1965–1995', *Applied Economics Letters*, Vol. 5, 11, pp. 727–31.
Arghyrou M.G. and Mourmouras I.A. (1999): 'The EMU INS, the EMU OUTS and the European Central Bank', in Beber M. and Kinsella R. (eds), *A Central Bank for Europe: The role of the European Central Bank in the creation and consolidation of EMU*, London: The Lothian Foundation.
Bernanke B. and Mishkin F. (1997), *Inflation Targeting: a new framework for monetary policy?*, NBER Working Paper, No. 5893, Cambridge, Massachusetts: National Bureau of Economic Research.
Brissimis S. and Gibson H. (1996), 'Monetary Policy, Capital Flows and Greek Disinflation', *Bank of Greece, Economic Bulletin,* No. 9, pp. 21–38.
Christodoulakis N. (1994), 'Fiscal developments in Greece, 1980–93', *European Economy*, No. 3/1994, pp. 99–134.
De Grauwe P. (1996), *Inflation Targeting to Achieve Inflation Convergence in the Transition Towards EMU*, CEPR Discussion Paper, No. 1457, London: Center for Economic Policy Research.
Giavazzi F. and Pagano M. (1988), 'The Advantage of Tying One's Hands. EMS Discipline and Central Bank Credibility', *European Economic Review*, Vol. 32, pp. 1055–75.
Giavazzi F. and Spaventa L. (1990), 'The New EMS', in De Grauwe P. and Papademos L. (eds), *The European Monetary System in the 1990s*, London: Longman.
Halikias D. (1993), 'Economic Stabilization and Growth: The Case of Greece', Greek *Economic Review*, Vol. 15, pp. 97–136.
Halikias D. (1996), 'The way to the European Monetary Union', *Epikaira Themata*, Series No. 11, Athens: Foundation of Economic and Industrial Studies (IOVE) [in Greek].
Hoover K. and Stephen S. (1992), 'Causation, Spending and Taxes: Sand in the Box or Tax Collector for the Welfare State', *American Economic Review*, Vol. 82, pp. 225–48.
Kanellopoulos C. (1992), 'The Underground Economy in Greece: What Official Data Show', *Greek Economic Review*, Vol. 14, pp. 215–36.
Katrakilidis C.P. (1997), 'Spending and revenues in Greece: new evidence from error correction modelling', *Applied Economics Letters*, Vol. 4, pp. 387–91.
Katseli L. (1990), 'Structural Adjustment of the Greek Economy', in C. Bliss and J.B. de Macedo (eds), *In Unity with Diversity in the European Economy: The Community's Southern Frontier*, Cambridge: Cambridge University Press.
Kenen P. (1995), *Economic and Monetary Union in Europe*, Cambridge: Cambridge University Press.
Larre B. and Torres R. (1991), 'Is convergence a spontaneous process? The experience of Spain, Portugal and Greece', *OECD Economic Studies*, No 16, pp. 169–98.
Lochmann S. (1992), 'Optimal Commitment in Monetary Policy: Credibility versus Flexibility' *American Economic Review*, Vol. 82, pp. 273–86.
Manage N. and Marlow M. (1986), 'The Causal Relation between Federal Expenditures and Receipts', *Southern Economic Journal*, Vol. 52, pp. 617–29.
Mourmouras I. A. (1994), *Why the Greek Government must grant political and economic independence to the Central Bank of Greece*, University of London, Queen Mary and Westfield College, Discussion Paper No. 320.
Mourmouras I.A. (1997a), *Central Bank Independence: A Review of the Theories*, Department of Economics, University of London, Queen Mary and Westfield College, Discussion Paper No. 360.
Mourmouras I.A. (1997b), *The Drachma and the ERM-2*, Athens: Kyriakatiki Kathemerini, February [in Greek].

Mourmouras I.A. and Arghyrou M.G. (1997), '*Greece and the European Union: An Explorative Essay*', Department of Economics, Queen Mary and Westfield College, Discussion Paper No. 362.

Mourmouras I.A. and Arghyrou M.G. (2000), 'Monetary Policy at the European Periphery: Greek Experience and Lessons for EU Candidates', *The European and Transatlantic Studies Series*, New York: Springer-Verlag.

Papademos L. (1990), 'Greece and the EMS: Issues, prospects and a framework for analysis' in De Grauwe P. and Papademos L. (eds), *The European Monetary System in the 1990s*, London: Longman.

Pavlopoulos P. (1987), *The Underground Economy in Greece*, Athens: Institute of Economic and Industrial Studies (IOBE) [in Greek].

Persson T. and Tabellini G. (1996), *Monetary Cohabitation in Europe*, NBER Working Paper No. 5532, Cambridge, Massachussetts: National Bureau of Economic Research.

Ram R. (1986), 'Causality between income and government expenditure: a broad international perspective', *Public Finance*, Vol. 1, pp. 393–413.

Ram R. (1988), 'Additional Evidence On Causality Between Government Revenue and Government Expenditure', *Southern Economic Journal*, Vol. 54, pp. 763–69.

Svensson L.E.O. (1997a), 'Optimal Inflation Targets, 'Conservative' Central Banks and Linear Inflation Contracts', *American Economic Review*, Vol. 87, pp. 98–114.

Svensson L.E.O. (1997b), 'Inflation forecast targeting: Implementing and monitoring inflation targets', *European Economic Review*, Vol. 41, pp. 1111–46.

Tsoukalis L. (1993), 'Country profiles: Greece', in *The New European Economy: The politics and Economics of Integration,* second edition, Oxford: Oxford University Press, pp. 253–57.

Vaitsos K. (1993), 'Central Axis of economic policy for an exit from the crisis', in Giannitsis A. (ed), *Macroeconomic management and the development deadlock*, Athens: Gutenberg, [in Greek] pp. 153–75.

Von Furstenberg G.M., Green J. and Jeong J.H. (1986), 'Tax and spend or spend and tax?', *The Review of Economics and Statistics,* Vol. 68, pp. 179–88.

Walsh C. (1995), 'Optimal Contracts for Central Bankers', *American Economic Review*, Vol. 85, pp. 150–67.

PART III
STATE MODERNISATION AND ADJUSTMENT

9 Greece and The European Union after Amsterdam

DIMITRIS N. CHRYSSOCHOOU, STELIOS STAVRIDIS AND ANDREAS MOSCHONAS

Introduction

The new Treaty of Amsterdam (AMT) which resulted from the 1996/7 Intergovernmental Conference (IGC) and is upgrading the Treaty on European Union (TEU) or Maastricht Treaty has now been signed (October 1997) and has been ratified (1st May 1999). This chapter aims to assess the latest treaty reforms both in their own merit and in relation to the Greek political scene.[1] In particular, the first section presents the main developments of the new treaty. The second considers the political debate in Greece prior to and following the 1996–97 IGC, while the final section looks at which of Greece's objectives have been fulfilled by the AMT.

As European Union (EU) member states remain the key actors in any treaty reform, it is important to focus on a specific case study for it offers not only insight in EU politics and policy making, but more importantly in the domestic politics of a member state. The Greek case in the 1996/7 IGC and the ensuing treaty are particularly relevant as Greece was especially concerned with possible reforms to the TEU in view of important internal and external challenges. Hence Greece's particular interest in reforming the Second Pillar of the TEU (Common Foreign and Security Policy), the future role of the Western European Union (WEU), and, by implication, that of the North Atlantic Treaty Organisation (NATO), as well as the implications of future enlargements to the East but also to the South (in particular Cyprus and Turkey).[2]

The State of Integration

The EU After Maastricht

The outcome of the 1996/7 IGC was a moderate step towards 'ever closer union'. Building on the TEU, the AMT preserves the three-pillar structure of the EU and with it the existence of two separate legal mechanisms: the Community Method based on the Commission's right of initiative and varying forms of the European Parliament's (EP) involvement in EU decision making; and the Intergovernmental Method based on the dominant role of the Council of Ministers, with the European Council providing for the EU's general direction.

As *The Economist* put it, the 1997 Amsterdam Summit 'produced more of a mouse than a mountain' (21 June 1997, p. 37). Arguably, as long as EU constitutional change is controlled by a management coalition of states, the prospects for substantive institutional reforms will remain particularly moderate. For the experience of EU treaty reform since the mid-1980s has shown that the proposals submitted to the various IGCs by the Commission and the EP are by far more advanced in terms of upgrading the level, rather than merely the scope of integration, than those submitted by individual states. It is also unclear whether these 'supranational' institutions *par excellence* can effectively impact on the choice made by member states when it comes to issues where national interests are at stake. The question of extending the EP's legislative and controlling powers over the Council perfectly illustrates the point: competence assertion on the part of the EP has occurred in areas where the states wanted to see progress – i.e., in non conflict-prone policy fields such as Article 100A of the Single European Act (SEA).

Equally, the extension of the level of integration with the TEU had much to do with the development of the Community's policy responsibilities, especially those centred around the four freedoms of movement and the creation of a 'single economic space' and, eventually, Economic and Monetary Union (EMU), rather than on the more sensitive issues surrounding the transfer of competences in the fields of Justice and Home Affairs (JHA) and in areas concerning the making of European foreign policy. By increasing the scope of integration – that is, bringing new policy arenas under the common management system – it was possible for the EU to sustain its expansionary policy regime, whilst at the same time to enhance the role of national governments both regionally and internationally. Although the creation of the Single Market has resulted in new forms of interest group organisation and patterns of large-scale civil society-formation, the member governments are still capable of exercising managerial control over integration. The result is the establishment of systems of common management based on positive-sum governing, rather than the creation of a new regional centre (Chryssochoou, 1997).

The spirit of intergovernmentalism has also survived, even when federal principles were included in the treaties, notably that of subsidiarity. The latter, originally hailed as a mechanism for facilitating the transfer of competences to EU institutions, has very much acted as a means of safeguarding the legislative autonomy of national authorities: the 'burden of proof' lies on the Community which has to justify that a particular action can be better achieved at the larger level. Similar points can be made about the following areas:

- the function of the co-decision procedure;
- the comitology phenomenon;
- the consensus-formation aspects of Qualified Majority Voting (QMV);
- the Presidency's agenda-identification and agenda-setting functions;
- the treaty-based nature of the EU's 'constitution';
- the still weak social legitimacy of EU institutions;
- the lack of openness and transparency in EU decision making;
- the retention of national vetoes (albeit of an accommodative kind);
- the marginal role of national parliaments in EU legislative processes.

All the above, which arguably lead towards a pragmatic interpretation of the EU, can be summarised in the form of the following five root assumptions about integration (Chryssochoou, 1998):

(1) EU treaty reform since the mid-1980s has produced a situation where the structural properties of the system determine both the 'scope' and 'level' of integration, and with it the possibilities for the emergence of a democratically organised Euro-polity.

(2) EU constitutional change, far from leading towards a diffusion of national sovereignty, maintains the institutional ability of governments to commonly manage their separate sovereignties through a process of 'co-determination' orchestrated by a 'cartel of elites'.

(3) A balance has been struck between interdependence and autonomy, in that the EU rests on the separate constitutional orders of states. This supports the idea about the reversal of the Mitranian logic to integration: instead of 'form follows function', it is the structural properties of the EU which allow the states to enjoy high levels of (territorial) segmental autonomy.

(4) The EU is best defined as a 'Confederal Consociation': a compound polity whose distinct culturally defined and politically organised units are bound together in a consensual form of 'Union' to further certain common ends, without either losing their sense of forming collective national identities, or resigning their individual sovereignty to a higher central authority.

(5) The 'burden of proof' lies more on federalism, rather than on intergovernmentalism, as method of achieving unification: integration is not about the subordination of states to a new regional centre, nor is it about a linear process towards a federal end. Rather, the EU remains a 'contractual union' sustained by an informal culture of consensus building at the elite level.

Reforming the Union

Whether a 'reasonable step' or one that is 'lacking ambition', the AMT represents the outcome of a largely managerial type of reform. Some areas previously falling in JHA will gradually be transferred to the Community (partial communitarisation), while the Schengen *acquis* is fully incorporated into the EU (with Britain and Ireland having secured an opt out). A new Employment Chapter is now part of the AMT (as a job-creating measure). It is also agreed that at the first enlargement the big countries will 'lose' their second Commissioner provided that they are compensated through a reweighting of votes in Council. But a decision has been deferred until a new IGC is convened at least one year before EU membership exceeds 20.

QMV has been extended in the fields of research, customs co-operation and fraud, and so has the (now simplified) 'co-decision procedure' in the areas of employment (incentive measures), social policy (equal opportunities and treatment), public health, transparency (general principles), statistics, and data protection (independent advisory authority). Further, the legislative procedures involving the EP are reduced to three: co-decision, consultation and assent; whilst a Chapter on Fundamental Rights and Non-discrimination is inserted in the treaty to strengthen the EU's 'human face', and safeguard the protection of human rights.

A new protocol is also enshrined in the AMT to define more precisely the criteria for applying the principles of subsidiarity and proportionality. These principles shall respect the *acquis communautaire* and the institutional balance, whilst taking into account that 'the Union shall provide itself with the means necessary to attain its objectives and carry through its policies'. Still, however, it is the Community that has to justify that the proposed legislation complies to these principles. *Ceteris paribus*, directives should be preferred to regulations and so should framework directives to detailed measures, thus leaving as much scope for national decisions as possible. The Commission should seek maximum consultation prior to initiating legislation; minimise administrative or financial burdens; and submit an annual report to the other EU institutions on the application of these principles.

Flexibility was finally included in the AMT, albeit precluding the creation of a *Europe à la carte* by introducing strict conditions for its application. Such a principle should further the objectives and protect the interests of the EU; respect the principles of the Treaties and the single institutional framework; be used only as a last resort; concern at least a majority of EU members; respect the *acquis communautaire*; not affect the competences, rights, obligations and interests of those members that do not wish to participate therein; remain open to all member states; and be authorised by the Council. It is also stated that the new 'flexible' arrangements will be governed by the same decision-making rules as in the TEU, adjusted accordingly for membership, and that the EP will be regularly informed by the Commission and the Council. Authorisation for such 'flexible' schemes 'shall be granted by the Council, acting by a qualified majority on a proposal by the Commission and after consulting the EP'. Any objection by a state on grounds of 'important and stated reasons of national policy' results in the whole matter being referred to the European Council for an unanimous decision.

Europe and the Greek Political Scene

There are two main pressures on political parties in Greece: Europeanisation and rationalisation. The following sections consider both phenomena in more detail. The first section covers the three main political streams in Greece since the restoration of democracy in 1974: New Democracy (ND), PASOK (socialists), and the Communists. The second section, which addresses the post-Maastricht debate leading up to Amsterdam, also includes POLAN (Politiki Anixi, liberals) and DIKKI (Demokratiko Koinoniko Kinima, radical socialists), both of which appeared on the political scene in the early to mid 1990s.

It is noteworthy that no fundamental debate has recently taken place within party political organisations concerning the European orientation of the country. Rather, and particularly after the coming into force of the TEU, there exists a widespread consensus among the major political forces on Greece's European destiny which makes the earlier confrontations between PASOK and ND, especially during the first Papandreou government (1981–85), part of history. Although there may well be some degree of differentiation among the two major parties on questions of Greece's European policy, these are essentially of a managerial, if not tactical, nature, often used for domestic political capital. Not surprisingly, therefore, what follows draws on the official party political positions vis-à-vis the 1996/7 IGC.

The Modernisation Effect of the EU

Over the years, the impact of Europeanisation on Greek political life has affected the structure and workings of political parties: they have moved from traditional clientelism based on personal ties and connections to a new system of party clientelism. This development has also had an impact in reducing populism in Greece although the personality of the Prime Minister remains important especially in foreign affairs (Ioakimidis, 1999, 1994).

Being a modern expression of traditional clientelism, the issue of party clintelism has become part of the Greek political culture and thus affected the entire party system of Greece. In this sense party clientelism has become a strategy for power of all political parties in Greece, particularly of those with the greater chance of coming to power. This political tradition is now facing a great challenge. As a matter of fact, the impact of European integration on PASOK's ideological stand became apparent from the mid-1980s, when the party dropped all of its previous reservations on EC/EU membership, while the organisational modernisation of the party along European lines is now a challenge facing PASOK under the new leadership of Kostas Simitis (Moschonas, 1997; Verney, 1993). The issues involved here centre mainly on the democratisation of its internal structure and the replacement of party clientelism by a more flexible mode of party contact with both civil and political societies.

Like PASOK, New Democracy has employed this electoral technique for many years and has now felt the pressure for modernising its practices in order to become a truly European party. This means that the commitment of ND to European integration and the subsequent cooperation with other European parties in the institutions of the EC/EU are factors which tend to reinforce the organisational modernisation of the party itself, i.e. the democratisation of its internal processes (Mouzelis, 1995).

Even for the Communists (KKE), the EC/EU institutions became an acceptable new field of struggle and a suitable ground for political cooperation. This new orientation still remains a valuable political option for the KKE in spite of the fact that in the 1990s the party has moved back to more traditional positions under the leadership of Aleka Papariga (Moschonas, 1997).

Besides the European pressures on the democratisation of their organisational structure, the parties are also engaged to follow a process towards the *rationalisation* of their policies including those related to the EU. By rationalisation of policies it is meant here that the parties must now try to persuade their electorate not so much on the basis of broad ideological aspirations (or biases) but rather on the direct relevance of their policy proposals to real social and political issues. The impact of this rationalisation requirement on each party depends on the proximity of their proposed policies to the reality as perceived by the electorate. In this sense KKE can no longer rely on a general opposition to European integration based on traditional ideological justifications, as the party did in the 1970s. The party must now rationalise its opposition to, and criticism on, European integration on the basis of tangible outcomes and reliable alternative solutions. To the extent that this happens, the party is forced to undergo a process of political adjustment as regards to the form and the content of its policies.

In a similar manner, the rationalisation impact of European integration on PASOK entails a drastic modification in the party's traditional commitment to populistic justifications and explanations. For ND, the rationalisation factor entails a drastic change in the traditional ideology of anti-communism and the practice of social populism employed in the past by the conservative forces of Greece. Even the ideological transition made by Karamanlis in the 1970s from anti-communism to Europeanism could hardly work in the 1980s, let alone in the difficult years of the 1990s. Today, ND, like PASOK, always tries to justify its policies not so much in relation to ideological dispositions but rather on the basis of their relevance to real socioeconomic and political issues.

This modernisation challenge derives from the fact that populism is no longer a credible political strategy for mass mobilisation because European integration itself makes imperative the rationalisation of the economic policies as a means of coping with the broader economic and social crisis. The danger here is that this rationalisation requirement may lead to a technocratic form of modernisation directed towards the simple improvement of average economic indices to the detriment of real social needs (Moschonas, 1997).

In the context of European integration, all these tendencies towards political modernisation make imperative the *political legitimisation* of the role of all the Greek parties irrespective of their ideological orientation. In the past, especially in the post-WWII period, the conservative forces of Greece had acquired for themselves a monopoly over the exercise of political power in government. This meant that the principle of political pluralism, upon which Western democracy is based, could be accepted in actual practice in Greece only to the extent that the conservative forces remained unchallenged not only in power but also in government. The post-Junta historical conjuncture undermined this kind of conservative authoritarianism, thereby making easier the transition to a more democratic political culture (Diamandouros, 1993; Charalambis and Demeztzis, 1993). However, even in the early 1980s the alteration of parties in government could not be considered a generally accepted political principle. The consolidation of this principle has been the outcome of an agonising process of social and political struggles wherein European integration gradually lost the characteristics of a crucial political issue. In this sense, European integration started to become an external stimulus for the elimination of all political discrimination, which entails the political legitimisation of party action irrespective of their ideological orientation. It is in this broad context that one must evaluate the positions of the political parties and of the Greek government on the post-Maastricht developments in the EU.

The Political Debate on Post-Maastricht Developments

'Europe' has always been an important ingredient in the political debate in Greece (Ioakimidis, 1994). Now that almost all of the Greek political parties have accepted EU membership, the debate tends to focus on the direct relevance of the parties' policy proposals for everyday social and political life. In other words, the fight over different ideological aspirations in the mid-1970s to the late 1980s is now over. The only exception remains that of the KKE-Communists (and probably to a certain extent DIKKI) who offer an alternative political scenario which is basically opposed to the mainstream of the EU policies, left and right, that is a social-market based liberal democracy. This will be clear from even a brief overview of the parties' positions on the 1996/7 IGC and on the resulting Amsterdam Treaty.

ND is the party which negotiated the Greek entry to the Community in 1981. Fourteen years later, the party reaffirmed its commitment to this European strategy in a declaration issued on the occasion of the 1994 Euroelections. It argued that ND strongly supports the deepening of European integration and the enlargement of the European Union. In keeping with the programme of the European People's Party, ND proposes the adoption of a European constitution based on the principles of democracy, efficiency and subsidiarity, and also the formation of a socially-sensitive European economic policy (New Democracy, 1994a, 1994b, 1994c).

The party's position on the 1996–97 IGC deals with the institutional organisation, foreign and security policy aspects, and the enlargement of the EU. The party supports the federal structure of the Union, the democratisation of its decision-making processes, and the strengthening of the role of the European Parliament and of the Commission. It also favours the development of a common foreign and security policy, within which the borders of the Union could be recognised and defended. Furthermore, the party believes that the further enlargement of the Union is a fundamental precondition to peace and stability in Europe (Papadogonas, 1996).

The party of POLAN was mainly formed along nationalist lines, namely in response to the issue of the Former Yugoslav Republic of Macedonia (FYROM), and thus assumed from its very inception a nationalist ideological flavour.[3] In spite of this right-wing nationalism, the party's programme on socioeconomic issues has centrist political connotations. On European integration, the party supports the federal political organisation of the European Union, but on the condition that the principle of subsidiarity and that of the national identity of the member states be respected. In this sense the European strategy of the party tends to assume ethnocentric connotations. POLAN also supports the democratisation of the Community institutions, the deepening of European integration and the enlargement of the Union, on the condition that the Community budget is increased, the financial resources are redistributed to the benefit of the less developed areas or countries, the Social Charter is implemented, and the social dimension of the internal market is strengthened (POLAN, 1994; Papdogonas, 1996).

The Maastricht Treaty on European Union found PASOK well advanced into the family of the West European socialist parties. Thus its position on European integration is now similar to that of the other parties grouped under the umbrella of the Party of European Socialists. In the 1994 European elections, the European Socialists declared their willingness to struggle for a Europe of the people, not of the economic interests, that is, a Europe with economic development and employment opportunities, a Europe democratic with a human face. In such a Europe, according to a party document, a strong PASOK means a strong Greece able to protect its national interests, economy, and society (PASOK, 1994).

On the 1996–97 IGC, PASOK proposed the deepening of political integration by introducing measures which could gradually lead to a federal structure, the strengthening of the role of the European Parliament, the creation of a Europe for the people (by safeguarding political and social rights for all and by fostering the economic and social cohesion of the Union), the development of the Union's security policy (by defining common external borders), and the enlargement of the Union (especially with the accession of Cyprus and Malta) (Papadogonas, 1996).

DIKKI, which was formed in 1995 on an ethnocentric political platform, is fundamentally opposed to the above. According to its leader, Dimitris Tsovolas, there are two national strategies which lead to diametrically opposed foreign, defence and economic policies. One is the European perspective centred on the belief that Europe will eventually become a single economic, political and security entity. Tsovolas casts doubts upon this eventuality and calls instead for an ethnocentric policy within the EU in support of the national interests. In such a policy, says Tsovolas, the modernisation of the economy becomes an integral part of the issue of national independence. As a result, DIKKI objected to the 1996–97 IGC process on the grounds that it undermined the sovereignty of the country and the role of the national parliament (Tsovolas, 1994a, 1994b; DIKKI, 1997).

To a certain extent, DIKKI's ethnocentric positions come close to those of the KKE. The Greek Communists adopted in the pre-entry period an ethnocentric strategy in relation to the proces of European integration, with emphasis on the issue of national independence. When accession became an accomplished fact, the party's policy changed from the previous slogan 'no to the EEC of the monopolies' to the new slogan 'total disengagement from the EEC of the monopolies'. But, until then, KKE has had to adjust to the 'new conditions of struggle'. In the EP in particular, the KKE made all these views quite clear. After a brief period of moderation during its participation in the progressive left coalition (SYN/*Synaspismos*), KKE returned to this ethnocentric interpretation in the early 1990s (KKE, 1993; Papariga, 1994; Rizospastis, 1994).

It came as no surprise, therefore, that on the 1996–97 IGC developments, while supporting the democratisation of the Union, KKE considered the further enlargement to the East as an effort on the part of the major powers of the Union to incorporate the former socialist countries into the capitalist system. At the same time, KKE stated its opposition to the development of a common foreign and security policy on the ground that such a measure cannot but further undermine Greece's national independence (Papadogonas, 1996).

The pro-European forces of the Left grouped around *Synaspismos* cannot possibly accommodate the above views. The party has repeatedly emphasised its determination to fight within the process of European integration, together with the social and political movements of contemporary left and the ecology, for a new Europe sensitive to the questions of social justice, ecological protection and democratic rights (Kanstandopoulos, 1994; POLAN, 1994b). On the 1996–97 IGC, in particular, the party supported a United Europe based on the basic principles of democracy, social solidarity, and peace and security. In keeping with these principles, the party proposed the federal and democratic organisation of the Union, so as to overcome the current democratic deficit, and facilitate the enlargement of the Union, the incorporation into the structure of the Union of all the questions of foreign and security policy, and the strengthening of the social dimension of the Union (Synaspismos, 1995). It came as no surprise,therefore, that the party decided to declare its dissatisfaction with the Amsterdam Treaty and to refuse to give a positive vote for it (Synaspismos, 1998).

In sum, the great majority of the political forces in Greece nowadays supports the process of European integration. This general agreement was reflected in the position of the Greek Parliament on the 1996–97 IGC. As a report by its Committee on European Affairs states clearly (IGC, 1997), the Parliament in Athens supports the federalisation of the EU, its democratic legitimisation (through a stronger EP role and a stronger role for national parliaments), the development of a truly common European identity in the world, a social Europe, and enlargement to the Central and East European countries plus the Balkans and Cyprus.

Greece and the New Treaty

Greece and the 1996–97 IGC [4]

Greece was among the first countries to realise the communicative, rather than negotiating role of the Reflection Group which soon after its creation established the groundwork of the IGC;[5] a clear enough indication of the cautiousness shown by the Greek government to identify first and then negotiate the various options for EU treaty reform. As for the nature of integration itself, Greece fears the possibility for a 'flexibility clause' to become a major operational principle of EU governance. Underlying this fear lies the idea that flexibility or 'enhanced co-operation' will lead to differentiated patterns of integration without, however, providing adequate legal/constitutional guarantees for those excluded to eventually form part of a 'hard core', or for that matter preserving the integrity of the *aquis communautaire*.

Similarly, if the real task of the IGC was to prepare for a smooth accession of Central and East European countries (and possibly others from the Mediterranean region) during the EU's next waves of enlargement, then the incorporation of a flexibility clause into the treaty presented considerable problems for the country to meet, even at a later stage (2001) the convergence criteria and become part of EMU. The January 1996 Memorandum of the Greek government makes an explicit link between the budgetary implications of enlargement and the principle of sufficient resources. A point also advocated by Spain with reference to the principle of additional resources: the accession of new members should not require the modification of the nature of EU policies, but rather would allow for flexible adaptation on the basis of transition periods. Here, the idea of 'reinforced solidarity' was put forward as an alternative to 'variable geometry', based on the following conditions: 'last-resort' status; openness; and accompanying measures to ensure the convergence of those lagging behind.

As regards the relationship between enlargement and EU decision making, it was expected that an enlarged EU of, say, 25 or so members, will upset further an already delicate balance in the Council. Hence, a new decision-making formula should be devised so as to ensure that the smaller states will not be alienated. But the idea of 'concurrent majorities' – taking into account the size of population as well as the number of state votes – was received with some scepticism from the Greek delegation – especially if the threshold would be 55 per cent. But Greece was clearly against a reweighting of votes in the Council for it could act in favour of the larger states. In connection to the above, it supported the idea of one Commissioner per member state, dismissed the possibility for a 'UN-type model' for the Council with a small number of permanent members and a rotating Presidency, as well as that of a 'directorate'.

The question of the communitarisation of JHA was treated with some cautiousness, although the Greek government favoured a solution of 'partial communitarisation' based on extension of the Commission's right of initiative and enhanced methods of judicial review. The introduction of QMV remained also an open possibility in some fields, however, such as anti-drugs action, whereas in other areas unanimity should prevail as the dominant mode of decision making. Greece also supported the idea of incorporating into the EU the Schengen *acquis*, as well as greater involvement of Community institutions in aspects relating to the crossing of the external frontiers such as the rules governing foreigners, immigration policy, asylum policy and joint rules for external frontier controls.

On the question of democratising the EU, Greece made it clear in the January 1995 document 'Towards a Citizen's Europe' that democratic reform should take the following forms: reinforcing the EP's powers of control in the EU's intergovernmental pillars; extending co-decision to almost all legislative acts produced in the first pillar whose adoption requires an absolute majority; simplifying existing decision-making procedures; accepting a ceiling of 700 MEPs; extending the policy initiation function of the Commission *in tandem* with an increase in EU parliamentary control; and institutionalising the Assizes meetings to improve parliamentary efficiency in scrutinising EU legislation.

In sum, the following amendments to the TEU were seen as positive developments or indeed 'gains' on the part of the Greek government:

- the inclusion in the Treaty of an Employment Chapter as a job-creating mechanism.
- the incorporation of the Social Protocol with a corresponding extension of the co-decision procedure, a strengthening of Article 119 on the equality of sexes, as well as that concerning 'social exclusion'.
- a specific reference to the Treaty on the 1989 Social Charter of fundamental rights and to the 1961 Turin European Social Charter.
- an additional reference to Article 130A and Declaration 30 for the development of 'island regions', with the EU being entitled to take special measures for their participation in the Single Market on equal grounds.
- the inclusion of the principle of 'sustainable development' in the preamble and Article B of the Treaty and its recognition as an explicit objective of the EU.
- strengthening the EU's 'human face' by incorporating a Chapter on Fundamental Rights and Non-discrimination, where Article 6A may form the basis for common action under unanimity.
- the incorporation of the Schengen Agreement and the protection of its *acquis*.
- the introduction of strict conditions for the use of flexibility.

What conclusions are to be drawn from the above reform package? The first is that the 1996–97 IGC provided for an intergovernmental mechanism of multilateral bargaining and negotiation. It is thus difficult to assess the extent to which Greece's original aspirations have been incorporated into the final text, although the above analysis generally indicates that what was actually achieved brings Greece closer to EU governance structures, whilst increasing the pressures for substantive domestic reforms towards modernisation.[6] But let us now turn to the more sensitive issue concerning the Greek position in relation to reforming the CFSP.

The External Dimension

This second sub-section concentrates both on the Amsterdam reforms in the external dimension of European integration, and, more particularly, on the changes in the CFSP provisions of the TEU. There are six main reasons for discussing in more detail the foreign policy and security dimension:

- Greece has always felt under threat from external aggression or interference and this is particularly true since the early 1990s due to recent developments on its Northern and Eastern borders (Balkans and Turkey);
- As a result, Greece remains a security demandeur which is reflected in the way Greek society puts international affairs high on its agenda. In particular the question of whether the IGC reforms would guarantee Greece's territorial integrity was given particular attention especially after the Imia incident of early 1996 and the killing of Greek-Cypriot civilians in mid-1996.
- As a small(er) state, Greece had experienced both the advantages and inconveniences of possessing a national veto on foreign and security issues. Again, the Imia incident comes to mind as the national veto, which had been used by Greece over the FYROM (Former Yugoslav Republic of Macedonia) saga a couple of years earlier (Stavridis, 1997), was utilised, this time by the UK, to prevent a common European declaration condemning the Turkish landing on one of the Greek islets (Valinakis and Pitsarou, 1996).
- By implication, as the foreign policy of the EU remains dominated by four or five big states, any changes to the way the CFSP works would be of crucial interest to Greece.
- Rightly or wrongly,[7] Greece's reputation within the EU has been tarnished by a nationalistic foreign policy behaviour which had damaged both the European credentials of the country and the effectiveness of its own foreign policy. This was particularly true of the early years of the first Papandreou administration (epitomised by widespread criticisms of the 1983 Greek Presidency), especially in relation to a number of problems in European Political Cooperation (Verney, 1996), but also more recently (in late 1993) with Pangalos's characterisation of Germany as a 'giant with a child's brain' (*The Independent*, 3

December 1993).

- Finally, and this is something which is conveniently overlooked in other member states, is the fact that the negative reactions to Greece's attitude by other member states and institutions (as epitomised by the European Commission's decision in early 1994 to bring Greece before the European Court of Justice over its unilateral embargo on the Former Yugoslav Republic of Macedonia or FYROM) have reinforced in Greece a sense of double standards and serious inconsistencies. As a result, Greece has tried to find support in the EU for its views on key issues for Greek foreign policy such as the Balkans, Turkey and the Cyprus problem. But, Greece has coupled it with a re-nationalisation of its foreign policy based on closer and better links with the USA where necessary (e.g. the 1991–95 conflict in former Yugoslavia; the 1996 Imia incident). As Valinakis and Pitsarou point out, 'the debacle of preventive diplomacy in former Yugoslavia [had shown]...the inability [of the EU] to defend common interests...and to alleviate Greece's fear of the conflict spilling over to encompass the entire Balkan Peninsula' (Valinakis and Pitsarou, 1996). Other examples would include the Dutch reluctance to ratify Greek membership of WEU; the refusal to grant Article 5 of WEU to Greece vis-à-vis Turkey, and CFSP Commissioner van den Broek's criticisms over Greece's 1994 embargo against FYROM.[8]

What follows consists of three parts, each addressing in detail Greece's position on the following issues:

- the institutional changes to the CFSP decision-making process;
- the future of European security arrangements and more specifically that of the future role of the WEU;
- the question of the protection of borders and the introduction of a mutual assistance clause.

Institutional Changes to the CFSP Decision-making Process

First, with regards to the role of the European Commission in CFSP, Greece was in favour of more Commission input as it believes that the interests of the small(er) states are better defended by a strong Commission. However, as noted above, Greece stopped short from accepting the possible 'de-nationalising' of the Commission (i.e. less Commissioners than member states) and argued for the continuation of at least one Commissioner for each member state.

Second, as for the use of QMV, the question of unanimity, and that of constructive abstention in the Council, Greece argued that unanimity had to be maintained if only for matters of vital national interest. Greece also argued against the extension of QMV to military and defence matters. The generalisation of QMV in the future is considered by Athens as a possible *quid pro quo* for a defence guarantee (c.f. territorial integrity, see below) in the future, but it is equally aware of the limitations of the current national veto as the already noted incident over Imia has shown (Valinakis and Pitsarou, 1996).

Third, changes to increase the visibility of the CFSP (the so-called 'Mr CFSP') were broadly supported by Greece.

Fourth, Greece favoured the setting up of a planning cell as this development would favour the emergence of a clear definition of the 'European interest', especially for crisis prediction and, eventually, a more active CFSP.

Fifth, as far as 'checks and balances' are concerned, i.e. the democratic control of the CFSP, Greece favoured an increased role for the EP in general, and supported an extended use of the EC budget in Pillar 2.

Security Issues and the Future Role of the WEU

One needs to refer briefly to the wider context: in 1995, Greece finally became a WEU member. But one needs to bear in mind that, despite WEU membership, the 1996–97 negotiations began when (as noted above) Greece had not received an automatic military guarantee because Article 5 had been revised with regards to NATO members (i.e. Turkey).

This meant that Greece's security needs were not fully satisfied by the new situation. It also meant that Greece would try to get as much security as possible out of a number of possible options: the proposed merger of the WEU into the EU; an EU guarantee for territorial integrity; and a political clause of solidarity. Greece pushed for all three but realised quite quickly that the first possibility was not on the cards as a coalition of the 'old neutralists' (Ireland and Denmark) had combined with the 'new neutralists'

(Austria, Sweden and Finland), with the support of the Atlanticists (e.g. the UK) to defeat such a development.

So Greece was generally in favour of more integration in the security and defence fields but did not harbour great hopes. As the merger of the WEU into the EU was not possible (at least not yet), Greece called in the meantime for a Common Defence Protocol, but this was not achieved either.

Greece was also in favour of the inclusion of the so-called 'Petersberg tasks' into the new EU Treaty (humanitarian, peace-keeping, crisis management: as defined in 1992 in a WEU meeting in Germany). These have been included in the AMT. Greece did not favour the extension of QMV to defence matters.

Which can only lead to the following conclusion: for the foreseeable future and irrespective of Amsterdam, Greece will see the USA as its best defence ally as far as Turkey is concerned, and NATO as its most important defence membership as far as its Northern borders are concerned (Albania, Yugoslavia, FYROM, Bulgaria). Of course, these layers are additional to a strong national defence which is confirmed by recent arms procurements decided by Athens.[9]

Protection of Borders and Mutual Assistance Clause

The protection of borders and the inclusion of a mutual assistance clause were the key objectives that Greece had as far as external reforms were concerned.

One needs to say that Greece's objectives would fit in the EU's rhetoric as a logical extension of economic and monetary union; they would also fall under the Schengen principle of internal borders and, finally, complete the concept of a European citizenship.[10] To what extent would all this lead in fact to a supranational and federal (or federalistic) political union does not concern us here but it falls in line with the Greek view that a federal Europe would satisfy its fundamental interests provided it is a genuine political union with a common defence.

Thus, both the question of borders and that of mutual solidarity were seen as vital objectives though they were accepted as difficult to achieve. Greece could find some solace in a number of new provisions in the Amsterdam Treaty but, on balance, it is not right in our view to say that the Treaty represents a breakthrough in either respect.[11] However, it is true that the new Treaty includes the word 'integrity' for the first time. Indeed, Article 11.1, the objectives of the CFSP include 'to safeguard the common values, fundamental interests, independence and integrity of the Union in conformity with the principles of the United Nations Charter...'. Article 11.2 adds that each member should ensure that they are not undermining the CFSP and that they all support each other in order 'to enhance and develop their mutual political solidarity...'.

All this might be read as a step in the right direction as far as Greek objectives were concerned, but they really fall short of these objectives and the clause for mutual solidarity could also possibly be read as a veiled criticism of Greece's stance on the Balkans during the conflict in former Yugoslavia in general, and the Macedonian question in particular.

Conclusions

Many of the proposals for reform supported by Greece were included in the AMT (See also Perrakis, 1998). However, the key objective of a territorial integrity clause failed to materialise, although some progress did occur. In the end, one relatively small(er) country can only input so much in the IGC negotiations where there are various combinations of possible package deals that cut across geographical and thematic boundaries.[12]

Soon after the signing of the AMT, Greece's attention shifted from the 'ratification question' (which commanded overwhelming parliamentary support) to the perennial issue of relations with Turkey. This time the approach was EU-wide as both Turkey and Cyprus were looking for full membership. This came to a fore at the 1997 Luxembourg European Council and is currently high on the agenda of the membership negotiations with these countries.

A final question is whether the 1996–97 IGC has indeed shown the limits of the reform process. Is it time for the EU to consider alternative options, less time-consuming, less heavy, more practical, and closer to (national) ways of minor constitutional reforms? Provided that small(er) states like Greece do not feel that their vital interests are affected by any such developments, it is perhaps time to find an alternative solution. Whatever approach is finally decided by the EU, Greece will continue to contribute constructively to its development.

Notes

1. For a comparative analysis of the positions of EU southern states during the IGC see Tsakaloyannis (1997).
2. Strictly speaking, enlargement was not on the IGC agenda and will not be discussed in any detail although it was clearly a reason for trying to reform the EU before the next round of accessions.
3. The actual relevance of POLAN as a political force in the future is unclear as it is no longer represented in the Greek parliament following the 1996 national election.
4. In this section, the Greek position is taken from the following documents: IGC (1995a, 1995b, 1996).
5. The term 'communicative' implies that the member states were not prepared to commit themselves to fixed pre-negotiating positions within the Reflection Group phase of the reform process. For more details see Tsinisizelis and Chryssochoou (1998).
6. On the wider issue concerning the relationship between Greece and the EU see Tsinisizelis and Chryssochoou (1996).
7. The merits of the cases either way are not discussed here, but suffice it to say that this is not necessarily meant as a criticism of Greece only: all EC/EU members engage in that kind of exercise at one point or another. In fact, empirical research on the way EC states voted at the UN General Assembly during the years of EPC show that the main 'culprits' for diverging from a common European line were the UK and France. For more details see Stavridis and Pruett (1996).
8. For a general background see Verney (1996).
9. Totalling $17bn over the next ten years, see Athanassopoulou (1997).
10. Especially with its external protection of European citizens in third countries: how is it indeed logical to argue that, say, the German embassy in Gambia would protect the interests of a Greek citizen but Germany would not be interested in doing the same when this same citizen is on his/her home soil! These examples are chosen at random and can be replaced by other ones of course.
11. For a different view see Tsatsos and Vigo (1997) and Papandreou (1997).
12. The question of whether or not there is a South European interest in the EU has not been discussed here. See Tsakaloyannis (1997).

References

Athanassopoulou, E. (1997), 'Blessing in Disguise? The Imia Crisis and Turkish-Greek Relations', *Mediterranean Politics*, Vol. 2, No. 3, Winter, pp.76–101.

Charalambis, D. and Demertzis, N. (1993), 'Politics and Citizenship in Greece: Cultural and Structural Facets', *Journal of Modern Greek Studies*, Vol. 11, pp. 219–40.

Chryssochoou, D.N. (1997), 'New Challenges to the Study of European Integration: Implications for Theory-Building', *Journal of Common Market Studies*, Vol. 35, No. 4, December, pp. 521–42.

Chryssochoou, D.N. (1998), *Democracy in the European Union*, London: Tauris Academic Studies.

Diamandouros, N.P. (1993), 'Politics and Culture in Greece, 1974–91', in Clogg, R. (ed), *Greece, 1981–89: The Populist Decade*, London: Macmillan, pp. 1–25.

DIKKI (1997), 'On the IGC for the Revision of the Treaties of the European Union', Athens,

May [in Greek].
IGC (1995b), 'Towards a Citizens' Europe – Democracy and Development', Memorandum for the 1996 IGC, January 1995.
IGC (1995c), *Conclusions of the Interministerial Committee of the Greek Government*, Athens, 7 June.
IGC (1996), *Memorandum of the Greek Government of 24 January 1996 on the IGC.*
IGC (1997), *Report of the Committee of European Affairs of the Greek Parliament on the IGC and the Revision of the Treaties of the EU*, 30 May [in Greek].
Ioakimidis, P.C. (1994), *Greece in the European Union: Problems and Prospects*, GSEIS Discussion Paper, No 52.
Ioakimidis, P.C. (1998), *The Treaty of Amsterdam: New Model of Integration or Disintegration?*, Athens: Themelio [in Greek].
Ioakimidis, P.C. (1999), 'The Model of Foreign Policy-Making in Greece: Personalities Versus Institutions', in Stavridis, S., Couloumbis, T., Veremis, T. and Waites, N. (eds), *The Foreign Policies of the European Union's Mediterranean States and Applicant Countries in the 1990s*, Aldershot: Macmillan, pp. 140–70.
Istituto Affari Internazionali (1996), 'Revision of Maastricht: Implementation and Proposals for Reform', Fifth Bulletin, Rome: Istituto Affari Internazionali, January–June.
Kanstandopoulos (1994), interview, in *Eleftherotypia,* 5 June.
KKE (1993), 'The Positions of the Central Committee on the West European Capitalist Integration', party documents, January.
Moschonas, A. (1997), 'European Integration and Prospects of Modernization in Greece', *Journal of Modern Greek Studies*, Vol. 15, No. 2, October, pp. 325–48.
Mouzelis, N. (1995), 'Greece in the Twenty-first Century: Institutions and Political Culture', in Constas, D. and Stavrou, T.G. (eds), *Greece Prepares for the Twenty-First Century*, Washington, D.C.: The Windrow Wilson Center Press, pp. 17–34.
New Democracy (1994a), 'For a Strong Greece in a Humane Europe', *Ta Nea*, 13 April [in Greek].
New Democracy (1994b), 'Strong Greece, Respected in Europe', *Euroelections*, 12 June [in Greek].
New Democracy (1994c), 'The Basic Positions of the European People's Party', *Euroelections*, [in Greek].
Papadogonas, N. (1996), 'The Greek Political Parties on the 1996 IGC', *Evropaiki Ekfrassi*, No. 19, pp. 31–6 [in Greek].
Papandreou, G. (1997), 'Intergovernmental Conference Conclusions', *Thesis: A Journal of Foreign Policy Issues*, Vol. 1, No. 2, Summer, Athens: Hellenic Ministry of Foreign Affairs, pp. 2–7.
Papariga, A. (1994), 'Capitalist Crisis and "European Union"', the daily *Eleftherotypia*, 17 April [in Greek].
PASOK (1994), 'Strong PASOK, Strong Greece in Europe', party document [in Greek].
Perrakis, S. (1998), *The European Union in Transition: From Maastricht to Amsterdam*, Athens: Ant. N. Sakkoulas [in Greek].
POLAN (1994a), 'We Represent Greece in Europe', party document [in Greek].
POLAN (1994b), 'Declaration on the European Elections of June 1994', *Avgi*, 20 February [in Greek].
Rizospastis (1994), 10 June [in Greek]
Stavridis, S. and Pruett, D. (1996), *European Political Cooperation at the United Nations: A Critical Assessment 1970–1992*, University of Reading Papers in Politics, No. 20, June.
Stavridis, S. (1997), 'The Common Foreign and Security Policy of the European Union: Why Institutional Arrangements Are Not Enough', in Stavridis, S. et al. (eds), *New Challenges to the European Union: Policies and Policy-Making*, Aldershot: Dartmouth,

pp. 87–112.

Synaspismos (1995), 'Proposals for the 1996 IGC', *Synaspismos*, 17–18 June [in Greek].

Synaspismos (1998), 'SYN votes "PRESENT" in Parliament on the Amsterdam Agreement', Decision of the Permanent Congress of SYN, 3–5 April.

Tsakaloyannis, P. (1997), 'The EU and the Common Interests of the South?', in Edwards, G. and Pijpers, A. (eds), *The Politics of European Treaty Reform: The 1996 Intergovernmental Conference and Beyond*, London: Pinter, pp. 142–58.

Tsatsos and Mendez de Vigo (1997), *Kyriakatiki Elefterotipia*, 30 November.

Tsinisizelis, M.J. and Chryssochoou, D.N. (1996) 'Images of Greece and European Integration: A Case of Uneasy Interdependence?', *Synthesis: Review of Modern Greek Studies*, Vol. 1, No. 2, pp. 22–33.

Tsinisizelis, M.J. and Chryssochoou, D.N. (1998) 'The European Union: Trends in theory and reform', in Weale, A. and Nentwich, M. (eds), *Political Theory and the European Union: Legitimacy, Constitutional Choice and Citizenship*, London: Routledge, pp. 83–97.

Tsovolas, D. (1994a), 'Political Positions' the daily *Ta Nea*, 28–30 March [in Greek].

Tsovolas, D. (1994b), *The Roads of Responsibility*, Athens: Kaktos [in Greek].

Valinakis, Y. and Pitsarou, E. (1996). 'Greece's Position on the Revision of the CFSP', in Kazakos, P. et al. (eds), I *Anathorisi tis Sinthikis tou Maastricht ke i Simasia tis ghia to Mellon tis Evropaikis Enosis/What is the Future of the European Union? The Maastricht Treaty Review* (bi-lingual), Athens: Sideris for ELIAMEP, pp. 155–76.

Verney, S. (1993), 'From the Special Relationship to Europeanism: PASOK and the European Community, 1981–1989', in Clogg, R. (ed), *Greece, 1981–89: The Populist Decade*, London: Macmillan, 1993, pp. 131–53.

Verney, S. (1996), 'Greece and the CFSP: Time to Resolve the Paradoxes' in Kazakos, P. et al. (eds), *I Anathorisi tis Sinthikis tou Maastricht ke i Simasia tis ghia to Mellon tis Evropaikis Enosis/What is the Future of the European Union? The Maastricht Treaty Review* (bi-lingual), Athens: Sideris for ELIAMEP, pp. 199–230.

10 The Changing Role of the Greek State in View of EMU

PANAGIOTIS LIARGOVAS[1]

Introduction

Since the late 1970s, when growth rates were still high and public deficits and public debt were low, Greek governments have embarked on unsustainable spending booms. Towards the end of the 1980s and the beginning of the 1990s, when the inevitable downturn arrived, Greek governments were resisting retrenchment. In addition, the state's effectiveness and efficiency has been poor for many years. Although necessary, economic and structural reforms were not imposed. It is only recently that public authorities undertook wide-scale economic and structural reforms.

The purpose of this paper is to seek explanations for the non-adoption of economic and structural reforms in Greece. It also tries to explain why Greek public authorities have finally started to implement structural reforms in order to improve the state's effectiveness and its efficiency. The next section makes a theoretical assessment of the political economy of state reforms, while the third section applies these theories in the case of Greece. The fourth section discusses the role of the European Monetary Union (EMU) on Greek political economy, while the final section offers some concluding remarks.

The Political Economy of State Reforms: Theoretical Assessment

In the past, traditional economic theory was not much concerned with analysing the behaviour of public agents. Most analysis concerned understanding of the behaviour of private agents (consumers, producers, investors etc.). Various rational assumptions were mainly based on the concepts of maximisation (utility, revenues etc.).

Public agents, on the contrary, were supposed to maximise social welfare without having self-targeted interests. Political behaviour not in compliance with this hypothesis was 'irrational' or 'beyond the scope of economic analysis'. Political scientists and sociologists used to offer explanations and therefore to cover this gap.

New political economy, however, has opened up the way to economic analysis. Economists can now offer realistic explanations for many issues, which relate to the state, such as the behaviour of policy makers, political parties and various interest groups in society. For analytical purposes, the same methodological tools – such as game theory – are used to analyse the behaviour of private agents.

According to the new political economy, governmental decisions which relate to the state are not exogenous, but can be explained as strategic decisions within the framework of the interrelationships which exists between governments and political parties or between governments and policy makers and organised interests. One topic of importance is that of structural and economic reforms. The main question here is why reforms that enhance the efficiency of the state or reforms that lead to a decrease in unsustainable spending are delayed or not adopted at all. That is, the new political economy tries to explain what was thought to be in the past 'irrational' or 'myopic behaviour'.

The large and growing literature on structural and economic reforms can be divided into three main categories: theories, which attribute governmental myopia or irrationality to (a) the behaviour of policy makers, (b) uncertainty and (c) interest groups. According to Alesina and Tabellini (1989), Ozler and Tabellini (1991) and Cukierman, Edwards and Tabellini (1992) governmental myopia in periods of political instability comes when groups in power realise that they might be replaced by future governments with different ideological or redistributing priorities. Therefore, they do not choose to implement reforms. According to these explanations a government having control over a macroeconomic variable will strategically try to use it to influence the choices of future governments. The uncertainty about which group will be in control in the future generates the 'political risk' which in turn influences the current economic decisions of private agents and of the government.

Person and Svensson (1989) claim that excessive government borrowing by a right-wing government might be a strategic decision because it makes future governments reduce spending. Alesina and Tabellini (1989) formalise the economic effects of political risk, which are consistent with the observation that budget deficits and debt are more likely to increase when the differences between parties are greater. The main conclusion of all these theories is that in periods of political instability, budget deficits and debt will tend to increase as each government borrows to finance its own preferred expenditures knowing that future governments will increase taxes or cut spending.

Rogoff (1990) developed another strand of literature based also on the behaviour of policy makers. He showed that even when voters are rational, governments tend to engage in pre-election spending.[2] They do so in order to influence voters. Voters on their side do not have enough information about the managerial abilities of policy makers. Furthermore, they can not distinguish between a short-term improvement of macro-economic conditions and a sustained improvement, which is attributed to the abilities of policy makers. Therefore, the latter have incentives to use expansionary policies so as to confuse voters and gain the next elections.

According to a completely different approach developed by Fernadez and Rodrik (1991), failure to adopt a particular reform is due to uncertainty regarding the distribution of resulting gains and losses. Individuals do not know how they themselves will fare under the reform. Therefore, aggregate support for reform can be lower than what it would have been under complete information, even when individuals are risk neutral, forward looking and rational and there is no aggregate uncertainty regarding the consequences of reform. Even if this is the case, the median voter does not vote to support the reform since she does not expect personal gain.

Suppose for example, that an economy consists of 100 workers, from which 60 are employed in the public sector and 40 are employed in the private sector. A reform might result in the following allocation: 60 workers will be employed in the private sector and 40 workers will be employed in the public sector. In addition, the income of those working in the private sector will increase by 20 units, while the income of those working in the public sector will decrease by 20 units. Obviously, the reform will increase total income by 40 units. In the absence of uncertainty, the majority of the workers would have backed it, with 40 votes difference. But the reform will never occur. The majority will reject it, because the majority takes into account the expected change in income. Individuals in the public sector know for sure they will gain, but the remaining individuals in the public sector do not know who among them will be winners and who will be losers. Ex-ante they consider it equally likely that any single one of them will be a winner. They know the aggregate number or the proportion of winners. The expected benefit equals the weighted average of the gains and losses, with the weights equalling the probability of each outcome occurring. The expected gain per public sector individuals can be calculated to be -6.667 which is a negative number [40/60 (-20) + 20/60 (+20) = -6.667]. The losses to the many public sector individuals are pulling down the gains to the few. The reform is not adopted even though (a) individuals are risk neutral, and (b) the majority would vote for the reform ex-post. The problem of implementing a reform becomes more difficult in countries where aggregate uncertainty is large, because in such cases individual uncertainty is larger.

In a similar fashion, Dewatripont and Roland (1991) point to the uncertainty regarding the preferences or other characteristics of those that gain and benefit. Under the existence of such uncertainty, gradual adjustment is the only strategy accepted by the median voter because the actual median position is unknown. A partial reform at the initial stage would induce only the highest-ability group to leave, while at the next stage the partial reform induces the next highest group to leave, with the process continuing until the reform has passed.

Finally, a third theoretical explanation of governmental myopia or irrationality is based on interest groups. According to Olson (1965), reform adoption is prevented by interest groups of different organisational ability. The gains from the status quo may be concentrated on a small number of individuals, while the losses are diffuse to the general public. Free riding hinders the lobbying efforts of the second group to a much greater extent. The group which gains from the status quo is relatively small and unhindered by free riders. In contrast, free riders hamper the lobbying efforts of the larger group to a much greater extent. Thus, as a result the status quo remains. The free riding problem experienced by the general public can be overcome by limiting the influence of interest groups through institutional reform or through political and economic integration.

Olson (1982, 1977) goes further by supporting that growth rates in capitalist countries are best explained by interest groups which act as retardants to growth.[3] The more developed the system of groups in a country, the more restrained the degrees of restrained growth will be. Olson argues that the private gains from pursuing growth-retarding policies exceed public losses from implementing these policies for the special interest groups concerned, though not for the society as a whole. Therefore, interest groups which act as retardants to growth are not offset by countervailing groups acting as stimulants to growth. These groups will tend to cause institutional sclerosis and economic stagnation.

In another approach, Alesina and Drazen (1991) state that delays in taking measures to stabilise and restructure the economy are due to the significant distributional implications which these reforms have on interest groups. Therefore socioeconomic groups and political parties may attempt to shift the burden of stabilisation or restructuring to other groups. Rational behaviour in this case is to wait because the group that gives in first is assumed to bear a larger part of the post-stabilisation tax burden.[4] Though each interest group knows the net benefit it would receive from the change under a proposed allocation of costs, it is uncertain about the net benefits other groups will enjoy, and hence about their willingness to pay for the reform. The process leading to reforms and stabilisation becomes a 'war of attrition', each group attempting to wait the others out and stabilisation occurs only when one group concedes and bears a disproportionate share of the burden. Concession may occur via legislative agreement, electoral outcomes, or ceding power of decree to policy makers. A political consolidation in this case leads to a resolution of the distributional conflict.[5]

To give an example, suppose that there are two groups in the economy. This economy is inefficient and there is a reform, which increases income of both groups, after the reform has taken place. But the reform entails a cost, which is distributed between the two groups in such a way that the group first initiating the reform bears greater cost. Therefore, there is uneven expected allocation of the costs of reform. Each group follows a strategic behaviour in a dynamic game setting. There are Nash equilibria, that is, points where the optimum decision of each group and the expectation of the other group coincide. The group which first abandons the game of waiting is the one that bears the greater cost. Concession occurs when the (group specific) cost of waiting just equals the expected benefit from waiting. A condition that makes the expected benefit greater, and therefore the reform come earlier, is the degree to which the policy maker has *commitment* to the plan – in that she is unlikely to give in to pressure to abandon reforms.

The Political Economy of State Reforms in Greece: Empirical Assessment

In this section Greece is used as an example to empirically support the explanations offered in the previous section regarding governmental myopia or irrationality.

We should first find out if there was governmental myopia or irrationality in Greece. According to Ranis and Mahmood (1992) governmental myopia exists when governments embark on unsustainable spending booms when resources are plentiful – due either to improvements in the terms of trade or the availability of external finance – later resisting retrenchment when the inevitable downturn arrives.[6] Table 1 presents real GDP growth rates, current account deficits, public sector expenses, public sector deficits and public debt in Greece from 1975 as evidence. It shows that the Greek state started to expand from 1979. In this year, the current account was in a slight surplus (0.8 per cent of GDP), public expenditures were at a low level (31.7 per cent of GDP) and the debt to GDP ratio was only 27.5 per cent. Growth rates during the 1975–79 period were quite high (5.3 per cent on an annual average). The expansion is reflected in the accelerating rates of public expenses, public deficits and public debts. Compared to 1979, public expenses had increased in 1989 by 37.5 per cent, public deficits by 500 per cent and public debt by 154 per cent. Growth rates during the 1980–89 period were disappointing and the current account accumulated large deficits. Government authorities in Greece were resisting retrenchment when the inevitable downturn arrived towards the end of the 1980s and at the beginning of the 1990s.

Governmental irrationality can also be depicted by the performance of the public sector and of public enterprises. Public sector inefficiency is reflected in the negative rates of productivity achieved during the 1980s and at the beginning of the 1990s. As the last column of Table 1 depicts, during the period 1975–79 labour productivity exhibited an annual average increase of around 4 per cent. In the 1980s the annual average was negative (-0.2 per cent). As shown in Table 2, in a thorough evaluation of the efficiency of public enterprises during the 1980s, the OECD (1990) reached the conclusion that public enterprise performance was extremely poor.[7]

It should be noted that the manufacturing sector (both state and non-state) instead of relying on its own dynamism to improve competitiveness or restructure its production, was over-subsidised during the relevant

Table 1 Basic Macroeconomic Indicators of Greece

	Rate of GDP Growth	Current account deficit (% of GDP)	Public expenses (% of GDP. General government)	Net government borrowing (% of GDP. General government)	Public debt (% of GDP. General government	Labour productivity (annual change)
1975	6.4	0.5	30.2	3.0	24.7	4.5
1976	6.9	0.5	30.7	1.7	24.6	5.7
1977	2.9	0.4	31.6	2.5	25.7	1.6
1978	7.2	0.2	32.0	2.9	28.0	7.1
1979	3.3	-0.8	31.7	2.4	27.5	1.8
1975–79	5.34	0.16	31.24	2.5	26.1	4.14
1980	0.7	-0.6	31.8	2.6	28.6	1.2
1981	-1.6	-1.7	38.0	9.1	34.5	-4.9
1982	-1.1	1.8	38.7	6.8	41.3	-1.6
1983	-1.1	2.8	40.5	7.6	41.9	-2.5
1984	2.0	2.5	42.4	8.4	48.0	1.5
1985	2.5	4.5	45.6	11.7	54.7	1.4
1986	0.5	3.6	44.1	9.5	55.9	-0.9
1987	-2.3	0.8	46.4	9.2	62.2	-3.0
1988	4.3	1.8	42.2	11.5	66.8	4.1
1989	3.8	4.3	43.6	14.4	69.9	2.7
1980–89	0.77	1.98	41.33	9.08	50.38	-0.2
1990	0.0	4.7	48.2	16.1	80.7	-2.2
1991	3.1	3.8	44.4	11.5	83.3	5.0
1992	0.7	2.0	46.5	12.8	89.0	-0.6
1993	-1.6	2.6	48.8	13.8	111.6	-2.6
1994	2.0	0.5	46.6	10.0	109.3	0.9
1995	2.1	2.4	48.3	10.6	110.1	1.3
1996	2.4	2.6	45.5	7.5	112.2	0.6
1997	3.2	2.6	42.9	4.0	109.5	3.5
1998	3.5	2.7	41.5	2.2	105.5	...
1999	3.7	2.7	40.5	1.9	105.3	...

Source: Ministry of National Economy.

Table 2 Comparative Performance of Public Enterprises (1985)

	Greece	Germany	France	Italy	Portugal	Spain	UK
Telecommunications							
Productivity*	15.8	29.8	26.0	...	12.6	35.2	21.7
Profitability#	3.3	7.5		...	1.7	9.4	3.1
Railways							
Productivity	4.2	25.3	22.4	...	4.6	11.7	25.5
Profitability	-173.9	13.2	-9.4	...	-2.6	-158.1	-11.1
Airlines							
Productivity	45.9	95.4	95.4	98.5	44.7	64.8	...
Profitability	-21.6	0.6	2.3	1.4	-5.9	-3.3	...
Electricity							
Productivity	48.0	198.3	114.9	97.1	43.5	180.1	95.8
Profitability	0.0	3.5	0.8	0.0	0.2	15.0	4.0

* Share of total sales in dollar terms to employment.
\# Ratio of after tax profits to total sales.
Source: OECD (1990). p. 62.

period.[8] At the beginning of the 1980s, the rate of protection for manufactured goods produced in Greece (tariffs, quotas, advance payments for imports and indirect taxes discriminating against imported goods) was between 20 and 25 per cent and there were also generous subsidies for manufactured exports. Also in 1987, the degree of import protection was still almost 15 per cent, while effective subsidies for exports amounted to 16 per cent of their value. Even though sharply declining after 1987, between 1988 and 1990 state aid to the manufacturing sector amounted to 1502 ecus per person employed per year (14.6 per cent of value added), putting Greece fourth in the EC.[9]

Despite these negative indicators, no state led initiatives to improve performance, efficiency or effectiveness were evident. The first section of the paper offered three explanations why this may be so. According to the

Table 3 National Elections in Greece

Election Date	% increases compared to previous year			Electoral outcome (% of votes)	
	Public spending	Budget deficit	Public debt	New Democracy	PASOK
20.11.1977	0.9	0.8	1.1	41.84	25.34
18.10.1981	6.2	6.5	5.9	35.87	48.07
2.6.1985	3.2	3.3	6.7	40.84	45.82
5.11.1989	1.4	2.9	3.1	46.19	40.68
8.11.1990	4.6	1.7	10.8	46.89	38.61
7.10.1993	2.3	1.0	22.6	39.30	46.88
22.9.1996	-2.8	-3.1	2.1	38.12	41.12

Source: Ministry of National Economy.

first, in periods of political instability governmental myopia comes from the realisation by groups in power that they might be replaced. Also, according to Rogoff (1990) at the pre-election periods governments increase public spending in order to attract more voters.

Table 3 indicates a rise in public deficits, spending and debt in the election year as compared to the previous year. The expansionary behaviour of governments during the 1980s can be attributed to the fact that the two main parties, the socialist PASOK and the conservative New Democracy had large ideological differences as regards the level and components of public expenditures. In periods of greater political instability (e.g. in 1981, in 1989 and in 1993 when the ruling parties lost control of the government) the rise in deficits and expenditures were among the largest. Figure 1 sketches the relationship between the rise in public expenditures and the fall in the electoral percentage of the ruling party compared to the previous elections. A positive correlation is revealed: the greater the expected loss of the ruling party, the greater the relaxation on public spending. The situation started to change in 1996 where, for the first time since the 1970s, public spending at the election year decreased compared to the previous year. This can be

Figure 1 Electoral Cycles in Greece

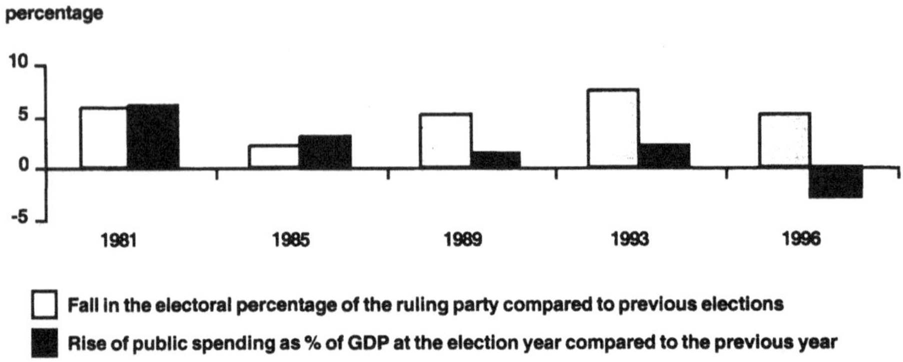

attributed to the ideological convergence, which has been achieved between the New Democracy and the PASOK parties and relates to matters of macroeconomic stabilisation (low inflation and interest rates, reduced budget deficits and debt) and of structural reforms (liberalisation, privatisation, greater efficiency of the state etc.). Previous studies regarding the existence of electoral cycles in Greece, e.g. Lockwood, Philippopoulos and Tzavalis (1997), Kapopoulos and Lazaretou (1996) and Prodromidis (1996) using various econometric techniques confirm our qualitative results.

Another explanation of governmental myopia was based on the uncertainty regarding the distribution of gains and losses from the reform. Uncertainty about the distribution of gains and losses existed whenever Greek governments expressed a will towards privatising public enterprises. Privatisation would create both gains and losses to the workers in the public sector. For example, a loss was to remain in the public sector with lower (real) incomes and social benefits and/or the danger of being laid off and becoming unemployed. However, the probabilities of both gains and losses led to an expected loss. Thus, workers in the public sector were against privatisation.[10]

Individual uncertainty regarding the distribution of costs and benefits was intensified due to increased aggregate macroeconomic uncertainty and the lack of credibility in economic policy in Greece during the past decades. Policy actions creating uncertainty in the 1980s were the high levels of inflation and interest rates (accompanied with large volatilities), the drachma devaluations of 1983 and 1985 and the large number of taxation laws. The lack of commitment in policy making led to the loss of credibility in policy actions and infused more uncertainty in the economy. The prisoner's dilemma helps us explain the negative consequences of the lack of credibility in policy making. Suppose that the government has announced the privatisation of public utilities. The government also announces that the privatisation programme will be accompanied with compensation measures and re-training of employees so as to convince the trade unions not to strike. But the government is not committed and is tempted not to honour promises after privatisation in order to avoid further increases in public spending. No matter what the government finally does the trade unions decide to strike, and therefore the final outcome includes a large social cost.

The final explanation offered of governmental myopia was based on the organisational ability of interest groups. Small pressure groups do not have the problem of free riding and they gain from the status quo. The existing literature on interest groups in Greece has focused mainly on their presence and specific characteristics. Interest groups in Greece are often synonymous with trade unions, as Greece did not experience the same development of civil societies as other countries in Western Europe. Trade unions were based on clientilistic practices which had their origins in the conditions created by the post-war right-wing governments and exemplified by PASOK governments. In particular, public sector unions had a special role and position created by patronage and state tutelage. This was due to the large size of workforce, which made them play a politicised public employment role. Their close relations with the state and with the party bureaucracy resulted in an increased number of privileges. In most cases they had special status relating to service, low tax rates, extended subsidisation of a wide range of staff activities and indirect payments. The origins of these privileges can be found in aspects of government-business relations in the 1950s and in the 60s. What is important, however, is that these strong, privileged trade unions of the wider public sector were able to influence the policies of the General Confederation of Workers, because such policies were formed bottom-up. Therefore, trade unions hindered the formation and implementation of effective state reforms.

Interest groups in Greece have also been analysed along the concept of state corporatism. According to Katseli (1990), state corporatism is, the voluntary cooperative regulation of conflicts over economic and social issues through a highly structured and interpenetrated set of political relationships by the state, banks and business augmented at times by unions and political parties being characterised by social partnership and relying on cooperative efforts of those concerned.[11]

Mavrogordatos (1988), Alexandropoulos (1990), Kioukias (1994) and Zarbaloukou (1997) present extensive analyses of (state) corporatism in Greece.[12] Lavdas (1997) exhibits an interesting triangle relationship between interest groups, bureaucratic agencies and party officials, based on reciprocal interactions and linkages,[13] while Kazakos (1991) talks about 'fragmented syntechniasmos', meaning the dominance of guilds.[14]

The case of Olympic Airways offers insights into the way interest groups affect the state. Olympic Airways has been (and still is) a loss making firm since 1975. An overstaffed company with low productivity and inefficient pricing policy, it has been losing market shares since late 1980s and has been accumulating large debts.[15] Between 1988–93, passengers fell by 22 per cent. It continues to lose passengers even today. Both the New Democracy government in 1993 and then the PASOK government in 1994 tried to implement a rescue package. In each case the trade unions opposed restructuring with the highest paid employees such as pilots and specialised engineers exhibiting the greatest hostility. Their opposition was concentrated mainly on matters pertaining to conditions of service, tax exemptions and indirect payments. Thus unions were defending a number of special status arrangements that had been granted by the state. The case of Olympic Airways is not the only one. Similar examples can be found in many other state-owned enterprises.

EMU as an External Pressure

In the previous section we tried to explain why for so many years structural and economic reforms – though necessary – were not undertaken. However, in the 1990s the situation has changed. Policy makers have (finally) started to implement economic and structural reform measures. The first (unsuccessful) effort appeared in 1993 with the Mitsotakis right-wing government. The next (recent) effort was by the Simitis social-democratic government in 1996. Why are Greek governments no longer myopic or irrational?

A simple answer might be 'crisis caused reform'. Krueger (1993) and Ranis and Mahmood (1992) have supported that economic reforms are undertaken when economic conditions deteriorate sufficiently so that there is a political imperative for better economic performance. Resistance to vested interests can be overcome when the system has no way of avoiding the required adjustment.[16]

This is a very tempting explanation for the case of Greece because at the beginning of the 1990s the economy was in a severe crisis (see Table 1). However, this explanation suffers analytically.[17] It is a tautology between reform and crisis. As Williamson and Haggard (1994) support, the fact that policy reform should follow a crisis, is no more surprising than 'smoke following fire'.[18] Therefore we should seek another explanation.

The one supported in this paper relates to European Monetary Union (EMU). EMU's effect on the Greek State is twofold. First, it has put pressure on the Greek governments to implement institutional reforms and therefore to increase the degree of commitment and credibility of policy makers, reducing thereafter the degree of uncertainty in the economy. Second, it has contributed to the ideological convergence among different political parties. Concepts such as 'macroeconomic stability', 'sustainability', 'efficiency', 'restructuring', 'flexibility', 'liberalisation' and 'privatisation' are now included in the 'dictionaries' of both right-wing and left-wing parties. Economic and real convergence, therefore, has resulted in an impressive ideological convergence.

Institutional reform creates obstacles to the influence of interest groups. EMU has put pressure on the Greek authorities to take measures regarding transparency and independence of governmental bodies. The creation of ASEP, an independent council responsible for the selection of public sector employees, the selection of high quality managers in public sector companies through public announcements, the introduction of public utilities in the Stock exchange, the independent evaluation of the performance of public sector companies, the independence of the Central bank and the introduction of drachma in the European Exchange Rate Mechanism (ERM) are some examples of institutional changes which relate to EMU and represent an effort to increase (self-) commitment.

Commitment is a condition that makes the expected benefit greater and therefore reforms come earlier. Commitments have the advantage of tying the governments' hands against unforeseen contingencies in which freedom of action would have been desirable ex ante. The Greek government is now committed to the EU and thus to implementing reforms so as to comply with the Maastricht criteria and become a member of EMU.[19] Commitment also works against the time-inconsistency problem for the government.[20] It does not allow public authorities to 'surprise' the private sector. It increases the credibility and reliability of the government. In addition, commitment increases diffusion of information to the public about the true objectives of the government in power.

Ideological convergence between political parties, on the other hand, is the result of the macro-economic policies followed, being in full accordance with the Maastricht convergence criteria and the requirements of the Stability and Development Pact. Take for example fiscal policy. Governments should maintain budgetary discipline in order to underpin the stability of the single currency and allow a more favourable policy mix. The Excessive Deficit Procedure establishes that member states shall avoid excessive deficits and provides two yardsticks for deficit and debt – namely 3 per cent and 60 per cent of GDP, respectively – on the basis of which the budgetary positions of the countries should be assessed. The Stability and Growth Pact recognises that, in order to respect the 3 per cent deficit ceiling even in unfavourable economic circumstances, government budgets should be close to balance or in surplus in the medium run.

Conclusions

This chapter has sought explanations for the non-adoption of structural reforms in Greece for many years and has tried to explain why Greek public authorities have finally started to implement necessary changes.

The large and growing literature on structural and economic reforms was divided into three main categories: theories, which attribute governmental myopia or irrationality (a) to the behaviour of policy makers, (b) to uncertainty and (c) to interest groups.

The chapter has confirmed the validity of all these theoretical explanations in the case of Greece crediting the recent implementation of economic and structural reforms in Greece to EMU. EMU has acted as an external shock, increasing public authorities' commitment to implementing changes and paving the way to institutional reforms, thus destroying the influence of interest groups in Greece. EMU has also contributed to the ideological convergence among different political parties.

Notes

1. I would like to thank two reviewers for helpful comments and suggestions on previous version of this paper. Any remaining errors are mine.
2. Before Rogoff (1990), Nordhaus (1975) was the first one to use this model. In his model voters did not have rational expectations.
3. See also Whiteley (1983, pp. 200–201).
4. Similar models have been developed by Laban and Sturzenegger (1994a and 1994b). These models try to explain the 'myopic' behaviour of governments by assuming rational and forward-looking behaviour of policy makers and interest groups which try to optimise their own objective function. They end up in a Nash equilibrium in which each group is doing the best it can, given the actions of others.
5. See Alesina and Drazen (1991) and Drazen and Grilli (1993).
6. See Ranis and Mahmood (1992, p. vi).
7. See also OECD (1993, pp. 33–35).
8. See OECD (1993, p. 35).
9. According to Patsouratis (1993), there were six different categories of state assistance to state enterprises.
10. A solution to this problem might be through calculation of cost and benefits. The state could compensate those who loose their status quo. For example the privatisation of the Olympic Airways could be achieved through compensation i.e. shares in the new airways so that the losers are not against.
11. See Katseli (1990, pp. 238–39).
12. Kioukas (1994), and Zarbaloukou question the concept of state corporatism since the late 1980s due to the liberalisation of the collective wage agreement framework. They prefer the term corporatism.
13. See Lavdas (1997, ch. 3).
14. See Kazakos (1991, pp. 60–62).
15. See Lavdas (1997, pp. 195–201).
16. The adoption of non-populist policies in Latin American countries is attributed to the fact that the crisis in these countries was so deep that even the costs of sticking to populist measures where higher than the costs of adjustment.
17. See Rodrik (1996).
18. See Williamson and Haggard (1994, p. 564).
19. The concept of commitment has been used widely as a strategic measure to decrease inflation in high inflationary countries. This process is analysed, among others, by Alogoskoufis and Manning (1988), and Giavazzi and Pagano (1987).
20. Its optimal ex-post strategy may differ from its optimal ex-ante strategy. In circumstances where the authorities have an ex-post incentive to renege on their promises, it is of course perfectly rational for private agents to discount announcements of future policy reforms.

References

Alesina, A. and Drazen, A. (1991), 'Why are Stabilizations Delayed?', *American Economic Review*, Vol. 81, No. 5, pp. 1171–88.

Alesina, A. and Tabellini, G. (1989), 'External Debt, Capital Flight and Political Risk',

Journal of International Economics, Vol. 27 No. 3/4, pp. 199–220.

Alexandropoulos, S. (1990), 'Tendencies of Corporatist Representation and Greek Reality', *Koinovouleftiki Epitheorisi 4* [in Greek].

Alogoskoufis, G. and Manning, A. (1988), 'On the Persistence of Unemployment', *Economic Policy*, Vol. 7, pp. 425–69.

Cukierman, A., Sebastian, E. and Tabellini, G. (1992), 'Seignorage and Political Instability', *American Economic Review*, Vol. 82, No. 3, pp. 445–502.

Dewatripont, M. and Roland, G. (1991), 'Economic Reform and Dynamic Political Constraints', *Review of Economic Studies*, Vol. 59, pp. 703–30.

Drazen, A. (1996), 'The Political Economy of Delayed Reform', *The Journal of Policy Reform*, Vol. 1, Issue 1, pp. 25–46.

Drazen, A. and Grilli, V. (1993), 'The Benefit of Crises for Economic Reforms', *American Economic Review*, Vol 83, June, pp. 589–607.

Fernadez, R. and Rodrik, D. (1991), 'Resistance to Reform: Status Quo Bias in the Presence of Individual Specific Uncertainty', *American Economic Review*, Vol. 81, No. 5, pp. 1146–55.

Giavazzi and Pagano (1987), 'The advantage of Tying One's Hands: EMS Discipline and Central Bank Credibility', *European Economic Review*.

Kapopoulos, P. and Lazaretou, S. (1996), 'Institutions, Political System and Economic Policy in Greece', *Studies in Economic Policy*, 2/96, Athens: IMOP, pp. 45–86 [in Greek].

Katseli, L. (1989), 'Economic Integration in the Enlarged European Community: Structural Adjustment of the Greek Economy' in Bliss, C. and Braga de Macedo, J. (eds), *Unity with Diversity in the European Economy: The Community's Southern Frontier*, Cambridge: Cambridge University Press.

Kazakos, P. (1991), *Greece Between Adaptation and Marginalization*, Athens: Diatton [in Greek].

Kioukias, D. (1994), *Organization of Interests in Greece*, Athens: Exantas [in Greek].

Krueger, A. (1978), *Foreign Trade Regimes and Economic Development.* Vol. 10. *Liberalization Attempts and Consequences*, Lexington: Ballinger.

Laban, R. and Sturzenegger, F. (1994a), 'Distributional Conflict, Financial Adaptation and Delayed Stabilization', *Economics and Politics*, Vol. 6, No. 3, pp. 257–76.

Laban, R. and Sturzenegger, F. (1994b), 'Fiscal Conservatism as a Response to the Debt Crisis', *Journal of Development Economics*, Vol. 45, No. 2, pp. 305–24.

Lavdas, K. (1997), *The Europeanization of Greece. Interest Politics and the Crises of Integration*, London: MacMillan Press.

Lohmann, S (1994), 'Information Aggregation Through Costly Political Action', *American Economic Review*, Vol. 84, No. 3, pp. 518–30.

Lockwood, B., Phillippopoulos, A. and Tzavalis, E. (1997), 'Politics and Fiscal Policy: Theory and Evidence from Greece', Athens University of Economics and Business, *Discussion Paper*, No. 97–05.

Mavrogordatos, G.T. (1988), *Between Pityokamptes and Prokroustes: Professional Associations in Today's Greece*, Athens: Odysseas [in Greek].

Nordhaus, W. (1975), 'The Political Business Cycle', *Review of Economic Studies*, Vol. 42, pp. 169–90.

OECD (1990, 1996), *Economic Surveys Greece*, Paris.

Olson, M. (1965), *The Logic of Collective Action*, Cambridge: Harvard University Press.

Olson M. (1982), *The Rise and Decline of Nations*, New Haven: Yale University Press.

Ozler, S. and Tabellini, G. (1991), 'External Debt and Political Instability', National Bureau of Economic Research Working Paper.

Person, T. and Svenson, L. (1989), 'Why a Stubborn Conservative Would Run a Deficit:

Policy With Time Inconsistent Preferences', *Quarterly Journal of Economics*, Vol. 104, pp. 325–45.
Prodromidis, K (1996), 'Basic Characteristics of Political Cycles in Greece', *Studies in Economic Policy* 2/96, Athens: IMOP, pp. 23–40 [in Greek].
Ranis, G. and Mahmood, S.A. (1992), *The Political Economy of Development Policy Change*, Cambridge: Basil Blackwell.
Rodrik, D. (1989), 'Promises, Promises: Credible Policy Reform Via Signaling', *The Economic Journal*, Vol. 99, September, pp. 756–72.
Rodrik, D (1986), 'Tariffs, Subsidies and Welfare with Endogenous Policy', *Journal of International Economics*, Vol. 21, November, pp. 285–99.
Rodrik, D (1991), 'Policy Uncertainty and Private Investment in Developing Countries', *Journal of Development Economics*, Vol. 36, pp. 229–42.
Rodrik, D (1996), 'Understanding Economic Policy Reform', *Journal of Economic Literature*, Vol. XXXIV, pp. 9–41.
Rogoff, K. (1990), 'Equilibrium Political Budget Cycles', *American Economic Review*, Vol. 80, pp. 21–36.
Whiteley, P. (1983), 'The Political Economy of Economic Growth', *European Journal of Political Research*, Vol. 11, pp. 197–213.
Williamson, J. (ed) (1994), *The Political Economy of Policy Reform*, Washington, D.C.: Institute for International Economics.
Zarbaloukou, S. (1997), *State and Labour Unions in Greece, 1936–90*, Athens: Sakkoulas [in Greek].

11 The Six Syndromes of Structural Adjustment. Or What Greek Privatisation Can Teach Us

GEORGE PAGOULATOS

The arguments advanced in this chapter lie on two premises:

(i) the *maximum* claim for a Greek 'contribution' to the EU can only be predicated upon an – at least – *minimum* contribution in the form of a consistent adherence of Greece to the country's obligations to the EU resulting from partnership, reciprocity, formal institutional and legal binding, and substantial convergence requirements.

(ii) after the painfully lost ground (in economic terms) of the 1980s, Greece in the 1990s, and particularly since the second half of the nineties, has been moving indeed more decisively on the adjustment path, creating the preconditions for a successful upgrade from the minimum to a potential maximum claim of contribution.

The Comparative Framework

As any other case studied within the realm of comparative politics and political economy, the Greek case should initially be allowed no special claim to exceptionalism. Greece's move into structural adjustment policies including privatisation parallels that of other countries inside and outside the EU, and as such should it be regarded. Thus, before entering the specific discussion of our case at hand, it would be worth placing it in its broader conceptual and policy framework.

Through the 1980s and early 1990s much of the academic and

technocratic debate on policy reform and innovation, including privatisation, was centred on the politics of imposing reform over and against societal group resistances. Through the conceptual lenses of the public choice school – occasionally and rather immodestly rebaptised into 'new political economy' – policy reform programmes were pessimistically viewed as being plagued by self-interested politicians, opportunistic bureaucrats, and rent-seeking coalitions, and generally ruled by the behavioural laws of neoclassical economics (Findlay, 1991; Grindle, 1991). Among others, the issues of the right 'packaging' and 'sequencing' of policy reforms appeared as prevalent in the academic and policy debate (Krueger, 1984).

While probably no other analytical tool has so far managed to effectively challenge the conceptual impact of public choice in the wider field of applied economic policy and political economy, the current state of the art represents a more sensitised and enriched version of the rationalist orthodoxy. While the considerations typically laid forth by public choice-type approaches remain robust, more recent experience, particularly from new democracies and middle-income countries, indicates that the major challenge regarding policy innovation and reform is not so much about imposing it as it is about sustaining it, making it 'stick' (cf. Haggard and Kaufman, 1992). In addition, the older 'social-democratic' prescriptions of building consensus around reforms and compensating losers have been strengthened (Maravall, 1997). What policy reformers have learned, and some have learned it the hard way, is that policy reforms are anything but irreversible, often lead to a backlash, and in any case cannot be imposed over and above the political system.

The cumulative experience from the application of economic adjustment programmes to developing and transition economies has led international policy communities to refocus attention to the pivotal role of institutions: rule of law, an independent and reliable judiciary, a clear delineation and protection of property rights, a non corrupt and effective administration, legal continuity, consistency and predictability especially in the areas that particularly affect the economic and market process (tax legislation and collection, economic and financial regulation, etc.), a strong central bank, a well-functioning financial system, and a social safety net to cushion the societal shocks of economic adjustment, are increasingly deemed indispensable for the viability of policy reform. 'Institutions' and 'good governance' are the new buzzwords of world 'technopols' and the new convergence points of the current economic policy orthodoxy (World

Bank, 1997; Michalski, Miller and Stevens, 1997; Haggard, Lafay and Morrisson, 1995: 23; cf. Bates, Haggard and Nelson, 1991).

The Six Syndromes of Greek Economic Adjustment and Privatisation

All that said, the Greek experience of structural adjustment policies, and privatisation in particular, contributes some possibly illuminating insights. To highlight those insights I will examine the Greek case in the 1980s and 1990s through the lenses of six syndromes which can be claimed to characterise government reforms. I will then discuss to what extent each syndrome accurately described the economic adjustment and privatisation policies of both ND (1990–93) and PASOK governments (1993 to present).

The Honeymoon Syndrome

The first is what, borrowing heavily from John Williamson (1994) and Dani Rodrik (1994), one might call: the *honeymoon syndrome*.

A government would choose to apply its most painful and politically costly reforms freshly upon its rise to power, in order to take advantage of the honeymoon period, before opposition builds up. A front-loaded sequencing of reforms is presumably a conventional wisdom among reformist policy makers.

However, the only recent Greek government which could be claimed to have applied that doctrine was, paradoxically, the re-elected 1985 Papandreou government. Three months after emerging victorious from the June 1985 election, the socialist government enrolled into the well-known and short-lived Simitis programme[1] (a Keynesian stabilisation which however – with the exception of financial deregulation – advanced very few structural reforms). Though the intention was to privatise loss-making bank and other state-controlled industrial subsidiaries,[2] no practical results were delivered in that area.

Though all governments in the 1990s have been committed to at least macroeconomic adjustment, no government has taken advantage of the honeymoon period by introducing its most serious of intended reforms during its early months in power. ND initiated the privatisation of large public utilities in as late as 1992, two years after its election. The PASOK governments, on the other hand, after a few timid privatisations, reinvigorated privatising ambition by expanding it to major public enterprises and promoted deeper labour and social insurance market reforms only until such policies were irrevocably imposed after the March 1998 drachma devaluation and entry into the EMS. Thus no government in the 1990s has rushed into a front-loaded privatisation programme.

Three possible hypotheses might explain this reluctance to take advantage of the honeymoon period. In a descending order of virtue, they are the following:

- 1st Hypothesis: there was a conscious attempt to trigger policy learning mechanisms, to habituate the public with the reforms through a step-by-step process. This was most probably the strategy selected by the 1996 Simitis government – but then some could argue that precious time was thus squandered as the applied macroeconomic policy mix had early on exhausted its potential and needed to be bolstered by additional microeconomic reforms.
- 2nd Hypothesis: governments were not exactly aware of the reforms they would later have to make, thus proceeding in a learning-by-doing manner.
- 3rd – and the gloomiest – Hypothesis: governments (for electoral reasons) have been committed to an extreme form of gradualism bordering on sheer procrastination.

This last possibility is music in the ears of reform radicals. However, the second hypothesis yields quite plausible assumptions too: governments rise to power in the hope that they will be able to eschew heavier and more costly structural reforms.

Due to the way Greek parties are organised, their lack of internal intelligence and policy formulation substructures (cf. Spourdalakis, 1988; Pappas, 1998), combined with the notorious deficiencies of the state's administrative machine (Spanou, 1992; Sotiropoulos, 1996), upon assuming government power both ND and PASOK have been more or less unprepared to exercise that power. By the time the new government is able to put itself together, study the problem, gather and analyse the data, weigh the alternatives, examine the strategic implications, define the operational goals, prepare the human resources, and begin implementing the reforms, the honeymoon is over. Then two options are left: either reforms begin too late, in which case they are often left incomplete, or they are cancelled on the run to the following election. Or they are simply postponed for the day after the following election.

Admittedly, the Greek governments' failure to take advantage of the honeymoon period is consistent with the experience of both Portugal and Spain in the 1980s (Bermeo, 1994; Bermeo and García-Durán, 1994), with one important difference: the relative delay of Spain and Portugal in implementing industrial restructuring and privatisation policies did not last as long as that of Greece, and as such was part of a South European postauthoritarian strategy of first consolidating democracy and then proceeding with the necessary economic and structural reforms. This strategy could possibly be invoked to justify the economic expansionism of the 1981 Papandreou government; however, it provides no convincing justification for the second half of the 1980s, by which time democracy had been clearly consolidated (Gunther, Diamandouros and Puhle, 1996; cf. Pagoulatos and Wright, 1999).

A more careful look at the mechanisms of Greek government policy making might suggest that governments have failed to take advantage of the honeymoon period not only because they chose not to do so (as could be claimed for the 1996 Simitis government) but because they were unable to do so (as could be the case with the 1990 government of ND).

Which were the characteristics of privatisation policy making in the 1990s? My own research of the 1990–93 period points to a number of conclusions most of which hold water for the post-1993 period as well.

For one thing, the public bureaucratic apparatus, particularly during the ND government, was seriously disengaged from privatisation-related policy making and implementation. Given the highly contentious political nature of privatisation as well as the ND's long period of alienation from power (not to mention the anti-public sector ideological zeal of some of its leading ministers), the ND government's mistrust of public bureaucracy is not difficult to explain. Policy making was dominated by the 'political leadership' of the ministries (ministers, underministers, secretaries general, and their advisers) and the managers of public corporations and state banks, which nevertheless were government/political appointees and outsiders of the public administration corps. Thus the bureaucracy was isolated from the radical change in policy direction, outside the 'policy spirit', and impaired when it came to serving as an effective executive instrument.

The exclusion of public bureaucracy from privatisation decision making was only one aspect of its relation with the government. The bureaucracy's unwillingness to become involved was the second and even stronger aspect. Public bureaucracy was always imbued with deep-rooted insecurity and suspicion toward its government superiors, dating back to traumatic experiences of partisan appointments, promotions and eliminations at the top echelons. If one policy domain probably mobilised those reflexes of civil service insecurity to extremes, that was privatisation. Career civil servants in governmental bodies involved in privatisation during the ND period probably felt weaker than any policy maker and totally unprotected from the political controversy privatisation invited.

The weaker the role of ministerial bureaucracies and the more top-centralised the process, the more different ministerial approaches and styles mattered. But the combination of top-centralisation and weak bureaucratic apparatuses also meant there were certain limits to the amount of output even the most committed privatiser-minister could produce. The larger and more important the projects (OTE, shipyards, AGET-Heracles, natural gas, Public Power Corporation) the heavier the complexity, the higher the stakes, the more forceful the resistances and competition of interests, the stronger the requirement for a personal involvement of the minister, and the weaker the possibility for delegation to the underminister or general secretary. Evidently, a minister could only afford to run a specific number of projects each time, given that privatisation was, after all, only one among many responsibilities for both the Economy and the Industry ministers. If important and urgent decisions had to be taken and could only be taken at the ministerial level or higher, then inevitably many significant issues would stall, and delay at the top level would induce similar delay at the lower echelons where decisions were implemented.

The natural combined consequence of policy overload at the top ministerial levels and general weakness, inflexibility and noncommittal disposition at the subsequent levels downward was a lack of executive follow-up and implementation of decisions. Repeatedly and on various issues decisions were taken in closed discussions between top government officials, which remained without any sort of follow-up action. Other times, tasks were initiated by the ministers and delegated to their assistants whereafter they were simply abandoned and forgotten buried under a load of pending jobs. Thus, the superimposition of a functionally 'alien' ministerial circle of political or technocratic appointees upon the ministry's tenure bureaucratic apparatus, and the feebleness of subsequent channels of communication between those two separate substructures, formed the organisational basis of executive discontinuity.

This organisational analysis helps explain why governments have not only chosen but have also probably not been able to take advantage of the honeymoon period in advancing serious structural reforms including privatisation.

The 'Things Cannot Get Worse' Syndrome

Here comes an 'iron law' of reform policy making: A government's ability to take advantage of its honeymoon period in order to advance serious reforms is associated with its capacity to persuade the public about the gravity of the economic conditions it was called to confront upon assuming power.

In other words, whenever different parties succeed each other in government (as it happened in 1989, 1990 and 1993) the honeymoon syndrome could be facilitated by another syndrome which I shall call *the 'things cannot get worse' syndrome*. The syndrome emphasises the regeneration and growth potential entailed in moments when things appear to be as bad as they could possibly get.

This is no untrodden ground in the literature. Authors from Schumpeter to Mancur Olson in his *Rise and Decline of Nations* have been captivated by the creative potential of otherwise destructive economic circumstances. In relative terms, the combination of inflation in the area of 20 per cent, public debt way over 100 per cent in GDP terms, an unstable payments balance and a government deficit rising out of control might qualify for the role. As we all know, a deficit is what you have when you don't have as much as you had when you had nothing. And by the end of the 1980s, Greek economic policy makers were heavily nostalgic of the times when they had nothing.

There are indeed moments when economic indices are so unambiguously dire that they simply stand beyond dispute. The salience of accumulated policy failure in these moments is such that economic malaise may end up releasing an overwhelmingly creative potential for recovery, by providing potent justification for policies advocating a radical break with the past.

A popular demand is created in such moments for strong government and a decisive shift of policy direction; the public is ready more than ever to accept painful structural reforms and the sacrifice of entitlements.

To take some well-known examples, such a moment was arguably the economic collapse of *Gonçalvismo* in Portugal after 1976, when radical socialism was abandoned for good; as was probably the 1982 alarming balance of payments crisis of Spain which allowed Gonzáles to launch his conservative economic policies that paved the way for Spain's model of supply-side socialism (Maravall, 1993). Such a moment was certainly France's exchange rate crisis following the failed expansionist experiment of 1981–82, which forced Mitterrand to make his famous *grand tournant* (Hall, 1986).

Such moments can provide an immensely valuable opportunity for long-due bold reforms provided that policy makers – as in all those cases mentioned – are both able *and* willing to ride on their wave. Since the 1980s, mainly two governments have been able to persuasively utilise the 'scorched earth' argument upon assuming power: the 1981 Papandreou government and the 1990 Mitsotakis government. The first was able but not willing to advance the type of structural modernisation required; the second was probably more willing but (not least because of its frail parliament majority) not able to do so. Thus, the 'things cannot get worse' syndrome was not very useful in enhancing bold structural reforms including privatisation.

Different is the case when the same party succeeds itself to power. Then, of course, the capacity to portray the inherited situation in the bleakest of terms is severely constrained. That was probably one of the main reasons why the 1985 stabilisation programme under Papandreou, though prompted by very similar circumstances to those of France and Spain in 1982 (mounting inflation and a severe balance of payments crisis), did not go as far as to include a biting microeconomic component. For the same reasons the 'things cannot get worse' syndrome has not been of much help to the 1996 Simitis government either. On the other hand, the 1993 Papandreou government, for well-known and rather trivial reasons, was not quite able to exhume the air of robustness and vigour required in order to successfully activate the 'things cannot get worse' syndrome.

The Unsustainability (or the 'Cannot Make it Stick') Syndrome

Speaking of the 1993 government succession of ND by PASOK, a few of the privatisation reforms initiated under the ND government were discontinued or uprooted by its successors (the Athens Bus Company, the privatisation of 49 per cent-cum-management of OTE). In fact, when in opposition, Papandreou's PASOK had threatened to reverse the entire privatisation programme of the Mitsotakis government.

This brings us to the third privatisation-related syndrome, which I will brand: *the unsustainability syndrome*, or, if you like, the *'cannot make it stick'* syndrome.

Indeed, several reformist governments have seen their reforms repealed as a result of intense political reaction and an ideological backlash.

Some have tried to apply strategies which make their reforms irreversible. They devise binding institutions and submit themselves to their binding effect. They establish a point of no return and then walk past it (viz, the Maastricht strategy). They try to pre-empt opposition forces through taking them by surprise with a 'short sharp shock' therapy (the Thatcherite strategy). Or they do exactly the opposite: they invest in building a gradual sociopolitical consensus in the hope that it is that which will finally render their reforms irreversible (this has been, to a certain extent, the strategy of current social democratic leaderships in the EU, including the Simitis government).

A brief parenthetical note is well due at this point. During the 1980s, shock therapy was extensively advocated by economists as the appropriate economic adjustment strategy. However, by the 1990s, the economists profession could claim to have benefited immensely from what might remain known as 'the Jeffrey Sachs screw-up' – from the Harvard economist who (in his earlier days) had advised a radical free market strategy for Russia without a previous build up of adequate institutions.[3] The threat of a social explosion in a number of adjusting countries (prominently among the transition economies of Eastern Europe) shifted the consensus in support of the gradualist strategy, which is by now probably the prevailing doctrine in international epistemic communities.[4] In other words, policy reformers have learned, and some have learned it the hard way, that if for the sake of policy reform you ignore politics, soon you will be left with a lot of politics but without any policy reform.

On the other hand, another fallacy has also been popular among certain economists, that authoritarian regimes – by being able to suppress sociopolitical opposition and trade unions – have been better equipped to implement economic reforms. There is no better proof of how erroneous this statement is than the 1998 financial collapse of what some had branded 'the bubble economies', Krugman's 'paper tiger' authoritarian regimes of South East Asia (Krugman, 1994). (Whether or not the 'Washington consensus' advocating free and ungoverned capital flows will crumble with them is another story and still too early to call.) The road to economic reform is and should only remain that of democratic politics – and it is only by good fortune that one can say this today fully aware of the truism being uttered.[5]

Having said that, however, one must also admit that democratic politics heavily constrains reformist policy makers. Such constraints are much stronger in adversarial systems – such as Greece – than they are in consensus-oriented sociopolitical systems, such as, say, the Rhine-capitalist democracies or even Spain.

Indeed, democratic politics in a highly politicised system exercises a paralysing effect on policy and institutional innovation. Politicisation is the shortcut word for adversarial politics and the latter's prevalence in the public sphere. It encourages the opposition to exaggerate its differences with government, it privileges a simplistic, heated ideological discourse averse to pragmatism. By promoting polarisation, politicisation fosters executive and institutional discontinuity, each administration reversing its predecessor's policies.

These particular features of the Greek political system, including the rent-seeking function of well-entrenched public sector trade unions, have constrained privatisation in two ways: policies are either not implemented at all or they are cancelled on the way by fear of political reaction (for example, the attempted restructuring of Olympic Airways in 1998); or policies are implemented only to be later reversed by the succeeding government (for example, the renationalisation of the Athens Bus Company by the 1993 Papandreou government).

This latter case corresponds to what I have branded the 'unsustainability syndrome' or the 'cannot make it stick' syndrome.

It is not difficult to agree that even the boldest of reforms are of little practical value if they cannot be made to stick (cf. Nelson, 1990). In a democratically politicised system the sustainability of reforms can be enhanced either by compensating the losers, or by accelerating the emergence of winners from the reforms. Much of that has to do with managing impressions: persuading vital interest categories that they stand to win; convincing the losers of reform that their losses are less than they consider them to be. There is thus a lot to be said about a government's vital stake in building a social acceptance and consensus for reform.

The 'Promised Land' Syndrome

Which brings us to our fourth syndrome. Borrowing again from Dani Rodrik (1994), I shall call it *the 'promised land' syndrome.*

As Rodrik has observed (1994: 214), 'when policymakers can articulate and communicate a sound vision of their model for society *and* there is widespread consensus in society about the desirability of this vision, it becomes easier to undertake and sustain comprehensive reform programs'.

Could that be the case with Greek privatisation policy?

Riding on the wave of the neoliberal ideological hegemony in Europe (cf. Wright, 1994), and in a process of gradual radicalisation of its privatisation ambition, the ND government tried to play first with the idea of identifying privatisation with an overhaul of the public sector; then it promoted privatisation as a choice-enhancing strategy of creating market opportunities and spreading property rights ('privatisation is the highest form of socialisation', the preamble to the 1991 privatisation framework law read); and finally, in its third most radical phase, the ND government tried to identify privatisation with the 'liberation' of citizens from the oppression of public monopolies and their trade unions.

However, the ND's privatisation programme was doomed to failure by its frail parliament majority and the lack of societal consensus to back it. That was not unrelated to the maximalist genre of opposition championed by PASOK under Papandreou.

The compelling pressure of public deficits in the 1990s has rendered privatisation a foremost revenue raiser for all governments, though the socialists have been clearly far more reluctant to surrender public control (with the exception of the banking sector), aiming instead mostly toward part privatisations (Table 1). The PASOK government's more moderate strategy particularly after 1996 has been to integrate privatisation into an overall vision of 'modernisation'. Such strategy could benefit from a higher degree of societal consensus, for a combination of reasons. First, because the learning process had substantially advanced: reasonable time had elapsed, policy makers, societal interests and the public had become relatively habituated to the desirability as well as to the inevitability of reform. Second, because the major opposition party (ND) – tactical inconsistencies notwithstanding – was *ipso facto* generally in support of that policy, which had not been the case when ND was in power. Third, because PASOK could easily contrast its own moderate privatisation policy to the more ambitious model

Table 1 Major Privatisations in Greece (1990–98)

Year	Enterprise and Holder	Sector	Percentage sold
1991	Bank of Piraeus (Commercial Bank)	Banking	66.67
1992	AGET-Heracles (IRO)	Cement	69.8
1992	Athens Bus Company (Government)*	Transport	100
1992	Eleusis Shipyards (Commercial Bank)	Shipyard	100
1993	Bank of Athens (National Bank)	Banking	66.67
1993	Hellenic Sugar Industry (Agricultural Bank)	Agro-industry	49
1994	Neorion Shipyards (National Bank and Industrial Development Bank)	Shipyard	100
1995	Hellenic Shipyards (Industrial Development Bank)	Shipyard	49
1996	OTE (Government) (first tranche)	Telecommunications	8
1997	Bank of Attica (Commercial Bank)	Banking	49.5
1997	OTE (Government) (second tranche)	Telecommunications	10
1998	Hellenic Petroleum (Government)	Energy	23
1998	Bank of Crete (Government)	Banking	97
1998	Bank of Central Greece (Agricultural Bank)	Banking	51
1998	Athens Stock Exchange	Financial	10
1998	OTE (Government) (third tranche)	Telecommunications	10

* The company was renationalised in 1994.

Source: National Economy Ministry; IRO and bank sources.

promoted by ND, and make even privatisation sceptics feel relieved for having being saved from the 'cruellest' Thatcherite version of the policy.

The 'Nixon Goes to China' Syndrome

A comparison of ND with PASOK in their privatisation and economic adjustment policies cannot fail to reveal another crucial advantage enjoyed by PASOK. According to a mainstream political science approach echoing Mancur Olson, most structural reform programmes are bound to generate losers whose accumulated political power probably exceeds that of the winners of the reforms, given the collective action problem. The higher 'reform dividend' gained, for example, through a more efficient allocation of resources is distributed among the broader public, accumulating over the medium and longer term. It thus cannot offset the distributive losses of particular interest groups deprived of their 'acquired rights', as those special interest groups are better organised and vocal whereas the general public is by definition dispersed and less well – if at all – organised.

The above conceptualisation has contributed greatly to our understanding of the political preconditions of economic reform. In fact, the Olsonian depiction might even be underplaying the bold redistributive content of structural adjustment.

In order to demonstrate the redistributional and power dimensions of structural reform, let us take two examples of such policy programmes, privatisation and financial deregulation. Both cases, if we are to take Giandomenico Majone seriously, form subcategories of regulatory reform (Majone, 1994).

Both deregulation and privatisation could be perceived as the outcome of the ascendancy of an economic rationality moulded by conditions of globalisation over a Keynesian or simply *dirigiste* status quo characterised by the domestic primacy of sociopolitical objectives. These objectives basically consisted of protecting socioeconomic groups deemed to be either 'productive' or weak (farmers, industry, small artisanship, the Greek periphery, later in the 1980s workers of ailing firms). They were thus motivated by considerations of economic development and/or redistributive justice. In a sense, both privatisation and financial deregulation expressed the incapacity of the postwar and postauthoritarian distributive order of state-assisted capitalist development to continue accommodating its sociopolitical objectives without detriment to its economic viability.

Alternatively viewed, both banking deregulation and privatisation manifested the rising economic importance of the financial sector, and corresponded to its long-held demand to be treated as an autonomous sector in its own right by being freed from the shackles of servicing development, fiscal, and other government priorities. European financial integration and the shift from a state-directed, development-oriented, pro-industry economic doctrine into a hands-off, market-based, inflation-dreading monetarist system of economic beliefs, exercised their belated impact by increasing the perceived importance and political muscle of the financial sector. This change merits attribution of a landmark significance as it amounted to uprooting a whole array of institutions and policies, and the perceptions on which they were founded. The modern postwar Greek economy was built on the premise of a strong industrial sector leading development, supported by an archipelago of small businesses acting in a complementary role to the larger industrial concerns, all of them generously financed by state-regulated banking. The overindebtedness of much of the state-protected industrial sector through the 1980s, combined with the alarming incapacity of small-scale enterprises (the backbone of the Greek business sector as it were) to survive cross-border competition, provided the banking elites championing a more 'efficient allocation of resources' with arguments for abandoning the state protectionist tendency to instrumentalise banking for the sake of industry. In that sense, banking reform at the domestic level signified nothing less than a distributive conflict, or the dynamic backlash of the financial sector and competitive business coalition against the previously protected industrial, small business, public sector, and agricultural interest groups.

Having said all that, and having pinpointed the inevitable losers of structural reform, the question is what type of government is better placed to undertake, diffuse or effectively confront the inherent sociopolitical cost of such policies. And the answer to that question leads us to the fifth syndrome, and a well-known one in the subdiscipline of international relations: *the 'Nixon goes to China' syndrome*. Thanks to his impeccable anticommunist credentials, Richard Nixon was the best fit President to reverse American foreign policy and embrace communist China.[6] Correspondingly, when a conservative/neoliberal government implements unpopular adjustment policies people will say it is doing so out of ideological zeal. On the contrary, if a pragmatic socialist government applies the same neoliberal-type policies, people will believe it has no other choice.

Benefiting from the momentum created by their conservative predecessors, and often in symbolic counterposition with them, reformist socialist governments have been able to apply economic adjustment policies and to often do so more effectively than their conservative predecessors. We have seen it by Gonzáles' socialists in Spain, we are seeing it by Tony Blair's New Labour in Britain (Hay and Watson, 1998), we are seeing it by the Olive Tree coalition in Italy (Della Sala, 1998); and we are finally probably seeing it by the current socialist government of Greece (at least in so far as the macroeconomic policy component is concerned) compared to the ND government of the early 1990s.

The 'Ulysses and the Sirens' Syndrome

Our analysis has so far singled out several reasons why PASOK has enjoyed a political advantage in the implementation of its economic adjustment and privatisation policies if compared to the 1990 ND government. Three of these factors stand out as most prominent, and can be summed up as follows:

- *Policy learning* (cf. Hall, 1993). Not only were the policy makers of the 1996 Simitis government able to draw on a more extensive record of experience with handling economic adjustment and privatisation policies; the elapsed time from the abandonment of state interventionism initiated in 1990 had also allowed the paradigm shift to mature both among policy makers and party apparatus and within the broader public.
- *The presumption of left-wing sensibility and undisputed social democratic credentials*, combined with the long-cultivated links of the Simitis government officials with the public sector trade unions afforded the 1996 PASOK administration the possibility to advance its structural adjustment programme against comparatively limited sociopolitical reaction.
- *The external constraint factor* was probably the most definitive of all. Privatisation and other structural reforms such as labour and insurance market liberalisation became a principal part of the government's actual agenda in earnest only after the March 1998 drachma devaluation and entry into the EMS. It was only then that the PASOK government

for the first time appeared relatively determined to directly implement these policies by almost defying political cost. The explanation for that brings us to what we might brand the *'Ulysses and the Sirens' syndrome.* In the famous Homerian metaphor signifying rational strategies for going round the imperfect rationality represented by weakness of will (Elster, 1984), Ulysses ties himself to the mast in order to avoid the temptations of the Sirens. Very much like the other EU countries had done by binding themselves to the Maastricht criteria, the Greek government chose to enter an externally imposed discipline mechanism which forced adjustment by rendering the cost of noncompliance insufferable. It was not only that privatisation was one of the terms under which Greece had been admitted to the EMS in March 1998. It was not even just that Greece's ambition of meeting the convergence targets in order to qualify for the second EMU wave of 1st January 2001 rendered privatisation inevitable, if only as a revenue raiser for the state budget. It was also that financial liberalisation multiplied the costs of any substantial derogation from the pursuit of healthy economic 'fundamentals' and of any serious stain on the government's policy 'credibility'. The entry of the drachma to the ERM in an environment of free capital movement and high interest rate differentials led to a massive inflow of mainly short-term capitals; these posed constant threat of a tantamount outflow (with devastating effects on the external account and the economy at large) if the first signals of government retreat from its announced policy targets were to be emitted.

Some Concluding Remarks

Perhaps the single most important lesson to be contributed from the European experience of structural adjustment is the unsustainability of unilaterally divergent national policies. This admission, however, of 'gloomy' pragmatism should not imply an uncritical acceptance of the currently orthodox conventional wisdom regarding economic adjustment. Certain items of the orthodox agenda such as the merits of trade liberalisation, the overhaul of insurance and pension systems, the need to ground social redistribution on sound public finances, the divestiture of state-owned business firms, the rationalisation and marketisation of a wide range of state-controlled activities followed by a clear delineation of the public-private boundary retain their robustness as policy prescriptions. Others have been laid bare to compelling dispute. Whereas liberalisation has rendered financial systems more efficient, and the dismantling of barriers for investment capitals has spread growth opportunities, the total deregulation of restrictions to the movement of purely speculative short-term capitals has left economies under the Damoclean sword of a financial collapse, transferring unprecedented power to the hands of collectively irrational global financial market players. Inasmuch as unilateral national opt-outs from this global financial disorder are hardly viable, the degree of absurdity of this particular dimension of financial globalisation has rightfully intensified calls for global-level universally coordinated action oriented towards 'governing' and 'taxing' short-term capital movements (Krugman, 1999).

However, the discussion about structural adjustment and privatisation up to a certain extent has indeed ceased to be a normative one. The most compelling justifications put forth for these policies in Greece concern not their intrinsic desirability but their pragmatic necessity in terms of a severely constraining international environment. Whereas consensus over the desirability question is still far from achieved, there is widespread agreement within expert policy communities that economic adjustment for a small, open, peripheral EU economy seeking to fully partake in the politico-institutional capital of the European Union, is inexorable. What remains debatable is the scope of such adjustment rather than its fundamental ingredients, and the tactical steps through which it may be brought about.

All that said, an additional word of caution is due. Privatisation should be followed by a strengthening and expansion rather than a weakening of public regulatory authority, through the creation of new regulatory bodies (safeguarding the rules of the game, market competition, and consumer protection) endowed with such statutory power as to render them independent not only from government but from the risk of becoming 'captured' by the private interests they are meant to regulate (cf. Vogel, 1998; Pagoulatos, 1999). If these new regulatory authorities fail to emerge (as has mostly been the case in Greece), then the redrawing of the public-private boundary resulting from liberalisation and privatisation will be lopsided, and the government clientelism traditionally exercised through the public enterprise sector will only be replaced by a concentration of oligopoly power in the hands of unaccountable and far more potent private interests.

Be that as it may, this was not a chapter about whether privatisation is desirable. It was about how, after the desirability question has been resolved, the policy can also be made possible. Suffice it to say that through a pragmatic and sensible application privatisation is not the ticket to a 'free for all' capitalism – which is neither desirable nor historically tenable. It is rather the necessary component of the transition from the interventionist to a new regulatory state, which, in the elegant phrase of Maravall, 'must become as small as possible and as large as necessary'. While this is increasingly settled, the exact politics of bringing it about remains a constantly inviting field of academic inquiry.

Notes

1. The stabilisation programme had been devised by the policy team of Kostas Simitis, then Economy minister. Simitis succeeded Andreas Papandreou as prime minister and chairman of PASOK after Papandreou's death in 1996.
2. These were mainly failed industrial firms which, during the first half of the 1980s, had come under the rather euphemistically named Industrial Reconstruction Organisation (IRO), a state holding company established with the purpose of overhauling these enterprises and returning them to the private sector. By the end of the 1980s, however, almost none of the IRO subsidiaries had been privatised or closed down; instead they were burdening the state budget with large deficits.
3. In a powerful paper Jeffrey Sachs himself (always influential but now a reform moderate and acute critic of 'big bang' adjustment strategies for transition economies) blames Russia's financial breakdown of the early 1990s on the failure of the IMF, the G-7 and other multilateral institutions to provide a financial lifeline of Marshall Plan proportions necessary to bring Russia back on its feet (Sachs, 1994).
4. Probably the strongest argument in support of shock therapy (or the 'big bang' strategy, as it is known) is derived from the rational expectations economic theory: shock therapy exercises a critical impact on market expectations, convincing actors that the government is determined to push ahead with the reforms; on the contrary gradualism, this argument maintains, may be interpreted as a signal of hesitance, thus inducing rent-seeking responses or systematic efforts by status quo interests to resist reform if they considered the government as prone to back out under the weight of sociopolitical opposition. However, there is no compelling evidence that sociopolitical resistance would be less adamant – and for that matter less successful – if market actors perceived the government as committed to a 'big bang' strategy. On the contrary, a shock therapy could promulgate even harsher reaction from the side of status quo interests, leading to a stand-off between government and, say, trade unions. If the government retreated as a result of this stand-off (a quite plausible outcome given the political/electoral cost gradualist or radically reforming governments invariably face), then the negative impact on the government's credibility would be more severe if the government had initially appeared as radical and uncompromising than if it had positioned itself as unbelligerent and gradualist.
5. Though the financial and economic collapse in South East Asia cannot be directly attributed to their authoritarian political regimes, the suppression of a dissenting opposition to their economic errors can. Suppression of political dissent in countries like Malaysia, Indonesia, Thailand and South Korea facilitated their adventurist subjection to a combi-

nation of ill-founded, doctrinaire economic recipes and crony capitalist management. (On the 1998 Asian crisis see Yotopoulos, 1998, as well as a collection of articles cited in Nouriel Roubini's homepage: www.stern.nyu.edu/~nroubini/asia/). The literature, however, tends to remain rather agnostic on the correlation between authoritarianism and economic growth (see Maravall, 1997: Appendix 2; Bertrand, 1998; also Haggard, 1990: 261 ff).

6. Drawing on other similar examples, the syndrome could be equally branded the 'De Gaulle solves Algerian problem', or the 'Rabin makes peace with the Palestinians' syndrome – and thanks to Mark Dragoumis for reminding me of the first.

References

Bates, R.H., Haggard, S. and Nelson, J.M. (1991), 'A Critique by Political Scientists', in G.M. Meier (ed), *Politics and Policy Making in Developing Countries: Perspectives on the New Political Economy*, San Francisco: ICS Press.

Bermeo, N. (1994), 'Comment', in J. Williamson (ed), *The Political Economy of Policy Reform*, Washington, DC: Institute for International Economics.

Bermeo, N. and García-Durán, J. (1994), 'Spain: Dual Transition Implemented by Two Parties', in Haggard, S. and Webb, S.B. (eds), *Voting for Reform*, Oxford: World Bank and Oxford University Press.

Bertrand, J. (1998), 'Growth and Democracy in Southeast Asia', *Comparative Politics*, April, 1998, pp. 355–75.

Della Sala, V. (1998), 'Politics Through Markets: The Italian Left Between the First Republic and EMU', paper at the Annual Meeting of the American Political Science Association (APSA), 3–6 September, Boston.

Elster, J. (1984), *Ulysses and the Sirens: Studies in Rationality and Irrationality*, Cambridge: Cambridge University Press.

Findlay, R. (1991), 'The New Political Economy: Its Explanatory Power for LDCs', in Meier G.M. (ed), *Politics and Policy Making in Developing Countries: Perspectives on the New Political Economy*, San Francisco: ICS Press.

Grindle, M.S. (1991), 'The New Political Economy: Positive Economics and Negative Politics', in G.M. Meier (ed), *Politics and Policy Making in Developing Countries: Perspectives on the New Political Economy*, San Francisco: ICS Press.

Gunther, R., Diamandouros, P.N. and Puhle, H.J. (eds) (1995), *The Politics of Democratic Consolidation: Southern Europe in a Comparative Perspective*, Baltimore: Johns Hopkins University Press.

Haggard, S. (1990), *Pathways from the Periphery. The Politics of Growth in the Newly Industrializing Countries*, Ithaca: Cornell University Press.

Haggard, S. and Kaufman, R.R. (1992), 'The Political Economy of Inflation and Stabilization in Middle-Income Countries', in Haggard and Kaufman (eds), *The Politics of Economic Adjustment*, Princeton: Princeton University Press.

Haggard, S., Lafay, J.D. and Morrisson, C. (1995), *The Political Feasibility of Adjustment in Developing Countries*, Paris: OECD.

Hall, P. (1986), *Governing the Economy: The Politics of State Intervention in Britain and France*, Oxford: Oxford University Press.

Hall, P. (1993), 'Policy Paradigms, Social Learning, and the State: The Case of Economic Policymaking in Britain', *Comparative Politics*, Vol. 25, pp. 275–296.

Hay, C. and Watson, M. (1998), 'Rendering the Contingent Necessary: New Labour's

Neo-Liberal Conversion and the Discourse of Globalisation', paper at the Annual Meeting of the American Political Science Association (APSA), 3–6 September, Boston.
Krueger, A.O. (1984), 'Problems of Liberalization' in Harberger, A.C. (ed), *World Economic Growth*, San Francisco: ICS Press.
Krugman, P. (1994), 'The Myth of Asia's Miracle', *Foreign Affairs*, Vol. 73 (6), pp. 62–78.
Krugman, P. (1999), 'The Return of Depression Economics', *Foreign Affairs*, Vol. 78 (1), pp. 56–74.
Majone, G. (1994), 'The Rise of the Regulatory State in Europe', *West European Politics*, Vol. 17 (3), pp. 77–101 (special issue on 'The State in Western Europe. Retreat or Redefinition?', edited by Müller, W.C. and Wright, V.).
Maravall, J.M. (1993), 'Politics and Policy: Economic Reforms in Southern Europe', in Bresser Pereira, L.C., Maravall, J.M. and Przeworski, A., *Economic Reforms in New Democracies: A Social-Democratic Approach*, Cambridge, Cambridge University Press.
Maravall, J.M. (1997), *Regimes, Politics and Markets*, Oxford: Oxford University Press.
Michalski, W., Miller, R. and Stevens, B. (1997), 'Economic Flexibility and Societal Cohesion in the 21st Century: An Overview of the Issues and Key Points of the Discussion', in *Societal Cohesion and the Globalising Economy*, Paris: OECD.
Nelson, J. (1990), 'Introduction: The Politics of Economic Adjustment in Developing Nations', in Nelson, J. (ed), *Economic Crisis and Policy Choice. The Politics of Adjustment in the Third World*, Princeton: Princeton University Press.
Pagoulatos, G. (1999) 'European Banking: Five Modes of Governance', *West European Politics*, Vol. 22 (1), pp. 68–94.
Pagoulatos, G. and Wright, V. (1999), 'The Politics of Industrial Privatization: Spain, Portugal and Greece in a European Perspective', *Rivista Trimestrale di Diritto Pubblico*, 3, pp. 613–62.
Pappas, T. (1998), *Making Party Democracy in Greece*, London: Macmillan.
Rodrik, D. (1994), 'Comment', in Williamson, J. (ed) *The Political Economy of Policy Reform*, Washington, D.C.: Institute for International Economics.
Sachs, J. (1994), 'Life in the Economic Emergency Room', in Williamson, J. (ed), *The Political Economy of Policy Reform*, Washington, D.C.: Institute for International Economics.
Sotiropoulos, D. (1996), *Populism and Bureaucracy: the Case of Greece Under PASOK*, Notre Dame: University of Notre Dame Press.
Spanou, C. (1992), 'Les politiques de recrutement dans l'administration hellénique: une modernisation impossible?', *Revue Française d'Administration Publique*, Vol. 62, pp. 313–24.
Spourdalakis, M. (1988), *The Rise of the Greek Socialist Party*, London: Routledge.
Vogel, S.K. (1998), *Freer Markets More Rules: Regulatory Reform in Advanced Industrialized Countries*, Ithaca: Cornell University Press.
Williamson, J. (1994), 'In Search of a Manual for Technopols', in Williamson, J. (ed), *The Political Economy of Policy Reform*, Washington, D.C.: Institute for International Economics.
World Bank (1997), *World Development Report* 1997: The State in a Changing World, New York: World Bank and Oxford University Press.
Wright, V. (1994), 'Industrial Privatization in Western Europe: Pressures, Problems and Paradoxes', in Wright, V. (ed), *Privatization in Western Europe*, London: Pinter.
Yotopoulos, P.A. (1998), 'Devaluation, Currency Crises and Exchange Controls', mimeo, Stanford University, September.

12 Public Infrastructure as a Determinant Factor of the Economic Performance of Greek Industrial Output

EMMANOUEL C. MAMATZAKIS[1]

Introduction

It is widely recognised that the efficiency of an economy is affected by the performance of public sector and its investment decisions. The aim of this chapter is to empirically estimate the effects of public capital stock on private sector productivity of the Greek industry.

Although the significance of public capital has been known for a long time, it is only recently that economists have endeavoured to evaluate its importance for productivity through different methodological approaches. If we seek to trace the starting point of the relevant literature then we have to mention Ashauer's research (1989a) that evoked a whole series of articles on the topic thereafter. His model, a production function, indicated a highly significant and positive effect of infrastructure on total factor productivity of US. In another study (1989b) he argues that the reduction of public investment in infrastructure was responsible, to a large extent, for the slow down of productivity in the majority of OECD countries in the 1970s. Munnel (1990a, 1990b, and 1992) reconfirmed Ashauer's findings by also estimating a positive output elasticity of infrastructure. Ford and Poret (1991) in a cross country analysis for eleven OECD countries found that countries with high infrastructure investment experienced high productivity growth. However, the very high estimated coefficient of public capital stock of these studies lead to serious criticism about the plausibility of the results. Evans and Karras (1994) found no evidence in their study, which took account of some of the points of the criticism, to support the idea that productivity is enhanced by public capital.

There are many issues that one has to consider about the possible causes of the above striking and conflicting results. In an attempt to identify some of them we will deal with the problem of having non stationary time series. It is known that the first two moments of non stationary time series are time dependent, causing spurious correlation in their estimated relations. Thus, after applying the appropriate tests for the order of integration of our variables, that is testing for the existence of unit roots, we examine if a long run relationship between public capital stock and private sector productivity exists. The long run relationship between the variables of our interest is then derived, taking the form of a linear combination that defines an equilibrium relationship with time invariant linear properties. In other words, a cointegration relationship, as defined by Engle and Granger (1987), between public capital stock and productivity.

The results of this study reveals the positive effect of infrastructure on productivity and also demonstrate that the causal relationship between them is rather running from the side of infrastructure to the side of productivity than the other way around.

Specific policy issues are, then, drawn. Especially in the case of Greece, which is an intermediate developed economy with increasing needs for modern infrastructure, partly because its position in the periphery of EU, and partly because of its anachronistic structure in many forms of infrastructure. The above findings identify the area that the government should be actively involved. Actually, the positive effect of infrastructure on private sector productivity is observed to be higher than other studies with reference to developed economies, demonstrating that the benefits of public investment in infrastructure projects are much higher in developing countries, like Greece.

In what follows, the next section provides a descriptive analysis of key macroeconomic figures of the Greek economy, especially mentioning the evolution of public infrastructure and productivity, followed by a presentation of our theoretical model – a Cobb-Douglas production function. Our data and unit root tests are then presented and cointegration techniques are used to examine the long run relationship between public capital stock and private productivity. Finally, some concluding remarks are mentioned.

Public Infrastructure and Productivity in Greece

The standard of living in an economy is defined to a large extent by its productivity performance. An increase in productivity, measured by the ratio of output to private purchased inputs, makes feasible from a technological point of view more output with the same quantities of inputs. In this event the overhead output will be shared among the individuals of the society. It means as well that more inputs characterised by scarcity are available to be used for social purposes. Most importantly, the economy as a whole enhances its international competitiveness with all the beneficial consequences, reduction of unemployment and increase of investment. It is, therefore, of significant importance to investigate to which extent infrastructure affects the productivity performance of the Greek economy.

The recent economic history of Greece manifests an outstanding economic performance soon after the end of 1950. The labour productivity, measured by the GDP per-man hour, annually increased by 6.6 per cent, while the same measure for EU and OECD was 3.7 per cent and 3 per cent respectively for the period 1960–79. At the same period the fixed investment was annually increasing by 6.7 per cent. A big part of the increase in fixed investment was covered by the share of public sector that counted for almost 30 per cent of fixed investment. It is evident that infrastructure investment formed one of the basic public priorities and constituted a basic tool for the development and industrialisation of the country, mainly in the sixties. These investments were concentrated in the immediate requirements of the economy for energy, transportation, telecommunications, health and education.

However, in the subsequent years a big decrease both in labour productivity and fixed investment was experienced. The annual percentage change of the fixed investment was actually negative in the period 1979–91. In the economic literature, it is frequently quoted the correlation between investment and growth of output. The descriptive statistics of Table 1 seem to verify this correlation. The growth of GNP dramatically fell from 5.6 per cent in the period 1969–79 to 1.3 per cent in the period 1979–91, at a period where fixed investment also declined sharply. This evolution negatively affected the per capita income that decreased in the years after 1979 by deteriorating the standard of living.

Moreover, the main point that can be derived from Table 1 is the common pattern of change of fixed investment, growth of output and labour

Table 1 Economic Development Indicators (annual average percentage change)

	Greece	EC	OECD
GNP			
1960–79	5.6	4.0	4.2
1979–91	1.3	2.1	2.6
Fixed Investment			
1960–79	6.7	3.9	4.6
1979–91	-0.8	1.6	1.4
Labour Productivity			
1960–79	6.6	3.7	3.0
1979–91	0.8	1.6	1.4
Average Per Capita Income as Percentage of OECD*			
1960	30	87	100
1970	41	89	100
1979	47	90	100
1991	44	92	100

*On the basis of the nineties current purchasing power parities.

Sources: OECD, Historical Statistics, 1960–94.

productivity. The acknowledgement that the rate of investment in an economy assists the development process and the growth of output is accepted to hold per se in most of the countries in the economic literature. The Greek case demonstrates that increases in capital formation contributed to a high growth rate of output in the 1960s and most of the 1970s, and supported the industrialisation of the economy.

But, in late 1970s a reversion of the development process was observed. As we can see in Table 2, the share of total industrial production in GNP dropped from 31.3 per cent in 1980 to 28.13 per cent in 1994. It seems that the industrialisation of the economy interrupted in the late 1970s, and it was never completed afterwards. On the other hand the share of agricultural sector steadily decreased, sustaining nevertheless a significant part of GNP, 12.4 per cent in 1994, while the share of the service sector was

Table 2 Changes in the Sector's Share as a Percentage of GNP

	Agriculture	Industry Total	Manufacturing	Services
1950	28.5	20.2	14.6	51.3
1960	22.8	25.7	16.3	51.4
1970	18.2	31.4	19.1	50.4
1980	17.7	31.3	19.5	51.2
1985	17.6	29.0	17.9	53.6
1990	11.6	30.1	18.5	58.2
1994	12.4	28.1	16.7	59.4

Source: National Statistical Office of Greece, National Accounts.

gradually increasing, capturing more than 50 per cent of GNP from 1950 to 1994.

There are many causes responsible for the deterioration of the industry in particular and of the Greek economy in general in the last two decades. The unfortunate economic policy manipulations can be identified as one of them. One specific area where the economic policy was poorly performed was the public infrastructure investment. Although the importance of providing the necessary infrastructure for easing the production process was known, it was disregarded in the event of soaring public deficits and imprudent increases in public consumption expenditure in the late 1970s and in the 1980s.

In Table 3 it can be observed that public expenditure as per cent of GNP sharply increased from 17.3 per cent in 1950 to 48.2 per cent in 1990. This increase mainly consisted of large public expenditures on goods and services, and transfer payments, that almost doubled and tripled respectively in this period. As a result, in an economy where public expenditure rose more than 30 per cent in the last thirty years, the public investment was steadily decreased from 5.7 per cent of GNP in the period 1958–66 to 4.4 per cent in the year 1990. Clearly, the dominant policy of cutting off public investment was based on the fact that the social-economic returns on public investment would take a long time to be realised, when an immediate reward to voters was required by subsequent governments in order to sustain their power.

Table 3 The Structure of Greek Public Expenditure, 1958-90

	Goods and Services		Public Investment		Transfer Payments		Total Expenditures
Years	Exp.	GNP	Exp.	GNP	Exp.	GNP	GNP
1958–66	47.5	11.3	24	5.7	28.4	6.7	23.8
1967–73	42.5	12.2	24.3	7.0	33.2	9.5	28.7
1974–81	46.7	15.3	16.6	5.5	37.7	12.8	33.7
1982–87	41.0	19.3	14.5	6.9	44.5	21.0	47.2
1988	46.7	17.5	12.9	4.9	47.7	18.0	46.1
1989	49.3	20.0	12.2	4.8	45.5	18.4	46.9
1990	45.2	20.2	9.9	4.4	50.5	22.6	48.23

Source: Bank of Greece, Monthly Statistical Bulletin..

Consequently, despite the needs of Greek economy for basic infrastructure, the public investment remained at very low levels, resulting in an insufficient capital stock to cope with the development process that the economy ought to have taken.

Specifically, Greece has a very poor motorway system, without further mentioning the anachronistic railways, airports incapable of dealing with an increasing number of tourists, and the low performance of the telecommunication network.

Table 4 shows that the core infrastructure captured 60 per cent of the total public capital stock, but only 22.5 per cent of the total capital stock, indicating how small is its share in the latter. Furthermore, the total public capital stock was counted around 28 per cent of the total capital stock in 1990 and was valued 471.521 million drachmas. The contradiction is that even though the public sector expanded, mainly in the 1980s, through extended nationalisation, its capital stock remained at very low levels. In US, for example, where presumably the role of government was not so active as it was in Greece, public capital stock counted for 36 per cent of the total capital stock in 1990.

The above descriptive analysis suggests that causal relationships between public investment, productivity, and subsequently growth of output may exist. One should observe that in the Greek case when public invest-

Table 4 Private and Public Capital Stock, 1990

Capital Stock	Million of Drachmas	Percentage of Total
Total	1,691,674	
Total Private Capital	1,220,108	72.2
Total Public Sector	471,521	27.8
Core Infrastructure*	381,325	22.5
Sanitary	10,768	0.63
Education	37,465	2.21

(*Core infrastructure includes ports, roads, rails, electricity, communications and transportation.)

Source: KEPE, Net Fixed Capital Formation, in: Skoutzos and Matheos, Athens 1991.

ment in infrastructure projects covered a significant part of total public expenditure the industrialisation of the country was rapid. It can be argued, therefore, that public infrastructure might form a capable macroeconomic tool that can assist the development of the Greek economy.

A Simple Theoretical Model

The aim of the current paper is to empirically investigate the relationship between public infrastructure and private capital productivity, adopting a neoclassical production framework where the former would be incorporated as an input of production. Specifically, following Ashauer (1989a), we adopt a Cobb-Douglas production function that treats infrastructure as a separate production factor:

$$Y_t = A_t K_t^{\alpha} L_t^{\beta} G_t^{\gamma} \tag{1}$$

where A_t is a measure of technology, Y_t is the private output, K_t is the private capital stock, L_t is the private labour, and G_t is the public capital stock. Because the private production is actually supported by the flow of services from public capital stock, we implicitly assume that these services are a stable proportion of public capital and they are represented in our model by the variable G_t.

The log transformation of equation (1) is given by:

$$\ln Y_t = \ln A_t + \alpha \ln K_t + \beta \ln L_t + \gamma \ln G_t + u_t, \qquad (2)$$

where u_t is an error term.

The coefficients α, β, and γ represent the private output elasticities with respect to private capital stock, private labour, and public infrastructure respectively. However, in the present study we are interested in the effect of public infrastructure on private capital productivity. Thus, we further transform equation (2) by simply subtracting from both sides private capital stock, K_t.

$$y_t - k_t = c_t + \beta(l_t - k_t) + \gamma g_t + u_t, \qquad (3)$$

where small letters represent logs, $y_t - k_t$ is the private capital productivity, $l_t - k_t$ is the ratio of labour to private capital, and g_t is the public capital stock.

Notice that the public capital stock enters in the production function as a complementary input, and it is assumed that there exist constant returns to scale over private purchased inputs (L, K) or increasing returns to scale over all inputs (IRS thereafter), that is $\alpha + \beta + \gamma > 1$.[2]

Empirical Estimations

Our data set is derived from the Annual Industrial Survey of Greece (AIS) and the Centre of Planning and Economic Research (KEPE). The sample of our empirical analysis covers the period from 1959 to 1993. The basic variables of our model are; value added (VA thereafter) of Greek industrial sector, private labour (L) measured as the number of employees, private capital stock (K), and public capital stock broadly defined (G).[3] All time series are expressed in real terms.

Table 5 presents the Augmented Dickey-Fuller test for inspecting whether our time series exhibit stochastic trends. The results of ADF tests suggest that our time series are not stationary, since they have one unit root

Table 5 Augmented Dickey-Fuller Test for Unit Root

Variables	Trended 1 lag	Trended 2 lags	Untrended 1 lag	Untrended 2 lags
$y_t - k_t$	-3.36	-2.99 -	1.57 -	1.88
$l_t - k_t$	-2.14	-2.07 -	2.51 -	2.45
g_t	-2.46	-2.64 -	2.69 -	2.61
$\Delta(y_t - k_t)$	-3.76 *	-4.11 **	-6.83 **	-4.09 **
$\Delta(l_t - k_t)$	-4.07 *	-3.66 *	-4.05 **	-4.00 **
Δg_t	-3.83 *	-3.6 *	-3.87 **	-3.59 **

An asterisk (*) indicates significance at 5 per cent level, while two asterisks indicate significance at 1 per cent level. The critical values are from Dickey-Fuller. The definition of variables are as follows: $y_t - k_t$ = log (value added/private capital stock), $l_t - k_t$ = log (number of employees/ priv. capital stock), g_t = log (broad definition of infrastructure).

and, therefore, they are integrated of order 1, I(1).

Subsequently, Johansen's maximum likelihood estimation method (Johansen 1988, 1991) of a system of equations is implemented. The advantage of this method is that allows us to investigate the existence of more than one cointegration relationship between our variables. Furthermore, we estimate equation (3) within a system of equations which takes the following vector error correction model (VECM) form:

$$\Delta X_t = \Gamma_1 \Delta X_{t-1} + \Gamma_2 \Delta X_{t-2} + \ldots + \Gamma_{K+1} \Delta X_{t-K+1} + \Pi X_{t-K} + E_t, \quad (4)$$

where $X_t = (y_t - k_t, l_t - k_t, g_t)$ is a (3 x 1) vector of variables, $\Gamma_i = -(I - A_1 - \ldots - A_i)$ contains information on the short run adjustment to changes in X_t (A_i, i = 1,...k, is a (3 x 3) matrix of parameters), and $\Pi = -(I - \Sigma A_i)$, a (3 x 3) matrix of parameters, contains information on the long run adjustment (see Appendix 1 for more technical details).

Testing for cointegration among the non stationary variables of equation (3) is essentially a search of how many 'r' linearly independent columns exist in Π matrix of the system of equations (4). The rank of Π matrix defines the number of cointegration vectors. Moreover, we apply Johansen (1991) maximum likelihood estimation method in order to derive estimations of the system of equations (4) subject to the hypothesis that Π has reduced rank.

In Table 6 the maximum likelihood eigenvalue statistics are reported, suggesting that there is one cointegration vector, r = 1 even when adjusted for the degrees of freedom. The null hypothesis is that there is no cointegration relationship, r = 0, and it is rejected at the 5 per cent level, indicating that the rank of Π is 1.

Table 6 Johansen's Maximum Likelihood Method Test for Cointegration Relationship (number of lags = 1)

Ho: rank=p	λ_{MAX}	using T-nm	95%	Trace	using T-nm	95%
r = 0	44.06 **	39.8 **	21	56.68 **	51.2**	29.7
r <= 1	11.84	10.69	14.1	12.62	11.4	15.4

An asterisk (*) indicates significance at 5 per cent level, while two asterisks (**) indicates significance at 1 per cent level (see Osterwald-Lenum (1992)). T-nm are λ_{MAX} and Trace statistics are adjusted for the number of degrees of freedom.

In this case the normalised parameter estimates of the cointgration vector are as follows:

$$y_t - k_t = 0.48\,(l_t - k_t) + 0.25\,g_t \qquad (5)$$

The effect of public infrastructure, g_t, on private sector capital productivity is positive, indicating that a 1 per cent increase in infrastructure results in an increase in private capital productivity by 0.25 per cent. This finding is similar to the one obtained by Christodoulakis (1993) using the two stage Engle and Granger method. The magnitude of this elasticity reveals the importance of infrastructure for the productivity of the industrial sector.

It is reasonable to expect that building up infrastructure enhances the productivity of the industrial sector, benefiting in this way the whole Greek economy. The findings of the present study provide empirical evidence in favour of this expectation. Alas, public investment expenditures have been heavily curtailed since the late 1970s.

However, we have to be sceptical as much as the underlying causality issues are concerned. Moreover, the cointegration analysis implies Granger-causality in at least one direction. In the way that we order the variables in the VECM, the causality runs from infrastructure to private capital productivity. But a feedback between these two variables is actually possible. In fact one of the main criticisms of the importance of public infrastructure is the feedback that might exist between output and public capital stock.

In terms of our analysis, if public infrastructure, g, is weakly exogenous, the third equation in model (4) with g as dependent variable will not include the error correction term, $\Pi\Xi_{t-K}$. Therefore, the long-run solution of public infrastructure, g, will not be affected by departures from the equilibrium defined by the cointegration vector. Public infrastructure will be, then, considered to be weakly exogenous and as a result neither private capital productivity nor the ratio of labour to private capital causes public infrastructure.[4]

An X^2 test was implemented in order to test the significance of α_3 in P matrix (see Appendix 1) for the Greek industrial sector. It gave a value of $X^2(1) = 1.04$ [0.25], p-value in brackets. Hence the null hypothesis is not rejected, and as a result we can treat public infrastructure as an exogenous variable. The normalised parameter estimates of model (4) with infrastructure treated as a weakly exogenous variable are:

$$y_t - k_t = 0.62\,(l_t - k_t) + 0.18\,g_t \qquad (6)$$

The effect of public infrastructure on private sector productivity is found again to be positive and quite big in magnitude, implying that a 1 per cent increase in public infrastructure will increase private capital productivity by 0.18 per cent.

The importance of the above empirical findings rests on the underlying policy suggestions. The low quality of, but also the low level of the services provided by, Greek infrastructure has become proverbial. Moreover, it is frequently quoted in the literature that one of the main inefficiencies, which the Greek economy has to overcome in order to converge with the remaining member states of EU, is the construction of an adequate level of public infrastructure. The outcomes of the present study necessitate an active government involvement in providing infrastructure.

Conclusion

In the present paper public capital stock is considered to be an input of production that, separately from the private capital stock, enters the well known Cobb-Douglas production function. Using the specific methodological approach we are able to examine the effect of infrastructure on private capital productivity of the two digit industrial production. Our results provide robust evidence in favour of the argument that public capital stock increases private sector productivity. Furthermore, a cointegration vector captures the long run relationship between infrastructure and private capital productivity. No evidence is found in favour of the argument that private capital productivity can cause public infrastructure.

Although, the results of our study cannot be said to take account of every aspect of the impact of infrastructure on productivity, they suggest that public investment in the former can positively affect the latter, and as a result can improve the performance of the industrial sector of the Greek economy.

Over the last twenty years Greece has faced a rapid de-industrialisation process, that has resulted in the creation of many economic inactive regions in the country. Public infrastructure investment might be, after all, the missing link of the macroeconomic policy, since infrastructure projects can directly enhance the attractiveness and the competitiveness of the Greek economy.

Furthermore, with Greece being a lagging member of EU, the economy confronts many impediments in its convergence procedure with the rest of the member states. The poor provision of services derived from infrastructure may be the Achilles' heel for the development of the economy. And besides the fact that policy makers in 1990s realise that the construction of infrastructure is a necessity for the economy, the size of the required public investment is so high that is extremely uncertain if it can be entirely financed only by the state.

Knowing the financial difficulties of countries like Greece, EU raised funds that can be used by the less favoured member states. More precisely, the EU support framework for Greece gives priority to the creation of the appropriate infrastructure as a necessary condition for the development of the country and its convergence to the European standards (see Appendix 2). As a result, a big part of EU funds that flow in Greece are invested in infrastructure projects. It is expected that these funds together with public funds can build up the necessary base for invigorating the economy.

In fact, currently, Greek infrastructure is being modernised with the help of grants from EU. The incoming European structural funds amount to more than 5 per cent of GDP yearly for the period 1993–99.

Moreover, it has been recently announced by economic policy makers that Greece's ambition for the 21st century is to become a business and transport hub, linking south-east Europe with EU markets. Infrastructure will play a determinant role in fulfilling these expectations and plans.

In conclusion, one of the major problems in Greece over the 1970s and the 1980s was low productivity growth, and resulting widening productivity gap between Greece and the EU. The stagnation of government investment in the 1980s meant that there was no substantial progress in the implementation of major infrastructure projects. This was despite the fact that there was widespread recognition of the importance of several major projects for the country's economic restructuring. It is generally believed, both in Greece and the European Commission, that an infrastructure policy will bring Greece closer to the EU. Therefore, obtaining quantitative estimates of the role played by public infrastructure may be of some usefulness for the efficient allocation of community resources.

Notes

1. I would like to thank Chris Martin and Jonathan Haskel for their comments on an earlier draft. I am also grateful to Ruth Baldry, and two anonymous referees.
2. Preliminary estimations showed that industrial production in Greece exhibits increasing returns to scale (IRS) over all inputs, (results are available on request, see also Mamatzakis (1998)). Additionally previous studies for the Greek industrial sector also found IRS to hold over all inputs, see Christodoulakis (1993).
3. We follow the definition of infrastructure given by Diewert (1986), which embodies capital stock in ports, railways, motor vehicles, civil aviation, roads, electricity, and communications. Notice that in the way we define infrastructure we deliberately exclude the capital stock that is directly used in the production of public goods.
4. Mosconi and Giannini (1992) showed that we can implement a test for weak exogeneity using the Johansen maximum likelihood estimation method, by setting restrictions in the α matrix. Private capital productivity does not Granger-cause public infrastructure if the α_3 element of the Π matrix is equal to zero.

References

Aschauer, D.A. (1989a), 'Is Public Expenditure Productive?', *Journal of Monetary Economics*, Vol. 23.

Aschauer, D.A. (1989b), 'Public Investment and Productivity Growth in the Group of Seven', *Economic Perspectives*, Vol. 13, No. 5.

Bank of Greece, (various issues), *Monthly Statistical Bulletin*, Athens.

Christodoulakis, N. (1993), 'Public Infrastructure and Private Productivity: A Discussion of Empirical Studies and an Application to Greece', Paper presented in 1993 in the Summer School of the University of Warwick.

Diewert, W. E. (1986), 'The Measurement of the Economic Benefits of Infrastructure Services', in *Lecture Notes in Economics*, Vol. 278, Springer, Berlin.

Engle and Granger (1987), 'Co-integration and Error Correction: Representation, Estimation and Testing', *Econometrica*, Vol. 55, pp. 251–76

ESYE, National Statistical Office of Greece, *Annual Industrial Survey* (various years), Athens.

ESYE, National Statistical Office of Greece, *National Accounts* (various issues), Athens [in Greek].

European Commission (1995), 'Greece: Community Support Framework 1994–1999', in *EC Structural Funds*, Brussels.

Evans, P. and Karras, G (1994), 'Is Government Capital Productive? Evidence from a Panel of Seven Countries', *Journal of Macroeconomics*, Vol. 16, Spring, pp. 271–79.

Ford, R. and Poret, P. (1991), *Infrastructure and the Private Sector Productivity*, OECD Working Paper, No. 91.

Harris, R.I.D. (1995), *Using Cointegration Analysis in Econometric Modelling*, Harvester Wheatsheaf.

Johansen, S. (1988) 'Statistical Analysis of Cointegration Vestors', *Journal of Economic Dynamics and Control*, Vol. 12, pp. 231–54.

Johansen, S. (1991), 'Estimation and Hypothesis Testing of Cointegration Vectors in Gausian Vector Autoregressive Models', *Econometrica*, Vol. 59, No. 6, pp. 15–21.

KEPE (1991), Centre of Planning and Economic Research, in Skoutzos and Matheos (eds) *Net Fixed Capital Formation*, Athens.

Mamatzakis, E.C. (1998), 'Dynamic Responses of Private Productivity to Public Infrastructure', QMW College Working Paper, No. 391.

Mosconi, R. and Giannini, C. (1992), 'Non-Causality in Cointegrated Systems: Representation Estimation and Testing', *Oxford Bulletin of Economics and Statistics*, Vol. 54.

Munnel, A.H. (1990a) 'Why Has Productivity Growth Declined? Productivity and Public Investment', *Federal Reserve Bank of Boston, New England Economic Review*, Jan–Feb, pp. 3–22.

Munnel, A.H. (1990b), 'How Does Public Infrastructure Affects Regional Economic Performance?', *Federal Reserve Bank of Boston, New England Economic Review*, Sep./Oct.

Munnel, A.H. (1992), 'Infrastructure Investment and Economic Growth', *The Journal of Economic Perspectives*, Vol. 6, No. 4.

OECD (various issues), *Historical Statistics*, Paris.

Osterwald-Lenum, M. (1992), 'A Note with Quantiles of the Asymptotic Distribution of the Maximum Likelihood Cointegration Rank Test Statistics', *Oxford Bulletin of Economics and Statistics*, Vol. 54.

Appendix 1

Analytically, the system of equations in (4) takes the form:

$$
\begin{matrix} y_t - k_t \\ l_t - k_t \\ g_t \end{matrix}
=
\begin{matrix} \gamma_{i11}\gamma_{i12}\gamma_{i13} \\ \gamma_{i21}\gamma_{i22}\gamma_{i23} \\ \gamma_{i31}\gamma_{i32}\gamma_{i33} \end{matrix}
\; x \;
\begin{matrix} \Delta(y-k)_{t-i} \\ \Delta(l-k)_{t-i} \\ \Delta(g)_{t-i} \end{matrix}
+
\begin{matrix} \alpha_1 \\ \alpha_2 \\ \alpha_3 \end{matrix}
\left[\beta_1 \beta_2 \beta_3\right]
\begin{matrix} y_{t-k} - k_{t-k} \\ l_{t-k} - k_{t-k} \\ g_{t-k} \end{matrix}
+
\begin{matrix} \varepsilon_{1t} \\ \varepsilon_{2t} \\ \varepsilon_{3t} \end{matrix}
$$

Furthermore, the matrix Π can be decomposed into $\Pi = \alpha\beta'$, where the matrix α is a (3 x r) adjustment matrix, representing the speed of adjustment to equilibrium; b is a (r x 3) cointegration matrix of long run coefficients, such that $\beta' X_{t-k}$ represents up to (n - 1) cointegration relationships, which ensure that the matrix X_t converge to the long run steady state solution.

The lag value in the VECM equals two, k = 2. The specific lag length ensures that the residuals of the multivariate system are Gaussian, and therefore they do not suffer from autocorrelation, heteroscedasticity. It has been observed that our variables have an inherent drift, thus our system of equations has an unrestricted constant which allows for non-zero drift in the unit-root processes. Two impulse dummies were included in the system for the years 1963 and 1979. These variables are exogenous and thus, they are not entering the cointegration space. The Π matrix contains information on the long run relationships between our variables. If β has only one column, r = 1, there is one cointegration relationship between our variables.

Appendix 2

Distribution of EU Resources to Big Infrastructure in the Period 1994–99 (8.27 billions ECU)

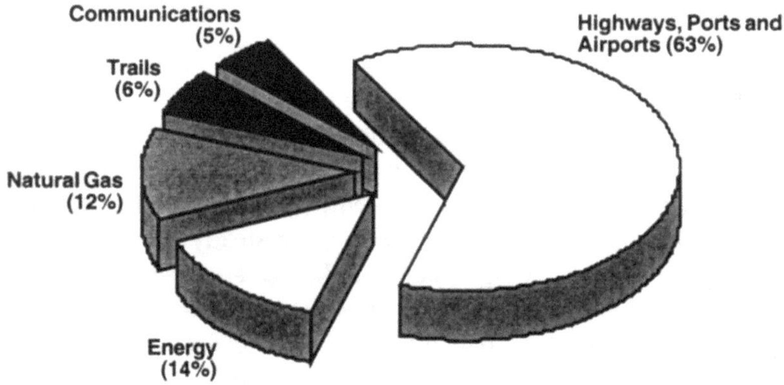

Source: European Commission, Brussels, 1995.

13 Institutional Networks, Learning and Greece's Adaptation within European Regional Policy

CHRISTOS J. PARASKEVOPOULOS

Introduction: Institutional Learning and Adaptation in European Regional Policy

The gradual Europeanisation of regional policy since the introduction of the Integrated Mediterranean Programmes (IMPs) in 1985, the reform of the Structural Funds in 1988 and, in particular, the operationalisation of the principles of partnership and subsidiarity, being considered as the main components of European structural policy, are seen as having far-reaching repercussions for the EU system of governance. In particular, although the development of European structural policy is viewed as a process of successive side-payments rounds in larger intergovernmental bargains aimed at buying off the agreement of the weaker member states in other policy areas, such as market integration or enlargement (Marks, 1992), the 'unintended consequences' (Pollack, 1995, p. 362) of the intergovernmental redistributive decisions should not be overlooked.

Thus, despite the coming back of the states in the post-Maastricht era through their upgraded role in the planning and implementation procedures of the Cohesion Fund (Mitsos, 1995), the empowerment of subnational governments across Europe is viewed as closely linked to the emergence of the system of 'multilevel governance' in the EU (Marks, 1993, p. 392), involving the 'outflanking' of the states (Marks, 1992, p. 212), by the transfer of authority on the one side to the supranational institutions and on the other to powerful regional bodies. The emergence of regionalism, however, is related to the increasing intensity of the changing, globalising political economy, which brings into question traditional functions of the nation states across Europe and emphasises the role of the endogenous political and socio-cultural resources in the development process. Moreover, there is evidence of a shift in the pattern of regional interests representation at the European level (that is, limited role of the Committee of Regions within the EU system of governance) from the well-known neo-corporatist system to a rather pluralistic and more competitive paradigm, that has been conceptualised as a system of 'competitive federalism' or 'disjointed pluralism' (Streeck and Schmitter, 1991, p. 159). Within this multi-layered policy-making environment, characterised by a great degree of interactions between actors, regional and local systems of governance are increasingly affected by the linkages with the supranational level and by their capacity to exploit the challenges those linkages present. Subsequently, in the era of globalisation the way in which the local is embedded into the global depends on the presence of a learning institutional infrastructure at the local level, rather than on the protective role of the state. Within the EU structural policy environment, this learning capacity is viewed as a crucial parameter that can improve the levels of effectiveness and efficiency in policy-making by facilitating the adaptation process.

The notion of 'learning', that has emerged recently within the theoretical framework of integration in Europe (Richardson, 1996, pp. 17–34; Kohler-Koch, 1996, pp. 370–71; Checkel, 1998; Paraskevopoulos, 1998b), is considered as a function of adaptable systems of 'governance under uncertainty' (Richardson, 1996, p. 20). It implies the process by which actors acquire new interests and identities and form their preferences through interactions with broader institutional contexts/norms (Checkel, 1998). Through these 'structure-actor' interactions, actors adapt their behaviour to meet the changes of the environment. As a predominantly interactive process, learning is crucially dependent on the way in which the system of intra-regional institutional interactions is shaped, on the adequacy of information and communication flows, and on the presence of fora for dialogue among the actors. The latter enable institutional actors, by their joint involvement in the processes of 'learning by doing' and 'learning by past successes and failures', to become adaptable, rather than adapted to changing conditions (Paraskevopoulos, 1998c). Learning in this environment is a function of past policy attempts (and the involved actors' interpretation of their successes and failures), of the capacities of institutions to design new activities, and of the changing ideas and shifting alliances and balance of power among the actors. Furthermore, within the EU structural policy environment, learning is viewed as significantly affected by the degree of decentralisation of the administrative structure of the state, which allows the stimulating of synergistic effects among the local actors. However, although the structure of the state may inhibit or facilitate the learning and adaptation processes at the local level, intergovernmental relations constitute a dynamic system that cannot be simply reduced to a symptom of the state structure (Klausen and Goldsmith, 1997). Hence, certain capacities for collective action that facilitate the shaping of the interactions and coalition-building among key social and economic actors at the local level are raised as the most important prerequisite for institutional learning and adaptation (Garmise, 1995b; Jeffery, 1997; Paraskevopoulos, 1998c).

In that sense, both formal and crucial informal institutional arrangements play the decisive role in determining the learning capacity of local systems of governance, their capability of adapting to changing conditions, and subsequently the degree of their mobilisation at the European level. This point has been strengthened by recent research outcomes, showing that the strength of associational culture and regional identity is the underlying factor of regional mobilisation at the European level, rather than a funding/resource focusing logic (Marks et al., 1996, pp. 61–3). This increasing importance of the capacities for collective action as a prerequisite for institutional learning and adaptation is underlined by the emergence of the network paradigm as an operational element of the institutional infrastructure at all stages of policy-making (Kenis and Schneider, 1991; Windhoff-Heritier, 1993; Kohler-Koch, 1996). The crucial question, however, refers to the old problem of what causes what structure or culture. Are the formal institutions the means to achieve collective action, or is their success dependent on the existence of important informal norms that evolve from culture, traditions and social behavioural codes? While existing empirical evidence suggests the differentiation of social norms is highly correlated with varying levels of institutional performance at the subnational level (Putnam, 1993), this chapter discusses this crucial issue within the framework of the EU system of governance.

The first section focuses on the role of institutional networks and social capital in resolving collective action problems through the processes of exchange and socialisation, thus facilitating learning and adaptation within the EU structural policy environment. Drawing upon the Greek specificities with regard to the Europeanisation process, the second section establishes the link between the presence of specific structural (network structure) and cultural (social capital endowments) features of the local institutional infrastructure on the one hand, and the existing inter-regional differentiation in the capacity of the local systems of governance for learning, adaptation and Europeanisation on the other. Based on evidence from Greece, the final section offers general conclusions for European structural policy and the EU system of governance.

Institutional Networks, Social Capital and Learning: Structuring Multi-Level Governance

The role of institutional networks and social capital in facilitating the learning and adaptation processes is related to their capacity for resolving dilemmas of collective action: by structuring the intra-regional institutional interactions the former, and by providing stable rules and procedures (social norms) that facilitate the exchange and flow of information and reduce uncertainty the latter.

Networks, in general, are based on relations or linkages and therefore they cannot be disassociated from the social or organisational system, which involves many other actors (Knoke and Kuklinski, 1982). Thus, institutional networks can be defined as systems of interactions involving both public and private institutional actors, which are linked around a certain policy domain or territory and hence bounded by it (Paraskevopoulos, 1998b,c). However, given that power within networks 'is the ability to attain higher levels of collective action' (Metcalfe, 1981, p. 504) and because of the high degree of resource interdependencies within inter-organisational networks, power relations are mainly based on the process of political exchange (Marin, 1990). Exchange relations involve a variety of resources (money, information, knowledge) and constitute one way to achieve collective action among the actors. In this respect, intra-regional functional networks, which tend to have a horizontal rather than a vertical structure and facilitate collective action by combining governmental and sectoral local actors and hence shaping the public/private relations and incorporating multiple type of resources, are considered as providing the appropriate organisational structure for learning and adaptation (Paraskevopoulos, 1998a,b,c).

The process of exchange, however, is profoundly influenced by the broad social context. Although it is based on actors' rational choices, the impact of the cultural factors cannot be ignored. While history and geography determine to a significant degree the way resources have been distributed, actors' choices with regard to the exchangeable resources are conditioned by norms, values, conventions and rules of behaviour. Thus, exchange relations do not depend on the availability of resources, but on actors' perceptions about their value and usefulness. Therefore, the value of the exchangeable resources and hence the shaping of the exchange process are determined through the socialisation function, within which social norms play the key role.

Within this theoretical framework, social capital has emerged as the crucial conceptual tool that, by facilitating 'certain actions of actors within the structure' (Coleman, 1988, p. 98), leads to the crossing of the old schism between structure and culture. As a resource for action available to an actor, it is one way of introducing the social structure into the rational choice paradigm (Coleman, 1988, p. 95; Ostrom, 1995). Although Coleman's (1990, pp. 300–302) definition of social capital as 'a set of inherent in the social organisation social-structural resources that constitute capital assets for the individual' implies it refers to individual actors (persons), it has been acknowledged as a crucial factor for facilitating collective action among corporate actors as well: 'because purposive organisations can be actors just as persons can, relations among corporate actors can constitute social capital for them as well' (Coleman, 1988, p. 98). Thus, social capital refers 'to features of social organisation, such as trust, norms, and networks that can improve the efficiency of society by facilitating coordinated action' (Putnam, 1993, p. 167) or, 'to internalised norms which stress the acceptance on the part of citizens of the positive role played by collective action in pursuing collective goods related to economic growth and social protection' (Leonardi, 1995b, p. 169). Hence, voluntary cooperation is easier in a community that has inherited a substantial stock of social capital, and the pursuit of collective goods is not seen as in contradiction with the pursuit of maximising individual wealth. In that sense, social capital points to the influence of social and cultural norms upon the rational or purposive action and sees social structure, institutional and economic performance as interactive systems. Trust constitutes the most important form of social capital, since it is viewed as the appropriate tool for resolving the inherent in the modern, volatile institutional settings uncertainty, by shaping the relations between partners (Storper, 1995; Sabel, 1993).

Although trust and inter-organisational networks are considered as factors that facilitate the restructuring process in areas of industrial decline, their use in the European regional policy environment is linked to the existing within the European policy-making environment similar needs for adaptation and adjustment (Paraskevopoulos, 1998c).

Under these considerations, the theoretical model of a learning institutional infrastructure in the European regional policy environment is based on a local functional network. Where there is lack of this type of networks, as in the Objective 1 regions of the smaller and more centralised member states, the adopted development strategies are usually driven by the central state administrative structures and therefore, irrespective of their effectiveness and efficiency, inhibit, rather than facilitate, the bottom-up learning and adaptation processes (Leonardi, 1995a).

On the other hand, European regional policy is considered a fundamental change in the system parameters that represents simultaneously a threat to the preexisting institutional arrangements in both the economic and political spheres, and an opportunity for institution-building and network-creation, especially in the less favoured Objective 1 regions. In particular, by challenging embedded structures and well-established interests at the regional and local levels, the Structural Funds programmes cause instability in the intra-network relations, which leads to the resistance to change on the part of some organisations for which change means loss of security and power. On the other hand, however, the EU programmes open up the process of institutional restructuring, especially in regions with poor institutional infrastructure, by weakening the position of firmly-established interests. This process facilitates the building of new institutions, because under specific conditions which are relevant to the Objective 1 regions, the process of institution-building presupposes the redundancy of the old institutional infrastructure (Storper, 1995).

Under these circumstances, the presence of multiple and collective leadership roles within the network can prevent the de-stabilisation of the intra-network relations, while, simultaneously, the collective response to the crisis can effectively moderate the local repercussions of the changes. Moreover, since institutional learning and adaptation are mainly processes of 'waking up and catching up' (Sabel, 1994, p. 137) and therefore usually undermine the stability of relations between the transacting institutional actors, an effective leadership functions as moderator of the tensions between learning and monitoring of the power relations that the changes may engender. Defined in this way, leadership requires the decentralisation of power and responsibility and a high level of involvement of the participants. On the other hand, trust provides the glue that cements and re-stabilises the relations among the actors and enhances the capacity of institutional networks to adapt to changing conditions (Paraskevopoulos, 1998b).

Figure 1 illustrates the way in which a learning institutional network at the local level, based on the processes of exchange and socialisation, can facilitate the learning and adaptation capacity of the region within the multi-level governance structure of European regional policy. In particular, the graph reveals the way in which the intra-regional interactions should be shaped. There is a group of actors (intra-regional functional network) linked with strong ties, while some of them (3,4,5) are loosely connected with other peripheral actors. This structure of the local interactions reflects both the need for local leadership involving public and private actors and the importance of the linkages with other peripheral local or non-local actors for access to new resources (information, knowledge, new ideas). Furthermore, the graph demonstrates the distribution of power among the actors based on

Figure 1 Learning and Adaptation in Multi-Level Governance Networks

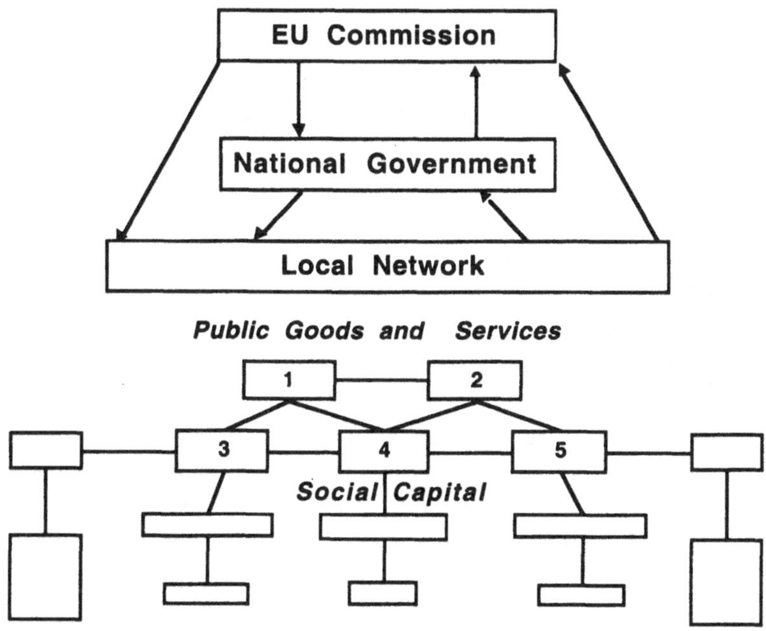

the process of exchange, whereby an actor's power is strengthened by his/her ability to combine external, as well as internal linkages and, therefore, access to multiple resources. Hence, the distribution of power within the network plays a key role in shaping the intra-regional interactions and achieving collective action. Finally, the role of social capital is to facilitate collective action among the actors through the socialisation process, which involves their active involvement in the provision of public goods and services that support the local productive system.

Therefore, social capital and institutional networks are identified as key components of the learning, adaptation and Europeanisation functions of subnational governments, by facilitating collective action among the actors through the processes of exchange and socialisation. Subsequently, exchange and socialisation constitute procedural components of the learning process. Within this framework, social capital, as the conceptual tool of the socialisation function, is considered a prerequisite for the learning process within networks. Thus, social capital, learning institutional infrastructure and adaptation are seen as interdependent concepts within European structural policy.

Greece and Europeanisation: The Response to an External Shock

Greece's centralised state structure and weak civil society are considered major impediments to both the exchange and socialisation functions at the regional and local levels and subsequently to the learning, adaptation and Europeanisation processes, by undermining the capacities for collective action (Paraskevopoulos, 1998a,c).

Indeed, despite the major reforms imposed by the Europeanisation process in the 1980s and 1990s, involving the establishment of the thirteen regions, the elected second tier of local government at the prefectural level and the creation of viable local government units by the compulsory merger of the communes ('Capodistrias plan'), the centralised administrative system, and the hierarchical intergovernmental networks are still considered identical characteristics of public policy making. This structure affects the distribution of resources and power among the local actors and subsequently constitutes a major impediment to the building of horizontal cooperative (functional) networks through the process of exchange at the regional and local levels, thus inhibiting Greece's adjustment to the European environment.

On the other hand, the question of civicness constitutes a crucial issue for the Greek socio-political structure, since both the administrative weaknesses and the clientelistic political system seem to be associated with an 'extremely weak civil society' (Mouzelis, 1995, p. 19) and the lack of social capital endowments (Paraskevopoulos, 1998a,c). The underpinnings of these mutually reinforcing processes are identified with the dominant in the modern Greek state-history cross-sectional cultural schism – the Diamandouros's *cultural dualism*[1] – between two powerful trends: the Western, which derives from the Enlightenment traditions of rule of law, constitutionalism and civicness, and the Byzantine-Ottoman, which is characterised by the combination of strong state, clientelism and the Orthodox Church (Diamandouros, 1994, p. 8; Mouzelis, 1995).

This cultural differentiation and the predominance of the 'underdog culture' during the transitional and post-civil war periods (Diamandouros, 1994, p. 15) have had far-reaching repercussions for Greece's capacity to adapt to the European environment, by obstructing the socialisation function. Additionally, the peculiar combination of populism and clientelism with elements of state corporatism after the emergence of PASOK in the 1980s (Mavrogordatos, 1988) led to what may be called 'state clientelist corporatism' (Paraskevopoulos, 1998c), that has deteriorated the state/society relations at the expense of the latter.

Under these conditions, the centralisation of regional planning, accompanied by the lack of formal or informal channels of information exchange and communication on intra or inter-regional basis, has constituted a major impediment to the implementation and monitoring of both the IMPs and the Regional Operational Programmes (ROPs) of the CSFs (Paraskevopoulos, 1998a,c).

Yet, notwithstanding the unfavourable circumstances, the Europeanisation process is interpreted as an external shock for the 'inward-looking political class' (Tsoukalis, 1993, p. 256), society and the economy by imposing pressures for change. Interestingly enough, these trends have brought about changes in the political system, which in the post-Papandreou era demonstrates signs of a 'from above' movement towards a more prompt structural adjustment to the European environment.

Additionally, existing evidence from the Aegean islands (Paraskevopoulos, 1998a,b,c) points to some signs of disassociation with the state structure differentiation in learning capacity and institution-building among regions and prefectures, which underlines the role of the local specificities in the adaptation process. In particular, qualitative features of the local institutional infrastructure in the regions of Southern and Northern Aegean islands, such as the structure of the local networks (density and centralisation measures of Tables 1 and 2)[2] and civic culture (social capital endowments) have played a key role in facilitating or inhibiting the capacities for collective action, learning and adaptation to the European environment.

Table 1 Density Measures for General Exchange and Policy Networks

	Networks of General Exchange	Policy Networks
Southern Aegean Islands	*0.367*	*0.414*
Dodecanese Prefecture	0.727	0.800
Cyclades Prefecture	0.545	0.636
Northern Aegean Islands	*0.237*	*0.277*
Lesbos Prefecture	0.418	0.564
Chios Prefecture	0.528	0.611
Samos Prefecture	0.595	0.667

Thus, despite the centralised structure of the state and subsequently the leading role of public actors (Regional Secretariat and Prefecture Councils), the local networks in the Dodecanese and Cyclades prefectures demonstrate a horizontal rather than vertical structure. What this structure reveals is that the institutional infrastructure of the prefectures is based on cohesive functional networks that combine public and private actors and constitute key components for the formation of the local institutional interactions. Additionally, these actors of the functional networks may provide alternative solutions for the leadership roles in the future, since the latest reforms lead to a less hierarchical structure of the intergovernmental relations. The horizontal structure of institutional interactions in Cyclades and Dodecanese seems to be related to the presence of some social capital endowments substantiated by civic participation in networks of civic engagement, and reflects the comparatively more balanced distribution of resources and power among the actors, which allows for horizontal exchange of valuable resources (knowledge, information) and facilitates the learning and adaptation processes (Paraskevopoulos, 1998a,b,c).

Table 2 Centrality Measures of General Exchange and Policy Networks

	Networks of General Exchange	Policy Networks
Southern Aegean Islands	*70.00%*	*64.74%*
Dodecanese Prefecture	33.33%	24.44%
Cyclades Prefecture	54.55%	43.64%
Northern Aegean Islands	*83.55%*	*79.22%*
Lesbos Prefecture	71.11%	53.33%
Chios Prefecture	60.71%	50.00%
Samos Prefecture	53.33%	46.67%

Conversely, the vertical structure of the networks in the prefectures of the Northern Aegean indicates the lack of core functional networks that would combine public and private actors and facilitate collective action and coordination of resources at the local level. Hence, the local system of governance is overwhelmingly dependent on the central state through the system of intergovernmental relations. This weakness of the institutional infrastructure in the prefectures of the Northern Aegean has led to a policy-making environment characterised by the dominant role of the Regional Secretariat as the leading actor within the institutional structure of each prefecture, since the local system of governance cannot provide an indigenous leadership. This vertical and hierarchical structure of the local system of governance has constituted a major impediment to the learning and adaptation processes in the Northern Aegean islands, which is illustrated by the problematic adjustment of their economic structures to the changing economic environment in the 1960s and 1970s. These structural features of the local institutional infrastructure, however, go hand in hand with an extremely weak civil society, substantiated by the lack of important networks of civic participation (Paraskevopoulos, 1998a,b,c).

These characteristics of the institutional networks played an important role in determining the adaptation capacity of the two regions to the European environment. Thus, whereas in the Southern Aegean their pre-existing institutional capacity facilitated their comparatively successful adjustment to European regional policy, illustrated by the improvement of the local institutional infrastructure, the high absorption rates in the sub-programmes of the ROP and the strengthening of the outward-looking orientation of the local networks, in the Northern Aegean the Europeanisation of regional policy signaled the start up of the process of institution-building, which led to a substantial improvement in local institutional capacity.

Concluding Remarks

This chapter has argued that social capital and institutional networks, by facilitating collective action among the actors through the processes of exchange and socialisation, constitute key components of dynamic political and economic governance at the regional level, which is closely linked to the learning capacity, adaptability and Europeanisation function of sub-national governments across Europe.

In the case of Greece, the combination of a centralised state structure and a weak civil society is considered the main obstacle for achieving politico-economic performance and adapting to the European environment. Thus, the prospects for adaptation and adjustment rely decisively on 'from above' initiatives towards the changing of the rules which, however, cannot sustain the process in the long run. The following lessons should be drawn from the case of Greece. First, local partnerships and networking, by enabling regional actors to be involved in cooperative relations and in the provision of public goods that support the productive system, constitute the crucial factors for institutional learning and adaptation in the less favoured regions of Europe and hence a criterion for the success or failure of the Structural Funds programmes. Second, although regional differentiation within centralised states is possible, it usually reflects a pre-existing differentiation in institutional capacity. Finally, even if the preexisting local capacity in terms of learning and institution-building is poor, the challenge of Europeanisation and the involvement in EU programmes and initiatives constitutes a positive external shock for the local systems of governance, which results to the improvement of the local institutional infrastructure.

Notes

1. The notion of 'cultural dualism', which in the Greek case has a cross-sectional nature in the sense that it is not exclusively identified with specific institution or structure but rather crosscuts every institution in Greek society, is used by Diamandouros under the conceptual framework of the 'critical juncture', that is a determinant of the developmental trajectory useful in both 'path-dependence analysis' and 'chaos theory' (Diamandouros, 1994, pp. 6–7).
2. The density measures refer to the degree of connectedness of the entire network, whereby zero indicates no connections between any actor and one means that all actors are linked to one another. Centrality measures, on the other hand, reveal actors' involvement in network relations and demonstrate the structure – horizontal or vertical – of the network. Hence, density and centrality measures together are used as indicators of the coherence and the structure of the networks.

References

Checkel, J.T. (1998), *Social Construction, Institutional Analysis and the Study of European Integration*, paper presented at the 26th ECPR–Joint Sessions of Workshops, University of Warwick, 23–28 March.

Coleman, J.S. (1988), 'Social Capital in the Creation of Human Capital', *American Journal of Sociology*, Vol. 94, Supplement, pp. 95–120.

Coleman, J.S. (1990), *Foundations of Social Theory*, Cambridge: Belknap Press of Harvard University Press.

Diamandouros, N. (1994), *Cultural Dualism and Political Change in Postauthoritarian Greece*, Estudio/Working Paper 1994/50, Juan March Institute, Madrid.

Garmise, S.O. (1995a), *Institutional Networks and Industrial Restructuring: Local Initiatives toward the Textile Industry in Nottingham and Prato*, Unpublished Ph.D. Thesis, London School of Economics.

Garmise, S.O. (1995b), 'Economic development strategies in Emilia-Romagna', in Rhodes, M. (ed), *The Regions and the New Europe: Patterns in Core and Periphery Development*, Manchester: Manchester University Press.

Jeffery, C. (1997), *Sub-National Authorities and European Integration: Moving Beyond the Nation-State?* Paper presented at the Fifth Biennial International Conference of the European Community Studies Association, Seattle, USA, May 29–June 1.

Kenis, P. and Schneider, V. (1991), 'Policy Networks and Policy Analysis: Scrutinizing a New Analytical Toolbox', in Marin, B. and Mayntz, R. (eds), *Policy Networks:*

Empirical Evidence and Theoretical Considerations, Colorado: Westview Press.
Klausen, K. and Goldsmith, M. (1997), 'Conclusion: Local Government and the European Union', in Goldsmith, M. and Klausen, K. (eds), *European Integration and Local Government*, Cheltenham: Edward Elgar.
Knoke, D. and Kuklinski, J.H. (1982), *Network Analysis*, California: Sage Publications.
Kohler-Koch, B. (1996), 'Catching up With Change: The Transformation of Governance in the European Union', *Journal of European Public Policy*, Vol. 3, No. 3, pp. 359–80.
Leonardi, R. (1995a), *Convergence, Cohesion and Integration in the European Union*, London: Macmillan.
Leonardi, R. (1995b), 'Regional Development in Italy: Social Capital and the Mezzogiorno', *Oxford Review of Economic Policy*, Vol. 11, No. 2, pp. 165–79.
Marin, B. (1990), 'Introduction', in Marin, B. (ed), *Governance and Generalized Exchange: Self-Organizing Policy Networks in Action*, Frankfurt: Campus Verlag, pp. 13–25.
Marks, G. (1992), 'Structural Policy in the European Community' in Sbragia, A. (ed), *Euro-Politics, Institutions and Policy-making in the 'New' European Community*, Washington D.C.: The Brookings Institution.
Marks, G. (1993), 'Structural Policy and Multilevel Governance in the EC' in Cafruny, A.W. and Rosenthal, G.G. (eds), *The State of the European Community: The Maastricht Debates and Beyond*, Vol. 2, London: Longman Group.
Marks, G., Nielsen, F., Leonard, R. and Salk J. (1996), 'Competencies, Cracks and Conflicts: Regional Mobilization in the European Union', in Marks, G., Scharpf, F.W. Schmitter, P. and Streeck, W. (eds), *Governance in the European Union*, London: Sage, pp. 40–63.
Mavrogordatos, G. (1988), *Between Pityokamptes and Prokroustes: Employers' Organizations in Contemporary Greece*, Athens: Odysseas [in Greek].
Metcalfe, L. (1981), 'Designing precarious partnerships', in Nystrom, P.C. and Starbuck, W.H. (eds), *Handbook of Organizational Design: Vol. 1; Adapting Organizations to Their Environments*, Oxford: Oxford University Press, pp. 503–30.
Mitsos, A. (1995), *The Community's Redistributive and Development Role in the Post-Maastricht Era*, Unpublished Manuscript.
Mouzelis, N.P. (1995), 'Greece in the Twenty-first Century: Institutions and Political Culture', in Constas, D. and Stavrou, T.G. (eds), *Greece Prepares for the Twenty-First Century*, Washington, D.C.: Johns Hopkins University Press and Woodrow Wilson Center Press.
Ostrom, E. (1995), 'Self-organization and Social Capital', *Industrial and Corporate Change*, Vol. 4, No. 1, pp. 131–59.
Paraskevopoulos, C.J. (1997a), 'Social Capital, Institutional Networks and the Adaptation of Greek Regions in European Regional Policy', paper presented to the *25th ECPR–Workshop on 'Social Capital and Politico-Economic Performance'*, Bern, Switzerland, February 27–March 4.
Paraskevopoulos, C.J. (1997b), 'Social Capital and Learning Institutional Networks: Making Sense of Subsidiarity in European Regional Policy', *TOPOS Review of Urban and Regional Studies*, Vol. 12, pp. 3–29 [in Greek].
Paraskevopoulos, C.J. (1998a), 'Social Capital and the Public/Private Divide in Greek Regions', *West European Politics*, Vol. 21, No. 2, pp. 154–77.
Paraskevopoulos, C.J. (1998b), 'Institutional Learning and Adaptation: Redefining the 'Limits' of the Integration Process in Europe with Evidence from Structural Policy', paper presented to the Workshop on Institutional Analyses of European Integration, 26th ECPR–Joint Sessions, University of Warwick, 23–28 March.
Paraskevopoulos, C.J. (1998c), 'Social Capital, Institutional Learning and European Regional Policy: Evidence From Greece', *Regional and Federal Studies*, Vol. 8, No. 3, pp. 31–64.

Pollack, M. (1995), 'Regional Actors in an Intergovernmental Play: The Making and Implementation of EC Structural Policy', in Rhodes, C. and Mazey, S. (eds), *The State of European Union, Vol.3: Building a European Polity?* Boulder: Lynne Rienner Publishers, pp. 361–90

Putnam, R.D. with Leonardi, R. and Nanetti, R. (1993), *Making Democracy Work: Civic Traditions in Modern Italy*, Princeton: Princeton University Press.

Richardson, J. (1996), *Actor Based Models of National and EU Policy-Making*, University of Essex, Dept of Government, Discussion paper No. 103.

Sabel, C. (1993), 'Studied Trust: Building New Forms of Cooperation in a Volatile Economy', in Swedberg, R. (ed), *Explorations in Economic Sociology*, New York: Russell Sage Foundation, pp. 104–44.

Sabel, C. (1994), 'Learning by Monitoring: The Institutions of Economic Development', in Smelser, N.J. and Swedberg, R. (eds), *The Handbook of Economic Sociology*, Princeton: Russell Sage Foundation, Princeton University Press.

Storper, M. (1995), 'The Resurgence of Regional Economies, Ten Years Later: The Region as a Nexus of Untraded Interdependencies', *European Urban and Regional Studies*, Vol. 2, No. 3, pp. 191–221.

Streeck, W. and Schmitter, P.C. (1991), 'From National Corporatism to Transnational Pluralism: Organised Interests in the Single European Market', *Politics and Society*, Vol. 19, No. 2, pp. 133–64.

Tsoukalis, L. (1993), *The New European Economy: The Politics and Economics of Integration*, Oxford: Oxford University Press.

Windhoff-Heritier, A. (1993), 'Policy Network Analysis: A Tool for Comparative Political Research', in Keman, H. (ed), *Comparative Politics: New Directions in Theory and Method*, Amsterdam: VU University Press, pp. 143–60.

14 Greek Orthodoxy and European Identity

EFTERPE FOKAS

Introduction

Easter is the most important event in Orthodox Christianity: it forms the central point of the ecclesiastical year, and the Holy Week services leading to it are marked by an especially reverential mood. Thus it came as quite a surprise when, after the service in an island village church, the priest read to a bewildered congregation a three-page encyclical warning against the threat the European Union's Schengen Agreement poses to 'our Orthodoxy'.[1] The proposed European census is a menace to the freedom of the individual Greek, the argument went, and its use of a computer system which somehow hinges on the number 666 is an offence to the faith. The Church is certainly not indifferent to Greece's place in the European Union. This is just one example of the ways in which the complex interrelationships between the political nation and the Orthodox tradition manifest themselves. Although the agenda of this conference was largely focused on politics and economics, questions of religion, culture and identity surfaced repeatedly: three out of four speakers on the panel that concluded the conference referred to religion both as a factor separating Greece from its EU partners and as a possible Greek contribution to Europe. A thorough examination of the place of Greece in the European Union, then, must also consider the role played by Orthodoxy as a large part of Greek identity in general,[2] and as a focal point for internal and external perceptions specifically about Greece and its relation to the West.

The role of the Church in contemporary Greek society has been explored through a number of issues. The scope here is limited to whether, how, and to what extent Greece's Orthodox identity affects the nation's place in the European Union. Even thus restricted the subject is vast, and space limitations allow only an introduction of certain complex issues which deserve deeper analysis. Thus the focus is further confined to those opinions, events, etc., which do represent an incompatibility between Orthodoxy and European identity. Religion and culture are, in many cases, deeply intertwined,[3] and the interplay between these factors and 'identity' is particularly salient in light of two political realities: the post-Cold War heightened attention to ethnicity, religion and identity; and the efforts at the EU level to establish a common cultural 'European identity'. In the context of contemporary Europe, where religious and cultural divisions are increasingly employed to draw borders in defining national identities, a critical question arises: does Greece's Eastern Orthodox faith – unique among its Catholic and Protestant, 'Western' European partners – affect the country's 'European identity'? One of the oldest divisions in Europe is that between Eastern and Western Christianity, and the cultural and political differences which developed between the two spheres have permeated their respective traditions. Certainly there is no inherent incompatibility between the Orthodox faith and the European unification project, nor with participation therein. In fact, the opposite could more easily be said: Orthodox leaders have substantially sanctioned the unification project and declared Orthodoxy's important role to be played in it.[4] Orthodoxy viewed as a national tradition, though – a preserver of ethnicity and a historical statement about Greece – has been portrayed by certain schools of thought, within and outside of Greece, as a barrier between Greece and the EU. It is through this second sense that Orthodoxy has been interpreted as an anti-European force proclaiming nonconformity to a unified Europe, and it is this interpretation of Orthodoxy which forms a focal point for this paper.

Clearly the EU has no official religious denomination: pockets of religious minorities exist within the fifteen member states, and references to religion in the context of the EU are usually controversial and tend to be avoided (particularly with reference to Turkey's application for membership). The post-Cold War struggles toward separatism, sovereignty and minority rights, however, have drawn international attention, academic and political, to issues of religion. Newly (re-) emerging identities and borderlines have introduced new conceptions of insiders and outsiders and have increased the already existing tensions generated by the movement of migrants, workers and refugees. Meanwhile, within this complex framework the European Union claims and hopes to be an entity beyond mere political and economic union, but also representative of a European identity reflecting a 'European civilisation'. The nine member states in 1973 signed the 'Declaration on the European Identity', proclaiming their 'same attitudes toward life' (Shore, 1993, p. 787). This declaration constituted the first significant step in a series of Community 'cultural policies' which, upon careful consideration, invoke the concern that they 'might...inadvertently promote new forms of xenophobia and cultural chauvinism' (Shore, 1993, p. 779). In as much as religion is a strong factor of culture and identity, religion plays a crucial, though difficult to elucidate, role in the developing 'European identity' of the European Union. To discern the implications for Greece, the relationship between religion and European identity must first be understood. From within such a framework we will address the case of Greece through perceptions – external and internal to Greece – of Orthodoxy as a factor dividing Greece from the West, Europe, and the European Union. Critical attention will also be paid to the historically and politically salient association between the faith and national identity. Finally, we will bring to light theoretical and empirical conclusions which follow from these facts.

European Identity and Religion

A scholar of European history has noted that 'the interweaving of the notions of Europe and Christendom is a fact of history which even the most brilliant sophistry cannot undo' (Hugh Seton-Watson, 1985, p.16). Indeed, 'ideas of Europe' have been permeated with references to Christianity and, more precisely, to a particular type of Christianity – that corresponding to the Western side of the Great Schism in the Christian Church.[5] The use here of the term 'religion' in the context of European identity consciously reflects these generalisations and biases which historically formed around it as both inclusive and exclusionary, both affirming and denying European identity.[6] Our current focus is those generalisations which carry implications for the Greek claim to European identity. In 'Religion in Contemporary Europe', David Martin writes that 'Religion is one reason why older maps exist like older paintings underneath contemporary configurations' (1994, p. 14). This remark highlights a point which is crucial for both the European and Greek contexts – Europe's religious history, including its unity and divisions, exists underneath conceptions of the meaning of Europe.

The connection between religion and European identity has been a prevailing factor in contemporary works on Europe written from historical, sociological and international relations perspectives. Introducing his ambitious work Europe: A History, Norman Davies suggests that 'geographical Europe has always had to compete with notions of Europe as a cultural community'(1997, p. 9). Where common political structures were absent, he contends, culture provided the criteria by which European civilisation could be defined, and Christianity especially filled this cultural role. Taking for granted that the East-West divide is a major marker of Europe not only in terms of geography but in terms of culture and 'civilisation', he proceeds to note that one of the most durable lines which have acted to divide Europe into East and West is that between Catholic (Latin) Christianity and Orthodox (Greek) Christianity (Davies, 1997, p. 27). Gerard Delanty's Inventing Europe: Idea, Identity, Reality (1995) explores both factors of religion and civilisation in their role as 'definers' of Europe. Giving considerable weight to the issue of religion, he does address the two halves of Western Christendom separately, but only before noting that 'what is to be stressed is that while the Reformation divided Europe between a Protestant north and a Catholic south, Christianity continued to be the principal source of cultural identity. It should not be forgotten that the divisions between Roman Catholic and Protestant regions in Western Europe were never as great as the gulf that separated Latin Christianity from Greek Christianity' (Delanty, 1995, p. 67). He contends that the idea of Europe as Occident fills the space left behind by Christianity as a unifying factor: 'When the idea of Europe replaced Christendom as the dominant cultural model, the notion of the Occident was retained as its referent. In this way the idea of Europe became a secular surrogate for Christendom' (Delanty, 1995, p. 68). Christianity relinquished its privileged position as the unifying theme in Western civilisation; it was in this space that the idea of Europe was first established as an autonomous idea. Arguably, though, the confessional frontier between Eastern and Western Christendom is not the sole definer of religious Europe. Though the focus on this division generally resonates in historio-sociological works on the 'idea of Europe', it underestimates the historical and contemporary significance of divisions within Western Christianity. The frontier between Catholicism and Protestantism may also be viewed as fundamental and consequential.[7] It is also simplistic to overlook the divisions internal to Europe created by religious minorities – 'les frontieres sont dans la ville' (Pieterse, 1995, p. 83). Better represented in the literature on the idea of Europe is the division between Islam and

Christianity and its important role in forging a conception of Europe as a religious and cultural entity (see Delanty, 1995; Halecki, 1950; Gerbod, 1977). Two concepts, in any case, largely shaped the idea of Europe – Western Christendom and Western Civilisation. To what extent are these historical ideas on European identity reflected in contemporary Europe?

According to David Martin, 'religion is currently providing one of the major markers of what is Europe' – any culturally viable interpretation of which thins out eastward.[8] This is clear, according to Martin, by the way faith interacts with the intimacies of life at religious borders: the different faiths 'there define worlds of difference' (Martin, 1994, p. 14). Though the terms 'Europe' and 'European' are imprecise, and the political and cultural identities of Europe indistinct, 'this is hardly an obstacle to making claims in everyday conversation about distinctively European practices or institutions...we can usually tolerate a wide margin of ambiguity and imprecision about things European. Is this true for religion in Europe?' (Beckford, 1994, p.160). Indeed, though ambiguity surrounds so much of what we discuss as 'European', and though religion in Europe is no more a precise phenomenon, yet discussion about it does tend to assume an air of precision. This phenomenon has given rise to the scholarly opinion that, in spite of a general decline in religious practice and the extent of religion's significance for public life in Western Europe, 'the continent's boundaries are becoming more sharply defined in religious terms' (Beckford, 1994, p. 167). Meanwhile, the continent's most recognised boundaries have come to be those drawn by the European integration project; for better or for worse, the EU is increasingly viewed as the indicator of what is 'European'.[9] Thus, the extent to which religion plays a role in contemporary 'ideas of Europe', particularly within the context of the EU project to create a common European identity, carries major significance for those nations which lie outside particular narrow definitions of such an identity.[10]

The View From 'the West'

Given these close linkages made between religion, civilisation and European identity, it is instructive to examine the possible role of Greece's Orthodox identity in the larger framework of post-Cold War Europe. The East-West divide during the Cold War was clear and convenient for theorists; the end of the Cold War, however, has re-introduced the difficult issue of how to understand, and where to draw geographically, the distinction between the two spheres.[11] NATO and EU expansion plans have politicised the issue, and the deeper questions of division – taking into account history, culture, and religion – have come to the forefront of popular consciousness. This new awareness of such issues, however, has also been spurred vividly by select, often radical theories which have emerged since the end of the Cold War. These have to be addressed here for the tremendous implications they carry for Greece.[12]

Samuel Huntington, Director of the Olin Institute for Strategic Studies and professor at Harvard University, has put forth one of the most prominent and controversial of these in his highly publicised 1993 Foreign Affairs articles and subsequent publication The Clash of Civilizations and the Remaking of World Order. Huntington articulates a theory concerning the patterns of conflict which will emerge through this transition in world politics after the end of the Cold War: although nation-states will continue to act as the most powerful actors in world affairs, 'The fault lines between civilisations will be the battle lines of the future' (1993b, p. 22). The concept is controversial, but what sparks especially heated debate, particularly amongst Greek intellectuals, is how and where Huntington draws his fault line in Europe. In defining civilisations as cultural entities which are based on villages, regions, ethnic groups, nationalities, and religious groups, Huntington identifies seven or eight major civilisations, two of which exist in Europe – 'Western' and 'Slavic-Orthodox'. The emphasis on religion as one of the most important factors shaping civilisations carries weighty implications for Greece, as the nation's religious orientation would place it in the non-Western camp of conflicting civilisations. Meanwhile, the other factors listed alongside religion as distinctions between civilisations are also significant in the case of Greece – history, language, culture and tradition; 'They [such differences] are far more fundamental than differences among political ideologies and political regimes' (1993b, p. 25). For, where identity is defined in ethnic or religious terms, an 'us' versus 'them' relation emerges in popular consciousness between peoples of different ethnicity or religion.[13] Huntington also sanctions the placement of Greece in the non-Western side of the European fault line with the contention that 'economic regionalism may succeed only when it is rooted in a common civilisation. The European Community rests on the shared foundation of European culture and Western Christianity' (1993b, p. 27). Huntington cites Jacques Delors, speaking as president of the European Community, as support for his civilisational paradigm: 'future conflicts will be sparked by cultural factors rather than economics or ideology' (1993a, p. 194).

Either Huntington is wrong, or there is some inconsistency in Eastern Orthodox Greece's membership in this (Western) European Union. The implications are enormous: 'The Cold War began when the Iron Curtain divided Europe politically and ideologically. The Cold War ended with the end of the Iron Curtain. As the ideological division of Europe has disappeared, the cultural division of Europe between Western Christianity, on the one hand, and Orthodox Christianity and Islam, on the other has reemerged' (1993b, pp. 29–30). That line dividing Western Christianity from Orthodox Christianity and Islam (which, in the Balkans, coincides with the geographic divisions between the Habsburg and Ottoman Empires), unites the Protestant and Catholic peoples of north and west in common experiences of European history (feudalism, the Renaissance, the Reformation, the Enlightenment, the French Revolution, the Industrial Revolution) against the peoples to the east and south, the Orthodox and Muslim, whose experiences under the Ottoman or Tsarist empires isolated them from the events that shaped the rest of Europe. Based upon these differences, 'the Velvet Curtain of culture has replaced the Iron Curtain of ideology as the most significant dividing line in Europe' (1993b, pp. 30–32). Greece's membership in the EU thus emerges as paradoxical, or as an unlikely exception at best.

Such views are by no means limited to Huntington. The age-old lumping together of 'Eastern', 'Balkan', 'Byzantine', and 'Greek' in terms of an 'other' is still quite prominent in political and academic thinking and serves to solidify a view of Orthodoxy as un-Western and un-European. Robert Kaplan's popular book Balkan Ghosts (1994), for instance, likens the friction between Catholicism and Orthodoxy with that between Communism and capitalism. According to Kaplan, before the end of the Cold War, only Westerners who were, like him, living in Greece could realise 'how Balkan Greece was' (1994, p. 239): 'They were Western only in the sense that they aspired to be Western…more a child of Byzantium and Turkish despotism than of Periclean Athens', stricken with 'the poison of eastern despotism and decline, seeping from Byzantium' (1994, p. 248). Keith Legg and John Roberts' Modern Greece: a Civilisation on the Periphery, puts forth the thesis that geography and culture have been and will continue to be central determinants of the Greek political, economic and social development, and especially in the context of the European Union: 'Greece's economic and political institutions are unlikely to adapt successfully to the demands of full participation' (1996, p. 2). The conclusion expressed in the final chapters is that the nation's geography and culture put into question the country's Cold War classification as European.[14]

Statements made by prominent media and political figures resonate these ideas. According to former Vice Chancellor Erhard of Austria, 'the WEU does not well understand the Orthodox portions of Europe'. George Kennan suggests that 'the roots [of the current Balkan problem] ...reach back, clearly, not only into the centuries of Turkish domination but also into the Byzantine penetration of the Balkans even before that time...thrusting into the southeastern reaches of the European continent a salient of non-European civilization that has continued to the present day to preserve many of its non-European characteristics' (Prodromou, 1997, pp. 126–127).

In a *Le Monde* article entitled 'In the Orthodox World, Religion Sacralises the Nation, and the Nation Protects the Religion',[15] the Greek Constitution's affirmation of Orthodoxy as 'the dominant religion in Greece' spurs the question: 'Is this compatible with the existence of a modern state and with participation in the European Union?'. And, according to a writer for The Spectator, Greece, 'from being one of us since the [Cold] War, has become one of them [the Balkans]. With the collapse of the Soviet Empire in eastern and Central Europe, Greece's usefulness [to the Western Alliance]...has disappeared' (Prodromou, 1997, p. 130). Former Secretary General of NATO Willy Claes echoed the same attitude: 'the events of recent years have demonstrated that human nature is profoundly influenced by the historical, cultural and social environment, whether it is short-lived, like the years of communism, or long-lasting, like the division of Europe into Latin and Byzantine worlds' (Carras, 1994). Thus, from a range of academic and political perspectives, Greece as an Orthodox Christian country is deemed un-European, un-Western, relegated to a civilisational camp different from that of its fellow members of the European Union and the rest of the West.

The View From Within

To what extent are such ideas reflected, or even spurred by, facts and opinions internal to Greece?[16] A reference to Orthodox doctrine shows that resistance to the West, Europe, or to the European Union specifically has no real theological basis. However, resistance to the West and to Europe is embedded in theological discourse, and it is in the intermingling of these realms – political and social convictions expressed in theological discourse – that we find Orthodoxy portrayed as a force hostile to the EU. A historical view reveals the powerful elements of anti-Westernism (highlighting the 1054 schism of the Christian Church, the experience under and following the Ottoman Empire, and the resistance to modernisation) and anti-Europeanism (emphasising distrust of the Roman Catholic and Protestant dominated Union). Meanwhile, the construction of the modern Greek state drafted Western, liberal political institutions onto the traditional Greek heritage.[17] The result was the emergence of two powerful and often sharply conflicting cultural traditions, 'embedded in the novel (Western) and antecedent (Byzantine-Ottoman) elements of the modern Greek historical experience, which, over time, reproduced themselves through ongoing and overlapping processes of interaction, accretion, assimilation, and adaptation'.[18] Greece's Orthodox identity has clearly been a powerful factor in these ideological developments, but this matter demands a measure of accuracy – a distinction, that is, between the official Orthodox Church position and individuals' opinions, in many cases expressed within neo-orthodox and fundamentalist movements and antithetical to the official Church position.[19] A careful examination reveals the anti-Western movement as multi-dimensional, shaped by particular time-periods, events, and people (including clerical figures, scholars, theologians, and political figures). In evaluating Orthodoxy's effect on Greece's membership and 'belongingness' in the European Union, it is instructive to distinguish between two factors involved: the role of the faith in politics (i.e. church-state relations), and the way the faith is perceived in relation to national identity (as a factor distinguishing Greece from the West and Europe).[20]

Church and State

The historical experience of Orthodoxy in Greece forged a relationship between church, state and ethnicity which established the faith as a strong force in political consciousness.[21] The extent to which this force still persists is much debated (Carras, 1994; Georgiadou, 1995; Lipowatz, 1993, 1995; Prodromou, 1995; Kitromilides, 1996). Traces of it are detectable, though, in today's church-state relations, in nationalist tendencies within Greek Orthodoxy, and in the place of Orthodoxy in the political sphere. The relationship between church and state in Greece has been explored from various perspectives, each applied to analyse the deep-rooted interdependence in establishing and maintaining Greek identity (Tsoucalas, 1993; Stavrou, 1995; Georgiadou, 1995; Herzfeld, 1985; Pollis, 1992; and Panagiotopoulou, 1997 provide historical, political, sociological and theological perspectives). The combination of these interdisciplinary perspectives is important for a deeper understanding of the many domains in which faith and identity are intertwined even in contemporary Greek society. Drawing on some of these, we shall focus on the realm of politics and particularly on how religion affects Greece's place in the European Union. This requires an awareness of the faith's connection to the nation – stemming from history and tradition – and of the state's tendency to play on this connection for purposes which have little to do with religion per se.

Perceptions of culture as a link between church and state persist, and Orthodoxy is still seen as a preserver and expression of national cultural identity (Georgiadou, 1995, p. 303). 'Whether 'national cultures' are direct outcomes of evolving ethnic traditions, deliberate products of ideological manipulation, or, rather, original blends of multiple historical factors, it remains a fact that national cultures constitute persistent and inescapable historical realities' (Tsoucalas, 1993, pp. 57–8); Greece, as a nation accused of obsession with its history and identity (Clogg, 1994; Malcolm, 1992), certainly reflects such attention to culture in the political domain. According to Constantine Tsoucalas, the perceived danger of 'losing one's cultural identity' because of foreign political and economic penetration leads to a backlash against 'antagonistic cultures' which forms a fundamental sociopolitical issue (1993, p. 61). The invocation of the faith in debates about national cultural identity in relation to Europe supports this sociological observation: 'Orthodox culture…has demonstrated enormous resilience and...whether or not it is studied, as a social and cultural force it carries with it serious political implications' (Stavrou, 1995, p. 35). Speaking about 'Orthodoxy's relation to the bearers of state authority', Stelios Papathemelis (while a Minister in 1995) highlighted the influence of Orthodoxy on Greek identity: no active politician can overlook or underestimate this fact, nor the historic experience of coordination between Orthodoxy and the state authority for hundreds of years (1996, p. 277). These words reveal a deep-seated awareness within Greek political consciousness of a special relationship between the Church and state, at least partly predicated upon the relationship between faith and nation forged during the time of Ottoman occupation. The 'millet' system of administration prevailing in the Ottoman empire granted the Patriarch (who was a Greek) both ecclesiastical and temporal authority over the Christian subjects of the empire (who were Serbs and Bulgarians as well as Greeks). This peculiarity of the Ottoman empire (the millet system) plus the fact that the Church's leadership has always been in the hands of Greeks, allowed the Church to help preserve the Greek language and a sense of 'belonging' and common ancestry among the Greek population. Thus, even at the fall of the Byzantine Empire, the status and function of the ecclesiastical hierarchy confused the spiritual and temporal 'to a degree that made it almost impossible for them to be disentangled' (Sherrard, 1995, p. 103). A case in point, exhibiting how Orthodoxy continues to be endowed with a social dimension: the then Minister Papathemelis proclaimed 'I am convinced that Orthodoxy, beyond that which concerns religious people and that which constitutes faith is, in the Greek space, civilisation' (1996, p. 276). Even beyond the perspectives of particular policy makers, though, there is an established structure for church-state relations: Orthodoxy is constitutionally recognised as the dominant faith of the Greek nation, and church leaders work closely with the Ministry of National Education and Religious Affairs, the department which provides for the state's formal association with as well as a degree of control over the Church (Stavrou, 1995, pp. 45–8). Meanwhile, the establishment of an autocephalous Church independent of the Patriarchate in Constantinople, soon after independence from Turkish occupation,[22] remains as a symbol of the belief that statehood requires a church of one's own.

Intimate church-state relations developed under a blending of nationalism and faith and have, in turn, served to perpetuate such a blending. Within the ecclesiastical hierarchy as well as in Greek society and political culture, Orthodoxy continues to be granted national character and is still acknowledged as the defender and perpetuator of the nation. Metropolitan Meletios of Nicopolis exclaims, 'It is a given that Greeks who forget the foundations of Orthodoxy isolate themselves from the Greek people – they cease, essentially, to be Greeks, whether we will it or not – and that Greek Muslims never existed. Those who became Muslim simply 'turkified'; they entered another nation' (1996, p. 86). And, from a lay-man professor-theologian, 'Orthodoxy serves the nationality. Nationalism is an ethnocratic expression of it. It was not chosen by the Church' (Feidas, 1996, p. 76). In the words of former President Constantine Karamanlis, 'The nation and

Orthodoxy...have become in the Greek conscience virtually synonymous concepts, which together constitute our Helleno-Christian civilization' (Stavrou, 1995, p. 39). The ties linking church and government are strong and are only heightened by such events as formal appearances by members of the Church or government in each other's domains. For instance, in 1986 Antonis Tritsis, as Minister of National Education and Religious Affairs, declared in an address to the Sixth Panhellenic Conference of Theologians, 'Orthodoxy constitutes the creative moment of the meeting...between Christianity and Hellenism…a whole new civilization whose first complete expression was given by Byzantium through which directly pass our own origins of modern Hellenism' (Stavrou, 1995, p. 37). Increased interaction between the two domains is also evident during the PASOK (Panhellenic Socialist Party) years of government in the 1980s (Prodromou, 1994, p. 134). Unlike their conservative predecessors, the 1981–87 PASOK governments advocated policies that aimed to shape a more secularised society (including policies introducing civil marriage, divorce by mutual consent, and greater lenience toward prosecution for adultery) (Georgiadou, 1995). But through the ensuing dispute with the Church, PASOK 'realized that the church had a diffuse influence over society...that the community of the Orthodox faith is not confined to a very small population of church-followers, but is rather a component of the nation's cultural identity' (Georgiadou, 1995, pp. 308–9). The party thus compromised and tempered its policy. These examples of a strong link between faith and nationalistic plans have thus given the impression that, both in its official and popular forms, 'Orthodoxy...sanctifies the socio-political Greek system' (Makrides, 1991, p. 68), and the state 'manipulate[s] Orthodoxy as part of the political-cultural project of nation-building' (Prodromou, 1994, p. 128).

The actual substance of church-state relations, though, seems to be quite shallow and limited to the ceremonial: there is little sincere interchange and influence over matters of importance to either sphere. Minister of National Education and Religious Affairs Gerasimos Arsenis (contrary to the impression given by his title), contends that the interaction between the institutions of church and state does not actually affect state policy. Asked about the influence of the Church on his policy decisions, he states that although Orthodoxy is taken into consideration and respected as a tradition that has shaped the Greek nation ('a part of our history and identity'), it does not have a formal political influence on the state.[23] Yet 'when all is said and done', as Theofanis Stavrou notes, 'church and state have on the whole supported each other as long as they both gained from the alliance' (1995, p. 47). Indeed, Orthodoxy as 'part of our history and identity' seems to have had, at times, a greater potential for influencing the state than other formal institutions.

National Identity, Faith and Europe

According to Constantine Tsoucalas, 'however deliberate and ideologized, the quest for national identity can only be founded on a real, if selective, historical and cultural past' (1993, p. 64). This point brings us to a second way in which the faith is salient in Greece's contemporary political situation in Europe: the invocation of Orthodoxy as an element of the national identity that resists the West and Europe. This widespread (though by no means uncontested) perspective on Greek national identity portrays the faith as a barrier between Greece and the European Union; it symbolises a conscious choice to embrace the Orthodox and Byzantine past of Greece while overlooking or perhaps even shunning those elements of Greek identity which are shared by Europe (for example, ancient Greek political philosophy). The language used to express such a distance felt from Europe is often quite powerful, even from highly authoritative figures. The following words were delivered by Metropolitan Dimitriados Christodoulos, now the Archbishop of Athens and All Greece and the focus of a great deal of controversy for his outspokenness in the political realm:

'The problem is very old. Directly after our liberation from the Turkish yoke the governing political and intellectual order in Greece became trapped in the perception that Hellenism could survive if it neglected its eastern mentality and if Greeks were to walk uninhibited in their course toward the West...I do not want to say that the integration of the EU is wrong. But it is dangerous...Today Hellenism is in danger of being absorbed into the European crucible...The Church should not isolate the Greek from Europe, nor though should it surrender him to Europe' (Christodoulos, 1997, p. A17).

It is in response to such applications of religion in the political realm – carrying an agenda consistently resistant of the West and Europe – that leaders and theorists who sought to shape the newly independent Greece along the lines of Western Europe often berated the Church's meddling in national affairs (Stavrou, 1995, pp.44–47). Today's leaders and theorists continue to face such issues: a conference on 'the role of Orthodoxy in the new international reality',[24] joined academics, theologians, religious and political leaders and media figures in discussion of various issues involving Orthodoxy on an international scale and more specifically, Orthodoxy in relation to Greek national identity. The concept that Greek identification with the West somehow constitutes a distancing from its Byzantine and Orthodox heritage was examined and revealed the traditional view of a strict either-or situation: either don the character of the West, or claim with fervour and historical, religious insight the Eastern Orthodox identity and the glory of Byzantium. According to Minister Arsenis, during the Cold War division of the world into East and West, Greece emphatically chose to belong to the West at the expense of its Orthodox heritage: 'We behaved as a member of the Western Community and Western Europe, and in our anxiety to be identified and act as Europeans we made an effort of passive adaptation to the European situation and [as the only Orthodox nation in unified Europe and a small nation at that], the less we spoke about our particularities and our Byzantine tradition and Orthodoxy, the better' (1996, p. 217). After the collapse of Communism and the Berlin Wall and the opening of the frontiers to the Balkans, however, 'Orthodoxy has re-emerged in the international and diplomatic forefront and, being a people of exaggeration, the nation swung from "we belong to the West" to "we belong to Orthodoxy"' (1996, p. 218).

Manifestations of this 'swing' are widespread and repeatedly analysed in the literature. A few noteworthy examples will suffice. In a short pamphlet entitled 1992: Threat or Hope?,[25] Georgios Metallinos, University of Athens professor of theology, fulfils the 'Apostolic Services' (Apostolikg Diakonia) request for an elucidation of the much-ignored spiritual side of the issue of European unity, 'in relation to, that is, the Greco-Orthodox identity of our People and its prolonged cultural presence' (Metallinos, 1992, p. 5). Recognising the need for a cultural and spiritual element for the success of the unification project, Metallinos questions what place Greece could have in such a 'spiritual geography' dominated by Roman Catholicism and Protestantism. He contends that, in its efforts to establish awareness of a 'common cultural and civilisational heritage', the European Community has found in history its desired answers concerning the components of such an identity and has proceeded to diffuse this idea through new historical education programmes (1992, p. 15). In what becomes an unashamed critique of religion in the West and a biased, self-congratulatory view of the strength and purity of the Eastern Orthodox faith, Metallinos proceeds to declare that Greek Orthodox identity is threatened by this European unification which demands cultural unity: 'The problem for Greece is not primarily economic or political...the problem is chiefly spiritual and cultural' (1992, p. 28). 'Our Greco-Orthodox tradition', he writes, 'is reflected and saved by means of its basic carriers which are: the religion (ecclesiastical life), the language and way of life (customs and communal practices)' (1992, pp. 29–30). Orthodoxy's antagonism to Western Christianity is thus deemed fundamental and unbridgeable. The pamphlet is a stereotypical example of anti-Europeanism related to Orthodoxy, involving the use of forceful language, us/them terminology, and mingling of culture and religion, ethnicity and faith. Intellectuals of the 'neo-orthodox' current of thought echo such concepts. In their project to rediscover the essence of Orthodoxy and its potential as an element of the Greek nation, Orthodox Christians are demarcated not only from non-Christian traditions but also from the Roman Catholics and Protestants. According to Christos Yiannaras, an influential theologian and professor in Greece and contributor to the neo-orthodox current, 'the whole problem of the Orthodox peoples at the moment is that they find themselves under the influence of the manner of everyday life, under the articulation and structure of the social life which European modernity has imposed' (Yiannaras, 1996, p. 80). Thus, European modernity is to be resisted in the name of Orthodoxy. It is important, however, to recognise that such hostility directed to Europe and the West does not necessarily carry political implications (or prescriptions) such, for instance, as does Huntington's theory. In fact, Yiannaras' fairly recent Culture, the Central Problem of Politics, opens with a chapter entitled 'The Second Provocation by Huntington'.[26] The piece is somewhat of a polemic against the conclusions Huntington draws with reference to Greece and a call for an academic counter-argument from the Greek perspective.

This distinction between sociocultural and political concerns becomes lost amidst much of the literature on contemporary Greek identity. Many sources reflect the common theme of a 'dichotomy in cultures' in Greece and present an interrelation between the ideas of modernisation, civilisation, the West, and Europe (Danforth, 1984; Panagiotopoulou, 1997; Herzfeld, 1985; Moschonas, 1997; Liakos, 1995). The result is the projection of a strict dichotomy between modern and primitive, progressive and 'underdog', elite and uneducated, wealthy and poor, urban and rural – often all related somehow to the descriptions of 'secular' and 'religious'.[27] Acceptance of this series of dichotomies and harsh division between them serves to perpetuate the view of Orthodoxy as a force opposing Greek modernisation, Europe, etc., and meanwhile fails to acknowledge the intricacies and contradictions involved. Indeed, aspects of the historical tradition and communal practice of Orthodoxy in Greece easily allow for its invocation in spheres beyond religion so that, in spite of relatively low church attendance (Georgiadou, 1995, p. 309), the faith's politicisation, the incorporative type of social inclusion the faith provides (the interplay between nationalism and religion is especially clear in this sense), and the high degree of religious and national homogeneity in Greece, combine to make Orthodoxy a strong force penetrating many aspects of national consciousness, especially with reference to the West and Europe.

Conclusions

Both external observers and the Church, state, and Greek population contribute to such continued appropriation of the faith in the political realm. The trend and its serious implications have sparked the fervent response of intellectuals both Greek and non-Greek. For example, Elizabeth Prodromou and Thanos Lipowatz have engaged in academic debate about the theological value of the relationship between Orthodoxy and Greek national identity (1993, 1995a, 1995b). According to Lipowatz's perception of Orthodoxy, the Church calls for the 'fusion' of the individual within an imaginary community and escape out of the world (rather than an active transformation of the world through responsible citizens). He interprets the modern-day role of the Church as 'fused' with the state and its refusal of historicity, rationality and the natural Right; church and state, religiosity and nationalism, reinforce one another. Greek mentality and political culture, therefore, inhibit modernisation and the development of a civil society. Lipowatz assumes that the Church has had such an effect on Greek mentality and political culture as to instill a defensive attitude towards Western Europe (Lipowatz, 1993, pp. 32–3, 38–9). Of course, the argument can be reversed: the Greek mentality and political culture may be considered to have had a larger effect on the Church's place in Greek society as primary hindrances to modernisation and civil society. In her response to Lipowatz's piece, Prodromou tries to dispel the necessary connection between faith and nationalism by looking at the faith itself, independent of nation and state (Prodromou, 1995). She thus elaborates on how Orthodoxy is, above all, a 'way of life' which understands personhood in terms of rationality and freedom in a way which indeed differs from Western faiths. Such differences, however, are not the stuff of which the relationship between faith and nationalism is made; nor do such distinctions between Eastern and Western Christianity surface significantly in those trends which project Orthodoxy as incompatible with the European Union. The debate raises some very important points. We must distinguish thoroughly between the various levels involved in Orthodoxy's role in contemporary Greek society – before, that is, we can fully understand how that role might, in turn, affect Greece's 'European identity' and place in the European Union. Orthodoxy as a Christian faith is, indeed, fundamentally different from Western Christian faiths in many doctrinal and traditional ways which also often carry socio-cultural effects. There is no doubt the Christian faiths affect the cultures where they are predominant – there is a Catholic culture as well as a Protestant and an Orthodox culture. But these even differ from case-to-case, from country-to-country. Thus, the diversity in cultures stemming from religious difference is to be acknowledged for what it is, and recognised for what it is not (necessarily): namely, a political map.

The drawing of the political map of Europe according to religion must be understood in light of the implications it carries for particular nations. In the case of Greece, Orthodoxy and the Church are identified with authoritarianism and reactionary nationalism and are thus deemed incompatible with modern, Western, pluralist democracy (Prodromou, 1996, p. 131). This 'orthodox' idea of Orthodoxy leads to what Prodromou describes as the 'orientalisation' of Orthodoxy, which serves as the primary marker for remapping the New European Order into cultural spaces – 'the civilized Europe of the modern West' and 'the Other European civilization of the non-West' (1996, p. 125). Highlighting media texts which 'reflect the emergence of a coherent standard of Eastern Orthodox Christianity that has been constructed for intellectual, policy and popular reference' (1996, p. 131), Prodromou emphasises something crucial to an understanding of the faith's contemporary place in shaping Greece's role in the European Union: such perceptions exist, and widely so, and they become tools for policy making, providing 'the intellectual basis for political decisions whereby a threatened non-Orthodox West would be justified in restricting membership in the new European political-economic and security architectures to promising modernizers of the Protestant-Catholic persuasion' (1996, p. 133). The peripheralisation of Orthodoxy is criticised by Costa Carras as well, with his argument that the faith 'is part of the wider pattern of historical experience that we call "Western" based on the same three roots, Judaic, Ancient Greek and Roman…and the attempts to create a fundamental distinction in other areas based on these religious differences inside Christianity are unsound' (1988, p. 32). He attributes certain clear weaknesses of the Orthodox position in relation to the Western (or, English-speaking) media to failings in specific Orthodox countries and Churches. It is central for the future, he argues, that broad sweeping judgements are avoided: though there are serious prejudices against the Orthodox, 'there is no unbridgeable external divide' (1988, p. 34).

There is clearly a lack of consensus over the relevance of the Orthodox faith to Greek national or European identity: the divergent perspectives of Lipowatz and Prodromou, Metallinos and Yiannaras attest to this. A view of Orthodoxy as a fundamental element of Greek national identity which is, effectively, a barrier between Greece and Europe to its West is, at best, representative of only one side of a 'dichotomy' in cultures in Greece – if such there be. From the European Union perspective, there is also a lack of consensus and clarity concerning European identity: an examination of opinions and official declarations on European identity reveals ambiguity over what it is to entail. The Commission has provided no real answers to these questions, as one European Commission report admits:

The term 'European' has not been officially defined. It combines geographical, historical and cultural elements which all contribute to the European identity. The shared experience of proximity, ideas, values and historical interaction cannot be condensed into a simple formula, and is subject to review by each succeeding generation. The Commission believes that it is neither possible nor opportune to establish now the frontiers of the European Union, whose contours will be shaped over many years to come (Shore, 1993, p. 786).

There is no official European Union cultural-religious agenda, but real political developments are not limited to official declarations and formulated agendas. Perceptions affect policy, and often the weightiest and most controversial of these are the ones which do so 'unofficially'. Indeed, an applied EU definition of 'European' could be detected, whereby 'the terms "non-EC nationals", "third countries" and "non-European" are being defined with increasing precision and thus, as if by default, an "official" definition of European is being constructed' (Shore, 1993, p. 786). Accordingly, the progression of the European Union toward a 'European identity' for its member nations should be considered in light of William Wallace's keen perception:

'Mental maps, imagined space, define political regions and communities. Such broad concepts as "the West" or "the Orient" cover no well-delineated territories; their appeal is in the associations they conjure up, mixing geographical space with economic and social interaction and with political and cultural identity to draw an imaginary – but nevertheless effectively recognized – divide' (1990, pp. 7–8).

Acute awareness of the existence and reinforcement of certain divisions in Europe is echoed at many levels, even in European leadership: at a meeting of European People's Parties in Brussels in March 1997, the Belgian Chairman Wilfried Martens declared that 'In our view Turkey cannot be a candidate for EU membership. We are in favour of extensive cooperation with Turkey, but the European project is a civilisational project. Turkey's candidature for full membership is unacceptable'.[28] Thus, individual nations can be seen to promote aspects of their identity which, they argue, are in line with this clear yet unspoken idea of the essence of Europe. 'It would be a very great mistake to make the EU a religious or cultural entity', declares the secretary-general of the Turkish Foreign Ministry Onur Oymen, 'We do not want a cultural or religious iron curtain to replace the political iron curtain that we fought for 50 years to remove'.[29] Yet even the vote in favour of Turkish future membership in the EU, a result of the recent Helsinki Summit of European leaders, was reported with headlines about the EU's first Muslim candidate and references to 'the Turk's' role in the Crusades nine centuries ago.[30] And, in Catholic Poland: 'The pope and bishops do not want the newly democratic Poland merely to "return to Europe". They want the new Poland to reassert its Catholic character, and in the process to invite Europe...to rediscover its common Christian roots' (Byrnes, 1997, p. 436). A recent article by Timothy Garton Ash makes clear the real political effects of (though ambiguous) ideas of what it is to be European – in the context of the EU – on individual nations:

In the first half of the twentieth century, the debate about who did or did not belong to Central Europe had real political significance. So it has today. For to be 'Central European' in contemporary political usage means to be civilised, democratic, cooperative – and therefore to have a better chance of joining NATO and the EU. In fact, the argument threatens to become circular: NATO and the EU welcome 'Central Europeans', so 'Central Europeans' are those whom NATO and the EU welcome.[31]

Or, to put it more provocatively and perhaps precisely, to be a member of NATO and the EU means to become (Central) European.

Indeed, trends towards a regionalisation of Europe on the basis of religion are evident, and theories such as that of Samuel Huntington only aggravate, and possibly quicken, the process. The political and economic Community of European nations knows no religious bounds; but does the European Union of Maastricht, that which sets forth a goal of cultural, social and ideological affinity between its members, remain untainted by a view of the religious ties which bind together and distinguish between nations? Surely as the developing Community strays further beyond strictly political and economic identity to cultural identity, religion will play a greater role in an understanding of European identity and what it takes to be 'European'. It is within this context that the uni-dimensional picture of Orthodoxy developed through popular media references to it in the political realm thus has great potential to designate the tradition as un-European and incompatible with the European Union.

The counterpart to these trends – the internal perceptions which view Greece's religious identity as a factor separating it from its Western neighbours – is equally potent through repeated references, by spiritual and political leaders, to a distinctive Hellenic Civilisation. As indicated above, the anti-Western and anti-Europe attitudes related to the Orthodox Church (at particular stages in the country's history and expressed through specific theologians, historians and sociologists) have had a significant effect on Greece's self-appraisal as Western and European, or not. The perception of the EU, the West, and of modern forces as a threat to Greek national identity is widespread and enduring enough to demand attention. In principle, and certainly from a religious perspective, this manipulation of religion in Greece as a factor in politics should be criticised. In political terms, though, and specifically with regard to Greece's place in European integration, such uses of Orthodoxy must be recognised for their damaging potential; 'It is precisely in its political message that the civilisational paradigm is most important as a standard for a particular idea of Orthodoxy and as a functional mechanism for building a regional Other Europe' (Prodromou, 1996, p. 133). Inherent in such perspectives on and uses of Orthodoxy is the potential for a self-fulfilling prophecy: a vicious cycle might emerge in which certain attitudes toward religious identity actualise the results predicted by particular theories, thus sanctioning such ideas of intrinsic distinctions based on religion. Regardless of the direction in which the prejudice is flowing (to or from the West), the potential results are the same: a regionalisation of Europe according to religious, cultural, and 'civilisational' differences, and the peripheralisation of Greece by these factors. An examination of perceptions of Orthodoxy, both internal and external to Greece, shows that neither is the Church indifferent to Greece's place in the European Union, nor is the European Union indifferent to the Church's place in Greece.

Notes

1. The bulletin is Circulation No. 2626 of the Holy Synod of the Church of Greece, 7 April 1997; for further discussion of this bulletin, see Konstantinos Kotsiopoulos, Orthodoxy and Europe (1998), p. 73.
2. That is, a focus on the relation between the Orthodox faith and Greek national identity as distinct from Orthodox theology and official Church practices. For attention to actual Orthodox doctrine and theology, see the works of Kallistos Ware and Philip Sherrard.
3. Peter Berger's The Social Reality of Religion (1969) provides a basic analysis of the interaction of religion and culture in the establishment of communal identity.
4. For example, in a lecture entitled 'A Christian Europe?' (1998), Metropolitan John Zizioulas argues that Europe cannot exist solely on economic or institutional bases and that there cannot be a union of Europe without an integration of spiritual forces. European culture is, at its best, a synthesis of the three cornerstones of European Christianity – Athens, Rome and Jerusalem; 'what we are experiencing today in Europe is a distortion of this synthesis…owing to the division between East and Western Christianity'. Likewise, in a meeting with the Roman Catholic Archbishop of Prague, the Ecumenical Patriarch Bartholomew stated, 'The unification of Europe, towards which we are heading and which we all pursue, cannot be limited to the military or the economic or the political sphere, but needs strong spiritual foundations. Within the pan-European family, we ask the Roman Catholic and Protestant brothers not to forget that the Orthodox Church too has a pivotal position', (Manginas, 1998, p. 8). And an article entitled 'Patriarch Bartholomeus, the Leader of Orthodoxy', cites the Patriarch's statement that 'Orthodoxy, acting silently, makes its presence felt in Europe and contributes strongly to the creation of the new European identity' (Courcoulas, 1999, p. 212).
5. Christopher Dawson's *Understanding Europe* (1952) and *The Making of Europe* (1946), Denis de Rougement's *The Meaning of Europe* (1963) and *The Idea of Europe* (1966), Oscar Halecki's *The Limits and Divisions of European History* (1950) and Bronislaw Geremek's *The Common Roots of Europe* (1996) draw, from different perspectives, common visions of Europe united in Western Christianity. Jean-Baptiste Duroselle's *L'Idee de l'Europe dans l'Histoire* (1965), and a text book entitled *The History of the Idea of Europe* (eds. K. Wilson and J. van der Dussen, 1993) offer summaries and analyses of such works.
6. Because European identity is an ambiguous concept, we rely on perceptions of it in our analysis. The intent here is neither to define nor to resist particular conceptions of

European identity, but rather to understand the prevalent conceptions and to address their related implications. By extension then, the works cited are not included here for their validity but rather for their reflection of prevalent ideas of Europe.

7. See J-C. Boyer, 'The Frontier between Protestantism and Catholicism in Europe', in *Annales de Geographie*, No. 588, Mar/Apr 1996; Henri Mendras, *The Europe of Europeans: Sociology of Western Europe* (1997); and Paul Gerbod, *Cultural and Religious Europe from 1815 to our time* (1977). For more specific attention to this issue, see Francis Castles (1994): he argues that the divide in Western Christendom has even current public policy outcomes, and he identifies a 'Catholic family of nations' in Western and Southern Europe based on analysis of voting behaviour. In a response to Castles, Goran Therborn (1994) argues that it is a religion's relationship to the state which truly determines variation. Thus Orthodoxy, Lutheranism, occasionally Calvinism, and especially Anglicanism are linked by their close relations to the state, while Catholicism is placed in a category of its own as a supranational bureaucracy. John Madeley (1982), like Castles, uses evidence of variance in voting behaviour to make the case that there is a distinction between Protestant and the rest of Europe. According to Madeley, 'despite rumours to the contrary, God is not dead so far as European politics is concerned' (p. 149).
8. Martin (1994: 14–15). Also, see William Wallace, *The Transformation of Europe* (1990), for a generally critical view of the various religious definitions of Europe.
9. As William Wallace (1990) notes, 'There has been a tendency since the optimistic years of the 1960s to identify "Europe" with the member states of the European Community' (p. 8).
10. The author is in no way making the argument that any viable 'European identity' for the EU must be rooted in old 'ideas of Europe' or in perceptions of a common European culture, as opposed to economic, political or even social efforts toward an identity based on future commonality. It is worth arguing, though, that where such a forward-looking project is weak or stagnant, past visions of Europe will be, and are, invoked to provide a much-needed foundation for unity. Certainly the ideas of the founders of the integration project were not limited to politics and economics: Jean Monnet is often quoted in saying that if he were to start all over again, he would begin with culture (Papcke 1992: 68). Furthermore, as noted above, the Community's early plans for establishing a 'European identity' were not limited to politics and economics either in their references to a common past and common culture.
11. See Orbis: *A Journal of World Affairs,* Vol. 41, No. 4, 1997, for the issue's focus on 'western civilisation in world politics'.
12. This does not claim to be a thorough selection of Western perceptions of Eastern Orthodoxy but, rather, consists of opinions which carry special importance for the case of Greece.
13. This is a point picked up in a great deal of scholarship on Greece. See Danforth (1984), 'The Ideological Context of the Search for Continuities in Greek Culture'; Panagiotopoulou (1997), 'Greeks in Europe: Antinomies in National Identities'; and Liakos (1995), 'The Canon of European Identity: Transmission and decomposition'.
14. See critique by Prodromou (1998).
15. Dhombres (1998). Interview with Francois Thual, expert in geopolitics and formerly employed in the French Ministry of Defence.
16. The perspectives offered here are neither representative of the general public opinion nor of the Official Orthodox Church. Rather, they reflect strong biases which are, nonetheless, considered important because they are enduring and expressed by prominent figures.
17. According to Liakos (1995: 130), 'transmission [or, transfusion, of Western European

achievements] becomes synonymous with modernisation and, in terms of territoriality, with Europeanisation and Westernisation'.

18. Diamandouros also emphasises the need to recognise the significance of Orthodoxy in the perpetuation of a certain cultural tradition (1995: 8).
19 Vasilios Makrides offers insight into and critical analysis of such movements in the following: 'Aspects of Greek Orthodox Fundamentalism' in *Orthodoxes Forum*, Vol 5, 1991; 'The Orthodox Church and the Post-War Religious Situation in Greece' in The Post-War Generation and Establishment Religion, eds. W.C. Roof, J.W. Carroll and D.A. Roozen (1995); 'Le Role de l'Orthodoxie dans la Formation de l'Antieuropeanisme at l'Antioccidentalisme Grecs' in *Religions et Transformations de l'Europe*, eds. G.Vincent and J-P. Willaime (1993); and 'Christian Orthodoxy Versus Religion: Negative Critiques of Religion in Contemporary Greece' in *The Notion of 'Religion' in Comparative Research*, ed. Ugo Bianchi, 1994.
20. These factors should, in turn, be distinguished from public opinion. According to opinion poll research conducted by Sophie Duchesne and Andre-Paul Frognier (1995), Greece, along with France, Portugal, Italy and Spain, is revealed as one of the 'most European' countries; a majority of Greeks feel they are not only citizens of their own countries but also of Europe. Meanwhile, according to a 1990 survey conducted by the National Social Research Centre, though church attendance in Greece is quite low compared to that of Italians, Spaniards and Portuguese, the Orthodox Church carries for the Greeks a greater influence than secular or political institutions (analysed by Georgiadou, 1995).
21. As with the opinions presented in the following section, the historical realities used here to elucidate the relationship between church and state are selected for their particular relevance to this relationship. That is, they are not to be interpreted as representative of a general history of Greek national identity as related to Orthodoxy. In fact, it could be more accurately said that there is no such thing as a representative 'general history' but, rather, a series of discontinuities – both in terms of church-state relations and in terms of the faith's perceived place in Greek national identity. In both cases there are major fluctuations depending on historical circumstances internal and external to Greece. For instance, the relationship between church and state and between faith and national identity seems to vary considerably between the experiences of the negotiations for accession to the European Community in the 1970s, on the one hand, and the 'Macedonia is Greek' campaign in the 1990s, on the other. As Georgiadou notes (1995: 304), 'the Greeks' collective representation of Orthodoxy and the Orthodox Church is unstable and subject to the political influences of the times'.
22. In accordance with a formal government declaration of July 23, 1833, and incorporated into the church constitution of the same year. See Stavrou (1995: 42).
23. Personal interview with Gerasimos Arsenis, 18 August 1997.
24. Organised by INERPOST, Institouto Erevnon kai Politikis Stratigikis, 1995. The proceedings of the conference were published by Gnosi in 1996.
25. Apeili i elpida; Ekdoseis Apostolikis Diakonias tis Ekklisias tis Ellados, 1992.
26. Yiannaras (1997); the chapter refers primarily to the 1996 Foreign Affairs article, 'The West Unique, Not Universal'.
27. See Diamandouros, 'Cultural Dualism and Political Change in Post-Authoritarian Greece', 1994. Diamandouros has explored Greece's cultural dichotomies in depth, focusing on the dynamics of late industrialisation and studying cultural dualism in south-eastern Europe in general. He posits that late industrialisation in Greece has led to the emergence of two competing and conflicting cultural traditions. Because neither has achieved permanent ascendancy over the other, a drawn out coexistence has developed: 'While facilitating its reproduction and ensuring its continued vitality, the capacity of

each culture to creatively adapt to changes in its domestic and international environments served to impede rather than to promote integration' (p. 5).
28. Quoted in Ayhin Tarihi, Jan/Mar 1997, pp. 144–5.
29. Quoted by Stephen Kinzer, 'Turks See Prejudice in EU's Closed Door', *International Herald Tribune*, 24 February 1997, p. 2.
30. See Stephen Kinzer, 'Turkey is still looking for its place in Europe', *International Herald Tribune* 10 December 1999, and Matthew Kaminski 'EU reaches accord with Turkey', *The Wall Street Journal Europe* 13 December 1999.
31. 'The Puzzle of Central Europe', *The New York Review of Books*, 18 March 1999, p. 18.

References

Arsenis, G. (1997), Personal Interview, 18 August.
Ash, T. G. (1999), 'The Puzzle of Central Europe', *The New York Review of Books*, 18 March, p.18.
Byrnes, T. (1997), 'The Catholic Church and Poland's Return to Europe', *East European Quarterly*, Vol. 30, No. 4, Jan., pp. 433–48.
Beckford, J. (1994), 'Final Reflections', in Fulton, J. and Gee, P. (eds), *Religion in Contemporary Europe*, New York: Edwin Mellen Press.
Berger, P. (1969), *The Social Reality of Religion*, London: Faber and Faber.
Carras, C. (1998), 'The Orthodox Church and Politics in a Post-Communist World', in Kitromilides, P. and Veremis, T., *The Orthodox Church in a Changing World*. Athens: Eliamep, pp. 15–38.
Carras, C. (1994), Byzantium as the Source of Modern Evil, Lecture delivered at the University of Birmingham Centre for Byzantine, Ottoman, and Modern Greek Studies, December.
Castles, F. (1994), 'On Religion and Public Policy: Does Catholicism Make a Difference?', *European Journal of Political Research*, Vol. 25, pp. 19–40.
Clogg, R. (1994), 'Greek-Bashing', *London Review of Books*, 18 August.
Christodoulos, D. (1997) 'O Ellinismos kai i Europi' (Hellenism and Europe), To Vima, 19 Jan, p. A17.
Circulation No. 2626 (1997), Holy Synod of the Church of Greece, 7 April.
Courcoulas, A. (1999), 'Patriarch Bartholomeus, the Leader of Orthodoxy', interview with Patriarch Bartholomeus, *God and Religion*, Vol. 1, March, pp. 211–19.
Danforth, L. (1984), 'The Ideological Context of the Search for Continuities in Greek Culture', *Journal of Modern Greek Studies*, Vol. 2, No. 1, pp. 53–85.
Davies, N. (1997), *Europe: a History*, London: Pimlico.
Delanty, G. (1995), *Inventing Europe: Idea, Identity, Reality*, London: Macmillan.
Dhombres, D. (1998), 'Dans le Monde Orthodoxe, la Religion Sacrilise la Nation, et la Nation Protégé la Religion', interview with Francois Thual, *Le Monde* 20 January, p. 13.
Diamandouros, N. (1993), Cultural Dualism and Political Change in Post-Authoritarian Greece, Working Paper 1994/50, presented at the Center for Advanced Study in the Social Sciences, 26 April.
Duchesne, S. and Frognier, A.P. (1995), 'Is there a European Identity?', in Niedermayer, O. and Sinnott, R. (eds), *Public Opinion and International Governance*, New York: Oxford University Press, pp. 193–277.
Dutu, A. (1990), 'New Ideas and Old Stereotypes Concerning the Common Roots of European Culture', *Dialog Westeuropa Osteuropa*, Dialogkongreb, des Osterreichischen

College in Alpbach.

Georgiadou, V. (1995), 'Greek Orthodoxy and the Politics of Nationalism', *International Journal of Politics*, Culture and Society, Vol. 9, No. 2, pp. 295–315.

Herzfeld, M. (1985), "Law and Custom': Ethnography of and in Greek National Identity', *Journal of Modern Greek Studies*, Vol. 3, No. 2, pp. 167–85.

Huntington, S. (1993a), 'If Not Civilizations, What?', *Foreign Affairs*, Nov/Dec, pp. 186–94.

Huntington, S. (1993b), 'The Clash of Civilizations?', *Foreign Affairs*, Summer. pp. 22–49.

Huntington, S. (1996a), *The Clash of Civilizations and the Remaking of World Order*, London: Simon and Schuster.

Huntington, S. (1996b), 'The West Unique, Not Universal', *Foreign Affairs*, Nov/Dec, pp. 28–46.

INERPOST (1996). Proceedings from a 1995 Conference of the Institute for Research and Political Strategy on 'The Role of Orthodoxy in the New International Reality', published in *O Rolos tis Orthodoxias sti Nea Diethni Pragmatikotita*, Athens: Gnosi, (the paper cites contributions to the conference by G. Arsenis, C. Yiannaras, M. Meletios, S. Papathemelis, and V. Feidas).

Kaplan, R. (1993), *Balkan Ghosts: a Journey Through History*, New York: Vintage.

Kinzer, S. (1997) 'Turks See Prejudice in EU's Closed Door', *International Herald Tribune*, 24 Feb, p. 2.

Konidares, G. (1965), 'Athens and Jerusalem: the Bond Between Christianity and Hellas', *Greek Orthodox Theological Review*, Vol. 11, No. 2, pp. 217–35.

Kotsiopoulos, K. (1998), *Orthodoxy and Europe*, Thessaloniki: Hellenic College of Thessaloniki.

Legg, K. and Roberts, J. (1996), *Modern Greece: a Civilisation on the Periphery*, Boulder: Westview.

Liakos, A. (1995), 'The Canon of European Identity: Transmission and Decomposition', *Journal of Modern Greek Studies*, Vol. 3, pp. 129–38.

Lipowatz, T. (1993), 'Orthodox Christianity and Nationalism: Two Aspects of the Modern Greek Political Culture', *Greek Political Science Review*, Vol. 2, Oct, pp. 31–47.

Makrides, V. (1991), 'Aspects of Greek Orthodox Fundamentalism', *Orthodoxes Forum*, Vol. 5, pp. 49–72.

Madeley, J. (1982), 'Politics and the Pulpit: The Case of Protestant Europe', *West European Politics*, Vol. 5, No. 2.

Malcolm, N. 'The New Bully of the Balkans', *The Spectator*, 15 August, p. 8.

Manginas, N. (1998), 'Ecumenical Patriarch Bartholomew Visits Czechia and Slovakia', Orthodox Observer, September, p. 8.

Martin, D. (1994), 'Religion in Contemporary Europe', in Fulton, J. and Gee, P. (eds), *Religion in Contemporary Europe*, New York: Edwin Mellen Press.

Metallinos, G. (1992), *1992: Threat or Hope?*, Press of the Apostolic Service of the Church of Greece.

Moschonas, A. (1997), 'European Integration and Prospects of Modernization in Greece', *Journal of Modern Greek Studies*, Vol. 15, No. 2, pp. 325–47.

Nederveen P. (1995), 'Europe Among Other Things: Closure, Culture, Identity', in von Benda-Beckmann, K. and Verkuyten, M. (eds), *Nationalism, Ethnicity and Cultural Identity in Europe*, Utrecht: ERCOMER.

Oikonomou, E. (1993), 'Foundations, Doctrine, and Politics of the Eastern Orthodox Church', *Mediterranean Quarterly*, Vol. 4, No. 1.

Panagiotopoulou, R. (1997), 'Greeks in Europe: Antinomies in National Identities', *Journal of Modern Greek Studies*, Vol. 15, No. 2, pp. 350–70.

Papcke, S. (1992), 'Who Needs European Identity and What Could it Be?', in Nelson, B., Roberts, D. and Veit, W. (eds), *The Idea of Europe: Problems of National and*

Transnational Identity, Oxford: Berg.
Pollis, A. (1992), 'Greek National Identity: Religious Minorities, Rights and European Norms, *Journal of Modern Greek Studies*, Vol. 10, pp. 171–95.
Prodromou, E. (1998) 'Essay Review', *Journal of Modern Greek Studies,* Vol. 16.
Prodromou, E. (1997), 'The Perception Paradox of Post-Cold War Security in Greece' in Graham, A. and Kalypso, N., *The Greek Paradox: Promise vs. Performance*, Cambridge, Mass: MIT.
Prodromou, E. (1996), 'Paradigms, Power, and Identity: Rediscovering Orthodoxy and Regionalizing Europe', *European Journal of Political Research*, Vol. 30, No. 2, Sept.
Prodromou, E. (1994), 'Toward an Understanding of Eastern Orthodoxy and Democracy Building in the Post-Cold War Balkans', *Mediterranean Quarterly*, Vol. 5, No. 2, Spring.
Seton-Watson, H. (1985), 'What is Europe, Where is Europe? From Mystique to Politique', *Encounter,* Jul/Aug.
Sherrard, P. (1995), *The Greek East and the Latin West: A Study in the Christian Tradition*, Evia: Denise Harvey.
Shore, C. 'Inventing the "People's Europe": Critical approaches to European Community "Cultural Policy"', *Man,* Vol. 28, No. 4, pp. 779–800.
Stavrou, T. (1995), 'The Orthodox Church and Political Culture in Modern Greece', in Constas, D. and Stavrou, T. (eds), *Greece Prepares for the Twenty-first Century*, Washington, D.C.: Woodrow Wilson Center.
Therborn, G. (1994), 'Another Way of Taking Religion Seriously', *European Journal of Political Research*, Vol. 26, pp. 103–10.
Tsoucalas, C. (1993), 'Greek National Identity in an Integrated Europe and a Changing World Order', in Psomiades, H. and Thomadakis, S. (eds), *Greece, the New Europe, and the Changing International Order*, New York: Pella.
Wallace, W. (1990), *The Transformation of Europe*, London: Royal Institute of International Affairs.
Yiannaras, C. (1997), *Culture, the Central Problem of Politics*, Athens: Indiktos.
Zizioulas, J. (1998), 'A Christian Europe?', Lecture delivered at the Hellenic Centre, London, 19 Jan.

PART IV
SOCIAL POLICIES

15 Social Protection in Greece in the Nineties: Reforming the 'Weak' Welfare State

MARIA PETMESIDOU

Introduction

The Greek welfare state developed with a considerable time lag in comparison to its European counterparts; it only weakly supported universalist criteria in social protection, and what is more, well before becoming firmly institutionalised, it faced a deep crisis. Major legal reforms, (that is, the establishment of a national health system) and the fast increase of social protection expenditure, in the first half of the eighties, did not succeed to bring about a balanced pattern of welfare. To this contributed the persistence of a number of qualitative internal contradictions of the Greek model of social protection (that is, fragmentation and deep inequalities of the income-maintenance system, extensive abuse of regulations, collusion of private and public interests in health care producing corruption and an enormous waste of public money), compounded by serious fiscal problems since the mid-eighties. The combined effect of a number of exogenous and internal factors, such as global economic restructuring and intensified international competition, sluggish economic growth in the country over the eighties and much of the nineties, significant demographic changes triggering off cost explosion of social welfare, and budgetary constraints intensified by the Maastricht criteria of EU integration, were equally important in precipitating an acute institutional and fiscal crisis.

As traditional support structures – based on family and kin ties – fade away, and in the absence of a strong culture of universalism and social citizenship (see Petmesidou, 1996a & b), the reform of the rather 'weak' Greek welfare state in the direction of balancing social welfare to fiscal stabilisation, promote competitiveness, but also effectively combat unemployment, social marginalisation and poverty turns out to be a rather difficult task. Moreover, such a reform necessitates thorough changes in economic governance in Greek society that will redraw the boundaries between the state and civil society, politics and the economy. For this to happen a new social balance needs to be achieved on the basis of wide social consensus, that, however, does not seem to be forthcoming.

In the following sections, the main features of the Greek model of social welfare in relationship to the trends of social protection expenditure are briefly discussed and its crisis characteristics are identified. The emphasis is on the reforms attempted in the areas of employment policy, social security, health and welfare particularly in the late nineties.

The Model of Social Welfare in Greece and its Crisis Dimensions

In comparative terms, the size of the Greek welfare state remained well below average European standards throughout the eighties and nineties. A fast expansion of social protection expenditure that took place in the first half of the eighties was not enough to close the gap between Greece and the other EU countries. In the first half of the nineties the ratio of current social protection expenditure to GDP exhibited a slight decline (from 22.6 per cent of GDP in 1990, it fell to 20.7 per cent in 1995, while the EU-15 average increased from 25.4 per cent to 28.6 per cent). Further, per capita social benefits, measured at constant prices, fell significantly in this period, while in all other EU countries a slight upward trend is observed (see Table 1).[1] As a result, the disparity between Greece (the lowest spender) and the countries which spent the most on social protection per capita in the European Union, measured in purchasing power standards, amounted to a ratio of 3.4 to 1 in mid-nineties (2250 PPS per capita in Greece, compared to 7725 PPS and 6391 PPS per capita in Luxembourg and Denmark which are the highest spender countries, Eurostat, 1998a, p. 15).

In comparison to the other South European countries, Greece embarked upon policies for expanding social citizenship quite late and at a time of low economic growth in the country, intensified globalisation trends, and large-scale restructuring of the European welfare states (Petmesidou, 1996a). Social protection expenditure grew rapidly in the early eighties, but this trend was soon reversed, manifesting a brief glimpse of the welfare state (Petmesidou, 1996b). Strong distributional imbalances, a huge public debt

Table 1 Per Capita Social Protection Expenditure at Constant Prices, 1990–96

	1990	1991	1992	1993	1994	1995	1996
EU-15	100	103	109	113	114	115	117
Belgium	100	104	106	111	114	118	121
Denmark	100	105	108	113	122	122	122
Germany *	100	96	103	104	106	110	114
Greece	100	98	94	96	99	104	109
Spain	100	110	117	122	119	119	120
France	100	103	107	111	112	114	114
Ireland	100	106	112	119	123	131	133
Italy	100	105	109	109	109	107	109
Luxembourg	100	108	112	120	124	129	134
Netherlands	100	101	103	104	102	101	100
Austria	100	104	107	110	115	117	118
Portugal	100	112	128	143	148	151	162
Finland	100	108	115	116	119	119	122
Sweden	100	100	105	104	105	104	103
UK	100	108	118	127	127	128	131

* 1990 data refer to the territorial situation before unification
Index 1990=100.

Source: Eurostat – ESSPROS Database according to the new methodology (ESSPROS Manual of 1996). Data obtained in November 1998.

Note: The table refers only to the first half of the nineties because there are no data available for Greece (as well as for some other EU countries) before 1990 according to the new methodology of the European System of Integrated Social Protection Statistics. Social protection expenditure data prior to 1990 draw upon the previously used ESSPROS methodology (1981 Manual); they extend up to 1993 and are not totally comparable to those based on the new ESSPROS methodology. On the basis of these data (ESSPROS Manual of 1981) social expenditure per head at constant 1985 prices is calculated here, in order to give a broader time perspective for Greece (Eurostat, 1995): 1980=62, 1985=100, 1990=107 and 1993=106.

(which shot up from about 40 per cent of GDP in early-eighties to 125 per cent in mid-nineties), as well as an alarming deficit incurred by the major social insurance funds attest to this.[2] Further, the pattern of development that Greece followed in the post-war period did not lead to extensive industrialisation, as the change was from a predominantly agrarian structure to a services-oriented economy (Petmesidou, 1996b, pp. 328–9). This severely limited the opportunities for a culture of contractual relationships and collective forms of interest organisation and social action to develop, which could promote social citizenship. Compared to the other South European countries, the change from pre-fordist to post-fordist socioeconomic structures was more rapid in Greece, while a tradition of contractual relations, collective solidarity and an active civil society was weakest (Petmesidou, 1996a, pp. 96–107; Petmesidou and Tsoulouvis, 1994). What is more, phenomena of statism and clientelism, (that is, an extensive intervention of the state in the economy and widely observed processes of creation and distribution of revenue on the basis of political credentials rather than market criteria) have traditionally been highly prevalent (Petmesidou, 1987). These conditions contributed to the maintenance and reproduction of a welfare philosophy focusing on individual, particularistic needs rather than on universal well being. This is also reflected on the mode of financing social welfare, which is based largely on contributions, while tax financing is particularly low (Petmesidou, 1996a, p. 110).

Greece has a mixed model of welfare sharing many characteristics with the other South European countries in terms of its structure and functioning.[3] Income maintenance benefits are provided by occupationally fragmented social security funds, while health care is delivered by a national health system (ESY). Though, in principle, ESY operates on the basis of universalism, up to now it has hardly succeeded to come close to a national health service of the type developed for instance in the UK, the Scandinavian countries, or even Italy. ESY was established as late as in 1983 and has been functioning since then in a way that has supported and maintained an extensive mediation of coverage by numerous occupational health schemes markedly uneven across social groups and geographic areas and chaotic in organisational terms. These conditions heightened polarisation of social protection, aggravated the organisational deficiencies of the system and hindered the development of a universalist culture.

The inherent distributional imbalances of the Greek social protection model can be illustrated with reference to: (a) the structure of social protection expenditure – a pension-heavy structure, in which old age, survivors and invalidity benefits predominate in the social budget; (b) the deeply fragmented pension system linked to a highly variegated contributory framework and to great inequalities in entitlements to as well as in the level of benefits; (c) the absence of a universalist income safety net; and (d) discretionary privileges in health care (Petmesidou, 1996b). Closely linked to these characteristics are also the inefficiency of public services and the 'deficit of legality'[4] in their operation well-documented in the relevant literature (e.g. large scale contributions and tax evasion, abuse of invalidity pensions, widely practised informal transactions by hospital doctors and patients, deeply penetrating private/public circuits in health care producing high commissions and profits contributing thus to perverse distribution of resources).

Figure 1 Percentage Constitution of Social Protection Expenditure (1990–95)

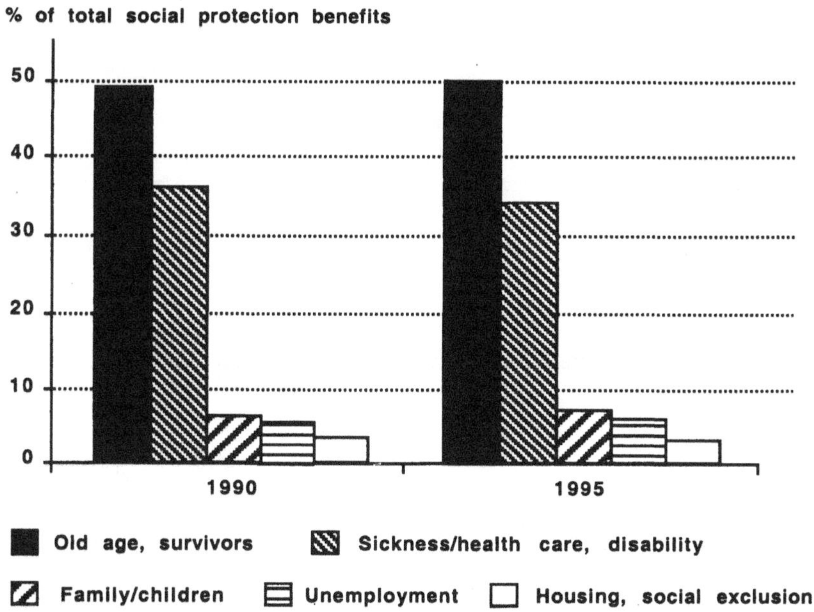

Source: Eurostat (1998b).

Pension schemes constitute the most developed aspect of the Greek social protection system, while other functions of social policy (family/maternity, housing and unemployment benefits) are less developed. Throughout the eighties and nineties old age benefits, together with invalidity benefits accounted for more than 50 per cent of the social budget (Figure 1).[5] The fast increase of family/maternity benefits particularly in the first half of the nineties (Figure 2) did not significantly change the structure of the social budget. Equally low is the share of unemployment benefits and expenditure for vocational training (5.9 per cent in 1995), despite the fact that unemployment rose with alarming rapidity in the last decade.

Greece constitutes an extreme example of high fragmentation in social insurance schemes: in 1998 there were eighty-four social insurance funds administering compulsory and supplementary pension schemes, about

Figure 2 Rates of Change of Social Protection Benefits (in drachmas, at constant 1985 prices)

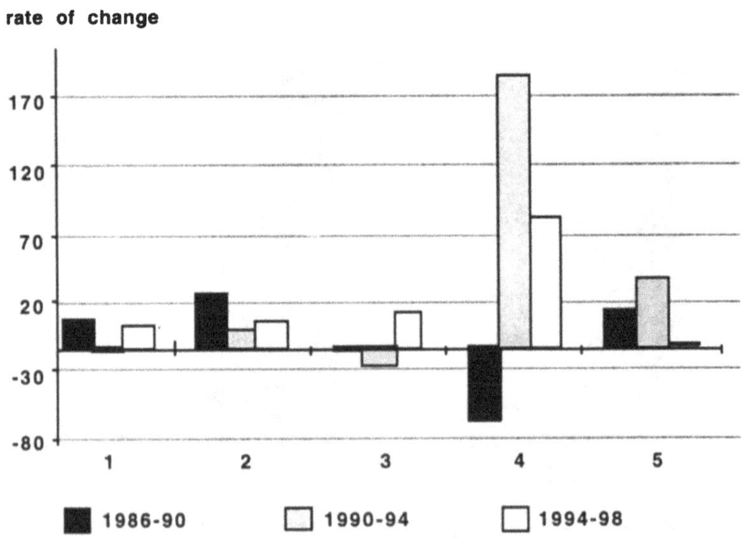

Source: Social Budgets 1986, 1990, 1994, 1998 (Ministry of Labour and Social Insurance).

[1 = old age, survivors and invalidity benefits; 2 = sickness benefits, 3 = social welfare benefits, 4 = family and maternity benefits 5 = unemployment benefits]

twenty health funds and more than one hundred organisations (under the control of five Ministries) providing various social welfare benefits. Organisational regulations, the rate of contributions, financial support by the state, and the types and level of benefits offered differ widely across the various funds. Polarisation of social protection appears to be high. A group of comparatively well-protected beneficiaries constituted by these socio-occupational categories whose members can secure a full and uninterrupted career in the formal labour market, as a precondition of becoming entitled to various benefits, is counterposed to a large number of unprotected persons, those who cannot secure such preconditions, given the absence of a universal income safety net. In the early nineties, the 'theoretical' earnings replacement rate for a worker with a full career in the manufacturing sector was even higher than the net average wage in this sector, while on the other hand, the minimum benefit for an elderly person with no contributive entitlements and no other means of support amounted to only 8 per cent of the net average wage in manufacturing (compared to an EU average of 36 per cent, European Commission, 1994a, pp. 54–5). Equally low is the minimum benefit for an invalid person who cannot work and has no other means of support (16 per cent of GDP per capita in 1992, the lowest rate among EU countries), while an unemployed person with no contributive entitlements and no other means of support cannot claim unemployment or any social assistance benefit.

In the early nineties, the deepening crisis of social security, reflected in the mounting deficit of IKA/TEAM reaching 52 billion drachmas in 1990, the diminishing ratio of employed workers to pensioners, the large public debt and the fast increasing budget deficit made a reform in the pensions field imminent. The three new pension laws (1902/1990, 1976/1991 and 2084/1992) were targeted to the above fiscal problems, but a thorough attempt to rationalise the social security system and overcome fragmentation was postponed.[6]

The legal reform increased pensionable age of civil servants and minimum requirements of working days for retirement under the general scheme of IKA/TEAM, raised contributions, discontinued the indexing of pensions to wages and introduced cuts in benefits for new entrants into the general scheme. Further, it attempted to tighten criteria of eligibility for invalidity benefits, without, however, strengthening social assistance policy (for instance, by introducing a universalist minimum income safety net).

The immediate effect of this reform was a deterioration of the level of minimum monthly pensions,[7] deepening polarisation of social protection even further. It was estimated that the pensioners of IKA lost approximately 290 billion drachmas in the period 1990–95 by the implementation of the aforementioned laws (Rombolis, 1996, p. 122). Thus, by mid-nineties about 1,000,000 pensioners[8] received minimum monthly benefits of less than 100,000 drachmas; these benefits were below 50 per cent of the average per capita income. Strong pressures by trade unions and pensioners' associations to bring into force again the indexing of pensions to wages were unsuccessful. Instead a means-tested meagre social assistance benefit was introduced in 1996 (EKAS) for pensioners 65 years and over receiving minimum benefits.[9]

Public expenditure on health care increased significantly from the mid-eighties to the late nineties. This brought Greece closer to EU standards in expenditure: 5.3 per cent of GDP in Greece, compared to an average of 6.5 per cent for EU-15, in 1997; if we also add private expenditure on health (2.9 per cent), Greece reaches the EU average and even surpasses the OECD average (7.1 per cent). Although in terms of the aggregate size of the health care sector there is not much distance between Greece and her European counterparts, there are great differences in qualitative terms, particularly as regards a persistent collusion of interests between the private and public sector, great inequalities in health care benefits across the numerous funds,[10] as well as the organisational deficiencies and poor performance of ESY, combined with its huge deficit. The financial problems of ESY are mainly due to escalating costs of medicines and fast increasing hospital fees and costs for diagnostic tests rather than to improvement of universal coverage and service standards.[11] As a matter of fact, citizens' dissatisfaction with health services in Greece is the highest among EU countries.[12] For about fifteen years since the establishment of ESY no major attempt was made to tackle the causes of inefficiency, corruption and perverse distribution of resources. Measures such as the introduction of co-payments for medicines and the drawing up of a positive list of medicines for prescription (concerning all health funds – law 2458/1997) partially addressed cost explosion. The recent law on *Modernizing ESY* (passed in 1997) introduced some ambitious institutional reforms and cost containment measures (e.g. the appointment of qualified management personnel in hospitals, the development of first-tier health care in urban centres, changes in the drawing up of hospital budgets, etc.), these have hardly been into force up to now though.

The high degree of centralisation of the social protection system constitutes another peculiarity of Greece.[13] Some minor reforms towards decentralisation in the eighties had no substantial effect on the scope of functions in social welfare undertaken by local authorities: among such changes were the establishment of open-care centres for the elderly at the local level and the transfer of responsibility for the operation of public nurseries to local authorities. The latter regulation, however, met the strong opposition of the relevant department of the Ministry of Social Welfare. The reluctance of the Ministry officials to decentralise public nurseries combined with the fiscal constraints experienced by local authorities greatly delayed this reform. It is only recently that a more substantial reform of local government was attempted (re-organisation of first-tier local authorities so as to create viable units, decentralisation of functions to local government and regional administration).

The peculiarities of social protection in Greece (fragmentation of social security, polarisation of protection, manipulation of benefits often on a clientelistic/particularistic basis) have for a long time been congruent with the overall structure of Greek society. They were closely linked to the statist/clientelistic model of social and political organisation consolidated in the post-war period. Moreover, as shown elsewhere (Petmesidou, 1996a, 1996b), familialism constitutes a crucial component of this model of social organisation and welfare provision: for a long time family and kin support, strongly linked with 'soft-budgeting practices' pursued by households, individuals and enterprises provided a substitute for the inadequate social welfare. In many respects, the crisis of the social protection system reflects the serious deadlocks to which the statist/clientelistic model of social organisation has led since the late eighties. Production of surplus income and wealth by political methods intensified antagonisms to an unprecedented extent undermining gradually the social legitimation of the system. In parallel, the malfunctioning of social protection eroded its material basis. In addition, changing trends in family patterns (i.e. increasing participation of women in the labour force, growing rates of divorce and one parent families) further limited the capacity of the traditional model of social protection based on family and kin support to tackle pressing social needs, due to growing unemployment (especially among the young), impoverishment and social exclusion. These social and institutional deadlocks compounded by the fiscal crisis of the state made urgent large scale institutional change. Greece's attempt to harmonise her institutions to the European Union and, particularly, to meet the target of joining the economic and monetary union (though with considerable delay) further accentuated the need for such a change.

However for any incisive reform to take place in the direction to a new model of welfare, building social consensus is crucial. This is a prerequisite for the country to face the most important challenges in social welfare, such as the need for effective and universal social assistance measures (including a universal income safety net); the shift from a welfare philosophy based upon centrally administered income-maintenance schemes to one favouring the provision of services which respond to local needs; as well as the need for an efficient employment policy to combat unemployment, restructure skills, and regulate casual labour and illegal migration.

Key Developments in the Late Nineties: Responding to the Crisis and to the New Challenges

In the first half of the nineties no major reform was enacted. The aforementioned pension laws of the early nineties aimed primarily to restore financial equilibria in the short and medium term. Similarly, not much progress was made in tackling the mounting problems of ESY. It is in the late nineties and mainly under the pressure of meeting the convergence criteria that a number of institutional reforms have been attempted. Among these, the launching of the social dialogue (in Spring, 1997) for building the required social consensus is of crucial importance. This was supposed to offer an opportunity for the social partners, together with government officials, to negotiate the terms of an agreement on social reform. The results have been rather poor up to now though and disagreement of the social partners has prevailed. Consequently, legal reforms were introduced more or less in a unilateral way by the government in its attempt to push through privatisation, austerity measures and labour market flexibility, in line with the budgetary and fiscal constraints set by the Maastricht criteria.

In this respect Greece differs from the other South European countries in which the nineties constitute a turning point with regard to social concertation. For instance, recent reforms in Italy and Portugal reflect wide social agreements for changing the pattern of economic governance, redrawing the boundaries between the state and society and strengthening civil society institutions. Such pacts, referred to in the relevant literature as 'regulatory' rather than 'redistributive',[14] gave rise to a phenomenon called 'competitive corporatism' (Rhodes, 1997, p. 17), in which a consensus building process 'assigns a renewed importance to public policies as a crucial factor in national competitiveness' (Regini and Regalia, 1997, p. 228). In contrast, social concertation is rather weak in Greece. Among other factors, the highly politicised and conflictual character of industrial relations considerably limited the possibility of wide social agreements on policy reform.

(a) The Social Dialogue

The first round of the social dialogue initiated by the government focused on issues of economic development, competitiveness and employment. The policy measures put on the agenda by public authorities concerned primarily employment and labour market flexibility. The major issues discussed were: work time flexibility; the possibility of part-time work in the public sector; a ceiling for the number of part-time workers in both the private and public sector; regulation of atypical work (subcontracting, tele-work, etc.); reduction in the non-wage labour cost for specific categories of workers (unemployed over 50 years, young unemployed, workers in sectors under crisis, such as textiles, steel industries and shipbuilding); the rate of severance payments; and local employment agreements.

The *Agreement of Trust* signed by the social partners and the government in November 1997, as the outcome of this dialogue, is a rather vague statement with no binding obligations. Disagreement on many of the above issues was strong. Especially the last two issues were firmly opposed by the representatives of the General Confederation of Greek Workers (GSEE). As regards the *Local Employment Agreements*, GSEE considered them as a way in which institutional changes in industrial relations leading to work and pay flexibility would be introduced, so to speak, by the back door, with wider repercussions at the national level.

A social dialogue on pensions reform (*Streamlining the Social Security Funds*) took place in parallel and also extended into 1998. The main issues of the agenda focused on: (a) merging social insurance schemes of similar socio-professional categories so as to reduce fragmentation; (b) managing the deficit-ridden funds; (c) developing ways of efficient use of the fixed assets and reserves of social insurance organisations; (d) introducing disincentives for retired persons to continue working; (e) regulating social security for new forms of work (part-time work, atypical forms of employment); (f) combating contributions evasion, and (g) containing cost in health care. A recently approved law (December, 1998), the so-called 'mini reform' of the pension system, partly drew upon this dialogue; however, once again, incisive changes were postponed.

(b) Employment/Unemployment

In the last few years, debate on labour market policy reform focused mainly on how to tackle employment and labour market rigidity, as a way of improving labour market performance and combating unemployment. Together with the other South European countries Greece was considered to have a highly restrictive employment protection legislation in the EU (strict rules for dismissals, high severance payments, strict job demarcations and work schedules). This was held to account for deteriorating economic performance and rapidly growing unemployment since the late seventies. The acute problem of youth unemployment (especially for women, as 41 per cent of the female labour force of 15 to 24 years were unemployed in 1996) and of long-term unemployment (amounting to 47 per cent and 63 per cent of the unemployed men and women respectively) is taken to be a strong indication of the inflexibility of the Greek labour market.[15] However, here, a crucial paradox should be noted. Institutional rules may exhibit a high degree of rigidity, yet from an informal point of view labour flexibility tends to be high in South Europe, even more so in Greece where the informal sector amounts to roughly 35–40 per cent of GDP (see Pavlopoulos, 1987; Negreponti-Delivani, 1990; Vavouras and Koutris, 1991; and Kalyvianaki and Xanthaki, 1993).[16] The circumventing of employment regulations, frequently practised by small firms which constitute the majority of enterprises in all sectors of the Greek economy, allows a great scope for work flexibility.[17] Since the late eighties illegal in-migration has further exacerbated phenomena of irregular and concealed work in South Europe; especially so in Greece, where a policy of integration of illegal immigrants only recently was introduced.

Policy measures in the early nineties, unilaterally decided by the government, aimed to austerity and labour market flexibility. In 1991 the automatic inflation indexation system for wages was abandoned. Further, in an attempt to tackle labour market rigidity the legal framework of industrial relations was substantially changed, so as to eliminate direct government interventions in collective negotiations; new legislation was introduced supporting part-time and fixed-term employment and making possible the use a fourth shift by firms, allowing thus for work time flexibility (European Commission, 1996a, p. 8). However very little use has been made of part-time and fixed-term employment contracts in Greece up to now (part-time and fixed-term employment amounted to 4.6 per cent and 11 per cent of the labour force in Greece in 1997, compared to the EU-15 average of 16.9 per cent and 12.2 per cent respectively). Further these measures were rather ad hoc and hardly set in the context of a coherent and effective employment policy.[18] The very low activity rates in Greece (among the lowest in the EU, particularly so for women), rising unemployment (especially long-term unemployment among the young and relatively high unemployment among tertiary-level education graduates), meagre expenditure on active labour market policies compounded by a waste of resources channelled to vocational training because of phenomena of corruption and fraud (see below) are indicative of employment policy deficiencies.

From the late seventies to the mid-eighties a very rapid increase of unemployment was recorded in Greece (from 2.1 per cent in 1977 – 1.1 per cent for men and 4.1 per cent for women – to 7.0 per cent in 1985 – 5.0 per cent for men and 10.6 per cent for women); it slowed down in the second half of the eighties but increased fast during the nineties. The annual average unemployment increase was higher for men than for women in the early nineties, a characteristic attributed to significant sectoral changes in employment (steadily declining employment in agriculture, significant restructuring in manufacturing and rapidly increasing tertiary sector employment). By the mid-nineties, the yearly increase of unemployment was higher for women. In 1997 total unemployment reached 10.4 per cent of the labour force (over 50 per cent of it being long-term unemployment).[19] Further, in 1997 even though the GDP increased by 3.5 per cent, total employment decreased by 0.5 per cent.[20] In the following year the trend was reversed as employment increased by 3.0 per cent; yet unemployment also increased quickly, reaching almost 12.0 per cent.

Despite the gravity of the problem, social policy for tackling unemployment is not very much developed.[21] Social protection of the unemployed relies heavily on family and kin support networks, given the fact that only a small number of the unemployed are eligible for benefit,[22] unemployment compensation is rather meagre (amounting to 50 per cent of the wage of the unskilled worker) and its duration is short (5 to 12 months, depending upon the number of days a person worked in the year before falling into unemployment). Further, the young unemployed, who enter into the labour market for the first time, are not entitled to unemployment benefit.[23] Greece also lacks any income support scheme for the long term unemployed; neither has there developed a policy of early retirement for those old-age workers experiencing long spells of unemployment. Obviously the Greek unemployment benefit system can hardly be considered as creating work disincentives or a risk of an unemployment trap as in other European countries.

What is more, until recently active labour market policy measures (that is, vocational training/re-training, subsidised employment) have been rudimentary (expenditure on such policies amounted to 0.4 per cent of GDP in 1994 and to 0.3 per cent in 1996). Undoubtedly, the resources for training courses and employment subsidies have increased in the last decade, due to the assistance by the structural funds of the EU to Greece, even in the absence of an efficient policy environment in the country. Yet, given the paucity of national resources for employment policy, the total budget is still meagre.

It is in the second half of the nineties that some significant legislative innovations were introduced in the direction of increasing privatisation and deregulation of the labour market (the law 2434/1996 on *Policy Measures for Employment, Vocational Education and Training*, and its follow-up, the law 2639/1998 on *Regulating Industrial Relations*). Although drawing upon the agenda of the social dialogue, these legal developments hardly reflected a consensual process of reform and some issues of the new legislation were vociferously opposed by trade unions (for example, work time flexibility). This hindered significantly their effective implementation.

Among the main aims of these laws were: increasing labour market flexibility and regulating atypical forms of work; linking passive to active labour market policies (so as to promote employability); upgrading OAED services (as a pre-condition for a more efficient labour market policy) in parallel with the establishment of private employment offices. Further, health insurance for the young unemployed (20 to 29 years of age) and provisions for the funding of health insurance contributions of long-term unemployed over 55 years of age were introduced.

The new legislation aimed also to facilitate the design and implementation of a long term employment programme that would redistribute resources between passive and active labour market measures through the implementation of continuing training and employment subsidisation programmes. The financing of these programmes utterly depends on resources by the European Social Fund. The absorption of Community Funding for human resources and vocational training, in the context of the Second Community Support Framework was rather low until the mid-nineties (12 per cent in September 1996). This slow rate of absorption was due to problems of inefficiency and large scale corruption that arose in the context of the First Community Support Framework with regard to vocational training programmes (Petmesidou, 1996b, p. 342). A recent law targeted to rationalising the vocational training system introduced stricter rules for the operation of training centres and the distribution of resources, and by the end of 1998 a number of programmes were resumed.

Closely linked with the aforementioned developments was also the passing of a law for the legalisation of illegal immigrants, in 1997, which was put in force in early 1998. About 376,000 illegal immigrants (roughly about two thirds of the estimated total number of illegal immigrants in Greece)[24] applied for getting a work permit – that is, the so-called 'green card' – which can be renewed for up to five years. As the procedure is still in progress, one can only estimate the number of successful applications: on the basis of available information by OAED about two thirds will finally satisfy the criteria for being granted a green card. The fact that a large number of illegal immigrants did not turn up for registration in OAED attests to the difficulties surrounding the legalisation procedure casting doubts on its effectiveness.

The National Action Plan for Employment drawn up in early 1998 on the basis of the EU Employment Guidelines – agreed upon in the European Jobs Summit of November 1997 – incorporated many of the above regulations and policy measures. Yet, as indicated in a Commission Report the Plan is wanting as regards an effective and coherent employment strategy geared towards a preventive rather than curative approach to unemployment. This is argued on the basis that it lacks an overall strategy; its multiannual perspective is unclear, as it does not provide an explicit time frame for meeting the stated objectives; the mechanisms of implementing and monitoring policy measures remain imprecise; and most importantly, the resources for its implementation are insufficient.[25]

(c) Social Security, Health Care and Welfare Policies

The pension system and health care face serious fiscal problems expected to be exacerbated by the turn of the century because of demographic ageing, system maturity, cost explosion of health care, combined with the aforementioned imbalances and organisational deficiencies of the social insurance system in Greece. As to demographic ageing, it is expected that the number of persons of pensionable age (65 years and over) will increase from 22.5 per cent of the population aged 15 to 64 years in 1995 to 25.7 per cent in 2000 and to 56.7 per cent in 2050 (Experts Committee, 1997, p. 11) with detrimental effects on the already burdensome dependency ratios.

Further, despite unremitting lip service to the need of combating contributions evasion and the enactment of successive regulations (see laws 2238/1994, 2559/1997 and 2519/1997) contributions evasion continues to be a major fiscal problem of the social insurance system estimated at 500 billion drachmas yearly for the period 1990 to 1997.[26]

As mentioned earlier, legal reform of the pension system and targeting measures introduced in the first half of the nineties had only a short-term positive fiscal effect. Moreover, the drastic cuts of old age benefits for the new entrants in the general scheme of IKA/TEAM (from 1.1.1993 onwards) to 60 per cent of their gross pensionable earnings (that is, revalued earnings of the last 5 years) led to acute social confrontations. Under this pressure the present government redefined minimum pensions for new entrants in the general scheme with a new legal act in early 1998.

Other regulations of law 2094/1992 were: (a) the fixing of supplementary pensions to 20 per cent of pensionable earnings (for those with a working career of 35 years), yet this regulation was also suspended by the present government given the lack of detailed information about the financial situation of the various supplementary funds; (b) the gradual increase of pensionable age; (c) the increase of employees' contributions with a parallel decrease of employers' contributions; (d) a ceiling set for the lump sum benefit paid to salaried workers at retirement; (e) the progressive decrease of employers' contributions for funding this lump sum benefit, so as to be abolished by the year 2003.

In the last few years a number of proposals were put forward by social policy experts and committees appointed by the government to develop plans for structural reforms in the pension field. A proposal by GSEE emphasised the need for a unified pension scheme, indexing pensions to wages, and tripartite funding of social security. The other proposals (by the Ministry of Social Insurance, the Institute of Economic and Industrial Research – IOBE – and top government advisers) more or less converge on the need for a reform establishing a mix of public and private pension schemes. The proposed system is based on three pillars: (a) a universal scheme granting a guaranteed minimum pension and funded by general taxation (or alternatively by the insured, the employers and the state), (b) a compulsory supplementary pension scheme operating on a contributory basis, and (c) a voluntary supplementary scheme based on private insurance (Leandros, 1996; see also Experts Committee, 1997).

In an attempt to reduce fragmentation and rationalise expenditure, proposals for unifying social insurance funds of similar socio-professional groups have been on the agenda of negotiations between the respective funds, government officials and trade unions over the last few years. Negotiations culminated in the amalgamation of three funds of self-employed workers (TEBE, the fund of self-employed artisans and small business owners; TAE, the fund of merchants, and TSA, the fund of owners of motor vehicles for public transport) covering about 800,000 insured persons, effected by the recent legal act in the pension field (the so-called 'mini reform' of social insurance, passed in December, 1998).

The proposal to create a unified fund for bank employees by abolishing the existing five different first-tier general schemes covering 27,000 people and to which also 23,000 bank employees (of the Commercial Bank of Greece and of various private banks) insured in IKA would be included, met the negative reaction of the association of employees of the Bank of Greece, as well as of IKA (given that IKA would lose resources in this way). As a result, the issue was postponed. Other less substantial changes, such as for instance the inclusion of some deficit-ridden supplementary pension funds, like the fund of workers in metal industry, into IKA have a more limited overall impact on overcoming fragmentation.[27]

Other provisions of the mini reform are: cuts in old age benefits for pensioners who have a job (and even suspension of benefits for pensioners less than 55 years who continue working); stricter rules for survivor benefits and graduation according to income; the establishment of a unified health organisation for monitoring health expenses of the funds; provision of preventive health services by the health funds; a decrease of co-payments for drugs for pensioners receiving the social assistance benefit (EKAS); the formation of a unified supplementary pension fund for public employees; as well as measures for the more efficient use of the resources of social insurance funds.

Equally important was the passing of law 2458/1997 (effective from January, 1998) for the social insurance of peasants. With this law, after thirty-six years of its establishment, OGA (the Organization of Agricultural Insurance) changed status and mode of operation: from a social security scheme financed through taxation, it became a contributions-based fund.[28] Given the huge deficit of OGA, it is held that moving from tax-based to contributions-based funding will help to overcome the financial crisis and raise minimum pensions.[29]

The financial management of the reserves of the various funds constitutes another vexed issue in the social insurance field, given the fact that until recently strict state control limited their profitable use.[30] Law 2216/1994 lifted some of the restrictions, allowing social insurance organisations to invest 20 per cent of their reserves (acting on their own or in collaboration with financial agents) in real estate, stocks, bonds, etc. Regulations that followed up redefined the above terms, making obligatory for social insurance organisations to deposit their reserves – if these are not invested by the funds themselves or through commercial banks – in the Bank of Greece. The aim was to pull resources so as to maximise returns by investing reserves in state bonds, mutual funds and other assets.[31] The provision of the recent pension law for a supervisory committee to be established in the Bank of Greece for overseeing investment of the reserves of social insurance organisations was strongly criticised by the trade unions because it was seen as re-strengthening state control (Petropoulos, 1998).

The fiscal problems of ESY constitute another facet of the predicament of the Greek welfare state. The deficit of hospitals was estimated to be about 70 billion drachmas in early 1998 (while the fifteen largest hospitals of the country incur a deficit of 350–650 million drachmas per month).[32] Deficits are largely due to: inefficiency in the organisation of health services, serious fiscal problems of the social insurance organisations, and the absence of a long-term strategy for ESY. In its report to the Ministry of Health an experts committee appointed for evaluating ESY stressed that:

'The Greek National Health System is in a process of development, yet it faces serious problems of unprofessional behaviour on the part of medical staff; it is characterised by an extremely large number of specialists but a very poor organisation of first-tier care undertaken to the largest extent by the out-patient departments of hospitals...Although one reform plan follows the other, none of them was decisively supported by successive governments' (Abel-Smith et al., 1994, p. 9).

It concluded that the government should develop a comprehensive reform plan giving emphasis to prevention and wide dissemination of health information. Its main suggestions were: (a) the establishment of a unified fund to which the revenue of all the existing health funds (as well as the state grants to the health funds and state subsidies to ESY) would be transferred; (b) the introduction of quasi-market relationships between public purchasers and providers (the unified fund acting as an association of purchasers); (c) the institutionalisation of family General Practitioner (paid by capitation); (d) the drawing-up of a positive list of medicines to be prescribed in ESY (doctors' prescriptions should be under continuous scrutiny); (e) financial and administrative de-centralisation of health services with the creation of Regional Health Councils; and (f) introduction of managerial criteria in hospital administration.

The law 2519 on '*Modernizing ESY*' which passed in late 1997 incorporated some of the above proposals. Its central provisions can be summarised as follows: (a) protection of citizens' rights in health services, (b) appointment of public health doctors and establishment of school health services at the central and regional level; (c) financial management of hospitals through closed global annual budgets; (d) the appointment of managing directors in hospitals; and (e) the promotion of first-tier health care through a plan of cooperation and coordinated action between out-patient hospital departments, existing clinics of the health funds, the health centres operating in the rural areas, and any existing municipal health centres (these will function as networks of health care provision linked to ESY hospitals).

However, the main provisions of this law have hardly been put into practice and there are serious doubts as to the extent to which the reform can tackle existing inequalities and inefficiencies in health care. There is no provision for a substantial development of first-tier public health care (especially in the urban areas). A network of cooperating first-tier health services was planned to function on a pilot basis, without substantial progress up to now though. On the other hand, in the rural areas, from a total of 170 health centres built in the eighties and nineties, a large part underfunction due to lack of medical staff and required equipment; and there are no guarantees for any improvement.

Inherent defects of the system (collusion of private and public interests and large scale corruption) are hardly tackled by the recent law. As stressed earlier, the large size of the private health sector in Greece (40 per cent of total health expenditure) and its strong links with the black economy are among the main causes of the system's inefficiency. There are no exact indicators about the size of the black economy of health services. According to various estimates for the first half of the nineties, it ranged between 1.1 per cent to 1.5 per cent of GDP (Kyriopoulos, 1992; Kyriopoulos et al., 1996; Gitona et al., 1997). Thus, in mid-nineties, roughly about 300 billion drachmas 'circulated' in the black economy of health services annually. Also, about 35,000 patients are 'channelled' for medical treatment abroad per year (the cost amounting to approximately 26 billion drachmas). The effective control of these phenomena constitutes a top priority for rationalising ESY.

Furthermore, with recent legislation (Law 2646/1998) a thorough restructuring of social welfare organisations is planned. The three major welfare organisations: the National Welfare Organisation (EOP), and two Child Welfare Institutions (PIKPA and METERA) are going to be amalgamated in a single institution (the National Welfare Agency) that will operate as a strategic agent for welfare policy development, while many of the functions performed by the above three welfare organisations (such as the running of public nurseries and child welfare centres) will be transferred to the first and second-tier local authorities.[33]

In the last couple of years, some other innovative welfare policies introduced as pilot schemes in certain localities are: the programme 'help at home' for the elderly (operating in a few localities but expected to be expanded to about one hundred local authorities in the near future); the establishment of open care centres for people with disabilities and for autistic children; a further revision of the rules for invalidity benefits (tightening medical criteria and drawing up common regulations across the funds).

In a nutshell, the reform of the rather weak welfare state in Greece in the 1990s was conditioned by factors such as the need to deal with the fiscal strains and organisational problems of a highly fragmented and unevenly developed social protection system; the requirement of fiscal discipline stipulated by the criteria of joining the European Monetary Union; and trends towards more selective care, common – to one degree or another – among EU countries and due to changing economic and social conditions in the post-fordist era.[34] Key issues in the rhetoric of reforms, particularly in the late nineties, were flexibilisation/deregulation of labour markets, modernisation of health and welfare institutions, and targeting considered to be appropriate responses to the changing socioeconomic conditions (i.e. changing labour markets, employment patterns, family structures and life courses). The extent to which this policy orientation can address new needs and risks related to new family arrangements, greater career uncertainty and high risks for atypical or non standard employment forms (part-time, fixed-term employment, subcontracting, etc.) to become life-cycle traps into poverty and marginalisation for some social groups is a highly contested issue.[35] As Esping-Andersen (1996, p. 25) argues with regard to flexibility in working life and labour market deregulation in post-industrial societies, if these policy options are not linked with an efficient strategy of social investment in education and active policies of training/retraining and life-long learning, it is highly likely that they will increase the chances of certain social groups to become chronic losers.[36] In the case of Greece, phenomena of persistently high long-term unemployment among the young, comparatively high risk of unemployment even among persons with tertiary-level education, and great inefficiencies in vocational training until the late nineties are indications of a deficient social investment strategy.

Further, changes in the pension field (as for instance stricter rules for entitlements to survivor benefits) point towards an individualisation of social security rights that is closely linked with increasing female participation in the labour market (European Commission, 1998c, p. 17). However, such a policy reform needs to be complemented by other measures as well. Compared to men, women face higher risks over their active adult-phase life courses, as they are more likely to be employed in non standard jobs and experience interruptions of their working career because of family responsibilities or unemployment. This makes pressing the need for social policy measures to harmonise women's employment with family formation and prevent phenomena of poverty among female-headed households. In addition, such policy measures are of utmost importance in order to tackle the acute problems of low fertility and demographic ageing.

Conclusion

Recent legal reforms in respect to the pension system, the labour market, health care and social welfare exhibit a decisive attempt by the present PASOK government to meet the challenges facing the Greek model of social protection. External pressures by the increasingly unified European economy and the wider context of globalisation coupled with internal factors of rapid cost increase of social protection and a comparatively large public debt put under great strain the Greek welfare state. Further, the in-build 'defects', contradictions and imbalances of the system seriously undermined its legitimacy leaving no room for the exercise of consistent social policy.

As repeatedly emphasised, reform for solving social and economic problems and removing deadlocks has to deal first with social consensus on a new mode of regulation of the economy and elaborate a new social contract with significant effects on the relationship between civil society and the state, political processes and the economy. The social dialogue and other current policies, such as the change in central-local relations, the attempt to restrict and control the *huge* informal sector and introduce a 'rational' decision-making process in public administration can operate in the direction of undermining the old world of individualistic/clientelistic social and political behaviour. Yet it remains to be seen how successful these policies can be to promote a broad consensus on the terms of a genuine (socioeconomic) regime transformation. Up to now, the change has clearly been slowest precisely with respect to working out a broad agreement among social actors for large scale and effective reform. There is no doubt that this incapacity of social partners to become significant forces of transformation – primarily due to the traditionally weak civil society in Greece – was further exacerbated by the one-dimensional focus on fiscal discipline stipulated by the Maastricht criteria of economic and monetary union. It is highly likely that a persistent policy along these lines will cause serious confrontations and a stalemate in the social dialogue in Greece.

Hopefully a chorus of academic and political pleas[37] for a concerted action to improve the Social Quality of Europe through 'a creative reciprocity between European economic and social policies' (Beck et al., 1997, p. 264) may provide fertile ground for a thorough and persuasive critique of economic domination over social goals. Important developments such as the inclusion of an *Employment Chapter* in the Amsterdam Treaty[38] and steps taken towards a more coordinated employment policy framework among EU countries may have a positive effect in the direction of a solidaristic supranational policy so as to fight against unemployment and unacceptable forms of social exclusion and marginalisation that many European citizens are experiencing. Such a development at the EU level might prove to be of crucial importance in mobilising actors towards social concertation for a thorough regime transformation in Greece, given the incapacity of internal social configurations to stimulate such a change up to now. Needless to say, European integration is still quite far from such an optimistic scenario.

Notes

1. One might claim that the downward trend in real social expenditure per capita in the early nineties was conditioned by the peculiar political and economic conditions in Greece in this period (i.e. high public spending in 1990, huge budget deficits, coalition governments after the crisis of the late eighties brought about by widespread corruption phenomena, and a recessionary economic trend in the first half of the nineties). Leaving aside the peculiarities in political developments in Greece in the late eighties – early nineties, we could stress that some other EU countries experienced a significant slow-down of economic output in the first half of the nineties; particularly so Spain (OECD, 1996a, p. 5), Portugal (OECD, 1996b, p. 132), and Italy (OECD, 1997, p. 150), which in terms of their social protection systems exhibit similarities with Greece. Yet, in these countries social expenditure per capita increased in the early nineties (the upward trend being more pronounced in Portugal).
2. By the mid-eighties the deficit of social insurance funds amounted to about 17 per cent of their total revenue and 3 per cent of GDP (Petmesidou, 1991, pp. 43–4; Petmesidou 1996b, p. 337).
3. For an analysis of the South European model of social protection see: Ferrera (1996); Katrougalos (1996); Petmesidou (1996a); and Rhodes (1997).
4. For a similar remark regarding the Italian welfare state see Ferrera (1997, p. 234).
5. Also, it is striking that in the early nineties about 50 per cent of all pensioners of the National Insurance Fund (IKA, the biggest social security fund for blue and white collar workers) received invalidity pensions (European Commission, 1994a, p. 30).
6. See on this issue also Venieris (1997, pp. 265–7).
7. Minimum monthly pensions fell from 20 to 16.8 wages of the unskilled worker.
8. About 70 per cent of the pensioners of IKA/TEAM and most of the pensioners of TEBE (the fund of self-employed artisans and small business owners), TSA (the fund of owners of motor vehicles for public transport) and other underprivileged funds belong to this category.
9. In 1997 provision of EKAS was extended to pensioners 60 to 64 years of age as well. Although an official poverty line does not exist in Greece, one could argue that a large group of pensioners receiving minimum benefits live in poverty (on this issue as well as on the problems regarding access to EKAS by elderly people receiving low pensions see Emke-Poulopoulou, 1998).
10. In 1997 per capita health expenditure of TEBE (42,124 drachmas) was about three times less than that of the health fund for the personnel of the Ionian Bank (130,574 drachmas) and roughly five times less than that of the health fund for the personnel of local authorities (about 204,000 drachmas – at constant 1994 prices), see Sissouras et al. (1998).
11. Expenditure for medicines increased by 85 per cent (at constant prices) between 1987 and 1995 (calculations by Farmetrica); while in 1997 health funds spent about 39 per cent of their budget on medicines.
12. In 1996 the percentage of people who declared that they were satisfied with the services offered by ESY amounted to 18.4 per cent ; it further decreased to 15.5 per cent in 1998.

13. Distinguishing her from the other South European countries, particularly Italy and Spain.
14. Manifesting the departure from a logic of an 'immediate exchange of benefits' between the state and social partners, that is, a quid pro quo logic that most often characterises corporatist agreements.
15. This is compounded by the high unemployment rate for university and higher technical education graduates (including persons with postgraduate qualifications): 23.3 per cent of the unemployed in 1997. From 1990 to 1997 unemployment among persons with tertiary level education increased by 67 per cent, that is faster than total unemployment (57 per cent); calculations are based on National Statistical Service of Greece (1990) and data of the 1997 Labour Force Survey available in electronic form.
16. According to an estimate by Eurostat Greece is ranked first among EU countries regarding the size of the informal economy (35 per cent of GDP), while lowest in the ranking is Finland where the informal economy amounts to only 2 per cent of GDP.
17. For a similar remark on the mix of labour market rigidity/flexibility in Italy and Portugal see Gualmini (1997, p. 83); OECD (1996b, p. 95); and European Commission (1996b: p. iv).
18. As argued elsewhere in respect to regional/urban and social planning in Greece (Petmesidou and Tsoulouvis, 1990a & 1990b), a major deficiency is the rudimentary development of a multi-stage policy process, in which policy measures are incorporated into coherent programmes whose implementation is strongly linked to monitoring, evaluation and review of the process. It is only recently – and partly because of stipulations of EU-funded programmes (or because of a set policy-process framework by the EU, as in the case of the National Action Plans for Employment) – that a policy framework linking forecasting/setting of objectives and priorities to monitoring, control, evaluation and review of programmes is attempted.
19. According to a recent research undertaken on behalf of the EU Employment Observatory, if we also take into account hidden unemployment (about 3 per cent), total unemployment amounts to 13.3 per cent of the labour force. Hidden unemployment refers to all those 'discouraged' unemployed who become inactive; it also has to do with the large number of self-employed persons in Greece (47 per cent of the labour force) among whom unemployment cannot be easily defined and detected (see Petmesidou, 1998).
20. That is, 18,000 jobs were lost in total (41,000 jobs were lost in the primary and secondary sectors, but only 23,500 new jobs were created in services). According to Ioakimoglou and Kritikides, 'this unusually small increase of employment in services in 1997' is most probably due to 'an increase in labour productivity.' And they pose the question whether this manifests a shift towards a regime of intensive accumulation in services with significant repercussions on the future of employment (1998, p. 25).
21. Little developed also is research on labour markets in Greece as an input to the policy process.
22. Of those registered as unemployed only a small percentage (roughly 50 per cent) get unemployment benefit; while of the total number of unemployed aged 25 to 64 about two thirds receive no unemployment benefit (European Commission, 1998a, p. 17).
23. A very meagre allowance of 25,000 drachmas per month is provided to the unemployed of 20–29 years of age who remain registered as unemployed for more than a year; this is provided by OAED (Organisation for the Employment of the Labour Force) for up to five months.
24. According to an OECD estimate illegal immigrants amounted to about half a million in 1995 (roughly about 13 per cent of the labour force), OECD (1996c, pp. 61–3); for other estimates concerning the period of the late eighties – early nineties see Petrinioti (1993) and Linardos-Rylmon (1993). Illegal immigrants work in the black market earning less

than 30 per cent to 50 per cent of normal wages (Fakiolas 1998). Of those who applied for work permit 43 per cent are Albanians, 12 per cent Egyptians, 11 per cent Pakistanis, 8 per cent Bangladeshis, 4 per cent Syrians and the rest are Romanians, Polish, Bulgarians and a few Indians; also 73 per cent of them are in the age group 18–37 years (provisional data obtained by OAED).

25. See European Commission, 1998b. Besides, from the 70,000 new jobs which were expected to be created on the basis of the 1998 National Action Plan (through subsidisation and training programmes) only 20,000 were materialised until the end of 1998, as confessed by the Minister of Labour.
26. Data obtained by the Greek Confederation of the Social Insurance Organisations Personnel.
27. About 65 small funds were affected by the recent reform; some of them were amalgamated with each other and others were abolished.
28. A few years ago, law 1754/1986 introduced a supplementary contributive pension scheme in OGA; this was upgraded into a main contributory pension scheme for 1,161,000 peasants in January 1998.
29. Law 2458/1997 introduced seven social insurance categories corresponding to seven pension levels, ranging from a minimum pension of 67,200 drachmas to a maximum of 194,180 drachmas (in 35 years of work).
30. Yet, on the other hand, when the social insurance funds incurred deficits they were forced to borrow money from the state-controlled banks on extremely unfavourable terms (Petmesidou, 1991, p. 42).
31. However, it is doubtful whether this regulation has up to now contributed to an efficient management of the reserves of social insurance funds, given the policy of the Bank of Greece to invest them in state bonds, thus, using them as a means of financing the state budget deficit.
32. As stated by the Experts Committee for the Study of Long-Term Economic Policy, there are no clearly defined rules for financing public hospitals; cuts in the budgets are made in an ad hoc way; funding is often delayed; while health funds cover only 20 per cent to 30 per cent of the real cost of hospital treatment.
33. Finally, responsibility of about one thousand five hundred nurseries is going to be transferred from the Ministry of Labour and Social Welfare to local authorities according to the new law.
34. For an analysis of the causes of these common trends see Esping-Andersen (1996).
35. Gender inequalities in this respect are very important as women are most often employed in precarious jobs (European Commission, 1994 and 1997).
36. For the catchwords of 'employability' and 'workfare' to have any positive effect in the policy field, they should not only be associated with an employment strategy of creating easy entries into the labour market (through low-wage, non standard jobs) but also with 'guarantees for mobility and improvement', so that these jobs do not become life cycle traps (see on this issue Esping-Andersen, 1996, pp. 25–6).
37. To mention here the report of the Comité de Sages (1996); the contributions to and debates in the two Conferences on the Social Quality of Europe organised by the Dutch Ministry of Social Affairs in Amsterdam (January, 1997 and June, 1998); as well as the signing of the *Amsterdam Declaration on the Social Quality of Europe* (June, 1998) and its presentation to the European Parliament.
38. As well as the incorporation of the Social Policy Agreement in the Treaty (as the British opt-out from social policy is over).

References

Abel-Smith, B., Calltorp, J., Dixon, M., Dunning, Ad., Evans, E., Holland, W., Jarman, B. and Mossialos, E. (1994), *Report of the Expert Committee on the Greek Health Services*, Athens: Ministry of Health, Welfare and Social Insurance [in Greek].

Beck, W., van der Maesen, L. and Walker, A. (eds) (1997), *The Social Quality of Europe*, The Hague: Kluwer.

Comité des Sages (1996), *For a Europe of Civic and Social Rights*, Brussels: European Commission, DG V.

Emke-Poulopoulou, E. (1998), *Greek Elderly Citizens: Past, Present and Future*, Athens: Ion.

Esping-Andersen, G. (1996), 'After the golden age? Welfare state dilemmas in a global economy', in Esping-Andersen, G. (ed), *Welfare States in Transition. National Adaptations in Global Economies*, London: Sage, pp. 1–31.

European Commission (1994a), *Social Protection in Europe*, Luxembourg: European Communities [in Greek].

European Commission (1994b), *Bulletin on Women and Employment in the EU* (Network of Experts on the Situation of Women in the Labour Market), No. 4, April, Brussels: DG V.

European Commission (1996a), *Labour Market Studies. Greece*, Luxembourg: European Communities.

European Commission (1996b), *Labour Market Studies. Portugal*, Luxembourg: European Communities.

European Commission (1997), 'Women and Employment in the European Union', *Equal Opportunities Magazine* (Medium-Term Action Programme on Equal Opportunities), No. 3, supplement, Brussels: DG V.

European Commission (1998a), *Social Protection in Europe*, Luxembourg: European Communities.

European Commission (1998b), *From Guidelines to Action: The National Action Plans for Employment*, Brussels: DG V.

European Commission (1998c), *Equal Opportunities for Women and Men in the European Union. Annual report 1997*, Brussels: DG V.

Eurostat (1995), *Social Protection Expenditure and Receipts, 1980–93*, Luxembourg.

Eurostat (1998a), *Social Protection Expenditure and Receipts, 1980–95*, Luxembourg.

Eurostat (1998b), 'Social Protection in the European Union', in *Statistics in Focus/Population and Social Conditions*, No. 14.

Experts Committee for the Study of Long-Term Economic Policy (1997), *Economy and Pensions*, Athens: National Bank of Greece [in Greek].

Fakiolas, R. (1998), *The Impact of Immigration to the Greek Labour Market*, conference paper presented at the Conference on Refugees and Immigrants in the Greek Labour Market, Greek Centre for European Studies (EKEM), (June) [in Greek].

Ferrera, M. (1996), 'The "Southern model" of Welfare in Social Europe', *Journal of European Social Policy*, Vol. 6, No. 1, pp. 17–37.

Ferrera, M. (1997), 'The Uncertain Future of the Italian Welfare State', *West European Politics*, Vol. 20, No. 1, pp. 231–49.

Ioakimoglou, E. and Kritikides, G. (1998), 'The Main Results of the 1997 Labour Force Survey of ESYE', *Labour Institute of the General Confederation of Greek Workers (INE) Newsletter*, No. 36, pp. 23–6 [in Greek].

Gitona, M., Kyriopoulos, J. and Karalis, G. (1997), 'The Informal Contribution to the Cost of Health Services', in Kyriopoulos, J. and Sissouras, A. (eds), *Unified Health Service: Necessity or Illusion*, Athens: Themelio, pp. 284–97 [in Greek].

Gualmini, E. (1997), 'Italy', in Compston, H. (ed), *The New Politics of Unemployment*, London: Routledge, pp. 68–86.

Kalyvianaki, K. and Xanthaki, M. (eds) (1993), *Tax Regime, Informal Economy and Tax Evasion in Greece*, Athens: Mediterranean Studies Foundation/Papazisis [in Greek].

Linardos-Rylmon, P. (1993), *Foreign Workers in the Greek Labour Market*, Athens: Labour Institute of the General Confederation of Greek Workers (INE) [in Greek].

Katrougalos, G. (1996), 'The South European Welfare Model: The Greek Welfare State, in Search of an Identity', *Journal of European Social Policy*, Vol. 6, No. 1, pp. 39–60.

Kyriopoulos, J. (1992), 'Formal and Underground Economy in the Health Sector in Greece', *Society, Economy and Health*, Vol. 3, No. 4, pp. 171–83 [in Greek].

Kyriopoulos, J., Gitona, M. and Karalis, G. (1996), 'Private Expenditure, Hidden Economy and Informal Co-payment in Health Care: The Role of Medical Manpower in Greece', paper presented at the FICOSSER Research Meeting, Patras-Delphi, (May) [in Greek].

Leandros, N. (1996), 'The Crisis of Social Insurance: Orientations for the Reform of the System', *Economic Subjects*, No. 3, Athens: Institute of Economic and Industrial Research [in Greek].

National Statistical Service of Greece (1990), *Labour Force Survey*, Athens: ESYE [in Greek].

Negrponti-Delivani, M. (1990), *The Economics of Informal Economy in Greece*, Athens: Papazisis [in Greek].

OECD (1996a), *Economic Surveys (1995–1996), Spain*, Paris: OECD.

OECD (1996b), *Economic Surveys (1995–1996), Portugal*, Paris: OECD.

OECD (1996c), *Economic Surveys (1995–1996), Greece*, Paris: OECD.

OECD (1997), *Economic Surveys (1995–1996), Italy*, Paris: OECD.

Pavlopoulos, P. (1987), *The Informal Economy in Greece*, Athens: Institute of Economic and Industrial Research [in Greek].

Petmesidou, M. (1987), *Social Classes and Processes of Social Reproduction*, Athens: Exantas [in Greek].

Petmesidou, M. (1991), 'Statism, Social Policy and the Middle Classes in Greece', *Journal of European Social Policy*, Vol. 1 No. 1, pp. 31–48.

Petmesidou, M. (1992), *Social Inequalities and Social Policy*, Athens: Exantas [in Greek].

Petmesidou, M. (1996a), 'Social Protection in Southern Europe: Trends and Prospects'. *Journal of Area Studies*, 9, pp. 95–125.

Petmesidou, M. (1996b), 'Social Protection in Greece: A Brief Glimpse of a Welfare State', *Social Policy and Administration*, 30, pp. 324–47.

Petmesidou, M. (1998), 'Social Change and Risks of Social Exclusion in Greece: How do the Middle Classes Fare?', in Berting, J. de Jong, M.J. and Steijn, B. (eds), *Economic Restructuring and the Growing Uncertainty of the Middle Class*, The Hague: Kluwer, pp. 115–33.

Petmesidou, M. and Tsoulouvis, L. (1990a), 'Planning Technological Change and Economic Development in Greece', *Progress in Planning*, Vol. 33, No. 3 (whole issue).

Petmesidou, M. and Tsoulouvis, L. (1990b), 'Aspects of State Policy in Greece: Historical Continuity and the Impact of the Crisis', in Sakis Karagiorgas Foundation, *The Functions of the State in the Period of Crisis*, Athens: pp. 288–301 [in Greek].

Petmesidou, M. and Tsoulouvis, L. (1994), 'Aspects of the Changing Political Economy of Europe: Welfare State, Class Segmentation and Planning in the Postmodern Era', *Sociology*, 28, pp. 499–519.

Petrinioti, X. (1993), *Immigration to Greece*, Athens: Odysseas Institute of International Relations [in Greek].

Petropoulos, A. (1998), 'Not in Line with EU Strategy the Control of Supplementary Funds', *Avgi* (Newspaper), (21st February) [in Greek].

Regini, M. and Regalia, I. (1997), 'Employers, Unions and the State: the Resurgence of Concertation in Italy', *West European Politics*, 20, pp. 210–30.
Rhodes, M. (1997), 'Southern European Welfare States: Identity, Problems and Prospects for Reform', in Rhodes M., (ed), *Southern European Welfare States. Between Crisis and Reform*, London: Frank Cass, pp. 1–22.
Rombolis, S. (1996), 'Social Insurance. Economic and Social Deficit', *Oikonomikos Tahydromos*, 51, pp. 118–24 [in Greek].
Sissouras, A., Karokis, A., Papaliou, O., and Fagadaki, A. (1998), *Health Expenditure of Social Insurance Funds*, Athens: National Centre for Social Research Research Report [in Greek].
Vavouras, J. and Koutris, A. (1991), *Informal Economy. Its Size in Greece and Abroad*, Athens: Papazisis [in Greek].
Venieris, D. (1997), 'Dimensions of Social Policy in Greece', in Rhodes, M., (ed), *Southern European Welfare States: Between Crisis and Reform*, London: Frank Cass, pp. 260–69.

16 Poverty and Anti-poverty Policies in Greece and a Comparison with Other Mediterranean EU Member States

PANOS TSAKLOGLOU[1]

Introduction

Until relatively recently few empirical studies of inequality and poverty in Greece could be found in the literature. This lack should be attributed to four factors. Firstly, between the early 1950s and the mid-1970s the Greek economy was growing rapidly. Therefore, even if it is assumed that inequality and (relative) poverty were rising, it is also safe to assume that both the average living standards and the living standards of the poorest segments of the population were improving during that period. Secondly, family links were strong and, in many cases, the family was substituting the rudimentary welfare state, thus, preventing the emergence of extreme cases of material deprivation. Thirdly, both before 1967 and, particularly, during the military dictatorship, the institutional framework was restricting the functioning of organisations that, usually, raise distributional questions in the public discourse (mainly trade unions). Last but not least, there was limited availability of statistical data for empirical distributional studies. As a result, until the mid-1970s there was limited interest in such studies.

The situation changed dramatically after the collapse of the dictatorship and, particularly in the 1980s. Following the two oil crises, the Greek economy slowed down and, then, entered a protracted period of stagnation, stop-and-go policies and stabilisation programmes. Questions of social justice, inequality, poverty and, for the first time, social exclusion gradually came to the forefront of the public discourse, whereas the availability of new statistical material allowed the in-depth examination of several aspects of inequality and poverty.[2] At the same time the first systematic attempts for the establishment of a modern welfare state were undertaken. In the ensuing debate several assertions were made about the 'uniqueness' of the Greek situation – a view challenged by a number of systematic comparative studies in several fields of social sciences.

The present paper aims to provide a short overview of the findings of empirical studies of poverty in Greece, outline the existing anti-poverty policies and compare Greece with other Mediterranean EU member states, contrasting their experience with the experience of the rest of the EU.

Poverty and Antipoverty Policies in Greece: An Overview

Before the main results of the empirical investigations of poverty in Greece are presented, a couple of methodological clarifications are essential. The first clarification concerns the distinction between poverty and social exclusion. The two concepts are frequently used interchangeably in the public discourse, even though they are not identical. By poverty, most theorists denote a situation of material deprivation, while social exclusion, although harder to define, can be viewed both as a state and as a process leading to material and non-material deprivation (Atkinson, 1997). Therefore, unlike poverty, social exclusion is better defined in terms of capabilities rather than commodities (Sen, 1998). A good example highlighting the distinction between the two concepts in the Greek context is, probably that of the elderly and the gypsies. The living standards of many elderly are low but, nevertheless, the great majority of them are not cut-off from the rest of the society. On the contrary, even though many gypsies are well-off, due to social prejudices most of them are de facto excluded from a number of social functions. The findings reported below are derived from empirical poverty studies only.[3]

The second clarification is more practical. Most empirical poverty studies utilise the data of the Household Budget Surveys. Such surveys are carried out by the National Statistical Service of Greece in regular intervals, cover the entire non-institutional population and collect information on several material indicators of the standard of living of the population (consumption expenditure, disposable income, housing amenities, consumer durables, etc.). However, two high poverty-risk groups are excluded or seriously under-represented in the samples of these surveys: the homeless and the legal and, particularly, illegal immigrants (especially those who do not speak fluent Greek). Although homelessness in Greece does not appear to be as serious a problem as in a number of EU member states (Avramova, 1997), the omission of the immigrants may 'distort' the results of the relevant studies carried out in the 1990s.

Although it is frequently emphasised that poverty is a multi-dimensional phenomenon, almost all existing studies rely on a single indicator; usually income or consumption expenditure. Further, most studies use 'relative' poverty lines; that is, the poverty line is defined as some fraction of the mean or median of the distribution under consideration. In recent years many researchers have adopted the methodology used in relevant publications of Eurostat, which sets the poverty line at 50 per cent of the mean equivalent disposable income or consumption expenditure of the population.[4] Using such a poverty line, the relevant studies report that the proportion of the population classified as poor is around 15 per cent – 20 per cent.[5]

The relevant studies show that throughout the last twenty five years some of the high poverty-risk population groups remained unchanged.[6] Irrespective of the choices made by the researchers regarding the concept of resources, the size of the equivalence scales or the level of the poverty line, members of households living in rural areas, or headed by unemployed persons or elderly persons or persons with low educational qualifications are always over-represented among the poor. It is interesting to note that a number of other population groups frequently cited in the public discourse as being at high risk of poverty – such as manual workers, families with children (unless they are very large families), mono-parental households, young unemployed tertiary education graduates, etc. – are either unambiguously classified as low poverty-risk groups or their position vis-à-vis the poverty line varies according to the concepts used.

An example of high poverty-risk identification is presented in Table 1, using the data of the most recent Household Budget Survey (1993/94). For the purposes of this table the population was initially grouped into mutually exclusive groups using five alternative criteria – region of residence, type of locality, household type, socioeconomic group of the household head and educational level of the household head. Then, the groups whose contribution to aggregate poverty was found to be higher than their population share according to all three welfare indicators – consumption expenditure, disposable income and a non-monetary deprivation index – were selected and the corresponding contributions to aggregate poverty are reported in Table 1. The poverty-risk of each group can be calculated by dividing the contribution of the group to aggregate poverty by its population share.

The estimates of Table 1 reveal that poverty has particular spatial dimensions; it is disproportionately concentrated in Northern Greece and is more prevalent in the rural rather than the urban areas. Further, poverty is associated with old age – particularly when the elderly live alone or with their spouses – low educational qualifications, unemployment and, to a lesser extent, employment in the agricultural sector. It should be noted that a number of these characteristics are likely to be interdependent. For example, a considerable proportion of the poor consists of elderly pensioners with low or no formal educational qualifications who live in rural areas. Using multivatiate techniques, it can be shown that the probability to fall below the poverty line is significantly affected by lack of educational qualifications, unemployment and, to a lesser extent, residence in rural areas, while old age and, particularly, employment in the agricultural sector, *ceteris paribus*, do not retain their statistical significance (Loizides and Giahalis, 1992; Mitrakos et al., 1998). Furthermore, it has been demonstrated that not only low educational qualifications are associated with higher probability of poverty from a static point of view, but that lack of educational qualifications contributes significantly to the inter-generational transmission of poverty (Papatheodorou, 1997).

Inter-temporal changes in poverty can be examined using the data of the four Household Budget Surveys which are currently available (1974, 1981/82, 1987/88 and 1993/94). At this point, a distinction needs to be made between changes in 'relative' poverty (that is, when the poverty line changes between surveys in line with the mean or the median of the distribution) and changes in 'absolute' poverty (that is, when the poverty line remains constant in terms of real purchasing power throughout the period under examination). Such estimates are reported in Figure 1 overleaf (base year 1974: 100.00). In this graph, apart from the inter-temporal changes of the poverty rate, which is not sensitive to the depth of poverty and the distribution of resources among the poor, estimates of the distribution-sensitive index of Foster et al. (1984) are also reported.[7] During the period 1974–82 poverty declined spectacularly in absolute terms, as a result of improvements in the average living standards and significant declines in inequality (Tsakloglou, 1990, 1993b). In absolute terms, poverty continued to decline

Table 1 Population Groups at High Risk of Poverty: Greece 1993/94

Population group (characteristic of the household or the household head)	Population share	Percentage contributions to aggregate poverty according to: Consumption expenditure	Disposable income	Non-monetary deprivation index
Region of Residence				
Eastern Macedonia and Thrace	6.27	8.66	9.61	13.34
Central Macedonia (excl. Greater Salonica)	8.38	14.82	13.78	13.63
Epirus	2.89	4.81	3.94	5.06
Thessaly	6.55	9.63	10.09	10.66
Type of Locality				
Rural areas (communes with pop. <2,000)	24.85	39.99	46.12	62.12
Household type				
One person aged 65 or more	3.80	9.50	6.97	12.82
Childless couple (at least one above 65)	8.98	17.77	15.90	19.08
Socioeconomic Group of Household Head				
Farmer or agricultural worker	12.38	17.77	19.89	24.76
Unemployed	2.70	4.69	5.08	2.70
Pensioner	24.17	37.71	33.84	39.27
Educational Level of Household Head				
Primary education not completed	17.69	41.00	36.40	55.28

Source: Tsakloglou and Panopoulou (1998b)

during the period 1982–94, but at a slower rate. With respect to relative poverty, the changes observed, followed the changes in inequality; that is, significant decline between 1974 and 1982, small increase between 1982 and 1988 and further decline during the period 1988–94. It is interesting to note that some of these results, are in stark contrast with assertions routinely made in the public discourse.

Figure 1 Inter-temporal Changes in Absolute and Relative Poverty in Greece

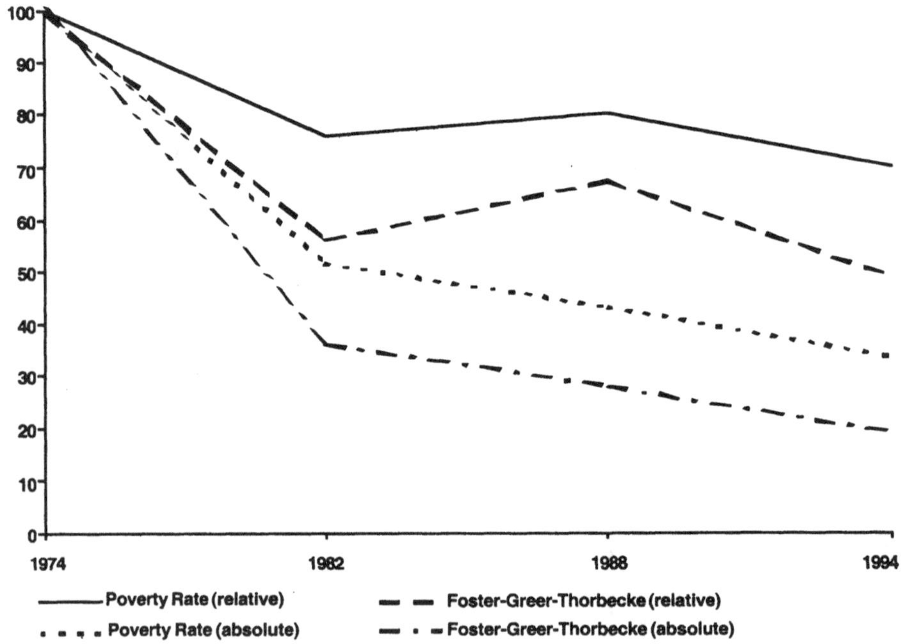

Source: Mitrakos and Tsakloglou (1998b).
Note: 1974:100.

Significant changes took place during the period under examination with respect to the composition of the poor. Traditionally, poverty in Greece was a predominantly rural phenomenon. Even though poverty is still more prevalent in the rural than in the urban areas of the country, the contribution of the rural population to aggregate poverty has declined significantly. This decline should be attributed primarily to two factors. Firstly, the higher prices that farmers enjoyed in the framework of the Common Agricultural Policy, contributed to a narrowing in the gap between the average living standards of urban and rural areas. Secondly, during the period under consideration, there was considerable internal migration, leading to a decline in the population share of the rural areas. A similar trend is also observed regarding the contribution of persons with low educational qualifications (illiterates or persons who did not complete primary education). Although the contribution of this group to aggregate poverty was and still is substantially higher than their population share, it declined considerably as a consequence of the continuous improvement in the educational qualifications of the population in the last three decades, which resulted in a decline in the group's population share. At the same time, two groups increased substantially their contribution to aggregate poverty: the unemployed and the elderly. Even though reliable unemployment data for the years before 1980 do not exist, it seems that in the early 1970s unemployment was not a significant problem in Greece, but it rose inexorably during the next two decades. As a result, and despite some improvements in the support provided to the unemployed, their contribution to aggregate poverty has risen considerably, although, as will be shown below, their poverty-risk in comparison with the rest of the population is not as high as in most EU countries.[8] However, the population group that replaced farmers as the group with the highest contribution to aggregate poverty are the elderly – in many cases elderly retired farmers. Even though the gap in the average living standards of elderly and non-elderly has not changed dramatically during the last twenty five years, the population share of the elderly and, consequently, their contribution to aggregate poverty have risen sharply.

Despite its decline after 1974, poverty in Greece still remains higher than in most EU member states in both relative and absolute terms, as demonstrated in Table 2. Naturally, the first column of the table shows that when a common poverty line is used for all member states, poverty in Greece (and the other 'cohesion countries') appears to be substantially higher than in the rest of the EU. Further, as the evidence of the next two columns of the table suggests, in the late 1980s relative poverty in Greece measured in terms of consumption expenditure was higher than in any other country apart from Portugal and Italy, whereas measured in terms of disposable income it was second only to the United Kingdom.[9] Unsurprisingly, the high level of relative poverty should be attributed to the fact that inequality in Greece is high in comparison with most EU countries, as shown in the last two columns of the table.

Table 2 Poverty and Inequality in EU Member States in the Late 1980s

Country	Poverty Rate			Index of inequality (Disposable Income)	
	Consumption Expenditure (EU poverty line) (1)	Consumption Expenditure (National poverty lines) (2)	Disposable Income (National poverty lines) (3)	Gini (4)	Atkinson (e=0.5) (5)
Belgium	0.101	0.074	na	0.235	0.049
Denmark	0.090	0.039	0.088	na	na
France	0.112	0.147	0.144	0.296	0.077
Germany	0.085	0.109	0.106	0.250	0.052
Greece	0.279	0.187	0.173	0.336	0.095
Ireland	0.294	0.157	0.169	0.330	0.093
Italy	0.240	0.211	0.130	0.310	0.080
Luxembourg	0.019	0.111	0.057	0.238	0.046
Netherlands	0.046	0.048	0.071	0.268	na
Portugal	0.477	0.245	0.172	na	na
Spain	0.292	0.169	0.137	na	na
UK	0.112	0.148	0.190	0.304	0.082

Sources:

Column (1) Hagenaars *et al* (1996),

Columns (2) and (3) Hagenaars *et al* (1994),

Columns (4) and (5) for all countries except Greece, Atkinson et al. (1995) – for Greece: own calculations.

As noted earlier, despite the fact that Greece never had a well-organised welfare state and anti-poverty policies are rather rudimentary, the still strong family links and, to a far lesser extent, actions of the Church and a few other social institutions, largely prevent the emergence of forms of acute poverty and social exclusion (Karantinos et al., 1992).[10] With respect to anti-poverty policies, Greece is the only member of the EU without a universal minimum social assistance benefit, despite the 1992 Council Recommendation on Sufficient Resources. In other words, poverty can be a 'free fall' experience in Greece. A number of existing categorical benefits, cover mainly the 'deserving' poor: elderly, invalid, large families and unprotected children, while social assistance for able-bodied unemployed persons after the exhaustion of their social insurance entitlements is conspicuously absent.

Table 3 overleaf reports the breakdown of the existing social assistance benefits for the fiscal year 1996. Social assistance benefits accounted for 0.84 per cent of GDP, but they were relatively thinly spread since the total number of potential beneficiaries was over 10 per cent of the population.[11] Most of the quantitatively important benefits which are received by a considerable proportion of the population were introduced in the 1990s (pensions to mothers of four or more children, social solidarity supplementary pensions, large family benefits, third child benefits). Further, it should be noted that three of the family benefits reported in Table 3 – pensions to mothers of four or more children, large family benefits, third child benefits – became means-tested in 1997, but the corresponding income thresholds are rather generous. Comparison of the potential recipients of these benefits with the population groups in high poverty-risk identified in empirical studies, reveals that these benefits are, indeed, directed towards some of the neediest members of the population.

Although social assistance may be one of the main instruments for alleviating poverty in the short run, other policies may also serve the purposes of anti-poverty policies by default. As such one can identify a number of social insurance benefits (particularly unemployment benefits), some of the breaks provided by the tax legislation (particularly those related to large families and medical expenses), as well as a number of active labour market policies (particularly policies aimed to fight exclusion from the labour market).[12] Naturally, in a broader perspective, initiatives in the fields of health, education, etc. also play a very important role in alleviating poverty.

Table 3 Social Assistance Benefits: Greece, 1996

Benefit	Total cost		Beneficiaries		Comments	
	in millions of drachmas	as % of GDP	Total number	as % of total population	Contributory	Means-tested
Pension to mother of 4+ children	65,969	0.222	238,074	2.26	No	No
Social Solidarity Supplementary Pension (EKAS)	43,649	0.147	305,986	2.91	Yes	Yes
Large Family Benefit	42,421	0.143	112,877	1.07	No	No
Disability Benefit	39,988	0.135	91,194	0.87	No	No
Family Allowance	16,634	0.056	300,898	2.86	Yes	Yes
3rd Child Benefit	13,085	0.044	25,459	0.24	No	No
Uninsured Elderly Pension	11,989	0.040	34,208	0.32	No	Yes
Housing Benefit	11,500	0.039	33,000	0.31	Yes	Yes
Orphan/Single Parent Benefit	4,994	0.017	34,684	0.33	No	Yes
Other Benefits	215	0.001	1,591	0.02	No	Yes
TOTAL	*210,456*	*0.844*	*1,177,971*	*11.19*		

Source: Matsaganis (1999).

Comparisons with other Mediterranean EU Member States

Are the above features uniquely Greek or can considerable similarities be found in other European countries? This section attempts to provide an answer to this question. Obvious candidates for comparison with Greece can be found among the other Mediterranean EU member states: Spain, Portugal and, to a lesser extent, Italy. In terms of GDP per capita in real Purchasing Power Parities, Greece does not differ substantially from Spain and, particularly, Portugal. The three countries experienced a transition from dictatorship to democracy in the mid-1970s and joined the then EC in the 1980s. Further, unlike most industrialised countries which experienced an increase in inequality since the early 1970s (Atkinson et al., 1995; Gottschalk et al., 1997), their levels of inequality declined during the same period (Tsakloglou, 1997; Guveia and Tavares, 1995; Ruiz-Castillo, 1998).

Since these countries have a lower GDP per capita than the rest of the EU, it is not surprising to find that, using a common poverty line, in 'absolute' terms poverty is higher in them than in the rest of the EU (apart from Ireland). However, the estimates of Table 2 show that relative poverty, too, is substantially higher in the Mediterranean EU member states than in the rest of the EU. Especially when distributions of consumption expenditure are utilised, the poverty rates of the four Mediterranean countries vary between 16.9 per cent and 24.5 per cent, whereas those of the rest of the EU are between 3.9 per cent and 15.7 per cent, with an unweighted mean of 10.4 per cent. Similar but less pronounced results are obtained when distributions of disposable income – which is usually considered a less reliable welfare indicator than consumption expenditure – are used instead. Moreover, it should be kept in mind that these distributions do not take into account social transfers in kind which, as shown in Table 5 below, are quantitatively more important in the non-Mediterranean EU member states as well as more likely to be targeted towards the bottom end of the distribution.

Turning to the structure of poverty, a number of considerable similarities across the Mediterranean EU member states and differences with the rest of the EU can be observed. This is clearly outlined in Table 4 overleaf. In this table comparisons are made between the four Mediterranean EU member states and the three big EU countries (France, UK and Germany).[13] Comparisons are performed with respect to the relative poverty risk and the contributions to aggregate poverty of eight non mutually exclusive high

Table 4 Population Groups at High Poverty-Risk and their Contribution

Population group	Poverty risk (group poverty rate/population poverty				
	GR	IT	ES	PT	FR
Households headed by farmers or agricultural workers	1.38	1.43	1.55	1.50	1.66
Households headed by unemployed persons	1.16	1.50	1.84	1.75	2.34
Households headed by retired persons	1.61	1.45	1.56	1.84	1.46
Households headed by persons aged 65+	1.87	1.69	1.66	1.87	1.75
One-member households (persons aged 65+)	2.13	1.83	2.15	2.26	2.25
Mono-parental households	0.84	1.04	1.30	1.05	1.22
Households headed by females	1.41	1.31	1.44	1.28	1.51
Households headed by persons who did not complete primary education*	2.12	na	1.92	2.16	2.01

GR: Greece, IT: Italy, ES: Spain, PT: Portugal, FR: France,
UK: United Kingdom, DE: Germany.

* Definition varies across countries. § Primary education or less. # Economically inactive.
Source: Hagenaars et al. (1994).

poverty-risk groups: households headed by farmers, unemployed, retired, all households headed by persons aged 65 or more, one-member households consisting of persons aged 65 or more, mono-parental households, households headed by females, and households headed by persons with no or low educational qualifications.[14]

The evidence of the first line suggests that in all Mediterranean countries (including France) the poverty risk of households headed by farmers is higher than that of the rest of the population. The opposite is observed in the UK and, especially, Germany. However, due to their higher population share in the poorer countries, these households contribute more than 15 per cent

to Aggregate Poverty in Selected EU Member States

rate)		Contribution to aggregate poverty						
UK	DE	GR	IT	ES	PT	FR	UK	DE
1.00	0.54	15.2	7.7	11.5	15.2	5.3	1.5	0.7
2.83	3.62	2.2	0.3	8.1	0.7	9.2	13.6	15.2
1.77	1.49 #	45.0	38.7	50.0	45.0	40.5	43.3	59.0 #
1.86	1.49	47.0	40.3	37.4	41.1	43.0	49.8	41.0
2.37	1.81	17.7	20.9	11.4	16.7	26.6	31.1	21.0
1.49	2.00	4.2	5.9	9.1	9.7	7.3	11.0	12.0
1.78	1.38	28.3	30.6	24.2	32.3	36.5	40.8	46.7
1.80 §	n.a.	38.2	n.a.	54.4	48.4	52.7	53.6 §	n.a.

to aggregate poverty only in Greece and Portugal, whereas the corresponding contributions in Germany and the UK are negligible. The striking feature of the next line is that even though households headed by unemployed persons are a high poverty-risk group in all countries under examination, the group's position vis-à-vis the rest of the population appears to be substantially worse in the more developed countries (Germany, UK, France). It is worth noting that despite the lack of a comprehensive protection system for the unemployed, the poverty situation of this group is far less pronounced in Greece than in the rest of the countries in Table 4. As a result of the discrepancy in the poverty risks and the fact that a considerable proportion of the unemployed in the Mediterranean countries (with the partial exception of Spain) consists of young persons living with their parents and wives of household heads, the contribution of the group to aggregate poverty appears to be substantially higher in the Northern than in the Southern EU countries of Table 4. The next three lines demonstrate that in all EU countries households headed by retired persons are a high poverty-risk group. The risk is higher if the household head is old (over 64) and particularly if he/she lives alone). No marked differences are observed between Northern and Southern EU countries with respect to this group. On the contrary, considerable cross-country differences are observed in the next line of the table. Unlike the rest of the countries in Table 4, mono-parental households in Greece appear to be a low poverty-risk group. The group's poverty-risk does not appear to be substantially higher than the national average in the other Mediterranean countries (including France), but it is quite high in the UK and, particularly, Germany. Similar cross-country differences are observed regarding the contributions of mono-parental households to aggregate poverty. The next line of Table 4 suggests that there is a sex bias in the poverty risk, since in all countries households headed by females – mostly elderly ladies living alone and heads of mono-parental households – are more likely to fall below the poverty line than male-headed households. Due to differences in population shares, the contribution of female-headed households to aggregate poverty is higher in the non-Mediterranean countries. Finally, the last line of Table 4 shows that in all countries for which data exist, the risk of falling below the poverty line is higher when the household head has low educational qualifications; the relevant risk being slightly higher in Greece and Portugal than in the other countries. In conclusion and despite some inevitable selectivity biases, the evidence of Tables 2 and 4 seems to suggest that Greece is not that notably different from the rest of the Mediterranean EU member states regarding her level and structure of poverty, whereas a number of differences can be observed between these countries and the rest of the EU member states.

Regarding policies aimed to alleviate poverty, after the recent introduction of a minimum income programme in Portugal, Greece is the only country in the EU without a general non-categorical social assistance benefit.[15] Before proceeding to examine social assistance in particular, it is important to look at the wider picture of social protection. Table 5 reveals a number of interesting similarities and differences across the EU in this field. According to the figures in the first column of the table, Greece's social

Table 5 Social Protection Expenditure in EU Member States (1991)

Country	Social Protection Expenditure as % of GDP	Ratio of cash to kind expenditures	Composition of Social Protection Expenditure by Type (%)				
			Sickness and Invalidity	Old Age	Family	Unemployment	Other
Austria	27.3	na	na	na	na	na	na
Belgium	27.6	3.1	34.8	44.0	8.5	11.2	1.5
Denmark	30.7	1.8	29.1	35.7	11.8	16.4	6.9
Finland	31.1	1.8	40.4	34.4	13.2	9.1	2.9
France	28.5	2.6	34.5	44.1	9.6	7.3	4.4
Germany	27.0	2.1	40.8	41.0	9.0	5.8	3.4
Greece	20.2	10.6	19.7	69.7	1.8	3.0	5.8
Ireland	20.9	1.9	35.6	28.2	17.4	13.6	5.2
Italy	24.6	2.6	33.4	60.5	4.2	1.8	0.0
Luxembourg	27.6	2.8	38.8	48.7	11.1	0.9	0.5
Netherlands	32.5	3.8	44.5	37.0	8.5	8.3	1.7
Portugal	16.9	1.9	42.3	39.1	5.9	4.8	7.8
Spain	21.7	2.9	36.9	41.0	1.6	18.3	1.9
Sweden	37.6	1.6	35.1	40.8	16.5	6.9	0.7
UK	24.7	2.0	33.8	41.4	11.0	6.7	7.0

Source: Eurostat (1994), Eardley et al. (1996).

protection expenditure as a proportion of GDP is the second lowest in the EU, after Portugal. Moreover, if the proportion of GDP devoted to social expenditure can be viewed as a rough indicator of a country's level of development of the social protection system – admittedly, a heroic assumption – then the four Mediterranean countries and Ireland appear to have the least developed social protection systems. Greece is also unusual regarding the limited importance of the in-kind transfers provided by the social protection system. The ratio of cash to non-cash (in-kind) social expenditure in Greece is 10.6, while in most other EU member states it hovers around 2.5.

The last five columns of Table 5 disaggregate social expenditure into its constituent components. These columns should be interpreted with caution, since the proportion of social expenditure devoted to particular purposes may be affected by both the institutional framework and the prevailing economic and demographic conditions.[16] The most striking result reported in these columns regarding Greece is that social protection is primarily protection for the elderly. Almost 70 per cent of the total social expenditure is devoted to the payment of old age and survivors pensions. This proportion is substantially higher than that reported in any other EU member state, apart from Italy, where the corresponding proportion is slightly above 60 per cent. On the contrary and despite the rhetoric in the public discourse, family benefits account for a small proportion of social expenditure, less than 2 per cent ; a feature shared with all Mediterranean EU member states.

Table 6 focuses on the social assistance benefits that are targeted primarily towards the poorest segments of the population. The data are from Gough et al. (1997) who define as social assistance benefits all means tested benefits in cash or in kind, including those which provide benefits to higher income groups. According to the figures reported in Table 6, in the early 1990s both social assistance expenditure as a proportion of GDP and the proportion of the population receiving social assistance in Greece were the lowest in the EU. Nevertheless, it should be also noted that within the EU means-tested expenditures appear to play a major role only in Ireland and the UK. At this point, a clarification is necessary. The estimates reported in Table 6 appear to contradict those reported in Table 3. The discrepancy is mainly due to the fact that the estimates of these tables refer to different years, since one of the most important means-tested benefits (social solidarity supplementary pension) was introduced after 1992, the reference year of Gough et al. (1997). In addition since, as noted earlier, a number of the benefits reported in Table 3 became means-tested but with

Table 6 Social Assistance in EU Member States (1992)

Country	Social Assistance recipients as % of population	Social Assistance expenditure as % of GDP	Social Assistance expenditure as % of Social Security expenditure
Austria	4.8	1.3	6.7
Belgium	3.6	0.7	3.0
Denmark	8.3	1.4	7.8
Finland	9.2	0.4	na
France	2.3	1.8	6.4
Germany	6.8	1.6	11.9
Greece	0.7	0.1	na
Ireland	12.4	5.1	41.2
Italy	na	1.5	9.1
Luxembourg	2.7	0.4	1.4
Netherlands	na	2.2	10.9
Portugal	2.1	0.4	3.8
Spain	2.7	1.2	8.4
Sweden	6.8	0.5	6.7
UK	15.3	6.4	33.0

Source: Gough et al. (1997).

generous income threshold in 1997, it is likely that adopting the definition of Gough et al. (1997) and assuming that the social assistance benefits in the rest of the EU remained roughly unchanged – another brave assumption – then, in the late 1990s Greece had moved somewhere in the middle of the range regarding the proportion of GDP devoted to social assistance benefits and close to the top end regarding the proportion of the population receiving social assistance.

The last table of the chapter, Table 7 overleaf, attempts to answer the question 'how effective are social transfers in reducing poverty in the

Table 7 Impact of Cash Transfers on Aggregate Poverty in EU Member States (1994)

Country	Percentage decline in poverty as a result of social transfers in cash		Percentage decline in poverty as a result of social transfers in cash (excluding pensions)		Index of poverty after all social transfers are accounted for	
	Poverty rate	Foster-Greer-Thorbecke (a=2)	Poverty rate	Foster-Greer-Thorbecke (a=2)	Poverty rate	Foster-Greer-Thorbecke (a=2)
Austria	62.4	87.7	36.5	59.8	0.170	0.026
Belgium	61.0	90.6	39.0	76.6	0.180	0.027
Denmark	72.3	95.8	62.7	90.7	0.107	0.009
France	63.5	92.3	42.7	77.2	0.158	0.017
Germany	56.6	87.7	25.6	61.0	0.177	0.029
Greece	44.0	82.7	6.8	22.3	0.207	0.035
Ireland	50.1	92.7	36.9	87.7	0.212	0.019
Italy	52.7	84.9	11.4	29.3	0.188	0.033
Luxembourg	66.0	90.2	44.7	68.2	0.143	0.020
Netherlands	73.6	92.6	57.0	83.2	0.099	0.017
Portugal	37.7	79.2	14.8	36.9	0.239	0.041
Spain	55.1	89.6	29.8	70.2	0.188	0.025
UK	52.3	92.0	39.4	85.4	0.204	0.022

Source: Heady et al. (1999).

member states of the EU?'. The analysis is performed for all transfers taken together and for the non-pension transfers separately, in an 'accounting' rather than behavioural framework. The data used for the purposes of this table are from the second wave of the European Community Household Panel (1994) and they refer to monetary incomes,[17] whereas, following the recently adopted practice of Eurostat, the poverty line is set at 60 per cent of the national median equivalent income. The poverty indices used are the poverty rate and the distribution-sensitive index of Foster et al. (1984). The last two columns of the table confirm that, on average, relative poverty in the Mediterranean EU member states is more acute than in the rest of the EU. This pattern becomes clearer when the index of Foster et al. is used instead of the poverty rate. The contrast is most vivid when the Mediterranean countries are compared with Ireland or the UK. The reason is that even though in the latter countries more population members – particularly elderly (Tsakloglou, 1996) – fall below the poverty line, they remain close to it, while the opposite is true for the Mediterranean member states.

The first two columns of Table 7 report the proportional reduction in poverty due to the impact of all social transfers. The figures in these columns should not be interpreted as the proportional increases in poverty in comparison with the poverty indices reported in the last two columns of the table if there were no transfers, but as the proportional declines in poverty due to the social transfers from the level of poverty that would have been encountered if these transfers did not exist.[18] Of course, this is a very unrealistic assumption since, in the absence of social transfers, population members would have behaved differently; hence, the analysis should be considered as 'accounting' rather than 'behavioural'. Nevertheless, such an approach is not uncommon in the literature and, undoubtedly, it can provide useful insights about the effectiveness of social protection systems. The estimates of the first two columns of Table 7 show that, in comparative terms, only in Portugal social transfers are less effective than in Greece in bringing people out of poverty. Once again, with the possible exception of Spain, a gap can be observed between the Mediterranean EU member states and the rest of the EU regarding the effectiveness of such transfers in alleviating poverty, with the former being less effective than the latter. Naturally, for both groups of countries, the impact of social transfers on poverty appears to be larger when the Foster et al. index is used instead of the poverty rate. This should be attributed to the fact that a number of social transfer recipients remain below the poverty line after the transfers, but their distance from it declines (in many cases substantially). The next two columns of Table 7 repeat the exercise for the non-pension transfers only. Since, as shown in Table 5, social transfers in Greece consist primarily of pensions, it is not surprising to find that the impact of the non-pension transfers to aggregate poverty in Greece is the lowest in the EU (followed closely by Italy and, to a lesser extent, Portugal). Furthermore, in these columns the difference between these Mediterranean countries and the rest of the EU regarding the relative efficacy of non-pension social transfers in alleviating poverty is even more striking than in the first two columns of the table.

The evidence presented in this section augurs well with the view of the authors who claim that there exists a distinct Southern European model of welfare and attribute the differences between these countries and the rest of the EU to a number of socioeconomic factors (Leibfreid, 1993; Ferrera, 1996; Gough, 1996). According to this view, in comparison with the rest of the EU, southern European countries are characterised by more 'dualistic' economic structures, with relatively high employment in the agricultural sector and considerable size of the 'hidden' economy. Family links are still strong and, in many cases, the Church and a few other voluntary bodies substitute the official welfare state. The origins of the South European welfare states are 'conservative-corporatist'. They are extravagant in their promises but rudimentary in their implementation, while social insurance is segmented. This segmentation creates various groups with conflicting interests. Despite their rhetoric, in many occasions, these interest groups, explicitly or implicitly oppose universalistic reforms; sometimes with the tacit support of other groups with vested interests against reform. These conditions favour the development of political clientelism and very frequently the situation is aggravated further by the endemically low efficiency in the provision of social services and the (real or alleged) corruption in the public sector. Social protection systems in these countries provide sufficient support only to those members of the population who have strong links with the formal labour market, while the rest of the population is covered with low and discretionary benefits or not covered at all. However, due to the existence of strong family links, if one family member is employed in the formal labour market and receives the associated social benefits, then a family safety net substitutes the rudimentary or non-existent public safety net, thus preventing the emergence of extreme forms of material deprivation and social exclusion. Finally, perhaps as a consequence of the relatively limited role of the social assistance, unlike many Northern European countries, the debate on the disincentive effects of social assistance policies (on labour supply, family formation, etc.) is rather limited in the public discourse of the Mediterranean EU member states.

Conclusions

The aim of the paper was to review the main results of empirical studies of poverty in Greece, outline the existing anti-poverty policies and compare Greece with other Mediterranean EU member states in these fields. It was shown that poverty in Greece is closely associated with old age, residence in particular regions and rural areas, low educational qualifications and, to a lesser extent, with lack of employment or employment in the agricultural sector. Since the mid-1970s poverty declined in both absolute and relative terms, but still remains higher than in most EU member states. Even though a number of policies aimed to alleviate poverty were introduced in the 1990s, Greece is still the only EU member state without a universal minimum social assistance benefit, whereas pensions account for over two thirds of social protection expenditure. Comparisons with other EU member states revealed a lot of similarities between Greece and other Mediterranean EU countries regarding both the level and the structure of poverty as well as the role and the impact of welfare state policies in the fight against poverty. Therefore, one can ask 'Is Greece really as different as sometimes claimed in the public discourse?' The evidence presented in this paper seems to suggest that at least in the fields of social policy in general, and poverty and anti-poverty policies in particular, the answer is negative. The similarities with other Mediterranean EU member states are too many to ignore.

Notes

1. Earlier versions of the paper were presented in seminars at the LSE and the 'Welfare State' Discussion Group. I would like to thank various seminar participants for useful comments and suggestions, particularly Manos Matsaganis, Christos Papatheodorou, Haris Symeonidou and an anonymous referee. Some of the results reported in the paper were derived in the framework of the research projects 'Family Structure, Labour Market Participation and the Dynamics of Social Exclusion' and 'EUROMOD: A European Tax-Benefit Model', funded by the European Commission under the Targeted

Socio-Economic Research Programme (TSER).

2. For a survey of empirical studies of inequality in Greece see Mitrakos and Tsakloglou (1998a); for surveys of poverty studies see Tsakloglou (1993a) and Petmesidou (1996a).
3. The single empirical investigation of social exclusion in Greece (National Centre for Social Research, 1996) adopts an ad hoc identification of the 'socially excluded' population groups rather than selecting a functional definition of social exclusion first and, then, identifying population groups at high risk of social exclusion.
4. Although such a poverty line is explicitly 'relative', very frequently in the public discourse the resulting poverty rate is erroneously called the 'proportion of population in absolute poverty'.
5. It should be noted, though, that since the distributions used are approximately lognormal (that is, skewed to the right), the estimates of the poverty indices are very sensitive with respect to the poverty line selected (Tsakloglou, 1990; Tsakloglou and Panopoulou, 1998a).
6. See Kanellopoulos (1986), Karayiorgas et al. (1990), Tsakloglou (1990), Eurostat (1990), Hagenaars et al. (1994), Tsakloglou and Panopoulou (1998a, 1998b), Mitrakos et al. (1998). A distinction should be made here between high poverty-risk population groups and population groups with high contribution to aggregate poverty. The two groups do not necessarily coincide, since several large population groups have a high contribution to aggregate poverty even though their poverty-risk is lower than the national average and vice versa.
7. The estimates in Figure 1 refer to the distribution of equivalent consumption expenditure per capita, after reconciling the consumption expenditure per capita estimates of the Household Budget Survey with the private consumption expenditure growth rates of the National Accounts. Similar trends are also derived using either income data or composite non-monetary indicators.
8. This is not evident in the estimates reported in Table 1; however, it becomes clear when the contribution of households with unemployed members to aggregate poverty is analysed.
9. The estimates reported in Table 2 were derived using common concepts of resources, reference units and equivalence scales across countries. Nevertheless, as will be discussed later, these cross-country comparisons may be a little misleading since, apart from the inevitable differences in information collection methods across countries, the poor – and, perhaps, the not-so-poor – in some countries may enjoy benefits in kind that are not available to the poor in other countries.
10. For a description of the Greek welfare state see Katrougalos (1996), Petmesidou (1996b) and Symeonidou (1997).
11. It should be noted that the distinction between social insurance and social assistance benefits is not always straightforward, while the number of actual benefit recipients was certainly lower than that reported in the bottom line of Table 3, 11.2 per cent, since some of them were receiving more than one benefit.
12. It is interesting to note that, especially in the case of the recently introduced policies aimed to fight exclusion from the labour market, most of the initiatives undertaken were supported by the EU in the framework of Structural Policies.
13. Initially, instead of France we considered Denmark, so as to have one country from each of the three representative welfare state paradigms of Esping-Andersen (1990) – liberal, conservative-corporatist and, social-democratic. However, the extremely low number of poor households in the Danish sample produced a number of paradoxical results and, hence, Denmark was left out of Table 4.
14. Even though the estimates of Table 4 refer to the late 1980s, a number of more recent national studies show that the situation was not different around the mid-1990s.

15. Portugal's programme is national, while those of Italy and Spain are regional. For a detailed discussion of minimum income schemes in the EU see Guibentif and Bouget (1997).
16. For example, high spending for the unemployed may be the result of high rates of unemployment, generous unemployment benefits, or both. Likewise, high spending for the elderly may be due to high pensions, large population share of older citizens or both.
17. The fact that the concept of resources used in Table 7 excludes incomes in kind overstates the extent and, particularly, the depth of poverty in Greece (and, probably, in the rest of the Mediterranean countries). This is due to two factors. The first is that outright home ownership is more prevalent in Greece than in the rest of the EU and imputed rents for owner occupied accommodation – the most important component of income in kind, accounting for around 15 per cent of disposable monetary income – are more equally distributed than monetary incomes. The second is that other incomes in kind, although quantitatively less important – they account for 3–4 per cent of disposable monetary income – are disproportionately concentrated at the bottom end of the distribution. On the contrary, the fact that benefits in kind are not included in the concept of resources used in this table, tends to understate the extent of poverty in Greece since, according to Table 5, these benefits are far more common in the rest of the EU than in Greece.
18. For example, in the first line of the table, 62.4 per cent denotes that if the poverty line in Austria was kept intact but there were no social transfers, the poverty rate would have been 0.452 rather than 0.170 and, therefore, the proportional decline in the poverty rate after the inclusion of social transfers is 62.4 per cent (62.4 = 100*(0.452 - 0.170)/0.452).

References

Atkinson, A.B. (1997), 'Social Exclusion, Poverty and Unemployment', in Atkinson, A.B and Hills, J. (eds), *Exclusion, Employment and Opportunity*, STICERD, LSE, CASE Discussion Paper No. 4.

Atkinson, A.B., Rainwater, M. and Smeeding, T. (1995), *Income Distribution in OECD Countries*, Paris: OECD.

Avramova, D. (1997), 'Research on Homelessness: State of the Art and Issues to be Tackled', Paper presented at the 33rd International Congress of Sociology, Cologne.

Eardley, T., Bradshaw, J., Ditch, J., Gough, I. and Whiteford, P. (1996), 'Social Assistance Schemes in OECD Countries', Department of Social Security Research Report 46, London: HMSO.

Esping-Andersen, G. (1990), *The Three Worlds of Welfare Capitalism*, Cambridge: Polity Press.

Eurostat (1990), *Poverty in Figures: Europe in the Early 1980s*, Luxembourg: Eurostat.

Eurostat (1994), *Basic Statistics of the Community*, 31st edition, Luxembourg: Eurostat.

Ferrera, M. (1996), 'The 'Southern Model' of Welfare in Social Europe', *Journal of European Social Policy*, Vol. 6, pp. 17–37.

Foster, J.E., Greer, J. and Thorbecke, E. (1984), 'A Class of Decomposable Poverty Measures', *Econometrica* Vol. 52, pp. 761–66.

Gottschalk, P., Gustafsson, B. and Palmer, E. (eds) (1997), *Changing Patterns in the Distribution of Economic Welfare: What happened During the 1980?*, Cambridge: Cambridge University Press.

Gough, I. (1996), 'Social Assistance in Southern Europe', *Southern European Society and Politics*, Vol. 1, pp. 1–23.

Gough, I., Bradshaw, J., Ditch, J., Eardley, T. and Whiteford, P. (1997), 'Social Assistance in OECD Countries', *Journal of European Social Policy,* Vol. 6, pp. 17–43.
Guibentif, P. and Bouget, D. (1997), *Minimum Income Policies in the EU,* Lisbon: Portuguese Union of Mutuals.
Guveia, M. and Tavares, J. (1995), 'The Distribution of Household Income and Expenditure in Portugal: 1980 and 1990', *Review of Income and Wealth,* Vol. 41, p. 1–18.
Hagenaars, A.J.M., de Vos, K. and Zaidi, M.A. (1994), *Poverty Statistics in the Late 1980s: Research Based on Micro-Data,* Theme 3, Series C Luxembourg: Eurostat.
Hagenaars, A.J.M., de Vos, K. and Zaidi, M.A. (1996), 'Patterns of Poverty in Europe', in Jenkins, S., Kapteyn, A. and van Praag, B.S.M. (eds), *The Distribution of Welfare and Household Production: International Perspectives,* Cambridge: Cambridge University Press.
Heady, C., Mitrakos, Th. and Tsakloglou, P. (1999), 'The Distributional Impact of Social Transfers in the EU: Evidence from the ECHP', Athens University of Economics and Business, Department of International and European Economic Studies Discussion Paper No. 99–04.
Kanellopoulos, C.N. (1986), *Incomes and Poverty in Greece: Determining Factors,* Centre of Planning and Economic Research, Scientific Studies No. 22, Athens [in Greek].
Karantinos, D., Ioannou, C. and Cavounidis, J. (1992), *The Social Services and Social Policies to Combat Social Exclusion in Greece,* Athens: EC Observatory on National Policies to Combat Social Exclusion, National Centre for Social Research.
Karayiorgas, D, Georgakopoulos, T., Carantinos, D., Loizides, I., Bouzas, N., Yfantopoulos, J. and Chrysakis, M. (1990), *Aspects of Poverty in Greece,* Athens: National Centre for Social Research [in Greek].
Katrougalos, G. (1996), 'The South European Welfare Model: The Greek Welfare State in Search of an Identity', *Journal of European Social Policy,* Vol. 6, pp. 39–60.
Leibfried, S. (1993) 'Towards a European Welfare State', in Jones, C. (ed), *New Perspectives on the Welfare State in Europe,* London: Routledge.
Loizides, I. and Giahalis, V. (1992), 'Poverty Profiles in Greece: A Probabilistic Approach', *Greek Economic Review,* Vol. 14, pp. 71–88.
Matsaganis, M. (1999), 'Social Assistance Benefits in Greece', National Centre for Social Research, Working Paper 1999/6.
Mitrakos, Th. and Tsakloglou, P. (1998a), 'Economic Inequalities in Greece: Survey of Evidence, Methodological Problems, Trends and Prospects', in Tsiakalos, G. (ed), *Social Inequalities and Social Exclusion,* Athens: Sakis Karayiorgas Foundation [in Greek].
Mitrakos, Th. and Tsakloglou, P. (1998b), 'Changes in Aggregate Inequality and Poverty in Greece after the Restoration of Democracy', Athens University of Economics and Business, Department of Economics Discussion Paper No. 97, 1998 [in Greek], forthcoming in *Meletes Oekonomikis Politikis.*
Mitrakos, Th., Panopoulou, G. and Tsakloglou, P. (1998), 'Economic Inequalities and Poverty in Greece: Quantitative Dimensions of the Problem', Athens University of Economics and Business, Department of International and European Economic Studies, Discussion Paper No. 98–02 [in Greek], forthcoming in Pakos, Th. (ed) *The 2/3 society,* Athens: Sakis Karayiorgas Foundation.
National Centre for Social Research (1996), *Dimensions of Social Exclusion in Greece: Principal Subjects and Determination of Policy Priorities,* Athens [in Greek].
Papatheodorou, C. (1997), 'Family Background, and Poverty in Greece: The Role of Father's Occupation and Education', Welfare State Programme, STICERD, LSE, Discussion Paper No. 133.
Petmesidou, M. (1996a), 'Greece, Turkey and Cyprus: Poverty Research in a Policy Vacuum', in Oyen, E., Miller, S.M. and Abdus Samad, S. (eds), *Poverty: A Global*

Review, Oslo-Stockholm-Copenhagen-Boston.: Scandinavian University Press.

Petmesidou, M. (1996b), 'Social Protection in Greece: A Brief Glimpse of a Welfare State', *Social Policy and Administration,* Vol. 30, pp. 324–47.

Ruiz-Castillo (1998), 'A Simplified Model for Social Welfare Analysis: An Application to Spain, 1973–74 to 1980–81', *Review of Income and Wealth,* Vol. 44, pp. 123–41.

Sen, A.K. (1998), 'Social Exclusion: Conceptual Problems and Measurement Issues', Paper presented at the 25th General Conference of the International Association for Research in Income and Wealth, Cambridge.

Symeonidou, H. (1997), 'Social Protection in Modern Greece', in Rhodes, M. (ed), *Southern European Welfare States: Between Crises and Before*, London: Frank Cass.

Tsakloglou, P. (1990), 'Aspects of Poverty in Greece', *Review of Income and Wealth,* Vol. 36, pp. 381–402.

Tsakloglou, P. (1993a), 'A Critical Evaluation of Empirical Investigations of the Phenomenon of Poverty in Greece', in Petralias, N. (ed) *Dimensions of Social Policy Today*, Athens: Sakis Karayiorgas Foundation [in Greek].

Tsakloglou, P. (1993b), 'Aspects of Inequality in Greece: Measurement, Decomposition and Inter-Temporal Change: 1974, 1982', *Journal of Development Economics,* Vol. 40, pp. 53–74.

Tsakloglou, P. (1996), 'Elderly and Non-Elderly in the European Union: A Comparison of Living Standards', *Review of Income and Wealth,* Vol. 42, pp. 271–91.

Tsakloglou, P. (1997), 'Changes in Inequality in Greece in the 1970s and the 1980s', in Gottschalk, P., Gustafsson, B. and Palmer, E. (eds), *Changing Patterns in the Distribution of Economic Welfare: What Happened During the 1980?*, Cambridge: Cambridge University Press.

Tsakloglou, P. and Panopoulou, G. (1998a), 'Who are the Poor in Greece? Analysing Poverty Under Alternative Concepts of Resources and Equivalence Scales', *Journal of European Social Policy,* Vol. 8, 1998, pp. 229–52.

Tsakloglou, P. and Panopoulou, G. (1998b), 'Poverty in Greece: Decomposition Analysis, Determining Factors and Inter-Temporal Change', Athens University of Economics and Business, Department of International and European Economic Studies (mimeo).

PART V
FOREIGN POLICIES AND EXTERNAL RELATIONS

17 The Europeanisation of Greece's Foreign Policy: Progress and Problems

PANAGIOTIS C. IOAKIMIDIS

One of the most remarkable developments over the past years has been the steady progress towards the Europeanisation of Greece's foreign and security policy. This phenomenon is in line with the most general trend for the Europeanisation of Greece's political system, economy and society as a whole (Ioakimidis, 1997). Europeanisation is seen as 'an incremental process reorienting the direction and shape of politics to the degree that EC's political and economic dynamics become part of the organisational logic of national politics and policy-making' (Ladrech, 1994).

In the case of the CFSP, Europeanisation can be taken to involve the internalisation of the objectives, policy styles, procedural and institutional requirements of the CFSP by an EU member state's foreign policy. This internalisation does not necessarily imply the downgrading of a country's foreign policy or the abandonment of distinctive national objectives. As Hill has aptly observed, 'CFSP should be seen as a collaborative framework of increasing solidity whose strength derives from the very fact that it permits national policies to continue in parallel' (Hill, 1997).

The Europeanisation of Greece's foreign policy has been a highly difficult and painful process. It has not yet been completed, nor has it encompassed all aspects and elements of the policy. But it is important that the basic elements, objectives and goals of the policy have acquired progressively a distinct European dimension and orientation.[1]

As noted, the Europeanisation of Greece's foreign policy forms part of the wider process referring to the Europeanisation of Greece's political system, economy and society. This in turn is evidently related to the wider trend for the adjustment of Greece's political, economic, social and institutional system to the requirements of the European integration process. The drive to accede to the single currency, the Euro, by 2001 highlights the significance of the whole process. The progress made in the process of adjustment is reflected in the fact that Greece has almost ceased being perceived as a 'heretical, awkward partner' in the EU framework. Until about 1995, Greece was viewed as a member state almost inherently incapable of internalising the esoteric logic of European integration and aligning its policy and behaviour to the EU's broad policy objectives and dynamics. Characteristically, writing in September 1994 about Greece's role in the Balkans, *The Economist* pointed out, among others, that:

> Despite 13 years in the European Union and hand-outs now worth $6 billion a year, Greece still seems to belong more to the volatile Balkans than to Western Europe. First the Greeks exasperated their EU partners by their casual approach to European obligations, their slowness in implementing directives and their hostility to better EU relations with Turkey. At one stage, a frustrated Jacques Delors, president of the European Commission, said 'he would be happy to see Greece leave'.[2]

Especially with regard to foreign policy coordination in the context of the European Political Cooperation (EPC), S.J. Nuttal observed in 1999 that '...it is generally admitted that the accession of Greece to the Community has made voting together more difficult because of the insistence of the Greeks in sticking to long-held national positions at the expense of Community solidarity...' (Nuttal, 1992). The same scholar as well as other authors have also accused Greece, along with UK and Denmark, of preventing the development of Europe's security identity in the mid-1980s (Nuttal, 1997).

The perception of Greece as an awkward, heretical EU partner was partly justified and partly exaggerated. In the field of foreign policy, it is true that Greece quite often pursued policy objectives clearly at odds with wider European goals. The most important characteristic example was Greece's policy over the diplomatic recognition of the Former Yugoslav Republic of Macedonia (FYROM) under the name 'Macedonia'.[3] Other cases over which Greece found itself diverting from European policy included East-West relations prior to the end of the cold war, the Middle East and terrorism.

It was, however, partly exaggerated especially with regard to the accusation levelled against Greece concerning its posture over EU-Turkey relations. In this area, Europe has shown inexcusable inability, or even unwillingness, to comprehend Greece's security concerns, interests and anxieties. It seems that in this particular area Greek and European interests, though converging on the macro-political level, are at odds on the micro-political level. At the macro-political level, both Greece and EU share the fundamental objective of the gradual integration of Turkey into the European institutional system, as that underlying condition for the democratic evolution and stability of the country. However, unlike most of its partners, Greece insists that Turkey's integration in the European system should follow the prior fulfillment of the conditions and criteria laid down by the Union itself for its enlargement.[4]

Progress towards Europeanisation of foreign policy has occurred at four different but interrelated levels:

(1) at the level of European policy

(2) at the level of foreign policy objectives

(3) at the level of policy instruments and style

(4) at the level of foreign policy making in terms of institutions, procedures and processes.

European Policy

At the level of European policy, the progress made has been by all accounts significant. When referring to European policy, we obviously mean the political objectives, positions and specific policy choices the country presents to European Union institutions for the development of the European Union. In the field of common foreign and security policy, Greece began to gradually modify its negative posture towards the priority of elaborating common foreign policy embracing security and defence at the European Union level in the mid-sixties. Faced with the prospect of being excluded from whatever arrangements the Union might agree for the security-defence policy either in the framework of the Single European Act or elsewhere, Greece realised that it had no other option but to participate actively in the process for the definition of the security/defence identity of the Union (Valinakis, 1994; Kazakos and Ioakimidis, 1994).

To that effect, Greece decided to seek full membership of the Western European Union (WEU) in February 1987 and, more importantly, to support the development of the European Union's security and defence identity. This posture took even a more positive dimension with the opening of the Intergovernmental Conference for drafting the Treaty on European Union (TEU). In a detailed memorandum and numerous other specific proposals submitted to the Conference, Greece advocated the development of common foreign policy by the Union.[5] Greece argued that a common foreign policy without a strong defence component would lack effectiveness and credibility. As a more concrete step, Greece linked its consent to the new treaty with the acceptance of its request to accede to the WEU. Indeed this request was granted by the nine member states of the WEU during the final stages of the negotiation for the TEU of Maastricht (Ioakimidis, 1993b, pp. 435–462). Greece signed the protocol for accession to the WEU in November 1992.

Since the signing of the TEU Greece has been an ardent advocate for deeper political integration including integration in the fields of security and defence, although it pursued certain foreign policy objectives perceived to be manifestly contradictory with deeper political integration (that is, the 'FYROM issue'). But it is characteristic that, with the exception of the 'FYROM issue', Greece has never invoked the veto in the context of EPC/CFSP in the period after 1992.

Greece's pro-integrationist stance culminated in the memorandum submitted in 1996 to the Intergovernmental Conference (IGC) convened to revise the Treaty on European Union (Ministry of Foreign Affairs, 1998). In that long text, Greece presented the most advanced proposals for deeper integration in the field of foreign policy and defence. In particular, Greece advocated the wholesale communitisation of the CFSP with the abolition of the pillar structure. Likewise, it supported the full incorporation of the WEU into the EU with the assumption of all TEU functions, be they political or military, by the EU. Although Greece was not given the opportunity to participate in the elaboration of the draft protocol for the phased integration of the WEU into the EU presented in March 1997 by six member states (Germany, France, Italy, Spain, Belgium, Luxembourg), it energetically supported the initiative. Moreover, Greece backed proposals for wider involvement both of the European Commission and the European Parliament in the CFSP. Similarly it endorsed the idea of the establishment of a Policy Planning and Early Warning Unit (PPEWU) while it objected to French proposals for appointing a 'high representative for the CFSP' outside the institutional framework of the Council, under the authority of the

European Council. On the contrary, it supported the elevation of the Secretary General of the Council to the post of high representative for the CFSP (Ioakimidis, 1998).

Nevertheless, while advocating the full communitisation of the CFSP, Greece expressed initial reservations about moving to qualified majority voting for decision making in the CFSP. However, it eventually accepted majority voting with the accompanying clause allowing countries to invoke 'important stated reasons of national policy' in order to thwart majoritarian decisions. But even in the question of majority voting, Greece appears by now prepared to side with the most pro-integrationist forces provided that it had a certain guarantee by the European Union for the protection of its external borders. Interestingly enough, the insertion of a clause in the CFSP provisions stipulating the protection of external borders was the only narrowly defined 'national objective' presented by Greece to the IGC.

Overall, therefore, as far as European policy is concerned, Greece has come to terms with the notion that its foreign policy objectives can coexist and indeed can be advanced by deepening policy and defence integration at the EU level. From this particular perspective, Greece can justifiably be described now as an 'orthodox' member state of the Union leaving pejorative descriptions like 'heretical' and 'awkward' well behind.[6]

Foreign Policy Objectives

As we have analysed elsewhere, participation in the EPC/CFSP has contributed decisively to broadening the scope of Greece's foreign policy (Ioakimidis, 1993a). Rather than dealing almost exclusively with the so-called 'national issues' ('ethnika themata'), issues referring to Greece's relations with its neighbouring countries, most notably Turkey, Greece has come to deal with a much wider foreign policy agenda largely because of its membership of the EU.

In the first place, Greek foreign policy has acquired a strong economic element and more generally elements of 'low politics'. While the Greek traditional foreign policy was interpreted as primarily implying the management of 'high politics issues' (relations with Turkey, Cyprus, NATO, etc.), the broadened policy agenda has embraced issues such as trade, environment, technology, culture and agriculture. The impact of the EU's external economic and trade relations on Greece's external relations and policy has been unquestionably catalytic in this respect.[7]

Coupled with the thematic expansion of the scope of Greek foreign policy, there has been a geographic broadening as well. More concretely, as a result of the dynamics associated with its participation in the EPC/CFSP, Greece has been forced to preoccupy itself for the first time in its history with the problems of remote countries or regions (that is, Latin America, Asia, Africa, etc.). Moreover, it has been forced to elaborate policies, strategies and positions to be presented to and negotiated at the relevant EU fora. In other words, Greek foreign policy has developed beyond the narrowly conceived and defined 'national interests' and 'national issues'. This trend has gathered momentum following the end of the Cold War and the historic changes that have transformed the political landscape in Eastern Europe, and more closely to Greece, changes in the Balkans. Although, initially Greece showed a marked inability to grasp the significance of the historic changes and take advantage of the opportunities unleashed for contributing to the political and economic transition of the region, it eventually adjusted its policy to new conditions thereby responding to pressures from the EU.[8] The new policy, especially as it was remoulded in 1996 by the Simitis government, aims at promoting the stabilisation of the region, interregional cooperation and even the integration of the Balkans in the EU (Hellenic Centre for European Studies, 1995). To that end, a series of policy initiatives have been launched for normalising Greece's bilateral relations with the countries of the region, the promoting of various schemes of interregional cooperation (Inter-Balkan Cooperation, Black Sea Economic Cooperation – BSEC, etc.). In this context the first ever summit of the political leaders of the countries of South East Europe was held in Crete in November 1997 thus inaugurating a process modelled on the EU summit meetings (European Councils).

The broadening of the thematic and geographic agenda has brought Greece in as yet unknown areas of foreign policy, something which has inevitably given rise to additional strains within the Greek Ministry of Foreign Affairs (MFA). This must be seen against the background of the day to day management of the EU affairs, which is carried out chiefly by the MFA, which constitutes a tremendous addition to the workload of the ministry and at the same time the most radical broadening of the policy agenda for the Greek foreign policy (Ioakimidis, 1995b). In a sense, it would not be an exaggeration to argue that Greece has acquired a full-fledged foreign policy as a result of the EU impact. Until the impact had materialised, Greece had no comprehensive foreign policy proper; it had only 'national issues' to deal with.

Policy Instruments and Style

The impact of the EPC/CFSP on the policy instruments and style of Greece's foreign policy has also been considerable. In a sense, it can be argued that EPC/CFSP has forced Greek foreign policy to embrace new policy instruments and adopt a new policy style for conducting policy more congruent with the EU requirements.[9] The style of policy progressively changed from a rhetorical, symbolic, nationalistic, formalistic and at times parochial and populistic to a more pragmatic, problem solving and issue oriented one. The interaction with the other member states in the context of EPC/CFSP has had a marked socialising impact upon decision makers and policy shapers in Greece. As a Greek diplomat has put it, 'participation in the EPC/CFSP has taught us the need to conduct foreign policy without making too much fuss'.[10]

The progressive shift of Greek foreign policy from the formalistic, rhetorical style to a pragmatic one is in line of course with a wider change in Greek political environment towards the same behavioural pattern.[11] The rise of C. Simitis to power in 1996 signifies this change. With Simitis in power, Greek politics have become less formalistic and more pragmatic, less symbolic and more issue oriented.

The emotionally heavy nationalistic language employed in foreign policy has given way to a more pragmatic lexicon. The most characteristic example is the near complete shedding from the vocabulary of such loaded phrases as 'ethnika themata' and 'ethika dikaia' (used to describe Greece's core foreign policy objectives). These almost untranslatable in any meaningful way phrases (literally 'national rights' and 'national issues') turned foreign policy objectives into sacrosanct national pursuits not subject to any sort of questioning, let alone negotiation and compromise. This change is accompanied by a wider attempt to redefine patriotism not merely as a constant drive to fulfil narrowly-conceived nationalistic objectives in foreign policy (objectives concerning primarily issues on Greek-Turkish relations) but as multi-faced situation leading to a 'stronger Greece'. According to the Prime Minister, C. Simitis, for instance, patriotism nowadays means a 'stronger Greece, stronger not merely in military terms but primarily in economic, political, institutional and cultural resources, a Greece fully integrated into the European Union'.

The change in style is not unrelated to substantive changes concerning the objectives and orientation of foreign policy. The waning nationalistic elements in foreign policy coupled with the ascendancy of the pragmatic elements feed into the public mind and contribute to gradually, if painfully, changing public perceptions and attitudes regarding Greece's position in the world and its relations with its external environment. In a country used to seeing itself as the centre of the whole world suffering from what has been termed as the syndrome of hellenecentrism, this change can hardly be underestimated.[12]

As regards the instruments and techniques of foreign policy, the impact of EU membership and the EPC/CFSP in particular has also been significant. First of all, participation has underlined the increasingly pivotal role of multilateral organisations, other than the UN, for building alliances and advancing foreign policy objectives. More importantly perhaps, it has also highlighted the intrinsic importance of negotiation and compromise as fundamental instruments for solving problems and promoting interests in the modern, interdependent world. Of course, conducting foreign policy and diplomacy revolves primarily around negotiations and compromise. Yet, in the Greek cultural tradition, negotiations were very often equated with an act leading inevitably to unacceptable surrender of national pride. Participation in the EU – which by definition involves constant, uninterrupted, day-to-day negotiations – has helped a great deal to legitimise the concept of negotiations and compromise as the principal diplomatic techniques of attaining objectives in the context of wider packages of negotiable items susceptible to trade-offs.

In the new techniques and instruments of conducting foreign policy imported from the EU to Greece one should also mention the new means of communicating views, positions and problems. Included in these are the COREU system and the network of contracts and exchanges in the framework of the Union and CFSP in particular.[13]

Policy-Making Structures

The pressures upon foreign policy from EU participation have led, somehow belatedly, to a radical reform of the institutional organisation of the

Greek Ministry of Foreign Affairs (Stoforopoulos and Makrydimitris, 1997). The new organisation of the MFA established by Law in 1998 was designed 'to meet the needs and challenges facing Greece, as a member of the European Union, whose foreign policy is increasingly intertwined with that of the European Union'.[14]

More specifically, the institutional restructuring of the Ministry aims at (i) bringing economics, trade and other 'low politics issues' into the mainstream of Greek foreign policy, (ii) enabling the Ministry to employ the new instruments and techniques for conducting foreign policy and to respond more effectively to the thematic and geographic broadening of Greece's foreign policy, (iii) establishing structures (Centre for Policy Analysis and Planning, Centre for Crisis management, Policy making units, etc.) enabling the Ministry 'to produce policy rather than merely procedures as has hitherto been the case' and (iv) enabling chiefly the Ministry to cope more effectively with the requirements and pressures emanating from Greece's participation in the EU. To that effect, new directorates have been created while independent economic and political directorates covering the same geographic areas have been merged into unified departments so that to deal in an overall, coherent, fashion with policy issues. In doing so, The Ministry clearly followed the example of the EU which, after the setting up of the CFSP in 1993, merged the various working groups and committees dealing with external economic issues and foreign policy in the context of the EPC/CFSP.

The impact of the EU on the institutional structures of foreign policy making is moreover emphasised by the setting up of the Centre of Analysis and Planning (imitating the Policy Planning and Early Warning Unit – PPEWU established by the Amsterdam Treaty). It is also reflected in the fact that the Directorate-General for European Union Affairs in the Ministry of Foreign Affairs has grown as the most sizable one in the terms of personnel and other resources. It has also come to occupy a central position in the policy-making process as it is the only directorate represented in practically all collective bodies of policy making in the ministry.

In a sense, structural reforms are aimed at institutionalising the process of policy making which has been largely dominated by personalities, notably the personalities of the Ministers of Foreign Affairs. But in the Greek case, one should always bear in mind that formal, legal reforms are not always translated into actual reforms in practice. What is provided on paper is not always what happens in reality.

The Sources of Europeanisation

The acceleration of the Europeanisation process and especially the Europeanisation of the foreign policy in the recent years can be ascribed to a number of factors. Besides the rise of C. Simitis and his team to power in 1996, a team forming the most pro-European government Greece has had since its accession to the EC in 1981, four underlying factors seem to account for the progress observed in the Europeanisation of Greece (Ioakimidis, 1995a):

Benefits from the EU The substantial and growing economic benefits, particularly budgetary benefits, that Greece has drawn from the European Union.[15] Budgetary transfers have contributed immensely to making the wider Greek public enthusiastically supportive of European integration. Indeed the Greek electorate registers the higher rates of support for European integration even though it tends to perceive the EU primarily as a 'cow to be milked'.

The end of the Cold War and the demise of the Soviet empire The dissolution of the Soviet system and the end of the rivalry between East and West eliminated even any theoretical possibility for Greece to look for an alternative framework for building alliances outside the western camp (Veremis and Couloumbis, 1997). Consequently, the EU appears to be the only institutional framework within which Greece can advance its interests and become integrated into the wider international system.

The EMU project The successful endeavour to establish the single currency (EURO) led Greece to realise that if it persisted with its earlier negative policy towards deeper integration and resisted the need to adjust its economy, society and policy to the EMU requirements, it ran the risk of finding itself marginalised not only economically but also politically and institutionally in the EU framework. Consequently, Greece has set as the overriding objective to join the single currency in the year 2001 by meeting the prescribed conditions ('the convergence criteria of the TEU') thereby further Europeanising its economy.[16]

The new enlargement of the European Union (Ioakimidis, 1996) The fact that practically all countries of Eastern Europe, indeed all countries surrounding Greece including Turkey, have set as their basic political objective to accede to the EU has highlighted the importance of Greek membership. It has also underlined the need for Greece to become deeper integrated and a more active player in the EU context.

All these factors have cumulatively contributed to the acceleration of the process for the Europeanisation of Greece. The single mindedness with which the 'Simitis government' pursues the 'EMU project' striving by all means to meet the 'convergence criteria' in order to bring Greece into the single currency reflects the centrality European Union has acquired for Greece. Indeed Europeanisation is now seen as the only realistic strategy for the modernisation of the Greek state and society. Inevitably, this has generated strong opposition by those traditional sectors of the society and well-entrenched vested interests which stand to lose from the modernisation process.

Greece and the Capability-Expectations Gap

The increasing Europeanisation of Greece's foreign policy by no means implies that Greece feels content with the performance and policy outputs of CFSP, especially with respect to the management of regional or international crises (that is, Bosnia, Kosovo, etc.). It feels even less satisfied with CFSP regarding its ability to address its fundamental security concerns, perceived or real threats and risks. On the contrary, Greece is bitterly complaining because, in its own view, the EU and CFSP in particular have failed to grasp the seriousness and intensity of its security problems, notably with respect to Turkey, or to realise the complicated problems and various sources of actual or potential conflict and instability in S.E. Europe, primarily in the Balkans.

To a certain degree, these complaints reflect different conceptions of regional problems and the role the Union can or must play in handling them. It also reflects different assessments of the evolving security and geopolitical environment in the wider S.E. Europe. For Greece, Turkey remains a dangerous source of instability in the region and an extremely acute threat to Greek territorial integrity. Nevertheless, in the long run Greece sees the European Union as the only factor which can provide the conditions and institutional instruments for resolving the problems of the region and cementing stability. The principal means for this appears to be of course the integration of the region including Turkey in the EU. Enlargement for Greece is 'an investment in democracy, security and prosperity'.

Looked at from a different, broader perspective, the Greek posture and complaints about the CFSP tend to highlight another dimension of the capability expectations gap associated with the operation of the CFSP.[17] In other words, it is not only third parties that might hold unrealistic, exaggerated expectations about the EU and its capability to perform certain tasks, but also individual EU member states, in this case, Greece.

More specifically, Greece appears to sustain much greater expectations about the capacity of the CFSP than the policy is capable of delivering in terms of intervening to prevent, manage and resolve crises and conflicts. Indeed, Greece gives at times the impression that it tends to view the EU in the old fashioned role of the 'protector power'. As is known, since its inception as a modern state in 1832 and until at least 1974, Greece used to be formally or informally under the tutelage of 'foreign powers' dubbed as 'protector powers'. This role was originally performed by Britain, France and Russia and subsequently by the United States. Greece opted for EU membership in 1975 in order, inter alia, to get rid of the regime of 'protecting powers'. The EU was seen as a substitute to the regime of 'protector powers'.

Despite the fact that considerable progress has been made over the past few years in the direction of narrowing the capability-expectations gap, it still remains yawning. CFSP has not yet acquired the institutional, political or military means and capabilities to perform the tasks that third parties or Greece expects from it (Hill, 1998). And it is highly doubtful whether it will ever acquire them. Consequently, what seems to be the reasonable approach for Greece is, first, to scale down its expectations adjusting them to the existing, real capabilities of the CFSP and, secondly, to strive for the strengthening of the policy in all its aspects, institutional, political, military.

Notes

1. On Greece's foreign policy in general see, Veremis, T. and Couloumbis, T. (1997), and

Papahadjopoulos, D. (1998).
2. *The Economist*, September 17, 1997. In May 1992, *The Economist* described Greece as 'The sick man in Europe', *The Economist*, May 9, 1992.
3. For this unfortunate episode see, Papahadjopoulos (1994).
4. On Turkey and the EU see, Muftuler-Bac, M. (1997). On Greece's policy in general see, Constas D. (1991).
5. The Text of this memorandum can be found in Perrakis, S. and Grigoriou, P. (1994).
6. Writing about the Balkans in January 1998 *The Economist* observed that 'Greece is more interested in joining Europe's monetary union than in pursuing nationalistic dreams', *The Economist*, January 24, 1998.
7. For a general discussion see, Kanellopoulos, A.K. and Frankonikolopoulos C.A. (1995).
8. This inability is reflected in the way Greece handled the so-called 'FYROM question', the veto of the EU financial assistance to Albania and the uncritical stance in favour of Serbia during the period of the Bosnia crisis.
9 On this aspect see, Ioakimidis, P.C. (1999)
10. Personal interview, Ministry of Foreign Affairs (September, 1998)
11. On Greek formalism see Mouzelis, N.P. (1978).
12. On the political aspects of Greek culture see Diamantouros, P.N. (1993).
13. It must be noted however that Greece has not yet made an extensive use of the COREU system as it registers the lowest number of telegrams sent through the system.
14. Law 2594, 24 March, 1998.
15. Net financial flows to Greece from the EU budget amount to approximately 4.5 per cent per year or 6 per cent of the Greek GDP.
16. For the impact of the EMU on Greek economy and policy see the relevant chapters in Kazakos, P. (1998).
17. The idea of 'capability-expectations gap' was elaborated by C. Hill (1993).

References

Constas, D. (ed) (1991), *The Greek-Turkish Conflict in the 1990s*, London: Macmillan.

Diamantouros, P.N. (1993), 'Politics and Culture in Greece 1974–91: An Introduction', in Clogg, R. (ed), *Greece 1981–89, The Populist Decade*, St. Martins Press.

Hellenic Center for European Studies (1995), *The European Community and the Balkans*, Athens: EKEM/Ant. Sakkoulas.

Hill, C. (1993), 'The Capability-Expectations Gap of Conceptualizing Europe's International Role', *Journal of Common Market Studies*, Vol. 31, No. 3, September.

Hill, C. (1997), 'The Actors Involved: National Perspectives' in Regelsberger, E., De Schoutheete de Tervarent, Ph. and Wessels, W. (eds), *Foreign Policy of the European Union, From EPC to CFSP and Beyond*, London: Lynne Rienner.

Hill, C. (1998), 'Closing the capabilities-expectations gap?' in Peterson and Sjursen, H. (eds), *A Common Foreign Policy for Europe*, London: Macmillan.

Ioakimidis, P.C. (1993a), 'Greece in the EC: Policies, Experiences and Prospects', in Psomiades, H.J. and Thomadakis, S.B. (eds), *Greece, the New Europe and the Changing International Order*, New York: Pella.

Ioakimidis, P.C. (1993b), *European Political Union*, Athens: Themelio.

Ioakimidis, P.C. (1995a), 'Contradictions Between Policy and Performance', in Featherstone, K. and Ifantis, K. (eds), *Greece in a Changing Europe, Between European Integration and Balkan Disintegration?* Manchester: Manchester University Press.

Ioakimidis, P.C. (1995b), 'The Greek Administration and the Shaping of European Policy', in Tsoukalis, L. (ed), *Greece in the European Community: the Challenge of Enlargement*, Athens: EKEM/Papazisis [in Greek].
Ioakimidis, P.C. (1996), *The New Enlargement of the European Union and Greece*, Athens: ELIAMEP/I. Sideris [in Greek].
Ioakimidis, P.C., (1997), *The European Union and the Greek State, The Consequences From the Participation in the Integration Process*, Athens: Themelio [in Greek].
Ioakimidis, P.C. (1998), *The Treaty of Amsterdam, A New Model of Integration or a Symptom of Disintegration*, Athens: Themelio.
Ioakimidis, P.C. (1999), 'The Model of Foreign Policy Making in Greece: Personalities Versus Institutions', in Stavridis, S., Couloumbis, T., Veremis, T., and Waites, N. (eds), *Foreign Policies of the EU's Mediterranean and Applicant Countries in the 1990s*, London: Macmillan.
Jopp, M. (1997), 'The Defence Dimension of the European Union: the Role and Performance of the WEU', in Regelsberger, E., De Schoutheete de Tervarent, Ph., and Wessels, W. (eds), *Foreign Policy of the European Union, From EPC to CFSP and Beyond*, London: Lynne Rienner.
Kanellopoulos, A.K. and Frankonikolopoulos, C.H. (eds) (1995), *The Present and Future of Greek Foreign Policy*, Athens: I. Sideris [in Greek].
Kazakos, P. (1998), *The New Agenda of the Left and Other Essays of Political Criticism*, Athens: Papazisis [in Greek].
Kazakos, P. and Ioakimidis, P.C. (eds) (1994), *Greece and EC Membership Evaluated*, London: Pinter.
Laddas, K.A. (1997), *The Europeanization of Greece, Interests, Politics and Crisis of Integration*, London: Macmillan.
Ladrech, R. (1994), 'Europeanization of Domestic Politics and Institutions: The Case of France', *Journal of Common Market Studies*, Vol. 32, No. 1, March.
Ministry of Foreign Affairs (1998), *For a Democratic European Union with Political and Social Content*, Athens: Themelio.
Mouzelis, N.P. (1978), *Modern Greece, Facets of Underdevelopment*, London: Macmillan.
Muftuler-Bac, M. (1997) *Turkey's Relations with a Changing Europe*, Manchester: Manchester University Press.
Nuttal, S.J. (1992), *European Political Cooperation*, Oxford: Clarendon Press.
Nuttal, S.J. (1997), 'Two Decades of EPC Performance', in Regelsberger, E., De Schoutheete de Tervarent, Ph., and Wessels, W. (eds), *Foreign Policy of the European Union, From EPC to CFSP and Beyond*, London: Lynne Rienner.
Papahadjopoulos, D. (1998), *Greek Foreign Policy in the Past Cold War Era: Implications for the European Union*, CEPS Paper No. 72, Brussels.
Perrakis, S. and Grigoriou, P. (1994), *Greece in the Process of European Integration (1981–1994)*, Athens: EKEM/An. Sakkoulas [in Greek].
Stoforopoulos, T. and Makrydimitris, A. (1997), *The System of Greek Foreign Policy: The Institutional Dimension*, Athens: EKEM/I. Sideris [in Greek].
Valinakis, Y. (1994), *Greece's Security in the Post Cold War Era*, Eberhausen/Isartal: Stiftung Wissenschaft Und Politic.
Veremis, T. and Thumann, M. (1994), *The Balkans and CFSP, The Views of Greece and Germany*, CERS Paper No. 59, Brussels.
Veremis, T. and Couloumbis, T. (1998), *Greek Foreign Policy, Dilemmas of a New Era*, Athens: ELIAMEP/I, Sideris [in Greek].

18 Greece in a Post-Cold War Environment

THEODORE A. COULOUMBIS

Following Mikhail Gorbachev's perestroika policies, we have witnessed the momentous events that led to the reunification of Germany, the disaggregation of the former Soviet Union, the dissolution of the Warsaw Pact and the Comecon, and the general collapse of the system of applied Marxism-Leninism in the European continent.

Despite the historic peace breakthroughs in the Israeli-Palestinian, South African, Northern Ireland and even the Bosnian questions, George Bush's optimistic vision of an emerging new world order of like-minded states was soon challenged by a long chain of crises – especially in Africa, the Balkans, and in some of the former Soviet republics of the Black Sea and Caucasus regions (See Fukuyama, 1992; Van Evera, 1991; Kegley, Jr., 1992, 1993; Kegley, Jr. and Raymond, 1994; Kupchan and Kupchan 1991, 1995). This, in turn, gave rise to a number of pessimistic assessments raising nightmarish images of a 'new world disorder', a 'return to history', 'from Sarajevo to Sarajevo' and so forth (See Mearshimer, 1990a, 1990b, 1995; Brzezinski, 1993; Kaplan, 1994).

Foreign policy analysts in Greece and elsewhere quickly reflected the schools of optimism and pessimism above.[1] The optimists highlighted global order, consensus among the permanent members of the UN Security Council, and collective international action undertaken against violators in places such as Iraq, former Yugoslavia, Somalia and Haiti as well as limited humanitarian assistance and action in Rwanda, Burundi, Bosnia and elsewhere.

In contrast, the pessimists viewed the world as moving back into a state of multipolar anarchy in which the strong do what they can and the weak suffer what they must. The optimists counselled the employment of political, diplomatic and economic leverage and placed special emphasis on Greece's institutional connections with multilateral mechanisms such as the EU, NATO, and the WEU. The pessimists, on the contrary, emphasised the military dimension of politics and recommended policies of temporary regional alliances and the taking of bold and decisive steps including the pre-emptive use of force in favourable but fleeting conditions.

One can label the optimists as multilateralists and internationalists who are guided by the philosophy of Jean Monnet. The pessimists, in turn, can be labelled as unilateralists and nationalists who are still inspired by the teachings of the Prussian general and theoretician Karl Von Clausewitz (1780–1831).

As post-cold war international conditions are unfolding, it appears that reality lies somewhere between the optimistic and the pessimistic projections. A new global bipolarity seems to be emerging, dividing the world into an advanced and stable 'North' (North America, Europe, Japan and Oceania) and a transitional, developing and unstable 'South' (the so-called Third World) which now includes portions of the former Soviet Union and of the post-communist Balkans.

Future political relations are likely to focus mainly on a North-South axis, but the informal global concert of powers will not automatically energise itself in every instance where there are threats to peace and/or violations of international law and norms. The stable North will probably continue to react to escalating conflicts in the unstable South according to criteria of interest, cost and capability. Accordingly, there will be zones of vital interest, such as the Gulf, where the likelihood of collective and decisive military responses against designated aggressors will be quite high. There will also be zones of moderate interest, for example, Bosnia and Kosovo, where peacekeeping, peacemaking and peacebuilding will be the order of the day. Finally, in a classic 'triage' fashion, there will be zones of indifference or benign neglect (such as the Sudan, Sri Lanka, Afghanistan, Rwanda, et al.) in which the international community will stand by sympathetically though helplessly and watch the bloody struggles for the survival of the fittest and the most ferocious.

This paper addresses two questions related to Greece's (and to a certain extent to Cyprus') foreign policy profile in the post-Cold War era. The first question relates to an assessment of the comparative stability/conflict quotient in the Balkans as old and newly born postcommunist states are navigating in the treacherous waters of transition to democracy and to market economy. The second question addresses Greek foreign policy vis-à-vis Turkey and assesses the cost/benefit ratios of mapping out a realistic strategy (and tactics) of tension reduction and conflict resolution which could, hopefully, lead to a historic reconciliation modelled on the Venizelos-Ataturk rapprochement of the early 1930s.

In the 1980s, it had been fashionable for scholars/practitioners such as Henry Kissinger and Jeanne Kirkpatrick to differentiate clearly between authoritarian regimes (for example, Latin American and Southern European variety military dictatorships) and totalitarian regimes (for example, communist systems such as those of the Soviet Union, Eastern Europe, Asia and the Caribbean). They viewed the former as less objectionable than the latter, despite their equally atrocious human rights records, because authoritarian regimes were considered reversible (in that under certain conditions they could evolve to democracy) while totalitarian regimes were pronounced permanent and irreversible. The post-perestroika collapse of European communist regimes exploded in the face of the Kirkpatrick/Kissinger thesis but has not necessarily destroyed its reasoning.

A number of political scientists have been recently asking themselves whether the processes of transition and consolidation of democratic institutions experienced by Southern European countries such as Portugal, Spain, Italy, Greece and Turkey could be considered as models for partial emulation by post-communist societies (see Chelabi and Stepan, 1995).

Before proceeding to respond to this question we should define for working purposes the concepts of transition and consolidation. Transition to democracy is normally a short-lived span of time involving the constitutional specification and the establishment of institutions which are designed to safeguard the separation of powers, the development and functioning of two or more political parties, the holding of regular elections (at least every four/five years), the functioning of representative parliamentary bodies, the protection of human rights and freedoms, and the development and operation of a genuine and pluralist press and other mass media.

The concept of consolidation of democracy is of special relevance to post-communist countries that are currently undergoing the difficult task of transition to democracy as well as to market economy. Democratic institutions may be considered to have been consolidated when at least three important preconditions are satisfied. First, the development of consensus among the political parties and groupings in a given country concerning the structure and the characteristics of democracy (for example, presidential republic, parliamentary republic or constitutional monarchy). Second, the successful rotation in power between parties and/or coalitions of the Right and the Left without military intervention and/or civil conflict. Third, the maintenance of an inter-party agreement regarding the external orientation (strategy) of a country. In the case of Greece, for example, the choice in the late 1970s was made, and was subsequently accepted by the whole spectrum of its political forces, that the country ought to seek membership in the European Community and maintain membership in NATO over the alternative option (vocally promoted in the 1970s by the Socialist and Communist parties) that Greece should have opted for a non-aligned/neutral status.

Based on the discussion so far, we can propose two working hypotheses regarding the path toward democracy of post-communist countries in Southeastern Europe (excluding from consideration for the time being three constituent states of former Yugoslavia, that is, Croatia, Serbia and Bosnia):

> Four post-communist countries, Albania, Bulgaria, the Former Yugoslav Republic of Macedonia (FYROM) and Romania are well into the stage of their transition phase, but we cannot, unfortunately, speak at this time about consolidated democratic institutions in any of the four. In all four cases, however, the rotation in power between Right and Left has moved these countries one notch closer to consolidation.

The transition and consolidation processes in metacommunist countries, unlike the case of transition/consolidation of southern European states, have faced the special and difficult to overcome problem of drastic and *simultaneous* changes taking place not only in the political system but also in the economic system. Resurrecting perhaps some old Marxist dialectics, we can appreciate how economic transition difficulties can spill over and complicate political developments. In sum, the creation of a civil society which is the *sine qua non* of every consolidated, pluralist democracy, presupposes the substantive functioning of a free market mechanism not only on the level of trade and consumption but also on the level of production which, in turn, calls for effective privatisation campaigns.

The major threat facing post-communist regimes in Southeastern Europe stems from extreme nationalism (chauvinism) and its Siamese twin, populism. The ideological vacuum that was created in the wake of the collapse of communism in Europe has been filled in the past few years by new or recycled politicians that have resorted to romantic, atavistic and attention-catching strategies. In their attempts to mobilise the disoriented masses, they have employed simplistic and divisive slogans. By waving the flags of ethnic separatism and irredentism these post-communist elites resurrected anachronistic visions regarding a 'greater' Albania, Bulgaria,

Croatia, Romania, Serbia, Macedonia and so forth.

These new politicians, by employing Manichean tactics and subdividing peoples and governments into angels and devils, have fed the fires and passions of political polarisation. Polarisation, in turn, blows up the bridges of consensus on fundamental questions of regime-type and external orientation, leading finally to internal conflicts (coups, revolutions and civil wars) and intervention by foreign antagonistic (regional or global) centres of power. The first victim of uncontrolled polarisation is democracy itself. The war in former Yugoslavia, especially the tragic butchery in Bosnia, was an example of the fate of a people without long democratic traditions undergoing acute economic crisis and being at the mercy of imprudent and populist politicians.

The more recent travails of Kosovo (NATO bombing and the Milosevic-engineered ethnic cleansing of Kosovar Albanians) are yet another case of the fragile balances in regions of former Yugoslavia including the potential for conflict in Montenegro, Vojvodina, the Sandzak and Tetovo (in the former Yugoslav Republic of Macedonia). The international agreement to restore Kosovo to a status short of independence but with enhanced autonomy under UN, NATO, EU, OSCE and G-8 auspices may – hopefully – pave the way for reconstruction, development and reintegration of the tried and tested 'black hole' of the Western Balkans into the Euroatlantic security architecture.

It will be the duty of the European Union and NATO (whose member states by and large enjoy consolidated democratic institutions) to continue safeguarding the peace agreements in Bosnia and Kosovo, ending all speculation about falling dominoes leading to another great European war. Our slogans should be 'no more Bosnias' and 'no more Kosovos'. The West's duty, further, is to promote democracy wherever social and economic conditions permit its growth and sustainability. This obligation is rendered imperative by what we might call the 'democratic paradox'. It has been argued, for instance, by careful social scientists such as Rudolph Rummel (1983), that the incidence of war had been lowest among democracies and virtually non-existent between what Rummel calls 'libertarian' states (that is, free-enterprise-oriented constitutional democracies). The paradox today is that we have been witnessing the rise of internal and international conflict taking place simultaneously with the transition to democracy in regions of former Yugoslavia and in parts of the former Soviet Union. Should this phenomenon, correlating democracy and conflict, be permitted to continue for long, the very reputation and legitimacy of democratic institutions will be seriously tarnished.

The solid foundations upon which a strong edifice of Southeast European peace and cooperation can be erected include respect for the inviolability of international boundaries, the consolidation of democratic institutions, comprehensive and demonstrated protection of the human rights of all citizens in each state (without discrimination against minorities on the basis of language, religion or other preferences) and a free-market economy (together with the mutually advantageous networks of interdependence the free market entails).

Peace and transnational cooperation will be cemented further as programmes of economic aid, technical assistance, free trade and investment become linked with the peaceful and democratic behaviour of recipients. The EU's, NATO's and the OSCE's strategies of 'preventive diplomacy' should, therefore, emphasise rewards (not only sanctions) which will contribute to the development and consolidation of an 'arc of peace and cooperation' in the Balkans and elsewhere in the former Warsaw Pact regions. Such a strategy will isolate disorienting conceptions/slogans that allude to the development of an 'Islamic arc' and an 'Orthodox arc' in the Balkan region.[2] 'Alliances', based on religious affinity and other exclusivist premises, would surely lead to the revival of bloody ethnic/religious conflicts and the self marginalisation of those involved. The task for consolidated democracies in the post-Cold War era is to pronounce a new doctrine of 'containment' where the object to be contained in the place of communism will be chauvinism and its ethnic-cleansing variants.

The nations and the peoples of Southeastern Europe in the post-cold war period must resist the siren-songs of a bygone era. They must avoid nationalist and irredentist claims at the expense of their neighbours, and must shy away from policies of subregional alliances, spheres of influence, revanchist campaigns, preemptive probes and disproportionate reprisals – all of which are remnants of a glorious but also self destructive past.

We should not forget that it took two world wars, and scores of millions of dead, for conditions to ripen and permit traditional European rivals (such as the French and the Germans) to move forward with the remarkable experiment of European integration that has gradually given birth to the European Union. In the post-cold war Balkans we have already suffered the tragedies of carnage and destruction in Bosnia and Kosovo. In addition to offering our hopes and prayers, we should try to support leaders who are cautious and prudent so that the Cassandran prophesy about the Balkans becoming once again the powder keg of Europe will not become self fulfilling.[3]

In the twenty-two years that have elapsed since the Greek Colonels' coup against Makarios and the Turkish invasion of Cyprus, the Greek and Cypriot governments have managed to keep the issue alive by employing strictly economic and political leverage on Turkey and the Turkish-Cypriots while avoiding recourse to the threat and employment of military means.

Turkey, given its apparent military superiority in the Cyprus region, has insisted on perpetuating the post-1974 partition, being the only country to have recognised the self-proclaimed Turkish Republic of Northern Cyprus (which unilaterally declared its independence in the Fall of 1983). Since then, the Turkish-Cypriot population has been prevented from reintegrating itself into the mainstream of a single and prosperous Cypriot economy.

Third parties (for example, the United States, Great Britain, Germany and, to a lesser extent, Russia), gauging, at times overestimating, the strategic and commercial importance of Turkey, have adopted a stance of benign neutrality on the Cyprus question, urging both sides to move quickly and decisively toward a mutually acceptable settlement of their prickly dispute.

In the view of this author, the negotiating position of Greece and Cyprus vis-à-vis Turkey has been enhanced since 1990 for (at least) the following three reasons:

- The end of the cold war and the gradual decline of Turkey's strategic importance in the security calculus of the US, EU and NATO.
- The convergence, in terms of domestic and foreign policy orientations, in the positions of Greece's political parties (Centre-Left and Centre-Right) following the healing of the wounds left by the Greek civil war (1946–49) and the reintegration of Greece's left (communist and socialist) into the political process after the restoration of democracy in 1974.
- The new European option of Cyprus and its policy of seeking accession to the EU. It should be remembered that in the 1960–90 period, Cyprus had openly identified its UN-focused foreign policy with the non-aligned movement.

Today, Greece and Cyprus are proposing a framework for the settlement of the Cyprus question which does not challenge the interests and objectives of Great Britain and the United States in the Eastern Mediterranean, given that the ultimate settlement package includes Cypriot membership in the EU and an increased role for NATO (Cyprus accession to NATO being the desired objective and a NATO post-settlement implementation force being the minimum).

Free of cold war servitudes (which among other things included a fundamental divergence of orientations, that is, a Euro-Atlantic membership for Greece and nonalignment for Cyprus) the two governments can easily follow a well orchestrated and diplomatically energetic foreign policy that will be founded on two pillars. The first pillar, strictly defensive, is designed to maintain a state of sufficiency in the balance of Greek-Turkish forces in the Aegean, Thrace and Cyprus.[4] It involves a defensive, strictly deterrent mission for the Greek and Cypriot armed forces designed to safeguard Greece's territorial integrity in the Aegean and Thrace and – in the case of Cyprus – to discourage any further extension of the Turkish armed forces beyond the so-called green line (that is, the line separating the occupied territories in the North from the rest of Cyprus). In sum, the first pillar involves a defence policy of two countries that want to avoid a war without losing in peace.

The second pillar covers the political/economic/diplomatic range of activity and it calls for flexibility, imagination and energy, combining the use of politico-economic instruments of leverage on Turkey and the Turkish Cypriot Community in Cyprus with a comprehensive and long-term set of proposals designed to reach mutually acceptable settlements in Cyprus and the Aegean. Abandoning single-issue, reactive policies of the past, Greece and Cyprus can take the initiative by identifying viable and mutually reassuring avenues of tension reduction and conflict resolution in a multilateral framework provided by the EU and NATO.

Since 1974 and the turbulent events in Cyprus that triggered the collapse of the military dictatorship, Greek foreign policy (in deeds if not always words) has been a synthesis of power and prudence. Despite occasional bursts of emotional and populist rhetoric – especially in pre-election periods – the Greek governments (whether formed by New Democracy or Pasok) have adopted a cautious and pragmatic set of external policies.

The fundamental premises, of what has been a consensual approach to external challenges and opportunities, can be summarised as follows:

> Greece – after 1974 – is perceived as facing a major revisionist challenge from neighbouring Turkey. This challenge calls for the maintenance of an adequate balance of military power sufficient to deter Turkey's employment of military force as an instrument of policy vis-à-vis Greece and Cyprus.

Greece is classified in the category of politically and economically developed states which have forged, since World War II, linkages of political and economic interdependence in accordance with the general principles of democracy and market economy. Accession to the European Community (Union) in 1981 has been the centre of gravity of a Greek strategy of continuing integration within a European region. Europe is viewed in Greece as an enlightened space which has abandoned since 1945 the modus operandi of formulating 'national interests' in terms of territorial expansion, irredentism, spheres of influence, unbridled ethnocentrism, economic protectionism, mercantilism and colonialism.

Greece's integration into a zone of global stability (EU, WEU and NATO) reinforces its already consolidated democratic institutions and contributes to diplomatic deterrence and the resultant safeguarding of the country's territorial integrity. Naturally, well-trained and well-equipped armed forces remain at the inner core of Greece's military deterrence mechanisms.

In the case of the Balkans, Greece has spearheaded policies of multilateral and multifunctional cooperation, even during the confining period of cold war bipolarity. These initiatives were an end in themselves, but they were also designed to improve Greece's bargaining power vis-à-vis Turkey by avoiding the creation of a multi-front diplomatic (and potentially military) confrontation. Unfortunately, Greek policies with respect to FYROM in the 1992–95 period almost managed to derail the country from this prudent course. However, the renormalisation of relations with Albania (early in 1995), the growing chances of a lasting settlement of Greece-FYROM difficulties with the mutual acceptance of a hyphenated name for FYROM, the continuation of excellent political and commercial contacts with Bulgaria and Romania and the rapidly improving relations with the new states of former Yugoslavia, are restoring Greece to its former course of an active peace contributor to the Balkans.

Greece, as a consolidated democracy with an advanced economy, has every reason to remain a *status quo* power and to avoid atavistic temptations (nationalist and irredentist) that have so brutally affected regions of former Yugoslavia and particularly Bosnia and Kosovo.

Together with its partners in the European Union and NATO, Greece can contribute to the reconstruction of war-torn former Yugoslavia by participating in peace-building projects, offering humanitarian assistance to all refugees, promoting principles and practices of inviolability of frontiers coupled with the protection of human rights of minorities, and emphasising the comparative advantage of economic interdependence. Active participation in peace-keeping and observation missions in Albania and Kosovo in the 1997-98 period is reflecting Greece's equidistant (vis-à-vis parties in dispute) and multilateralist policies in the Balkans.[5]

A successful strategy of peace and mutually advantageous cooperation in the Balkans is likely to ameliorate the troubled Greek-Turkish relationship once Greek and Turkish elites realise that a war between the two countries would be catastrophic and that the perpetuation of high levels of tension in their diplomatic relations ultimately hurts their multilateral nexus of relationships.

Greece and Turkey have been involved in the past twenty-five years in a costly and protracted diplomatic and economic confrontation reaching at times the brink of outright warfare. With the peace process in full swing in critical areas such as the Middle East, Northern Ireland, South Africa and former Yugoslavia, it is imperative to address the complicated issues separating Greece and Turkey with the aim of devising tactics and strategies toward tension reduction and reconciliation.

If we were to move forward with this line of reasoning we should accept two major premises: The first premise is that a Greek-Turkish war is unthinkable and unwinnable because, to begin with, it would isolate both belligerents from their Western institutional affiliations. Even if, after the first battles, one of the two countries were to secure marginal territorial gains at the expense of the other, a chain of revanchist conflicts would surely follow classifying both Greece and Turkey as high risk zones with a devastating impact on their economies and societies.

The second premise is that perpetuating the current Cold War atmosphere does not serve the interests of either Greece or Turkey. Among other costs, both countries are being obliged to maintain disproportionately high military expenditures (on the average around 5 per cent of their GNPs) at the expense of vital economic stabilisation and development programmes.

A climate of reconciliation, cooperation and friendship cannot be restored as long as the Cyprus question remains unresolved. A genuine settlement of the Cyprus problem would exclude 'enosis' (union of Cyprus with Greece) and 'taksim' (partition of Cyprus into Greek and Turkish segments). A historic compromise, therefore, calls for *independence* in he form of a federal, bizonal and bicommunal state as specified in the Makarios-Denktash (1977) and Kyprianou-Denktash (1979) summit agreements.

The federal state of Cyprus that will emerge after settlement, will be given an excellent chance to survive and prosper if at the time of its genesis it were to become *simultaneously* a member of the European Union and – if deemed acceptable – NATO. EU membership, together with genuine collective guarantees, demilitarisation (except for the British sovereign base areas), and a NATO-commanded multinational implementation force (until mutual confidence is securely established), will allow the troubled Cypriots to forge a long-lived unity based on all rights, duties and freedoms that democracy entails.[6]

Shifting to the Aegean area, we can project a rapid process of reconciliation following a Cyprus settlement. For this to happen, both sides have to abandon maximalist aspirations and accept what is feasible (and mutually acceptable), rather that what is deemed individually desirable.

A much needed historic compromise between Greece and Turkey in the Aegean must rest on two general and two operational principles of foreign policy. The first general principle involves the mutual denunciation of the use of force by both Greece and Turkey. The second general principle provides that the Greek-Turkish differences in the Aegean will follow the road of peaceful settlement involving time-tested methods such as bilateral negotiations and – in case of deadlocks – conciliation, good offices, mediation, arbitration and adjudication. The two operational principles apply to Turkey and Greece respectively. For the benefit of Turkey, it must be understood that the Aegean will not be transformed into a 'Greek lake'. For the benefit of Greece, it must be also understood that the Aegean will not be *partitioned* or *subdivided* in a fashion that *enclaves* Greek territories (the eastern Aegean and the Dodecanese islands) into a Turkish zone of functional responsibility.

Following a potential grand settlement, both Greece and Turkey will increase significantly their trade, tourism, investment and joint ventures at home and abroad. Greece will, also, abandon its policy of 'linkage' vis-à-vis Turkey's accession strategy to the European Union and will, in fact, seek to facilitate Turkish entry. Simply, a European Turkey will be for Greece a much easier neighbour to live with than an isolated and militaristic Turkey.

Notes

1. For a useful survey of the foreign policy debate in Greece along realist (pessimist) and

pluralist (optimist) lines, see Contantinides (1996). On the same debate see also Fatouros, (undated). The literature on Greece's political, economic, social cultural and diplomatic profiles in the English language is quite rich and steadily growing. For an inclusive and useful annotated bibliographical guide see Veremis and Dragoumis (1998).

2. For gloom and doom scenarios regarding the Balkans, with strong recommendations that this conflict-prone region be left alone to cope with its self-made and inevitable conflicts, see Kaplan (1993) and Huntington (1996).
3. For a powerful chronicle of mediating efforts that led to the Dayton Peace accords in 1995, see Holbrooke (1998).
4. Government of Cyprus' efforts to add to its defence capabilities are designed to nudge the island toward a process of mutually agreed arms reductions and, ultimately, demilitarisation. Turkey retains an unquestioned military superiority in the Cyprus region, especially in terms of naval and air capabilities.
5. Despite a huge wave of anti-war sentiment in Greece's public opinion during the recent NATO operations in Kosovo and the Federal Republic of Yugoslavia, the Greek government adopted a careful policy of working within the NATO ranks for a peaceful settlement of the intractable problem that would permit all Kosovar – Albanian refugees to return in safety (under UN authorised auspices) to their homes while paving the way for Kosovo to gain a status of enhanced autonomy which however, would fall short of independence.
6. It should be understood that although a fair and mutually acceptable settlement of the Cyprus problem would facilitate immensely the country's EU accession, the outcome of final accession cannot be indefinitely subject to a veto of the most intransigent side.

References

Brzezinski, Z. (1993), *Out of Control: Global Turmoil on the Eve of the 21st Century*, New York: Scribner.

Chelabi, H.E. and Stepan, A. (eds) (1995), *Politics, Society and Democracy: Comparative Studies, Vol. 3 of Essays in Honour of Juan J. Linz*, Boulder, Colorado: Praeger.

Contantinides, S. (1996), 'Greek Foreign Policy, Theoretical Orientations and Praxis', *Hellenic Studies/Etudes Helleniques,* Vol. 4, No. 1, pp. 43–62.

Fatouros, A.A. (undated), 'O Polemos ston Kolpo kai oi Ellines Diethnologoi' in *Diethnes Dikaio kai Diethnis Politiki*, Thessaloniki, Vol. 21–22, pp. 221–92 [in Greek].

Fukuyama, F. (1992), *The End of History and the Last Man*, New York: Free Press.

Holbrooke, R. (1998), *To End a War*, New York: Random House.

Huntington, S.P. (1996), *The Clash of Civilizations and the Remaking of World Order*, New York: Simon and Schuster.

Kaplan, R.D. (1993), *Balkan Ghosts: A Journey Through History*, New York: St. Martin's.

Kaplan, R.D. (1994), 'The Coming Anarchy', *The Atlantic Monthly*, Vol. 273, No. 2 (February), pp. 44–76.

Kegley, C.W., Jr. (1992), 'The New Global Order: The Power of Principle in a Pluralistic World', *Ethics & International Affairs*, Vol. 6, pp. 21–42.

Kegley, C.W., Jr. (1993), 'The Neoidealist Moment in International Studies? Realist Myths and the New International Realities', *International Studies Quarterly*, Vol. 37, No. 2 (June), pp. 131–46.

Kegley, C.W., Jr. and Raymond, G.A (1994), *A Multipolar Peace? Great-Power Politics in the 21st Century*, New York: St. Martin's.

Kupchan, Charles A. and Kupchan, Clifford A. (1991), 'Concerts, Collective Security and the Future of Europe', *International Security*, Vol. 16, No. 1 (Summer), pp. 114–161.

Kupchan, Charles A. and Kupchan, Clifford A. (1995), 'The Promise of Collective Security', *International Security*, Vol. 20, No. 1 (Summer), pp. 52–61.

Mearshimer, J.J (1990a), 'Back to the Future: Instability in Europe After the Cold War', *International Security*, Vol. 15, No. 1 (Summer), pp. 5–56.

Mearshimer, J.J. (1990b), 'Why We Will Soon Miss the Cold War', *The Atlantic Monthly*, Vol. 266, No. 1 (July), pp. 35–50.

Mearshimer, J.J. (1995), 'The False Promise of International Institutions', *International Security*, Vol. 19, No. 3 (Winter), pp. 5–49.

Rummel, R.J. (1983), 'Libertarianism and International Violence', *Journal of Conflict Resolution*, Vol. 27, No. 1 (March), pp. 27–81.

Van Evera, S (1991), 'Primed for Peace: Europe After the Cold War', *International Security*, Vol. 15, No.3 (Winter), pp. 7–57.

Veremis, T. and Dragoumis, M. (1998), *'Greece'*, Oxford: World Bibliographical Series, Clio Press (revised version).

19 Kosovo: A Greek Appraisal

THANOS VEREMIS

Western policy makers are in agreement that the rights of Albanians have been violated in Kosovo and that they deserve autonomous status in this province. Unlike other places in the world however, where similar violations are only decried, in the case of Kosovo NATO members were determined to force the Serb authorities to comply with Western demands of withdrawal. How the Serbs, along with the Iraqis, became the favourite villains of Western mass-media, constitutes a case study of the failure of small and middle-ranking states to come to terms with the reality of great power politics. Today Western predisposition against Serbia is so entrenched in the media that books hostile to the Serbs are usually well received even by scholarly reviewers.[1] The Kosovo issue however defies facile explanations.

Kosovo was the first to disturb the sleep of Yugoslavia's leadership. A carry-over of nineteenth century irredentist nationalism (Jelavich, 1977, pp. 224–27), it festered throughout the twentieth century and became the harbinger of Yugoslavia's dissolution shortly after the death of Joseph Broz Tito (Woodward, 1995, pp. 94–5). The architect of the postwar state of the Southern Slavs, had taken special precautions. Having turned down Kosovo's demand for Republican status, Tito offered more autonomy, financial aid and recognition to the Albanians. The constitutional amendments of 1968 and 1971 granted Kosovo some of the prerogatives of the Republics and the status of a Socialist Autonomous Province. This process of political decentralisation crystallised in the 1974 constitution was pushed through by Tito and his Slovene deputy, Edvard Kardelj. Kosovo, recognised as a constituent element of the Yugoslav federation, was granted the right to fly the Albanian flag with the black eagle on a red background and gained policy-making rights. Furthermore, the crash programme for economic development gave it priority over other areas (Montenegro, Bosnia-Herzegovina). From 1971–75, 70 per cent of Kosovo's budget and investments came from federal sources (Pavlowich, 1988, p. 82).

The 1974 constitution granted Kosovo a direct voice at the federal level, principally through representation to federal instruments of government and state and party leaderships. The new constitution diminished Serbian control over Kosovo, and signified a generalised process of decentralisation in the federation, bringing about a certain 'localism', which soon led to friction. Instead of restraining the centrifugal forces, the ruling Communist party became the carrier of conflicts.

The *League of Communists of Yugoslavia* was divided into ethnic segments but was not democratised. It was the arena of a bitter contest between regional groups professing a communist identity but representing above all regional and ethnic interests. Thus the 1974 constitution laid the institutional ground for the trend of ethnic division which gradually alienated the peoples of Yugoslavia from Yugoslavism. It could be argued that the seventies are especially important in understanding, not only the subsequent break-up of Yugoslavia but also the nature of the Kosovo problem as it stands today. The most salient elements of Albanian Kosovar nationalism developed in those years.

The acute economic crisis in Yugoslavia of 1980 hit Kosovo hard and unemployment soared. The authorities responded with a massive expansion of education and the promotion of capital-intensive industries which did little to solve the problem. By 1981 Pristina University had 51,000 students, the highest concentration of young people in any Yugoslav institution. Harsh economic conditions and the grim prospects of job opportunities for students prolonged their university studies and contributed to the formation of an intelligentsia embracing nationalism as an outlet for its discontent. The movement for a Federated Republic of Kosovo as well as 'pan-Albanism' attracted widespread grass-root support among students and intellectuals, sparking demonstrations across Kosovo between 1968 and 1979 (Pavlowich, 1982). Whereas class cleavages were acknowledged by the Communist doctrine, ethnic cleavages were deemed the result of state of 'pseudo-consciousness' by any Marxist regime. The federal state, therefore, chose to address the problem by throwing more funds into the turbulent province.

It is evident that liberalisation, instead of pacifying the Albanians, strengthened their ethnic identity and resolve. It is equally evident that Serb nationalism draws upon this period to allege that the Serbs suffered hardships under Albanian rule. Serbs accuse ethnic Albanians of using discrimination, intimidation and even violence between 1974 and 1989 to drive them out of the region in order to create an 'ethnically pure' Kosovo. According to the estimates of Serbian Academy of Science and Arts, the extent of emigration varied from 78,000 to 102,000 in the period 1971–81 (Macura, 1982). Ethnic Albanians would claim that such emigration was due to the harsh economic conditions and the discomfort of the Serbs at the shift of power from the Serbian minority to the Albanian majority.

Tito's death in 1980 ushered in the crisis of Yugoslavia's loss of authority. Ethnic nationalism was on the rise and the Serb variety was revived out of a sense of victimisation rooted in medieval history. Tito was accused of deliberately weakening Serbia by removing 'Vardar Banovina' and Montenegro from its realm and turning the former into the Socialist Republic of Macedonia, and the latter into the Federated Republic of Montenegro, while Kosovo and Vojvodina were made autonomous provinces.

Kosovo exploded in March and April, 1981 bringing about a 'reversal of fortunes' for Kosovo Albanians. Unrest was sparked by students in Pristina, Prizren and Projujevo, protesting over their living conditions. Tensions escalated with Albanians demanding that Kosovo be accorded the status of a Federated Republic; some even calling for union with Albania and the Albanian populated region of Tetovo in the Socialist Republic of Macedonia. The Federal Army used brutal force to establish order. The number of dead varied between 500 to 1000, depending on which side was doing the reporting, but the official number of those convicted for conspiracy and irredentism was 658 and on lesser charges 2000 (Ramet, 1992, p. 196). The event caused much soul-searching in Belgrade over the 1974 reforms. Albania was singled out as the source of irredentism and the lines of communication between Tirana and Pristina were cut.

In the late 1985, the condition of the Serbs in Kosovo began to feature increasingly in the mainstream public opinion of Serbia. Some 200 prominent Belgrade intellectuals petitioned to the Yugoslav and Serbian national assemblies in January, 1986 about the plight of their brethren. By 1987, Kosovo had become the cornerstone of Serb nationalism with 60,000 Serbs signing a petition alleging 'genocide' against their kind. Slobodan Milosevic's rise to power in the Serb Communist Party exploited the nationalist tide and put an end to Tito's multiethnic politics (Glenny, 1993, p. 33).

On 28 June, 1987 – the 598th anniversary of the 1389 Kosovo battle – Milosevic, addressing a crowd at the 'field of Blackbirds', declared that the Serbs would never be vanquished again raising this national issue to the top of his agenda. By doing so he gained support among such nationalist intellectuals as Dobrice Cosic and created a firm power base to assault the leadership of the *Serbian League of Communists*. His nationalist campaign to bring Kosovo under Serb control and alter its autonomous status granted by the 1974 constitution, was a harbinger of future developments (Ramet, 1991, pp. 93–105, 99).

In March, 1989, Kosovo lost the authority to pass its own laws and on 5 July, 1990, the Serbian parliament assumed full and direct control of the province. Ethnic Albanians reacted to the seizure by boycotting the Serbian take-over and building their own parallel set of political and social institutions. Kosovo's parliament and government refused to be dissolved and went underground. On 7 September, 1990 the Kosovo Albanian legislature met in Kacanic and approved a constitution that gave Kosovo republican status within the Yugoslav federation. A year later (26–30 September, 1991), Albanians endorsed the Kacanic constitution with a self-styled referendum and on 19 October the legislature met and declared Kosovo a 'sovereign and independent state'. (This state was recognised by Albania on 22 October). On 23 December, Kosovo appealed unsuccessfully to the EU for recognition and by February, 1992 Albanian organisations claimed to have collected half a million signatures for a petition to the UN Commission of Human Rights protesting against the situation in the province, but no action was taken by the Commission.

In May, 1992, Albanian Kosovars went to the polls to elect their President and 143 Members of Parliament. While the police prohibited voting in public places, they did not make a serious effort to stop the elections altogether and the turnout was high. Ibrahim Rugova, leader of the Democratic League of Kosovo (LDK) was elected, his party winning 96 out of the 143 seats (Biberaj, 1993). Tore Bogh, head of the CSCE mission to Kosovo, soon after the expulsion of the organisation stated that the only authority recognised by ethnic Albanians in Kosovo was the 'parallel' Rugova government.[2]

The implacable Kosovo problem led to a proposition for the partition of the region and the idea of partition was repeated by the president of the Serbian Academy of Sciences and Arts, Aleksandar Despic.[3] In his speech to the Academy's annual assembly in July, 1996, Despic warned that Kosovo represented the most significant strategic problem for the future of the Serbian nation. According to him, the higher birth rate of ethnic Albanians meant that 'in twenty or thirty years (Serbia will) become a country of two nations with approximately equal numbers of people'. He concluded his speech with a proposal that talks begin 'with those who are insisting on secession of Kosovo, about a peaceful, civilised separation and demarcation in order not to repeat the tragic experiences of recent history' (Maliqi, 1996, p. 14). The shape of peace in Bosnia would also determine the future of Kosovo: If Bosnia were ultimately partitioned between Croats and Serbs, the latter would adopt a similar solution for Kosovo, as part of a Serbian ethnic consolidation. But such a development would require redistributing territory and people, a process that could involve violence.

The Dayton Agreement had profound implications on Kosovo's politics. The lessons drawn from it by many Albanian Kosovars, were the following:

- the territorial spoils of the Bosnian war were validated,
- the international position of former Yugoslavia's external borders stood firm,

Rugova's non-violent appeals to the world community for independence proved to be futile. Adem Demaci, a political dissident of the 1960s who spent many years in prison under the communist regime and subsequently became leader of the *Human Rights Council of Kosovo*, argued that Rugova's policy merely sustained the status quo while the clue to a solution of Kosovo's problem was in negotiations with Belgrade. According to Gasmend Pula, President of the *Kosova Helsinki Committee*, 'Demaci's past and his pronounced personal activism and charisma, includes remaining within the rump Yugoslav federation and despite publicly stated words of great respect for certain Serbian features, provide him also the support of more radical organisations domestically…' (Pula, 1996, pp. 4–5). On the radical side of the political spectrum there were voices calling for violent activism.

August, 1996, however, held a pleasant surprise for Kosovo. Milosevic and Rugova, agreed to end the six-year Albanian boycott of schools. If the agreement had materialised, about 300,000 children and teachers would have returned to Kosovo's schools and 12,000 students to the University (Silber, 1996). The *Memorandum of Understanding* between the two men also signified that, albeit unofficially, both leaders recognised each other's authority.[4]

A major impediment to a solution was the reluctance of the two sides to come to the negotiating table on anything but their own terms. The Kosovo Albanians shirked from any bilateral meeting that could be interpreted as an acceptance of the Serbian regime and insisted in international mediation. The Serbian government considered this a domestic dispute and overruled the presence of an international mediator.

The talks could materialise if Milosevic, or the President of Serbia, Milan Milutinovic was convinced that a third party in the discussions need not compromise the Serbian position if it was not the representative of a major Western power, but rather a nongovernmental organisation from a state in the region. A nongovernmental organisation that enjoyed the confidence of both sides could go a long way toward breaking the impasse. The role of the 'San Egidio' community in Rome in facilitating the education agreement of 1996, is an example of how small actors succeed in mediation where great powers fail (Veremis, 1998).

The cleavage between Albanians and Serbs widened in the Spring of 1998 as the Kosovo Liberation Army (KLA – UCK) made its violent entry demanding independence and refusing any communication with the authorities. The KLA shared with Kosovo's President elect, Ibrahim Rugova, a claim to independence, but unlike him, the armed rebels were not willing to wait for the prodigious demographic increase of the Albanians to overtake the Serbs. In this respect they coincided with Milosevic who was also unwilling to wait for Albanians to challenge Serb authority at the polls when they attain a critical voting mass.

Western preference for a solution of autonomy convinced both the KLA and Milosevic, although from different perspectives, that they ought to present the world with a *fait accompli*.

If Kosovo was to be partitioned, the future demarcation line drawn by the Serbs would probably circumvent Pristina to include as many Serb monuments and mining areas as possible. The percentages would be settled in the field while NATO and the EU would attempt to discourage the FYROM Albanians from following the Kosovo example. Despite US envoy Richard Holbrooke's dire predictions, Greece is in no danger of being entangled in a proverbial Balkan war, but is opposed to any anomaly that would destabilise the region and, will have to devise ways of assisting FYROM to maintain its status quo. Mr. Gligorov is confronted with difficult decisions concerning the survival of FYROM.

On 13 October, 1998, American Secretary of State, Madeleine Albright, summoned all NATO foreign ministers to approve the Activation Orders (ACTORDS) that would allow air strikes against Serb targets in Kosovo and elsewhere in Serbia, if President of FRY, Milosevic, failed to comply with UN Security Council decision (1199) of withdrawing his forces from the field of battle.

Although there is little doubt as to who the West considered the villain in this conflict, there were certain factors that inhibited such a radical undertaking.

First of all the attack directed against the forces of a sovereign state exercising (albeit in a brutal manner) authority within its territory, would create a problematic international precedent. In the case of Bosnia, the government of that state invited the air strikes, not so in Serbia. The UN Security Council decision no doubt offered legitimacy to the act, but then scores of UN decisions in Cyprus were ignored throughout the past twenty-four years. The humanitarian principle would have been an undisputed legitimiser if the bombing of states perpetrating atrocities against their citizens had occurred consistently against friend and foe, weak and strong, alike.

The Serbian authorities (although in the wrong) were a convenient target. They have a death wish which they exhibit consistently, they have no friends in the West (thanks to Western mass media) and they represent a weak state. Attacking them risked only the discontent of a former superpower which has come to bad days.

A serious factor, which inhibited Western military action until March, 1999, was FYROM. US Ambassador to Skopje, Christopher Hill, who authored the various versions of the *Interim Accord*, was preoccupied with the impact of any Kosovo solution on FYROM. Independence would most likely activate the process of fusion between Kosovo and the Western part of FYROM which is populated by Albanians. A secession of the FYROM Albanians with a little help of the KLA, would cripple that state and could set in motion its eventual dissolution.

The Kosovar Albanians have nurtured a just cause but their leader's peaceful resistance since 1989 when their autonomous status was cancelled, failed to alert Western attention. The KLA introduced tactics which in other occasions were identified by Western governments as acts of terrorism and predictably attracted both massive Serb reprisals and Western attention. Even Mr. Holbrooke appeared in a photograph with KLA representatives and by doing so he acknowledged its role in the solution of the Kosovo problem. Unlike the West however, which to this day insists on autonomy for the Albanian Kosovars, President Rugova and the KLA insisted on independence (Caplan, 1998, p. 789).

The 13 October, 1998, agreement between Richard Holbrooke and Slobodan Milosevic that averted NATO strikes in Kosovo was yet another reminder to the European onlookers that they had once again remained on the sidelines of Balkan developments (International Herald Tribune, 1998, p. 1). As with Bosnia, Kosovo sharpened tensions between the US and the EU over security issues and many Europeans felt that the American envoy did not even take the trouble to send them a copy of the agreement with the Serb Leader. (The Germans waited for two days before a copy of the accord was obtained through the Embassy of the FRY in Bonn.) To add insult to injury, Mr. Holbrooke failed to attend a meeting of the *Contact Group* on 15 October, two days after the agreement had been concluded in Belgrade. It was, after all, that group – made up of Britain, France, Germany, Italy, Russia and the United States, that had given him his mandate to speak with the Yugoslav president (Cohen, 1998).

With the withdrawal of the Serb forces the KLA predictably made progress in resuming control of Kosovo. By mid-November, 1998 approximately one third of the countryside was patrolled and policed by the guerilla forces, which secured passage to travellers or arrested and detained Serbs. The President of the FRY threatened the Albanians with renewed hostilities if movement in Kosovo was not restored according to the provisions of his accord with Holbrooke.

The cleavage between the autonomy that the international community was willing to offer the Kosovar Albanians, and the full independence they demanded, could have been bridged by the ELIAMEP proposal of June, 1998. Evangelos Kofos who was responsible for drafting the proposal, introduced a timeframe that would allow a careful transition from one phase to another with a minimum of friction.[5] The pacification of the region and the solution of the problem, according to the proposal, evolves in four phases:

Phase One During the first phase, to be concluded on a predetermined time limit, the parties would agree on the reorganisation of the province as an Autonomous Region, composed of Albanian and Serb cantons. The Serb cantons would include areas of strong symbolic value to the Serbs. Percentages of land distribution would be an issue of mutual agreement, but it could not surpass the limit of 30 per cent for the Serb cantons. Some minor movement of population on a voluntary basis – with strong incentives for those moving – might be necessary to ensure that the respective ethnic groups – Albanians and Serbs – enjoy relative majority in their respective cantons.

Phase Two Upon finalisation of the arrangements agreed upon, the second phase of the agreement would come into force by the admittance of the 'Autonomous Kosovo Region' (AKR), as a self-ruled administrative entity within the Republic of Serbia. There will be three layers of administration: cantonal, regional and republican. Specific lines of self-rule will be drawn by negotiations. The AKR and its cantons would enjoy extensive self-rule in all domains, including public order, with exception of national defence and foreign policy.

Phase Three In phase three, the AKR would be allowed, following a period of up to 10 years, to decide to join the Yugoslav Federation as a federated 'Republic of Kosovo', (RK) sharing equal rights with Serbia and Montenegro, which do not include the right of secession.

Phase Four After an additional period of 10–15 years, phase four would come into effect, whereby the cantons of the Republic of Kosovo by plebiscite could exercise the right of self-determination for establishing an independent state. Those cantons deciding against independence could choose to join one or the other remaining constituent states of the Yugoslav federation. Constitutional provisions, reinforced by international guarantees, would ensure that the putative independent state would commit itself not to opt for union with another state.

Understandably, the provisions of such an agreement would require the solemn and binding guarantee of an international treaty, endorsed either by the Security Council of the United Nations, or by other relevant international bodies.

If this proposal had been adopted then, (in some miraculous way), the subsequent trials and tribulations of Serbia, Kosovo and the USA, perhaps would not have taken place.

The negotiations over the Rambouillet accord in February and March, 1999 were eminently successful with the Kosovar Albanians because their leaders, and more specifically, Veton Surroi, grasped the opportunity of an autonomy guaranteed by the West to overcome the deadly stalemate. Their hope, according to Surroi, was that a recovery of functional autonomy for Kosovo would generate a quantum leap in Serbo-Albanian relations and would establish new rules of the game in the region.

Although their serve was masterful, the Albanians failed to anticipate the combination of responses by Milosevic and their NATO supporters. The outcome was in keeping with a Quentin Tarantino script rather than the Dayton accord. The prospect of an autonomy for Kosovo that would allow the Albanians to prosper within Serbia and even acquire a demographic edge in a few decades, was certainly not an option welcome to the Serbs. Milosevic's priority had been either to dominate Kosovo, or partition it and preserve for Serbia whatever could be salvaged of the Serb heritage.[6] His chance to evade the likelihood was provided by NATO and the US with their insistence that the ground troops of the implementation force in Kosovo would be provided by the Atlantic Alliance, rather than any other institution involving Russia. In fact the make-up of the implementation forces was less important than the substance of the accord: the autonomous status of Kosovo as seen by the accord was not a lasting arrangement. Independence through a referendum would in time occur creating a precedent for FYROM.

The protracted NATO bombing of Yugoslavia hastened the process that the alliance professed it would arrest. In fact President Clinton's second and third aim (the first being, 'to demonstrate the seriousness of NATO's purpose') to prevent further violence against the Kosovan population and to preserve regional stability, were not served by NATO's action. Milosevic was prepared to take the punishment while proceeding to ethnically cleanse North-Western Kosovo and at the same time consolidated his authority at home. His view that the West tricked him into signing the Dayton accord with a guarantee of Yugoslavia's territorial integrity, has now become common currency in Serbia.

Western governments have used various arguments to justify NATO action in legal terms. The most credible is that Milosevic has violated a Security Council resolution adopted last October, that imposed a ceasefire in Kosovo and set limits on the Yugoslav forces in the province. The resolution threatened action if Belgrade resisted and invoked chapter VII of the UN Charter, which calls for the use of force to uphold international peace and security (Taylor, 1999). The question that lingers is why did the Alliance choose to enforce this resolution among many that remain inert?

The post-Milosevic era that Western governments hoped to accelerate through NATO action might witness either the disintegration of Yugoslavia into a number of non-viable micro-states, or a decimated Serbia with its present leadership still lodged into power. Milosevic's survival has been predicated on the continuation of the string of anomalies that bedevil his federation and postpone the prospect of reconstruction in this Balkan backwater. The question now is whether the rest of Southeastern Europe can pursue its development and its linkage with the European Union and NATO without Yugoslavia. The stabilisation and consolidation of boundaries among Serbia and its southern neighbours ought to become a major priority of the West because a disintegration of Yugoslavia could release a chain-reaction of similar phenomena in the region.

The 'day after' the imbroglio, poses a formidable challenge to our Alliance and our European community. If we do not tend to a speedy reconstruction of Serbia and Kosovo so that they may resume their ability to support their respective populations, we run the risk of being on the receiving end of a new wave of economic refugees and a surge of criminality that will affect the development of South-Eastern Europe.

The displacement of people within the southern Balkans, already threaten the integrity of the Former Yugoslav Republic of Macedonia and the precarious stability of Albania. Furthermore, the Kosovo Liberation Army (KLA – UCK) will loom large in Kosovo. Its Western trained forces will not easily come to terms with Pristina's political moderates and will strive for the Greater Albania at the expense of stability in Skopje and Tirana. We should beat them to their game by emancipating Kosovo now.

All the suffering and damage caused by these two wars (or a war within a war) will have come to naught if any settlement of this long standing problem reverts to a fragile concept of autonomy under Serbian sovereignty. The horrors of ethnic cleansing have excluded the possibility of symbiosis and therefore it may be wiser to look for a formula that would reestablish the two communities apart. A bizonal, bicommunal trusteeship of the UN could in five or ten years evolve, if the two communities choose, into a small part that will unite with Serbia and a larger one that may constitute an independent Kosovo.[7]

The Atlantic Alliance and the European Union will have to guarantee the integrity of the state's boundaries with FYROM and Albania so that no irredentist claim will affect relations with its neighbours. In the process of state-building, a new security force will replace the KLA which was groomed by NATO as a substitute for Western reluctance to commit ground troops against the Serb army in Kosovo. The KLA, according to the Petersburg agreement, will be disarmed after Kosovo is evacuated from Serb forces. The future regime of the bizonal and later, independent entity will greatly depend on the return of the politicians (Rugova, Surroi, Shalla,

Kosumi, Tahiri, etc.) to counter the monopoly of the KLA warlords who are now calling the shots.

The prospect of reconstruction does not look bright for Serbia. Besides the fact that NATO and the EU will continue to keep the Serbs isolated from the rest of the world so long as they don't overthrow their leader, the country has no collateral (besides 'collateral damage') to offer in order to finance the rebuilding of its infrastructure.

The outcome of any solution in Kosovo and its impact on the region will also enhance or diminish NATO's credibility. In the meantime we are confronted with a multifaceted catastrophe that the spokesmen of this war do not fully convey to their public. Some supporters of the NATO team were mainly concerned with the outcome of this match, regardless of its long-term effects on the terrain. Today the terrain has become unable to support its population.

Those of the team who are uncomfortably situated closer to the catastrophe and will reap its consequences much quicker than the rest of Europe, are also fearful of NATO's future. If its vocation and the role of its European partners are not clearly defined, this unique institution runs the risk of becoming the plaything of decision makers who will evoke moral principles to justify an unbridled activism.

Notes

1. Malcolm (1998), is probably the most explicit case of one-sided analysis. The book enjoyed warm reception by reviewers in the *Times Literary Supplement*, the *Economist*, the *New York Review of Books*, etc. The sole exception was Aleksa Djila's scathing review in *Foreign Affairs* (September–October, 1998) in which, among others, he points out the inconsistency of Malcolm's views on Bosnia and Kosovo. Whereas he is a strong advocate of restoring a unified state in the former, he pleads the cause of secession for the latter.
2. The CSCE mission was expelled from Kosovo by the Serb authorities after the expulsion of the FRY from the organisation.
3. Kristic (1995), is discussed by Islami, H. (1995), pp. 3.
4. For the text of the Milosevic-Rugova agreement, see ELIAMEP, Kosovo, pp. 40–41
5. For a detailed expose see, Kofos, E. and Veremis (1998, pp. 131–46).
6. For an early view on the partition of Kosovo see Kristic, B. (1995).
7. See Veremis and Triantaphylou (1999).

References

Biberaj, E. (1993), 'Kosovo. The Balkan Powder Keg', *Conflict Study*, Research Institute for the Study of Conflict and Terrorism, February.

Caplan, R. (1998), 'International Diplomacy and the Crisis in Kosovo', *International Affairs*, Vol. 74, No. 4, October.

Cohen, R. (1998), 'Kosovo Crisis Strains Relations Between the US and Europe', *The New York Times*, November 10.

ELIAMEP (1998), *Kosovo. Avoiding Another Balkan War*, Athens.

Glenny, M. (1993), *The Fall of Yugoslavia*, London: Penguin Books.

Greenwood, C. (1999), 'Yes, But is the War Legal?', *Observer*, March 28.

International Herald Tribune (1998), 'Tallying the Kosovo Deal', November, p. 1.

Islami, H. (1995), 'Albanophobia and the Great-Serbian Interests', *Koha*, 3 May.

Jelavich, C. and Jelavich, B. (1977), *The Establishment of the Balkan National States 1804–1920*, Seattle: University of Washington Press.

Kofos, E. and Veremis (1998), 'Kosovo: Efforts to Solve the Impasse', *The International Spectator*, Vol. 33, No. 2, April–June, pp.131–46.

Kristic, B. (1995), *Kosovo between the Historical and Ethnic Rights*, Belgrade.

Macura, M. (ed) (1982), 'The Migration of Serbs and Montenegrins from Kosovo and Metohija' in *Serbian Academy of Science and Arts, Demographic Studies*, Vol. III, Belgrade.

Malcolm, N. (1998), *Kosovo. A Short History*, London: Macmillan.

Maliqi, S. (1996), 'Jettisoned to Keep SS Serbia Afloat?', *War Report*, No. 43, July.

Pavlowich, S.K. (1982) 'Kosovo: An Analysis of Yugoslavia's Albanian Problem', *Conflict Studies*, no. 137/38, December.

Pavlowich, S.K. (1988), *The Improbable Survivor. Yugoslavia and its Problems. 1918–1988*, London: C. Hurst & Co.

Pula, G. (1996), 'Modalities of Self Determination – The Case of Kosova as a Structural Issue for Lasting Stability in the Balkans', *Sudeosteuropa*, 45 Jhg.

Ramet, P. (1991), 'Serbia's Slobodan Milosevich: A Profile', *Orbis*, Foreign Policy Research Institute , Vol. 35, Winter, pp. 93–105.

Ramet, S.P. (1992), *Nationalism and Federalism in Yugoslavia*, Indiana University Press.

Silber, L. (1996), *Financial Times*, 3 September.

Taylor, P. (1999), 'NATO Action Rests on Dubious Legal Grounds', *Athens News*, 25 March.

Veremis, T. (1998), 'How Mediation Could Help Resolve the Kosovo Crisis', *International Herald Tribune*, 13 March.

Veremis, T. and Triantaphyllou, D. (1999), *Kosovo and the Albanian Dimension in Southeastern Europe*, Athens: ELIAMEP.

Woodward, S. (1995), *Balkan Tragedy. Chaos and Dissolution after the Cold War*, Washington DC: The Brookings Institution.

20 Greece's Contribution to European Political Cooperation Policies Towards Former Yugoslavia, June 1991–January 1992: An Institutional Analysis

ARISTOTLE TZIAMPIRIS

Introduction

The disintegration of Yugoslavia has been the most violent event in Europe since the conclusion of the Greek Civil War in 1949. The resolution of the conflict eventually required the active involvement of several countries and organisations. Beginning in the Summer of 1991, and for a significant period of time, European Political Cooperation (EPC) was exclusively or primarily responsible for addressing the many problems emanating from the war. As an EPC member state neighbouring Yugoslavia, Greece had undisputed and significant security and foreign policy interests in the region, as well as the power to veto all EPC decisions.

Despite the seriousness of the crisis and its importance to Greece, the actions of the country's government have been severely criticised, and often portrayed as extremely non-cooperative and counter-productive.[1] The perception is that Greece hampered efforts to contain and end the Yugoslav War primarily because of its dispute with the Former Yugoslav Republic of Macedonia (FYROM).[2] This dispute essentially constituted the more recent episode of the Macedonian Question.[3]

A closer examination of Greece's behaviour reveals that the country's government pursued politics of cooperation towards former Yugoslavia during the brief but important period of June 1991–January 1992, thus contributing substantially to EPC's efforts to resolve the conflict. It is the purpose of this essay to describe and explain on the basis of institutionalist theory, Greece's cooperative foreign policy record during those months. At this point, it should be clarified that EPC will be viewed as a regime, thus allowing the application of theory of institutionalism.[4] Furthermore, cooperation will be taken to occur 'when actors adjust their behaviour to the actual or anticipated preferences of others, through a process of policy coordination'.[5]

Yugoslavia Disintegrates, EPC Mediates, and Greece Cooperates

The end of the Second World War found Marshall Tito and his communist partisans in control of Yugoslavia. The country was divided into six republics: Bosnia-Herzegovina, Croatia, Macedonia, Montenegro, Serbia, and Slovenia.[6] Yugoslavia became a particularly stable and prosperous (by socialist standards) country, 'with an average annual economic growth [for the years 1965–89] of 6.3 per cent'.[7] However, despite its apparent affluence and stability, Yugoslavia was actually travelling along a perilous path. During the 1990 elections, nationalists came to power in almost all of the republics, and tensions greatly intensified.[8]

Given the prospects for instability, EPC member states adopted a stance advocating a '*united* and democratic Yugoslavia' and offered substantial economic incentives.[9] However, the process of Yugoslavia's disintegration soon became irrevocable. Thus, on 25 June 1991, Croatia and Slovenia declared their independence. The war in Yugoslavia began two days later, when the Serb-controlled Yugoslav National Army (JNA) attacked Slovenia. On the same day, EPC's Foreign Ministers were meeting at Luxembourg, and it was immediately decided that the Troika be dispatched to Yugoslavia.[10] It proposed a plan that included the suspension of all declarations of independence for three months, the return of the army to its barracks, as well as other measures that aimed at solving the country's constitutional crisis.[11] Although all sides agreed to these measures, none of them were implemented, and the Troika was forced to go back on 30 June, this time threatening the suspension of aid.

While hostilities continued in Slovenia, the republic's army proved surprisingly successful in its operations against the JNA. In order to increase the pressure and achieve a meaningful settlement, the Extraordinary EPC Ministerial meeting of 5 July 1991 decided that EPC would impose an arms embargo on all Yugoslav republics.[12] Greece endorsed this decision, as well as the warning that unless agreement was reached, the Second and Third Financial Protocols with Yugoslavia would be suspended. These protocols constituted 'the largest aid package which the EC has ever given to an individual state', worth some $1 billion.[13]

On 5 July, the Committee of Senior Officials (CSO) of the Conference on Security and Cooperation in Europe (CSCE) accepted the EPC plan, which primarily called for the cessation of hostilities.[14] This acceptance also signalled the fact that the CSCE was essentially relinquishing its responsibilities for the resolution of the war in Yugoslavia. Perhaps for the first time in several decades, EPC's members were being assigned the leading and almost exclusive role in dealing with an important international crisis.

EPC efforts to reach a settlement seemed to culminate with the signing of the Brioni Accord on 7 July.[15] The agreement provided for the withdrawing of the JNA forces from Slovenia, and thus marked the end of what was a limited war that had lasted ten days. Furthermore, it was decided to introduce an EPC sponsored mission to monitor ceasefires, while there was agreement to begin negotiations on all aspects of the future of Yugoslavia before 1 August.

The Troika missions and Brioni Accord bought a brief period of time. The war had ended in Slovenia and had not yet moved to any other of the Yugoslav republics. Nevertheless, it had become apparent to most observers that, in the words of Jacques Delors: 'the Yugoslav federation in its present form has had its day.'[16] On 13 July the Dutch Presidency sent a telegram to the other EPC members, suggesting that they move towards the 'voluntary redrawing of internal borders as a possible solution'.[17] The Greek government disagreed, but its negative assessment did not cause any problems. The Dutch proposal to tinker with borders prior to recognition failed to win any EPC adherents, and was thus not pursued any further.

During the month of August, war broke out in Croatia. There the JNA proved more efficient than in Slovenia, achieving the control of almost a fourth of the country by early September. Faced with this development, Greece agreed with the 27 August EPC Ministerial meeting resolution to express its dismay. The meeting made perfectly clear that the Serb irregular forces in Croatia and the JNA were being considered as responsible for the outbreak of violence in Croatia.[18] The Greek Foreign Minister Antonis Samaras also decided with his counterparts to establish a Peace Conference and an Arbitration procedure within this larger framework.[19] The procedure was supposed to consist of a five member Arbitration Commission (AC), with two members being appointed by the Yugoslav Federal Presidency. The Yugoslav representation failed to materialise, and the AC eventually consisted solely of EPC member state appointees, who were also Presidents of their country's Constitutional Court. It was chaired by the French Robert Badinter.[20]

During the 27 August EPC meeting, Samaras expressed his government's concern over what eventually became an extremely contentious issue by submitting a Memorandum on Yugoslav Macedonia.[21] It began by suggesting that Kosovo and Yugoslav Macedonia might require different EPC approaches than the ones pursued in Slovenia and Croatia. In an academic-like, diplomatic but ultimately alarmist tone, it argued that a declaration of independence by Yugoslav Macedonia would create serious problems. The state would not be economically viable, while its huge Albanian minority would be a source of instability and perhaps even war.

Given this perception of a potentially explosive situation, it became evident that the Greek government did not welcome a declaration of independence. However the Memorandum did not propose to block or postpone such actions as they were seen as imminent. Rather, the document was intended to clarify possible actions that would have been considered unfriendly and provocative by Greece. Thus, the issue of the new state's name came to the forefront:

> The Greeks also strongly contest the use of the traditionally Greek name of Macedonia for identifying a *Slavic people*...the Greeks believe that the Macedonian name is part of their own historical heritage and should not be used to identify, *in an ethnic sense*, another nation.[22]

Although Greek sensitivity about the name Macedonia was emphasised, the Memorandum did not indicate a precise Greek position on the name issue. The objection to the ethnological use of the name Macedonia, together with the fact that on five occasions the document describes the inhabitants of Yugoslav Macedonia as Slav-Macedonians, possibly suggested that Greece might have been open to a compromise name that would have included the term Macedonia.[23]

The Intensification of Greek Cooperation

On 8 September 1991, the Yugoslav Republic of Macedonia held a referendum on its independence. According to the official results, the turnout was 72.16 per cent, and of those voting 96.44 per cent expressed their support for a 'sovereign and independent state of Macedonia, with the right to enter in a future union of sovereign states of Yugoslavia'.[24] On the basis of this referendum, the Assembly of the Yugoslav Republic of Macedonia declared the state's independence on 17 September.[25]

Greek Prime Minister Konstantinos Mitsotakis responded to the referendum results by emphasising that 'the position of the Greek government, as regards the name that [the inhabitants of the Yugoslav Republic of Macedonia] use is given, self-evident and shared by the entire Greek nation.'[26] This statement sent a strong message that the name of the new republic was of importance to both the Greek people and government. At the same time, it did not reject or propose any specific name, thus allowing substantial scope for negotiation and a possible compromise.[27]

Meanwhile, Greek cooperation within EPC both continued and intensified in several key issue areas. The first involved the singling out and verbal condemnation of the Serbian side as responsible for the atrocities and the spreading of the war to Croatia. Instances of Greek cooperation on this issue are numerous, and include the 6 October 1991 informal meeting of the Ministers of Foreign Affairs that condemned the JNA, as well as the 27 October EPC declaration on Dubrovnik which consisted of a strongly worded and largely justified attack on Serbian military actions.[28]

EPC's condemnation of the Serbs was not only limited to verbal accusations, as it soon incorporated the application of additional economic sanctions, while simultaneously giving preferential treatment to the cooperating republics including FYROM. Thus, on 6 October 1991 EPC's Foreign Ministers threatened to terminate the Cooperation and Trade agreement with Yugoslavia;[29] and on 8 November, there was an EPC decision on the imposition of a series of economic sanctions.[30] EPC's intention to request a UN Security Council imposed oil embargo was also stated. Again, it was made perfectly clear that these punitive actions would be taken only against the parties that were not cooperating 'in a peaceful way towards a comprehensive political solution on the basis of the EC proposals'.[31]

The cooperating republics were eventually rewarded in the 2 December General Affairs Council meeting which decided a series of positive measures that reversed most of the 8 November sanctions.[32] On the same day, a Council Regulation was issued, 'concerning the arrangements applicable to the import of products originating in the Republics of Bosnia-Herzegovina, *Macedonia*, Slovenia and Croatia'.[33] Given Greece's Memorandum on Yugoslav Macedonia and subsequent actions, it is striking to see that the term Republic of Macedonia is used in an official Council document. This did not suggest a Greek intention to recognise the state with this name, since Foreign Minister Samaras had made his agreement to these measures conditional upon the incorporation of the following statement: 'the Twelve [are] anxious to point out that the adoption of these measures was entirely without prejudice to the question of recognising the Republics.'[34] As will be demonstrated, this was a deliberate decision that fitted well with Greece's cooperative strategy.

Another area of Greek cooperation involved decisions that encouraged various Yugoslav republics to request EPC recognition. On October 6, Greece and its EPC partners:

> Agreed that a political solution should be sought in the perspective of recognition of the independence of those republics wishing it, at the end of a negotiating process conducted in good faith and involving all parties.[35]

Undoubtedly, these statements paved the way for FYROM to request recognition. The Greek government though, did not attempt to utilise this early opportunity, in order to express concerns or insert conditions relating to a possible application by FYROM.

On 7 December, 1991, the AC published its first opinion, which concluded that 'the Socialist Republic of Yugoslavia is in the process of dissolution'.[36] Consequently, it was becoming increasingly difficult for the EPC member states to avoid facing the issue of recognising at least some of the Yugoslav republics.

The Issue of Recognition

The issue of recognition was confronted by the Greek government during a 4 December 1991 Cabinet meeting.[37] According to the minutes, there was a decision to support the continuation of a united Yugoslavia. Furthermore,

> The government set three conditions to the Skopje Republic [FYROM], which must be accepted, if recognition is wanted: First, [it must] change the name 'Macedonia' *which has a geographic but not an ethnic basis*, second, [it must] acknowledge that it has no territorial claims against our country, and, third, [it must] acknowledge that no 'Macedonian Minority' exists in Greece.[38]

As the Maastricht Summit approached, German pressure for the recognition of Croatia and Slovenia intensified. In response to this pressure, an Extraordinary EPC Ministerial Meeting was convened in Brussels on 15 December 1991.[39] The agreement that was eventually reached early in the morning signalled the official and irreversible end of the Socialist Federal Republic of Yugoslavia. The German Foreign Minister's adamant stance to unilaterally recognise at least some of the Yugoslav republics was instrumental in determining the outcome of the meeting. Thus, it seems that in order to at least preserve a semblance of the principle of solidarity, EPC's Foreign Ministers accepted Germany's position. More specifically, a common position was adopted on the conditions to be satisfied before preceding to recognise the various republics.[40] Applications were to be submitted by 23 December, and it was agreed that the AC would provide advice concerning the merits of the various applications.

Samaras has never denied that he had serious misgivings about the consequences of the 16 December meeting. Because of the circumstances however, the Greek Foreign Minister believed that vetoing all of the decisions would have been counter-productive. In order to adequately address his country's concerns, he forcefully insisted that a paragraph stating additional conditions that would apply to FYROM's probable application for recognition be inserted. Italian Foreign Minister de Michelis insisted that FYROM be recognised, but was rebuffed by Samaras who thus became the target of an undiplomatic verbal assault. He claims that de Michelis angrily yelled at him: 'You are a pirate and a blackmailer! This is piracy!'[41]

Eventually, there was agreement on the following three conditions:

> The Community and its member States also require a Yugoslav Republic to commit itself, prior to recognition, to adopt constitutional and political guarantees ensuring that it has no territorial claims towards a neighbouring Community State and that it will conduct no hostile propaganda activities versus a neighbouring Community State, *including the use of a denomination which implies territorial claims*.[42]

Of these conditions, the last proved ambiguous, controversial, and consequential.

Samaras claims that during the 16 December meeting, he fulfilled his government's 4 December instructions about FYROM. This claim is accurate in regards to the new republic's name, since the phrasing of the third condition is consistent with both the 4 December Cabinet meeting decision and the Memorandum on Yugoslav Macedonia. The former Foreign Minister though underestimated or misunderstood the possibility that according to these documents, a name with a geographic and not an ethnic designation for the new republic, in the line of Upper Macedonia or Vardar Macedonia, was at the very least debatable, if not acceptable.[43]

News of the 16 December agreement on the three conditions was met with enthusiasm in Greece. The government announced 'a great national success', while the Panhellenic Socialist Movement (PASOK) which was the main opposition party, declared that the agreement constituted a 'positive event'.[44] Importantly, the official and celebratory Greek statements did not include a *restrictive* interpretation of the third EPC condition, according to which the use of the term Macedonia would have been excluded in every possible way from FYROM's name.[45]

On 22 December 1991, the Foreign Ministry's press spokesperson, Ambassador Kalamidas was asked 'if our [EPC] colleagues pressure us for a synthetic name [i.e. one including the term Macedonia], will we deny it?'[46] He replied that 'it is self-evident, there is no issue of us retreating. What does a synthetic name mean?' This exchange constitutes the first indication of a possible hard-line and restrictive interpretation of the third EPC condition. However, there was an element of vagueness in Kalamidas' response. Furthermore, such an interpretation could not have possibly been deduced from any document, Cabinet decision or statement that the Prime Minister had made following the 16 December EPC meeting. In other words, this was not the official position of the Greek government.

Meanwhile, FYROM had applied for Community recognition on 20 December, announcing its intention to satisfy all necessary conditions.[47] The new republic's Parliament inserted two amendments to the constitution on 6 January 1992. The first denied that FYROM harboured any territorial ambitions towards neighbouring states, while the second promised that 'The Republic shall not interfere in the sovereign rights of other states and their internal affairs'.[48] In addition to these amendments, FYROM provided a series of answers and documents to the Badinter Commission.[49]

While the AC was deliberating, Greece gave further indication of the importance that was being placed on the new republic's name. In a 3 January 1992 letter to the Community Heads of Government, Greek President Konstantinos Karamanlis wrote that the Republic's name was of '*fundamental importance* to Greece...This republic has absolutely no right, neither historical nor ethnological, to use the name Macedonia'.[50] Significantly, this phrasing did not endorse a restrictive interpretation of the third EPC condition.

On the same day, a meeting took place in a central Athens Hotel between representatives of FYROM's and Greece's Foreign Ministries. It was the first instance of the two states talking directly and publicly since the disintegration of Yugoslavia had begun. The reason is related to the 16 December 1991 EPC meeting, where Samaras had agreed that Greece would make an effort, at a bilateral level, to resolve the dispute with FYROM.[51] Hence, the decision to hold this meeting can be viewed as another example of the politics of cooperation and relative flexibility that were pursued by Greece. However, FYROM's representatives had specific instructions not to address the third EPC condition. Ambassador Kalamidas who was also present (but not a direct participant), called Samaras to inform him of developments. He then proceeded to give a press conference announcing that because of the inability to discuss the new republic's name, talks were being abandoned.

A few days later (11 January), the AC ruled that FYROM fully complied with EPC's guidelines for recognition, and emphasised the republic's undertaking to refrain from the conduct of hostile propaganda.[52] Most importantly, the AC took the view

> That the Republic of Macedonia has, moreover, renounced all territorial claims of any kind in unambiguous statements binding in international law; [and] that *the use of the name 'Macedonia' cannot therefore imply any territorial claim against another State*.[53]

The Badinter Commission's ruling dealt a serious blow to Greek arguments on this issue. However, by also ruling against the recognition of Croatia and Bosnia-Herzegovina, it presented Greek diplomacy with an opportunity.[54] Seeking EPC support, Mitsotakis flew to Rome and Bonn on 14 January and met with Prime Minister Andreotti and Chancellor Kohl. He seems to have pledged that Greece would support the recognition of Croatia, and in turn gained their agreement that there would be no EPC recognition of FYROM unless the republic complied with EPC's three conditions. Given these developments, on 15 January 1992, EPC decided to largely ignore the advice of the AC and recognise Slovenia and Croatia, but not FYROM.[55]

This decision marks the end of a period during which the Greek government practised politics of cooperation and moderation towards former Yugoslavia and FYROM. Between June 1991 and January 1992, Greece cooperated consistently within EPC on almost all the issues that arose from the dissolution of Yugoslavia, thus contributing to efforts to contain and end the war. The country's veto power was not utilised and essentially never even threatened. Greece supported the June 1991 position to maintain a united Yugoslavia, but also signed the 16 December 1991 EPC declaration that formalised the acceptance of Yugoslavia's disintegration. The Greek government agreed to the verbal condemnation of Serbia, as well as on the selective application of sanctions that primarily targeted the Serbs. Furthermore, Greece agreed to the establishment of the Peace Conference, the creation of the Arbitration Commission and the recognition of Croatia and Slovenia.

Greek behaviour towards FYROM was primarily marked by moderation and a willingness to cooperate. On the most contentious issue that involved the republic's name, Greece made evident its disagreement on the name Macedonia. Nevertheless, the possibility of reaching a compromise on a name with a geographic designation for FYROM was consistently left open in almost all major Greek decisions, documents and statements. They include the 27 August 1991 Memorandum on Yugoslav Macedonia, Mitsotakis' response to FYROM's referendum on independence, the 4 December 1991 Cabinet meeting decisions and Karamanlis' 3 January 1992 letter to the Community's Heads of Government. Significantly, some possibility of a compromise on FYROM's name was allowed under the conditions agreed in the 16 December 1991 EPC meeting. Finally, Greece organised a bilateral meeting between Foreign Ministry representatives of the two states on 3 January 1992, and even signed a Council document that referred to the Republic of Macedonia on 2 December 1991.

Institutionalist Relevance

Institutionalist theory emphasises the role of institutions and essentially ignores domestic politics.[56] As regards this approach, the theory seems to be vindicated in explaining Greece's foreign policy during the June 1991–January 1992 period. In these months, domestic politics simply did not play a significant role.

More specifically, there were almost no particular domestic developments that determined or influenced to any important degree the politics of Greek cooperation and moderation. The one major exception is related to Greece's failure to present an acceptable nominee to the AC. The country lacks a Constitutional Court, and the closest equivalent is the Council of the State (Semvouleo tis Epikrateias). Its President Mr. Botopoulos, although perfectly qualified, was considered to be affiliated with PASOK and as a result was side-stepped. Mitsotakis nominated a more politically friendly Vice-President of the Council, Mr. Degleris.[57]

Not surprisingly, given the stipulation of the EPC decision that only Presidents of Constitutional Courts were to be nominated, Mr. Degleris failed even to be considered for appointment, thus depriving Greece of a chance to have a national representative on the AC. However, even if a proper candidate was nominated, there would have been no guarantee of appointment.

In analysing institutionalist relevance, it is crucial to stress that Greek decision makers including the then Prime Minister and Foreign Minister, believed that it was essential that their state be viewed by its EPC partners as contributing to the solution of the Yugoslav conflict. They also desired to portray Greece as a country with legitimate concerns in the region. The ultimate goal was to create a reputation of trustworthiness and responsibility, as well as a sense of debt, goodwill and understanding.[58]

These reputational concerns and goals were ultimately produced by the 'shadow of the future' cast by the EPC regime.[59] Greek officials were fully aware that the regime would be responsible for many subsequent decisions that would almost certainly be of considerable importance to their country.[60] Such anticipated regime decisions covered developments in Yugoslavia, as well as a series of Greek foreign policy goals that primarily included monetary compensation for losses suffered by the war in Yugoslavia, the establishment of the Cohesion Fund and accession to the Western European Union (WEU).[61]

Greek decision makers aimed at ensuring that their country not acquire the reputation of contributing, or being a part of the region's problems.[62] This prudent goal dictated a series of cooperative decisions. Hence, the government never considered vetoing the establishment of the Hague Peace Conference, or of the Arbitration Commission. However, the latter's creation produced certain and relatively easily foreseen problems for Greece in its dispute with FYROM.

The same rationale explains Greece's participation in EPC's condemnation and penalisation of Serbia, despite the fact that history, religion, fears, interests and geopolitical outlook were shared among the two states to a considerable extent. In other words, reputational concerns superseded what amounted to a kind of a Greek-Serbian special relationship. As Mitsotakis explained while referring to this issue:

> [Within EPC] there exists an interesting balance. No country can actually follow exclusively its policies. One must often compromise or even follow policies with which one disagrees, in order to attain other more important goals *in the future*.[63]

Another example of Greek behaviour being influenced by reputational concerns and EPC's 'shadow of the future', was related to the goal of gaining Community compensation for damages to the national economy due to the Yugoslav War.[64] The government considered its EPC behaviour and reputation as a key test and condition for gaining such aid. It was believed that more compensation could be secured by demonstrating a consistent willingness to cooperate, even if this meant cooperating on issues with negative consequences. In this way, the existence of the regime EPC with its continuous decision-making function created incentives for cooperation.[65]

Greece's 'gentle' stance towards FYROM was partly influenced by concerns that the possible descent into war and the disintegration of the new republic would probably have detrimental effects for both Greece and the region.[66] However, EPC's 'shadow of the future' also influenced the flexibility on the issue of FYROM's name, to the extent that a compromise name in the line of Upper Macedonia was at the very least not rejected. Furthermore, it helps explain the Greek failure to block FYROM from applying for EPC recognition.

In interviews with Samaras, the former Foreign Minister boasted and kept repeating essentially the same rationale behind such cooperative decisions. An example is illustrative. Concerning the 2 December 1991 Council document referring to the 'Republic of Macedonia', Samaras emphasised that

> I did not want to take what would have been perceived as an extremist position. Such a position could have created the impression that Greece could have territorial ambitions against Skopje....Furthermore, I wanted to create a positive climate [for Greece] with our European partners; and there were also our goals at Maastricht.[67]

Thus, it can be concluded that the institutionalist prediction that regimes 'link the future with the present', create reputational concerns and thus ultimately increase pressure for cooperation, stands vindicated.[68] Considerations of reputational concerns and the 'shadow of the future' though, do not suffice to explain entirely the politics of Greek cooperation. An analysis of the 2 December 1991 document suggests additional regime-related reasons of crucial importance. More specifically, it has already been mentioned that Samaras referred in an interview to his government's goals at Maastricht. A telegram of the Greek Ministry of Foreign Affairs also explained that *'although Greece did not agree with this [2 December 1991] decision, it would not block a decision, because of the upcoming Maastricht Summit'.*[69] This implied link between cooperation and the Treaty on European Union (TEU) that was negotiated at Maastricht deserves examination.

Institutionalist theory argues that goods uniquely provided by a regime, high issue density and the possibility of side-payments help achieve and foster cooperation.[70] All of these regime-produced incentives were present at the Maastricht Summit. WEU membership and the establishment of the Cohesion Fund were 'goods' that could have been uniquely provided by EPC. In addition to the support of the other 'poor' EPC members, the Greek government also believed that the reputation of a cooperative state would increase the chances of achieving greater monetary allocations from the Structural Funds.[71] Furthermore, it was hoped that a positive reputation and a cooperative stance on Yugoslavia and on other issues would suffice to gain accession to the WEU.[72]

The granting of Greece's Maastricht foreign policy goals can be viewed as an important side-payment which facilitated the signing of the TEU. According to Greek decision makers, it also represented a reward for their country's cooperation on Yugoslavia.[73] Institutionalism predicts that the existence of high issue density facilitates such side-payments and thus increases the chances for cooperation.[74] This was undoubtedly the case during the TEU negotiations, when issue density reached a peak.

Furthermore, institutionalist theory emphasises the importance of reciprocity.[75] This helps explain the agreement to EPC's 15 January 1992 decision on the recognition of the former Yugoslav republics.[76] Greece did not veto the recognition of Croatia on the condition that this cooperative action be reciprocated by the Community's refusal to recognise FYROM.

Reciprocity can perhaps also be used in explaining Samaras' agreement to sign the 16 December 1991 EPC declaration. For endorsing a document that he believed would produce negative results for the region, the former Foreign Minister achieved the three EPC conditions on the recognition of FYROM. Samaras claims that he was essentially presented with a *fait accompli* because of Germany's intransigence, and argues that vetoing the declaration would have bestowed upon Greece the reputation of a non-cooperating member, and would have also incurred the wrath of Germany.[77] Possibly then, reputational concerns played a role in this decision as well.

On the basis of the above analysis, it can be argued that the politics of Greek cooperation during the period of June 1991–January 1992 are largely explained by the theory of institutionalism. Institutionalist concepts such as the 'shadow of the future', high issue density, side-payments, reciprocity, goods uniquely offered by regimes and regime-related reputational concerns, are central in understanding Greek foreign policy towards former Yugoslavia and FYROM. Also, the fact that domestic politics played only a marginal role, further contributes to the vindication of institutionalist analysis.

It can also be concluded that at least partly due to the increased possibility of side-payments, EPC – and contrary to some recent scholarship, Inter-Governmental Conferences and Summit meetings – may offer the opportunity for substantive cooperative agreements.[78] This was undoubtedly the case during the Maastricht Treaty negotiations, when issue density had reached a peak.

Finally, regarding Greek foreign policy, it has been shown that a series of cooperative actions contributed to EPC's attempt to end the Yugoslav War, and also secured some of the country's major foreign policy goals. However, after mid-January 1992, a process began that was defined by the rise of intense popular passions, increased partisanship, as well as the public and acrimonious split between Mitsotakis and Samaras on the handling of the dispute with FYROM. As a result, a restrictive position on the new republic's name was adopted, that eventually became non-negotiable and paramount to almost all other foreign policy considerations. This development contributed substantially to the decline of the politics of cooperation, and to the pursuit of politics of confrontation towards FYROM and limited cooperation within EPC. However, the analysis of this fascinating process belongs to another inquiry.[79]

Notes

1. For example, see Gow (1997, p.78, fn. 32).
2. The term FYROM will be utilised, for the purposes of this essay. It must be admitted that the use of any term concerning the new republic is susceptible to attacks of bias. However, this approach has the advantage of conforming to the 1993 United Nations (UN) Security Council Resolution 813, according to which 'this state [will be] referred to for all purposes within the United Nations "the Former Yugoslav Republic of Macedonia" pending settlement of the difference that has arisen over the name of the state'. See Valenakes and Dales (1994, p. 147).
3. The modern phase of the Macedonian Question probably begins with the establishment of the Bulgarian *Exarchate* in 1870, which initiated an educational, religious and ultimately armed rivalry within Ottoman Macedonia primarily between Bulgarians and Greeks. See Daikin (1966). During the 1912 First Balkan War, the alliance of Greece, Bulgaria, Serbia and Montenegro managed to overthrow the Ottoman yoke from the Balkan Peninsula. See Carnegie Endowment, 1914/1993. Committing a tremendous military blunder, Bulgaria attacked its former allies in 1913, causing the Second Balkan War and ending up with a mere 10.1 per cent of Macedonia. Greece and Serbia gained 51.5 and 38.4 per cent respectively. See Kofos (1964, p. 44). Bulgaria thus became a revisionist power, siding with Germany in both World Wars, and thus managing to temporarily occupy parts of Greek Macedonia. Following the end of the Nazi occupation, the Macedonian Question played a central role in the Greek Civil War. See Kofos (1989). Significantly, in the war's final dramatic stages, and before their total defeat, the Greek communist forces were largely comprised by Slav-Macedonians. See Woodhouse (1976, p. 262). After 1949, the Macedonian Question continued mostly in the sensitive and sometimes passionate arguments between Greece and Yugoslavia concerning human rights issues and irredentist claims. See Kofos (1986) and Mertzos (1992, pp. 403–46).
4. For the most widely used definition of an international regime, see Krasner (1983a, p. 2). For a comprehensive examination of how EPC can be viewed as a regime, which is beyond the confines of this essay, see Tziampiris (1999, Chapter 3).
5. Keohane (1984, p. 51). This definition 'is now [the] consensus...definition of cooperation', Milner (1992, p. 467).
6. 'Serbia [also] contained…the autonomous province of Vojvodina and the autonomous region of Kosovo-Metohija', Singleton (1985, p. 209).
7. *The Economist*, 2 February 1991, p. 45.
8. For an analysis of the 1990 elections, see Woodward (1995, pp. 117–25).
9. EPC Press Release P. 35/91, 26 March 1991; emphasis added. See also the terms of the Third Financial protocol that was signed between the Community and Yugoslavia on 24 June 1991, in the Official Journal of the European Communities (hereafter OJ), No C 134/6, 25 May, 91.
10. See Bull, EC 6–1991, p. 8.
11. See Gow and Freedman (1992, p. 102).
12. See EPC Press Release P. 61/91, 5 July, 1991.

13. *The Times*, 6 July, 1991, p. 10.
14. For further details of EPC's plan, see Gow and Freedman (1992, p. 105–6).
15. For the text of the Brioni Accord, see European Political Cooperation Documentation Bulletin (hereafter EPCDB), Vol. 7, 1991, pp. 334–8.
16. See OJ No. 3-407/68, 9 July, 1991.
17. The text of the telegram can be found in Owen (1995, pp. 2–3).
18. For the relevant declaration produced by this meeting, see EPCDB, Vol. 7, 1991, pp. 389–90.
19. Samaras was Foreign Minister from 11.4.1990 to 14.4.1992. As regards the Peace Conference, it commenced at the Hague on 7 September, 1991, and was chaired by former British Foreign Secretary Lord Carrington.
20. This is why the Arbitration Commission is often referred to as the Badinter Commission. Badinter was joined by colleagues from Belgium, Spain, Germany and Italy.
21. For the text of the Memorandum (in English), see Skilakakis (1995, pp. 258–60).
22. See Skilakakis (1995, p. 260; emphasis added).
23. See Skilakakis (1995, p. 42–3).
24. Cited in Valenakes and Dales (1994, p. 38). The official results can be found (in English), in Valenakes and Dales (1994, pp. 38–9).
25. For the text of FYROM's declaration of independence (in English), see Valenakes and Dales (1995, p. 40–2).
26. See Skilakakis (1995, p. 46). Mitsotakis was Greece's Prime Minister from 11 April, 1990 to 13 October, 1993.
27. Mitsotakis made several similar statements before the 4 December 1991 Cabinet meeting. See Lygeros (1992 pp. 104–5) and Tarkas (1995, p. 64).
28. See the statement made by EPC's Ministers of Foreign Affairs on 6 October 1991. It can be found in EPCDB, Vol. 7, 1991, pp. 476–7. For the EPC's declaration on Dubrovnik, see EPC Press Release P. 105/91, 27 October, 1991.
29. See EPCDB, Vol. 7, 1991, pp. 476–7. See also Woodward (1995, p. 468, fn. 104).
30. See EPC Press Release P. 109/91, 8 November, 1991.
31. Ibid.
32. See Council of the European Communities General Secretariat (hereafter Council) 9558/91 (Presse 220-G), 2 December, 1991. For further positive measures that also included Montenegro, see Council 4392/92 (Presse 12-G), 3 February, 1992.
33. OJ No. L 342/1, 12 December 1991; emphasis added.
34. Council, 9558/91 (Presse 220-G), 2 December 1991.
35. See EPCDB, Vol. 7, 1991: 476; emphasis added. A similar statement was included in the EPC Declaration of 28 October 1991. See EPC Press Release P. 106/91, 28 October 1991.
36. *International Legal Materials* (hereafter ILM), Vol. 31, No. 6, December 1992, p. 1494.
37. For important accounts of this meeting, see Skilakakis (1995, pp. 62–3) and Petridis (1997, p. 391).
38. Papaconstantinou (1994, p. 419; emphasis added).
39. The account of this meeting is partly based on interviews with Mr. Kofos, Mr. Mitsotakis, Mr. Samaras and Mr. Skilakakis, as well as on Genscher's account, which can be found in Genscher (1997, pp. 797–9). See also Skilakakis (1995, pp. 63–4) and Tarkas (1995, pp. 67–9). As regards information about the positions held by people who were interviewed for the purposes of this chapter, see the end of the references section.
40. See EPC Press Release P. 128/91, 16 December, 1991.
41. Interview with Mr. Samaras.
42. EPC Press Release P. 128/91, 16 December, 1991; emphasis added.
43. For example, the 4 December, 1991 Cabinet meeting had decided that the name

Macedonia 'has a *geographic*...basis', Papaconstantinou (1994, p. 419; emphasis added). This wording clearly permitted the discussion of names such as Upper Macedonia.

44. *Eleftherotypia*, 18 December, 1991, p. 4. The official government announcement is quoted in Tarkas (1995, p. 70).
45. For Mitsotakis' and Samaras' statements, see *Makedonia*, 18 December 1991, p. 1.
46. Cited in Tarkas (1995, p. 77).
47. See *Makedonia*, 21 December, 1991, p. 20.
48. See 31 *ILM*, 1992, p. 1511 .
49. For FYROM's answers (in English), to the most important questionnaire that was sent by the AC, see Valenakes and Dales (1994, pp. 54–62).
50. For Karamanlis' letter, see Ioannou (1992: pp. 101–2; emphasis added).
51. Interviews with Mr. Kofos and Mr. Samaras.
52. For the AC's opinion, see 31 *ILM*, 1992, pp. 1507–12.
53. See 31 *ILM*, 1992, p. 1511; emphasis added.
54. For the AC's opinions on Croatia and Bosnia-Herzegovina, see 31 *ILM*, 1992, pp. 1501–7.
55. See EPC Press Release P. 9/92, 15 January, 1992.
56. The seminal work of institutionalist theory is Keohane (1984).
57. This account is partly based on interviews with Mr. Lengeris, Mr. Papaconstantinou, Mr. Papathemelis, Mr. Tarkas and Mr. Vrahatis.
58. Based on interviews with Mr. Kofos, Mr. Mertzos, Mr. Mitsotakis, Mr. Papaconstantinou, Mr. Samaras, Mr. Skilakakis and Mr. Tzounis. The degree of agreement among them is remarkable.
59. On the 'shadow of the future,' see Axelrod (1984, p. 174).
60. Based on interviews with Mr. Kofos, Mr. Mertzos, Mr. Mitsotakis, Mr. Papaconstantinou, Mr. Samaras, Mr. Skilakakis and Mr. Tzounis.
61. Based on interviews with Mr. Kofos, Mr. Mertzos, Mr. Mitsotakis, Mr. Papaconstantinou, Mr. Samaras, Mr. Skilakakis and Mr. Tzounis. The Cohesion Fund was seen as a new stage in the Community's regional polices that aimed at reducing regional disparities and problems. The practical implications of these policies for a country like Greece were immense. For example, some funds were targeted to what were called Objective 1 regions, defined as areas in which the per capita Gross Domestic Product (GDP) was less than 75 per cent of the Community average. Greece as a whole fell under this category, and thus Objective 1 appropriations for the period 1989–93 were ECU 6,667 million, which represented 69.4 ECUs per inhabitant, as well as 18.4 per cent of all such allocations. See Urzainqui and de Andres (1992, p. 93). As regards the WEU, it must be explained that Greece had applied for membership in 1987, primarily because it was believed that the organisation's Article V would provide important security guarantees against a possible attack by Turkey. These guarantees were impossible under NATO rules where both countries are members. For the text of the entire WEU Treaty that includes Article V, see Bloed and Wessel (1994, pp. 1–6).
62. Based on interviews with Mr. Kofos, Mr. Mertzos, Mr. Mitsotakis, Mr. Papaconstantinou, Mr. Samaras, Mr. Skilakakis and Mr. Tzounis.
63. Interview with Mr. Mitsotakis; emphasis added.
64. 'With 40 percent of Greece's trade passing through Yugoslavia, Athens estimate[d] losses up to $18 million per day' (*The New York Times*, 9 November, 1991, p. A1).
65. Based on interviews with Mr. Kofos, Mr. Mertzos, Mr. Mitsotakis, Mr. Papaconstantinou, Mr. Samaras, Mr. Skilakakis and Mr. Tzounis.
66. This point was made in interviews with Mr. Mitsotakis, Mr. Papaconstantinou and Mr. Samaras. See also Glenny (1996, p. 143) and Kyrkos (1994, p. 19).

67. Interview with Mr. Samaras.
68. Axelrod and Keohane (1993, p. 94).
69. Skilakakis (1995, p. 57); emphasis added. In an interview, Mr. Skilakakis revealed that although not in quotation marks in his book, this is the exact wording of the telegram.
70. See Keohane (1984, Chapter 6).
71. The Structural Funds included the European Regional Development Fund (ERDF), the European Social Fund (ESF) and the European Agricultural Guidance and Guarantee Fund (EAGGF).
72. Based on interviews with Mr. Mitsotakis and Mr. Samaras.
73. Interviews with Mr. Mitsotakis, Mr. Papaconstantinou and Mr. Samaras.
74. For example, see Keohane (1983, p. 155) and Keohane (1984, p. 91).
75. For a definition of reciprocity, see Keohane (1986, p. 8).
76. See EPC Press Release P. 9/92, 15 January, 1992.
77. Interview with Mr. Samaras.
78. For an example of such scholarship, see Smith (1996, p. 9).
79. See Tziampiris (1999, Chapters 7 and 8).

References

Axelrod, Robert (1984), *The Evolution of Co-Operation*, New York: Basic Books.

Axelrod, Robert and Keohane, O. Robert (1993), 'Achieving Cooperation Under Anarchy: Strategies and Institutions', in Baldwin, David (ed), *Neorealism and Neoliberalism*, New York: Columbia University Press.

Baldwin, David (ed) (1993), *Neorealism and Neoliberalism*, New York: Columbia University Press.

Bloed, Arie and Wessel, A. Ramses (eds) (1994), *The Changing Functions of the Western European Union (WEU)*, Dordrecht: Martinus Nijhoff Publishers.

Carnegie Endowment (1914/1993), *The Other Balkan Wars*, Washington DC: Carnegie Endowment for International Peace.

Daikin, Douglas (1966), *The Greek Struggle in Macedonia 1897–1913*, Thessaloniki: Institute for Balkan Studies.

Danchev, Alex and Halverson, Thomas (eds) (1996), *International Perspectives on the Yugoslav Conflict*, London: Macmillan.

Genscher, Hans-Dietrich (1997), *Memoirs*, Athens: Laverenthos [in Greek].

Glenny, Misha (1996), 'The Macedonian Question', in Danchev and Halverson (eds) *International Perspectives on the Yugoslav Conflict*, London: Macmillan.

Gow, James and Freedman, Lawrence (1992), 'Intervention in a Fragmenting State: the Case of Yugoslavia', in Rodley, S. Nigel (ed), *To Loose the Bands of Wickedness*, London: Brassey's.

Gow, James (1997), *Triumph of the Lack of Will*, London: Hurst and Company.

Hannequart, Achille (ed) (1992), *Economic and Social Cohesion in Europe*, London: Routledge.

Ioannou, Krateros (1992), *The Issue of Skopje's Recognition*, Athens: Sakkoula [in Greek].

Keohane, O. Robert (1994), 'The Demand for International Regimes', in Krasner, D. Stephen (ed), *International Regimes*, London: Cornell University Press.

Keohane, O. Robert (1984), *After Hegemony*, Princeton: Princeton University Press.

Keohane, O. Robert (1986), 'Reciprocity in International Relations', *International Organization*, Vol. 40, pp. 1–27.

Kofos, Evangelos (1964), *Nationalism and Communism in Macedonia*, Thessaloniki: Institute for Balkan Studies.
Kofos, Evangelos (1986), 'The Macedonian Question: The Politics of Mutation', *Balkan Studies*, Vol. 27, No. 1, pp. 157–72.
Kofos, Evangelos (1989), *The Impact of the Macedonian Question on Civil Conflict in Greece (1943–1949)*, Hellenic Foundation for Defense and Foreign Policy (Occasional Paper No. 3), Athens.
Krasner, D. Stephen (ed) (1983), *International Regimes*, London: Cornell University Press.
Krasner, D. Stephen (1983a), 'Structural Causes and Regime Consequences: Regimes as Intervening Variables' in Krasner, D. Stephen, *International Regimes*, London: Cornell University Press.
Kyrkos, Leonidas (1994), *The No-Exit Step of Nationalism*, Athens: Themelio [in Greek].
Lygeros, Stavros (1992), *Skopje*, Athens: Livani [in Greek].
Mertzos, I. Nikos (1992), *We the Macedonians*, Athens: I. Sideris [in Greek].
Milner, Helen (1992), 'International Theories of Cooperation Among Nations', *World Politics*, Vol. 44, No. 3, pp. 466–96.
Owen, David (1995), *Balkan Odyssey*, London: Victor Gollancz.
Papaconstantinou, Michalis (1994), *The Diary of a Politician*, Athens: Vivliopolion tis Estias [in Greek].
Petridis, B. Pavlos (1997), *The Politician Theodorakis*, Athens: Proskinio [in Greek].
Pijpers, E. Alfred, Regelsberger, Elfriede and Wessels, Wolfgang, (eds) (1998), *European Political Cooperation in the 1980s*, Dordrecht: Martinus Nijhoff Publishers.
Pijpers, E. Alfred (1998), 'The Twelve Out-of-Area: A Civilian Power in an Uncivil World?' in Pijpers, E. Alfred, Regelsberger, Elfriede and Wessels, Wolfgang, (eds), *European Political Cooperation in the 1980s*, Martinus Nijhoff Publishers, Dordrecht.
Rodley, S. Nigel (ed) (1992), *To Loose the Bands of Wickedness*, London: Brassey's.
Skilakakis, Thodoros (1995), *In the Name of Macedonia*, Athens: Elleneke Evroekdotike [in Greek].
Smith, E. Michael (1996), *The 'Europeanization' of European Political Cooperation*, Berkeley: Center for German and European Studies.
Tarkas, Y. Alexandros (1995), *Athens-Skopje* (Volume 1), Athens: Laverenthos [in Greek].
Tziampiris, Aristotle (1999), *Greece, European Political Cooperation and the Macedonian Question, June 1991–December 1992*. London School of Economics and Political Science, London (unpublished PhD thesis).
Urzainqui, Elvira and de Rosario, Andres (1992), 'The Lagging Regions of the Community' in Hannequart, Achille (ed), *Economic and Social Cohesion in Europe*, London: Routledge.
Valenakes, Yiannis (ed) (1992), *Yearbook of Defence and Foreign Policy '92: Greece and the World, 1990–9*, Athens: ELIAMEP [in Greek].
Valenakes, Yiannis and Dales, Soteres (eds) (1994), *The Skopje Question*, Athens: Sideris [in Greek].
Woodhouse, M. Christopher (1976), *The Struggle For Greece, 1941–9*, London: Hart-Davis and MacGibbon.
Woodward, L. Susan (1995), *Balkan Tragedy*, Washington DC: The Brookings Institution.

Interviews

Arsovski, Ljupco (FYROM's Head of Mission to Greece, 3 February 1997).

Kofos, Evangelos (former Greek Ambassador, 5 January 1997).
Lengeris, Elias (member of the Central Committee of the Greek Communist party, 27 August 1997).
Mertzos, Ioannis (journalist and former Advisor for Macedonian-Thrace Issues to Mitsotakis, 18 December 1996).
Mitsotakis, Konstantinos (former Prime Minister of Greece, 10 April 1997).
Papaconstantinou, Michalis (former Greek Foreign Minister, 23 December 1996 and 10 January 1997).
Papathemelis, Stelios (former Minister of Northern Greece, 11 January 1997).
Samaras, Antonis (former Greek Foreign Minister, 24 December 1996 and 3 February 1997).
Skilakakis, Thodoros (author and former Aide to Mitsotakis, 15 April 1997).
Tarkas, Alexandros (journalist and former Aide to Samaras, 9 April 1997).
Tzounis, Ioannis (former Ambassador and Greece's former junior Minister of Foreign Affairs, 14 April 1997).
Vrahatis, Yiannis (Chief of Staff to Mr. Konstantopoulos, Leader of the Greek party Synaspismos, 30 August 1997).

21 Greece and the EU-Turkish Relationship

HARRIS C. GEORGIADES

Following the December 1997 decisions of the European Council at Luxembourg, relations between the European Union (EU) and Turkey have become the focus of considerable attention and the subject of a controversial debate. One line of argument holds that Turkey was unjustly and unwisely shunned by the Union, which is ignoring its own strategic and commercial interests and is, instead, guided by cultural and religious considerations and subjective notions about democracy and human rights. The counter-argument is that the EU has expressed what are nothing more than the self-evident prerequisites for membership and that Turkey, rather than feeling left out, should grasp the opportunity and make those changes that will eventually enable its accession to the Union.

This debate is not, of course, entirely new since the EU-Turkish relationship has its origins in the early 1960s – a relationship that on the whole has been difficult and problematic. Within this relationship Greece has a very particular role which deserves special attention. Greece is the only member state which borders Turkey and relations between the two countries have been mostly poor. As the second decade of Greek membership approaches its completion, the time is right for an overview of the role of Greece in the shaping of EU relations with Turkey.

Background

The relations of Turkey with the then, European Community (EC) were inaugurated in 1959 when the Turkish government applied for an association with the EC. Interestingly, the 'Greek factor' was of determining importance even back then. Turkey had actually submitted its application only sixteen days after a similar Greek application. Even though this was part of the wider Turkish orientation to the West and a follow-up to the membership of NATO, the Council of Europe and the OECD, most analysts agree that the Turkish move was prompted by the fear of 'the possible damage that Greece could inflict on Turkey in the Western alliance if it were allowed to monopolise the European arena which was thought to be an important prospective site for Turkish-Greek rivalry'.[1]

The Association Agreement with Greece was signed in 1961 and was, at the time, the most encompassing agreement signed by the Community. Progress on the Turkish application was held down by the Turkish military coup of May 27, 1960. This was the first time that the domestic politics of Turkey would hamper the development of its relations with the EC, but it would not be the last. Eventually, Turkey was granted a similar status as Greece by a Community seeking an even-handed approach towards the two allies.[2]

The Ankara Agreement, completed by the Additional Protocol signed in 1973, included a commitment for the creation of a Customs Union by the year 1995. However, from then on the EC-Turkey Association faced trouble. The 1970s were years of economic difficulties for Turkey and these were attributed by both the industrialists and sections of the government to the terms and conditions of the Association Agreement. In essence there was a change in the way that Ankara viewed its relations with the EC, with economic considerations taking prominence over political ones (Eralp, 1993, pp. 28–9). Eventually, in October 1978, Prime Minister Bulent Ecevit froze the Association with the Community.

During these years Greece was recovering from seven years of military rule and from the blow of failing to prevent the 1974 Turkish invasion and occupation of the northern part of Cyprus. However, in contrast to Ankara's approach, the government of Constantine Karamanlis saw Greece's relations with the EC through a political rather than an economic lens. Karamanlis actually shared many of Ecevit's misgivings over the terms of the Association agreement, but believed that the best way to alleviate such problems was for Greece to participate fully in the decision-making process of the Community. More importantly, the Greek Prime Minister believed that membership of the Community would consolidate the remarkably smooth transition to democracy and would improve the Greek position vis-à-vis its eastern neighbour. Indeed, Karamanlis had become firmly convinced that 'Greece's destiny would have been bleak outside the greenhouse of democracies that had been carefully erected by the master builders of

European integration' (Couloumbis and Yannas, 1996, p. 163), and formally applied for full membership in 1975.

Even though Turkey was moving towards a severing of its relations with the Community, it did nevertheless realise that Greece would attain an advantage once it joined the EC and reacted angrily to the prospect. It has been maintained that the purpose of the expedition of the Turkish Navy survey ship *Sismik 1* in the Aegean Sea in July 1976 was to provoke a crisis in Greek-Turkish relations and make visible to the Community the dangers involved in accepting Greece as a member state (Tsakaloyannis, 1989, p. 47). Despite the Turkish reactions, accession negotiations were successfully completed in 1979, and on January 1, 1981, Greece formally joined as the tenth member of the Community.

The Greek Stance in the 1980s: Dead-Ended Denial

Before the effective accession of Greece, the Community had adopted a flexible attitude towards Turkey in an obvious attempt to 'compensate' Ankara for the acceptance of Greece. Among other gestures, the intention of the Nine was to proceed with the phased dismantling of the remaining duties on Turkish agricultural products (Stephanou and Tsardnides, 1991, p. 210), while the then Italian presidency reassured Turkey that Greece's accession would not affect the development of EC-Turkey relations. On its part, the Turkish government announced in June 1980, its decision to make a formal application for membership on the autumn of that year (Bac, 1997, p. 62).

Had these plans proceeded, Greece would have no doubt found itself in an urgent need to formulate a policy regarding EC-Turkish relations. However, developments within Turkey led to a different turn of events. On September 12, 1980, the military once again took over the Turkish government. The result was that the Council of Ministers froze all relations with Turkey, including the disbursement of 600 million ECUs that were allocated to Turkey under the Fourth Financial Protocol. For Greece this meant that for the time it would suffice if it could just align itself with the Community stance.

The real test for Greek policy came after 1985 when the EC began to normalise its relations with Turkey in response to the return of the country to civilian rule. For most of the remainder of the decade the Greek stance was one of reservations, objections and outright denial towards any movement on the field of EC-Turkish relations. Greece had originally refused to undersign the Ankara Agreement of 1963, that was necessary if Greece was to become a contracting party to the EC-Turkey Association. It only did so after receiving concessions by Turkey on the issue of the Greek properties in Turkey. Greece also objected to the reactivation of the institutional bodies of the Association. The strongest objections however, came on the issue of the financial co-operation with Turkey. Greece remained firm in vetoing the activation of the Fourth Financial Protocol and even resorted to the European Court of Justice in protest to the granting of a special 10 million ECU assistance to Turkey (Perrakis, 1996, pp. 181–2).

On April 1987, just one month after a serious crisis in Greek-Turkish relations, the Turkish government of Turgut Ozal submitted an application for full membership. Once again Greece reacted negatively, citing the poor record of Turkey on the issue of human rights, as well as the Turkish aggressive policy against Greece and the lack of progress on the issue of Cyprus. In fact, all these issues were consistently being put forward by Greece as conditions to any further development of EC-Turkish relations.

One tangible result of the Greek policy was that Athens was portrayed as the sole culprit for the lack of progress in EC-Turkish relations. Indeed in the minds of many Turks, Greece was the only obstacle to the accession of their country into the Community. This, however, was a misperception, albeit one that was of convenience to Greece's partners and one that the Greek side did not try hard enough to correct. The fact is that the EC partners had absolutely no intention of accepting the Turkish application for full membership. The size of Turkey and its low level of economic development would 'wreak havoc' on the Community, not to mention the political and social shortcomings of the country. Thus the opinion of the Commission on the Turkish application, published in 1989, left little prospect for Turkish membership.

On the other hand, Turkey continued to have a major geostrategic and economic significance due to its location and the size of its economy. Thus the member states, excluding Greece, were unwilling to upset Ankara further by insisting too much on issues such as progress on the problem of Cyprus or the respect of human rights and democratic procedures by the Turkish government. On the contrary, the priority of the European partners was to find ways to placate the feelings of the Turkish leadership by offering verbal reassurances and compensation packages that would, of course, stop short of full membership. It was in this spirit that, in the aftermath of the essentially negative opinion of the Commission, the creation of a Customs Union and the extension of a comprehensive financial assistance package to Turkey were proposed.

In assessing Greek policy, one cannot fail to note that the inflexible and absolute stance taken by Greece denied the country the opportunity to influence the EC policy towards Turkey in any constructive way. 'Conditionality' ought to have meant the search for those criteria that, once met, would enable a healthy and sound EC-Turkish relationship. However, the impression is that for the Greek government conditionality meant that the road to the normalisation of relations and the eventual accession of Turkey to the EC went through Athens and not according to standard criteria. And Athens had not even answered the question if it really wanted a European Turkey or a Turkey isolated from Europe and the unification process.

So the inability of Greece to rally the support of its partners to the extent that it wished, was not only the result of the significance and value of Turkey to the member states but also a result of the Greek actions within the Community. Greece bears the responsibility for failing to offer a credible proposal regarding Turkey. In addition, for most of its tenure, the socialist government of PASOK (1981–89) had failed to portray the necessary commitment to the European unification process and all that is entailed by this process. The irresponsible economic policy, the foreign policy rhetoric of Prime Minister Andreas Papandreou and the policy of 'footnotes' and 'reservations' severely damaged Greece's standing in the Community. So Greece could hardly expect Community solidarity in this two way process when it had often failed to demonstrate its own solidarity on a number of issues involving the interests of its partners.[3]

The Greek Stance in the 1990s: A New Approach…Eventually

The coming into power of the more pro-European New Democracy party led by Constantine Mitsotakis in 1990, raised prospects for an improvement of the Greek position within the Community as well as expectations for an active and responsible Greek role in the formulation of an EC policy that would face the challenges of a new European state of affairs. The economic and foreign policy of the new government was no doubt more akin to what would be expected from an EC member state.

However, Mitsotakis proved unable to prevent the engagement of the country in a dispute over the name of the Former Yugoslav Republic of Macedonia (FYROM). This development once again led to a deterioration of Greece's relations with its EC partners, cancelled, to a very large extent, the European role that Greece could undertake in the troubled Balkans and reduced the ability of Greece to implement its policy of conditionality regarding EC-Turkey relations.

At the European Council meeting in Lisbon at the end of June, 1992, the main preoccupation of the Greek government was the stance of the Community on the issue of FYROM. Consequently and in order to get all the other member states to accept the Greek views on the FYROM issue, the Mitsotakis government was led to adopt a more conciliatory approach towards EC-Turkey relations by accepting the release of funds slated for Turkey under the Renewed Mediterranean Policy and not objecting to a British initiative aimed at enhancing Turkey's ties to the EC (Yannas, 1994, p. 219).

In 1993 a politically transformed but physically frail Andreas Papandreou and a PASOK harbouring strongly pro-European views were returned to power. On the field of EU-Turkish relations, however, the old negative approach resurfaced once the proposal for the completion of the Customs Union with Turkey was brought to the fore.

But this time, there were also calls for a different more positive approach which stressed that the EU-Turkey Customs Union was a contractual obligation for the EU, was something that was considered to be in the interest of each and every one of the remaining member states and was something that Greece alone could not prevent without itself facing a major cost. Eventually, under the stewardship of the French presidency and with the involvement of the Greek and Turkish ambassadors to Paris, a package deal was reached on March 6, 1995: the Greek veto on the Customs Union was lifted in exchange for a commitment on the opening of accession negotiations with the Republic of Cyprus.[4]

On January 1996, Prime Minister Papandreou stepped down and was succeeded by Costas Simitis. In a matter of days, Simitis was faced with a very serious Greek-Turkish crisis which broke out when the Turkish government of Tansu Ciller challenged the sovereignty of the uninhabited rocky islet of Imia, in the Eastern Aegean. As part of its response to what it considered to be a Turkish aggressive policy incompatible to European norms,

Greece reinstated its objections to the financial package that was part of the Customs Union deal.

However, Prime Minister Simitis, a moderate leader with a commitment to the modernisation of the economy and politics of Greece, appeared determined to approach the European partners and cover the ground that Greece had 'lost' during the previous decade. The participation of the country in the hard-core of European Monetary Union became a priority, while on the field of foreign policy Greece played down the dispute with FYROM and tried to improve its general standing in the Balkans. Within this new setting, the Greek government has, since 1996, showed signs of a new and more constructive approach regarding EU-Turkish relations. Despite the ambivalence of Greek government public statements, it has been repeatedly explained that the Greek wish is for Turkey to be a part of European integration rather than excluded from it.[5]

This new attitude resulted in a markedly improved Greek position within the Union. During the European Council at Luxembourg on December 1997, at which crucial decisions were taken regarding the enlargement of the Union, Greece, making good use of its improved standing, was for the first time able to contribute decisively towards the formulation of a strategy for EU-Turkish relations which is essentially based on the policy of conditionality.

At the Luxembourg summit, Greece expressed its support to Turkey's European perspective and its eventual participation in the EU. It was pointed out that for Greece the 'religion factor' was not considered to be a criterion for the participation of any country to the Union. It was explained that being Turkey's neighbour, Greece stood to benefit from a Turkish participation more than any other partner. On the other hand, Greece more than any other partner, was aware and was often on the receiving end of Turkish policies that certainly did not meet up to European expectations and values. Thus the Greek wish was for a frank and sound relationship between the EU and Turkey based on European values and practices.[6]

The result was that the European leaders eventually clarified and codified a set of rules and principles, mainly the respect of human rights, democratic institutions, borders and international law, that once met by Ankara would enable the further development of EU-Turkish relations. The reaction of the Turkish government which refused to see the prospects in this decision, was one of rejection, threats and ultimatums.[7] This was hardly surprising given that the government of Mesut Yilmaz had actually campaigned for an acceptance of the Turkish membership application.

Conclusion: The Way Forward for the EU, Greece and Turkey

The view that what is bad for Turkey is good for Greece is not uncommon among Greeks, but is nonetheless mistaken. Greece would be far better off having a democratic, prosperous and Europeanised eastern neighbour. While this would not resolve all Greek-Turkish problems, it would mean that Turkey would pose far fewer problems than an unstable, highly nationalistic, or strongly Islamic Turkey. What then is required from Greece, is the substitution of the negative stance on EU-Turkish relations with a proactive stance designed to influence and change for the better the behaviour and policy of Turkey. Greece must have realised by now that the European Union is still not so much about the upholding of democracy and justice, as it is about diplomacy; a diplomacy requiring intelligence and foresight.

The lifting of the Greek veto on the EU-Turkey Customs Union in 1995, was an example of the intelligent diplomacy expected from Greece. Not only did it satisfy the economic interests of its partners, but also of Greece itself.[8] In addition, by adopting this new approach, Greece managed to commit the EU to the opening of accession negotiations with Cyprus as well as a much more decisive and rigorous scrutiny of Turkish policy and behaviour by the European Parliament.

Greece must also realise that it needs to be a reliable EU partner, able and willing to contribute to the widening and deepening of the Union. During the last few years Greece has moved in this direction and can already enjoy an improved position within the Union. This is not just the result of a more constructive foreign policy aiming to achieve regional stability and co-operation, but also a result of what is to be considered a determined and honest Greek effort for economic convergence – despite the Greek failure to join the European Monetary Union on its inauguration. The Greek success at Luxembourg, a result of this improved position, should not be viewed as the Greek will being imposed upon its partners, but rather as an active contribution of Greece toward clarifying the principles that should characterise EU-Turkish relations.

Many Turks no doubt still resent the Greek stance within the EU. However, it will be much more difficult for them, or for anyone else, to accuse Greece of blocking Turkey's European perspective, when other

European leaders, such as the German Foreign Minister Klaus Kinkel, are openly stating that 'the Turkish train remains on the rail line to Europe, but the path to full membership goes via the human rights situation, the Kurdish situation, relations with Greece, the Cyprus situation and naturally over several economic problems'.[9]

The Greek role regarding the development of EU-Turkish relations has not, of course, ended with the adoption of the conditionality policy by the EU. Various member states already appear eager to side-step these self-evident prerequisites and Greece must be ready to defend its position. At the same time, however, it has to be ready to show the necessary flexibility on such issues as the release of the financial assistance to Turkey.[10]

In the opinion of the authors of an article published in *Foreign Affairs*, 'a prosperous, democratic, tolerant Turkey is a beacon for the entire region, a Turkey engulfed by civil wars and racial and religious hatreds, or nursing ambitions to interfere abroad, would hurt American interests in innumerable ways' (Chase et al., 1996, pp. 47–8). Greece must find ways to convince its partners that the same is true for European interests and that this view should guide the search for criteria for the development of EU-Turkish relations. In the last few years Greece has shown encouraging signs that it is willing to be at the forefront of this effort. What remains to be seen is whether the Turkish leaders themselves will share this vision for their country and their region as a whole.

Notes

1. Mehmet Ali Birand, *Turkiye' nim Ortak Pazar Macerasi 1959–1985* (Istanbul: Milliyet yayinlari,1985), pp. 56–57, cited in Atila Eralp, 'Turkey and the European Community in the changing post-cold war international system' in Canan Balkir and Allan M. Williams (eds), *Turkey and Europe*, (London & New York: Pinter, 1993, p. 27).
2. The Ankara Agreement was signed on September 12, 1963 and came into force on December 1, 1964.
3. For a critique of the foreign and European policy of PASOK see John C. Loulis, 'Papandreou's Foreign Policy', *Foreign Affairs*, Vol. 63, No. 2, (Winter 1984/85).
4. The EU-Turkey Customs Union came into force once it was ratified by the European Parliament on December 13, 1995, after the EP received reassurances and a commitment by the Turkish government for an improvement on the issue of human rights in Turkey.
5. See for instance the statements of Greek President Stephanopoulos in Munich on June 1996 ('...Greece is a country that seeks peace and that is why it wishes to see Turkey join the Union', *Oikonomikos Tachydromos*, June 20, 1996), of Prime Minister Simitis just one day before the Imia crisis ('...we acknowledge the necessity of Turkey's European orientation', *Athens News Agency*, December, 29, 1996) and the article by

Alternate Foreign Minister George Papandreou in the Athens weekly *To Vima* on June 1, 1996 ('We have every interest in co-operating and seeing Turkey developing into a European Union partner').

6. For an outline of the Greek stance during the Luxembourg summit see George Papandreou, 'After Luxembourg. The time of truth for the EU-Turkish relationship', *To Vima*, December 21, 1997 [in Greek].
7. For more details on the Turkish reactions see *BBC, Summary of World Broadcasts*, 16, 17 & 19 December, 1997.
8. For the economic impact of the Customs Union on the involved parties, including Greece, see *Ta Nea* May 27, 1998 (Greek daily newspaper).
9. Turkish Daily News, October 1, 1997.
10. The opinion of the New Democracy party as expressed by such leading figures as Costas Karamanlis (*Ta Nea*, November 19, 1997) and Dora Bakoyianni (*Phileleftheros*, June, 7, 1998) raises the prospect that, under certain conditions, the government will not face severe criticism by the opposition if it proceeds with such a move.

References

Bac, M. (1997), *Turkey's Relations with a Changing Europe*, Manchester: Manchester University Press.

Birand, M.A. (1985), *Turkiye' nim Ortak Pazar Macerasi 1959–1985*, Milliyet yayinlari, Instanbul.

Chase, R., Hill, E. and Kennedy, P. (1996), 'Pivotal States and US Strategy', *Foreign Affairs*, Vol. 75, No. 1, January/February.

Constantine, S. and Tsardanides, C. (1991), 'The EC Factor in the Greece-Turkey-Cyprus Triangle', in Constas, D. (ed), *The Greek-Turkish Conflict in the 1990s: Domestic and External Influences*, MacMillan Press.

Couloumbis, T. and Yannas, P. (1996), 'Greek Foreign Policy Priorities for the 1990s', in Featherstone, K. and Ifantis, C. (eds), *Greece in a Changing Europe. Between European Integration and Balkan Disintegration*, Manchester: Manchester University Press.

Eralp, A. (1993), 'Turkey and the European Community in the Changing Post-cold War International Syștem', in Balkir, C. and Williams, A.M. (eds), *Turkey and Europe*, London and New York: Pinter.

Loulis, J.C. (1985), 'Papandreou's Foreign Policy', *Foreign Affairs*, Vol. 63, No. 2, Winter.

Papandreou, G. (1997), 'After Luxembourg. The Time of Truth for the EU-Turkish Relationship', *To Vima*, December 21 [in Greek].

Perrakis, S. (1996), 'Greece and the European Community-Turkey Relations', in *Greece in the European Union. An Assessment of the First Fifteen Years of Membership*, Papazisis, Athens [in Greek].

Tsakaloyannis, P. (1989), 'The European Community and the Greek-Turkish Disputes', *Journal of Common Market Studies*, Vol. XIX, No. 1, September.

Yannas, P. (1994), 'The Greek Factor in EC-Turkey Relations', in Kazakos, P. and Ioakimides, P.C., *Greece and EC Membership Evaluated*, London: Pinter.

22 Greece and the Balkans: Economic Relations

AXEL SOTIRIS WALLDÉN*

Greece's economic relations with its Balkan neighbours[1] receive considerable publicity. Within the country, there is hardly a minister who resists the temptation to include some Balkan initiative in his/her programme, and the public is apparently very happy to hear that in one area at least Greece performs and even leads. Also foreign observers are keen to highlight this aspect of Greek activity, in a pedagogic effort to show the benefits of regional cooperation, as opposed to the country's unfortunate recent political adventures in the area.

But how much substance is there behind the rhetoric? Does the economic future of Greece lie in the Balkans? Can Greece play an important role in its Balkan neighbours' 'road to Europe' – meaning to the European Union? This chapter attempts a quick overview of the state of Greece's economic relations with the Balkans, drawing some conclusions related to the prospects.[2]

Trade and Investment

The Balkans are still a relatively minor trade partner of Greece. In 1997, trade with Balkan countries reached $2.1 billion, with exports at $1.3 billion and imports at around $750 million. This represents 6 per cent of Greece's total trade as compared to 61 per cent for Greek trade with EU partners. In exports, Greece's Balkan share is higher (13 per cent), but still considerably lower than its EU share (50 per cent) (see Annex, Tables 1–3).

---

* Views expressed are personal and do not in any way engage the European Commission.

Figure 1 Balkan Share in Total Greek Trade (1950–97)

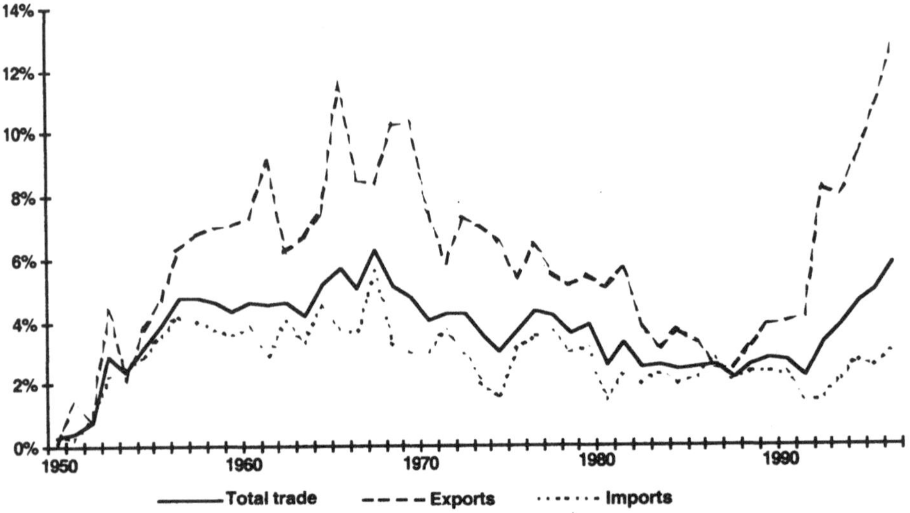

Source: Greek national statistics and EUROSTAT.

Figure 2 Greek Trade with the Balkans, 1997 (Total Value $2.1 bn)

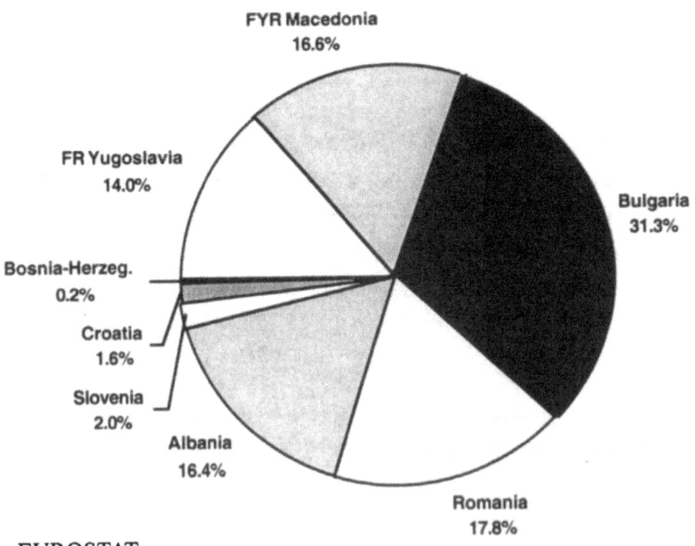

Source: EUROSTAT.

However, Greek trade with the Balkans in the 1990s has been particularly dynamic: its share in total Greek trade has been steadily rising, especially in exports, where it has quadrupled since 1989 – reaching an all-time peak in 1997 (see Figure 1). By contrast, the EU share in Greek exports has dropped by almost 20 percentage points over the same period. The Balkans are one of the few areas with which Greece runs a trade surplus (export/import ratio of 171 per cent in 1997, compared to 31 per cent in trade with the EU and 41 per cent in total Greek trade). Also, the Balkans cover 55 per cent of Greek trade with transition countries, while the same figure for the EU-15 is a mere 16 per cent (for Italy, which comes second in the EU, it is 33 per cent).

Bulgaria is by far the most important Balkan trade partner of Greece, answering for almost 1/3 of the country's Balkan trade (Figure 2). Romania, Macedonia, Albania and the FR Yugoslavia follow (with shares in the 14–18 per cent range). Trade with Croatia, Slovenia and Bosnia is negligible. If we look at exports only, Albania ranks first, followed closely by Macedonia and Bulgaria (each of them absorbing around $300 million).

On the whole, the Greek share in EU exports to the Balkans is modest, around 6 per cent, though it has tripled since 1989, and is more than 10 times higher than Greece's share in EU exports to the rest of the world.

Figure 3 Greek Share in EU-15 Exports to the Balkans 1989, 1997

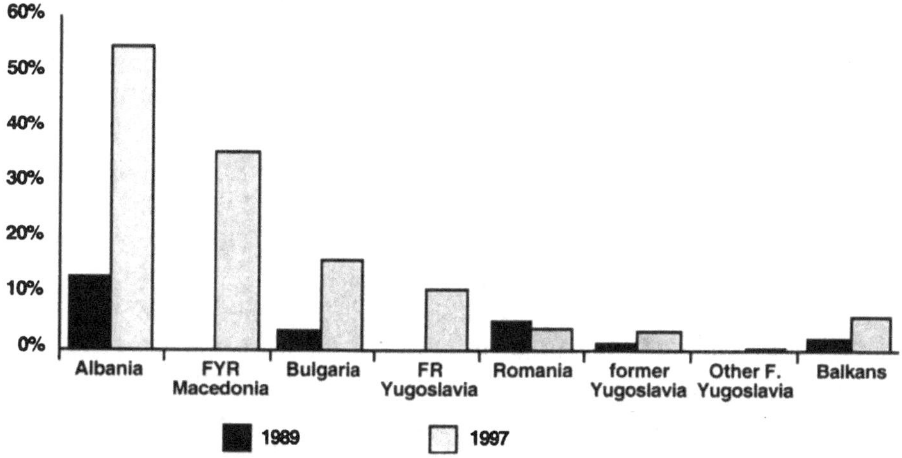

Source: Table 1.

Figure 4 Greek and Turkish Exports to the Balkans, 1997

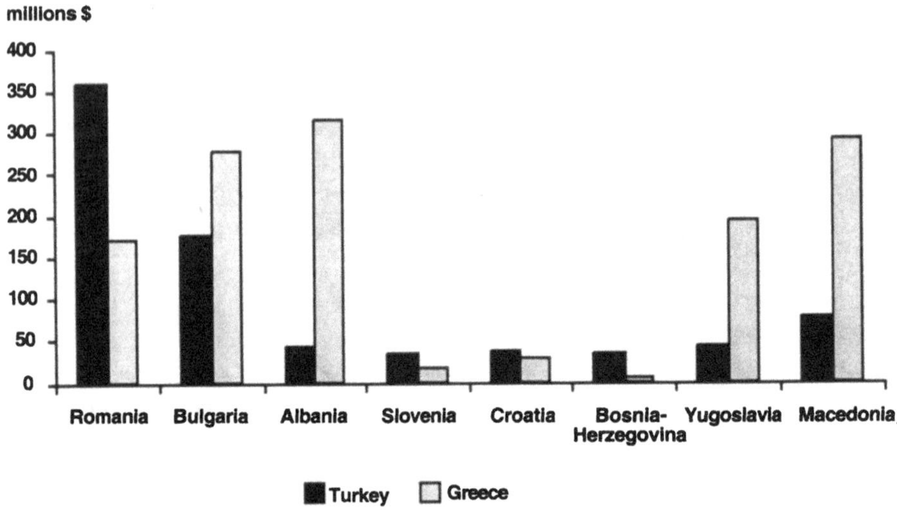

Source: Greece-EUROSTAT, Turkey-COMTRADE.

However, Greek trade presence in the southern part of the peninsula is spectacular. Greece is the first exporter to Albania and Macedonia, and answers for 55 per cent and 36 per cent of total EU exports to those two countries, respectively. Its share in EU exports to Bulgaria and Serbia is also very high, 16 per cent and 11 per cent respectively. In 1997, an estimated value of $150 of Greek exports corresponded to each inhabitant of Macedonia, while the same figure for Albania was around $95. These sums amount to substantial parts of those countries' GDPs (10–15 per cent at current exchange rates). On the other hand, Greek exports to Romania answer for less than 4 per cent of EU exports to that country, and this share has been dropping, despite an important increase in its $ value (Figure 3 on previous page).

A comparison of Greek and Turkish trade with the Balkans (Figure 4 and Annex, Table 4) shows that in terms of turnover, Greece is slightly above Turkey (+20 per cent), and this is due to substantially higher Greek exports (+64 per cent), while Turkish imports from the area slightly exceed the Greek imports (+19 per cent). Turkey is clearly better positioned in Romania (2.1 to 1), but Greece performs much better in Albania (almost 8

Figure 5 Main Greek Exports to the Balkans, 1997

Source: EUROSTAT.

to 1), Yugoslavia (4.1 to 1), Macedonia (3.2 to 1), and in exports to, though not in imports from, Bulgaria. The situation in the Balkans is in stark contrast to that in the NIS where Turkey leads with 6 to 1 (12 to 1 in the Transcaucasian and Central Asian Republics), but even in the non-Balkan EU candidate countries, where the ratio is 1.8/1 in favour of Turkey.

Product-wise, Greek *exports* to the Balkans are quite diversified (Figure 5 and Annex, Table 5): they are comprised of food and industrial consumption goods, intermediate industrial goods and raw materials, as well as fuels. A striking post–1989 feature has been the increasing share of a multitude of consumer goods; more recently, there are also considerable flows in improvement trade, especially in textiles and clothing. The Balkans absorb substantial shares of Greek exports of oil products and road vehicles (30–40 per cent), and to a lesser degree, of essential oils and perfumes, cereals and articles of metal (20–30 per cent). Greece answers for more than 60 per cent of EU exports to the Balkans of tobacco and its products, and for

Figure 6 Main Imports to Greece from Balkans, 1997

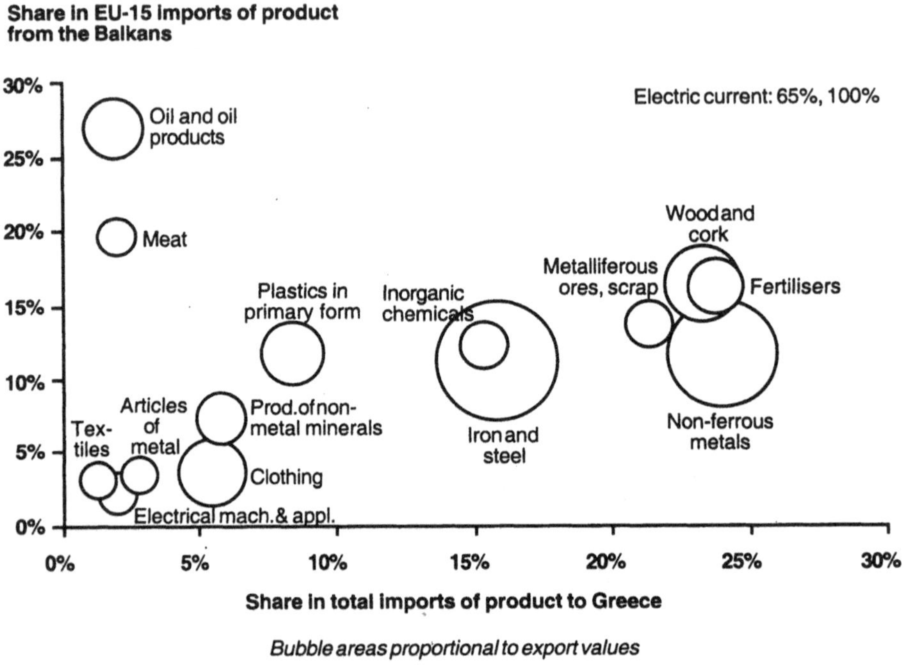

Source: EUROSTAT.

around 50 per cent of EU exports of oil products. The Greek share is also very high in EU exports of textile fibres and vegetable and fruit (30–40 per cent).

Imports from the Balkans comprise mostly of intermediate industrial goods and raw materials (Figure 6 and Annex, Table 6). The area answers for substantial shares of total Greek imports of non-ferrous metals, wood, fertilisers, and metalliferous ores and scrap (20–25 per cent) and to a lesser extent, steel products and inorganic chemicals (around 15 per cent); also the bulk of electric current imports originate from neighbouring Balkan countries. Greece represents an important market for Balkan country exports of oil products and meat (20–30 per cent of EU imports from the area), but also of fertilisers, wood, metalliferous ores, non ferrous metals, steel, inorganic chemicals and plastics in primary form (10–20 per cent).

With respect to *investment*, Greece has been very active in the Balkan area, initially in Bulgaria, Albania and Romania, and more recently in Macedonia and the FR Yugoslavia. Cited figures are not always reliable, but it appears that the Greek presence in FDI is important in the above countries. Greek investment is usually of very small scale and focuses on commercial activities, often of an ephemeral nature. There are however some notable exceptions where large Greek firms have been involved: ice-cream, Coca-Cola, oil products, non-ferrous metals, marketing of western cars, and 'Lotto' games. Recently the Greek state telecom organisation (OTE) acquired an important stake in the Yugoslav telecom organisation, in alliance with its Italian counterpart.[3] Greek banks have been very active, many of them opening branches, representation offices or joint ventures in Balkan countries.

Other Economic Relations

Apart from trade and investment, economic relations with the Balkans present an interest to Greece in a number of areas:

Massive Albanian (mostly illegal) *immigration* has substantially modified the labour market structure in Greece and has boosted economic activity in a number of sectors; at the same time it has brought serious social problems and tensions, including arms and drug trafficking, particularly after the 1997 events in Albania. For Albania, migration to Greece is a major source of foreign exchange (emigrant remittances reportedly exceed the country's total export receipts) and a safety valve for its labour market. Attempts by the Greek authorities to regulate these flows, not the least in view of the country's integration in the Schengen area, raise doubts as to their eventual efficiency. There is also some migratory pressure from other Balkan countries, but it is better contained. *Visitor* flows from former Yugoslavia were traditionally important for northern Greece's tourist and retail sectors. These flows were curtailed during the Macedonian and Yugoslav crises, but have since resumed both from Serbia and from Macedonia. However, Schengen regulations could prove an obstacle.

The post-1989 and post-Dayton geopolitical environment in the Balkans has modified the situation regarding cooperation in the *transport* sector. Growth of intra-Balkan flows necessitates better connections, both in terms of capacity and of density of networks. Greece – especially in the northern Greek ports – is now in a better position to attract transit flows to and from its northern neighbours, mainly Macedonia, Serbia, and Bulgaria. On the other hand, it would appear that many obstacles still prevent the full resumption of Greek transit to Central and Western Europe through the Balkans. The shift in these flows towards the Greek-Italy axis may last beyond the recent crises. Nonetheless, investment in Balkan transport networks, with assistance from the EU and the IFIs, seems a rational long term policy. There is also apparently some scope for the Balkans as a transit route between adjacent areas, though the potential of this dimension is often exaggerated, especially with respect to the role of Greece in this context. A regional approach to Balkan transport networks, superseding national antagonisms which lead to overlaps and irrational options is a necessity.

The Balkans are poor in *energy* resources and hence net importers of energy. Greece imports some electric energy from its northern neighbours, while its northern ports, especially Thessaloniki, are gateways for energy supplies to Macedonia and elsewhere. Russian gas imports to Greece pass through Romania and Bulgaria and there are plans to extend the gas pipeline network from Greece to Albania – although an alternative route to Albania through Macedonia is also under consideration. There is certainly scope for improving cooperation between Greece and its Balkan neighbours in a number of energy-related areas: interconnection of grids; pipeline networks; and exploitation of local energy resources, including hydroelectric potential. Given the expected increased weight of Caucasus and Central Asian energy, the Balkans could be called to play a role in the transit of this energy to the West. The potential role of Greece in this context is probably rather limited, except for the Burgas-Alexandroupoli oil pipeline project, intended to bypass the bottleneck of the Straits. Evidently, this route is of particular political and economic interest to Greece, though its viability and merits would have to be objectively assessed, also taking into account possible environmental impact.

Until 1990, Greece's northern borders counted among the less open in Europe. Since then, the situation has somewhat improved, reflecting the opening up of the neighbouring countries, the end of the Cold War, as well as availability of funds for *cross-border cooperation* from the EU. However, cooperation between border regions of Greece and of its northern neighbours is still lagging:

- Relations with Macedonia are being restored, after four years of practical interruption, but Greece is apparently still reluctant to develop cross-border cooperation for reasons related to ethnic minorities.

- Cooperation between border regions with Bulgaria is constrained by the terrain, by the economic crisis in Bulgaria, but also by Greek opposition to contacts between Muslim populations living on both sides of a large segment of the Greek-Bulgarian border. An announced policy-shift in official attitudes towards the Muslim minorities in Thrace has apparently not yielded substantial practical results.
- Finally, organised cross-border cooperation with Albania is severely constrained by the general collapse of the state and the economy in that country. However, in this case Greece is highly interested in contacts with the southern part of Albania, where a Greek minority lives. Indeed, what is happening here, is a process of integration of southern Albania to the Greek economy (through trade, investment, official and NGO aid, remittances, movement of persons, and illegal activities), which, if not managed with utter prudence, could endanger the unity of the Albanian territory, with obvious repercussions on interstate relations and on regional stability.

Summing up, the following concluding remarks can be made:

- Greek post-1989 economic performance in the southern Balkans has been remarkable. A zone of major Greek economic influence comprises the three neighbouring countries and Serbia. This zone is clearly distinct from a zone of poor Greek performance which includes the Visegrad and the Baltic countries, but also Slovenia and Croatia, and from a zone of intermediate Greek presence, which includes Romania, the Ukraine, Moldova, the Transcaucasian Republics, and, probably, Southern Russia. Geographic vicinity, but also cultural affinities, would seem important factors in this differentiation.
- Greek economic performance in the southern Balkans is all the more impressive, if one considers the country's recent disastrous political record in the area, but also the unfavourable political and economic climate in most of the neighbouring countries during most of the post-1989 period. Indeed, it would appear that politics have not been able to arrest the development of economic relations, and that Greece has apparently performed best in countries where the political and economic environment was the worst. True, this statement should be qualified in terms of even larger opportunities that were probably lost, while there are also limits beyond which politics and the environment

obviously do obstruct economic relations: the Yugoslav war, the Greek embargo against Macedonia, as well as the more recent economic collapses in Bulgaria and Albania, provide some evidence on this point – although illegal or semi-legal economic activities flourished during these events.

- The economics of Greek performance in the Balkans are sensible but cast some shades on the prospects. Greece has exploited its comparative advantages, which beyond geography and history, include such factors as flexibility in a volatile political and economic environment, and intermediate prices and qualities in conditions of limited incomes and domestic productions recovering from collapse. These latter factors are likely to erode with time, and Greek exporters and investors will meet increasing competition from domestic Balkan and other Western producers. Greece has a lead-time, which it should put to use for achieving a higher quality presence; however, there are doubts as to the extent this lead-time has been exploited, not least because political factors diverted the necessary efforts.
- The economic opening to the Balkans, also has some negative aspects for Greece. Adjustment strains from increasing integration are generally small, though there is an important issue of delocalisation of the clothing industry, which needs to be addressed.[4] Nevertheless, such strains are usually part of much broader global processes, and could not be solved through a regression to protectionism. On the whole, Greece profits from economic integration with the Balkans. The real problem, however, is that the Greek economy seems to be turning away from the demanding EU market to find easier outlets in the Balkans and the NIS. There is thus a risk that the Balkan 'opening' takes the form of a qualitative downgrading of Greek production. Such a process could in the long run have serious economic and also political consequences, as Greece would seem to seek refuge in a marginalised Balkan area. A related partial but important problem is the substantial increase of 'grey economy' activity, including criminal activity, which has accompanied the Balkan opening and has been favoured by the embargoes, and the breakdown of law and order in neighbouring countries.
- In the fields of transport, communications and energy, there is undoubtedly scope for intensified cooperation between Greece and its neighbours, since here history, both distant and recent, has not allowed things

to develop in the way they developed in other parts of Europe. There are also probably some opportunities for cooperation in promoting transit of energy and goods. However, over-ambitious plans in this latter area do not always seem grounded on a long-term assessment of the region's and especially the country's comparative advantages, and often reflect antagonistic approaches to neighbours.

- There is a strong regional dimension in Greece's economic relations with the Balkans. Not surprisingly, both benefits and risks from their intensification are concentrated in the northern part of the country. On balance, this region and especially Thessaloniki seems to be profiting from the opening, though the above mentioned 'downgrading' effect concerns very much the economy of Northern Greece which was traditionally closely linked to Germany. Another problem in this context is that the northern border regions have not been sufficiently involved in the country's Balkan opening, for reasons including, as explained, political reluctance related to ethnic minority issues. Market-led cross-border integration in conjunction with restrictive attitudes towards organised cross-border cooperation could have a serious negative impact on the country's border regions.

- It is now clear that the European Union's enlargement process will focus in the coming years on countries where Greece's stakes are insignificant; inversely, those transition countries where Greece has important interests are either wholly excluded from the enlargement process, or seem less promising within that framework. This situation presents a number of risks for Greece, which will have to be studied and addressed. The economic – apart from the political and strategic – importance for Greece of a European perspective for the Balkans is more pressing than ever. The issue whether this area is converging to Europe or drifting away from it has apparently yet to be solved. To Greece, this dimension of the enlargement process is vital and should not be overshadowed by the unavoidable, but sometimes excessive focus on Cyprus – for one could not expect the country to escape in the long-run from a regional process of marginalisation.

- The much publicised issue of Balkan regional cooperation is closely related to the above-mentioned problem of a European perspective for the area. Despite the rhetoric, prospects for regional cooperation in the Balkans are in fact bleak, for a number of reasons related to history, politics and economics. They would be definitely non-existent if this cooperation were conceived by some of its promoters as a substitute rather than a vehicle for the rapprochement of the Balkans to the Union. Overlaps or even outright antagonisms – reminiscent of pre-World War power politics – between various initiatives and sponsors are an additional obstacle. Political and economic common sense would plead for better coordinated and eventually fewer fora, without third party sponsors, and with a predominant European dimension.

- Finally, to return to the initial questions of this chapter – 'Is the economic future of Greece in the Balkans?' and 'Does the road to Europe for Balkan countries pass through Greece?' The economic future of Greece lies of course in Europe, the EMU and in global competitivity. Nevertheless an enhanced Greek role in a Balkan region, which itself would be moving closer to the Union, could be a precious asset, while at the same time it would benefit both the Union and its Balkan partners. There are however some prerequisites:
- A minimum of political and economic stability in the area. As mentioned above, there are obviously limits to the ability of Greece to profit economically from chaos in the neighbouring area. Hence, there is additional reason for concern over the growing tension in the Albanian-populated regions of former Yugoslavia.
- Overcoming the consequences of the very negative recent political record of Greece in the region. Fortunately, it would seem that a new spirit prevails now in Athens in this respect. Nevertheless, some thorns have still to be removed for Greece to be able to play its full role in the area: full normalisation with Skopje, abandoning of sectarian anti-Turkish reflexes, more open attitudes towards minorities, for example.
- In the economic field, just as in politics, it is important that Greece will show the Balkans the way to Europe, rather than be drawn by them away from it. Resisting the 'downgrading effect' of the Balkan and Eastern opening is a major priority for the country, and basically can only be addressed by improving the overall efficiency of the economy.
- Finally, in its economic approach to Balkan neighbours, Greece should resist a certain arrogance, which usually accompanies erroneous assessments on its potential regional role. Greece is of course not the only, and as a rule not even the main channel of the Balkans to Europe, and

should act accordingly. The country would have much to gain if its regional economic initiatives were less subordinated to traditional power politics, and better worked-out and implemented.

Notes

1. Throughout this paper, relations with the Balkans include all Balkan transition countries (Albania, Bulgaria, Romania and the five successor states of former Yugoslavia); relations with Turkey are excluded, although that country, historically, politically, and in part geographically as well, belongs to the Balkans.
2. A more detailed overview of Greek economic relations with the Balkans can be found in Walldén, A.S. (1996) and Petrakos, G. and Christodoulakis, N. (1999).
3. According to recent reports, the implementation of this deal is meeting severe obstacles.
4. See for instance, Lambrianidis, L. (1996).

References

Lambrianidis, L. (1996), 'The Opening of the Balkan Markets and Consequent Economic Problems in Greece', in *Modern Greek Studies Yearbook*, Vol. 12, University of Minnesota.

Petrakos, G. and Christodoulakis, N. (1997), *Economic Developments in the Balkan Countries and the Role of Greece: From Bilateral Relations to the Challenge of Integration*, Centre for Economic Policy Research, Discussion Paper Series No. 1620, London: International Macroeconomics, April.

Walldén, A.S. (1996), 'La Grèce dans les Balkans', in *L'Europe Centrale et Orientale*, Paris: Les études de la Documentation Française, pp. 69–90.

Walldén, A.S. (1999), 'Greece and the Balkans: Economic Relations' in Cofoudakis, V., Psemiades, H. and Gerolganatos, A. (eds) *Greece and the New Balkans: Challenges and Opportunities*, New York: Pella Publishing Company Inc, pp. 71–121.

Annex: Table 1 Greek Trade with Balkan Countries 1989–97

	Total Balkans	Bulgaria	Romania	Albania	former Yugoslavia	Slovenia	Croatia	Bosnia-Herzeg.	FR Yugoslavia	FYR Macedonia
Exports million $										
1989	239.1	68.6	42.3	18.8	109.5					
1990	310.1	53.0	59.3	17.8	180.0					
1991	344.7	87.8	84.8	12.2	159.9					
1992	406.3	167.2	107.4	41.3	90.5					
1993	692.5	303.4	89.3	126.3	173.6	10.5	8.1	15.3	0.0	139.6
1994	750.8	412.9	93.3	213.1	31.5	7.4	9.4	0.5	0.0	14.2
1995	1005.9	447.3	180.4	261.2	117.1	44.6	13.8	0.2	21.8	36.7
1996	1237.2	312.2	173.9	323.0	428.2	12.5	13.7	1.4	168.5	232.1
1997	1298.6	278.3	170.0	314.8	535.4	18.4	27.2	4.0	192.9	292.8
Annual change										
90/89	30%	-23%	40%	-5%	64%					
91/90	11%	66%	43%	-31%	-11%					
92/91	18%	90%	27%	238%	-43%					
93/92	70%	81%	-17%	206%	92%					
94/93	8%	36%	5%	69%	-82%	-30%	17%	-97%	+++	-90%
95/94	34%	8%	93%	23%	272%	505%	46%	-51%	+++	159%
96/95	23%	-30%	-4%	24%	266%	-72%	0%	460%	673%	533%
97/96	5%	-11%	-2%	-3%	25%	48%	98%	196%	14%	26%
Imports million $										
1989	384.9	70.0	79.4	7.5	228.1					
1990	469.9	109.1	72.0	12.3	276.5					
1991	486.1	155.8	92.2	11.9	226.3					
1992	332.5	161.0	70.9	18.1	82.5					
1993	324.7	198.3	47.8	15.4	63.2	13.7	17.1	3.3	0.0	29.1
1994	442.0	317.5	47.4	35.3	41.8	21.0	14.1	1.9	0.0	4.8
1995	716.6	483.8	134.2	37.5	61.0	29.9	14.2	1.2	1.1	14.7
1996	702.3	368.4	143.8	35.9	154.2	26.5	10.6	0.5	77.5	39.2

1997	757.8	364.4	196.9	22.2	174.3	23.7	6.6	0.8	94.3	49.0
Annual change										
90/89	22%	56%	-9%	64%	21%					
91/90	3%	43%	28%	-3%	-18%					
92/91	-32%	3%	-23%	52%	-64%					
93/92	-2%	23%	-33%	-15%	-23%					
94/93	36%	60%	-1%	129%	-34%	54%	-18%	-42%	...	-84%
95/94	62%	52%	183%	6%	46%	42%	1%	-37%	+++	208%
96/95	-2%	-24%	7%	-4%	153%	-11%	-26%	-60%	+++	167%
97/96	8%	-1%	37%	-38%	13%	-11%	-38%	71%	22%	25%
Trade balance million $										
1989	-145.8	-1.5	-37.1	11.3	-118.6					
1990	-159.8	-56.2	-12.7	5.5	-96.5					
1991	-141.4	-68.0	-7.3	0.3	-66.4					
1992	73.8	6.2	36.5	23.2	8.0					
1993	367.9	105.1	41.5	110.9	110.3	-3.2	-9.0	12.0	0.0	110.6
1994	308.8	95.4	46.0	177.8	-10.3	-13.6	-4.7	-1.4	0.0	9.4
1995	289.3	-36.5	46.1	223.7	56.0	14.7	-0.4	-1.0	20.7	22.0
1996	534.9	-56.2	30.1	287.1	274.0	-14.1	3.2	0.9	91.1	192.9
1997	540.8	-86.0	-26.9	292.7	361.1	-5.2	20.7	3.2	98.6	243.9
X/M ratio										
1989	62%	98%	53%	250%	48%					
1990	66%	49%	82%	145%	65%					
1991	71%56%	92%	103%	71%						
1992	122%	104%	152%	228%	110%					
1993	213%	153%	187%	818%	275%	77%	47%	459%	...	480%
1994	170%	130%	197%	604%	75%	35%	67%	26%	+++	298%
1995	140%	92%	134%	696%	192%	149%	97%	20%	2007%	250%
1996	176%	85%	121%	899%	278%	47%	130%	278%	218%	592%
1997	171%	76%	86%	1421%	307%	78%	414%	480%	205%	598%

Source: Greek national statistics;1997: EUROSTAT.

Annex: Table 2 Greek Exports to the Balkans and to Other Regions: Developments since 1989

	1989	1992	1996	1997	1997 Index (1989 = 100)	Change 1996–97 (%)
		(million $)				
Romania	42.3	107.4	173.9	170.0	402	-2
Bulgaria	68.6	167.2	312.2	278.3	406	-11
Albania	18.8	41.3	323.0	314.8	1675	-3
former Yugoslavia	109.5	90.5	428.2	535.4	489	25
FYR Macedonia			232.1	292.8		26
FR Yugoslavia			168.5	192.9		14
Other			27.5	49.7		80
Baltic countries			12.3	26.3		113
Russia			360.6	319.1		-12
Other NIS			211.4	185.8		-12
Balkans	239.2	406.4	1237.2	1298.6	543	5
Visegrad countries	80.7	169.2	194.6	202.2	251	4
former USSR	139.8	124.7	584.3	531.2	380	-9
CEECs and NIS	460	700	2016	2032	442	1
Other third countries	2401	2385	3345	3017	126	-10
EU-15	5250	6777	6078	5093	97	-16
World	7579	9862	11439	10142	134	-11

Source: Greek statistics. EUROSTAT COMEXT for year 1997 data. EUROSTAT and COMTRADE from COMEXT for EU-15 data.

1989	1992	1996	1997	1989	1992	1996	1997	Greece's rank in EU 1997
Share in total Greek exports				Share in EU-15 exports				
(%)	*(%)*	*(%)*	*(%)*	*(%)*	*(%)*	*(%)*	*(%)*	
0.6	1.1	1.5	1.7	5.2	6.0	4.1	3.9	7
0.9	1.7	2.7	2.7	3.6	13.3	18.5	16.3	3
0.2	0.4	2.8	3.1	12.9	9.6	42.0	54.7	1
1.4	0.9	3.7	5.3	1.2	1.4	3.3	3.6	
		2.0	2.9			27.3	35.7	1
		1.5	1.9			12.5	11.0	4
		0.2	0.5			0.3	0.4	
		0.1	0.3			0.3	0.4	
		3.2	3.1			1.7	1.2	
		1.8	1.8			3.4	2.4	
3.2	4.1	10.8	12.8	2.0	4.1	6.2	6.1	
1.1	1.7	1.7	2.0	0.7	0.7	0.4	0.3	
1.8	1.3	5.1	5.2	0.8	0.7	1.8	1.3	
6.1	7.1	17.6	20.0	1.1	1.4	1.9	1.7	
31.7	24.2	29.2	29.7	0.48	0.49	0.61	0.73	
69.3	68.7	53.1	50.2	0.65	0.51	0.46	0.39	
100.0	100.0	100.0	100.0	0.61	0.53	0.58	0.51	

Annex: Table 3 Greek Imports to the Balkans and to Other Regions: Developments since 1989

	1989	1992	1996	1997	1997 Index	Change 1996–97
			million $		*1989 = 100*	*(%)*
Romania	79.4	70.9	143.8	196.9	248	37
Bulgaria	70	161	368.4	364.4	521	-1
Albania	7.5	18.1	35.9	22.2	295	-38
former Yugoslavia	228.1	82.5	154.2	174.3	76	13
FYR Macedonia			39.2	49.0		25
FR Yugoslavia			77.5	94.3		22
Other			37.6	31.1		-17
Baltic countries			5.0	3.7		-27
Russia			694.2	488.6		-30
Other NIS			178.2	139.0		-22
Balkans	385.0	332.5	702.3	757.8	197	8
Visegrad countries	247.4	261.3	335.5	292.1	118	-13
former USSR	309.6	435.2	877.4	631.3	204	-28
CEECs and NIS	942	1029	1915	1681	178	-12
Other third countries	4491	6881	8082	7014	156	-13
EU-15	10733	15603	17678	16327	152	-8
World	16166	23513	27675	25022	155	-10

Source: Greek statistics. EUROSTAT COMEXT for year 1997 data. EUROSTAT and COMTRADE from COMEXT for EU-15 data.

1989	1992	1996	1997	1989	1992	1996	1997
Share in total Greek imports				Share in EU-15 imports			
(%)	*(%)*	*(%)*	*(%)*	*(%)*	*(%)*	*(%)*	*(%)*
0.49	0.30	0.52	0.79	2.7	5.1	4.6	5.5
0.43	0.68	1.33	1.46	10.6	15.8	20.6	18.2
0.05	0.08	0.13	0.09	5.8	25.1	34.2	24.2
1.41	0.35	0.56	0.70	2.7	1.3	2.0	2.2
		0.14	0.20			9.8	11.7
		0.28	0.38			15.3	10.1
		0.14	0.12			0.6	0.5
		0.02	0.01			0.1	0.1
		2.51	1.95			2.5	1.7
		0.64	0.56			5.0	2.9
2.38	1.41	2.54	3.03	3.1	3.7	5.5	5.5
1.53	1.11	1.21	1.17	2.0	1.5	0.9	0.7
1.92	1.85	3.17	2.52	1.2	1.6	2.5	1.7
5.8	4.4	6.9	6.7	1.91	1.96	2.27	1.81
27.8	29.3	29.2	28.0	1.07	1.52	1.42	1.27
66.4	66.4	63.9	65.2	1.32	1.50	1.40	1.32
100.0	100.0	100.0	100.0	1.26	1.52	1.45	1.30

Annex: Table 4 Greece and Turkey in the Balkans: Trade in 1997

TRADE WITH:	EXPORT Turkey (*million $*)	Greece (*million $*)	Turkey/Greece
Romania	358.8	170.0	2.11
Bulgaria	175.9	278.3	0.63
Albania	41.1	314.8	0.13
Slovenia	34.3	18.4	1.86
Croatia	36.1	27.2	1.33
Bosnia-Herzegovina	31.9	4.0	7.91
Yugoslavia	42.8	192.9	0.22
Macedonia	77.4	292.8	0.26
Total Balkans	798.3	1298.6	0.61
in % of total	3.5%	11.4%	
in % of total CEC+NIS	20%	64%	
Visegrad-4+Baltic-3	562	228	2.46
NIS	3512	505	6.96
– *Russia*	2057	319	6.45
– *Ukraine*	337	117	2.88
– *Caucasus+Central Asia*	1089	55	19.91
Total CEEC+NIS	4074	2032	2.00
in % of total	17.7%	17.8%	
EU-15	12248	5093	2.40
in % of total	53.1%	44.5%	
World	23048	11439	2.01

Source: Greece-EUROSTAT, Turkey-COMTRADE (EUROSTAT COMEXT data base).

IMPORT			TOTAL TRADE		
Turkey (*million $*)	Greece (*million $*)	Turkey/Greece	Turkey (*million $*)	Greece (*million $*)	Turkey/Greece
394.1	196.9	2.00	752.9	366.9	2.05
408.9	364.4	1.12	584.7	642.7	0.91
3.4	22.2	0.15	44.5	337.0	0.13
30.0	23.7	1.27	64.3	42.1	1.53
8.6	6.6	1.30	44.7	33.8	1.32
1.3	0.8	1.55	33.2	4.9	6.81
27.0	94.3	0.29	69.9	287.2	0.24
30.2	49.0	0.62	107.6	341.8	0.31
903.4	757.8	1.19	1701.8	2056.3	0.83
1.9%	3.0%		2.4%	5.6%	
23%	45%		21%	55%	
391	296	1.32	953	524	1.82
3615	628	5.76	7127	1133	6.29
2174	489	4.45	4231	808	5.24
918	53	17.34	1255	170	7.39
469	77	6.08	1557	132	11.8
4006	1681	2.38	8080	3713	2.18
8.2%	6.7%		11.3%	10.2%	
24870	16327	1.52	37118	21420	1.73
51.2%	65.2%		51.8%	58.7%	
48585	25022	1.94	71633	36461	1.96

Annex: Table 5 Greek Exports to the Balkans 1997 by Main Categories of Products

SITC	Product	Balkans			Share in total Greek exports to Balkans		Share in total Greek exports of product
		$m	*$m*	*1989=100*			
		1997	*1989*	*1997*	*1997*	*1989*	*1997*
33	Oil and oil products	344.7	15.9	2172	26.5%	6.6%	34.7%
05	Vegetables and fruit	98.7	28.5	346	7.6%	11.9%	9.7%
12	Tobacco and products	65.7	6.6	994	5.1%	2.8%	14.0%
84	Clothing	55.7	6.7	827	4.3%	2.8%	3.8%
04	Cereals	45.8	0.5	8498	3.5%	0.2%	20.2%
66	Prod of non-metallic min.	45.4	12.8	355	3.5%	5.3%	9.8%
26	Textile fibres	41.8	32.9	127	3.2%	13.8%	12.2%
55	Essential oils, perfumes	35.3	0.1	32118	2.7%	0.0%	28.6%
78	Road vehicles	35.2	0.1	41805	2.7%	0.0%	39.9%
65	Textiles	32.3	18.3	176	2.5%	7.7%	8.8%
69	Articles of metal	31.8	7.9	402	2.5%	3.3%	20.7%
77	Electrical mach. + appl.	30.9	0.2	13674	2.4%	0.1%	11.3%
68	Non ferrous metals	30.4	2.1	1428	2.3%	0.9%	7.7%
67	Iron and steel	29.4	6.6	447	2.3%	2.8%	12.2%
89	Misc. industrial products	26.9	1.3	1994	2.1%	0.6%	4.7%
28	Metallic ores + scrap	22.7	32.7	69	1.7%	13.7%	17.5%
64	Paper and products	17.7	21.1	84	1.4%	8.8%	20.0%
51	Organic chemicals	10.9	4.1	269	0.8%	1.7%	29.5%
99	Secret	4.8	7.9	61	0.4%	3.3%	2.7%
27	Non metallic ores	4.7	4.9	96	0.4%	2.0%	4.2%
21	Hides, skins, raw	0.5	8.3	6	0.0%	3.5%	1.5%
	First 15	949.9	215.3		73.1%	90.0%	13.2%
	Other	348.7	23.9		26.9%	10.0%	11.8%
	Total	1298.6	239.1	543	100.0%	100.0%	12.8%

Included are the fifteen first products in 1997 and 1989.
Source: EUROSTAT (COMEXT data base). 1989 – Greek statistics.

Share in EU-15 exports of product to Balkans	Romania $m	Bulgaria $m	Albania $m	FR Yugo-slavia $m	FYR Mace-donia $m	Slovenia $m	Croatia $m	Bosnia Herze-govina $m
1997	*1997*	*1997*	*1997*	*1997*	*1997*	*1997*	*1997*	*1997*
48.1%	19.24	31.82	*92.37*	*38.05*	*161.04*	0.04	2.13	0.01
32.2%	*22.35*	*16.76*	*13.34*	*17.49*	*20.41*	2.14	5.59	0.61
61.4%	*11.82*	2.06	*23.37*	*17.10*	4.56	0.85	5.44	0.54
11.2%	1.02	*39.03*	1.55	4.27	*9.50*	0.22	0.06	0.02
16.4%	1.74	*5.73*	*32.81*	1.88	2.69	0.08	0.39	0.44
9.1%	3.22	*11.28*	*21.42*	*4.87*	3.00	0.01	1.48	0.07
34.7%	*6.47*	*28.01*	0.08	3.16	3.21	0.54	0.36	0.00
8.9%	*6.93*	*5.50*	*4.69*	*6.79*	*3.88*	2.85	*3.86*	0.81
1.5%	1.73	*8.97*	2.03	*17.56*	*4.26*	0.50	0.00	0.11
2.8%	2.49	*8.68*	*5.50*	*6.11*	*8.62*	0.05	0.86	0.00
3.9%	8.48	*7.65*	*8.15*	*4.41*	3.02	0.08	0.02	0.01
2.4%	*6.74*	*11.04*	*4.90*	*5.01*	1.56	1.20	0.33	0.07
10.4%	4.39	17.48	2.66	*4.03*	1.80	0.00	0.00	0.00
5.6%	1.75	2.84	*19.39*	1.12	*4.32*	0.01	0.00	0.00
3.6%	*5.18*	*5.50*	*7.50*	*3.41*	*4.54*	0.23	0.43	0.08
36.1%	12.03	1.43	0.00	0.20	0.01	7.58	1.47	0.00
3.4%	1.30	6.27	3.02	2.36	4.42	0.09	0.18	0.04
3.2%	0.31	0.82	3.28	3.87	1.30	0.00	1.34	0.00
17.9%	0.79	0.51	0.87	1.57	1.02	0.04	0.01	0.0027
7.1%	0.11	0.82	1.18	0.39	1.75	0.03	0.39	0.01
7.0%	0.00	0.02	0.34	0.09	0.01	0.00	0.00	0.00
9.5%	103.5	202.4	239.7	135.3	236.4	8.8	20.9	2.8
	61%	*73%*	*76%*	*70%*	*81%*	*48%*	*77%*	*69%*
3.0%	66.5	76.0	75.1	57.6	56.4	9.7	6.3	1.2
6.1%	170.0	278.3	314.8	192.9	292.8	18.5	27.2	4.0

Annex: Table 6 Greek Imports from the Balkans 1997 by Main Categories of Products

SITC	Product	Balkans *$m*	*$m*	*1989=100*	Share in total Greek imports from Balkans		Share in total Greek imports of product
		1997	*1989*	*1997*	*1997*	*1989*	*1997*
67	Iron and steel	132.8	22.6	587	17.5%	5.9%	15.8%
68	Non-ferrous metals	106.3	36.2	294	14.0%	9.4%	24.1%
24	Wood and cork	54.6	24.7	221	7.2%	6.4%	23.3%
84	Clothing	48.0	2.6	1832	6.3%	0.7%	5.5%
57	Plastics in primary form	40.8	16.0	255	5.4%	4.2%	8.4%
35	Electric current	37.7	3.6	1038	5.0%	0.9%	65.0%
33	Oil and oil products	35.4	18.5	192	4.7%	4.8%	1.9%
56	Fertilisers, chemical	29.2	4.9	596	3.9%	1.3%	23.8%
66	Prod. of non-metallic min.	26.2	12.1	216	3.5%	3.2%	5.8%
52	Inorganic chemicals	21.1	7.9	269	2.8%	2.0%	15.4%
28	Metallic ores, scrap	20.7	2.5	832	2.7%	0.6%	21.4%
77	Electrical mach. + appl.	18.8	12.7	149	2.5%	3.3%	2.0%
01	Meat	16.0	28.0	57	2.1%	7.3%	2.0%
69	Articles of metal	15.2	12.6	121	2.0%	3.3%	2.8%
65	Textiles	14.3	12.2	118	1.9%	3.2%	1.3%
63	Wood manufactures	12.7	15.7	81	1.7%	4.1%	9.9%
00	Live animals	11.2	44.5	25	1.5%	11.6%	17.5%
64	Paper and products	10.9	11.3	97	1.4%	2.9%	1.7%
72	Machinery for spec. ind.	4.8	9.1	53	0.6%	2.4%	0.5%
78	Road vehicles	3.5	21.0	16	0.5%	5.5%	0.2%
	First 15	617.3	297.0		81.5%	77.2%	
	Other	140.5	87.9		18.5%	22.8%	
	Total imports	757.8	384.9	197	100.0%	100.0%	3.0%

Included are the fifteen first products in 1997 and 1989.
Source: EUROSTAT (COMEXT data base). 1989 – Greek statistics.

Share in EU-15 imports of product from Balkans	Romania *$m*	Bulgaria *$m*	Albania *$m*	FR Yugo-slavia *$m*	FYR Mace-donia *$m*	Slovenia *$m*	Croatia *$m*	Bosnia Herze-govina *$m*
1997	*1997*	*1997*	*1997*	*1997*	*1997*	*1997*	*1997*	*1997*
11.1%	46.98	76.45	0.06	3.60	5.40	0.24	0.11	0.00
11.5%	40.19	13.21	0.41	44.43	7.95	0.12	0.00	0.00
16.3%	11.68	28.25	1.10	9.80	2.34	0.12	1.20	0.10
3.5%	1.76	32.98	2.27	3.76	7.19	0.05	0.01	0.00
11.8%	12.35	16.92	0.00	8.58	2.38	0.00	0.50	0.02
100.0%	4.65	28.50	0.75	0.00	3.83	0.00	0.00	0.00
26.8%	21.04	14.26	0.03	0.09	0.00	0.00	0.00	0.00
16.2%	3.38	25.74	0.00	0.02	0.05	0.00	0.01	0.00
7.3%	4.56	14.04	0.20	3.66	0.58	1.98	1.16	0.03
12.1%	2.32	15.28	0.13	2.11	1.26	0.03	0.00	0.00
13.7%	4.11	9.18	7.08	0.20	0.14	0.00	0.00	0.00
2.3%	1.48	4.56	0.05	1.50	0.80	10.00	0.40	0.05
19.6%	0.85	8.68	1.19	0.45	4.74	0.00	0.03	0.09
3.3%	3.03	7.01	1.49	1.13	0.21	2.24	0.10	0.00
3.0%	1.37	6.99	0.13	1.64	3.23	0.84	0.10	0.00
4.1%	1.57	8.95	0.37	1.31	0.13	0.14	0.26	0.00
23.3%	10.74	0.49	0.00	0.00	0.00	0.00	0.00	0.00
4.9%	1.16	5.04	0.56	0.30	0.12	3.36	0.35	0.00
2.5%	1.40	2.34	0.16	0.24	0.53	0.15	0.00	0.00
0.4%	0.54	0.62	0.13	1.68	0.43	0.06	0.01	0.00
	159.8 81%	302.0 83%	14.9 67%	81.0 86%	40.1 82%	15.6 66%	3.6 55%	0.3 36%
5.5%	196.9	364.3	22.2	94.3	49.0	23.7	6.6	0.8

23 Are Greek Companies that Invest in the Balkans in the 1990s Transnational Companies?

LOIS LABRIANIDIS[1]

Introduction

The conditions created in the Central and Eastern European Countries (CEECs) after the collapse of the communist regimes led many Greek companies to invest in these countries. This article attempts to interpret this novel phenomenon, where in a very short time a large number of investment projects were initiated abroad. Indeed, until the opening of the CEECs there were extremely few Greek companies with investments abroad (such as Petzetakis, Metaxas and Titan), while in the 1960s and mainly the 1970s a number of construction companies (such as Edok-Eter, Archirodon, Odon kai Odostromaton, Skapaneas, Elliniki Techniki and Meton) showed some activity in the Middle Eastern countries. Since then the situation has changed drastically and now we are dealing with a very large number of Greek companies with activities abroad. So, while in 1989 there were only three Greek companies with investments abroad, within less than a decade (in 1998) the number of these companies had increased to well over 500 with more than 1,200 projects in the CEECs.

The main goal of this article is to initiate a theoretical debate regarding whether the investment plans developed by Greek companies in the CEECs resemble conventional types of Transnational Companies ('true transnationals') or Transnational Companies (TNCs) from Underdeveloped Countries (UDCs) ('new transnationals') or something else.[2] This theoretical debate is not simply concerned with the classification of Greek investment projects into one or the other category, but with the understanding of the mechanisms causing this internationalisation. Most important of all, the article attempts to reveal the comparative advantages of Greek investments in the CEECs that render their realisation feasible and whether they can be sustained in the long-run.

A more thorough analysis of the possible consequences of this phenomenon with respect to the Greek economy is not offered here as it is readily available elsewhere.[3] In these articles it was asserted that the recent opening of the markets of the CEECs was, and to a great extend still is, a significant opportunity for the Greek economy. The current 'strong' position of Greek firms in the Balkans is mainly due to the fact that investors from advanced industrialised countries are maintaining a 'wait and see' stance. The opening of the Balkan markets, where there is demand for products of not so high quality is allowing the Greek economy more time to modernise its productive base. There are also significant negative effects from the flow of Greek investment in the Balkans. In the short term there is a reduction of employment in certain industrial sectors and areas of the country. In the long term, the most important threat is the undermining of the effort to restructure Greek industry towards the production of high quality, internationally competitive products. Moreover, as soon as the economies of these countries will be restored there might be a move, of goods and capital, in the opposite direction.

Internationalisation and TNCs

The Internationalisation of Markets and the Creation of TNCs

During the Post-War period the degree of interdependence of national economies started to increase and took the form of peripheral zones of free trade, as well as global production systems (Vernon, 1966). These tendencies – and particularly the second – have accelerated during the last 25 years leading to the acclaimed internationalisation or globalisation of the world system. The term internationalisation, which is adopted here, suggests that despite the increasing interdependence of economies, their 'focal point' remains the various 'national' economies, and considers an independent economic policy acceptable and efficient, even though in some cases national policy may be opposed by international trends and choices. On the other hand, the term globalisation implies that the economic system has been unified into a global economy, which renders independent economic policies impossible.[4] There is undoubtedly an exaggeration about the term 'globalisation' since, as Krugman (1995), estimated for the USA the main market remains the domestic for 90 per cent of the products and 97 per cent of the companies.

The last 15 years have been characterised by two significant qualitative changes in the deeper forms of internationalisation of production. Firstly, while in the previous periods Foreign Direct Investment (FDI)[5] was aiming at exploiting the natural resources and the traditional industrial branches of the developing countries, since 1980 it has mainly turned to technologically advanced industries, and particularly services (Ozawa, 1992; UN, 1995). Secondly, there have been significant changes in the countries of origin of the FDI. During the 1930s and the early post-war period, the USA replaced Great Britain as the most important source of FDI. Since 1960 Japan has emerged as a rapidly developing source of FDI, while during the last decade UDCs such as Korea, Malaysia etc. have become increasingly important. However, despite the changes which have been occurring in the relative importance of FDI from various source countries and the very fast growth of the share of FDI from UDCs (4.3 per cent in 1985 – 9.7 per cent in 1997, UNCTAD, 1998), the fact remains that a small number of Developed Countries (DCs) generates almost all the FDI in the world economy.

Even though there is a long standing discord regarding the use of the terms Multinational (MNC) and Transnational (TNC) corporations, the term TNC is applied here in a broad sense, following Dicken (1992, p. 47), Lall (1983, pp. 1–2), UNCTC (1978, p. 158), Wells (1983, pp. 7–9) and others, to mean any firm:

- that invests abroad. This is at variance to the Harvard Business School's Transnational Enterprise Project definition, according to which a US based firm was not counted as a TNC unless it had manufacturing subsidiaries in six or more foreign countries.
- that involves active participation of the investor in the management and operation of the enterprise, hence a TNC is distinguished from portfolio investment.
- that enjoys geographical flexibility, in the sense that it has the ability to shift its resources and operations between locations on a global scale hence taking advantage of differences in factor endowments,

government policies etc. between countries.

- that is characterised by technological intensity, advanced marketing, concentrated market structures, high levels of skill, economies of scale, the prevalence of multiplant operations and, of course, it is large in size.
- that its overseas operations have some kind of ownership tie to the parent firm in the home country. This requisite is the differentiating factor of TNCs and MNCs, with the latter not being tied to any national entity.
- that invested abroad with management and know-how to do something similar to what it was doing at home.
- that invested in any sector (primary, secondary and tertiary) and not just in manufacturing activities as some authors suggest (e.g. Hood-Young, 1979, p. 3).

An enterprise to be considered as a parent firm, must be owned by nationals of that country and its management must reflect the domestic culture. The emigrant entrepreneur who decides to try his fortune abroad – such as the Indian, Lebanese, Syrian and overseas Chinese businessmen who have for decades migrated to a number of UDCs and carried with them their skills and sometimes, capital – is not considered as a TNC.

The TNC originating from a DC is the 'ideal type', which is termed as 'true transnational'. The firms from UDCs that are creating FDI can be called 'new transnationals' (see among others Wells 1983).

Why Firms Choose to Exploit Their Skills Through Direct Investment Abroad

In the world of neo-classical economics, there is little place for FDI since trade will equalise factor prices. With no barriers to trade, and with costless information, international trade is the only form of international involvement. However, FDI does exist and firms that are involved must have some sort of special assets that give them a competitive edge abroad over other firms.

The product life-cycle theory proposes a model to explain the creation of TNCs. Firms innovate for their home market, generating skills and knowledge that, in some cases, are then exploitable abroad. Since managers are responsive to their home markets, the nature of a particular firm's advantage is influenced by the characteristics of that firm's national market.

Hymer's (1976) theory of the 'monopolistic advantages' traces the existence of TNCs to market failures in the generation, diffusion and exploitation of intangible assets such as technology, brand names and marketing or organisational skills (which Caves (1982) terms 'ownership advantages'). The 'monopolistic advantages' possessed by firms are very similar to the barriers to entry of new competition.

When a firm intends to profit from the use of its 'monopolistic advantage' overseas, it might choose either to export its product and services or to subcontract it, or sell its skills to an enterprise located in a foreign market which might involve sale of machinery, licence, turnkey plants, management contracts, technical service agreement, etc. Finally, a firm might choose to establish a foreign branch or subsidiary, i.e. to 'internalise' its advantage within the firm, which is the issue of this paper. The internalisation strategy can contribute, as Dicken (1992, p. 145) suggests, to both parts of the firm's profit equation (i.e. it can increase revenues, and minimise costs).

However, the 'monopolistic'/'owner-specific' advantage (such as certain types of knowledge, organisation and human skills), according to Dunning (1993), is one of the three closely related conditions that have to be satisfied for a firm to become engaged in international production. The second is that such advantages are most suitably exploited by the firm itself rather than by selling them or leasing them to others; and the third that it is more profitable for the firm to exploit its assets overseas, rather than domestically.

The choice of form for the exploitation of a 'monopolistic advantage' depends, as Lall (1983, pp. 16–20, p. 253) argues, firstly on location costs for serving given foreign markets which include transport, labour, overheads, tariff and non-tariff barriers (e.g. protectionist policies to foster import substitution). Second, it depends on the profitability of internalising an advantage by FDI vis-à-vis that of selling it to an unrelated firm. In fact, the newer and more profitable the technology, the more FDI is preferred over licensing. The larger the firm, the more it is able to profit from a 'package' of technology, marketing, managerial and other advantages and the less vulnerable it is to risks from particular mistakes, so the more it would prefer FDI. Intangible advantages (i.e. contained in the skills and experience of people), rather than those embodied in a brand name, blueprint or patent, are better exploited by FDI, since selling them is difficult, costly and not particularly rewarding.

What are the Comparative Advantages of TNCs From UDCs

Two schools of thought, not necessarily contradictory, have emerged. The first, based on the 'product-cycle approach', treats TNCs from UDCs as relatively passive recipients of mature technologies and traces their ownership advantages to labour intensity, small-scale operations, lack of differentiation and low overheads. The main proponent of this school is Wells (e.g. see Wells, 1983).

The internationalisation of UDC firms may be seen as a stage in the product-life-cycle or a 'technological gap' model to explain trade and investment flows. The countries currently manufacturing the product export it down to those that do not yet have plants. Not only may the source of exports in world trade move down that order as the product matures, but the source of FDI might follow a similar pattern. The source of exports might move down the order because of the availability of technology plus the differences in production costs. The source of investments moves down the order because many products have been adapted to the needs of a somewhat lower-income consumer as they have been produced abroad (smaller cars, refrigerators etc. in Europe than in US).

The second school of thought, derived from the analysis of technological development, looks directly at the process by which enterprises acquire competitive competence, the main proponent of this school is Lall (e.g. see Lall et al., 1983).

TNCs from UDCs cannot possess competitive advantages in frontier technologies and sophisticated marketing. However, even the possibility that proprietary advantages can arise at lower levels of technology, size, or skill may at first sight seem surprising. How can firms without an innovative edge or a powerful brand name out-compete firms from a high technology DC? How can firms from UDCs which are not technologically active even in narrowly specialised branches of industry, discover an internationally exploitable advantage in technologies which are well-diffused and products which are relatively unsophisticated?

Their advantage lies in some special edge they have built up in widely diffused technologies, special knowledge of marketing relatively undifferentiated products, or special managerial or other skills. This edge may arise from some adaptation or improvement in the process or product technology (minor innovation) which would be costly for other firms to reproduce, or from a simple cost advantage in providing a standard technology.

But if a technology is well-diffused how can a firm from an UDC innovate for itself a unique proprietary asset? The answer must be to the 'localisation' of technical change at the micro level and the irreversibility of such change. That is, while in abstract neo-classical theory technological knowledge is not localised, in practice it is. Firms, as Lall (1983, pp. 4–5) argues, only know and understand a very limited range of techniques, and to shift to a different one requires considerable cost and effort. Their technical progress is localised around this point and proceeds in a direction governed by given market conditions and scientific advance. Moreover, since technological advance encompasses not just the innovator but a whole range of linked actors (component and material suppliers, distributors, users etc.), it moves all the related activities with it, each enterprise innovating in the locality of its own known techniques. The process is irreversible. Older technologies, while they may be known in some abstract sense, cannot be efficiently reproduced or transferred once the entire industrial system has moved on to new technologies.

Many of the UDCs investors appeared to have gained their initial advantage when they adapted large scale technologies of the industrialised countries for manufacture at small scale in their home countries which gives them a skill that is exportable to other countries with small markets.

Moreover, there are also push factors too that led firms from UDCs to invest outside their home country such as, according to Wells (1977, p. 136), strict foreign-exchange controls, requirement to earn their own foreign currency in order to make some imports, legal constraints imposed on the growth of firms at home (e.g. antitrust action) and the small size of home market.

TNCs From UDCs vs. TNCs From DCs

TNCs from DCs enjoy advantages closest to barriers to entry that lead to concentration and large firm size, i.e. very advanced technology and marketing, large size, high levels of skill, and a propensity to seek out very concentrated markets. Hence, they are able to avoid tough price competition, since production costs are not generally critical to their success. This lack of attention to cost minimisation, leaves a market niche for the firms of UDCs.

TNCs from UDCs tend to thrive in industries or segments of the market where cost competition is severe and the advantages of economies of large scale do not overwhelm small scale manufacturers. They usually operate in industries with mature technologies. They derive their competitive advantages from the technologies that enable them to manufacture at low cost. The 'descaling' of technology is generally more labour-intensive than the large scale technology employed by 'true transnationals', hence capital-labour ratios for subsidiaries of 'new TNCs' are much lower than those of 'true TNCs'. Moreover, they have small expenditures on managers and engineering personnel as well as on buildings. Finally, they can reduce costs to substitute locally available materials and components for specialised inputs through abilities acquired in their home country.

The ability of new TNCs to reduce costs, enhances their advantages over the 'true transnationals' in market segments where price competition is a viable strategy. It is only few of them that have developed strong trade names for their products even at home. Hence, TNCs from UDCs are quite unlike the true TNCs that have been so skilled in creating the image of differentiated products, in controlling distribution channels, in providing service, or even in building a strong reputation.

Subsidiaries of UDC parent companies are almost all in other UDCs, usually in countries with a lower level of development than the home country, while those from the DCs are spread all over the world though they tend to concentrate more on other DCs. Moreover most subsidiaries of UDC firms are located within the region of the home firm and they reveal a very strong 'neighbourhood' character, (this was particularly acute during the first wave of TNCs from UDCs).[6]

Usually it is important for the true TNC to maintain a close relationship with its subsidiary. Because the subsidiary has a role to play in the global strategy of the parent company (e.g. provide raw materials, parts for manufacture elsewhere, a market for components), its prices and its image may affect the prices or image of products sold by the firm elsewhere. A TNC from a DC has some preference for importing from its affiliates so as on the one hand to gain the option of manipulating transfer prices and on the other hand to secure the inputs that it wants. Local inputs, with their varying standards, are likely to pose particular problems for firms that emphasise brand name and are, thus, concerned with having a product of very standardised quality. On the contrary the subsidiary of the UDC is often 'on its own', after a brief period of assistance from the parent.

The vast majority of UDC investors enter foreign markets through the use of joint ventures with partners of the host country. Aware of the feelings raised by wholly foreign ownership in their own countries, investors from UDCs are more sensitive to this issue when they invest elsewhere than are their counterparts from the advanced countries.

'New' TNCs are, in general, small and have a very limited number of overseas affiliates compared with true TNCs. They are basically in resource-based sectors and in distribution. Within manufacturing industry itself, the emphasis is on relatively unsophisticated, low-technology products with high labour-intensity.

Since TNCs from UDCs are often more independent of their parent firms, they tend to remit a smaller proportion of their profits to their home countries. In this sense, they offer alternatives to excessive dependence from the TNCs from DCs. However they have also some drawbacks compared to TNCs from the DCs such as their greater proneness to bribing officials, keeping more expatriates in managerial and skilled professional jobs and competing more intensely with local enterprises.

The differences between TNCs from UDCs and those from DCs, though existent, have been overstated. Some of them are due to the weak early state of evolution of TNCs from UDCs, which gives them fewer monopolistic advantages.

Advantages and Disadvantages of TNCs Compared to Local Firms

When a firm from one country operates in another country, it incurs a set of costs that are not faced by local firms. It has the extra burdens caused mainly by the language barrier, by geographical and cultural distance, by unfamiliarity with local conditions, by the need to communicate between the subsidiary and the home office and by the fact that the remuneration of managers and technicians brought from home is more costly. Finally, policies of many host governments discriminate against the foreign investor in subtle or even in overt ways. TNCs have encountered hostility and resentment in all countries that host substantial FDI, but nowhere more than in UDCs, where they were blamed for the national economy's manifest shortcomings (things have changed in the '80s). In order for a TNC to be able to offset all the above mentioned disadvantages, it must have an asset or skill that is not possessed by a local firm.

The magnitude of the disadvantage towards host country firms is smaller for the TNC from UDCs compared with those from DCs because the former are often familiar with a somewhat similar political and socio-economic environment. However, TNCs from UDCs, are found in industries where price competition is typical, they lack the technological and managerial advantages of DC firms and they operate in industries where competition makes it difficult to retain any advantage that does exist. It is thus logical to assume that in this sense they are most likely to engage in direct competition with local enterprises.

Investment Activity of Greek Companies in the CEECs[7]

Geographical Proximity Constitutes an Important Component in the Development of Greek Investments in the CEECs

There are 1,269 investment projects of Greek companies in 20 of the 27 CEECs.[8] Their great majority (81.7 per cent) is concentrated in just three countries (i.e. Bulgaria 41.1 per cent, Albania 20.3 per cent and Romania 20.3 per cent). Furthermore there is a significant concentration in Russia (6.9 per cent), while Poland (2.9 per cent), FYROM (2.6 per cent), Ukraine (1.5 per cent) and Yugoslavia (1.2 per cent) account for smaller proportions. In the remaining 12 countries the presence of Greek companies is negligible. Investment activity of Greek companies in CEECs started in Bulgaria (1989), followed by Albania and Russia (1992) and Romania (1993) while in the remaining countries it represents a post-1994 phenomenon (Labrianidis et al., 1998, p. 146, p. 171).

From a total of 521 Greek companies that have invested in CEECs, 35 companies (6.7 per cent of the total) had activities in more than one country. Seventeen of those companies invested in 2 countries, 12 in 3 and the remaining six companies in more than three countries. The country which is present in almost all combinations is Bulgaria, while Romania, Russia, Albania and Yugoslavia are also involved in a variety of combinations (Labrianidis et al., 1998, p. 162).

Within CEECs Greek companies tend to concentrate in the capital city of each country (Bucharest 91.2 per cent, Moscow 83.3 per cent, Skopje 80 per cent, Warsaw 71.4 per cent, Sofia 48.5 per cent, Tirana 41.4 – Labrianidis et al., 1998, 172–8). The relatively low concentration of Greek investment projects in Sofia and Tirana as a percentage of the total in Bulgaria and Albania can be attributed to geographic proximity with Greece. This leads to considerable concentration of investment in the Southern parts of the two countries which border with Greece. These are mainly investments originating from companies located in Northern Greece.

Sectoral Distribution of Investments in the CEECs

The majority of Greek investment projects in the CEECs are in trade (47.2 per cent) and industry (36 per cent) while there is a significant percentage of service related companies (13.2 per cent). Industrial companies are mainly in clothing (47.9 per cent) and food-beverages (25.5 per cent), while trading companies are concentrated in food (27.2 per cent), general trading (22.1 per cent), clothing (5.8 per cent), oil products (5.1 per cent), beverages (4.1 per cent) and furniture (3.4 per cent – Labrianidis et al., 1998, 167–8).

Most (71.8 per cent) of the Greek companies do not change sectors when they invest in the CEECs. The great majority of Greek companies with activities in the CEECs have parent companies in Greece which are mainly industrial firms (67.9 per cent), a smaller part (15 per cent) of them is involved in trade industries while the contribution of service related (9.1 per cent), technical (5.4 per cent) and mining (2.7 per cent) companies is significantly lower. Most of the industrial companies are in clothing (44.1 per cent), followed by food (20.5 per cent), metal products (4.3 per cent), beverages (3.5 per cent) and footwear (3.5 per cent). Regarding the trading companies, the largest number of firms is in food (26.3 per cent), electronics (12.3 per cent), general trade (10.5 per cent) and oil products (8.8 per cent) (Labrianidis et al., 1998, pp. 165–6).

Structure of Ownership and Type of Equipment Used by the Greek Ventures in the CEECs

A small part of the productive companies in the CEECs is wholly owned by the Greek company (31.3 per cent), whereas in most cases there is participation of local business people (43.8 per cent) or even the state (21.9 per cent – Labrianidis et al., 1988, p. 188). This is partly due to the fact that

Greek businesspeople face significant problems when they decide to operate independently in an extremely 'difficult' environment language, bureaucracy, frequent changes of the legal framework, corruption etc.). Another reason behind the decision to build partnerships is that the 'new' company ceases to look 'foreign' to the local population, thus creating a more positive 'climate'.

A significant proportion of the companies in the CEECs either use old equipment of the parent companies in Greece (57.4 per cent), or new equipment purchased in Greece (35.3 per cent). In both cases the consequences for the Greek economy are positive. In the first case it leads (in 58.1 per cent of the cases) to the renewal of equipment in production facilities within Greece. In the second case it may lead to the strengthening of some machinery industries (e.g. packaging and sorting machinery, tobacco and wine processing machinery) in which there is a tradition in Greece.

A Considerable Proportion of the Greek Companies in the CEECs are Directly Related to TNCs

One could distinguish four basic types of Greek companies operating in the CEECs: (1) Large (further subdivided into (1a) subsidiaries of TNCs, (1b) with participation of foreign capital, (1c) agents of TNCs, (1d) Greek companies), (2) Medium size, (3) Subcontracting and (4) Small.

(1) a. Some TNCs assign to their subsidiaries in Greece the task of operating in the CEECs in the context of the global location strategy of the TNC. This decision can be attributed to the fact that these countries constitute small, difficult and dangerous markets, and are near Greece. Such a strategy offers significant prospects for the Greek subsidiaries of TNCs. There are numerous such examples.[9]

b. A significant proportion (11.1 per cent) of the productive companies in the CEECs belongs to companies in Greece which have foreign apital in their structure. The above figure is rather high in relation to the average in Greece, and indicates an increasing dynamism by this type of company.

c. Many Greek companies entered the CEECs as agents of foreign firms. They are assigned by TNCs the task of 'entering' the Balkans, since this is a rather small market and therefore not interesting to a

TNC, whereas the Greek agent can benefit from economies of scale in distribution. Furthermore, the Balkans is a difficult market in which 'informal' relations and practices are predominant and the Greek businessperson is used to operating in such an environment. Working within such markets is also facilitated by the Greek tax legislation.[10] Finally, geographic proximity is of great importance. The entrance of Greek companies as agents, apart from the increase in their profits has no significant benefits for the Greek economy and has certainly no long term prospects, since in a later stage the agency is likely to be assigned to a local company, before the establishment of a subsidiary.

d. The majority of large companies investing in the CEEC's are Greek (among them some stately owned banks and communication companies). A significant number of large companies operating in the Balkans had previously strengthened their positions through a process of mergers and acquisitions.[11] There was a remarkable 'wave' of mergers and acquisitions in the Greek market after 1987. This was due to a number of reasons such as: the process towards the unification of the European market; the gradual relaxation of import tariffs (1985–92); the Greek market started to look appealing to the TNCs; the gradual departure from the traditional Mediterranean diet; the strengthening of the role of super-markets; the significant investments in the food industry during the previous years which led to the development of attractive target companies; finally the opening of the Balkan markets which gave a serious advantage to Greek companies. A significant part of mergers and acquisitions (46.8 per cent) took place in the food and beverage industry in the 1987–93 period (90.6 per cent), mainly between already existing Greek companies in the sector (61.9 per cent – Labrianidis et al., 1998, 123).

From a total of 521 Greek companies operating in the CEECs, 140 (26.8 per cent) are large by Greek standards, in terms of employment as well as turnover. An exception here is the clothing industry, in which companies have many employees but a relatively small turnover (Labrianidis et al., 1998, Appendix Table 7.21). The large size of these companies in Greece can also be supported by a number of other indices, such as their legal status (most of them are limited liability companies), and their relatively 'long' history, as 63.5 per cent have been operating for more than 18 years, while according to Giannitsis (1996), only 54 per cent of the companies in

Greece are more than 12 years old. These companies in Greece are mainly in the food industry (18.6 per cent), construction (12.1 per cent), clothing (10 per cent), computers-communications (5.7 per cent), tobacco (5 per cent), oil products (5 per cent), metal products (3.6 per cent) and beverages (3.6 per cent – Labrianidis et al., 1998, p. 189).

(2) The medium size Greek companies exhibited the least dynamism regarding the penetration of the CEEC markets.

(3) A significant proportion of the industrial companies in the CEECs (43.8 per cent) belongs to industrial companies in Greece which operate exclusively as subcontractors on behalf of large foreign firms, mainly in the garment industry. These companies in Greece are very diverse ranging from very large (more than 300 employees) to very small ones (less than 20 employees) and from financially healthy to bankrupt.

The companies in the garment industry were developed in Greece mainly in the 1970s on the basis of subcontracting ordered by EU companies, taking advantage of the relatively cheap labour, the high export subsidies provided by the Greek governments, as well as the existence of the Multi-Fibre Agreement. The relocation to the CEECs is part of a continuous, however meaningless, effort to minimise labour costs, whose effects are mainly negative to the Greek economy. Very soon more parts of the production process will be transferred to the CEECs, (today, only the sewing stage takes place there). Moreover, the foreign firms which subcontract to Greek producers are likely to demand further adjustment of the costs to the conditions of the CEECs markets, or assign the subcontracting to local producers themselves. However, if this relocation is based on the reduction of the average cost of the Greek firm (parent and subsidiary) and an effort to move towards producing brand-named, high quality products, with just in time methods etc., it will be positive to the Greek economy (Labrianidis, 1996c).

(4) There is a great number of small companies with activities in the CEECs, most of which are mainly trading or subcontracting companies. In many cases these companies were not created as subsidiaries (there are no parent companies), or their parent companies were rather small and ceased operations due to the existence of better prospects in the

CEECs. Moreover, the number of small commercial companies which was significant in the first period of the opening of the CEECs markets is constantly declining, as local entrepreneurs are starting to take over.

The Small Size of Greek Firms that Invested in the CEECs is a Handicap

Greek firms that invested in the CEECs are small compared with TNCs, which means that they have two crucial disadvantages, i.e. shortage of capital and management skills (Buckley et al., 1988). Furthermore, Greek firms have no history in FDI and hence risks are perceived to be greater since they have no international experience on which to draw. Finally, most investment projects by Greek firms in the CEECs occurred through the 'direct' route (i.e. by directly establishing an overseas production subsidiary). They did not follow more long term strategies before establishing a subsidiary (Buckley et al., 1988, pp. 44–68). That is: a) exporting to a country; b) first exporting to a country, then appointing a foreign agent; c) first exporting to a country, then setting up an overseas sales subsidiary; and d) first exporting to a country, then appointing a foreign agent there, then setting up an overseas sales subsidiary (the 'full' route). Needless to say that the 'direct' route is the less successful one, since each step gives information to the firm, offers an opportunity for reassessing the overall strategy and forms a base from which the next step can be taken.

Character and Categorisation of Greek FDI

Why do Greek Companies Invest in the CEECs

The basic factors pushing (push factors) Greek companies away from the domestic market, leading them to initiate projects in the CEECs are the saturation of the Greek market and the intensification of competition, which is mainly caused by the intense import penetration, particularly in some specific sectors, as well as the high costs in labour intensive industries (such as clothing and footwear).

The basic reasons attracting (pull factors) Greek companies to undertake FDIs in the CEECs are first, the opportunity to reduce production costs, mainly through the reduction of labour costs, which is of primary importance to labour intensive industries (e.g. clothing, fur, footwear). Second, the opportunity to exploit the natural resources (minerals, agricultural and animal products). Third, many companies have entered these markets, knowing that they will operate under loss for a certain period of time, since the markets are still unshaped, hoping that these losses will be compensated for by the strong positions they will have gained when the markets will start improving. Fourth, the avoidance of tariff or non-tariff (custom delays) impediments. Fifth, the exploitation of existing relations within CEECs, in the sense that an investment in one CEEC can be used as a base for the expansion to other CEECs, due to reduced tariffs, existing traditional trade channels etc. Sixth, the fact that they are relatively unshaped markets, in the sense that competition is still based on prices and not on quality/differentiation of the product. Finally, the existence of Greek companies, as well as the existence of Greek communities in these countries brought about the establishment of other Greek companies ('following the customer' – banks, insurance companies, labelling products, dyeing, packaging products etc.). As Dicken (1992, p. 87) points out, a most important by-product of TNCs in manufacturing industry in the last few decades has been the closely related development of TNCs in business services (banks, advertising agencies, hotel chains, car rental firms, insurance, legal corporations etc.), that have followed the lead of their corporate clients in establishing a global network.

The lack of strategy from Greek firms and the priority of labour cost reduction as a pulling factor is easily depicted in the choice of the recipient countries of Greek FDI.

One of the most significant aspects of Greek FDI is its extreme concentration in CEE. Developed countries directed only an insignificant proportion of the volume of their FDI to CEECs (e.g. Spain 0.5 per cent, UK 1.2 per cent, Denmark 1.4 per cent, France 2.3 per cent and Belgium and Luxembourg 2.5 per cent). The only exception being Austria with an important share (42.5 per cent) of its FDI addressed to CEECs (OECD, 1998). Hence Greece, having more than 95 per cent of the volume of its FDI in CEECs, constitutes a significant exception in the above pattern.

Another aspect of Greek FDI which differentiates it from almost every developed European country is its geographical spread within this specified area. That is, Greek affiliates are concentrated in their neighbouring countries (i.e. Bulgaria 41.1 per cent, Albania 20.3 per cent, FYROM 2.6 per cent) or in their vicinity (i.e. Romania 20.3 per cent). This is actually one of the most significant characteristics of the 'new multinationals' which tend to invest to neighbouring countries. Nevertheless, historical and cultural ties are not irrelevant to even more developed economies. In this context Spanish FDI is mainly directed towards Latin America, while France and the UK have significant interests in most parts of the world, most possibly because of their colonial past. The only other European country with a relatively high concentration in CEE is Austria, another country with very close historical ties with the countries of the region.

On the other hand Greek investment is relatively important only in these countries, whilst in the more 'mature' markets (viz. The Czech Republic, Hungary and Poland) (Table 1 overleaf), as well as in the CEECs which are not as mature as those three but are further away from Greece than the Balkan countries, the Greek presence is relatively insignificant. There is, nevertheless, some evidence that whatever investment in those countries, which are not the main recipients of Greek investment in terms of either the number of projects, or their value, generally tends to exclude immigrant capital and concern larger investments by the largest and most dynamic Greek companies.

Overall it can fairly easily be concluded that Greek FDI is of primary importance and significant in absolute figures only for Bulgaria, a country which only very recently accomplished a certain stability and advancement of transition. This implies that for a rather long period Bulgaria (as in fact the remaining of the Balkan countries) had largely been excluded from the plans of the large MNCs. The remaining two neighbouring countries (Albania and FYROM) are still perceived as extremely immature and risky and in any case are very small. Regarding Romania, the overall data provided by the authorities is very problematic and could not lead us to safe conclusions.[12]

The Monopolistic Advantages of Greek Companies that Permit the Establishment of Investment Projects in the CEECs

In order to realise all these investment projects, Greek companies in CEECs must enjoy certain monopolistic advantages towards both the host country firms and the TNCs ('true' and 'new'). The main monopolistic advantages of Greek investment projects in the Balkans towards the host country firms are that they have substantial capital, (though very small if compared with FDI from DCs); established relations with the Western market; parent firms

Table 1 Origin of FDI in Romania, Bulgaria, Hungary, Poland and the Czech Republic

Romania[1] (1997)			Bulgaria[2] (1997)		
FDI origin	FDI inflows		FDI origin	FDI inflows	
	$USm	%		$USm	%
Netherlands	514.4	15.3	Belgium	251.6	21.1
Germany	355.5	10.6	Germany	233.4	19.6
Italy	285.0	8.5	Netherlands	92.6	7.8
France	264.2	7.8	USA	73.4	6.2
USA	235.4	7.0	UK	71.1	6.0
Korea	234.1	6.9	Austria	53.8	4.5
Turkey	171.6	5.1	Cyprus	51.7	4.3
Austria	161.1	4.8	Greece	51.1	4.3
UK	156.7	4.6	Korea	45.7	3.8
Luxembourg	136.2	4.0	Spain	44.7	3.7
Hungary	85.9	2.5	Luxembourg	42.0	3.5
Greece	82.1	2.4	Switzerland	23.5	3.0
Cyprus	76.9	2.3	Russia	30.9	2.6
Switzerland	72.1	2.1	Ireland	17.6	1.5
Syria	57.7	1.7	EBRD	17.5	1.5
Others	480.8	14.3	Others	80.2	6.7
Total	3,369.5	100.0	Total	1,192.8	100.0

Sources

1. Romanian State Ownership Fund.
2. Bulgarian Foreign Investment Agency.
3. OECD, Migration, Free Trade and Regional Integration in Central and Eastern Europe, 1997.

Hungary[3] (9/1995)

FDI origin	FDI inflows $USm	%
Germany	1,872.9	28.5
USA	1,384.3	21.0
Austria	1,042.7	15.8
Netherlands	371.4	5.6
France	312.8	4.8
UK	258.2	3.9
Italy	258.2	3.9
Belgium	212.5	3.2
Japan	168.8	2.6
Switzerland	128.1	1.9
Others	573.0	8.7
Total	6,582.9	100.0

Poland[3] (9/1995)

FDI origin	FDI inflows $USm	%
USA	1,815.0	30.6
International	912.0	15.4
Germany	614.0	10.3
Italy	390.0	6.6
France	335.0	5.6
Netherlands	362.0	6.1
Austria	248.0	4.2
UK	350.0	5.9
Switzerland	196.0	3.3
Others	711.0	12.0
Total	5,933.0	100.0

Czech Republic[3] (9/1995)

FDI origin	FDI inflows $USm	%
Germany	1,423.3	27.0
Switzerland	828.6	15.7
Netherlands	771.9	14.6
USA	745.2	14.1
France	534.4	10.1
Austria	277.9	5.3
Belgium	221.5	4.2
Others	472.3	9.0
Total	5,275.1	100.0

originating from an EU member state and management with experience in operation in a market economy. Greek investment projects will retain the above mentioned monopolistic advantages only for a short period of time. It will only be a matter of a few years until local firms develop similar skills themselves.

As for the main monopolistic advantages of Greek investment projects in the CEECs towards TNCs ('true' and 'new') these are first, knowledge of working in an unstable environment. In fact, TNCs from both DCs and UDCs, due to the economic and social instability in the countries where

Table 2 Average level of FDI by country of origin and economic sector ($ US)

	Industry	Construction	Agriculture	Transport
Belgium	35,759,710	50,000	364	48,230
Netherlands	6,539,005	330	0	87,016
Germany	1,483,486	347,885	137,020	4,265,083
UK	2,000,351	1,145	7,150	22,310
USA	838,520	20,000	13	365
Switzerland	2,159,641	305	241,223	363,825
Cyprus	21,224	178,715	0	0
Austria	586,962	832,651	0	108,134
France	881,165	36,892	36,965	833
Czech Republic	427,213	600	3,200,300	0
Russia	66,482	147,113	382	20,182
Greece	526,854	93,049	4,596	1,624
Israel	358,875	3,500	8,905	0
Italy	129,850	125	69,387	103,036
Ukraine	39,048	177	0	331
Lebanon	1,041	10,000	0	426
Syria	179,955	0	0	0
Armenia	133,819	0	0	0
Turkey	4,998	27,057	1,795	224
Total	2,744,116	102,914	309,008	264,296

Source: Bulgarian Foreign Investment Agency.

Greek investment projects have been established, have maintained a 'wait and see' attitude. Second, the geographic proximity. Third, they have access to, compared to the other European countries, cheap skilled labour in their home country. In a sense Greek engineering companies, are involved in the export of factors of production: technical and manual work force while firms from DCs have to face much more expensive labour costs and, for typical projects, no longer have a technological edge. Finally, the traditional Greek firm owned by a business family has the advantage of being able to risk more and hence grab all the opportunities.

Communications	Commerce	Tourism	Services	Others	Total
1	7,373	0	0	13,545	2,287,516
0	619,615	0	120,922	20,009	881,440
2,675	270,129	7,592,604	537,543	5,437	625,838
2,496,996	89,481	1,042	1,234,010	8,898	430,933
25,908	241,136	880,117	562,241	90,481	346,325
1,821	105,465	391,500	44,221	12,163	341,651
0	103,843	297,522	899,594	222,338	277,924
427	107,740	1,554	899,894	10,999	222,224
53,960	27,561	212	4,641,796	9,565	152,996
0	9,587	2,174	44,043	213,511	119,056
0	14,255	97,109	2,011,970	6,673	51,524
353,166	3,744	31,674	710,482	20,654	40,064
0	18,562	20,860	63,043	5,817	38,131
0	5,372	0	485,000	5,600	17,244
0	2,236	0	0	14,530	5,906
0	3,228	0	67,991	227	3,526
0	2,179	0	0	0	2,935
0	1,417	0	0	2,830	2,342
0	1,264	34,229	0	1,076	1,479
366,869	86,010	779,216	880,196	36,908	307,845

The Size of Greek Companies

Since we do not have overall data concerning the countries of origin of FDI in CEECs we offer some provisional conclusions derived from partial data. That is, first Greek FDI projects in CEECs are large in number but quite small in volume of investment. Regarding Romania,[13] according to the Romanian State Ownership Fund, in November 1998, there were 1569 Greek projects with a capital invested amounting to US$ 82 million, while for Bulgaria according to the Bulgarian Foreign Investment Agency, these figures were in September 1997, 1274 and US$ 51 million respectively. The resulting average size of the Greek companies was US$ 52,304 in Romania and US$ 40,064 in Bulgaria. Both figures seem to be compatible with the Greek level of development and the size of Greek companies.

In a sense the Greek presence in Bulgaria seems to have two significantly different faces.[14] On the one hand it appears similar to that of some less developed countries (Turkey, Lebanon, Syria, etc.), since the average investment in commerce, where about 90 per cent of all Greek firms are operating, is not much higher than that of the countries mentioned above (Table 2 previous page). On the other hand the average investment in industry is not much lower than that of the most developed economies, despite the fact that Greece has the largest number of industrial affiliates. Moreover, this figure would be significantly higher, had the Greek offshore companies been included.

However, even this remark should be viewed with extreme caution. During various visits in Bulgaria, as well as to a number of other CEECs, a significant number of informal Greek affiliates were detected, which were literally non-existent for the Bulgarian authorities. With the inclusion of such companies in the database the average investment of Greek manufacturing would be significantly smaller, possibly even reaching the levels of the less developed countries mentioned above.

Perhaps, to follow Kobrin (1997, pp. 158–59) when he speaks for investments abroad from UDCs, the phenomenon of investment in CEECs by most Greek firms could more accurately be described as immigration rather than as FDI. Many Greek investment projects in the CEECs are of the emigrant entrepreneur type who decides to try his fortune abroad. That is, businessmen who migrate carrying with them their skills and sometimes, capital.

Concluding Remarks

From the analysis that preceded it could be argued that Greek investment projects in the CEECs, with a few exceptions, cannot be classified either as 'true' or 'new' transnationals. They are labour intensive, small scale operations, they are in industries with mature technologies, they pay low overheads, they compete on price rather than product differentiation, they don't have an established brand name, they don't invest heavily in advertising, they are established in UDCs, they are established in neighbouring countries, their subsidiaries are left on their own, they form joint ventures with local entrepreneurs. Needless to say that only a handful of them have a chance of becoming new TNCs and even less so 'true TNCs'.

However, the large companies (type 1 – that constitute the 27 per cent of firms with investment projects in the CEECs) do resemble, more to new transnationals. In fact, a handful of those companies (e.g. Titan, Petzetakis, Chipita, Thrace Paper Mills etc.) – and this too is a rather novel phenomenon – seem to resemble more to 'true' TNCs rather than 'new' ones. These four and a few more companies have invested in countries which are more developed than Greece, often in other continents, with highly competitive markets. Furthermore, their affiliates are under strict control from the parent company. Finally, it seems that the choice of location is not random or opportunistic as in the majority of Greek firms, forming an essential part of the strategy of the companies and their global positioning.

Notes

1. I would like to thank my friend Dr. Chrysafis Iordanoglou for his comments on an earlier draft of this paper.
2. The term 'Developing country' according to the UNCTC refers to the countries with market economies in Latin America, Africa (except South Africa), Oceania (except New Zealand and Australia), and Asia (except Japan). In a similar way one might use the term Third World Country or Newly Industrialised Economies. All the above terms imply that the process of development is linear and that it simply happens that some firms are at the moment lagging behind. The use of the term UDCs is based on the conception that there are structural differences between developed and UDCs and it is not necessary that UDCs ultimately will become developed. This term does not refer to low-income European countries such as Portugal, Spain and Greece; Israel or the centrally planned economies of the USSR, of Eastern Europe and the People's Republic of China.
3. That is, Labrianidis (1996 a, 1996b, 1996c and 1997).
4. Globalisation has a long history both in Orthodox Economics and Political Economy.

Older versions of the theory in Political Economy were the theories of International Systems (Wallerstein, 1979) and the New International Division of Labour (Frobel et al., 1980). The more modern versions are numerous such as in Economics by Ohmae (1995), Dicken (1992), Dunning (1993) while in Political Economy by Lash-Urry (1994). The opposing theory has been developed, inter alia, by Hirst-Thompson (1992) and Jenkins (1987).

5. FDI may be defined as the transfer by a firm of resources – including capital, technology and personnel – into a foreign business venture with the objective of acquiring control of the venture (EBRD, 1994, p. 122).
6. The Asian firms invest in Asia Hong Kong firms in southern China. Indian firms rarely venture beyond the Indian Ocean. (Sri Lanka, Malaysia and Kenya), L. American firms within South or Central America (Argentine in Brazil, Chile and Uruguay) (Dicken 1992, pp. 81–87; Wells, 1977, p. 133 and 1981, p. 4, p. 24). Between 1965 and 1978, as Whitmore et al. (1989, p. 5, p. 18) estimates, 99 per cent of Argentine and 95 per cent of Chilean investment was in other L. American countries. Yugoslav TNCs invest mainly in Germany, Austria, Italy and Switzerland (Artisien et al., 1992, pp. 38–40)
7. This section is based on two research projects coordinated by the writer (see Labrianidis et al., 1997 and 1998).
8. This figure is not exhaustive of the Greek activity in the area. In fact this was one of the most significant problems we were faced with (i.e. the lack of any systematic data collected by official sources regarding the activity of Greek companies in the CEECs). In order to overcome this obstacle, a new database was created using a large number of diverse sources (i.e. Reports of the commercial attaches of the Greek Embassies, Law 1892 concerning the realisation of investments in CEECs, Catalogue published by the Association of Industries of Northern Greece, of firms exporting to at least one CEEC, Catalogue published by ICAP, of 5,000 firms exporting to at least one CEEC, Economic Chamber of Greece (1993), index of daily and periodical press (Imerisia, Express, Kerdos, Ikonomicos Tachydromos, Ependytis etc.), interviews (snow ball sampling)). Even though this database is rather comprehensive it remains problematic in two senses: First, the number of Greek companies is underestimated, since there are many (mainly small) investments, impossible to trace. Second, the data is not always comparable due to the different sources used. However despite the insufficiencies, the data allows the formulation of some basic arguments regarding the Greek entrepreneurial activity in the CEECs.
9. Some of these companies are: Elliniki Yfantourgia, Athinaiki Zithopyia, 3ε, ALICO, Olympic DDB Needham Advertising, Molinger, Henkel, Knorr, Laureal, Ciba Geigy Hellas, Zeneca Hellas, Rhone Poulenc Hellas, Dow-Flanco Hellas, Yamaha Hellas.
10. Greek tax legislation allows companies to treat a part of their total export revenue as 'export promotion expenses without receipts'. This allows them to use informal instruments to promote their interests.
11. Such as: food industries (Delta, Papadopoulos, Fage, Pavlidis, Goody's, Chipita, Best Foods, Ion), Beverages (Boutaris, 3ε), Tobacco (Michailidis), Electric appliances (Fourlis), Packaging (Mailis), Textile mills (Magrizos), Software (Intracom, Singular), Construction (Michaniki, Sarantopoulos), Advertising (Olympic).
12. See footnote 13.
13. It should rather emphatically be stressed that the Romanian registration system is still uncoordinated and problematic rendering the resulting data extremely overestimated (at least with regards to Greek FDI) and significantly less reliable than the Bulgarian registration system. The actual figures could be less than half of those reported by the RSOF. Unfortunately, this data is the only available.
14. Unfortunately the same conclusions cannot be safely drawn for the other CEECs due to insufficient data.

References

Artisien, P., McMillan, C.H., Rojec, M. (1992), *Yugoslav Multinationals Abroad*, Macmillan.

Buckley, P., Newbould, G., Thurwell, J. (1988), *Foreign Direct Investment by Smaller U.K. Firms*, Macmillan.

Dicken, P. (1992), *Global Shift*, P. Chapman.

Dunning, J. (1981), *International Production and the Multinational Enterprise*, Allen & Unwin.

Dunning, J. (1993), *Multi-National Enterprises and the Global Economy*, Addison-Wesley.

EBRD (European Bank of Reconstruction and Development) (1994). *Transition Report.*

Frobel, F., Heinrichs, J., Kreye, O. (1980), *The New International Division of Labour*, Cambridge.

Hirst, P., Thompson, G. (1992), 'The problem of 'globalisation', *Economy and Society*, Vol. 21 (4),

Hood, N., Young, S. (1979), *The Economics of Multinational Enterprise*, Longman

Hymer, S. (1976), *The International Operations of National Firms*. MIT Press.

Hymer, S. (1979), *The Multinational Corporation*, Cambridge.

Jenkins, R. (1987), *Transnational Corporations and Uneven Development*, Routledge.

Kobrin, S. (1997), 'Comment', in Agmon, T. and Kindelberger C.P. (eds), *Multinationals From Small Countries*, MIT Press, pp. 157–165.

Krugman, P. (1995), *The Age of Diminishing Returns*, Polis [in Greek].

Labrianidis, L. (1996a), 'Thoughts on an Industrial Policy in View of the Opening of Greek Firms to the Balkans', *Cahiers of the Institute of Labour*, Vol. 6–7, 75–85 [in Greek].

Labrianidis, L. (1996b), 'The opening of the Balkan Markets and Consequent Economic Problems in Greece', *Modern Greek Studies*, Vol. 12/13, pp. 211–235.

Labrianidis, L. (1996c), 'Subcontracting in Greek Manufacturing and the Opening of the Balkan Markets', *Cyprus Journal of Economics*, Vol. 9 (1), pp. 29–45.

Labrianidis, L. (1997), 'The opening of the Greek Companies to the Balkan Markets Might Have Important Negative Consequences in the Development of the Country', *The Hellenic Review of Political Sciences*, Vol. 9, pp. 65–101 [in Greek].

Labrianidis, L., Kalantaridis Ch., Karagianni St., Katsikas I, Kourtessis, Ar. (1997), *The Greek Industry and Developments in Central and Eastern Europe*, Research Report Financed by the Ministry of Industry [in Greek].

Labrianidis, L., Kalogeresis Th., Karagianni St., Katsikas I., Mavroudeas St. (1998), *The Economic Implications for the Development of Greece and Northern Greece in Particular, Due to the Opening of the Greek Industry to the Balkans*, Research Report Financed by the General Secretary of Research and Technology [in Greek].

Lall, S. (1974), 'Less-Developed Countries and Private Foreign Direct Investment', *World Development*, Vol. 2, pp. 4–5.

Lall, S. (1983), 'The Theoretical Background', in Lall S. (ed), *The New Multinationals*, J. Wiley & Sons, pp. 1–20.

Lash, S., Urry, J. (1994), *Economies of Signs and Space*, Sage.

OECD (1998), *International Direct Investment Statistics Yearbook 1998.*

Ohmae, K. (1995), 'Putting Global Logic First', *Harvard Business Review*, Jan/Feb.

Ozawa, T. (1992), 'Foreign Direct Investment and Economic Development', *Transantional Corporations*, Vol. 1 (1), pp. 27–54.

Petrakos, G. (1996), *The New Geography of the Balkans: Cross-Border Cooperation Between Albania, Bulgaria and Greece*, University of Thessaly.

UN (1995), 'Evaluating the Uruguay Round', *World Economy.*

UNCTC (1978), *Transnational Corporations in World Development*, UN.

UNCTAD (1993), *World Investment Report: Transnational Corporations and Integrated International Production.*

Vernon, R. (1966), 'International Investment and International Trade in the Product Cycle', *Quarterly Journal of Economics*, Vol. 80, pp. 190–207.

Wallerstein, I. (1979), *The Capitalist World Economy*, Cambridge.

Wells, L.T. (1977). 'The Internationalization of Firms From Developing Countries', in Agmon, T. and Kindelberger C.P. (eds), *Multinationals From Small Countries*, MIT Press, pp. 133–56.

Wells, L.T. Jr. (1981), 'Foreign Investors From the Third World' in Kumar, K. and McLeod, M.G. (eds), *Multinationals From Developing Countries*, Lexington Books, pp. 23–36.

Wells, L.T. Jr. (1983), Third World Multinationals, MIT Press.

Whitmore, K., Sanjaya, Lall, Jung-Taik, Hyun (1989) 'Foreign Direct Investment From the Newly Industrialised Economies', *World Bank Working Paper*, No. 22.

FSC
www.fsc.org
MIX
Papier | Fördert
gute Waldnutzung
FSC® C083411

Kolibri 360 GmbH
Ferdinand-Jühlke-Straße 7
99095 Erfurt, Deutschland
produktsicherheit@kolibri360.de